New Apelleses and New Apollos
Poet-Artists around the Court of Florence (1537–1587)

Diletta Gamberini

New Apelleses and New Apollos
Poet-Artists around the Court of Florence (1537–1587)

DE GRUYTER

This publication was generously supported by the Alexander von Humboldt Foundation.

Unterstützt von / Supported by

Alexander von Humboldt
Stiftung / Foundation

ISBN 978-3-11-074355-5
e-ISBN (PDF) 978-3-11-074366-1

Library of Congress Control Number: 2021949431

Bibliographic information published by the Deutsche Nationalbibliothek
The Deutsche Nationalbibliothek lists this publication in the Deutsche Nationalbibliografie;
detailed bibliographic data are available on the Internet at http://dnb.dnb.de.

© 2022 Walter de Gruyter GmbH, Berlin/Boston

Cover design: Kerstin Protz, De Gruyter
Cover illustration: Giorgio Vasari, *Cosimo I de' Medici Surrounded by his Architects, Engineers and Sculptors*, fresco, 1555–1558, Florence, Palazzo Vecchio, Sala di Cosimo I.
Layout and typesetting: Andreas Eberlein, aromaBerlin
Printing and binding: Beltz Grafische Betriebe GmbH, Bad Langensalza

www.degruyter.com

Contents

Preface and Acknowledgments	11
Introduction: The Artist as a Poet	13
Geographical and chronological scope of the book, and a brief prospect of the history of poet-artists in Renaissance Italy	19
Nature of the sources; specifics and relevance of the cultural context under consideration	25
Purpose and structure of the book	28
Looking at Michelangelo	33
The example of the universal artist	33
Antecedents and historical background of the model	37
A special paradigm for Florentine artists?	41
Memory, reception, imitation: Michelangelo's poetry among the artists of the Medici court	46
How to imitate Michelangelo?	52
Cellini and Michelangelo	57
The imitation of Michelangelo between Vasari and Bronzino	61
A Literato's Recognition	71
Varchi, the artists, and the Accademia Fiorentina	71
Of pens, brushes, and hammers: the presence and dignity of the artists' poetry in Varchi's dialogues in verse	79
The main historical occasions for Varchi's dialogue in verse with artists	83
Patron, broker, dedicatee: Varchi and the Florentine arts in light of his sonnet exchanges with artists	92
Disavowing art	112

Between Praise and Vituperation — 119

- The poetic triumph of the *Perseus* — 119
- General public, connoisseurs, and artists: categorizing the sculpture's audience — 123
- Artists' poems in praise of the *Perseus* — 131
- "sì come s'usa nelle grandi scuole" — 141
- The history of vituperative poems by artists and the example of Cellini — 147
- Self-defense poems — 155

The Problem of Patronage — 165

- The gray areas of propaganda — 165
- When art and poetry do not suffice: the case of Pilucca — 168
- Polemical streaks in Bronzino's reflection on Cosimo's patronage — 176
- Between courtly panegyric and artistic self-exegesis — 192

Appendix — 201
Bibliography — 251
Plates — 279
Credits — 287
Index of Names — 289

"I was touched to see that you had truly paid attention to some pages that I showed you. I did not take from that that they deserved attention. I regard that attention as a gift freely and generously given on your part. Attention is the rarest and purest form of generosity."

Simone Weil, letter to Joë Bousquet (April 13, 1942)

Preface and Acknowledgments

The generosity of three institutions made this book possible. Research for the project was initiated during the tenure of a Melville J. Kahn fellowship at Villa I Tatti – The Harvard University Center for Italian Renaissance Studies, in 2015/2016, and carried on during the following semester, when I was a fellow at the Kunsthistorisches Institut in Florenz. Finally, a postdoc at the Art History Department of Ludwig-Maximilians-Universität in Munich (2018–2020), supported by the Alexander von Humboldt Foundation, allowed time for thinking through the materials I had collected and for writing. Each of these periods has given me the opportunity to engage in a dialogue with colleagues from different disciplinary backgrounds, whose questions and observations contributed much to broadening the horizons of the project I had initially envisioned. For the exchanges we had at I Tatti, favored by both the Villa's lunches and the walks in the garden that are necessary to work them off, I would particularly like to thank Alina Payne, Marco Simone Bolzoni, Luisa Capodieci, John Christopoulos, Elsa Filosa, Allen Grieco, Christian Kleinbub, Pamela O. Long, Mariano Pérez Carrasco, Courtney Quaintance, David Rosenthal, Jennifer Sliwka, Luka Špoliaric, Giulia Torello-Hill and Henk van Veen. At the KHI, I benefited from conversations with Alessandro Nova, Bobby Brennan, Dario Donetti, Fabian Jonietz and Luca Palozzi. In Munich, Ulrich Pfisterer has been a really welcoming and thought-provoking academic host. He, Chiara Franceschini, Cloe Cavero de Carondelet, Erin Giffin and Rahul Kulka read significant parts of the book, and gave most valuable feedback. Over the years leading up to the completion of this work, Michael Cole, Jonathan Nelson, Deborah Parker and Jane Tylus did not only exchange ideas with me on topics related to this project, but also often provided support for me to pursue research – this path has not been an easy one, and their help was fundamental. For conversations in various ways focused on themes covered in these pages, thanks go to Cristina Acidini, Lorenzo Amato, Maurizio Arfaioli, Francesco Bausi, Dario Brancato, Arnaldo Bruni, Giuseppe Capriotti, Eliana Carrara, Paolo Celi, Alice Collavin, Claudia Conforti, Frédérique Dubard de Gaillarbois, Bruce Edelstein, Benjamin Fellmann, Giovanni Ferroni, Francesca Fantappiè, Antonio Geremicca, Simon Gilson, Carlo Alberto Girotto, Bernhard Huß, Joseph Kopta, Francesca Latini, Florian Mehltretter, Émilie Passignat, Anne Proctor, Giovanna Rizzarelli, Massimiliano Rossi, Cristina Ruggero, Morten Steen Hansen, Patrizia Tosini and Sanne Wellen. At last, I would like to thank Academic Language Experts (www.aclang.com) for their contribution to the manuscript, as well as Bobby Brennan for his most generous help with proofreading my English.

The writing and (long) editing of the book were completed in February 2021, and the bibliography aims to be updated to that point.

Munich, July 2021

Introduction: The Artist as a Poet

Scholars of early modern European culture have long highlighted the prominent role played in that intellectual landscape by the *doctus artifex*, the creator whose accomplishments as a painter, sculptor or architect were fleshed out by many other skills, often rooted in the canon of liberal arts. Their work has emphasized, in particular, how these figures acted as powerful catalysts of that long process of social ascent of the artist that was one of the distinctive phenomena of the age. Much attention has thus been paid to the pivotal role that the literary output of those who mainly practiced the arts of drawing played in this historical transformation, especially in the Italian context.[1] At least since the Renaissance and Mannerism chapters of Julius von Schlosser's *Kunstliteratur* (1924), criticism has typically focused on the various genres of prose production of these authors (e. g. biography, autobiography, memoir, dialogic, treatise, periegesis), devoting just an episodic and marginal attention to their poetic output.[2]

---

[1] Valuable introductions to the interrelated themes of artists' education, intellectual ambitions, and literary endeavors in early modern Europe include, to name just a few major works: Martin Wackernagel, *Der Lebensraum des Künstlers in der florentinischen Renaissance: Aufgaben und Auftraggeber, Wekstatt und Kunstmarkt*, Leipzig 1938, pp. 363–368; Rudolf and Margot Wittkower, *Born under Saturn: The Character and Conduct of Artists. A Documented History from Antiquity to the French Revolution*, London 1963, pp. 14–16 and pp. 93–96; Charles Dempsey, Some Observations on the Education of Artists in Florence and Bologna during the Later Sixteenth Century, in: *The Art Bulletin* 62 (1980), pp. 552–569; Sergio Rossi, *Dalle botteghe alle accademie: realtà sociale e teorie artistiche a Firenze dal 14° al 16° secolo*, Milan 1980; Department of Art, Brown University (ed.), *Children of Mercury: The Education of Artists in the Sixteenth and Seventeenth Centuries*, Providence, RI 1984; Jan Białostocki, Doctus Artifex and the Library of the Artist in XVIth and XVIIth Century, in: Abraham Horodisch (ed.), *De Arte et Libris: Festschrift Erasmus, 1934–1984*, Amsterdam 1984, pp. 11–22; André Chastel, L'artista, in: Eugenio Garin (ed.), *L'uomo del Rinascimento*, Rome 1988, pp. 253–263; Thea Vignau-Wilberg, *Pictor Doctus*: Drawing the Theory of Art around 1600, in: Eliška Fučíková (ed.), *Rudolph II and Prague: The Court and the City*, London 1997, pp. 179–188; Francis Ames-Lewis, *The Intellectual Life of the Early Renaissance Artist*, New Haven, CT 2000; Bodo Guthmüller, Berndt Hamm, and Andreas Tönnesmann (eds.), *Künstler und Literat: Schrift- und Buchkultur in der europäischen Renaissance*, Wiesbaden 2006, and Heiko Damm, Michael Thimann, and Claus Zittel (eds.), *The Artist as Reader: On Education and Non-Education of Early Modern Artists*, Leiden / Boston 2013. These topics are also at the core of the forthcoming monograph by Angela Dressen, *The Intellectual Education of the Renaissance Artist 1450–1550*, Cambridge 2021.

[2] See Julius von Schlosser, *Die Kunstliteratur, ein Handbuch zur Quellenkunde der neueren Kunstgeschichte*, Vienna 1924, pp. 85–406. In his book, Schlosser discussed a few poetic compositions by Italian Renaissance artists. In particular, he took into consideration Giovanni Santi's *Cronaca Rimata* (ca. 1478–1494), the *Antiquarie prospettiche Romane* by the so-called "Prospettivo Milanese depintore" (published in 1500), Francesco Lancillotti's *terza rima* composition of the *Lamento della pittura* (published in 1509), and Giovan Paolo Lomazzo's poetic autobiography and anthology of the *Grotteschi* (1587). On the whole, however, this typology of artists' writings remains a peripheral subject in his paramount work.

As a result, scholarship has underestimated the implications of an argument that is a recurrent refrain in those artists' most-studied writings. Over and over again, such texts proclaimed the liberal status of artistic activity by leaning on an ancient constellation of ideas asserting the similarity between the practices of art and verse composition, from Horace's *ut pictura poesis* to Simonides of Ceos's concept of painting as "mute poetry," with such pronouncements sometimes leading to the notion that nearly every painter was also a talented poet.[3]

By virtue of their author's prestige, Michelangelo's poems were the first compositions by an Italian Renaissance artist to receive more than superficial interest. The growing focus on these texts, which has come about in recent years as an increasingly penetrating examination of their relationship to their creator's visual arts,[4] has in turn helped rescue the poetry of other such writers from critical oblivion. The sonnets and epic poems of the Carrara-born sculptor, medalist, and architect Danese Cataneo, who worked in the Veneto region from the 1530s and until his death (1572) was in contact with the most distinguished literati of that society, have for example provided fodder for a sophisticated analysis of the interferences that could occur between the artistic and poetic output of a successful professional of the disciplines of drawing.[5] In recent years, however, it is mostly the compositions of some leading painters and sculptors of Cosimo I's Florence that have enjoyed a certain scholarly rediscovery. Divided into a lyric, Petrarch-inspired canzoniere and a body of burlesque verse, the extensive

---

[3] For the sources of these ideas, see Horace, *Ars Poetica*, l. 361, and Plutarch, *Moralia* (*De gloria Atheniensium*), 346f. A vast scholarly literature has addressed the revival of these notions during the Italian Renaissance: it will suffice here to mention the classic study by Rensselaer W. Lee, "Ut Pictura Poesis": The Humanistic Theory of Painting, in: *The Art Bulletin* 22.4 (1940), pp. 197–269; the elegant treatment by Leonard Barkan, *Mute Poetry, Speaking Pictures*, Princeton, NJ 2013, and the recent discussion by Émilie Passignat, *Il Cinquecento: le fonti per la storia dell'arte*, Rome 2017, pp. 76–78 and pp. 273–278, with further bibliography. In his *Trattato dell'arte della Pittura* (1584), Giovan Paolo Lomazzo claimed that nearly every painter possesses a poetic talent: for his argument see *infra*, fn. 28. It's useful to remember that some recurrent motifs in the biographies of Renaissance artists were indebted to topoi that we find in the biographies of prominent poets: see Catherine M. Soussloff, *The Absolute Artist: The Historiography of a Concept*, Minneapolis / London 1997, pp. 47–61, and Johannes Bartuschat, Dalla vita del poeta alla vita dell'artista: tendenze del genere biografico nel Quattrocento, in: *Letteratura & arte* 1 (2003), pp. 49–57.

[4] Among the most illuminating treatments of Michelangelo's poetry and its relation to his artistic oeuvre are Glauco Cambon, *Michelangelo's Poetry: Fury of Form*, Princeton, NJ 1985; Grazia Dolores Folliero-Metz, *Le Rime di Michelangelo Buonarroti nel loro contesto*, Heidelberg 2004; Leonard Barkan, *Michelangelo: A Life on Paper*, Princeton, NJ 2011; Oscar Schiavone, *Michelangelo Buonarroti: forme del sapere tra letteratura e arte nel Rinascimento*, Florence 2013; Ida Campeggiani, *Le varianti della poesia di Michelangelo: scrivere per via di porre*, Lucca 2012; Sarah Rolfe Prodan, *Michelangelo's Christian Mysticism: Spirituality, Poetry, and Art in Sixteenth-Century Italy*, Cambridge 2014; Ambra Moroncini, *Michelangelo's Poetry and Iconography in the Heart of the Reformation*, London 2019, as well as the magisterial critical and annotated edition of Michelangelo Buonarroti, *Rime e lettere*, eds. Antonio Corsaro and Giorgio Masi, Milan 2016.

[5] Massimiliano Rossi, *La poesia scolpita: Danese Cataneo nella Venezia del Cinquecento*, Lucca 1995. On Cattaneo's poetic activity, see also Rosa Maria Galleni Pellegrini, "Ut sculptura poësis": Danese Cattaneo "non meno ne lo scrivere che ne lo scolpire eccellente", in: Giovanna Baldissin Molli, Rosa Maria Galleni Pellegrini, Cristina Andrei, and Luisa Passeggia (eds.), *Danese Cattaneo da Colonnata, scultore, poeta, architetto: Collezione = Sculptor, Poet, Architect: Collection (Colonnata 1512–Padova 1572)*, Fosdinovo 2013, 1, pp. 320–345, and Tancredi Artico, Danese Cataneo, "felicissimo spirito" nelle carte tassiane. L'*Amor di Marfisa* e la *Gerusalemme liberata*, in: *Italianistica Debreceniensis* 23 (2017), pp. 8–20.

poetic production of Bronzino has received the lion's share of this renewed attention.[6] The first critical and annotated editions of the poems of Giorgio Vasari and Benvenuto Cellini, and some targeted contributions on the verse of sculptors and goldsmiths like Vincenzo Danti and Domenico Poggini, have subsequently shed light on how revealing these writings can be with regard to the intellectual contacts, cultural interests, and aesthetic ideals of their creators.[7] In the case of Cellini, it was also possible to understand that poetry was the author's most durable literary pursuit and the forge for crafting the main polemical and self-apologetic motifs

---

[6] This renewed interest came from literary scholars and art historians in almost equal measure. See for example the editions Agnolo Bronzino, *Rime in burla*, ed. Franca Petrucci Nardelli, Rome 1988, and Bronzino, *I Salterelli dell'Abbrucia sopra i Mattaccini di ser Fedocco*, ed. Carla Rossi Bellotto, Rome 1998, as well as the critical treatments of Deborah Parker, Towards a Reading of Bronzino's Burlesque Poetry, in: *Renaissance Quarterly* 50 (1997), pp. 1011–1044; eadem, *Bronzino: Renaissance Painter as Poet*, Cambridge 2000; eadem, The Poetry of Patronage: Bronzino and the Medici, in: *Renaissance Studies* 17 (2003), pp. 230–245; eadem, Bronzino and the Diligence of Art, in: *Artibus et historiae* 25, no. 49 (2004), pp. 161–174; Maurice Brock, *Bronzino*, trans. David Poole Radzinowicz and Christine Schultz-Touge, Paris 2002, pp. 7–17 and *passim*; Wolf-Dietrich Löhr, "E nuovi Omeri, e Plati": Painted Characters in Portraits by Andrea del Sarto and Bronzino, in: Thomas Frangenberg (ed.), *Poetry on Art: Renaissance to Romanticism*, Donington 2003, pp. 48–100; Giuliano Tanturli, Formazione d'un codice e d'un canzoniere: *Delle rime del Bronzino pittore libro primo*, in: *Studi di filologia italiana* 62 (2004), pp. 195–224; idem, Il Bronzino poeta e il ritratto di Laura Battiferri, in: Marco Ariani, Arnaldo Bruni, Anna Dolfi, and Andrea Gareffi (eds.), *La parola e l'immagine: studi in onore di Gianni Venturi*, Florence 2011, 1, pp. 319–332; Stephen J. Campbell, Counter Reformation Polemic and Mannerist Counter-Aesthetics: Bronzino's *Martyrdom of St. Lawrence* in San Lorenzo, in: *RES: Anthropology and Aesthetics* 46 (2004), pp. 98–119; idem, Bronzino, Aemulatio und die Liebe, in: Anna Kathrin Bleuler, Fabian Jonietz, Jan-Dirk Müller, and Ulrich Pfisterer (eds.), *Aemulatio: Kulturen des Wettstreits in Text und Bild (1450–1620)*, Berlin 2011, pp. 193–230; Stefania Pasti, La produzione letteraria, in: Claudio Strinati (ed.), *Bronzino*, Rome 2010, pp. 201–237; Massimiliano Rossi, "… Quella naturalità e fiorentinità (per dir così)." Bronzino: Lingua, carne e pittura, in: Carlo Falciani and Antonio Natali (eds.), *Bronzino: pittore e poeta alla corte dei Medici*, Florence 2010, pp. 177–193; Antonio Geremicca, *Agnolo Bronzino: 'la dotta penna al pennel dotto pari,'* Rome 2013; idem, "Damone" per "Crisero" e gli altri: Benedetto Varchi e gli artisti (prima e dopo l'Accademia Fiorentina), in: Carla Chiummo, Antonio Geremicca, and Patrizia Tosini (eds.), *Intrecci virtuosi. Letterati artisti e accademie nell'Italia Centrale tra Cinque e Seicento*, Rome 2017, pp. 11–26; idem, Inedite corrispondenze in versi tra Benedetto Varchi e Agnolo Bronzino, in: *Italique* 22 (2019), pp. 59–80; Stuart Lingo, Looking Askance: Agnolo Bronzino's *Martyrdom of San Lorenzo* between the Medici, Mercury and Machiavelli, in: *Rivista di letterature moderne e comparate* 68, no. 3 (2015), pp. 217–242; Carla Chiummo, Bronzino e l'Accademia Fiorentina, in: Jane E. Everson, Denis V. Reidy, and Lisa Sampson (eds.), *The Italian Academies 1525–1700: Networks of Culture, Innovation and Dissent*, Abingdon 2016, pp. 258–276; Carla Chiummo, Burlesque Connotations in the Pictorial Language in Bronzino's Poetry, in: *Renaissance and Reformation/Renaissance et Réforme* 40, no. 1 (2017), pp. 211–237; Sefy Hendler, *Un mostro grazioso e bello: Bronzino e l'universo burlesco del Nano Morgante*, Florence 2016. The new critical and annotated editions of the painter's lyrical verse and a selection of five burlesque compositions are also the subject of unpublished doctoral dissertations by Paulo Celi, *Delle rime del Bronzino pittore Libro primo*, PhD diss., Università di Pisa 2018, and Francesca Latini, *Edizione e commento di cinque capitoli in burla del Bronzino*, PhD diss., 2 vols., Università Europea di Roma 2015.

[7] Giorgio Vasari, *Poesie*, ed. Enrico Mattioda, Alessandria 2012, and Benvenuto Cellini, *Rime*, ed. Diletta Gamberini, Florence 2014. For the poetic works of Danti and Poggini, see Michael W. Cole and Diletta Gamberini, Vincenzo Danti's Deceits, in: *Renaissance Quarterly* 69 (2016), pp. 1296–1342, and Diletta Gamberini, A Bronze Manifesto of Petrarchism: Domenico Poggini's Portrait Medal of Benedetto Varchi, in: *I Tatti Studies in the Italian Renaissance* 19 (2016), pp. 359–383, with further references.

that run through his autobiography as much as his technical treatises and discourses on art.[8] Despite this relative blossoming of research into the verse of individual painters or sculptors, and short but invaluable studies that have reviewed the *status quaestionis* for sixteenth- and seventeenth-century Florence, there has still been no attempt at a more organic examination of the function that this type of writing held for those who primarily practiced the visual arts at that time.[9]

Still, the recognition of this gap does not in itself justify the need for such an attempt. As Guido Mazzoni observes in a crystalline analysis of the evolutionary trajectories of modern poetry, all reconstructions of prior stages of the history of literature tend to suffer "of fetishism: even in the most accurate studies […], the texts that the interpreter takes into consideration represent a very low percentage of the works composed in a certain cultural space and in a certain epoch."[10] The ambition to provide a more organic picture of a phenomenon that, in quantitative terms, involved few exponents of the Italian artistic scene of the early modern period would therefore ultimately be in service to an idle erudite curiosity if these authors' poetic output were not, as this book aims to demonstrate, emblematic of dynamics that transformed some basic structures of that cultural system. Another reason to undertake this endeavour is the need to overcome two interrelated limitations of the generally accepted approach to the poems of Italian Renaissance artists. These are errors of perspective that tend to project a modern conception of poetry onto the past and that conflate that literary form with what is now the lyric genre.[11]

---

[8] Along with the commentary of Cellini 2014 (as in fn. 7), relevant works include Gerarda Stimato, *Autoritratti letterari nella Firenze di Cosimo I: Bandinelli, Vasari, Cellini e Pontormo*, Bologna 2008, pp. 154–183; Giada Guassardo, Una nota sul tema del carcere nella *Vita* e nelle liriche di Benvenuto Cellini, in: *Rassegna europea di letteratura italiana* 48 (2016), pp. 91–109; Marcello Ciccuto, Il pregiudizio dell'alterità. Per Benvenuto Cellini biografo "in figura", in: Maria Pia Sacchi and Monica Visioli (eds.), *Scritti autobiografici di artisti tra Quattrocento e Cinquecento: seminari di letteratura artistica*, Pavia 2017, pp. 89–99, Antonio Corsaro, Dinamiche relazionali nella *Vita* di Benvenuto Cellini, ibid., pp. 101–119, and Giovanna Rizzarelli, Disegnare con le parole. La doppia creatività di Benvenuto Cellini, in: *Italique* 22 (2019), pp. 39–58.

[9] Two insightful assessments of the presence of poet-artists in the Florentine context are the essays by Massimiliano Rossi, L'artiste en tant que poète dans le milieu florentin, in: Elena Fumagalli and Massimiliano Rossi (eds.), *Florence au grand siècle entre peinture et littérature*, Cinisello Balsamo 2011, pp. 27–31, and idem, Le réseau des arts. Les artistes en tant que poètes face au portrait, in: Carlo Falciani (ed.), *Florence: Portraits à la cour des Médicis. Bronzino, Salviati, Pontormo*, Brussels 2015, pp. 149–155. The only broad-ranging monographic work on the poetry of artists in Renaissance Italy dates back to over a century ago, but it is compilatory and descriptive rather than critical in nature: see Ada Berti, *Artisti-poeti italiani dei secoli XV e XVI*, Florence 1907. In many passages, Berti's book closely follows the historical reconstruction that we read in Albertina Furno, *La vita e le rime di Angiolo Bronzino, studio*, Pistoia 1902, pp. 3–25, the first monograph devoted to Bronzino's literary activity. On a more personal note, the limits of the available research in the field and the heuristic possibilities inherent in a more organic approach to it became clear at the end of my monographic study of Cellini's poetry, which first led me to envision the present project.

[10] Guido Mazzoni, *Sulla poesia moderna*, Bologna 2005, p. 17 (my translation).

[11] For a sense of how widespread this mistaken assumption is in critical discussions of pre-modern poetry, see esp. Claudio Giunta, *Versi a un destinatario: saggio sulla poesia italiana del Medioevo*, Bologna 2002, pp. 16–30, and Mazzoni 2005 (as in fn. 10), pp. 36–42. In their analyses, both Giunta and Mazzoni build upon a set of ideas that Theodor Adorno first articulated in his *Rede über Lyrik und Gesellschaft* (1951), which underlined how the

First, the disinterest or scant consideration with which much academic literature continues to treat the poems of this kind of writers arises from the unspoken assumption that verse is the space of expression of an ego folded in on itself, intent on probing its own thoughts and most intimate feelings. The corollary of this axiom is the notion that such compositions cannot say anything meaningful about the professional practice and interests of their authors, and that if they do, they should be dismissed as alien to the authentic spirit of poetry. Telling, for example, are Bernd Roeck's silence on the poetic genres in his agile monograph on artists' writings in the early modern period, and the pages that Francis Ames-Lewis devotes to verse in his classic book on the intellectual life of early Renaissance practitioners of the arts of drawing.[12] In brief discussions of rhymed works like the *Cronaca* of Urbino painter Giovanni Santi (ca. 1478–1494), the father of Raphael who was himself not averse to occasionally penning a sonnet, or the *Antiquarie prospettiche romane* of the anonymous "Prospettivo Milanese Dipintore" (ca. 1500), the latter study lends support to those who had labeled these compositions as coarse and utterly unpoetic.[13] While noting that such writings can sometimes provide insights into the artistic life of the time, Ames-Lewis also seems to place their main draw elsewhere: he emphasizes that the verse of Renaissance artists reveals, above all, the authors' desire for the intellectual prestige traditionally accorded to poets.[14] The literary universe to which

modern idea of lyric poetry has little similarity to pre-modern examples of the genre. See esp. Theodor Adorno, *Notes to Literature, Volume 1*, ed. Rolf Tiedemann, trans. Shierry Weber Nicholsen, New York 1991, pp. 38–40: "The lyric work hopes to attain universality through unrestrained individuation […]. But the manifestations in earlier periods of the specifically lyric spirit familiar to us are only isolated flashes, just as backgrounds in older painting occasionally anticipate the idea of landscape painting. They do not establish it as a form. The great poets of the distant past […] whom literary history classifies as lyric poets are uncommonly far from our primary conception of the lyric. They lack the quality of immediacy […] which we are accustomed, rightly or not, to consider the criterion of the lyric and which we transcend only through rigorous education."

[12] Bernd Roeck, *Gelehrte Künstler: Maler, Bildhauer und Architekten der Renaissance über Kunst*, Berlin 2013, and Ames-Lewis 2000 (as in fn. 1), pp. 168–172.

[13] On the art historical relevance of Giovanni Santi's *Cronaca*, see the discussion by Kim E. Butler, La 'Cronaca rimata' di Giovanni Santi e Raffaello, in: Lorenza Mochi Onori (ed.), *Raffaello e Urbino: la formazione giovanile e i rapporti con la città natale*, Milan 2009, pp. 38–43; on the five surviving autograph sonnets by Raphael, their main literary models and linguistic features, see now Lucia Bertolini and Francesco P. Di Teodoro, "Al mio gran foco": Raffaello poeta tra passato prossimo, Petrarca e l'antico, in: Marzia Faietti and Matteo Lanfranconi (eds.), *Raffaello: 1520–1483*, Milan 2020, pp. 287–293, with further references. On the *Antiquarie* and their debated attribution to Bramante, see Giovanni Agosti and Dante Isella (eds.), *Antiquarie prospetiche romane*, Milan 2006², and the considerations of Massimo Giontella and Riccardo Fubini, L'uomo con il compasso e la sfera: note sulla recente edizione delle *Antiquarie prospetiche romane* attribuite a Bramante, in: *Archivio storico italiano* 164 (2006), pp. 325–334.

[14] Consider in particular Ames-Lewis 2000 (as in fn. 1), pp. 168–169: "Some Renaissance painters sought to exercise their inventive abilities by writing poetry themselves. They sought recognition as poets because, in spite of Alberti's defence of painting and Leonardo's arguments for the painter's affective superiority, throughout the early Renaissance poets were more highly regarded than painters in intellectual circles […]. Some early Renaissance artists themselves aspired to write poetry, although their early products should perhaps be described as 'verse' rather than 'poetry.'" According to Ames-Lewis, the only accomplished poetic compositions by early Renaissance artists are those penned by Raphael, Bramante, and the young Michelangelo. A more neutral evaluation of the poetry of early Renaissance artists, from Andrea Orcagna to Bramante and Raphael, is that of Christiane J. Hessler, *Zum Paragone: Malerei, Skulptur und Dichtung in der Rangstreitkultur des Quattrocento*,

those compositions belonged, however, was founded on an idea of poeticity very different from the one that took hold in the Romantic period. While modern poetry favors subjective, inward-looking forms geared toward a strictly individualistic, egocentric expression of self (what Adorno called the "unrestrained individuation" of lyric work), outward-looking forms referencing the external reality still played a vital role in the poetry of the Italian Renaissance.[15] Even at a time when Petrarch's *Canzoniere* held sway over the rules of writing in verse, the range of subjects that lent themselves to poetic treatment had remained far broader than the spectrum crystallized in that paradigm: it was therefore perfectly acceptable for poets of the age to choose content we would now surely relegate to the realm of prose.[16] As we will often see in the pages of this book, for those authors it was also perfectly acceptable to pen compositions expressing their roots in historical circumstances that to our eyes seem essentially unpoetic.

Second, the recent interest in the poems of prominent artists of the Italian Renaissance has shifted the modern bias toward a subjectivistic poetry on another plane. Often portraying an image of the isolated genius working within a cultural vacuum, studies on those authors have lost sight of the fact that verse writing was usually, at the time, anything but a monological practice. Especially since the mid-1500s, in conjunction with that expansion of Italian literary society that Carlo Dionisotti described so masterfully,[17] it was actually more of a dialogical and frequently even choral activity. That communicative dimension largely took the form of a conversation with a small or large circle of associates, aimed at reinforcing friendship or personal regard through mutual declarations of approval, solidarity, or shared ideals in domains such as political or aesthetic sensibility. In other cases it took the form of an author's attack on adversaries guilty of holding different opinions in those fields.[18] Because the vast majority

---

Berlin / Boston 2014, pp. 228–230. Rather than focusing on the supposedly unpoetic nature of these texts, Hessler emphasizes the extent to which these works reflect their authors' aspirations to be recognized as learned and universal artists.

[15] The fortune of these extroflected or outward looking forms of poetry dates back to the first centuries of Italian literature and represents the unifying thread of the broad-ranging study of Giunta 2002 (as in fn. 11) on the poetic traditions of medieval Italy. Compare also Mazzoni 2005 (as in fn. 10), p. 212: "L'egocentrismo della poesia moderna non ha equivalenti in nessun'altra forma letteraria, neppure nell'autobiografia posteriore a Rousseau […]: i poeti moderni di solito scrivono in uno stile distante dalla frase di grado zero, prestando poca attenzione all'aspetto reale del mondo che la voce descrive. Le opere in versi degli ultimi secoli sembrano incapaci di porre dei limiti all'io […]. L'immagine del mondo che la maggior parte delle poesie moderne rinvia al lettore è di tipo narcisistico." For Adorno's remarks, see *supra*, fn. 11.

[16] Consider, for instance, Giunta 2002 (as in fn. 11), p. 225, which discusses some medieval examples of "identità di funzione e conguaglio della poesia sulla prosa," and observes, with reference to the poems by Giovanni Dondi dall'Orologio (ca. 1330–1388): "Il messaggio può […] essere quello banale, privato, quotidiano, privo di qualsiasi valore e intenzione artistica che normalmente (vale a dire in un'altra età della poesia: quella presente, ad esempio) verrebbe giudicato incompatibile coi versi."

[17] See Carlo Dionisotti, La letteratura italiana nell'età del Concilio di Trento, in: idem, *Geografia e storia della letteratura italiana*, Turin 1971², pp. 227–254.

[18] On sociability as one of the most distinctive features of sixteenth-century Italian poetry, see especially Giulio Ferroni, *Poesia italiana del Cinquecento*, new ed., Milan 1999, pp. xi–xxi; Arnaldo Di Benedetto, Un'introduzione al petrarchismo cinquecentesco, in: *Italica* 83 (2006), pp. 170–215, pp. 179–180, as well as Brian Richardson, *Manuscript Culture in Renaissance Italy*, Cambridge 2009, pp. 95–137. Richardson stresses the centrality of this feature in connection with his analysis of manuscript cultures in Renaissance Italy, as this form of dissemination

of poet-artists of the Italian Renaissance participated fully in this process of socialization of poetry, a study aspiring to provide a more detailed reconstruction of their writing practices must stress the importance of the dialogic impetus that informed them.

Geographical and chronological scope of the book, and a brief prospect of the history of poet-artists in Renaissance Italy

While this book aims to sketch a more integrated picture of the poetic output of Italian Renaissance figures who were chiefly practitioners of the arts of drawing, it does not claim to be a thorough compendium of that corpus. The assumption, nonetheless, is that the works selected can indicate some of the main tendencies that defined a broader historical phenomenon. Steering such a choice has been a geographical and chronological principle of synecdoche, of focalization on a part as representative of the whole.

Geographically, the book focuses on Florence and does not touch on other scenes where individual poet-artists were active during the Renaissance, such as Urbino where Giovanni Santi worked, or Milan where Donato Bramante penned his sonnets.[19] It also excludes cities that during the same period nurtured small communities of verse-writing painters, sculptors, architects, and goldsmiths. One of the earliest such milieux seems to have been Bologna at the turn of the sixteenth century, where two local artists took part in a multilingual poetic sylloge that was published on the death of the poet Serafino Aquilano (1504): the University of Bologna law professor, scholar, antiquarian, and renowned goldsmith Tommaso Sclarici del Gambaro, and the not yet surely identified "Hercule depintore bolognese," whose compositions join those of an eminent sculptor and medalist then in the service of Isabella d'Este in Mantua, Gian Cristoforo Romano.[20] But the list of Bolognese poet-artists who were active at the time may also include the most acclaimed painter of that scene, Francesco Francia, who in Carlo Malvasia's *Felsina Pittrice* (1678) is credited with a sonnet celebrating the young Raphael as a model of painterly excellence.[21] Caution is however necessary because, as with

---

was typically associated with "dialogic" verse. Once again, this social dimension of poetic production found an antecedent in the medieval tradition, for which see Giunta 2002 (as in fn. 11), pp. 71–266.

[19] On Bramante as a poet, see Carlo Vecce's introduction to his edition of the artist's twenty-five preserved sonnets (Donato Bramante, *Sonetti e altri scritti*, ed. Carlo Vecce, Rome 1995), Luciano Patetta, *Bramante e la sua cerchia a Milano e in Lombardia: 1480–1500*, Milan 2001, pp. 77–81, as well as Dante Isella, *Lombardia stravagante: testi e studi dal Quattrocento al Seicento tra lettere e arti*, Turin 2005, pp. 27–37.

[20] These considerations are indebted to Giovanna Perini, Poems by Bolognese Painters from the Renaissance to the Late Baroque, in: Frangenberg 2003 (as in fn. 6), pp. 3–28. The focus of Perini's essay extends up to and including three Baroque Bolognese painters who also penned verse: namely, Lionello Spada, Giovanni Luigi Valesio, and Agostino Mitelli.

[21] The text of the sonnet *All'Eccellente Pictore Raffaello Sanxio, Zeusi del nostro secolo*, whose incipit runs *Non son Zeusi, né Apelle, e non son tale*, was first published in Carlo Cesare Malvasia, *Felsina pittrice, vite de' pittori bolognesi* […], Bologna 1678, 1, p. 46.

other poems that Malvasia ascribes to artists, the attribution remains otherwise unproven and therefore controversial in the academic community.[22]

Another geographical context that seems to have witnessed an early flourishing of poet-artists was Rome just before the traumatic sack of the city in 1527. Indirect evidence in this case derives from Benvenuto Cellini's autobiography, in which the author writes of belonging at that time to a "compagnia di pittori, scultori, orefici, li meglio che fussino in Roma," whose entertaining social gatherings would often incorporate music and poetry performances.[23] The group of artists (including personalities of the caliber of Giulio Romano, Giovan Francesco Penni, and Francesco Ubertini *alias* Bachiacca) would on such occasions improvise sonnets that were then inked on loose sheets of paper and read aloud by the other guests. Given the extent to which these compositions retained a strong link to oral performances and participated in a taste for poetic improvisation that in those decades operated across socio-cultural divides,[24] it comes however as no surprise that no written trace of such a production has come down to us.

In many of his letters, on the other hand, Pietro Aretino mentions with praise less extemporaneous poetry-writing practices among contemporary artists. The first of these references appear in his epistles of the late 1530s, but such indications become numerous for the 1540s and 1550s, and concern an array of names that are often little-known today but at the time were active on the Veneto scene. Along with extolling the poems of a first-rate artist like Danese Cataneo, Aretino compliments the poetry of the goldsmiths Alessandro Caravia, Paolo Crivelli, and Battista Baffo, the painter Gigio Artemio Giancarli from Rovigo, and the Florentine sculptor Paolo Geri, on occasions with the aim of encouraging these artists to pursue their interest in verse composition despite the criticisms they had received for it.[25]

---

[22] One such text is a programmatic sonnet purportedly by Agostino Carracci (incipit: *Chi farsi un buon pittor cerca, e desia*), which compiled a set of rules for achieving greatness in the art of painting: see ibid., p. 159. For a review of the modern critical debate on both the sonnet that Malvasia attributed to Francia and the one he ascribed to Agostino Carracci, see Perini 2003 (as in fn. 20), pp. 8–9.

[23] The detailed account of the gatherings of this group, whose founder was the Sienese sculptor Michelagnolo di Bernardino, can be read in Benvenuto Cellini, *La vita*, ed. Lorenzo Bellotto, Parma 1996, pp. 105–109 (1.30), p. 105 for the quote.

[24] On poetic improvisation in the first decades of the sixteenth century, see Luca Degl'Innocenti, Brian Richardson, and Chiara Sbordoni, eds., *Interactions between Orality and Writing in Early Modern Italian Culture*, London 2016, as well as Blake Wilson, *Singing to the Lyre in Renaissance Italy: Memory, Performance, and Oral Poetry*, Cambridge 2019, pp. 406–421.

[25] Relevant are the letters in which Aretino (Pietro Aretino, *Lettere sull'arte*, eds. Ettore Camesasca, Fidenzio Pertile, and Carlo Cordié, 4 vols., Milan 1957–1960, 1, pp. 76, 81, 206–207, 220–221, and 2, pp. 333–334) paid homage to the poetry of the goldsmiths Paolo Crivelli (whom he defined a "non mediocre poeta" in a letter of November 7, 1537, and praised for nourishing his intellect with "dolci frutti de la poesia" in a letter of July 21, 1542), Battista Baffo (November 16, 1537: "Io ho visto i vostri sonetti, e vi giuro che non fu mai maestro di zecca né orefice miglior poeta di voi"), and Alessandro Caravia (letters of March 12, 1542, and May 1550). He also praised the verse of Gigio Artemio from Rovigo, "poeta non men famoso che pittore valente" (letter to Graziano da Perugia of February 1546: see Aretino 1957–1960, 2, p. 151), of the Florentine sculptor Paolo Geri alias il Pilucca (in many exchanges spanning from 1545 to 1553), and of Danese Cataneo. On Aretino's recognition of the latter's poetic activity, see Rossi 1995 (as in fn. 5), *passim*. On the biography, artistic activity, and three long

The literary Accademia della Val di Blenio, created in Milan in 1560, also enlisted several poet-artists in prominent roles.[26] The founders and earliest officials of the institution, which was programmatically geared toward the composition of rustic poetry in a Lombard dialect, included for example the painter, engraver, sculptor in bronze, and rhymester Ambrogio Brambilla. In 1568 he was succeeded in the office of chancellor by the painter, poet and future art theorist Giovan Paolo Lomazzo, and at least one other practitioner of the arts and member of the academy, the architect Girolamo Maderno, was quite assiduous at writing verse. Bearing witness to these authors' poetic endeavors are some texts published in the *Rabisch* (1589), the collection of dialect poems by Lomazzo, who had already displayed his ambitions as an Italian language poet in the monumental edition of *Rime [...] ad imitatione de i Grotteschi* of 1587.[27] What's more, to validate his theory that almost every painter had some "spirito di poesia," in the *Trattato dell'arte della pittura* (1584) Lomazzo had mentioned the poetry writing of several artists who had worked in Milan in the preceding decades. His pantheon of the most acclaimed painter-poets of the Renaissance thus included Gaudenzio Ferrari and Bernardino Luini alongside Bramante, Leonardo (who made it onto the list because of the mistaken attribution of a composition by Antonio di Meglio and of other, unspecified "sonetti, che sono difficili a ritrovare"), Michelangelo, and Bronzino.[28] We do not know today whether the first two mentions

poemetti in dialect by Alessandro Caravia, today mostly known for being charged in a trial for heresy on the part of the Santo Uffizio (1557–1559), see now Enrica Benini Clementi, *Riforma religiosa e poesia popolare a Venezia nel Cinquecento: Alessandro Caravia*, Florence 2000. Aretino's encomia of the verse of contemporary poet-artists are grounded in his celebrations of universal talent. See, for instance, his letter to Diego Hurtado de Mendoza of January 1546 (Aretino 1957–1960, 2, pp. 140–141): "Ma, in quanto al giovare ai bei ingegni con lo essempio del vostro pellegrino ispirito, bisogna adorarvi conciosia che i cieli hanno infuso più virtù nel vostro solo intelletto che in mille degli altri insieme. Tal che non è scienza di studio immortale, né costume di nobiltá eroica, che non vi adorni il nome di lode e l'anima di gloria, per il che apparite signor in la splendidezza, gentiluomo in la creanza, prelato in la religione, cavaliero in la spada, poeta in la penna, filosofo in la cognizione, pittore nel giudicio, cortigiano in la pratica, commune persona in la universalità."

[26] An updated discussion on the place of artists within the Academy is offered by Barbara Tramelli, Artists and Knowledge in Sixteenth Century Milan: The Case of Lomazzo's Accademia de la Val di Blenio, in: *Fragmenta* 5 (2011), pp. 121–138. Many useful considerations of the institution's activity can also be found in Giulio Bora, Manuela Kahn-Rossi, and Francesco Porzio, eds., *Rabisch: il grottesco nell'arte del Cinquecento*, Milan 1998.

[27] For the former work, see Giovan Paolo Lomazzo, *Rabisch*, ed. Dante Isella, Turin 1993; for the latter collection, which includes the *Vita del auttore descritta da lui stesso in rime sciolte* and a second book largely devoted to the celebration of sixteenth-century artists, see Lomazzo, *Rime ad imitazion de i grotteschi usati da' pittori: con la vita del auttore descritta da lui stesso in rime sciolte*, ed. Alessandra Ruffino, Manziana 2006. A valuable introduction to Lomazzo's poetic activity is that of Edoardo Taddeo, I grilli poetici di un pittore: le 'Rime' di G. P. Lomazzo, in: *Il contesto* 3 (1997), pp. 140–181.

[28] Consider what the author writes in the second chapter of the text, with regard to the matter of pictorial compositions (Giovan Paolo Lomazzo, *Scritti sulle arti*, ed. Roberto Paolo Ciardi, 2 vols., Florence 1973–1975, 2, pp. 244–246): "E se pure in parte alcuna si vuol variare, si ha d'avvertire alla convenevoleza et anco all'accrescimento dell'effetto, ad imitazione de' poeti, a quali i pittori sono in molte parti simili, massime che così nel dipinger, come nel poetare, vi corre il furor di Apolline, e l'uno e l'altro ha per oggetto i fatti illustri e le lodi de gl'Eroi da rappresentare. Onde soleva dir alcuno che la poesia era una pittura parlante e la pittura era una poesia mutola. Anci pare, per non so quale conseguenza, che non possa essere pittore che insieme anco non habbia qualche spirito di poesia; e di rado s'è ritrovato pittore che abbia potuto cosa alcuna dipingere, che subito anco non sia stato indotto dal genio naturale a cantarla puramente in versi, ancora che per aventura non sapesse

were historically more accurate than the references to the phantasmatic da Vinci poems, but what matters most for our purposes is the acknowledgment of a Lombard tradition of artists accustomed to frequenting the muses of poetry like many of their Florentine colleagues.[29]

Chronologically, this book highlights a portion of the centuries-long historical trajectory of the Florence-based practioner of the arts who was also a poet. While it would eventually extend to prominent representatives of twentieth-century Italian culture, such as the painter and man of letters Ardengo Soffici,[30] this trajectory begins in a bit of a haze, for a lack of secure documentary evidence makes it difficult to distinguish between real data and the fabulized edification of the myth of the *artifex* blessed from on high with a multitude of talents. It is at any rate significant that the earliest Florentine artist with a poem to his name is the man who, in Renaissance historiographical tradition, was credited with having inaugurated the modern rebirth of the arts: three fifteenth-century manuscript collections of poetry are the testimonies that Giotto would have penned a canzone against that glorification of poverty that took root in the spiritual-leaning circles of Franciscanism of his time.[31] Though the copyists who assembled two of these codices were probably humanists, the news of Giotto's supposed poetic activity does not seem to have circulated widely in the early modern period.[32] In fact, the critical rediscovery of the *Chançon Giotti pintori de Florentia* did not occur until the nineteenth century, stirring a debate over its authorship that in recent years has tended to accept the paternity its title suggests.[33]

---

leggere né scrivere. Sì come tra gli altri fa fede quello enimma de i dadi di Bramante […]. Così si trova che il dotto Leonardo da Vinci soleva molte volte poetare, e fra gli altri suoi sonetti, che sono difficili a ritrovare, si legge quello: *Chi non può quel che vuol, quel può voglia* […]. Se ne leggono anco de gli altri gran pittori gimnosofisti [i. e. 'savvy', 'learned'], come furono il Buonarotti, il Ferrari, il Lovino et il bernesco Bronzino […]." On Lomazzo's attribution of Antonio di Meglio's sonnet to Leonardo, see here chapter 1, fn. 82. This interest in the poetry of painters also led Lomazzo to mention, with praise, the written "capitoli, et stanze amorose" by Raphael (Lomazzo, *Idea del tempio della pittura*, Milan 1590, p. 58).

[29] It is worth noting the apparent absence of Southern cities among the Italian centers that witnessed a flourishing of poetic vocations among visual artists. This absence is all the more relevant if we consider that the most prominent poet-painter of Seicento Italy, Salvator Rosa, was of Neapolitan origin, although his famous verse *Satire* mostly date to the artist's sojourn in Florence. On Rosa's literary activity, see especially Oreste Ferrari and Ferruccio Ulivi, *Salvator Rosa, pittore e poeta nel centenario della morte (1615–1673)*, Rome 1975; Floriana Conte, *Tra Napoli e Milano: viaggi di artisti nell'Italia del Seicento. Volume 2: Salvator Rosa*, Florence 2014, and Daniela De Liso, *Salvator Rosa tra pennelli e versi*, Florence 2018.

[30] On Soffici as a poet, see, among others, Antonio Pietropaoli, *Poesie in libertà: Govoni, Palazzeschi, Soffici*, Naples 2003.

[31] For a detailed discussion of the manuscript transmission of the poem, a critical edition of its text, and a review of the scholarly literature available on it, see Stefano Ugo Baldassarri, Alcuni appunti su Giotto e la poesia, in: *Lettere italiane* 49 (1997), pp. 373–391.

[32] The only notable exception to this general silence seems to be a mention of Giotto's poetic activity in Giovan Battista Armenini's *De' veri precetti della pittura* (1586). See Armenini, *De' veri precetti della pittura*, ed. Marina Gorreri, Turin 1988, p. 237: "Ma quel pittore che fu quasi un miracolo, che accompagnò con l'architettura e con l'istorie la pittura, la musica e la poesia fu primieramente Gi‹o›tto fiorentino, dal quale si vide uscire la prima luce da quelle orrende tenebre in che sepolta era."

[33] Baldassarri argues for the reliability of the poem's attribution (see Baldassarri 1997 [as in fn. 31], pp. 387–389), as do two of the few other modern studies of the composition: Marcello Ciccuto, Un'antica canzone di Giotto e

Starting with the *Libro di Antonio Billi* (ca. 1506–1530), on the other hand, there are several Renaissance-era mentions of poetry by the painter, sculptor, and architect Andrea di Cione, better known as Orcagna.[34] That source attributed to the versatile fourteenth-century artist a sonnet sequence which modern scholarship has usually identified as twenty-six "Sonetti delorcagnolo" that have survived in manuscript form – some of them of great literary interest as they are among the earliest examples of the "alla burchia" genre, the comic manner of poetry that would become famous with Domenico di Giovanni alias "Il Burchiello."[35] Yet the attribution of the poems is once again controversial, since several scholars have supported the theory that their author, "Orcagnolo," was not Andrea di Cione but rather his grandson, Mariotto di Nardo.[36] This possibility would in any case point to another early Florentine example of poet-artist, as Mariotto di Nardo was chiefly active as a painter.[37]

Critical debate over how reliable the documentary evidence truly is has also extended to Antonio Manetti's account that Filippo Brunelleschi wrote poems as a form of *ad hominem* attack.[38] The most in-depth study of three sonnets that various manuscripts of poetry collections

i pittori di Boccaccio. Nascita dell'identità artistica, in: *Intersezioni* 16 (1996), pp. 403–416, and Michael Viktor Schwarz and Pia Theis, *Giottus Pictor*, 2 vols., Vienna 2004, 1, pp. 63–69.

[34] See Antonio Billi, *Il libro di Antonio Billi*, ed. Fabio Benedettucci, Anzio 1991, p. 72, for which Orcagna "dilettossi di comporre, e ancora si truova de' sua sonetti." Starting from the first edition of the *Vite* (1550), Vasari drew on this source to ascribe familiarity with poetic composition to Andrea di Cione. For a discussion of the passage, see below, chapter 1, n. 80.

[35] For the most recent and philologically thorough assessment of the tradition of the poems, see Fabio Carboni, L'Orcagna e il Frusta, in: *Cultura neolatina* 69 (2009), pp. 111–165, which concludes that the author of the texts was indeed Andrea di Cione. Francesco Trucchi, ed., *Poesie Italiane inedite di dugento autori: dall'origine della lingua infino al secolo decimo-settimo*, 4 vols., Prato 1846, 2, p. 24; Antonio Lanza, *Polemiche e berte letterarie nella Firenze del primo Rinascimento (1375–1449)*, Rome 1989², pp. 337 and pp. 365–366; Paolo Orvieto and Lucia Brestolini, *La poesia comico-realistica: dalle origini al Cinquecento*, Rome 2000, p. 189, and Gert Kreytenberg, *Orcagna, Andrea di Cione: Ein universeller Künstler der Gotik in Florenz*, Mainz 2000, pp. 13–14, are of the same opinion.

[36] Among the studies that uphold this thesis are Vittorio Rossi, *Il Quattrocento*, rev. ed., Milan 1938, p. 265; Lewis Hall Gordon, Burchiello Inedito (A Propos of M. Messina: Domenico Di Giovanni Detto Il Burchiello. Sonetti Inediti. Firenze, Olschki, 1952), in: *Italica* 33 (1956), pp. 128–129; Francesco Bausi, Orcagna o Burchiello? (Sul sonetto 'Molti poeti han già descritto amore'), in: *Interpres* (1993), pp. 275–293, p. 277, and Mauro Cursietti, Alle radici della poesia burchiellesca: l'Orcagna pittore e lo Za buffone, in: *La parola del testo* 6 (2002), pp. 109–131.

[37] On Mariotto di Nardo as a painter, see most recently Dillian Gordon, Two Newly Identified Panels from Mariotto Di Nardo's Altarpiece for the Da Filicaia Chapel in S. Maria Degli Angeli, Florence, in: *The Burlington Magazine* 155.1318 (2013), pp. 25–28, and Valentina Baffi and Giacomo Guazzini, *Due pittori tardogotici fiorentini per Pistoia: Mariotto di Nardo e Rossello di Jacopo Franchi*, Pistoia 2015, with further references.

[38] Manetti mentioned Brunelleschi's use of the sonnet as a means of conducting diatribes in two passages of his biography of the artist. In the first, he was reconstructing the origins of an enmity between the architect and Donatello, on the occasion of the completion of the latter's sculptural works for Brunelleschi's Old Sacristy in the Florentine Basilica of San Lorenzo. See Antonio Manetti, *Vita di Filippo Brunelleschi*, Milan 1976, p. 110: "Le quali cose sue della sagrestia […] non ebbono mai la grazia di Filippo. Il che veggendo ed intendendo Donato, furono cagione di grande indegnazione verso Filippo; e detraeva Donato alla fama ed all'opra di Filippo quant'e' poteva, essendo sollevato da qualcuno, ché era un poco leggieri; ma Filippo se ne ghignava e faceva poca stima di sue parole. Pure, […] perseverando Donato nelle sue prosunzioni, e per purgarsi Filippo pe' tempi, che le porticciuole de' macigni che hanno per usci e bronzi non fussino sue, né nulla che fussi in quelle facciuole delle porticciuole tra pilastro e pilastro, dalla cappella alle mura de' canti, costrinse Filippo a fare certi sonetti, che an-

place under the architect's name gives however credit to his biographer,[39] thus reinforcing the theory that the creator of Florence Cathedral's dome did not disdain to hurl intellectual and professional invective through verse. Also worth noting is the fact that one of these compositions makes deliberate reference to the stylistic mastery of Orcagna,[40] as if building a specific line of fealty between Florentine poet-artists of different generations.

After these sporadic and at times dubious examples from the fourteenth and fifteenth centuries, the special local fortune of the visual artist who penned verse would not be established until the mid-Cinquecento. This book will focus on the unprecedented flourishing of poetic vocations among artists working in Florence during the fifty years from Cosimo I de' Medici's ascent to power as Duke of the city (1537) until the death of his son Grand Duke Francesco I (1587), but several studies have now clarified that poet-artists continued to thrive in the capital of the Tuscan grand duchy during the Baroque era: the painters Andrea Boscoli, Cristofano Allori, Andrea Commodi, Giovanni da San Giovanni, Francesco Furini, Baccio del Bianco, Sebastiano Mazzoni, and Lorenzo Lippi; the sculptors Giovanni Angelo Lottini and Agostino Ubaldini; and the engineer and architect Cosimo Lotti account for a corpus of verse that varies in terms of quality, quantity, and literary ambition but is solid evidence of the importance that poetry writing had assumed for many seventeenth-century Florentine artists. Having dispensed with the composition of prose that was typical of many of their colleagues from earlier generations, the literary activism of these authors was at this point limited almost exclusively to the genre of burlesque verse.[41] It is even possible that the high standing their comic verse

---

cora se ne truova qualcuno, che lo purgano di tutto." In the second passage, the author related that Brunelleschi similarly responded to the ongoing criticism of a detractor regarding his works for the Opera of Santa Maria del Fiore (ibid., p. 114): "E essendo Filippo ragguagliato di queste cose, e provatosi di farlo stare cheto per più modi, e non gli giovando nulla, e' gli fece un sonetto, ch'io udi' già, e non l'ho potuto ritrovare, el quale costui tenne a mente non tanto quant'e' visse Filippo, ma quanto visse lui medesimo." On the art historical relevance of the first passage, see Ulrich Pfisterer, *Donatello und die Entdeckung der Stile 1430–1445*, Munich 2002, p. 284.

[39] See Giuliano Tanturli's preface to Filippo Brunelleschi, *Sonetti di Filippo Brunelleschi*, eds. Domenico De Robertis and Giuliano Tanturli, Florence 1977, pp. 5–19, with a review of the previous literature on the poems and of the erroneous attributions that have sometimes dogged studies on the topic. For instance, in his monograph on Brunelleschi, Eugenio Battisti (*Filippo Brunelleschi: l'opera completa*, Milan 1976, p. 324) had expressed doubts on the attribution of the sonnets to the architect.

[40] See the *Sonetto d'uno che contraffà l'Orcagno*, in Brunelleschi 1977 (as in fn. 39), p. 23.

[41] On the poetic output of these artists, see esp. Nadia Bastogi, *Andrea Boscoli*, Florence 2008, pp. 367–373; Claudio Pizzorusso, *Ricerche su Cristofano Allori*, Florence 1982, pp. 93–98; idem, *A Boboli e altrove: sculture e scultori fiorentini del Seicento*, Florence 1989, pp. 63–71 and 125–185 (on Agostino Ubaldini); Igino Baffoni, *Il conte Giovannandrea Commodi pittore e poeta fiorentino (1560–1638)*, Gubbio 1955², pp. 12–17; Guia Fantuzzi, Giovanni da San Giovanni e il cinismo, in: *Artista* (2003), pp. 130–149, p. 149; Morten Steen Hansen, Butchering the Bull of St. Luke: Unpublished Writings by and about the Painter-Poet Giovanni Da San Giovanni, in: *Analecta Romana Instituti Danici* 40/41 (2016), pp. 63–89 (the latter article also with reference to manuscript sources on Baccio del Bianco and Cosimo Lotti's poetry); idem, "Pro bono malum": Francesco Furini, Ludovico Ariosto, and the Verso of Painting, in: *The Art Bulletin* 99 no. 3 (2017), pp. 62–92, pp. 82–83; Massimiliano Rossi, Furini poeta and Testi editi e inediti di Francesco Furini, in: Mina Gregori and Rodolfo Maffeis (eds.), *Un'altra bellezza: Francesco Furini*, Florence 2007, pp. 107–119 and pp. 295–306; idem, Il tempo ritrovato di Sebastiano Mazzoni, in: *Paragone / Arte* 51 (2001), pp. 64–78; Eva Struhal, *La semplice imitazione del naturale: Lorenzo Lippi's Poetics of Naturalism in Seventeenth-Century Florence*, PhD diss., John Hopkins University 2007; eadem,

enjoyed among contemporary local intellectuals not only strengthened the biographical topos of the quirky artist, for instance in Filippo Baldinucci's *Notizie de' professori del disegno*,[42] but also encouraged the fabrication of textual forgeries. This might be the case for the mock-heroic poem *La guerra dei topi e dei ranocchi*, an Italian translation in octaves of the pseudo-Homeric *Batracomyomachia*, originally published in 1788 under Andrea del Sarto's name and with a note that the text was first recited in 1519 before the Compagnia del Paiuolo, the Florentine *brigata* that was founded by the sculptor Giovan Francesco Rustici and was devoted to organizing festive convivial events.[43] Under close scrutiny, however, the poem seems to reveal the markings of one of the many seventeenth-century literary hoaxes penned by the polymath Francesco Redi.[44]

Nature of the sources; specifics and relevance of the cultural context under consideration

When not linked to oral performances, the poetic compositions of early modern Italian artists typically circulated in manuscript form and seldom saw the press during that age. Far from necessarily indicating a disengaged approach to writing, this appears to be the consequence of these authors' predilection for the kind of exchange, occasional, burlesque or licentious poems that at the time were more often passed around through scribal dissemination.[45] As Massimiliano Rossi has observed, this would at any rate suggest the need, in future studies of this kind of literary output, to conduct a census of the many manuscript texts that surely lie unprobed in the collections of Italian libraries.[46]

Reading with *acutezza*: Lorenzo Lippi's Literary Culture, in: Damm, Thimann, and Zittel 2013 (as in fn. 1), pp. 105–127; Alessandro Filippo Piermei, *Memorabilium sacri ordinis Servorum B. M. V. breviarium [...]*, Rome 1934, 4, pp. 226–230 (on Giovanni Angelo Lottini). The greater part of this list was first compiled by Rossi 2007, which emphasizes how Giovanni da San Giovanni, Furini himself, Baccio del Bianco, Sebastiano Mazzoni, Cosimo Lotti, and Lorenzo Lippi embody "una vera e propria poetica neoburlesca." The only true exception to this trend of comical poetry among early seventeenth-century Florentine artists is the Servite friar and religious dramatist Lottini, a former pupil of the sculptor, friar, and poet Giovann'Angelo Montorsoli, as his extensive manuscript poetic output (over 300 compositions, including sonnets, madrigals, and *canzoni*) consists entirely of moral and devotional texts.

[42] For the connection that Baldinucci established between the artists' active engagement with comic poetry and the topical motif of the *bizzarria* long associated with artistic professions, see Rossi 2007 (as in fn. 41), p. 107.

[43] On the Compagnia del Paiuolo, see esp. Tommaso Mozzati, *Giovanfrancesco Rustici: le Compagnie del Paiuolo e della Cazzuola. Arte, letteratura, festa nell'età della Maniera*, Florence 2008.

[44] Such is the thesis of Gabriele Bucchi, *La Guerra de' topi e de' ranocchi* attribuita ad Andrea del Sarto: un falso di Francesco Redi?, in: *Filologia italiana* 4 (2007), pp. 1–46, which is based on the presence of many linguistic and historical anachronisms in Andrea del Sarto's alleged text. After a revision of the long scholarly debate on the poem's attribution, Sanne Wellen, *La guerra de' topi e de' ranocchi*, Attributed to Andrea del Sarto: Considerations on the Poem's Authorship, the Compagnia del Paiuolo, and Vasari, in: *I Tatti Studies in the Italian Renaissance* 12 (2009), pp. 181–232, maintains on the contrary that the *Guerra* has probably come down to us in the form of an eighteenth-century revision of a composition originally by Andrea del Sarto.

[45] For a discussion of how these were the poetic genres most often circulated in manuscript form, see Richardson 2009 (as in fn. 18), pp. 95–137.

[46] Rossi 1995 (as in fn. 5), p. 7.

Introduction: The Artist as a Poet

Starting from just such an exploration that has uncovered a wealth of relevant material, and from a careful rethinking of other, often little-known sources, this book is therefore focused on one segment of the longer, more geographically diverse history of the poetry of artists who were active in Renaissance Italy. The decision to concentrate on the Florentine milieu in the mid and late decades of the sixteenth century was, however, not arbitrary. The Florence of Cosimo I and Francesco I de' Medici is a uniquely suited setting to casting light on the role that poetic writing held in the intellectual life of such authors, for this was the early modern milieu with the most widespread tendency for painters, sculptors, architects, and goldsmiths to use writing as a means of self-fashioning and a space for theoretical, historical, or didactic reflection on the practice of art.[47] In the domain of prose, these writers produced some of the works that have most shaped our understanding of the period's artistic culture: Giorgio Vasari's *Vite* and *Ragionamenti*; Benvenuto Cellini's autobiography, his *Trattati dell'oreficeria e della scultura*, and his discourses on art; Jacopo Pontormo's so-called *Diario*; Vincenzo Danti's *Trattato delle perfette proporzioni*; Alessandro Allori's *Ragionamenti delle regole del disegno* and Bartolomeo Ammannati's letter to the members of the Accademia del Disegno are the most conspicuous and influential fruits of these artists' extraordinary commitment to the pen.[48] That most of these authors, along with many other important names from the Florentine art scene of the time, also composed poetry gives us the chance to observe from a new perspective how their primary professional interests informed their writings.

---

[47] See, among others, the considerations of Joanna Woods-Marsden, Introduction: Collective Identity/Individual Identity, in: Mary Rogers (ed.), *Fashioning Identities in Renaissance Art*, Aldershot 2000, pp. 1–15, p. 5, which connect the relative paucity of visual self-portraits by Florentine artists of that milieu to their extensive use of literary media: "Exceptionally for the culture, all these Florentine artists [Bandinelli, Pontormo, Bronzino, Vasari, Cellini, and Allori] wrote something, most of them for publication. To say that they privileged the word is an understatement. Bandinelli, for instance, declared that his real passion was literary, not artistic, creation: 'I wish to immortalize my name with my pen, this being a truly congenial and liberale pursuit.' His enemy Cellini did precisely that by producing no visual self-likeness, not even a medal, to place beside his incomparable literary self-representation. Such cultural values […] were a key determinant underlying the veritable explosion of artistic biography, autobiography and autobiographical treatises in Florence in the 1550s and 1560s." In their introduction to Buonarroti's poems (Michelangelo 2016 [as in fn. 4], p. VII), Antonio Corsaro and Giorgio Masi similarly emphasize how mid-sixteenth-century Florence witnessed an extraordinary "assembramento di pittori e scultori conterranei che compongono in un breve torno d'anni un buon numero di versi e di prose" and how this concentration of artist-writers represents an unusual phenomenon in the history of Italian literature.

[48] Out of caution, I am excluding Baccio Bandinelli's so-called *Memoriale*, which Louis Alexander Waldman first argued to be an early seventeenth-century forgery by the artist's grandson, Baccio Bandinelli il Giovane (see Louis Alexander Waldman, *Baccio Bandinelli and Art at the Medici Court: A Corpus of Early Modern Sources*, Philadelphia 2004, pp. X–XII.) While Waldman's thesis is grounded in codicological and archival evidence, a documentary discovery has recently been made that suggests that we should question some of his conclusions about the late fabrication of the *Memoriale*. In a forthcoming contribution, Carlo Alberto Girotto (written communication) discusses a previously unknown text by Anton Francesco Doni, a distant relative of Baccio Bandinelli and one of the artist's few fervent supporters in the Italian literary scene of the age, which contains *in nuce* some of the contents that we read in the *Memoriale*. According to Girotto, it is plausible that Bandinelli (who might have played a role in the ideation of the text) preserved the document, which must have remained in the family's archives after Baccio's death. Baccio il Giovane probably only recovered the source and used it as the basis for his rewriting.

In the context of their broad-ranging devotion to the written word, what fostered so much enthusiasm for verse composition among these artists was the convergence of various lines of development of the Medicean cultural field. First of all, Florence was certainly one of the major epicenters of the opening of Italian literary society that reached its apex during the years of the Council of Trent (1545–1563), mostly affecting categories of writers such as women and, to our point, practitioners of the arts of drawing.[49] As Dionisotti first reconstructed, this phenomenon was closely entwined with the simultaneous rise of an increasingly resourceful publishing industry intent on conquering new shares of the market.[50] We can imagine, then, that the proliferation of printed materials designed to make poetic composition an accessible technique to ever larger swathes of the population (rhyming dictionaries, glossaries, guides to meter, etc.) might have provided even those artists who were a bit lacking in literary education with the rudiments necessary to turn out a few sonnets, satisfying what had become nearly a must for those who strove to see their intellectual stature socially recognized.[51] Another trend that seems to have nurtured the spread of the poetry-writing painter or sculptor was the imitation of illustrious ancient paradigms. In the *Naturalis Historia*, for instance, Pliny the Elder referred to the poems with which artists like Zeuxis, Apollodorus, and Parrhasius supposedly glorified their own art or criticized that of their rivals.[52] As we will see, some textual clues offer reason to suspect that many sixteenth-century Florentine artists were familiar with these anecdotes and even took them as a model for their own self-justificatory or argumentative use of the poetic medium.

While these two factors exherted an influence that went beyond Medici society, other, more specifically local aspects helped create a multitude of versifiers among Florentine practitioners of the arts of drawing.[53] Above all was the intensification of those tight exchanges between art-

---

[49] Dionisotti 1971 (as in fn. 17), p. 243, and see also Stefano Carrai, Italian Poetry of the Renaissance: Recent Studies and New Perspectives, in: *I Tatti Studies in the Italian Renaissance* 17 (2014), pp. 207–215, p. 212.

[50] Dionisotti 1971 (as in fn. 17), pp. 244–246.

[51] Compare the following remarks by the same scholar (Carlo Dionisotti, Leonardo uomo di lettere, in: *Italia Medioevale e Umanistica* 5 [1962], pp. 183–216, p. 189): "Il Vasari scriveva quando letteratura e arti belle, dipingere e far versi, erano diventate abilità facilmente cumulabili, di che egli stesso era esempio, e quando il pieno trionfo della poesia italiana cinquecentesca faceva sì che un'abilità poetica fosse fra le decorazioni ambite da ogni persona d'ingegno, nonché di genio." For the commercial fortune of editorial instruments such as the *rimari* in Cinquecento Italy, see esp. Giovanni Presa and Alessandra Uboldi, *I rimari italiani*, Milan 1974, and Amedeo Quondam, *Il naso di Laura: lingua e poesia lirica nella tradizione del Classicismo*, Modena 1991, pp. 123–150. For a discussion of the relevance that such books could have had in the literary instruction of artists, see Cole and Gamberini 2016 (as in fn. 7), pp. 1318–1323.

[52] For an account of Pliny's anecdotes about short poetic compositions by ancient artists, see here, ch. 3, fn. 408 and 409.

[53] My use of the expression "arts of drawing" and the deriving identification of the four main categories of practitioners considered in this book (painters, sculptors, architects, and goldsmiths) refer to a classification that was typical of the Florentine artistic tradition up to the foundation of the Accademia del Disegno (1563). As Marco Collareta has demonstrated (see, for instance, his essay Benvenuto Cellini ed il destino dell'oreficeria, in: Alessandro Nova and Anna Schreurs [eds.], *Benvenuto Cellini. Kunst und Kunsttheorie im 16. Jahrhundert*, Cologne 2003, pp. 161–169), the institution's policy marked the demotion of goldsmithery to the rank of artisanal activity, following Giorgio Vasari's evolving ideas on the subject. The same scholar has shown that several

ists and literati that had distinguished the city's cultural scene since at least the previous century.[54] Decisive in this sense was the fact that many painters and sculptors became members of the local literary academy over the period spanning from its founding in 1541 until its radical institutional reform in 1547, side by side with all the leading names of the Medicean intelligentsia. During those years the Accademia Fiorentina seems to have fostered the reinforcement of a "trading zone," in the meaning that the historian Pamela Long has given to the notion. In other words, the institution greatly intensified the rate of communication and circulation of different abilities between people with a traditional university education and those who had mostly learned their craft in workshops.[55] Though not devoid of conflict, this interchange would have been equally fruitful for both such groups: just like many artists fine-tuned their writing skills by interacting with the Academy's men of letters, the latter came out of such exchanges with a better-informed interest in the visual arts, and perhaps a heightened inclination to dabble in drawing themselves. Finally, the way many Florentine artists worshiped Michelangelo seems to have sparked a widespread desire to emulate his engagement with poetry.[56]

Purpose and structure of the book

Central to my research has been the concern to understand how the practice of art shaped the poetic voices of painters, sculptors, architects and goldsmiths, distinguishing them from within the proliferation of verse-writing that occurred in late Renaissance Italy. In this regard, my work builds upon an argument set forth by the literary scholar Christian Bec, who identified in a high degree of meta-professional reflectivity the most defining feature of the writings of fifteenth- and sixteenth-century Italian artists.[57] This book thus breaks new ground by sorting out the ways in which these practitioners of the arts exerted their agency on the poetic

---

Florentine artists, with Benvenuto Cellini in first place, voiced their opposition to this demotion and continued to hold goldsmithery firmly among the arts of drawing.

[54] On the peculiar degree of interconnection that characterized the worlds of visual artists and literati in Quattrocento Florence, see, among others, Dionisotti 1962 (as in fn. 51), p. 201; Gene A. Brucker, *Renaissance Florence*, New York 1969, pp. 215–222; Giuliano Tanturli, Rapporti del Brunelleschi con gli ambienti letterari fiorentini, in: Franco Borsi, Arnaldo Bruschi, Guglielmo De Angelis d'Ossat, and Giovanni Spadolini (eds.), *Filippo Brunelleschi: la sua opera e il suo tempo*, Florence 1980, 1, pp. 125–144.

[55] On the concept of "trading zones" and its relevance for the study of the culture of sixteenth-century Italy, see Pamela O. Long, Multi-Tasking 'Pre-Professional' Architect/Engineers and other Bricolagic Practitioners as Key Figures in the Elision of Boundaries between Practice and Learning in Sixteenth-Century Europe: Some Roman Examples, in: Matteo Valleriani (ed.), *The Structures of Practical Knowledge*, Cham 2017, pp. 223–246, with further references.

[56] For a discussion of the ramifications of these last factors, see chapters 1 and 2.

[57] See Christian Bec, Artisti scriventi e artisti scrittori in Italia (secondo Trecento – primo Novecento), in: Antonio Franceschetti (ed.), *Letteratura italiana e arti figurative: Atti del XII Convegno dell'Associazione internazionale per gli studi di lingua e letteratura italiana (Toronto, Hamilton, Montreal, 6–10 maggio 1985)*, Florence 1988, 1, pp. 81–100, p. 87. Compare, in particular, his observations that writing was never, for these authors, "un atto gratuito […], un piacevole svago," nor was it the fruit of an elementary desire for self-memorialization, since these practitioners of the visual arts were generally using the written word as a site in which "riflettere

medium – adapting, transforming, and appropriating it in order to tackle issues that were central to these authors' chief activities. Drawing on the critical acquisition that Italian poetry was at that time mainly conceived as an interpersonal pursuit, the study also gives due emphasis to the social dimension that was embedded in these writers' compositions. The reconstruction of the relational framework and discursive communities within which their verse originated will result, it is hoped, in a more fine-grained picture of how context-specific cultural debates, patterns of power, and lines of artistic evolution informed such a literary output.

Aiming to shed light on the intersections of artistic and poetic practices in the milieu at issue, the book tackles afresh a set of crucial yet previously unexplored questions: what does the poetry that these artists penned reveal about their key intellectual reference models and interlocutors? What about their professional relations and patronage networks? Each chapter addresses one salient aspect of this nexus of problems, unraveling its implications at both the literary and art-historical levels. Close textual analyses of these writers' verse compositions represent the foundational building blocks of the monograph's critical discourse and the unifying thread running through its four sections, while the appendix that closes the volume provides the edition of the texts under consideration.[58]

The first chapter considers the extent to which Medicean artists engaged in verse-writing to fashion for themselves intellectual personae in the image of Michelangelo, the most revered poet-artist of the Renaissance, as well as to participate in the heated contemporary debates on the artistic imitation of that paradigm. This section of the book is grounded in the analysis of the poems that these writers dedicated to their "divine" colleague, but also of a variety of intermedial sources (e. g. paintings, drawings, written testimonies by Florentine literati, etc.). Methods of analysis that have already proven fruitful for the study of other painters and sculptors from early modern Italy will help lay bare how an imitative stance towards the towering model of Michelangelo, who remained voluntarily absent from Florence over the final three decades of his life (1534–1564), shaped these authors' identity-construction both as artists and as writers. The inquiry will chiefly rely on scholarly works that have elucidated how the desire of several sixteenth-century painters and sculptors to outwardly project a Michelangelesque image was predicated on ideals discussed in earlier Renaissance controversies on literary *imitatio*, which also provided the conceptual foundations for early-modern disputes over artistic imitation.

---

sulla funzione ed il significato dell'arte e dell'artista," as well as "definire i loro rapporti nei confronti degli altri intellettuali e […] situarsi in seno ad una società urbana o cortigiana."

[58] Only when necessary for the argument will excerpts from longer artists' texts be quoted in the body of the chapters. This is particularly true for Bronzino's burlesque *capitoli*: since these compositions typically run for hundreds of lines, I have chosen to quote only those passages that were most relevant to my reasoning. When quoting directly from sixteenth-century manuscript or printed sources, the following criteria have been adopted: abbreviations have been expanded without using round brackets; *j* has been rendered as *i*, *ſ* as *s*, and *&* as *et* (which would be read as *ed* before a word beginning with a vowel, or *e* before a word beginning with a consonant); *u* and *v* have been separated; word divisions have been modernized and punctuation has been rationalized in order to clarify the syntactical structure of the sentences. Apostrophes, accents, quotation marks and capital letters all follow modern usage; accents have also been used to distinguish the voices of the verb *avere* (e. g. *ò*, *ài* etc.) when the writer did not use the etymological *h*.

Introduction: The Artist as a Poet

The second chapter concentrates on the compositions that exponents of the Florentine art scene exchanged with one of the most distinguished members of the local intellectual elite – the philosopher, man of letters, and art theorist Benedetto Varchi. As is suggested by his soliciting the written responses of eight artists to his momentous 1547 academic enquiry on the relative merits of painting and sculpture, Varchi advocated for the participation of such professionals in the literary arena. This section of the monograph will reveal that it was especially in the domain of poetry that he endorsed these authors' engagement with writing, to the point that his verse of correspondence is by far the richest testimony of the diffusion among them of poetic practices. From these exchanges it will emerge that painters, sculptors, architects, and goldsmiths found in the humanist not only an authoritative figure who gave recognition to their aspirations as writers, but also an educated art-lover who appreciated their professional capacities, and a cultural broker who could facilitate their bid for ducal commissions. Scrutiny of these materials will mainly draw upon the findings of literature scholars on the role of poetry in cementing ideal and material solidarity among writers of the age. Along the lines of recent developments in word and image studies, as well as of theories on how literary representations filter historicity, the acknowledgment of the high level of conventionality of several exchanges between Varchi and Medicean artists will also lead to probing how these texts' use of long-established poetic topoi on artworks could intersect with real contemporary practices of art production.

The third chapter has two interrelated focuses. On the one hand, it concentrates on the poems that exponents of the local artistic community wrote to praise or lampoon the visual creations of fellow members of the same professional circle. On the other hand, it takes into account verse that such authors seem to have penned to defend their own artworks from vitriolic poetic attacks. Drawing on specific argumentations that Benvenuto Cellini developed in his prose writings, my discourse will initially cast light on the strategic functions that an artist from that milieu could ascribe to those forms of poetic discourse. The discussion will show how the central role that the sculptor attributed to the encomiastic or vituperative texts penned by colleagues was predicated on ancient and Renaissance aesthetic theories about the legitimacy of artistic judgment. Having established such a critical framework, the chapter will move on to closely inspect a number of these verse compositions. Their scrutiny will point out that this textual corpus offers a privileged cross-section of the alliances and rivalries that oriented the "horizontal" relations within the Florentine arts community of these years. The relevance of these materials as understudied sources on artistic allegiances often born out of workshop genealogies, as well as on clashes among competing aesthetic options in that scene, will thus be given due attention.

The fourth chapter focalizes on a selection of poems that our authors addressed "vertically" to the ruler and supreme arts patron of the city. This section begins with the assessment of Duke Cosimo's artistic and literary patronage that we read in one of the age's most insightful writings on the society of mid-Cinquecento Florence, namely, Anton Francesco Doni's *I marmi* (1552–1553). The work's depiction of the Florentine cultural policy of those years, which undermines its panegyrical remarks on Cosimo's generosity with some oblique allusions to his thriftiness and to the hardships that the best artists faced in his duchy, paves the way for a discussion of the similarly ambivalent picture of Medici patronage that emerges from the artists' own verse. It will become clear that this production complicates one of the most recurring and influential motifs of the visual and textual propaganda of ducal Florence, that is to say the idea that a new golden age of arts flourished under the egis of Cosimo. The verse of the Florentine sculptor and academician Paolo Geri will for instance reveal a struggling artist's (losing) attempt to win the duke's favor by poetic means, as well as a lyrical presentation of Cosimo's munificence that was more hortatory than descriptive. A poorly-known poem that Bronzino addressed to the duke will then allow us to delve into the painter's reflection on the nexus between the quality of art produced and the conditions of economic support that artists enjoy – a hotly debated topic in sixteenth-century artistic literature. Notwithstanding Bronzino's fame as a visual and verbal eulogist of Medici power, the analysis will highlight how his poetic pondering was tinged with protest against a perceived decadence in contemporary painting that also Cosimo's patronage seemed to promote. The last section of the chapter will shift its focus to a sonnet that the sculptor Domenico Poggini addressed to the duke. The artist's literary communication with his patron was in this case functional to a celebration of his merits that was also a means of introducing an encomiastic artwork created for him. What will emerge as particularly noteworthy here is a use of the poetic medium that seems to concretize several sixteenth-century ideas about the *doctus artifex* and about competence in verse composition as a most desirable cultural asset for practitioners of the arts.

Ultimately, the book aims to challenge the long-standing marginalization of poetry in scholarly discourse about the intellectual ambitions of Italian Renaissance artists. By revealing how verse was a strategic factor of the engagement with the written word of many painters, sculptors, architects, and goldsmiths from ducal and granducal Florence, but also sometimes a writing practice that was at risk of losing its cultural prestige due to its very success, the monograph will illuminate an aspect of these authors' literary pursuits that has not yet received the attention it deserves. It will also demonstrate that these poetic materials provide many fresh insights into art-theoretical debates, patronage questions, workshop cultures, issues of professional identity, and networks of personal relations in one of the most bustling and competitive arts scenes of sixteenth-century Italy.

Looking at Michelangelo

The example of the universal artist

Time and time again in the course of his long life (1475–1564), Michelangelo was celebrated by contemporary literati as the paradigm of the artist blessed by heaven with a genius that expressed itself at the highest level in different media, and encomiastic references to his activity as a poet soon became a central tenet of such tributes. Before him, there had certainly been other painters, sculptors or architects whose poetry had been praised by foremost men of letters. At the end of the previous century, for instance, a leading humanist of the Milanese court like Gasparo Visconti could pay sustained homage to the verse of Donato Bramante.[59] Especially after leaving Florence for good in 1534, Michelangelo nonetheless received a level of recognition as a poet-artist that was unprecedented in the Italian Renaissance.[60] Some of the most influential literati of the age lined up to celebrate his verse, while the addressee of such complimentary remarks lost no occasion to reaffirm the "amateurish, awkward and rough" character of his compositions.[61]

In 1534, for example, Francesco Berni penned a soon-famous *capitolo in terza rima* that offered a first acknowledgment of the literary stature of Michelangelo's poetic output, praising the "new Apollo and new Apelles" who could imbue his verse with philosophical ideas of Platonic origin, creating a poetry of "things" that was incomparably superior to the evane-

---

[59] See the introduction to Donato Bramante, *Sonetti e altri scritti*, ed. Carlo Vecce, Rome 1995, p. 15.

[60] It is only in these decades that poetry writing, a practice Buonarroti had started at least since the beginning of the century but often desultorily and with an experimental attitude, became a central occupation for the artist. See esp. Enzo Noè Girardi, *Studi su Michelangiolo scrittore*, Florence 1974, pp. 34–47.

[61] Answering to Francesco Berni's tribute to his poetry (see fn. 62), Michelangelo wrote that he was ashamed of writing back to his literarily cultivated interlocutor: "Mentre la scrivo a verso a verso, rosso / divengo assai, pensando a cui la mando, / sendo il mio non professo, goffo e grosso" (Michelangelo 2016 [as in fn. 4], *Rime comiche, d'occasione e di corrispondenza*, p. 281, n. 11, ll. 46–48). If such a *declaratio modestiae* is certainly also a rhetorical trope, Michelangelo's awareness of the non-professional character of his own poetic practice was probably sincere and shaped many of his written reflections on such creative activity, especially in his letters. See, for instance, what he wrote in a 1557 letter to Giorgio Vasari (Michelangelo, *Il carteggio di Michelangelo*, eds. Giovanni Poggi, Paola Barocchi and Renzo Ristori, 5 vols., Florence 1965–1983, 5, pp. 105–106): "Io scrivere m'è di grande affanno, perché non è mia arte." Some remarks on the topos of the writer's affected modesty in Vasari's *Vite* are especially useful here (Patricia Lee Rubin, *Giorgio Vasari: Art and History*, New Haven, CT 1995, p. 148): "A self-effacing stance was a prescribed rhetorical form […]. Vasari's disclaimers were not, however, empty phrases; they were selected forms of address. With his professions of inadequacy Vasari states a fact in a way that poses and resolves a paradox: he is an author who is not a writer. With such statements he shows himself to be qualified to undertake the work, because he is familiar with the rules."

scent "words" of so many contemporary Petrarchists.[62] Berni's critical judgment seems to have opened the gates to a flow of similar homages to the artist's literary activity. One of the most relevant among these was Donato Giannotti's *Dialogi de' giorni che Dante consumò nel cercare l'Inferno e 'l Purgatorio*, which bears witness to the fame Michelangelo had achieved as a poet by 1546, and the extent to which his admirers had begun circulating his verse in manuscript form.[63] Members of Buonarroti's closest circle of friends in Rome, Giannotti and Luigi del Riccio also planned to publish an extensive anthology of the artist's poems. Even though their project was never carried out, it gave a decisive impulse to the initiative that was most consequential to establishing the fame of such a poetic corpus in Cinquecento Italy: namely, the lecture that Benedetto Varchi gave at the Accademia Fiorentina on Michelangelo's sonnet *Non ha l'ottimo artista alcun concetto* (March 6, 1547).[64]

Read "publicamente […] con gran concorso di popolo et con piacere di tutti,"[65] Varchi's sophisticated exegesis gave the artist a place within the literary elite of the time. Before

---

[62] See Francesco Berni, *Rime*, ed. Danilo Romei, Milan 1985, p. 184, cap. 65, ll. 25–31: "Ho visto qualche sua composizione: / son ignorante, e pur direi d'avélle / lette tutte nel mezzo di Platone; // sì ch'egli è nuovo Apollo e nuovo Apelle: / tacete *unquanco, pallide viole* / e *liquidi cristalli* e *fiere snelle*: / e' dice cose e voi dite parole." For an excellent analysis of Berni's Capitolo, and of Michelangelo's response to it, see Matteo Residori, Sulla corrispondenza poetica tra Berni e Michelangelo (senza dimenticare Sebastiano del Piombo), in: Daniel Boillet and Michel Plaisance (eds.), *Les années trente du XVIe siècle italien*, Paris 2007, pp. 207–224.

[63] Consider for instance Donato Giannotti, *Dialogi di Donato Giannotti, de' giorni che Dante consumò nel cercare l'Inferno e 'l Purgatorio*, ed. Deoclecio Redig de Campos, Florence 1939, pp. 43–44: "[M. Donato]: 'non solamente io non opererò che costoro non vi vestino di quegli ornamenti [the recognition as the greatest painter, architect and sculptor ever existed], li quali voi dite che non sono vostri, ma ve ne aggiugnerò ancora un altro, affermando che voi siete così gran poeta come qualunque altro de' tempi nostri […]. Negherete voi quel che è noto a tutto il mondo? Non si leggono tutto il giorno vostri sonetti, vostri madriali, con diletto e maraviglia di ciascuno? Non sentiamo noi cantare dai più eccellenti musici, tra gli altri, quel vostro madrialetto: *Deh, dimmi Amor, se l'alma di costei* […]. Quello epigramma che voi ultimamente faceste sopra la vostra Notte […] potrìa esser meglio tessuto, più sentenzioso, più dilettevole?'"

[64] On Giannotti and Riccio's project of edition of a selection of Michelangelo's verse see Antonio Corsaro, Intorno alle rime di Michelangelo Buonarroti: la silloge del 1546, in: *Giornale storico della letteratura italiana* 185 (2008), pp. 536–569, which also reconstructs the earlier scholarly debate on the macrotextual nature of the poetic florilegium. For a convincing discussion of how such a project played a pivotal role in the genesis of Varchi's lecture see Frédérique Dubard de Gaillarbois, introduction to Benedetto Varchi, *Deux leçons sur l'art*, Paris 2020, pp. 19–27. More generally, Dubard's introduction to the latter work (pp. 1–90) is the most insightful and updated study of the *Due Lezzioni*, of the two parts' organic interdependence and of their being the most paradigmatic expression of Varchi's articulated cultural profile and interests. Other recent and useful examinations of the humanist's lecture on Michelangelo's sonnet include Salvatore Lo Re, Varchi e Michelangelo, in: *Annali della Scuola Normale Superiore di Pisa. Classe di Lettere e Filosofia* s. 5 4 (2012), pp. 485–516 and 613–614, pp. 485–489; Raymond Carlson, "Eccellentissimo poeta et amatore divinissimo": Benedetto Varchi and Michelangelo's Poetry at the Accademia Fiorentina, in: *Italian Studies* 69 (2014), pp. 169–188; Vittorio Scardamaglia, Benedetto Varchi e Michelangelo "scultore di versi", in: *La Rivista. Études culturelles italiennes Sorbonne Universités* 5 (2017), pp. 113–135 (https://etudesitaliennes.hypotheses.org/files/2017/05/7ScardamagliaFiniNouveau.pdf, last accessed 31/01/2021) and Tommaso Mozzati, "È dunque Artista vocabolo non Latino, ma Toscano": Michelangelo poeta nelle lettere fiorentine da Francesco Berni a Benedetto Varchi, in: Carlo Falciani and Antonio Natali (eds.), *Il Cinquecento a Firenze: "Maniera moderna" e Controriforma*, Florence 2017, pp. 41–51, pp. 46–49, all with further bibliography.

[65] With these words the event is recorded in the manuscript annals of the institution (Florence, Biblioteca Marucelliana, cod. B.III.52, c. 40v): see Carlson 2014 (as in fn. 64), p. 172.

Michelangelo, only such prominent poets as Pietro Bembo, Vittoria Colonna and Luigi Alamanni had received the honor during their lifetime of becoming the subject of lectures at the Florentine Academy, an institution mainly devoted to illustrating the most revered Tuscan writings of Dante and Petrarch.[66] The choice to focus on the poetry of a contemporary author who did not primarily profess letters or philosophy was indeed so groundbreaking that Varchi felt the need to justify it. He did this by presenting Michelangelo as an example of a perfect genius, whose versatility was a manifestation of the classic homology between *pictura* and *poesis*:

> E coloro, che si maravigliano come ne' componimenti d'un uomo, il quale non faccia professione di lettere, né di scienze, e sia tutto occupatissimo in tanti, e tanto diversi esercizi, possa essere così grande e profondità di dottrina ed altezza di concetti, mostrano male, che conoscano o quanto possa la natura, quando vuole fare uno ingegno perfetto e singolare, o che la pittura e la poesia sono secondo molti non tanto somigliantissime fra loro, quanto poco meno che una cosa medesima.[67]

Following an interpretive approach that had often been used in previous lectures at the Accademia Fiorentina, Varchi made reference to numerous other texts by the author to cast light on all the meanings of the commented poem, citing from no less than twenty-seven of Michelangelo's compositions.[68] In his discussion, he argued that those sonnets and madrigals proved to be the work of a true philosopher, a wise connoisseur of the difficult art of love, and above all a writer of extraordinary verse, on par with his masterpieces in painting, sculpture and architecture.[69] In the sonnet concluding the lecture, Varchi once again paid homage to the artist's universality, extolling Michelangelo as a heavenly paradigm to which the rest of humanity could aspire but never equal, a supreme model (literally, a *speglio*, i.e. a mirror) of what art and nature could achieve:

---

[66] See Michel Plaisance, *L'Accademia e il suo principe: cultura e politica a Firenze al tempo di Cosimo I e di Francesco de' Medici*, Manziana 2004, p. 275.

[67] Benedetto Varchi, *Opere*, eds. Giovanni Battista Busini and Antonio Racheli, 2 vols., Trieste 1858–1859, 2, p. 613. The apologetic tone is even more explicit ibid., pp. 614–615, where the author states that he had decided to lay out the doctrine and utility of Michelangelo's verse "per non essere tenuto da certi, i quali tanto hanno avuto a male, e tanto mi sono iti biasimando della elezione di questo sonetto."

[68] This suggests that Michelangelo's poetry must have already had a significant degree of manuscript circulation in the Florentine milieu: on this question, see esp. Corsaro, Intorno alle rime di Michelangelo Buonarroti, pp. 287–288. We can also assume that, thanks to its web of references, the 1547 lecture further contributed to the dissemination, knowledge and appreciation of that body of verse.

[69] Varchi 1858–1859 (as in fn. 67), 2, p. 626: "Da questo sonetto [*Non vider gli occhi mai cosa mortale*] penso io, che chiunque ha giudizio, potrà conoscere quanto questo Angelo, anzi Arcangelo, oltra le sue tre prime e nobilissime professioni architettura, scultura e pittura, nelle quali egli senza alcun contrasto non solo avanza tutti i moderni, ma trapassa gli antichi, sia eccellente, anzi singolare nella poesia e nella vera arte dell'amante […]. Della qual cosa niuno si debbe maravigliare; perciocchè, oltra quello che apparisce manifesto a ciascuno, che la natura volle fare, per mostrare l'estremo di sua possa, un uomo compiuto, e, come dicono i Latini, fornito da tutte le parti." On the author's peculiar emphasis on the worth and depth of Michelangelo's philosophy see Dubard de Gaillarbois's introduction to Varchi 2020 (as in fn. 64), pp. 29–30 (also with reference to the development of the same set of ideas in Varchi's funeral oration for Buonarroti, in 1564), 40–41 and *passim*; on his socratic interpretation of Michelangelo's theory of love see esp. Carlson 2014 (as in fn. 64).

> Ben vi potea bastar, chiaro Scultore,
>   Non sol per opra d'incude e martello
>   Aver, ma co'i colori, e col pennello
>   Agguagliato, anzi vinto il prisco onore:
> Ma non contento al gemino valore,
>   C'ha fatto il secol nostro altero e bello,
>   L'arme e le paci di quel dolce e fello
>   Cantate, che v'impiaga e molce il core.
> O saggio e caro a Dio ben nato veglio,
>   Che 'n tanti, e sì bei modi ornate il mondo,
>   Qual non è poco a sì gran merti pregio?
> A voi, che per eterno privilegio,
>   Nasceste d'arte e di natura speglio,
>   Mai non fu primo, e non fia mai secondo.[70]

This praise of the versatility of Michelangelo's talent found a privileged audience among the many painters and sculptors who were members at the time of the Accademia Fiorentina.[71] Though not enrolled in the institution, one who almost certainly must have heard the lecture, and probably would have had access to a manuscript of the text that was to be printed in January 1550, was Giorgio Vasari.[72] Studies have in fact demonstrated how, in the Torrentino edition of his *Vite* (1550), Vasari re-used many of the ideological tenets of Varchi's *Lezzione*, and in particular his idea of the excellence of Michelangelo's poetry as an indication of the artist's universality.[73] Such an intellectual debt left several traces in the Torrentiniana: when, for instance, Vasari exhorted his readers to consider, as proof of Michelangelo's supernatural gifts, his "bellissime canzoni" and the "stupendi suoi sonetti, gravemente composti," the superlatives and the use of the stylistic category of *gravitas* closely recall similar considerations in Varchi's lecture.[74] Even the hagiographic opening image of the biography of Buonarroti

---

[70] Varchi 1858–1859 (as in fn. 67), 2, p. 627.

[71] On the expulsion of artists from the Florentine Academy that took place in the summer 1547, see the following chapter.

[72] As it is well known, Varchi's lecture was published together with his *Lezzione* on the paragone debate, which took place at the Accademia Fiorentina just a week after the public exegesis on Michelangelo's sonnet (March 13, 1547). Being one of the artists who in 1547 had submitted their written responses to Varchi's "poll" on the superiority of either painting or sculpture, Vasari probably had access to a manuscript copy of the *Due Lezzioni*, which were eventually published by Lorenzo Torrentino in January 1550 (1549 in Florentine style).

[73] See the commentary by Paola Barocchi in Giorgio Vasari, *La vita di Michelangelo nelle redazioni del 1550 e del 1568*, ed. Paola Barocchi, 5 vols., Milan 1962, 2, pp. 25–26 and Rubin 1995 (as in fn. 61), pp. 182–183. Of a different opinion Dubard de Gaillarbois, introduction to Varchi 2020 (as in fn. 64), p. 60. It is important to stress how the notion of the artist's universality, which Vasari applies to Michelangelo, had been current in earlier celebrations of Raphael. On sixteenth-century praises of Raphael as the universal artist, and particularly on funerary poems that celebrated him as an architect, an antiquarian, and sometimes even a sculptor, see Ulrich Pfisterer, *Raffael. Glaube, Liebe, Ruhm*, Munich 2019, p. 222. These compositions were often the work of humanists of the Roman Curia, who were certainly familiar with the fact that Raphael had started penning verse in the same milieu: see ibid.

[74] Compare Giorgio Vasari, *Le vite de' più eccellenti pittori scultori e architettori: nelle redazioni del 1550 e 1568*, eds. Rosanna Bettarini and Paola Barocchi, 8 vols., Florence 1967–1997, 6, p. 111 (1550), and Varchi 1858–1859 (as in fn. 67), 2, p. 613, which described Michelangelo's sonnet as "bellissimo" and as "pieno di […] antica purezza e Dantesca gravità." Vasari's contextual reference to the "molti dotti" who had "comentate e lette pub-

followed in the wake of the same model, which had celebrated a talent equally versed in the disciplines of drawing as well as in poetry and moral philosophy. Taking from the *Lezzione*'s final sonnet the image of an artist who was the supreme "mirror" of arts and nature, Vasari for instance underlined how verse belonged to the array of Michelangelo's earthly manifestations from which the world had to draw inspiration:

> […] il benignissimo Rettor del cielo […] si dispose mandare in terra uno spirito che universalmente in ciascheduna arte et in ogni professione fusse abile […] a mostrare che cosa siano le difficultà nella scienza delle linee, nella pittura, nel giudizio della scultura e nella invenzione della veramente garbata architettura; e volse oltra ciò accompagnarlo de la vera filosofia morale, con l'ornamento della dolce poesia, acciò che il mondo lo eleggesse et ammirasse per suo singularissimo specchio nella vita, nell'opere, nella santità dei costumi e in tutte l'azzioni umane […].[75]

Antecedents and historical background of the model

Already in the 1550 edition of his *Vite*, Vasari's literary depiction of Michelangelo's poetical practice therefore showed a close dependence upon Varchi's *Lezzione* of 1547. Departing from that model, however, Vasari interpreted these suggestions according to a hermeneutical grid that posits Buonarroti as the culmination of a history that since antiquity had seen artists dedicate themselves to verse writing. The reference to the "ornament" of poetry, in the opening paragraph of Michelangelo's biography, served in this regard to confirm an idea already articulated in the preface to the *Vite*. It was here that the author observed how "sempre fur quasi tutti e' pittori e gli scultori eccellenti, dotati dal cielo il più delle volte non solo dell'ornamento della poesia, come si legge di Pacuvio, ma della filosofia ancora, come si vide in Metrodoro, perito tanto in filosofia quanto in pittura."[76] In referring to these ancient *exempla*, Vasari echoed a famous passage from the *Naturalis Historia* in which Pliny had mentioned Pacuvius, painter and tragedian, and Metrodorus, philosopher and sculptor, as proof that in the past only people of high social and intellectual standing dedicated themselves to the visual arts.[77] Even so, it is

---

blicamente nelle più celebrate Accademie di tutta Italia" Michelangelo's poems serves also to indirectly refer to Varchi's lesson.

[75] Vasari 1967–1997 (as in fn. 74), 6, pp. 3–4 (1550).

[76] Ibid., 2, p. 7 (1550). Pietro Aretino had already compared Vasari's own versatile *ingegno* as "istorico, poeta, filosofo e pittore" to the Plinian example of Metrodorus in the letter of June 7, 1536: see Vasari, *Der literarische Nachlass Giorgio Vasaris*, eds. Karl Frey and Herman-Walther Frey, 2 vols., Munich 1923–1930, 1, p. 70. Notably, however, for Vasari poetry had to remain a non-time-consuming activity, because one possible risk associated with an intensive literary practice was a decreased productivity in the artistic field. In his introduction to the Torrentiniana biography of Leon Battista Alberti, the author thus argued that "Grandissima comoditate arrecano le lettere universalmente a tutti coloro che di quelle piglian diletto, ma molto maggiore la apportano elle senza alcuna comparazione agli scultori, a' pittori et agli architetti, abbellendo et assottigliando come elle fanno le invenzioni che naturalmente nascono in quelli," but also added that Alberti "se bene attese a far opere […] fu ancora molto più inclinato a lo scrivere che a lo operare" (Vasari 1967–1997 [as in fn. 74], 3, pp. 283 and 285 [1550]).

[77] See respectively Pliny the Elder, *Naturalis Historia* 35.19 and 135 for references to Pacuvius ("Apud Romanos quoque honos mature huic arti contigit, siquidem cognomina ex ea Pictorum traxerunt Fabii clarissimae gentis […]. Proxime celebrata est in foro boario aede Herculis Pacuvi poetae pictura") and Metrodorus ("Ubi eodem tempore erat Metrodorus, pictor idemque philosophus, in utraque scientia magnae auctoritatis"). Pacuvius was

important to note how the Renaissance author adapted these references to support a thesis that is quite different from that of his ancient source: anticipating an idea that Giovan Paolo Lomazzo was to develop in his *Trattato dell'arte della Pittura*, he argued for the existence of an almost necessary connection between excellence in painting and sculpture, on the one hand, and philosophical knowledge and poetic writing, on the other.[78]

In the teleological structure of the Torrentiniana, classic antiquity is therefore concisely framed as a sort of prehistory of the model of poet-artist that culminates in Michelangelo. A more sustained attention was however paid to modern antecedents of this figure, by way of references to the poetic activity of artists like Andrea Orcagna, Filippo Brunelleschi, Bramante and Benedetto da Rovezzano.[79] In the introductory paragraph to Orcagna's biography, for instance, Vasari presented this fourteenth-century Florentine painter, sculptor, architect, and poet in terms that project onto him the role of precursor of Michelangelo's versatility. He made this point particularly clear when he wrote that excellence in any of the domains of the *ingegno* inevitably involves a capacity to achieve similarly excellent results in other fields of knowledge, with an argument that echoes a programmatic passage from Varchi's academic lecture on the "paragone" between painting and sculpture.[80]

---

not the only poet-artist in Pliny's influential history of art: for other such examples, see the discussion here in ch. 3. For the importance of Pliny's stories on the high social and intellectual status of ancient painters during the Renaissance see most recently Sarah Blake McHam, *Pliny and the Artistic Culture of the Italian Renaissance: The Legacy of the Natural History*, New Haven, CT 2013, pp. 45–46, with further bibliography. For the place that the ancient source had in the two editions of the *Vite*, see ibid., pp. 273–285, as well as Giovanni Becatti, Plinio e Vasari, in: Istituto di storia dell'arte dell'Università di Napoli (ed.), *Studi di storia dell'arte in onore di Valerio Mariani*, Naples 1971, pp. 173–182; Rubin 1995 (as in fn. 61), pp. 54 and 147; Patricia A. Emison, *Creating the "Divine" Artist: From Dante to Michelangelo*, Leiden 2004, pp. 19–58.

[78] In the sixth book of his *Trattato dell'arte della Pittura*, Lomazzo takes Vasari's thesis as a point of departure for arguing – in the name of the *ut pictura poesis* principle – that every painter, even the one who is otherwise illiterate, is always imbued with a "spirit of poetry" and ready to compose verse on the subjects of his paintings. See the introduction to this book, fn. 28.

[79] The author records how some Florentine rivals of Brunelleschi "erano stati con sonetti fatti da Filippo svergognati" (Vasari 1967–1997 [as in fn. 74], 3, p. 185 [1550]). On Bramante, see ibid. (4, p. 84), with the statement that the artist "Dilettavasi de la poesia e volentieri udiva e diceva improviso in su la lira, e componeva qualche sonetto, se non così delicato come si usa ora, grave almeno e senza difetti." For Benedetto da Rovezzano, see ibid., p. 289: "Si è medesimamente dilettato delle cose di poesia, et è stato non meno vago di poeteggiare cantando che di fare statue co' mazzuoli e con gli scarpelli lavorando: onde gli diamo lode egualmente in tutte due le virtù."

[80] Ibid., 2, p. 217: "Rare volte è uno ingegnoso e valente che non sia ancora accorto e sagace, né mai la natura partorì uno spirto in una cosa eccellente che ancora in molte non operase il medesimo, overo delle altrui non fusse almeno intelligentissimo, come fece nell'Orgagna il quale fu pittore, scultore, architetto e poeta." Compare Varchi's words from the published text of the *Lezzione sulla maggioranza delle arti* (Benedetto Varchi and Vincenzo Borghini, *Pittura e scultura nel Cinquecento*, ed. Paola Barocchi, Livorno 1998, p. 33): "confermatomi nella credenza mia che chiunche è eccellentissimo in un'arte nobile, non sia del tutto privato di giudizio nell'altre." For more on this, see the following chapter. For Vasari's representation of Orcagna as a precursor of the model of the "universal artist" see Mario Pozzi and Enrico Mattioda, *Giorgio Vasari storico e critico*, Florence 2006, p. 340 (with reference to the Giuntina), with a discussion of some other references to artists as poets in the *Vite*. This image was later revised by Lomazzo's *Libro dei sogni*: see Lomazzo 1973–1975 (as in fn. 28), 1, p. 148, on which see also Hessler 2014 (as in fn. 14), p. 228, fn. 658.

In the Giunti edition of the *Vite* (1568), comments on the poetical leanings of modern artists become even more widespread than in the 1550 book. The Giuntina's references to painters, sculptors and architects who had composed poetry included precursors, contemporaries and successors of Michelangelo: alongside two living Florentine artists, Bronzino and Domenico Poggini, the author thus mentioned figures like Buffalmacco, Leonardo da Vinci, Silvio Cosini, Sebastiano del Piombo or Bartolomeo Genga.[81] We now know that Vasari's information on these artists' poetic practices is not always historically reliable.[82] What matters more for our purposes is, at any rate, his desire to present a model that was brought to perfection in Michelangelo, and could serve as inspiration for contemporary practitioners of the visual arts who represented a crucial part of the reading public of the *Vite*.

The author's emphasis on the liberal status of painting, sculpture and architecture helps explain why he gave so much attention to the figure of the poet-artist. Such a construct embodied the ideas promoted by an illustrious array of didactic texts, according to which the full mastery of any of the *artes liberales* required a preparation that went beyond the confines of disciplinary specialization. If the model of encyclopedic knowledge made famous by Cicero

---

[81] Consider the famous remarks on Bronzino's poetic activity (Vasari 1967–1997 [as in fn. 74], 6, p. 237 [1568]): "Si è dilettato costui e dilettasi assai della poesia; onde ne ha fatto molti capitoli e sonetti, una parte de' quali sono stampati. Ma sopra tutto (quanto alla poesia) è maraviglioso nello stile e capitoli berniesschi." On Poggini, see infra. On the earlier names consider in order ibid., 2, p. 172, transcribing an explicatory sonnet that Buffalmacco would have inserted in his frescoes for the Camposanto of Pisa; ibid., 4, p. 24, for the declaration that Leonardo, while working in the Milanese court, "fu il migliore dicitore di rime a l'improviso"; the remark (ibid., p. 261) on Silvio Cosini, who "si dilettò di comporre sonetti e di cantare all'improviso;" the words on Sebastiano del Piombo, who was the addressee of Francesco Berni's *capitolo Padre, a me più che gli altri reverendo*, "al quale rispose fra' Sebastiano con un altro assai bello, come quelli che, essendo universale, seppe anco a far versi toscani e burlevoli accomodarsi" (ibid., 5, pp. 100–101; the *capitolo* to which Vasari alludes, *Com'io ebbi la vostra, signor mio*, was in truth the work of Michelangelo, who penned it in the name of Sebastiano), as well as the consideration (ibid., p. 355) that Bartolomeo Genga "Dilettossi di fare sonetti et altri componimenti di rime e di prose, ma niuno meglio gli riusciva che l'ottava rima, nella qual maniera di scrivere fu assai lodato compositore."

[82] Vasari drew the mentions of Orcagna and Brunelleschi's poetic activity respectively from the *Libro di Antonio Billi* and Antonio Manetti's biography of the architect. For references to modern scholarly debates on the reliability of these claims, see the introduction to the present book, pp. 23-24 and notes. Particularly controversial is the depiction of Leonardo as a "dicitore di rime a l'improviso," i. e. as the author of the compositions he recited impromptu. Vasari probably derived this information from Paolo Giovio's life of the artist (ca. 1527) or from Benedetto Varchi's funeral oration for Michelangelo (1564). In the former source, we read that Leonardo "ad lyramque scite caneret" (see Paolo Giovio, *Scritti d'arte: lessico ed ecfrasi*, ed. Sonia Maffei, Pisa 1999, p. 234, and also Hessler 2014 [as in fn. 14], p. 230, fn. 664), but this most concise information did not specify whether the artist was also responsible for the creation of the verse that accompanied the music. The latter source, on the other hand, stated that Leonardo was by all means a poet: "un nipote di ser Piero da vinci, chiamato al Battesimo Lionardo [...] haveva oltra l'Architettura, oltra la scultura; per sua principale Arte [...] la Pittura. Era costui Aritmetico, era Musico, era Geometro, e cosmografo; era Astrologo, e Astronomo; era Versificatore, e Poeta; era Filosofo, e Metafisico" (Benedetto Varchi, *Orazione funerale di m. Benedetto Varchi: fatta, e recitata da lui pubblicamente nell'essequie di Michelagnolo Buonarroti in Firenze [...]*, p. 54). Giovan Paolo Lomazzo eventually resumed Vasari's image of Leonardo as a poet in his *Trattato dell'arte della pittura*, where he even transcribed and attributed to the artist the poem *Chi non può quel che vuol, quel che può voglia*, which in truth was the work of the Florentine rhymester Antonio di Matteo di Meglio (Lomazzo 1973–1975 [as in fn. 28], 2, p. 245.) On this, see esp. Dionisotti 1962 (as in fn. 51), pp. 189–190, which dismisses Vasari and Lomazzo's claims on the basis of several considerations, first of all the absence of any authentic poem among the thousands of autograph papers by the artist.

in *De Oratore* had inspired much pedagogic literature in the Renaissance, culminating with Baldassarre Castiglione's *Libro del Cortegiano* (1528) and its theories about the broad-ranging competences that a perfect courtier should possess, the professionally-specific need for an artist to have multifarious disciplinary skills was an idea largely influenced by Vitruvius. Specifically, a passage in the first book of *De Architectura* offered early modern readers the model of an *artifex* who was capable of combining technical knowledge with basic literary and philosophical notions.[83] Such benchmarks of Renaissance art theory as Leon Battista Alberti's *De Pictura* (whose Latin version dated back to 1435), Lorenzo Ghiberti's *Commentarii* (ca. 1448–1454), or Pomponius Gauricus's *De Sculptura* (1504) demonstrate that fifteenth- and sixteenth-century Italian artists eagerly embraced and propagated these ideas.[84] Unlike Vasari, however, none of these authors had included writing verse among the necessary skills for artists.[85] A comparison between the *Vite* and *De Pictura* is telling in this regard.[86] Alberti too had

[83] Vitruvius, *De Architectura*, 1.1. On the ideal of the cultural training of the architect that was proposed by Vitruvius see esp. Pierre Gros's introduction to Vitruvius, *De Architectura*, eds. and trans. Antonio Corso and Elisa Romano, 2 vols., Turin 1997, 1, pp. 7–9, as well as the editors' detailed commentary to the passage, pp. 68–81, fnn. 39–139.

[84] Compare Rubin 1995 (as in fn. 61), pp. 54–55: "The first lines of Vitruvius's book declare that 'the architect should be equipped with the knowledge of many branches of study and varied kinds of learning.' Ghiberti paraphrased this in his *Commentaries*." For the relationship between Vitruvius's *De Architectura* and Alberti's *De Pictura*, see esp. Gàbor Hajnóczi, Principî vitruviani nella teoria della pittura di Leon Battista Alberti, in: Arturo Calzona (ed.), *Leon Battista Alberti: teorico delle arti e gli impegni civili del De re aedificatoria. Atti dei convegni internazionali del Comitato Nazionale VI centenario della nascita di Leon Battista Alberti: Mantova, 17–19 ottobre 2002, Mantova, 23–25 ottobre 2003*, Florence 2007, pp. 189–202, with further references. On Gauricus's indebteness to the ancient source see the commentary to Pomponius Gauricus, *De sculptura*, ed. and trans. Paolo Cutolo, Naples 1999, p. 265.

[85] Vitruvius, *De Architectura* 1.1.3–4, in broad terms indicated *litterae* and *litteratura*, a general literary culture, as part of the architect's knowledge. In a similar vein, Ghiberti does recommend a basic philosophical training for the artist, but does not mention poetry as part of the ideal education of those who practiced the art: "conviene che [il]literato sia, perito della scrittura et amaestrato di geometria, et abbia conosciute assa' istorie, o diligentemente abbia udito phylosofia […]" (Lorenzo Ghiberti, *I commentarii: Biblioteca Nazionale Centrale di Firenze, II, I, 333*, ed. Lorenzo Bartoli, Florence 1998, p. 47; the editor of the book points out that the manuscript's "illiterato" is a mistake for "litterato"). Another text that had become familiar to Vasari by the time of the second edition of the *Vite*, Cennino Cennini's *Libro dell'arte*, argued for a genetic connection between painting and poetry on the basis of the classical principle *ut pictura poesis*, but did not prescribe poetry writing for painters. See Cennino Cennini, *Il libro dell'arte*, ed. Fabio Frezzato, Vicenza 2003, p. 62 (I 1), in which the author states that painting "con ragione merita metterla a·ssedere in secondo grado alla scienza e choronarla di poexia". As for Gauricus, his work argued at length the need for the sculptor to possess a broad-ranging education, also in the field of literature and antiquarianism (see Gauricus 1999 [as in fn. 84], pp. 138–147), but did not touch upon the topic of poetic composition. Although not belonging to the genre of artistic treatises and certainly unknown to Vasari, we might here also record the position that Jacopo de' Barbari articulated in his letter to Friedrich the Wise, Elector of Saxony (ca. 1502). In the document, which addressed the topic of the kind of education that is necessary to achieve excellence in painting, the artist stated that the painter "necesita la poesia per la invention de le hopere, la qual nase da gramatica e retorica ancor dialetica" (Paul Kirn, Friedrich der Weise und Jacopo de' Barbari, in: *Jahrbuch der Preußischen Kunstsammlungen* 46 [1925], pp. 130–134, p. 134). In this case, however, it is not entirely clear whether such a remark referred to a passive knowledge of poetry or to an active commerce with it.

[86] Vasari was well familiar with the work. He mentioned Ludovico Domenichi's vernacular translation of the *De Pictura* in his biography of Alberti (e.g. Vasari 1967–1997 [as in fn. 74], 3, p. 285 [1568]), and several passages

used Pliny's examples of Pacuvius as poet and Metrodorus as philosopher: as in the ancient source, however, these references served to generally affirm the status of painting as a liberal art.[87] Furthermore, when Alberti did speak of poetry as part of the painter's necessary cultural background, he mentioned only a *passive* fruition of verse, recommending regularly reading and frequenting poets so as to gain inspiration for the painting's *istoria*.[88]

To fully understand why Vasari heralded the figure of the poet-artist, we should also keep in mind that an authentic cultural revolution was under way by the time he was writing. Between the 1540s and 1560s, the intellectuals hierarchies that had traditionally dominated the Italian literary scene were loosened to an unprecedented degree, and this encouraged ever more artists to take part, both as poets and as prose writers, in a broader and more inclusive republic of letters.[89] In indicating verse writing as a highly recommendable, if not outright necessary, complement to the practice of the visual arts, Vasari proved to be fully aware of the novel opportunities for intellectual promotion that painters, sculptors and architects could find in such a renewed cultural scenario.

A special paradigm for Florentine artists?

While reflecting a profound historical change that was transforming the literary scene of the Peninsula, the importance that Vasari's *Vite* attributed to the construct of the poet-artist and to the verse writing of Michelangelo was also particularly consistent with the function that the model had on a more local scale. It is indeed possible to prove how the poetic practice of many artists who were active in Florence in the second half of the Cinquecento was the result,

---

in the *Vite* rely on that source. See, most recently, Robert W. Gaston, Vasari and the Rhetoric of Decorum, in: David J. Cast, *The Ashgate Research Companion to Giorgio Vasari*, Burlington, VT 2014, pp. 245–260, p. 252.

[87] Compare Leon Battista Alberti, *La pittura di Leonbattista Alberti tradotta per m. Lodovico Domenichi*, Venice 1547, c. 20r (corresponding to Leon Battista Alberti, *On Painting and On Sculpture: The Latin Texts of "De ictura" and "De statua,"* ed. and trans. Cecil Grayson, London 1972, pp. 62–63 [2.27]): "i buoni pittori furono sempre lodati, et tenuti in grandissimo honore appresso ogniuno; di modo che non pure nobilissimi, et prestantissimi cittadini, ma philosophi, et Re anchora, non solo si dilettarono di cose dipinte, ma grandissimamente etiandio di dipingere […]. Pacuvio poeta Tragico, nipote d'una figlia d'Ennio poeta, dipinse uno Hercole in piazza. Socrate, Platone, Metrodoto [sic], et Pirrhone philosophi furono eccellenti ne la pittura."

[88] Alberti 1547 (as in fn. 87), cc. 37v–38r (corresponding to Alberti 1972 [as in fn. 87], p. 94 [3.53]): "Ma ben vorrei, che 'l pittore fosse dotto, quanto possibil fosse, in tutte l'arti liberali […]. Appresso non sarà fuor di proposito, se si diletteranno de' poeti, et de gli oratori. Perciochè costoro hanno molti ornamenti comuni col pittore. Et molto anchora gli gioveranno quei letterati copiosi con la cognitione di molte cose a ordinar bene la compositione de l'historia; tutta la quale lode specialmente sta ne l'inventione."

[89] Dionisotti 1971 (as in fn. 17), p. 243: "I rapporti e scambi fra la letteratura e le altre discipline diventano in questo periodo molto più facili e frequenti. Così anche fra la letteratura e le arti. Non si ha più una aristocrazia letteraria che, dall'alto dell'enciclopedia umanistica allestita fra Quattro e Cinquecento, interviene e giudica in cose che direttamente non la riguardano. Scienziati e artisti cominciano a ritrovarsi, se non proprio come a casa loro, certo a loro agio, in una società letteraria più larga, più cordiale e più aperta. In tali condizioni si spiega la stesura delle *Vite* del Vasari, dell'autobiografia e dei trattati del Cellini, un contributo insomma, fornito da artisti, che non ha forse riscontro in alcun altro periodo della letteratura italiana."

or was interpreted as the result, of a specific imitative approach to the "divine" artist. In order to cast light on the extent and implications of such a mimetic stance, two types of documentary materials will be discussed: first, contemporary testimonies that referred to the poetry writing of several Medicean painters and sculptors as a deliberate imitation of Michelangelo, and second, references to that model that were present in the verse of the same artists, where they function as an "element of deliberate shaping in the formation and expression" of their identity as poets.[90]

The writings of some prominent literati of ducal Florence testify to the idea that the poetic engagement of Medicean artists was inspired by the model of Michelangelo. The most explicit of such testimonies is a sonnet by the satirical poet Alfonso de' Pazzi, alias "l'Etrusco."[91] In the poem (ca. 1551–1555), the author addressed Agnolo Bronzino to ask him for a copy of one of the burlesque *capitoli in terza rima* which the painter, following the popular example of Francesco Berni's paradoxical eulogies, had written in praise of the mosquito.[92] After paying homage to the painting style of his addressee, Pazzi stated his own desire to learn from Bronzino's "capitol […] della zanzara," which he declared superior to the works of Berni himself and of Pietro Aretino, the two most influential comic poets of the century. Significantly, the author then proceeded to interpret Bronzino's choice to engage with both painting and poetry not as a simple, intrinsically-motivated will to practice different media, but rather as an act of volition to acquire a kind of versatility that Michelangelo had already demonstrated to possess. Borrowing our categories from René Girard's mimetic theory, we might say that l'Etrusco presented Bronzino's ambition to cumulate artistic and literary skills as a manifest case of a "desire according to Another" rather than one "according to Oneself," with Michelangelo acting as the admired mediator who shapes and directs all of his faithful subject's preferences and most defining aspirations:[93]

---

[90] Stephen Greenblatt, *Renaissance Self-Fashioning: From More to Shakespeare*, Chicago 1980, p. 1.
[91] On the author, see esp. Giorgio Pedrotti, *Alfonso de' Pazzi, accademico e poeta*, Pescia 1902; Domenico Zanrè, *Cultural Non-Conformity in Early Modern Florence*, Aldershot and Burlington, VT 2004, pp. 111–139; the introduction and commentary to Alfonso de' Pazzi, *Nuovi canti carnascialeschi di Firenze: le "canzone" e mascherate di Alfonso de' Pazzi*, ed. Aldo Castellani, Florence 2006, and Giorgio Masi, Politica, arte e religione nella poesia dell'Etrusco (Alfonso de' Pazzi), in: Antonio Corsaro, Harald Hendrix, and Paolo Procaccioli (eds.), *Autorità, modelli e antimodelli nella cultura artistica e letteraria tra Riforma e Controriforma. Atti del seminario internazionale di studi, Urbino-Sassocorvaro, 9–11 novembre 2006*, Manziana 2007, pp. 301–358.
[92] I first published and discussed the sonnet, which had previously remained unknown, in Diletta Gamberini, "Antica purezza e dantesca gravità": forme dell'appropriazione della poesia di Michelangelo nella Firenze di Cosimo I, in: *Italique* 21 (2018), pp. 199–233, pp. 209–210 and 228, fnn. 43–44. Pazzi's poem refers to one of Bronzino's two Bernesque capitoli on mosquitos (*A messer Benedetto Varchi in lode delle zanzare* and *Esortazione del Bronzino pittore alle zanzare*: see Bronzino, *Rime in burla*, 45–64), whose composition Francesca Latini has persuasively dated to the period ca. 1551–1553 (see Latini 2015 [as in fn. 6], 1, pp. 178–180). If this is the *terminus post quem* for the sonnet, its *terminus ad quem* is November 3, 1555, the date of Alfonso de' Pazzi's death.
[93] For the theoretical framework underpinning the present argument see René Girard, *Deceit, Desire, and the Novel: Self and Other in Literary Structure*, trans. Yvonne Freccero, Baltimore 1965 (first ed. 1961), pp. 1–52. According to such a framework, we can probably define the dynamics between Michelangelo and Bronzino that is portrayed by Pazzi's sonnet as one of "external mediation." In this typology, the subject is willing to fully acknowledge his imitation of the mediator or role-model. For the fundamental difference, see ibid., pp. 9–10:

Per il Bronzino
Per che da ciaschedun sempre si impara,
   o sia vulgare o greco o ver latino,
   io ti prego e suprico, Bronzino,
   che in pittura ài manier sì rara,
che del capitol tuo della zanzara
   copia mi mandiate con stil divino.
   Lo tratti tal che 'l Berna e l'Aretino
   perderian se facessin teco a gara.
Il Buonarroti ti veggo imitare,
   che poesia agiung'alla pittura,
   con la qual vivo al ciel si innalza a volo:
or cimental ancor nella scultura,
   et fama avrai fin l'un et l'altro polo,
   et di questo ti prego non mancare.[94]

Particularly meaningful is the last tercet of the sonnet.[95] The idea that Bronzino chose to dedicate himself to poetry as a way of imitating Michelangelo leads Pazzi to invite the painter to compete with Buonarroti also in sculpture. The exhortation is important because it illuminates the equivalence established between poetry and the arts of drawing as media in which Medicean artists could emulate the recognized "father" of the Florentine artistic community. If, as Paul Joannides and Francis Ames-Lewis have written, "a collective psychobiography of Italian sixteenth-century artists" took on the traits of "an Oedipal drama" precipitated by the need to confront oneself with the "towering artistic personality" of Michelangelo,[96] this proved to be all the more true in ducal Florence. The fact that Michelangelo spent the last three decades of his life away from the city did not prevent the Medicean scene from becoming the artistic milieu most sensitive to his example.[97] It was especially in this scenario that the relation to

"We shall speak of external mediation when the distance is sufficient to eliminate any contact between the two spheres of possibilities of which the mediator and the subject occupy the respective centers. We shall speak of internal mediation when this same distance is sufficiently reduced to allow these two spheres to penetrate each other more or less profoundly. Obviously it is not physical space that measures the gap between mediator and the desiring subject. Although geographical separation might be one factor, the distance between mediator and subject is primarily spiritual [...]. The hero of external mediation proclaims aloud the true nature of his desire. He worships his model openly and declares himself his disciple."

[94] The text is preserved by the cod. Capponi 134 of the Biblioteca Nazionale Centrale di Firenze (hereafter BNCF), on p. 341. This is an anthology that one of the author's sons, Luigi de' Pazzi, assembled in the early 1570s by transcribing hundreds of compositions by his father; see Giorgio Masi, Pazzi, Alfonso de', detto l'Etrusco, in: *Dizionario Biografico degli Italiani* (hereafter *DBI*) 82, Rome 2015, pp. 1–3. Given the nearly illegible character of Alfonso's handwriting, errors in Luigi's transcriptions are quite common, and the sonnet to Bronzino contains what appear to be two such mistakes, which have been conjecturally emendated in the text: at l. 10, the manuscript reads "che poesia agiunt'alla pittura;" at l. 14, "et di quanto ti prego non mancare."

[95] Also interesting, at l. 6, is Alfonso's choice to label as "divino" Bronzino's writing tool (the "stilo"). With such wording, the poet reinforces the parallel between the Florentine painter-poet and Michelangelo, who had conquered his own "divinity" by mastering poetry as well as painting (ll. 10–11).

[96] Quoted from the introductory remarks of Francis Ames-Lewis and Paul Joannides (eds.), *Reactions to the Master: Michelangelo's Effect on Art and Artists in the Sixteenth Century*, Aldershot 2003, p. 1.

[97] For a general introduction to the place that Buonarroti had in Florentine arts after 1534 see Marco Chiarini, Alan P. Darr, and Cristina Gianni (eds.), *L'ombra del genio: Michelangelo e l'arte a Firenze, 1537–1631*, Milan

that model was played out also in terms of the media with which an artist chose to measure up. Confronted with an artist capable of excelling in all three the arts of drawing, sculptors like Bartolomeo Ammannati or Giambologna, for example, chose to limit the media in which they sought to claim his artistic inheritance.[98]

Read against this background, the implications of the last tercet of Pazzi's poem become less paradoxical than at first glance. After all, other sixteenth-century writings testify to the idea, clearly stated in the sonnet by l'Etrusco and in other instances discernible behind a network of intertexual allusions, that an artist could pen verse as a way to fashion for himself a Michelangelesque public persona. These writings also bear witness to how contemporaries saw Bronzino as the leading figure among those Florentine practitioners of the visual arts whose engagement with poetry was modeled after Buonarroti's. For example Varchi, who at the end of his academic lecture on the sonnet *Non ha l'ottimo artista alcun concetto* had cited Berni's definition of Michelangelo as a "nuovo Apollo e nuovo Apelle,"[99] repeatedly used similar expressions to pay homage to Bronzino. Consider the first tercet of his sonnet *Bronzino, ove sì dolce ombreggia e suona* (for the full text see Appendix, no. 49):

> Hor voi, che, nuovo Apelle e nuovo Apollo,
>   Con doppio honore hornate e doppio stile
>   Hor di rime il bell'Arno hor di colori.

Varchi was here adapting to his new addressee some of the expressions already used in the sonnet *Ben vi potea bastar, chiaro scultore*, at the end of his 1547 academic lecture on Buonarroti's poetry. The mention of Michelangelo's versatile talent adorning the world ("O saggio e caro a Dio ben nato veglio, / che 'n tanti e sì bei modi ornate il mondo") was thus reworked in the sonnet in honor of Bronzino to refer to the city of Florence ("il bell'Arno"), which the

---

2002; for an insightful analysis on the special reverence that Florentine writers, theorists on art, and artists had for the master see Eugenio Battisti, *Michelangelo: fortuna di un mito. Cinquecento anni di critica letteraria e artistica*, ed. Giuseppa Saccaro del Buffa, Florence 2012 (but the essay in question, *La critica a Michelangelo dopo il Vasari*, was first published in 1956), pp. 63–70, which emphasizes (p. 63) how these figures generally saw in Michelangelo "un modello d'umanità, cosicché gli scrittori s'impegnano a mettere in luce diversi aspetti della sua vita, della sua cultura, della sua educazione." Elizabeth Pilliod, The Influence of Michelangelo: Pontormo, Bronzino and Allori, in: Joannides and Ames-Lewis 2003 (as in fn. 96), pp. 31–52, p. 31, also remarks on the special cult that the artistic scene of ducal Florence had for the "divine" artist. Of a "Dominanz Michelangelos beherrschte Stadt Florenz" speaks Campbell 2011 (as in fn. 6), p. 194. Also relevant are Claudia Lazzaro, Michelangelo's Medici Chapel and Its Aftermath: Scattered Bodies and Florentine Identities under the Duchy, in: *California Italian Studies* 6 no. 1 (2016), pp. 1–35, and the introduction to Marco Simone Bolzoni, Furio Rinaldi, and Patrizia Tosini (eds.), *Dopo il 1564: l'eredità di Michelangelo a Roma nel tardo Cinquecento*, Rome 2016, pp. 7–11. Bolzoni, Rinaldi and Tosini compare the Roman and Florentine receptions of Michelangelo after his death in 1564 and contend that the devotion to the "divine" master of the Medicean artists was characterized by pedantic excesses that found no correspondence in Roman art of the age.

[98] On this see the considerations of Michael W. Cole, *Ambitious Form: Giambologna, Ammanati, and Danti in Florence*, Princeton, NJ 2011, p. 39.

[99] Varchi 1858–1859 (as in fn. 67), 2, p. 626: "mi basti allegare un sonetto solo, il quale […] mostrerà, come disse quello ingegnosissimo Poeta di ciance e da trastullo, che egli è nuovo Apollo e nuovo Apelle, e non dice parole ma cose, tratte non solo del mezzo di Platone, ma d'Aristotile."

twofold talent of the painter was embellishing with both colors and verse. In a sonnet dating to the last years of his life, Varchi similarly coined a new variation of Berni's words, describing Bronzino as "sì grande Apelle e non minore Apollo."[100] Also other literati of the *sodalitas* of Bronzino deployed the same eulogistic strategy: Laura Battiferri degli Ammannati thus addressed her painter friend noting how much grace "a voi novello Apelle Apollo infonda," while the now unknown Cavalier Sellori celebrated him as "un nuovo Apollo, un nuovo Apelle."[101] In their evident echoes of the wording originally used to praise Michelangelo, these and other formulas all tended to promote the image of a Florentine artist who, in his literary activity, was taking up the baton of Michelangelo's versatility.[102]

But Bronzino was not the only artist of the Medici milieu whose poetry was associated with the example of the "Divine." Another passage from the Giunti edition of the *Vite* is telling in this regard. In describing the statue of Poetry, which on the occasion of the Florentine exequies for Michelangelo had been created to pay homage to his literary activity, Vasari noted that the work had been made by "Domenico Poggini, uomo non solo nella scultura […] ma ancora […] nella poesia parimente molto esercitato."[103] A remarkable engagement in verse writing represented in other words a trait that associated Poggini to the deceased, but perhaps also an element that made the former artist a good choice for commemorating the latter *qua* poet.[104]

---

[100] Sonnet *D'ogni cosa rendiam grazie al Signore*, v. 10 (ibid., p. 992.) The poem was included among the author's *Sonetti spirituali*, which were published posthumously (see here ch. 2). The author's re-use and adaptation of Berni's words for Michelangelo in the present text are noted, among others, in Tanturli 2004 (as in fn. 6), p. 196, and Carla Chiummo, "Sì grande Apelle, e non minore Apollo": il nonsense del Bronzino manierista, in: Giuseppe Antonelli and Carla Chiummo (eds.), *"Nominativi fritti e mappamondi." Il nonsense nella letteratura italiana*, Rome 2009, pp. 93–124.
[101] See Battiferri's sonnet *Sì come in al fonte ebb'io larghe e seconde*, l. 4 (in Laura Battiferra, *Laura Battiferra and Her Literary Circle: An Anthology*, ed. and trans. Victoria Kirkham, Chicago 2006, p. 174), and Sellori's *Cinga le tempie a te, saggio Bronzino*, l. 14 (in Agnolo Bronzino, *Sonetti di Angiolo Allori detto il Bronzino ed altre rime inedite di piu insigni poeti*, ed. Domenico Moreni, Florence 1823, p. 18).
[102] Another relevant example is provided by Michele Capri's sonnet *O mio terreno Apollo, o nuovo Apelle*, which the author addressed to Bronzino and was included in the small anthology of funeral verse *Poesie di diversi authori latine e volgari, fatte nella morte di Michel'Agnolo Buonarroti* (Florence 1564, c. Biiiv). In the same anthology, also the friar and literato Giovan Maria Tarsia emphasized Bronzino's status as Michelangelo's ideal heir, though he did not explicitly mention poetry. Consider how his sonnet *Poi che'l saldo motor della gran mole* (ibid., c. Aiiiv) celebrates the deceased at ll. 9–11: "Perché gito se nè […] quel mostro, / quel miracol, quel vanto di natura / l'Angiol, di cui voi Angiol sète herede."
[103] Vasari 1967–1997 (as in fn. 74), 6, p. 237 (1568). The passage also makes reference to Giovanni Maria Butteri's painting depicting "Michelagnolo tutto intento a scrivere alcuna composizione, et intorno a lui […] le nove Muse et innanzi a esse Appollo […] con un'altra corona in mano, la quale mostrava di volere porre in capo a Michelagnolo."
[104] In the following century, something comparable happened when Michelangelo's grandnephew, Michelangelo il Giovane, commissioned a painting commemorating *Michelangelo and Poetry* for Casa Buonarroti (1615). Probably also in consideration of his activity as a poet, Cristofano Allori was chosen to provide the design for the work that was eventually executed by Zanobi Rosi: see Pizzorusso 1982 (as in fn. 41), p. 13.

Memory, reception, imitation: Michelangelo's poetry among the artists of the Medici court

The aforementioned sources highlight how the poetic activity of several artists of the Medicean milieu was repeatedly seen as a deliberate imitation of Michelangelo. Other documents instead illustrate the different ways in which painters and sculptors from the same scene presented themselves as privileged heirs of that model. A first set of relevant testimonies concerns those artists who preserved and disseminated his verse compositions, including artists who did not write poetry themselves. We know for example that Michelangelo Buonarroti il Giovane, while collecting manuscript materials in view of the *editio princeps* of the compositions of his great-uncle (1623), solicited and received from the heirs of Bernardo Buontalenti (1531–1608) some handwritten comic poems and poetical fragments by Michelangelo. The future editor of the *Rime* did this because Buontalenti had carefully preserved several papers in which, alongside sketches of human figures, statues and architectural elements, Michelangelo had penned verse attested nowhere else (Table 1).[105] Michelangelo il Giovane also acquired a similar document, which along with sketches and designs of mouldings bore a madrigal by the master's hand, from the sculptor Cristofano Stati (1556–1619).[106] A native of Bracciano, in northern Latium, Stati had received his training in Florence, and it was probably here that he had obtained this precious "relic."[107]

In the above cases, we can reasonably assume that Buontalenti's and Stati's desire to preserve Michelangelo's poems took second place to that of collecting the drawings in the same papers.[108] In another circumstance, however, it is possible to attest an exclusive intent to save

---

[105] For the list of the poems that were part of Buontalenti's collection of drawings, which included the *ottave* of *Tu ha' 'l viso più dolce che la sapa*, see Cesare Guasti, *Le Rime di Michelangelo Buonarroti, pittore, scultore e architetto*, Florence 1863, p. LXII; on the ironic ways in which the comic and low intonations of the poem engage with the lofty subjects of the drawings in the same sheet, representing three groups featuring a Madonna with Child, see Barkan 2011 (as in fn. 4), pp. 167–172 (Barkan's book offers, in general, a perceptive analysis of the recurrent co-presence, in Michelangelo's papers, of drawings and poems). On Buontalenti's collection see also Antonio Corsaro in Michelangelo 2016 (as in fn. 4), p. LVII, with reference to Michelangelo Buonarroti il Giovane's transcription of these compositions in what is now the ms. Archivio Buonarroti XV of the Museo Casa Buonarroti, in Florence. In the manuscript, the poems are preceded by the note "Da disegni di Ms Bernardo Buontalenti, oggi miei."

[106] Michelangelo il Giovane transcribed the poem, *Quanto sare' men doglia il morir presto*, in the same manuscript that included the transcriptions from Buontalenti's papers, i.e. the ms. Archivio Buonarroti XV. To the composition, he added the annotation "Da una carta di schizzi di Michelagnolo in man di Cristofano da Bracciano scultore. eravi scritto questo madrigale > anzi ballata < pareva di mano di Michelag.lo stesso." See Guasti 1863 (as in fn. 105), p. LXII; the original sheet appears to have gone missing: see Paul Joannides, *The Drawings of Michelangelo and His Followers in the Ashmolean Museum*, Cambridge 2007, p. 41.

[107] On Stati's career in Florence, see especially Charles Avery, *Studies in Italian Sculpture*, London 2001, p. 323, with further references.

[108] In his funeral oration for the artist, Benedetto Varchi made several references to the huge monetary value that contemporaries already ascribed to Michelangelo's drawings – something that certainly encouraged painters and sculptors to collect these precious relics of the master's art. See, for instance, Varchi 1564 (as in fn. 82), p. 16, which recounts how Michelangelo's pupil, Antonio Mini, had donated to Francis I Valois "infiniti […] varii disegni, e diversi modegli di tutte le sorti, che valevano un mondo."

the memory of Buonarroti's poetical compositions on part of a Medicean artist. The episode is documented by the presence, among the materials that Michelangelo il Giovane collected for his edition of the *Rime,* of a small codex containing almost fifty compositions by his great-uncle.[109] The annotation that opens the manuscript, today in the Archivio Buonarroti, states the following (Table II):

> RIME di MICHEL, più che mortale, ANGEL divino; scultore, pittore e architettore fiorentino, / di messer Accursio Baldi / scultore dal Monte a San Sovino, il quale le copiò da un quadernetto in mano a una donna, di mano di Michelagnolo con varie lezioni e rassettatici di sua mano come scrive Michelagnolo di Lionardo.

Up to the word "Fiorentino" the note is in the hand of Accursio Baldi himself. A goldsmith, as well as engraver and sculptor of Florentine training, Baldi was here echoing the famous lines with which Ariosto had paid homage to Michelangelo, "[…] quel ch'a par sculpe e colora, / Michel, più che mortale, angel divino" (*Orlando Furioso* 33.2.3–4). His literary reference to the "Divine"'s talent in the three arts of drawing opened a collection of compositions that was a most remarkable document of Michelangelo's excellence in his fourth art, namely, poetry, whose personification is perhaps identifiable with the woman which Baldi roughly sketched alongside the citation.

The rest of the introductory note, written by Michelangelo il Giovane and by his descendant Filippo Buonarroti, bears evidence to the fact that Baldi had transcribed his collection directly from Michelangelo's autograph papers. Another document in the same archive confirms this, stating that the sculptor from Monte San Savino "tutte queste [poesie] in Roma copiò da un quadernetto in mano a una donna che non glielo volle dare et era della stessa mano di Michelangelo."[110] While the dearth of biographical information on Baldi makes it impossible to date precisely his trip to Rome, the paleographic comparison with other writings in his hand allows us to date his transcription of Michelangelo's compositions to the early years of his activity, documented in the Medicean milieu from 1579.[111] A minor name in the Florentine

---

[109] Florence, Casa Buonarroti, Archivio Buonarroti, ms. XIV.4 (the original manuscript is today a codicological unity bound in a miscellany containing different poetic materials on and for Michelangelo). For a description of the codex and its contents, which often overlap with the contents of the florilegium of Buonarroti's verse assembled by Donato Giannotti and Luigi del Riccio, see Antonio Corsaro in Michelangelo 2016 (as in fn. 4), pp. LII–LIII.

[110] On the latter note, which is taken from the ms. XV (c. 37v) of the Archivio Buonarroti (a collection of Michelangelo's poems that Michelangelo il Giovane compiled as he was preparing the 1623 edition), see Corsaro in Michelangelo 2016 (as in fn. 4), p. LVII.

[111] Daniela Bruschettini's entry on Accursio's bronze candelabra for the Siena cathedral (in: Fiorella Sricchia Santoro [ed.], *L'arte a Siena sotto i Medici: 1555–1609. Mostra: Siena, Palazzo Pubblico 3 maggio–15 settembre*, Rome 1980, pp. 264–265) and Anna Maria Massinelli, Accursio Baldi e la statua di Sisto V a Fermo, in: Paolo Del Poggetto (ed.), *Le arti nelle Marche al tempo di Sisto V*, Cinisello Balsamo 1992, pp. 232–235, provide concise but useful introductions to Accursio Baldi's life and professional career. Bruschettini hypothesizes that the artist's Florentine formation took place around the circle of Giambologna, and that around 1585 the relationships between the two had deteriorated (see the 1585 letter in which Baldi complains for the Flemish sculptor's low estimate of his two bronze candelabrum-bearing angels for the altar of the Hospital Church of Santa Maria della Scala, in Siena, in Giovanni Gaye, *Carteggio inedito d'artisti dei secoli XIV, XV, XVI*, 3 vols., Florence 1839–1840, 3, pp. 464–468). She also records the earliest document of the artist's activity, namely, Raffaello Gualterotti's

artistic scene, Baldi developed in that environment a certain talent for verse composition.[112] It was thus certainly as a poet-artist that he looked up to the one artist who had been able to achieve supreme results in writing as much as in the disciplines of drawing. What's more, in assembling a collection of poems by Michelangelo, he probably intended not only to preserve memory of a relevant portion of his unpublished corpus of verse, but also to prepare a repertory of materials that he could imitate and re-use in his own poetical exercises. Similarly to the painters and sculptors who copied works by the greatest masters as a fundamental part of their invention process, Renaissance poets typically transcribed other authors' compositions as a preliminary step for the creative re-use of those materials.[113]

The small corpus of poems by Baldi that has come down to us does not offer much textual evidence of Michelangelesque traces, but the case is different in several poems by Medicean artists of the previous generation. Investigation of such literary echoes in their verse is sometimes only circumstantial, insofar as it is impossible to prove with certainty that these sculptors and painters were familiar with their artistic and intellectual model's writings. Still, both the academic lecture delivered by Varchi and the presence of Buonarroti's poems in miscellaneous collections of the time suggest that his compositions had a remarkable manuscript circulation in ducal Florence,[114] and point to the concrete possibility that a number of textual affinities between the verse of Michelangelo and that of other artists working in Florence were the result of imitation rather than polygenetic resemblances.

---

description of the *Feste delle nozze del Serenissimo D. Francesco Medici Granduca di Toscana e della Serenissima sua consorte la Signora Bianca Cappello* (published in Florence by Giunti in 1579), which Baldi and Sebastiano Marsili illustrated with sixteen etchings. Massinelli's contribution focuses on Baldi's activity in Fermo, where the artist arrived in 1588 and two years later completed the bronze statue of pope Sixtus V and the bust of the jurist Marco Antonio Severo. Her study indicates in 1607 the year of Accursio's death, which on the contrary occurred in 1609. See Florence, Archivio di Stato (hereafter ASF), Guardaroba Medicea, 301, c. 12r (a list of the *Diversi huomini di Architettura, Pittura et altri Magisteri* who received salaries from the Granduke Ferdinando de' Medici), where the name «Accurso Baldi scultore» is followed by the note «morse 26 settembre 1609». Relevant for the proposed dating of Baldi's note in the manuscript XIV.4 of the Archivio Buonarroti is the fact that the handwriting is much closer to the sculptor's autograph sonnet *Ecco per libertà darne e vittoria* (BNCF, cod. II.I.397, c. 81), which he composed in 1579 on the occasion of Francesco de' Medici's marriage with Bianca Cappello, than to his autograph letter to Ippolito Agostini and sonnet to Scipione Bargagli (Siena, Biblioteca Comunale degli Intronati, codd. D. V.2, c. 32r and D.VII.10, c. 161r), which date to the final years of the sixteenth century.

[112] Along with the compositions listed in the previous note, Baldi was the author of a sonnet published in the volume *Rime del signor Raffaello Gualterotti. Al serenissimo don Francesco Medici*, Florence 1581, unnumbered page. He also authored several sonnets in the self-celebratory anthology *Prima parte delle rime toscane et de' versi latini da diversi autori composti, in lode di Sisto V et della statua di bronzo dalla M. Illustr. Città di Fermo dedicata a S. Santità, et fatta da Accursio Baldi Sansovino*, Fermo 1590, which he curated upon the completion of his bronze statue of Sixtus V. On Baldi's poetic output see Jean Balsamo, Franco Tomasi, and Carlo Ossola (eds.), *De Dante à Chiabrera: Poètes italiens de la Renaissance dans la bibliothèque de la Fondation Barbier-Mueller*, 2 vols., Geneva 2007, 1, p. 80.

[113] For the role of manuscript transcriptions of poetry among Renaissance writers, see Richardson 2009 (as in fn. 18), p. 133.

[114] For a full list and a description of the Florentine poetic anthologies that preserve poems by the artist see Corsaro in Michelangelo 2016 (as in fn. 4), pp. LXIV–LXXVII and *passim* for the manuscripts of the Archivio Buonarroti.

In the corpus of poetry by Benvenuto Cellini, for instance, there are various pieces that suggest a deliberate re-use of Michelangelesque tesserae.[115] One such example is a fragment of a sonnet that dates to the final months of 1560, when Cellini had lost hope of getting the coveted commission for the Neptune Fountain in the Piazza della Signoria. After the death of Baccio Bandinelli, to whom the work had been originally committed, and after an open competition was held among the foremost sculptors of the Florentine court, the Duke had just allocated the prestigious artistic task to Bartolomeo Ammannati.[116] For the circumstance, Cellini wrote an embittered poem of which only the tercets now survive, *io fo modegli, altrui à l'opre e 'l vanto* (Appendix, no. 1). What deserves particular attention is the burlesque passage in which the author characterized his verse writing as a sign of senile foolishness, for this excerpt closely reminds the way in which Michelangelo, in a letter to Giorgio Vasari, had described his own decision to pen poetry as a confirmation of the rumors that in his old age he had become a bit of a dotard: "Messer Giorgio amico caro, voi direte ben che io sie vechio and pazzo a vole' far sonecti; ma perché molti dicono ch'i' son rinbanbito, ò voluto far l'uficio mio."[117] Writing to an anonymous addressee "Voi mi terrete fuor d'ogni sapere, / che come un rinbanbito così canto" (ll. 4–5), Cellini thus seemed to be echoing Buonarroti's ironic self-deprecation. The use by both of the second person plural pronoun "voi," of the future tense to predict the derisory reaction to an old artist's decision to write poetry, and especially of the comic term "rinbanbito," all suggest more than a casual resemblance between the two texts. Furthermore, Michelangelo's declaration of poetics was contained in a document that, although unpublished at the time, was probably well known to Cellini for reasons of court diplomacy, being a letter in which Buonarroti declined the invitation to return to Florence proffered to him by Duke Cosimo through Vasari (1554).[118]

The above example presents us with the case of an artist who seems to have purposely used an intertextual memory of Michelangelo to construct his own image as poet. In his autobiography, Cellini wrote that his early artistic training had taken place "continuamente in Firenze […] sotto la bella maniera di Michelagnolo," and that he had never betrayed that lesson: it is in this regard all the more interesting that in his poems, too, he repeatedly proved himself

---

[115] Another relevant example comes from the sonnet *Signiore eccellentissimo et divino*, which seems to contain a memory from Michelangelo's *capitolo I' sto rinchiuso come la midolla*: see my discussion in Cellini 2014 (as in fn. 7), pp. 69–70.
[116] For the history of the commission see Loretta Cammarella Falsitta and Alessandro Falsitta, *Cellini, Bandinelli, Ammannati: la fontana del Nettuno in Piazza della Signoria a Firenze*, Milan 2009, with further references.
[117] Michelangelo 1965–1983 (as in fn. 61), 5, p. 21 (19 September 1554).
[118] Also in 1560, Cellini had written to Michelangelo to convince him to return to Florence and thus please Duke Cosimo (see his letter of March 14, 1560 ibid., pp. 208–209). It seems likely that Cellini was aware of the answer his addressee had given to Vasari's own attempt to induce him to go back to Florence. Michelangelo's letter, on the other hand, was a semi-official document, which addressed Vasari as ducal emissary, and it probably circulated among the several painters and sculptors who were involved in Cosimo's reiterated efforts to persuade Buonarroti to return to his hometown. For a reconstruction of such efforts see the rich commentary of Paola Barocchi in Vasari 1962 (as in fn. 73), 4, pp. 1598–1614.

a skillful imitator of that model.[119] This is perhaps less true of Giorgio Vasari, notwithstanding the fact that he was the only Medicean artist who had the honor to exchange verse with the "divine" master. Although in his poetry there are a number of echoes from Michelangelo's compositions, these often appear as mannered but rather superficial homages.[120]

The ideological import of this form of literary imitation was particularly crucial for Bronzino. In the Spring of 1561, the artist whom so many Florentine literati celebrated as the spiritual heir of "new Apollo" and "new Apelles" wrote to Michelangelo a letter which supported the same notion of an ideal filiation between the two. After claiming he was seizing the occasion offered by his recent meeting with a member of the Buonarroti family to finally express his feelings for his addressee, Bronzino went on to state in para-religious terms his devotion to Michelangelo. Acknowledging himself as a disciple and metaphorical child or fruit ("creatura") of his addressee, the Florentine painter emphasized how he owed all that he knew and was capable of doing, albeit it little, to his model. He then invited Michelangelo to graciously accept the sonnet included in the letter, *O stupor di natura, Angelo eletto* (Appendix, no. 2), as a testimony of the same devotion:

> […] Messer Michelagnolo mio, sallo Iddio quanto io ho sempre amato et reverito le grandissime ed incomparabili virtuti vostre et come sempre ho desiderato che Vostra Signoria mi comandi, e quanto io habbi havuto sempre voglia di scriverle […]; ma non mi parendo essere né degno a ciò né in parte alcuna sufficiente, me ne sono stato, riserbandomi solo l'amore nel mezzo del cuore inverso di voi e lo stupore de' vostri altissimi meriti […]. Ma hora, essendomi venuta questa troppo grandissima occasione, non me ne sono potuto tenere, perché non mi pare però ragionevole che, havendo io sempre riconosciuto da voi tutto quello, ancora che per mio difetto sia poco, che io so e vaglio, e perciò tenermi, anzi essere, e sua creatura e discepolo ed insomma tutto suo, che almeno, stimulato dalla sì grande humilità vostra, io non gl[i]ele facessi […] sapere […]. Io non voglio più tediare il modestissimo animo vostro né occuparlo con lungo scrivere, ma solo pregarla che non li sia grave ancora di leggere il presente sonetto, che io con questa le mando e che l'altissima humilità di quella in salutare così bassa persona m'ha tratto della penna, offerendomi per quanto io vaglio, mentre harò vita, a Vostra cortesissima Signoria […].[121]

---

[119] Cellini 1996 (as in fn. 23), p. 46 (*Vita* 1.13.) For the author's literary framing of his own imitation of Michelangelo, with special reference to Cellini's autobiography, see Jane Tylus, Cellini, Michelangelo and the Myth of Inimitability, in: Margaret A. Gallucci and Paolo L. Rossi (eds.), *Benvenuto Cellini: Sculptor, Goldsmith, Writer*, Cambridge 2004, pp. 7–25, and Pasquale Sabatino, "Imparare sotto la bella maniera di Michelangelo": l'imitazione nelle opere di Benvenuto Cellini, in: *Chroniques italiennes web* 16 (2009): http://chroniquesitaliennes.univ-paris3.fr/PDF/web16/Sabbatinoweb16.pdf, last accessed 31/01/2021.

[120] The two had been exchanging compositions since the early 1550s, while they were both in Rome: see Vasari 2012 (as in fn. 7), p. 53. For the presence of memories from Michelangelo's poetry in Vasari's verse, see for instance Enrico Mattioda's commentary ibid., pp. 39–40. For an analysis of the sonnet exchange that originated from Vasari's 1554 invitation to Michelangelo to leave Rome for Florence, and of the deep stylistic differences between the two artists' compositions, see Gamberini 2018 (as in fn. 92), pp. 214–215.

[121] Michelangelo 1965–1983 (as in fn. 61), 5, pp. 255–256 (May 3, 1561). On the letter see Pilliod 2003 (as in fn. 97), p. 36; Antonio Geremicca, Sulla scia di Agnolo Bronzino, Alessandro Allori sodale di Benedetto Varchi. Un ritratto 'misconosciuto' del letterato e un suo sonetto inedito," in: *La Rivista. Études culturelles italiennes Sorbonne Universités* 5 (2017), pp. 87–113 (https://etudesitaliennes.hypotheses.org/files/2017/05/6GeremiccaFiniNouveau.pdf, last accessed 31/01/2021), p. 98, and esp. Robert W. Gaston, Towards a Post-Modernist Bronzino?, in: Andrea M. Gáldy, Agnolo Bronzino: Medici Court Artist in Context, Newcastle upon Tyne 2013, pp. 107–127, p. 114: "the intepretation of Bronzino's fulsome poetic and theoretical expressions of subservience to Michelangelo's artistic genius needs to be tempered with an understanding of the decorous rules of contemporary

The sonnet, which the author conventionally downplayed as the proof of his inferior intellect, was in truth a most sophisticated manifesto of integral Michelangiolism.[122] Its initial reference to the angelic nature of the addressee and to the fact that he combined perfect goodness ("il Buono arroto", with a play on words on the participle of the verb *arrogere*, 'to add') with equally perfect virtue represents a variation of the etymological witticisms on the artist's name that were so common among his contemporaries.[123] The idea of religious reverence that underlies the first quatrain, however, takes on less conventional traits in the second stanza. Resorting to a sacramental vocabulary ("vi feci voto," "devoto / vi consacrai"), in reference to the status of his addressee as "terrestre dio," the author stated that from an early age he had devoted both his person and his work to the cult of Michelangelo. To do this, Bronzino chose to echo Michelangelo's most famous poem in the Florentine milieu: the one that had been the object of Varchi's academic lecture. As Deborah Parker has first noted, the dichotomy of "mano" and "intelletto" that Bronzino claimed he had devoted to the master is clearly modeled after Michelangelo's sonnet on the "ottimo artista," there described as the sculptor who possesses "la man, che ubbidisce all'intelletto."[124] What deserves to be underscored is the twofold function of such a reference. On the one hand, the intertextuality indicates Bronzino's desire to present himself as a painter who solely through his dedication to Buonarroti had been able to fully develop his intellectual and manual capabilities, the Michelangelesque conditions for excellence in art. On the other hand, the modeling of the author's persona after Michelangelo extends to the literary sphere as well as to the visual arts. In short, Bronzino here declared his faith in his addressee both as a poet and as a painter: a faith affirmed despite the great formal differences that, in reality, separate the poetical languages of the two artists.[125]

---

poetic genre and letter-writing […]. When Bronzino sent Michelangelo a sonnet in 1561 he accompanied it with a letter that seems to us today to overflow with cringing hyperbole […]. In fact, if one is familiar with the decorous language of courtly letter-writing of the period, there is nothing excessive about these expressions of ritualised submission that would accompany the sending of an unsolicited poem and letter by a person of lesser fame and standing." As Richardson 2009 (as in fn. 18, pp. 27–29) illustrates, in Cinquecento Italy the enclosure of a letter was a frequent medium of scribal publication for single sonnets or small numbers of poems.

[122] Discussions of the present text, as well as of the second sonnet that Bronzino addressed to Michelangelo (*Come l'alto Michele Angel, con forte*, on which see *infra*), have consistently emphasized how the poems represent the author's most explicit declarations of devotion to Buonarroti: see Janet Cox-Rearick, *Bronzino's Chapel of Eleonora in the Palazzo Vecchio*, Berkeley 1993, p. 106; Parker 2000 (as in fn. 6), pp. 91–96; Campbell 2011 (as in fn. 6), pp. 207–208.

[123] On the fortune of the rhetoric devices that stressed the angelic nature of Michelangelo, see esp. Romeo De Maio, *Michelangelo e la Controriforma*, Rome 1978, pp. 447–451 and 463–465; Stephen J. Campbell, "Fare Una Cosa Morta Parer Viva": Michelangelo, Rosso, and the (Un)Divinity of Art, in: *The Art Bulletin* 84 (2002), pp. 596–620, p. 599, fn. 9 and 620, fn. 109; William E. Wallace, *Michelangelo: The Artist, the Man and His Times*, Cambridge 2010, pp. 32–33, and Diletta Gamberini, "Divine" or Not? Poetic Responses to the Art of Michelangelo," in: Claudia Swan (ed.), *Tributes to David Freedberg*, Turnhout 2019, pp. 431–441, with further bibliography.

[124] Parker 2000 (as in fn. 6), p. 95.

[125] On the differences in style and language between Michelangelo's and Bronzino's lyrical corpus see Andrea Emiliani, *Il Bronzino*, Busto Arsizio 1960, pp. 96–97. Compare also Campbell 2011 (as in fn. 6), p. 209, which rightly contrasts Bronzino's Petrarchism, its "puristischen, reinen Form" and "subtil-delikaten Sprache", to Michelangelo's "komplizierte Dichtungen, deren Metrum oft recht anspruchsvoll ist, die nicht selten mit einer

These instances of literary self-fashioning, then, particularly resonate with some enlightening remarks on the forms that the imitation of Michelangelo took among sixteenth-century Italian practitioners of the visual arts, also outside the milieu of Florence. In the words of Morten Steen Hansen, for painters of the likes of Daniele da Volterra or Pellegrino Tibaldi "imitation after other artists could be a means to shaping an artistic persona in the image of predecessors."[126] Notably, such an imitative attitude often extended outside the boundaries of professional activity and affected such aspects as the imitator's ideals of behavior or even exterior image, for an assimilation of models of unique artistic and intellectual prestige was functional to the social aspirations of those who practiced this kind of imitation.[127] In the Florentine milieu, the writing of poetry became one privileged option for artists to create and "perform" a self of the Michelangelesque type, and thereby to obtain a recognition comparable to the master's.[128]

How to imitate Michelangelo?

The theme of *imitatio*, at the center of Bronzino's letter and sonnet of 1561, underpins a larger constellation of poems that various artists of ducal Florence addressed to Michelangelo or dedicated to a reflection on his art. A discussion of this literary output can usefully begin with a composition by a painter who was not yet in the service of Duke Cosimo, but which anticipates the ideological chores of this constellation of texts. Between the end of 1550 and the beginning of 1551, Giorgio Vasari wrote to Michelangelo the sonnet *Angel, fra noi più che Michel divino* (Appendix, no. 3), in response to one that the old master had addressed him out of gratitude for sending him the Torrentino edition of the *Vite*.[129] Given the circumstances of the composition of the sonnet, it comes as no surprise that a dense network of references connects Vasari's poem to the Torrentiniana's biography of Buonarroti. The messianic tone that informs the latter text's opening, with its celebration of the artist who proved to be a "cosa celeste e divina più che mortale," for instance distinguishes the incipit of Vasari's lyric. This text then presents Michelangelo as the guide who, through his example, made it possible for

---

gewissen grammatikalischen Unberechenbarkeit strukturiert sind, und deren Grundstimmung häufig […] in einem groben Tonfall vermittelt wird."

[126] Morten Steen Hansen, *In Michelangelo's Mirror: Perino Del Vaga, Daniele Da Volterra, Pellegrino Tibaldi*. University Park, PA 2013, p. 9. Important are also the discussions of how contemporary writers linked the reputation of seventeenth-century artists such as Gian Lorenzo Bernini to the model of Michelangelo, and how the artists themselves fashioned their own public persona and works to encourage this kind of association and artistic genealogy: on this, see Catherine M. Soussloff, Imitatio Buonarroti, in: *The Sixteenth Century Journal* 20 (1989), pp. 581–602, and Carolina Mangone, Like Father, Like Son: Bernini's Filial Imitation of Michelangelo, in: *Art History* 37 (2014), pp. 666–687.

[127] Steen Hansen 2013 (as in fn. 126), p. 55.

[128] For the notion, see Richard Poirier, *The Performing Self: Compositions and Decompositions in the Languages of Contemporary Life*, New York / Oxford 1971.

[129] For Buonarroti's poem (incipit: *Se con lo stile o coi colori*), see Michelangelo 2016 (as in fn. 4), *Rime liriche e amorose*, n. 93 (p. 253).

the author to take a journey towards artistic perfection and eternal fame. Notably, Vasari used literary memories from Dante – an author which he knew to be very dear and "famigliarissimo" to Michelangelo[130] – to construct his own manifesto of devotion to the master. To make just two examples, his wording "sereno e chiaro / Lume" echoes the way in which Dante had paid homage to Virgil, "de li altri poeti onore e lume" (*Inferno* 1.82), and the images of the "scorta" and of the path, which since antiquity had been associated to the discussion of imitative practices, similarly evoke Dantean representations of the exemplarity of the same author of the *Aeneid*.[131] These textual references, then, outline an ideal scheme in which Michelangelo takes on the role of a modern Virgil, and Vasari that of a new Dante: just like the latter poet had presented his first guide to the underworld as the source of all that was worthy in his work ("Tu se' lo mio maestro e 'l mio autore; / tu se' solo colui da cu' io tolsi / lo bello stilo che m'ha fatto onore;" *Inferno* 1.85–87), so did Vasari attribute all his success and fame as an artist to the exclusive imitation of Michelangelo.

In the lines describing his own emancipation from the darkness of artistic ignorance to the light of knowledge under the guide of the addressee, Vasari was also deploying a kind of imagery which he had already used in the Torrentiniana. Consider how, in the final biography of the book, he had exhorted artists to imitate Michelangelo "in all things:"

> O[h] veramente felice età nostra, o[h] beati artefici, che ben così vi dovete chiamare, da che nel tempo vostro avete potuto al fonte di tanta chiarezza rischiarare le tenebrose luci degli occhi e vedere, fattovi piano, tutto quel ch'era difficile da sì maraviglioso e singulare artefice! Certamente la gloria delle fatiche sue vi fa conoscere et onorare, da che ha tolto da voi quella benda che avevate inanzi gli occhi della mente, sì di tenebre piena, e v'ha scoperto il velo del falso, il quale v'adombrava le bellissime stanze dell'intelletto. Ringraziate di ciò dunque il cielo e sforzatevi d'imitar Michel Agnolo in tutte le cose.[132]

The sonnet's argument that it was possible to acquire artistic fame only by imitating the "Angel, fra noi più che Michel divino" similarly echoes the ideological tenets of the concluding passage in the 1550 biography:

> Però, come nel principio dissi, il Cielo per essempio nella vita, ne' costumi e nelle opere l'ha qua giù mandato, acciò che quegli che risguardano in lui possiano, imitandolo, accostarsi per fama alla eternità del nome, e per l'opere e per lo studio alla natura, e per la virtù al cielo.[133]

In other compositions written in Rome in the early 1550s, Vasari likewise developed his image as an artist devoted to the imitation of Michelangelo,[134] and also after moving to Florence he

---

[130] Quoted from the Giuntina's biography of Buonarroti: Vasari 1967–1997 (as in fn. 74), 6, p. 73.
[131] For the metaphors of the path and the guide in ancient and Renaissance debates on imitation see G. W. Pigman, Versions of Imitation in the Renaissance, in: *Renaissance Quarterly* 33.1 (1980), pp. 1–32, pp. 19–21. For Dante's definition of Virgil as "la mia scorta" see *Inferno* 12.54.
[132] Vasari 1967–1997 (as in fn. 74), 6, pp. 48–49 (1550).
[133] Ibid., p. 119.
[134] For example, in the *capitolo in terza rima* addressed to his wife Niccolosa Bacci, Vasari described Buonarroti as "gran vecchio mio, / Qual pasce noi di cose alte e divine," a mirror in which men could observe "Di quanto ben ci abbi dotato Iddio." In inviting his newly wed bride, living in Arezzo, to continue to bear their separation, Vasari then confided his hope of soon becoming one of the followers of Michelangelo. See Vasari 2012 (as in

continued in this literary construction of his artistic persona. Addressing a poem to the old master (*Gl'anni che visse quel che fece l'arca*: Appendix, no. 4), in the attempt to convince him to leave the corrupt Roman curia and join him in the heavenly court of Duke Cosimo, the author for instance presented himself as a disciple who had lamentably lost, and needed to find once more, the Michelangelesque path to excellency. Such a *topos modestiae*, on the other hand, served Vasari to depict himself as the first member of that Florentine artistic community which was following the same path and was anxious to show Michelangelo its unconditioned devotion.[135]

Notably, a number of the ideological tenets of the Torrentiniana's biography of Michelangelo had a shaping impact on the compositions of other Medicean poet-artists. Deborah Parker has for instance emphasized how the incipit of Bronzino's sonnet *Come l'alto Michele Angel, con forte* (1561; Appendix, no. 5), celebrating the Archangel Michael as the celestial alter ego of Buonarroti for defeating the rebel angels and dissipating the shadows that threatened Paradise, is reminiscent of the opening of Vasari's account.[136] And the ideological and lexical affinities between the texts are particularly close when one considers other passages from the Torrentino edition of the *Vita* of Michelangelo, starting from this work's emphasis on the supernatural destiny that would have been inscribed in the name imposed upon the artist, which finds correspondence in Bronzino's typical punning on the angelic nature of the addressee.[137]

---

fn. 7), p. 57 (capitolo *Per dar riposo alla mia mente stanca*), ll. 62–70. Michelangelo was celebrated as an ethical as well as artistic model also in another *capitolo* by Vasari. In the text, the author addressed the older master as a "d'arte e di senno eterno specchio," and asked for his advice on how to deal with his own professional difficulties as an artist in service of an ungenerous client like Pope Julius III. See ibid., p. 59 (*capitolo Consiglio, a voi messer che siate vecchio*).

[135] For a lengthier discussion of the poem, see Gamberini 2018 (as in fn. 92), pp. 213–215. Vasari voiced similar ideas almost a decade later, in a letter in which he presented to Michelangelo the newly founded Accademia del Disegno. In the document, the institution was depicted as a community of artists united in their devotion to the addressee – a devotion of which Vasari claimed to be the main representative. See the document in Michelangelo 1965–1983 (as in fn. 61), 5, pp. 298–305 (March 17, 1563), with regards to the Academy's projects for the pictorial and sculptural decoration of the Sacristy of San Lorenzo. For the strategic role that the association with Michelangelo had for the new-born institution see Marco Ruffini, *Art without an Author: Vasari's* Lives *and Michelangelo's Death*, New York 2011, pp. 35–38; for Vasari's representation of Michelangelo as the father of arts see Paul Barolsky, *Giotto's Father and the Family of Vasari's* Lives, University Park, PA 1992, pp. 131–132.

[136] Consider in particular Vasari 1967–1997 (as in fn. 74), 1550, 6, p. 3: "il benignissimo Rettor del Cielo volse clemente gli occhi a la terra; e veduta la vana infinità di tante fatiche, gli ardentissimi studii senza alcun frutto, e la opinione prosuntuosa degli uomini, assai più lontana dal vero che le tenebre dalla luce […]." See Parker 2000 (as in fn. 6), pp. 93–94, for a discussion of the relation between this text and Bronzino's poem.

[137] See Vasari 1967–1997 (as in fn. 74), 6, pp. 4–5 (1550): "Nacque dunque […] un figliuolo a Lodovico Simon Buonarroti, al quale pose nome al batesimo Michele Agnolo, volendo inferire costui essere cosa celeste e divina più che mortale." Although the wordplays on Michelangelo's name were very common among the poets who paid homage to the artist, such a rhetorical device might – in the case of the present sonnet – also have an indirect relation to Bronzino's activity as a painter. As Janet Cox-Rearick (1993, as in fn. 122, p. 105) first observed, the emphasis on the identification between Michelangelo and the Archangel Michael linked the sonnet to the visual depiction of the latter subject on the vault of the Chapel of Eleonora di Toledo in Palazzo Vecchio. The figure itself was conceived as a homage to the master, given that "St. Michael's elegant head and his contrived posture seem to refer to Michelangelo's *Victory* of 1530–32, one of the first sculptures to exhibit the fully developed characteristics of the Maniera […]. In evoking this work (which, like St. Michael, represents the victory of

Another such passage was the paragraph in the Torrentiniana that exhorted contemporary artists to imitate Michelangelo "in all things:"[138] the text's metaphorical constellation, which stresses how the world of arts was shrouded in obscurity before the saviour of the arts removed the veil covering the artists' eyes of the mind, anticipates the one used by Bronzino when he describes the Archangel Michael removing the veil of error from the paradisaical court, with an image that also echoes the way in which Vasari emphasized how lucky were the artists who, thanks to Michelangelo, were able to see "squarciato il velo delle difficultà di quello che si può fare et imaginare nelle pitture e sculture et architetture."[139]

A pervasive intertextuality to Vasari's Torrentiniana helps illuminate another aspect of the poem by Bronzino. While in *O stupor di Natura, Angelo eletto* the author described his own personal devotion to Michelangelo, in *Come l'alto Michele Angel, con forte* he extends a monotheistic Michelangelesque cult to a plurality of followers. When the painter speaks of a "noi" who had the opportunity to follow Buonarroti and leave behind the errors of earlier artistic practices (ll. 5–6: "Tal voi, di nome e d'opre, a noi per sorte / Dato scopriste il ver […]"), the plural pronoun is not a *plurale maiestatis*[140] but rather designates a community of artists, basically coinciding with the one indicated by Vasari: the lucky chosen who lived in an age illuminated by the "Divine."

Like many passages in the Torrentiniana, Bronzino's sonnet assumed Michelangelo to be the only object worth imitation. According to the poem, the virtues, intellectual qualities and artistic capabilities of the old master made him the source of all that was worthy to be achieved in the arts: any other model was, quite simply, superfluous and to be excluded. Indeed, in light of the literary debates on imitation that fixed the critical categories through which sixteenth-century art criticism discussed the topic, Michelangelo emerges from the last compositions we have examined as the type of supreme model that Pietro Bembo, in his letter-manifesto *De Imitatione* (1513), had presented as the only example necessary to imitate in order to excel.[141]

---

good over evil), Bronzino declared an admiration of Michelangelo's art that informs the chapel's Moses frescoes, the chapel's altarpiece and his mature art in general."

[138] Compare the already mentioned passage in Vasari 1967–1997 (as in fn. 74), 6, pp. 48–49 (1550): "da che ha tolto da voi quella benda che avevate inanzi gli occhi della mente, sì di tenebre piena, e v'ha scoperto il velo del falso." Deborah Parker discusses similar images in Bronzino's capitolo *Secondo delle scuse*; see Parker 2004 (as in fn. 6), p. 166: "Like Vasari, Bronzino depicts Michelangelo's effect on the arts in allegorical terms: throughout his vita of the sculptor Vasari refers to the darkness which had shrouded the arts before Michelangelo's birth." Speaking of the advancement of Florentine sculpture in the aftermath of Michelangelo's example, Cosimo Bartoli voiced similar ideas in his *Ragionamenti*. After mentioning two beautiful statues created by the seventeen-years-old sculptor Santi Camilliani, the author declared (Bartoli, *Ragionamenti sopra alcuni luoghi difficili di Dante*, Venice 1567, c. 20r): "non sto niente in dubbio che elle sono così fatte, che da cinquanta anni a dietro non le harebbero sapute condurre tali, quei maestri che havessero atteso alla arte quaranta o cinquanta anni; et tutto mercè di Michelangelo che ha aperti gli occhi a questa età di maniera, che hora mai per molti non ha più invidia a gli Antichi."

[139] Vasari 1967–1997 (as in fn. 74), 6, p. 75 (1550).

[140] This can be proven when we consider that, in the previous sonnet, the authorial voice only speaks in the first person.

[141] The literature on sixteenth-century literary debates on imitation is huge: among the key works on the topic see especially Lee 1940 (as in fn. 3), pp. 203–210; Pigman 1980 (as in fn. 131); Thomas M. Greene, *The Light in*

In the field of visual arts, Michelangelo was, in other words, here represented as the equivalent of Cicero and Virgil, the *auctores* whom Bembo labeled as the highest peaks of Latin prose and poetry. According to the *De Imitatione*, the principle of the imitation of the best possible model was after all true for literature as much as for painting or sculpture, as proven in antiquity by the supreme examples of Apelles and Lysippus.[142] Additionally, the role these poems attributed to Buonarroti as the only one capable of guiding his followers away from a path dense with dangers and errors, the only one who could ensure that the artists after him might achieve true glory, was related to the same set of ideas. Bembo had asserted, for instance, that every voyage is made safer by the presence of a guide, and that the shining example of masters is for men the most formidable encouragement to achieve fame.[143]

Notably, it was this same theoretical system that advocated the kind of integral imitative approach which led Vasari to argue that Michelangelo had to be imitated "in all things," and pushed several Medicean artists to fashion for themselves a public persona after their master. Ever since the controversies on imitative practices of the early sixteenth century, this approach had been considered typical of the Ciceronianists (i. e. the upholders of the imitation of Cicero as the single best possible example of Latin writing), as opposed to those who chose to follow a plurality of models. This approach could take the form of a chameleonic ability to conform to one's model, as an anonymous sixteenth-century biographer suggested when he stated that Pietro Bembo "era nato singolarmente all'imitazione […], di maniera che quando prendeva ad imitare uno si trasformava in lui, e a lui si rendeva tutto simile."[144] On the contrary, those

---

Troy: Imitation and Discovery in Renaissance Poetry, New Haven, CT 1982, pp. 171–196; Martin McLaughlin, *Literary Imitation in the Italian Renaissance: The Theory and Practice of Literary Imitation in Italy from Dante to Bembo*, Oxford 1995, esp. pp. 249–274. A number of studies have addressed these theories' interferences with contemporary art criticism: especially relevant are Eugenio Battisti, *Rinascimento e Barocco*, Turin 1960, pp. 175–215; Pasquale Sabbatino, *La bellezza di Elena: l'imitazione nella letteratura e nelle arti figurative del Rinascimento*, Florence 1997, and James Ackerman, Imitation, in: Alina A. Payne, Ann L. Kuttner, and Rebekah Smick (eds.), *Antiquity and Its Interpreters*, Cambridge 2000, pp. 9–16.

[142] See Bembo's letter to Pico (in: JoAnn DellaNeva, ed., *Ciceronian Controversies*, Engl. trans. Brian Duvick, Cambridge, MA 2007, p. 49): "if one author is by far the best and most excellent of all those we consider good, such that all the qualities each of the others has are even finer and more splendid in that one writer, will we gain nothing by rightly imitating the greatest and best of all, unless we also imitate those that we consider only moderately good? It is as if an artist who has learned to paint in the style of Apelles – whose skill the other painters so admired that they awarded him first place without contest – also was made to consult the paintings of Polygnotus and Timanthes by whom Apelles was taught; or a sculptor who imitated Lysippus's excellent and famous art of statuary also had to contemplate the stiff figures of Calamis or the even stiffer ones of Canachus." On this passage see also Greene 1982 (as in fn. 141), p. 174.

[143] Compare Bembo's letter to Pico (DellaNeva 2007 [as in fn. 142], p. 69): "As we travel more confidently when we find a guide, so we show more readiness to engage in other matters when we have teachers and masters; and nothing excites in us every fine desire for praise and glory more than the emulation of others." See also p. 75: "just as the runners who avoid stumbling will finish the race sooner than the ones who repeatedly slip, so those engaged in literary imitation will reach their goal more swiftly themselves if they avoid stumbling. To be sure, this sometimes seems to depend on fortune and chance. So many things […] summon one's soul from its designated pathway and lead it in the wrong direction. But those who will take delight in the study of oratory or poetry will be obliged to stick to this path and try to complete it to the best of their ability."

[144] The quote is from Battisti 1960 (as in fn. 141), p. 187.

who favored an eclectic imitative approach had attacked the idea that a sole model should be imitated "in all things." Against Bembo, Giovan Francesco Pico had for instance maintained that it was essential to avoid following a single example "omnibus […] in rebus." According to Pico, the desire to "completely imitate" ("omnino imitari") another human being, "almost as if he were better than God almighty" ("quasi ille Deo praestaret optimo maximo,") was a pernicious form of idolatry: a position that further evidences the similarity between the para-religious character of Ciceronianist reverence and the monotheistic devotion towards Michelangelo that several poet-artists of ducal Florence openly professed.[145]

Cellini and Michelangelo

The fact that various Medicean painters and sculptors presented Michelangelo as their sole model and argued for the existence of a community of artists sharing this devotion should not obfuscate the agonistic element associated with this stance. In an artistic scene as competitive as the Florentine one in the 1550s and 1560s, their ambition to present themselves as privileged followers of that example was a form of self-promoting strategy that was anything but solidaristic.[146] Indeed, the claimed heritage of Michelangelo was one of the terrains on which took place the clash among artists competing for Medici commissions and embodying different stylistic trends, whose fortune fluctuated in ducal Florence.

The desire to assert the author's preeminence within the community of Florentine disciples of the revered master is, for instance, central in a series of poems by Cellini. Let us consider his sonnet *Solo una fronda della tua corona* (ca. 1560; Appendix, no. 6), with its new and uncompromising assertion of exclusive devotion to Michelangelo's teachings. The poet admitted here that he lacked the universal talents of his model, the only one who, as argued in the Torrentiniana, had achieved the greatest perfection in all the three arts of drawing, as well as in poetry and moral philosophy. Nevertheless, Cellini proudly identified the one field in which he could assert his status as heir of the "Divine:" of the laurel crown that metaphorically adorned Michelangelo's head as painter, sculptor, architect, poet and philosopher, the single branch of sculpture sufficed to make the author illustrious. All his fame as a sculptor, he argued, he owed to Buonarroti, and this included both the medium of marble and of bronze (one that Michelangelo notoriously did not favor).

---

[145] Quotes from the first of Giovan Francesco Pico's two letters on imitation, in DellaNeva 2007 (as in fn. 142), pp. 17 and 41. With reference to Italian arts of the sixteenth century, compare Rona Goffen, *Renaissance Rivals: Michelangelo, Leonardo, Raphael, Titian*. New Haven, CT 2002, p. 27: "Michelangelo may be seen as the 'Ciceronian' model for the visual arts of his time, as Giotto had been for an earlier age." On the religious undertones that characterize the arguments of several early-modern upholders of the literary imitation of the best model compare Battisti 1960 (as in fn. 141), p. 191: "Nell'atto d'imitare […] chi imita non solo deriva i valori del modello, ma si sottopone ad una rigida gerarchia. Il suo atteggiamento è culturale e morale insieme […]."
[146] On the topic, see esp. Cole 2011 (as in fn. 98), with further references.

The artistic genealogy that Cellini traced in the following lines can be read – to draw on Steen Hansen's discussion of the forms of Michelangelesque imitation among sixteenth-century Italian painters – as "a series of ideological and self-defining positions taken in relation to given (art) historical situations through which artists retroactively constructed their own past."[147] Thus the sonnet equates for example, as corollaries of the author's and addressee's activities as sculptors, Michelangelo's excellence in painting and Cellini's greatness in goldsmithery. The poet referred to his goldsmith art as something belonging to his professional past, an area in which he had achieved outstanding results, but which had been completely replaced by sculpture. His reference to Michelangelo served in this sense to proclaim his own eminence as a sculptor as well as to justify his past conversion from jewels and gold ("gioie" and "horo") to bronzes and marbles.[148] The analogy between Cellini's personal artistic development and that of Michelangelo is also part of a discourse for which both the artists received a divine investiture: the artistic greatness of the two, so runs the argument, was a sign of God's grace, which gave them both talents unavailable to other men. In this fashion, Cellini was appropriating for himself the image of the artist sent by Providence on earth which characterized Vasari's biography of Michelangelo. At the same time, he maliciously noted the vanity of other contemporary artists, who also aspired to be acknowledged as heirs to Michelangelo while lacking that "amplio tesoro" of virtues that Heaven had granted the author and his addressee.

Even after Michelangelo's death (1564), Cellini continued to affirm that the heights reached by the departed were inaccessible to other artists of the Medicean milieu. In the sonnet *Virtuosi, gentili spiriti santi* (Appendix, no. 7), written when the controversy on the paragone between painting and sculpture was re-sparked by Buonarroti's exequies,[149] the

---

[147] Steen Hansen 2013 (as in fn. 126), p. 6. A similar, ideological construction of an artist's past can be found in Vincenzo Danti's preface to his *Trattato delle perfette proporzioni* (1567; text from Paola Barocchi, ed., *Trattati d'arte del Cinquecento, fra Manierismo e Controriforma*, 3 vols., Bari 1960-1962, 1, p. 211): "Essendo stato parere quasi di tutti gli uomini intendenti, che Michelagnolo Buonarroti sopra ciascun moderno e forse antico, che intorno all'arti del disegno si sia con lungo studio essercitato, abbia con eccellente perfezzione condotto a fine l'opere sue, così di scultura come di pittura et architettura […], avendo già passato ventidue anni e quasi il fiore della mia prima giovanezza quando, mediante la cognizione e grandezza di tant'uomo, ad attendere a quest'arti e all'imitazione di lui mi disposi […]. Dintorno alla quale […] quanto per me si potrà nel rimanente della mia vita ho proposto esercitarmi, tenendo sempre come uno specchio dinanzi agli occhi, sì come ho fatto insin qui con ogni diligenza, le bellissime opere sue, e quelle con la mente contemplando e, quanto mi fia conceduto, con l'opere imitando."

[148] For related ideas, compare the letter that Cellini addressed to Michelangelo at about the same time as the sonnet (September 3, 1561), in Michelangelo 1965-1983 (as in fn. 61), 5, p. 266.

[149] On this famous polemic see Alessandro Del Vita, Giorgio Vasari e Benvenuto Cellini, in: *Il Vasari* n. s. 15, 4 (1957), pp. 124-134; Rudolf and Margot Wittkower (eds.), *The Divine Michelangelo: The Florentine Academy's Homage on His Death in 1564*, London 1964; Piero Calamandrei, *Scritti e inediti celliniani*, ed. Carlo Cordié, Florence 1971, pp. 99-123; Andrea Gareffi, Le 'Esequie del divino Michelangelo' o del manierismo consacrato: la misura dell'eternità, in: *Biblioteca Teatrale* 23/24 (1979), pp. 39-69; Zygmunt Waźbiński, *L'Accademia medicea del disegno a Firenze nel Cinquecento: idea e istituzione*, 2 vols., Florence 1987, 1, pp. 95-103; Eliana Carrara, La nascita dell'Accademia del Disegno di Firenze: il ruolo di Borghini, Torelli e Vasari, in: Marc Deramaix, Perrine Galand-Hallyn, Ginette Vagenheim, and Jean Vignes (eds.), *Les académies dans l'Europe humaniste: idéaux et pratiques*, Geneva 2008, pp. 129-162; François Quiviger, Célébrations académiques et débats sur l'art: Benvenuto Cellini et l'"Oratione in lode della pittura" di Lionardo Salviati, ibid., pp. 187-196; Frédérique Dubard

author appropriated another topos contained in the Torrentiniana biography of the master. Addressing the poets who had written verse in praise of the departed, Cellini affirmed that no one would ever achieve the superb quality of his sculpting and drawing, and this idea that Michelangelo's perfection could never be replicated echoed similar considerations in the 1550 edition of the *Vite*, such as the passage where Vasari described the reaction of contemporary artists to the carton of the *Battle of Cascina*:

> Per il che gli artefici stupidi e morti restorono, vedendo l'estremità dell'arte in tal carta per Michele Agnolo móstra loro. Onde veduto sì divine figure, dicono alcuni, che le videro, di man sua e d'altri ancora non s'essere mai più veduto cosa che della divinità dell'arte nessuno altro ingegno possa arrivarla mai.[150]

By the time Cellini wrote his sonnet, this motif had turned into a recurring topos in the literature on Buonarroti, such as Ascanio Condivi's biography (1553) and Varchi's funerary oration (1564).[151] The basic assumptions of this ideological construct reflected, once again, the Ciceronian controversies on imitation. A forerunner of Bembo in advocating the need to imitate a single perfect model, Paolo Cortesi had for instance argued that the force and excellence of Cicero's eloquence could never be reached, no matter how hard one tried to approximate him.[152] What deserves to be here underlined is how Cellini adopted for his own purposes the critical commonplace of the impossibility of imitating Michelangelo: his verse compositions declared that this impossibility concerned all other artists, but certainly not the author himself. Behind his professed reverence for Michelangelo, one discerns then the ambition to compete with him while at the same time denying this possibility to other artists.[153] This feature is therefore entirely consistent with a recurring

---

de Gaillarbois, Le *cagnaccio* et le *botolo*: dialogue d'artistes ou portrait croisé de Cellini et de Vasari, in: *Chroniques italiennes web* 16 (2009): http://chroniquesitaliennes.univ-paris3.fr/numeros/Web16.html (last accessed 31/01/2021); Corinne Lucas Fiorato, Cellini, Vasari et Borghini: un trio problématique, ibid. On the artistic and symbolic programs of the funerals, see most recently Ruffini 2011 (as in fn. 135), pp. 11–38.

[150] Vasari 1967–1997 (as in fn. 74), 1550, 6, p. 24. As for sculpture, the notion of the impossibility of imitating Michelangelo informed Vasari's ecphrastic descriptions of the Vatican *Pietà* and of the *Moses* for the Tomb of Julius II. For the *Pietà* see ibid., p. 16: "Alla quale opera non pensi mai scultore né artefice raro potere aggiungere né di disegno né di grazia, né con fatica poter mai di finitezza, pulitezza e di straforare il marmo tanto con arte quanto Michele Agnolo vi fece, perché si scorge in quella tutto il valore et il potere dell'arte." For the *Moses*, see ibid., p. 28: "E similmente finì un Moisé di cinque braccia, di marmo: alla quale statua non sarà mai cosa moderna che possa arrivare di bellezza, e de le antiche ancora si può dire il medesimo."

[151] See, for instance, Ascanio Condivi, *Vita di Michelangelo Buonarroti*, Rome 1553, c. 40v: "Che così sia, lo mostran le sue figure, nelle quali tant'arte e dottrina si ritrova, che quasi sono inimitabili da qualsivoglia pittore," and Varchi 1564 (as in fn. 82), p. 7: "Ora che un huomo solo […] fosse non solamente buono Pittore, ma solo, non solamente buono Scultore, ma singolare; non solamente buono Architettore, ma unico; e cosa tanto nuova, tanto indisusata, tanto inudita in tutti secoli, in tutti i paesi, in tutte le storie."

[152] See Paolo Cortesi's letter to Agnolo Poliziano, in DellaNeva 2007 (as in fn. 142), p. 11: "Let me add that to have available the brilliant richness of the divine man's speech leads one to believe that it can be imitated, but snatches away all such hope from anyone that actually attempts it."

[153] The ambitions that shaped Cellini's artistic practice as well as his writings were, from this point of view, comparable to those that had characterized the professional parables of contemporary artists who were active in other parts of Italy. Fundamental here is Steen Hansen 2013 (as in fn. 126). See, among others, his considerations on Daniele da Volterra, p. 55: "From the mid-1540s onward, the overriding concern of Daniele da Volterra was

motif in the author's autobiography: as noted by Jane Tylus, in his *Vita* Cellini set out to present himself and his art as inimitable, thus appropriating for himself a recurrent critical refrain in the literary mythology on Michelangelo, and even arrived at re-interpreting his creation of the *Perseus* as a demonstration of his capacity to surpass his master.[154]

This way of presenting Michelangelo as the supreme artistic touchstone as well as an exemplar which had to be outdone corresponded to the assumptions of the Bembian theory of imitation. Whereas Cortesi saw the imitative practices of the Ciceronianists as exercises that while meritorious were nevertheless doomed to fail, Bembo affirmed the possibility of emerging victorious from a challenge with the paradigm of stylistic excellence. He even identified the drive to compete with this kind of model as an essential element of the process of *imitatio*:

> In fact, just as Cicero became eminent among Latin speakers […] and alone surpassed all the fine masters of rhetoric who came before him, certainly a great and divine feat, so it is perfectly possible that another will someday become eminent and surpass everyone else, including Cicero himself. The easiest way that can happen, however, is by imitating most the person we want most to excel […]. If we shall ever equal those whom we shall have most imitated, at that point we should try to surpass them. But first we should apply all our effort, all our labor, all our thought to equaling our models. For it is not so difficult to overcome and defeat those whom you have equaled as it is to equal those whom you are imitating.
>
> So this […] can be our rule in everything of this kind: first, that we set before ourselves for imitation the best of all models; then, that we imitate that person with the aim of equaling him; and finally, that all our efforts have in view outstripping the man we have equaled. Thus we should harbor in our minds those two distinguished accomplices in most great affairs – emulation and expectation. But we should always couple emulation with imitation.[155]

It has been convincingly argued that the third step in this process of imitation, equaling and surpassing of the supreme paradigm was purely virtual in the eyes of Bembo, who remained skeptical that his contemporaries could actually outshine the examples of perfect style found in Lat-

---

to be seen as Michelangelo's elect follower, artistic inheritor, and the one who would eventually take his place and even surpass him."

[154] According to its creator, the *Perseus* was for instance an artwork that Buonarroti would have been able to realize only in his youth, and certainly not in his late years. See Cellini 1996 (as in fn. 23), p. 725 (*Vita* 2.97): "il mio maestro Michelagnolo Buonarroti, sì bene e' n'arebbe fatta una così, quando egli era più giovane, et non arebbe durato manco fatiche che io mi abbia fatto; ma ora che gli è vecchissimo, egli no·lla farebbe per cosa certa; di modo che io non credo che oggi ci sia notizia di uomo che la sapessi condurre." On this, see especially Tylus 2004 (as in fn. 119), p. 12: "Cellini is intent on confining Michelangelo's greatness to a previous era; and now that Michelangelo is too old to create works requiring fatica it is up to Cellini to carry on."

[155] DellaNeva 2007 (as in fn. 142), p. 81. For a classical discussion of the genetic connection between imitation and emulation, see Thomas Greene's considerations on a passage from Dionysius of Halicarnassus's book *On the Ancient Orators* (Greene 1982 [as in fn. 141], p. 58) "the term 'imitation' (mimesis) is coupled with a second term that would frequently accompany or replace it throughout its history, namely 'emulation', zelos, defined felicitously as 'an activity of the soul impelled toward admiration of what seems to be fine.' In his actual comparisons of the Greek historians and orators, Dionysius employs zelos or its cognates at least as often as mimesis." Useful is also the discussion of *aemulatio* as one of the most defining aspects of the literary and artistic life of early-modern Europe in the introduction by Jan-Dirk Müller and Ulrich Pfisterer to Müller, Pfisterer, Bleuler, and Jonietz 2011 (as in fn. 6), pp. 1–22 (see p. 4 for a discussion of the example of Michelangelo).

in literature.[156] These categories nevertheless provide the ideological coordinates within which were positioned the competitive relations established by artists like Cellini with Michelangelo, whom they typically heralded as their example in art and the subject of an absolute devotion.

The imitation of Michelangelo between Vasari and Bronzino

Although in less explicit terms than in Cellini's writings, an emulative stance towards Michelangelo also informs the works of other artists active in ducal Florence. That contemporaries recognized such a stance as not only legitimate but also particularly praiseworthy is demonstrated, among other sources, by a sonnet by Jacopo Marsuppini which we read among the papers of Vasari, for the text openly argued that "Giorgio immortal" had achieved a divine status and even proved his versatile talents superior to those of Michelangelo.[157] But also Bronzino, the most eloquent advocate of the Michelangelesque cult among Medicean artists, justified and commended the ambition of surpassing the object of his devotion.

Let us consider the sonnet *Poi che la luce mia, da mille chiare* (Appendix, no. 8), belonging to a series of poems the painter wrote upon the death of his beloved master Jacopo Pontormo (1557). Bronzino celebrated here the pictorial testament of the departed, namely, the now lost fresco cycle for the choir of the Florentine basilica of San Lorenzo, presenting it as a supreme paradigm of how an artist should approach his models.[158] According to the poet, having demonstrated in his previous artistic enterprises his exceptional skills as draftsman and colorist and having shown "quanto arte può fare" (l. 3), Pontormo had managed to almost complete a work of singular beauty and nobility when he dedicated himself to the decoration of Duke Cosimo's "temple." The author argued that the beautiful wall painting was full of horror, marvel and art, and bore the mark of Pontormo's desire to overcome the limits of human nature, as well as to surpass himself and *any other artist* ("cercò […] tutti altri avanzare;" ll. 7–8). Bronzino, who was

---

[156] See McLaughlin 1995 (as in fn. 141), p. 264. In his treatise *De Imitatione* (1541), Bartolomeo Ricci similarly identifies three phases of the imitative process, which he labeled "sequi," "imitari" and "aemulari." On this, see Pigman 1980 (as in fn. 131), p. 3.

[157] The poem is preserved in Florence, Biblioteca Riccardiana, ms. Ricc. 2948, c. 34r, following the rubric *A m. Giorgio Vasari Iacopo Marsoppini*: "Voi stupir fate, come io scrivo in carmi, / natura e l'arte, et con eterno ingegnio / lo spirto date al dotto disegno, / alle carte, alle tele, a' legni, a' marmi; // Il Buonarroto mai seppe mostrarmi / sì stupendo artifitio, altero e degno, / ond'io per celebrarvi in questo regno / un Pindaro, un Apollo vorrei farmi. // Giorgio immortal, che dal mar Indo al Tile / cercando il tutto non trovate il paro, / che già fate stupir huomini e Dei, // hor goda Arezzo, città signorile, / ch'ha partorito sì divin tesauro, / di cui veggio ogn'hor quaggiù trofei // sopra la piena d'Arno / […]" (the last line of the poem is illegible).

[158] In its representation of the way in which Pontormo had approached his models, the sonnet appears to contribute to Bronzino's broader discourse on the exemplarity of his former master's artistic activity, on which see Larry J. Feinberg, *From Studio to Studiolo: Florentine Draftsmanship under the First Medici Grand Dukes*, Seattle 1991, p. 75: "It is likely that Bronzino promoted, verbally and by example, the Pontormo revival that took place in the last four decades of the century."

commissioned to complete the frescoes of the choir,[159] did not explicitate who these artists were, and yet contemporary readers would have known that the one model that Pontormo, throughout the last years of his life, had most tenaciously striven to emulate was Michelangelo.

In light of the above, the comparison between the expressions used by Bronzino to celebrate Pontormo's last artistic enterprise and the words with which Vasari, a decade later, condemned the same work becomes revealing of the sort of schism that took place among the self-proclaimed Florentine followers of Michelangelo on the question of how to emulate that example. In praising the Laurentian frescoes, Bronzino underlined the positive stimulus of emulation that had characterized Pontormo's approach to his models, Michelangelo above all, in an anticipation of what were to be the main tenets of the contemporary critical re-evaluation of that lost pictorial work. Recent scholarship has in fact interpreted those paintings as the "final and most extraordinary homage to Michelangelo's example in its basic concentration on the nude,"[160] and the result of a tenacious drive to surpass that example.

In the Giuntina biography of Pontormo, Vasari on the contrary described the Laurentian frescoes as a complete failure and the proof of how pernicious it was to attempt outdoing Michelangelo by imitating him and him alone. Indeed, Pontormo's aspiration "in quest'opera di dovere avanzare tutti i pittori e forse, per quel che si disse, Michelagnolo" constituted the critical premise for one of the author's sharpest critiques of an artwork: having discussed Pontormo's emulative approach, Vasari notoriously proceeded to attack all aspects of his work for the San Lorenzo choir, from a supposed lack of order in the *istoria* to the absence of rules, of proportions, of an adequate perspectival arrangement of the figures.[161] According to the biographer, those frescoes had been the scene of a final confrontation between Pontormo and who for decades had been the touchstone of all his ambitions as a painter, and such a contest necessarily ended with the total defeat of the imitator, though he was once an excellent artist.[162]

The polarization between Bronzino's praise for Pontormo's emulative stance and Vasari's condemnation of that same stance in 1568 reflects the loss of a shared faith in the place of Michelangelo as the perfect and sole model to be followed. At the time of the 1550 edition of the *Vite*, Vasari's own theoretical position was after all not entirely consistent, for the passages in which he invited his readers to follow the old master's example "in all things" coexisted with

---

[159] The paintings were unveiled on 23 July 1558: see Massimo Firpo, *Gli affreschi di Pontormo a San Lorenzo: Eresia, politica e cultura nella Firenze di Cosimo I*, Turin 1997, p. 14.

[160] David Franklin, *Painting in Renaissance Florence 1500–1550*, New Haven, CT 2001, p. 202. On the positive role of effort in the imitation of the perfect model, compare Bembo's letter to Giovan Francesco Pico in DellaNeva 2007 (as in fn. 142), p. 73: "But really, nothing is so very difficult and so hard that it seems we cannot conquer and overcome by our efforts, especially if we try as hard as we can. I therefore applied myself with the greatest diligence. After I had completely erased from my memory those stylistic traits, which by then had become deeply seated from imitating inferior writers, I turned all my efforts on the greatest and best."

[161] Vasari 1967–1997 (as in fn. 74), 1568, 5, p. 332. On Vasari's treatment of Pontormo's final work, see most recently Sharon Gregory, The Unsympathetic Exemplar in Vasari's Life of Pontormo, in: *Renaissance Studies* 23 (2009), pp. 1–32, pp. 24–32, and Ruffini 2011 (as in fn. 135), pp. 40–48, with further references.

[162] The author traced back the origin of Pontormo's choice of Buonarroti as his unique model to the time (ca. 1532) when the former artist painted the panel of *Venus and Cupid* for Bartolomeo Bettini after some designs by Michelangelo: see Vasari 1967–1997 (as in fn. 74), 5, p. 326 (1568).

somewhat different considerations. In both the biographies and the theoretical chapters of the Torrentiniana, Vasari for instance warned artists about the dangers of imitating too faithfully a single model. Moreover, he praised Raphael for adopting an eclectic imitative practice in his painting, based on the assimilation of the best qualities of a wide range of examples.[163] However, these ideological oscillations occurred solely outside the specific discussions of Michelangelo as the messiah and guiding light of the arts. The cracks in the Torrentiniana's teleological structure did not, to put it differently, prevent Vasari from generally advocating an imitation centered on Michelangelo, whom he presented as the one artist who had shown his fellow practitioners of the arts how to approximate perfection, but also as the one model which was impossible to surpass or even equal. The trajectory of progress that underpins the design of the 1550 *Vite* thus led to the same dead end as Cortesi's theory when it had prescribed the imitation of a sole perfect model, while also asserting the impossibility of equaling its excellence.[164] As modern scholars have noted, the ascending parable of Vasari's historiographical construct was in this way undermined by a paradoxical "crisis of perfection," after which a decadence of the arts was presented as inevitable.[165]

In response to this dead end, in the Giuntina Vasari notoriously opted for a different imitative theory, and while he did not systematize all his reflections on the subject he did generally champion a more eclectic imitation, typical of Raphael's art.[166] Appropriating arguments

---

[163] Gregory 2009 (as in fn. 161), pp. 9–11, and eadem, Vasari on Imitation, in: Cast 2014 (as in fn. 86), pp. 223–243, p. 233; but see also Battisti 1960 (as in fn. 141), pp. 180–181, which already discussed Vasari's presentation of Raphael's imitative method in light of literary theorizations of eclectic imitation. We should keep in mind that Raphael's early works (e.g. the Pala Baglioni of 1507) demonstrate that he, too, had sometimes practiced an imitation essentially based on the the best possible model – in the case of the Pala Baglioni, Michelangelo himself: see Pfisterer 2019 (as in fn. 73), p. 81. This is not entirely in contrast with Vasari's argument in the Giuntina edition of the *Vite* (Vasari 1967–1997 [as in fn. 74], 4, pp. 204–206). The author in fact maintained that Raphael had understood, in the first years of his professional maturity, the need to abandon his previous ways of imitating other masters.

[164] Ascanio Condivi articulated a similar position. In a long passage of his biography of Michelangelo, he argued that any artist living after Buonarroti would have to content himself with the role of an epigone, since it was impossible to reach, let alone surpass, that model's perfect qualities. See Condivi 1553 (as in fn. 151), c. 40v: "lo mostran le sue figure, nelle quali tant'arte et dottrina si ritruova, che quasi sono inimitabili, da qual si voglia pittore […]. Quanti […] poeti doppo Homero e Vergilio? E se pur qualch'uno ce n'è stato che […] sia stato subietto attissimo di poter da sé arrivare al primo luogo, non dimeno costui, per haverlo trovato occupato, et per non essere altro il perfetto che quello […] s'è dato all'imitatione di que' primi, come ideal del perfetto […]." On this passage see Steen Hansen 2013 (as in fn. 126), p. 4. On the Torrentiniana's biography of Michelangelo see, along with the fundamental commentary of Paola Barocchi to Vasari 1962 (as in fn. 73), also Laura Riccò, *Vasari scrittore: la prima edizione del libro delle Vite*, Rome 1979, pp. 150–172.

[165] James Clifton, Vasari on Competition, in: *The Sixteenth Century Journal* 27 (1996), pp. 23–41, p. 25. Compare the famous passage from the *Vite*'s *Proemio* to the third age of art (Vasari 1967–1997 [as in fn. 74], 3, pp. 6–7 [1550]): "Questa lode certo è tócca alla terza età, nella quale mi par poter dir sicuramente che l'arte abbia fatto quello che ad una imitatrice della natura è lecito poter fare, e che ella sia salita tanto alto, che più presto si abbia a temere del calare abasso che sperare oggimai più augumento."

[166] Classical studies on the shift of imitative paradigms and teleological structures between the Torrentino and the Giunti edition of the *Vite* include Schlosser 1924 (as in fn. 2), p. 257; Svetlana Alpers, Ekphrasis and Aesthetic Attitudes in Vasari's Lives, in: *Journal of the Warburg and Courtauld Institutes* 23 (1960), pp. 190–215, pp. 206–209; Battisti 1960 (as in fn. 141), pp. 192–193; Paola Barocchi's introduction to Vasari 1962 (as in fn. 73),

used in the literary field against strict Ciceronianists, the author therefore criticized those who had once been his co-religionists in the "church" of Michelangelo, attacking several artists who had made him the sole model of their art.[167] For Vasari, those who did this had not understood that Michelangelo's unattainable excellency in the pictorial rendition of the nude meant it was possible to compete with him only in different domains of art, such as coloring, and only if one imitated (like Raphael did) a variety of masters.[168] This explains why Bronzino's lyrical praise for Pontormo's "soverchi studi" of a strenuous emulative stance, which the poet presented as the cause of his master's death but also as the seal of his artistic greatness (Appendix, no. 8, ll. 12–14), left space in the Giuntina for condemnation of an artist who did not have any chance of ever emerging victorious from his final confrontation with Michelangelo, and whose blind drive to outdo that example brought only suffering and shame.[169]

esp. pp. xix–xxxiii, as well as Rubin 1995 (as in fn. 61), pp. 397–401. A differently nuanced account of the question on Raphael as a model of imitation in the Giuntina is that of Pozzi and Mattioda 2006 (as in fn. 80), pp. 250–254, which argues that in the book "Vasari si è convinto che alla perfezione si può giungere in vario modo, ma ci sono perfezioni di grado diverso e quella di Raffaello è di grado più basso" (p. 254), also because (p. 395) "la perfezione di Michelangelo […] era […] dinamica. Non aveva un punto d'arrivo: quando, dopo aver dipinto le storie bibliche della Sistina, dipinge le *Sibille* e i *Profeti* è ancora più perfetto; l'esperienza accumulata ha affinato la sua virtù, ha permesso un grado di perfezione superiore […]. Quando poi dipinge il *Giudizio universale* si supera nuovamente." Along the same lines is the discussion of Enrico Mattioda, introduction to Giorgio Vasari, *Le vite de' più eccellenti pittori, scultori e architettori*, ed. Enrico Mattioda, Alessandria 2017–, 1, pp. 26–30. For a recent assessment of the different treatments of the question of imitation in the two editions see also Gregory 2009 (as in fn. 161), with further bibliography.

[167] As Lionello Venturi first suggested (Venturi, *Storia della critica d'arte*, Florence 1948², pp. 162ff.), such a critical re-orientation was perhaps in part due to Dolce's *Dialogo della pittura* and to its criticisms, through the character of Pietro Aretino, against the multitudes of those slavish "pittorucci, che sono scimie di Michelagnolo" (Dolce in Barocchi 1960–1962 [as in fn. 147], 1, p. 148). Such wording was modeled after the derogatory label that the upholders of eclectic imitation had often used against the strict and unintelligent Ciceronianists, that of *simiae Ciceronis*. On this, see Ernst Robert Curtius, *European Literature and the Latin Middle Ages*, trans. Willard R. Trask, New York 1953, pp. 538–540; Pigman 1980 (as in fn. 131), p. 8, and McLaughlin 1995 (as in fn. 141), p. 136.

[168] Compare Pozzi and Mattioda 2006 (as in fn. 80), p. 396: "La straordinaria eccellenza di Michelangelo risiede anche e soprattutto nel fatto che egli 'non ha voluto entrare in dipingere altro che la perfetta e proporzionatissima composizione del corpo umano e in diversissime attitudini', cioè quanto di più difficile e di alto un artista possa proporsi di rappresentare: infatti secondo il racconto biblico è stato plasmato da Dio […]. Tralasciò tutti gli altri soggetti," and p. 398: "Sono moltissimi i campi in cui Michelangelo non si è provato."

[169] Most useful for a better understanding of the implications of Bronzino's poetic eulogy of Pontormo are the considerations of Franklin 2001 (as in fn. 160), p. 211: "For Tuscans like Pontormo, seeking to create the perfect style – following Michelangelo above all – involved a selective process, very much concentrated on the powerfully conceived human figure. And so, in contrast to the Raphael of his Roman period, Tuscan artists of this kind attempted seemingly endless variations on the constricted universal of the male body in action […]. In the final analysis, nothing could be more central to the concerns of a Florentine Renaissance artist than the search for invented perfection, the difficult and the unexpected […]. In that he was the last great painter to sustain the most outstanding of Tuscan artistic traditions valuing graphic force and unconventionality, it is perhaps not too farfetched to claim that Pontormo's death most truly represents the end of the Florentine Renaissance in its purest manifestation. What would co-exist in stylistic terms in Florence primarily through the examples of Vasari and Salviati would be a more cosmopolitan art, dominated by earlier Roman models as in Raphael especially, but more open to influences from the entire peninsula. Artists working in Florence towards 1550 were faced with stark choices."

This difference between Vasari and Bronzino is indicative of a shifting in the approach, in the Florentine artistic scene of the 1550s and 1560s, to imitative theories and practices. On the one hand, artists like Bronzino (like his master Pontormo before him) and Cellini continued to champion the imitation of Michelangelo as the supreme and only model in art.[170] The writings we have examined demonstrate how these figures translated their reverence towards the "Divine" in an attitude that was far from submissive or epigonic, but that was instead characterized by the eristic ambition of equaling and surpassing their purported (though not necessarily actual) only standard of perfection.[171] On the other hand, after having maintained the importance of following only Michelangelo as the ultimate touchstone of artistic excellence, Vasari eventually came to advocate an eclectic imitation. In the Giuntina he thus exhorted artists not to concentrate their imitative efforts exclusively on the representation of the nude – the domain that painters like Pontormo and Bronzino had traditionally favored – in order to avoid being crushed by the greatness of that model. According to recent scholarship, his new position was strictly related to the founding of the Florentine Accademia del Disegno (1563), for eclectic imitation best served the institution's mission.[172] Such an imitative stance seemed in particular less prone to the "excessive studies" in which Pontormo had engaged in his last confrontation with Michelangelo, and therefore more functional to training young artists who would be able to work productively and efficiently on Medicean commissions.

At the height of his maturity, Bronzino himself became fully aware of the epochal change brought about by the adoption in Florence of an artistic pedagogy based on eclectic imitation. In this regard, the testimony of his *Secondo capitolo delle scuse* is of great import.[173] Of uncertain date, the poem documents Bronzino's very critical response to the diffusion of new imitative trends among the younger generations of painters active on the local scene and, as such, is probably to be interpreted as his contentious stance on the didactic ideals that were promoted within the Accademia del Disegno.[174] In a passage of the capitolo (ll. 145-162; Appendix, no. 9), inserted in the context of a more general discussion of the excuses that artists

---

[170] The character of Pietro Aretino, in Ludovico Dolce's *Dialogo della pittura* (1557), notoriously attacked and described such an approach as typically Florentine. See Dolce in Barocchi 1960-1962 (as in fn. 147), 1, p. 147: "Ma non è maraviglia che, essendo voi fiorentino, l'amor che portate a' vostri vi faccia talmente cieco, che riputiate oro solamente le cose di Michelagnolo e le altre vi paiano piombo vile. Il che quando non fosse, vi raccordereste che la età di Alessandro Magno inalzava insino al cielo Apelle, né però rimaneva di lodare e di celebrar Zeusi, Protogene, Timante et altri eccellenti pittori." On this, see Paola Barocchi's introduction to Vasari 1962 (as in fn. 73), 1, pp. xix-xx, and Mark W. Roskill, *Dolce's Aretino and Venetian Art Theory of the Cinquecento*, New York 2000, pp. 12-13.
[171] For the concept of eristic imitation, characterized by a competitive attitude towards one's models, see Pigman 1980 (as in fn. 131). Pigman registers (p. 20) how "one of the few points of agreement between Pico and Bembo in their exchange of letters on imitation is a preference for striving to surpass rather than for following."
[172] See Gregory 2009 (as in fn. 161), p. 32, with further references.
[173] On the poem see the considerations of Brock 2002 (as in fn. 6), pp. 312-313, and especially of Parker 2004 (as in fn. 6).
[174] Brock 2002 (as in fn. 6), p. 312 dates the poem to the years between 1549 and 1551; Parker 2004 (as in fn. 6), p. 163 more convincingly suggests a dating between the 1550s and the 1560s, while Gregory 2009 (as in fn. 161), p. 32, suggests 1568 as the *terminus post quem* for its composition. In my opinion, it is not necessary to infer (as Gregory does) that Bronzino's poem was written after the second edition of the *Vite*: the author might have

made to justify their own sloppy creative practices and culpable lack of *diligenza*,[175] the author specifically addressed his pedagogical concerns for the loss of centrality of the Michelangelesque paradigm in contemporary artistic education. He thus insisted on the need for painters to take Michelangelo as their only guide of their art, and then moved on to an attack against those bad pedagogues who, with the excuse that the path shown by that master was too steep and impossible to follow, encouraged young artists to abandon that supreme model in favor of lesser ones. Bronzino's polemic goes as far as comparing these nefarious teachers, who in the text go unnamed and yet somewhat suspiciously resemble Vasari's ideological profile, to someone who jumps into a cesspool and then invites others to follow him. According to the author, the choice not to follow Michelangelo as the only guide to perfection was a recipe for artistic disaster, for such an option turned painting into a most futile thing ("frasche"), dramatically undermined by the lack of study and of proper drawing skills.

One last time, we might observe how these reflections on the despicable consequences of a painting pedagogy grounded in eclectic imitation closely echo a Bembian set of ideas. In his letter to Paolo Cortesi *De Imitatione*, Bembo had criticized the late Agnolo Poliziano for having advised young writers, who found themselves incapable of imitating the eloquence of Cicero, to follow a number of less difficult authors. He argued that he had been able to prove the fallacy of this method when, discouraged by the difficulty of competing with the best examples of oratory art and classic literature, he had initially opted for models that "seemed

---

contested those positions that Vasari had been championing in the context of the Accademia del Disegno, and that were eventually theorized in his book.

[175] Diligence, "one of the most despised critical criteria in the Western tradition" (Gaston 2013 [as in fn. 121], p. 110), is an aesthetic tenet that Bronzino extolled throughout his literary work (for instance in his letter in verse to Duke Cosimo, *Hor che voi siete, o mio signore, andato*, on which see ch. 4). It has also been noted (Fredrika H. Jakobs, Vasari's Bronzino: The Paradigmatic Academician, in: Anne B. Barriault, Andrew Ladis, Norman E. Land, and Jeryldene M. Wood [eds.], *Reading Vasari*, London 2005, pp. 101–115, p. 103) that "diligenza" is the characteristic that Vasari singled out as the most defining feature of the colleague's pictorial language. See, for instance Vasari 1967–1997 (as in fn. 74), 1568, 6, pp. 231-232: "In Santa Trinita pur di Firenze si vede di mano del medesimo in un quadro a olio […], un Cristo morto, la Nostra Donna, San Giovanni e Santa Maria Maddalena, condotti con bella maniera e molta diligenza […]; ritrasse Bonacorso Pinadori, Ugolino Martelli, messer Lorenzo Lenzi, oggi vescovo di Fermo, e Pierantonio Bandini e la moglie […]: tutti furono naturalissimi, fatti con incredibile diligenza, e di maniera finiti che più non si può disiderare. A Bartolomeo Panciatichi fece due quadri grandi di Nostre Donne con altre figure, belli a maraviglia e condotti con infinita diligenza." Jakobs 2005 argues (p. 101) that Vasari's considerations on Bronzino's artistic activity, located in the opening section of the collective chapter of the Giuntina devoted to the works of the Accademici del disegno, "stands as a primer to academicism, its subject paradigmatic of all that inheres in that term", and that the emphasis on diligence should be understood within the same framework. In this sense, her essay concludes by observing (ibid., p. 115): "To imitate, rather than simply replicate, the works of Michelangelo implies by the very nature of the term a process of stylistic progression, an advancement requiring diligenza. Vasari's *Life of Bronzino* stresses this point, proffering the example of this 'most important' of academicians as a model for younger Academy members to heed and reminding them of the need to be diligent." The latter claim, I believe, holds true only if one adds that Vasari typically balances an appreciation for *diligenzia* with a great emphasis on the opposite value of *prestezza* (for more on this see chapter 4 of this book). In this sense, Vasari highly praised the young academician Battista Naldini for being "spedito" in his creations (Vasari 1967–1997 [as in fn. 74], 6, p. 240 [1568]). Furthermore, it is significant that nowhere in his biographical piece on the colleague does Vasari discuss Bronzino's imitative approach to Michelangelo.

more accessible and convenient to imitate than did the best."[176] He maintained that this choice had betrayed his aspirations and prevented him from excelling, while also claiming that it was this defeat that eventually spurred him to take a different and better route – one that made it possible for him to efface the mediocre stylistic traits that imperfect models had instilled into his mind. For Bembo, on the other hand, the difficulty of embarking on a path towards perfection could not obfuscate the fact that "nothing is so very difficult and so hard that it seems we cannot conquer and overcome by our efforts, especially if we try as hard as we can." Presenting his own process of literary refinement as a pedagogic paradigm, he concluded by stressing that he had not once regretted his decision to apply himself, "with the greatest diligence," to the imitation of the best writers, leading Cortesi to take on the same approach to composition.

What is important to pinpoint is how founded were the concerns that Bronzino voiced in the *Secondo capitolo delle scuse*. Indeed, by the early 1570s (also in the aftermath of Counter-Reformation attacks on Michelangelo's art which culminated in Giovanni Andrea Gilio's criticism of the *Last Judgment* of 1564),[177] the supporters of an exclusive imitation of that model had become a minority in the Florentine artistic scene. The excuse of the impossibility of imitating Michelangelo, of which Bronzino had denounced the growing popularity, was by that time orienting the new tendencies among local painters. Just a few years after the creation of works that embodied a paroxysmal form of Michelangiolism, such as Alessandro Allori's *Last Judgment* in the Montauto Chapel of the church of the Santissima Annunziata (1560–1564; Fig. 1) and Bronzino's *Martyrdom of Saint Lawrence* in the basilica of San Lorenzo (1565–1569; Fig. 2),[178] these new trends were already prevailing. Recent studies have noted, for

---

[176] For Poliziano's position, which was the subject of his *Oration on Quintilian and Statius*, see DellaNeva 2007 (as in fn. 142), p. XVIII. This and the following quotes from Bembo's response are from ibid., pp. 71–73.

[177] For contemporary polemics on the *Last Judgement* see especially Eugenio Battisti, La critica a Michelangelo prima del Vasari, in: *Rinascimento* 5 (1954), pp. 117–132, and La critica a Michelangelo dopo il Vasari, in: *Rinascimento* 7 (1956), pp. 135–157, as well as Bernadine Ann Barnes, *Michelangelo's Last Judgment: The Renaissance Response*, Berkeley 1998, and eadem, *Michelangelo and the Viewer in His Time*, London 2017.

[178] On the extent of Bronzino's imitation of Michelangelo in the San Lorenzo painting, see most recently Brock 2002 (as in fn. 6), pp. 313–324, which sees in the work a manifestation of the artist's "art of reference", and Ruffini 2011 (as in fn. 135), pp. 55–58. On the character of that imitation, which was not devoid of ironic and parodic tones, see Campbell 2004 (as in fn. 6), pp. 98–119; Carlo Falciani, Della pittura sacra, ma anche di 'fianchi, stomachi ec.', in: Falciani and Natali 2010 (as in fn. 6), pp. 277–295, p. 290; and Lingo 2015 (as in fn. 6), with further bibliography. Most relevant are also the remarks of Gaston 2013 (as in fn. 121), pp. 111–112: "it should be obvious to us, watching contemporary art feeding off both traditional and recent art movements, that Bronzino's art-making can be usefully compared to the processes of citation, quotation, appropriation, and parody that are at the core of postmodernist art and theory […]. But what is most likely to trouble the postmodern critic of Mannerist art's ever-s-finely tuned imitation process is the respect it apparently exhibits towards the work of preceding artists […]. In some of the twentieth-century scholarship on Bronzino such respect (a decorum concept related to the Latin term *reverentia*) was seen to be slavishly imitative." Vasari's short biographic text on Alessandro Allori, included in his chapter on the Accademici del Disegno of the Giuntina, already signalled the indebteness of the paintings of the Montauto Chapel to Michelangelo. See Vasari 1967–1997 (as in fn. 74), 6, p. 238 (1568): "Ha dipinta e condotta tutta di sua mano con molta diligenza la cappella de' Montaguti nella chiesa della Nunziata […]. Nella tavola è Cristo in alto, e la Madonna, in atto di giudicare, con molte figure in diverse attitudini e ben fatte, ritratte dal Giudizio di Michelagnolo Buonarroti […]; e nella volta sono alcune Sibille e Profeti, condotti con molta fatica e studio e diligenza, avendo cerco imitare negli ignudi Michelagnolo." Allori

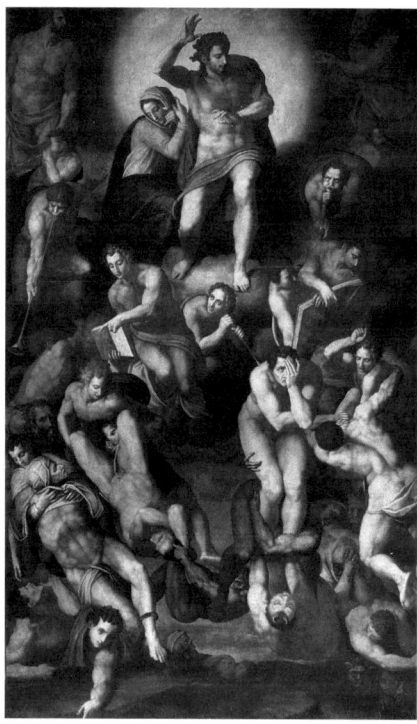

1 Alessandro Allori, *Last Judgment*, oil on panel, 1560–1564, Florence, Santissima Annunziata, Montauto Chapel.

example, how the paintings for the Studiolo of Francesco I (1570–1574) marked a clear break with Michelangelo's figurative language.[179] In the same way, scholars have emphasized how the pictorial works that between the late 1560s and 1570s changed the aspect of so many Florentine churches, such as Girolamo Macchietti's *Martyrdom of Saint Lawrence* in the basilica of Santa Maria Novella (1573; Fig. 3), were clearly the product of a new generation of painters and sculptors who had been trained in the Accademia del Disegno and who "reconciled their undoubted reverence for Michelangelo with their avoidance of his style."[180] Along with the

---

himself, after all, had explicitly declared his intention to imitate Michelangelo with his signature of the *Last Judgment* ("Alexander Allorius civis Flor. Bronzini alunnus inventum optimi pictoris Bonarrotae haec sedulo pinxit"). On the Michelangiolism of the Montauto paintings see the considerations of Simona Lecchini Giovannoni, *Alessandro Allori*, Turin 1991, pp. 218–219; Pilliod 2003 (as in fn. 97), pp. 36–43 (also with reference to other works by Allori); Ruffini 2011 (as in fn. 135), pp. 59–63. Ruffini emphasizes, however, how Allori's imitation of Michelangelo was of a different nature than Pontormo's or Bronzino's: "He did not try to surpass or even to equal the Roman masterpiece, but offered instead an example of its many possible translations […]. Allori created a new manifesto of Michelangiolism: not a free, individual interpretation of his work, following Pontormo's and Bronzino's examples, but one drawing on the vocabulary of linear forms already provided by the master."
[179] Marcia B. Hall, *After Raphael: Painting in Central Italy in the Sixteenth Century*, Cambridge 1999, p. 238.
[180] Ibid. (also quoted in Parker 2004 [as in fn. 6], p. 173, fn. 9), with reference to earlier observations by Waźbiński 1987 (as in fn. 149), 1, p. 213. See also the editors' introduction to Falciani and Natali 2017 (as in

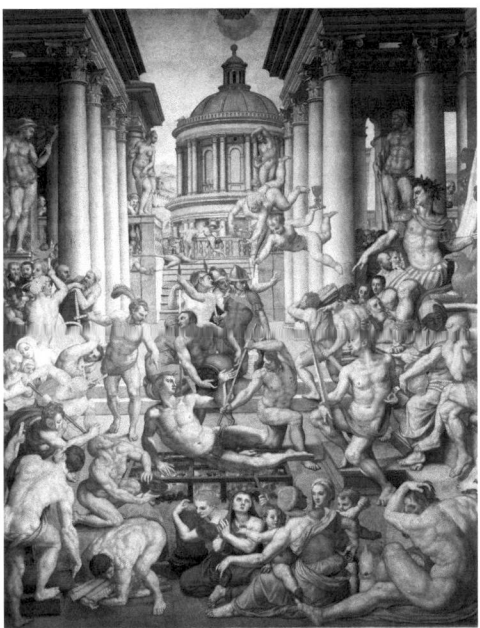
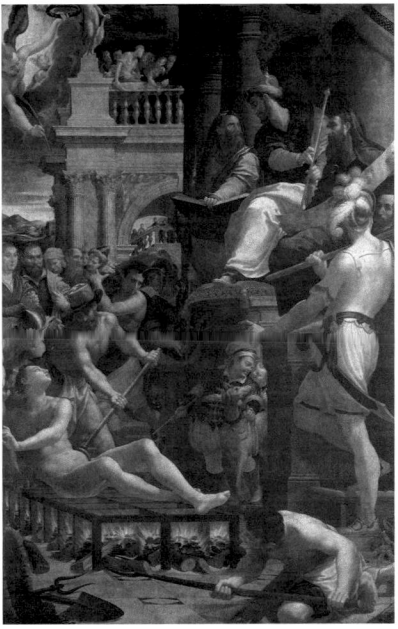

2 Agnolo Bronzino, *Martyrdom of Saint Lawrence*, fresco, 1565–1569, Florence, San Lorenzo.

3 Girolamo Macchietti, *Martyrdom of Saint Lawrence*, oil on panel, 1573, Florence, Santa Maria Novella, Giuochi Chapel.

deaths of some of the artists who in their writings and professional activity had been so concerned with the problem of Michelangelesque imitation in diverse ways (Cellini died in 1571, Bronzino in 1572 and Vasari in 1574), these works marked the transition of Florentine arts to an age that looked with different eyes at that model.

fn. 64), pp. 18–19, which introducing the works of artists such as Santi di Tito, Mirabello Cavalori and others, stated: "Quelle voci rifulgono dunque in esordio per dare ragione di quale sia l'origine degli artefici (essi pure grandi e ingiustamente negletti) che a Firenze, appunto nella seconda metà del Cinquecento, sulle orme dei padri camminarono, liberamente nondimeno esprimendosi, talora arrivando perfino a sviare quegli esempi o comunque a liberarsi dalla loro tutela." Commenting on Bronzino's *Martyrdom of St. Lawrence*, Maurice Brock has similarly stressed how the painter's display of Michelangeloism was "quite simply passé" (Brock 2002 [as in fn. 6], pp. 312–314): "Bronzino's resourcing, occurring as it did at a time when the Florentines, despite their tireless admiration for Michelangelo […], were distancing themselves from Michelangeloism, was patently out of step with the age. It might be tempting to look to Bronzino's advanced age to explain his reversion to the art of reference […]. We prefer a less reductive explanation […]. In all probability, the painter had passed through a short phase of doubt; but now he was more convinced than ever that Michelangeloism constituted both a cast-iron guarantee of fiorentinità and the style best-adapted to conveying beauty, meaning, and emotion […]. Bronzino was inciting artists of the rising generation […] to continue advocating the forza of Florentine art, and to strive like him to keep to the arduous path of artistic truth that Michelangelo had blazed."

A Literato's Recognition

Varchi, the artists, and the Accademia Fiorentina

As soon as he left behind his Republican past and six years as a *fuoruscito* to enter the service of Duke Cosimo, in early March of 1543,[181] Benedetto Varchi was able to resume frequenting artists who were active in and around the Medici court. Coming from a family directly tied to the practice of the visual arts,[182] he had long since forged an important intellectual fellowship with figures at the forefront of that artistic milieu. He had known Agnolo Bronzino at least since the late 1520s, and in a letter written approximately a decade later the painter would qualify, on a par with the sculptor Niccolò Tribolo, as "amicissimo" of Varchi and dedicatee of his translation of Book XIII of Ovid's *Metamorphoses*.[183] The letter's closing salutations also

---

[181] On the years that Varchi spent as a *fuoruscito*, mostly between Padua and Bologna, see esp. Salvatore Lo Re, *Politica e cultura nella Firenze cosimiana: studi su Benedetto Varchi* (Manziana 2008), pp. 129–256; on the circumstances and chronology of his return to Florence, see also Firpo 1997 (as in fn. 159), p. 266.

[182] One of Varchi's biographers, Giovan Battista Busini, writes that "Benedetto del Grillandaio [i. e. Ghirlandaio, 1458–1497], eccellentissimo dipintore di que' tempi" was the first husband of the humanist's mother: see ibid., p. 205, n. 187; Lo Re 2008 (as in fn. 181), p. 93. Another biographer, Baccio Valori, specifies that Varchi was even named after the painter ("Nacque pertanto Benedetto Varchi […] di madonna Diamante, di Lionardo d'Urbano artefice, e prima moglie d'un Benedetto Ghirlandai, da cui prese il nome"): see ibid., p. 117. Frédérique Dubard de Gaillarbois's introduction to Varchi 2020 (as in fn. 64), p. 5, adds the consideration that Varchi himself mentioned this kinship in his funeral oration for Michelangelo (1564).

[183] Compare Varchi's words in his dedicatory letter: "L'ho indirizzata a voi duoi […] perciò che oltra l'essermi ciascuno di voi egualmente amicissimo e oltra la pari e grandissima eccellenzia vostra, dell'uno nella scultura e dell'altro nella pittura, vi dilettate ambo duoi e intendete nelle cose poetiche" (quoted from Parker 2000 [as in fn. 6], pp. 171–172). On this document, see also Leatrice Mendelsohn, *Paragoni: Benedetto Varchi's "Due Lezzioni" and Cinquecento Art Theory*, Ann Arbor, MI 1982, pp. 181–182, and esp. Geremicca 2017 (as in fn. 6), pp. 17–20, which takes the epistle as a starting point for a thorough reconstruction of Varchi's artistic networks around the Accademia Fiorentina. Geremicca 2013 (as in fn. 6), pp. 86–96 provides the best account of Bronzino's long-lasting friendship with Benedetto Varchi. On Tribolo's intellectual networks and his familiarity with Varchi, who might have provided him with the iconographic program for the Medici Villa of Castello, see the important studies by Alessandro Cecchi, Il Tribolo, la corte medicea, i letterati e gli artisti suoi amici, in: Elisabetta Pieri and Luigi Zangheri (eds.), *Niccolò detto il Tribolo tra arte, architettura e paesaggio*, Poggio a Caiano 2001, pp. 29–36, and Alessandra Giannotti, *Il teatro di natura. Niccolò Tribolo e le origini di un genere: la scultura di animali nella Firenze del Cinquecento*, Florence 2007, pp. 75–115. Varchi once again connected the names of his friends Bronzino and Tribolo in a letter to Carlo Strozzi dated October 25, 1539, which he wrote in the aftermath of Pietro Bembo's passage to Florence (see Benedetto Varchi, *Lettere, 1535–1565*, ed. Vanni Bramanti, Rome 2008, pp. 75–77 for the full text): "Mi par di vedervi hora quando eravate con Luca [Martini], col Tribolo et col Bronzino a considerare gli occhi et gli atti del reverendissimo Bembo, et non so mai come Luca si potè tenere, sappiendo quanto io l'adoro et quanto egli è cortese, d'andare a baciargli la mano." A detailed and

reveal other members of Cosimo's artistic entourage who were part of the humanist's inner circle: there is mention of the woodcarver, sculptor and soon-to-be-architect Giovan Battista di Marco del Tasso; of a modest bronzesmith who would find his fortune making essences for the Lord of Florence, Bastiano di Francesco di Jacopo or Ciano *profumiere*, and of the sculptor Raffaello da Montelupo, who was probably passing through Florence at the time.[184]

With the exception of Raffaello da Montelupo, for Varchi these were important contacts in the context of the Accademia Fiorentina, which he entered just days after his homecoming to Florence.[185] Even more significantly, they were a trusted group of allies when the humanist found himself at the center of a war within that very institution. Spurred by rivalries in which

updated account of the dense network of artistic relations in Florence, with a special but non-exclusive focus on his relations with the artists who responded to the humanist's "poll" on the relative merits of painting and sculpture, is offered by the introduction to Varchi 2020 (as in fn. 64), pp. 54–67.

[184] See the conclusion of the letter (in Parker 2000 [as in fn. 6], p. 172): "State sani e salutatemi col buon Tasso e con il nostro Ciano e tutti gli amici e specialmente il nostro non men buono e amorevole che valente messer Raffaello da Montelupo." On Tasso's professional career, see especially Marco Collareta, Una restituzione al Tasso legnaiolo, in: *Paragone / Arte* 35 (1984), pp. 81–91, and Emanuele Barletti, Ipotesi di lavoro su Giovan Battista del Tasso, in: *Critica d'arte* 6 (1990), pp. 55–61; for the hostile representation that Vasari provided of his activity as an architect, see Alessandro Cecchi, Il maggiordomo ducale Pierfrancesco Riccio e gli artisti della corte medicea, in: *Mitteilungen des Kunsthistorischen Institutes in Florenz* 42 (1998), pp. 115–143, pp. 118–124. Thanks to Tasso's skills as a woodcarver, Varchi had suggested him in a letter dating from December 1539 as the ideal person to create the pawns in a chess set that Bronzino was later intending to paint: see Jonathan K. Nelson, Creative Patronage: Luca Martini and the Renaissance Portrait, in: *Mitteilungen des Kunsthistorischen Institutes in Florenz* 39 (1995), pp. 282–303, pp. 283 and 300, n. 4, and Plaisance 2004 (as in fn. 66), p. 46. On the versatile activity of Bastiano di Francesco, see esp. Alessandro Nesi, *Ciano profumiere: un personaggio stravagante della corte di Cosimo de' Medici*, Florence 2015, which draws attention to the artist's cooperation with Zanobi Lastricati on a bronze statue of *Mercury* (1549–1551), now in the Walters Art Gallery of Baltimore. For Raffaello da Montelupo, who around 1539 was mainly working in the Orvieto cathedral but frequently traveled elsewhere, see Raffaello da Montelupo, *Vita di Raffaello da Montelupo*, ed. Riccardo Gatteschi, Florence 1998, pp. 46–48. An affectionate letter that the artist sent to Varchi in 1550 (quoted in full in Giovanni Gaetano Bottari and Stefano Ticozzi, eds., *Raccolta di lettere sulla pittura, scultura ed architettura scritte da' più celebri personaggi dei secoli XV, XVI e XVII*, Milan 1822, pp. 112–114, and mentioned also in Geremicca 2017 [as in fn. 6], p. 21) demonstrates that this friendship was a long-lasting one, while also revealing that the humanist attempted to convince the duke to employ Raffaello in Florence. Other documents illustrating this close association are Lorenzo Scala's letter to Varchi from February 20, 1546, and the latter's mention of Raffaello's statue of St. Cosma within his lecture on Michelangelo's sonnet: see Mendelsohn 1982 (as in fn. 183), p. 182, n. 433; Vanni Bramanti, ed., *Lettere a Benedetto Varchi, 1530–1563*, Manziana 2012, p. 244, and introduction to Varchi 2020 (as in fn. 64), p. 57.

[185] Varchi enrolled in the institution on March 8, 1543, whereas Tribolo and Bronzino's enrollment dated back to February 11, 1541, at the time of the Accademia degli Humidi's transformation into the Accademia Fiorentina. Giovan Battista di Marco del Tasso, on the other hand, became an academician on November 4, 1544. The records are preserved in the manuscript of the *Annali* of the institution (Florence, Biblioteca Marucelliana, ms. B III 52, cc. 3r, 13r, and 21r), on which see Alessandro Cecchi, Il Bronzino, Benedetto Varchi e l'Accademia Fiorentina: ritratti di poeti, letterati e personaggi illustri della corte medicea, in: *Antichità viva* 30 (1991), p. 23; Plaisance 2004 (as in fn. 66), p. 88, and Annalisa Andreoni, *La via della dottrina: le lezioni accademiche di Benedetto Varchi*, Pisa 2012, p. 11 (with reference to Varchi's enrollment). For a survey of artists' enrollment in such institutions see François Quiviger, The Presence of Artists in Literary Academies, in: David Chambers and François Quiviger (eds.), *Italian Academies of the Sixteenth Century*, London 1995, pp. 105–112. For a broad-ranging assessment of academic cultures in early modern Italy see Jane E. Everson, Denis V. Reidy and Lisa Sampson (eds.), *The Italian Academies 1525–1700: Networks of Culture, Innovation and Dissent*, London 2016.

personal jealousies compounded deep differences of opinion in matters of religion, philosophy, language and literature, some leading intellectuals of the academy (first and foremost the "Aramei" Giovan Battista Gelli, Pier Francesco Giambullari, Cosimo Bartoli, and Carlo Lenzoni) were quick to falsely accuse Varchi of rape of a young girl, landing him in prison in March 1545.[186] Relatively isolated from many of the institution's other literati, Varchi found support among the artists who gravitated around it. Once he was released from prison and even appointed academic consul on April 12, 1545, he thus took advantage of his position to further open the ranks of the leading Florentine cultural institution to the practitioners of the visual arts. During his consulship the academy admitted an artist with long-standing ties to the humanist, Benvenuto Cellini, who at the time was still in the service of Francis I of France but would soon return definitively to his native city, and soon thereafter also the sculptor Baccio Bandinelli and the painter Francesco Salviati were enrolled as academicians.[187]

Some poetry exchanges published in the collection *De' sonetti di m. Benedetto Varchi colle risposte, e proposte di diversi parte seconda* (1557) document how artists active in Florence were an important part of the humanist's *sodalitas*, i.e. the social group bound to him as much by friendship as by solidarity and intellectual collaboration,[188] and how they were in fact among those quickest to defend Varchi when he found himself at the center of a flare-up of the controversy with the Aramei in 1546. The longest and most intense poetic dialogue between Varchi and a local artist, in this case Agnolo Bronzino, originated precisely against this backdrop. It was Bronzino who began the correspondence by sending his friend the sonnet *Varchi, ch'a par dei più saggi e migliori*, to which Varchi replied with the homometrical *Bronzino, io*

---

[186] The main reasons for this hostility were Varchi's religious proximity to Valdesian ideas in the 1540s, his fidelity to the legacy of Pietro Bembo, which many Florentine intellectuals perceived to be alien to the city's literary tradition, and several aspects of his philosophical positions, which were informed by his Paduan training at the Accademia degli Infiammati and which collided with some of the prevailing Neoplatonic inclinations of the Aramei. For an account of Varchi's incarceration, see Baccio Valori's biography of the humanist in Lo Re 2008 (as in fn. 181), pp. 125–126. Excellent reconstructions of the circumstances of this academic war are provided by Antonio Sorella in Benedetto Varchi, *L'Hercolano*, ed. Antonio Sorella, Pescara 1995, pp. 91–92; Firpo 1997 (as in fn. 159), pp. 272–282; Plaisance 2004 (as in fn. 66), pp. 133–146; Andreoni 2012 (as in fn. 185), pp. 148–151, and Simon A. Gilson, *Reading Dante in Renaissance Italy: Florence, Venice and the "Divine Poet,"* Cambridge 2018, pp. 119–132.

[187] Cellini matriculated into the Academy on April 23, 1545 (Florence, Biblioteca Marucelliana, cod. B III 52, c. 25r) and arrived in Florence in the second half of July (Eugène Plon, *Benvenuto Cellini, orfévre, médailleur, sculpteur: Recherches sur sa vie, sur son oeuvre et sur les pièces qui lui sont attribuées*, 2 vols., Paris 1883, 2, p. 71). His friendship with Varchi dated back to at least 1535 (the sculptor's autobiography, Cellini 1996 [as in fn. 23], pp. 305–306, *Vita* 1.84, testifies that the humanist had then penned a sonnet mourning the artist's alleged death). Around that time, Varchi also mediated between Pietro Bembo and Cellini on several occasions in the complex negotiations regarding the making of Pietro Bembo's portrait medal: see Davide Gasparotto, La barba di Pietro Bembo, in: *Annali della Scuola Normale Superiore di Pisa. Classe di Lettere e Filosofia* 4 (1996), pp. 183–206; Varchi 2008 (as in fn. 183), pp. 5–9 and 19–25. Bandinelli and Salviati's enrollment is recorded on May 21, 1545: see Florence, Biblioteca Marucelliana, B III 52, c. 25r and Cecchi 1991 (as in fn. 185), p. 25.

[188] On the notion of Renaissance *sodalitas* and how such a classically conceptualized community often found expression in poetic discourses, see the editors' introduction in: Ingrid De Smet and Paul White (eds.), *Sodalitas litteratorum: Le compagnonnage littéraire néo-latin et français à la Renaissance. Études à la mémoire de Philip Ford = Studies in Memory of Philip Ford*, Geneva 2019, pp. 19–26.

cercai sol dietro i migliori (Appendix, nos. 10–11).[189] The *proposta*, first in a thematically compact series of eight exchange-poems published in the 1557 volume, celebrated Varchi's literary fame and also mentioned his ultimate victory over his enemies' envy, with a reference to the impassioned lecture *Sopra l'invidia* that Varchi had given during a private session of the academy on March 21, 1546.[190] Bronzino's sonnet openly referred to the themes of that lecture, in which Varchi had alluded polemically to the adversaries who had sullied his name: the idea behind the first tercet, for example, that the glory and stature of genius are bound to unleash the malevolence of inferior individuals, condenses the content of the entire third chapter of Varchi's lecture.[191] The ideological welding of these texts is invaluable for understanding the role artists played in the conflicts that pervaded the Accademia Fiorentina in 1545–1546, as confirmed also by the correspondence in verse between Varchi and the sculptor, architect and engineer Francesco da Sangallo, once again published in the 1557 volume of *Sonetti* (*Quei tre spirti del ciel pregiati e chiari*; Appendix, no. 12). Like Bronzino, soon after the spring of 1546 Sangallo expressed his unqualified esteem and support for Varchi, congratulating him on his victory over a bevy of envious rivals.[192]

Even once the academic dispute had abated, Varchi continued to cultivate important relationships with the artists that gravitated around the Medici court. Although his friendship with Bandinelli (as witnessed by the latter's admission to the academy in 1545) quickly deteriorated,[193] by the end of the 1540s the network of alliances that tied the literato to Florentine practi-

---

[189] It is useful to recall that, in pre-modern Italy, a typical characteristic of sonnet exchanges was the fact that each line of the poetic *risposta* had the same rhyming words (or, less frequently, the same final consonances) as the *proposta*.

[190] Andreoni 2012 (as in fn. 185), p. 14, n. 1; see also Firpo 1997 (as in fn. 159), pp. 275–281. Firpo was the first to trace references to Varchi's academic war in Bronzino's poetry. For example, he has interpreted the sonnet *Certo omai, che non possa il torto crine* in the painter's canzoniere as alluding to the humanist's liberation from prison. In his careful monograph on Bronzino's poetry, Antonio Geremicca emphasizes the relevance of the theme of envy in a group of sonnets, including those published in the 1557 edition of Varchi's *Sonetti*, and interprets these texts in light of Varchi's academic lecture on the same topic: see Geremicca 2013 (as in fn. 6), p. 36. For the relevance that Varchi's lecture on envy had on Vasari's *Vite*, see Vincenzo Caputo, *"Dar spirto a' marmi, a i color fiato e vita": Giorgio Vasari scrittore*, Milan 2015.

[191] Compare, for instance, ll. 9–11 of Bronzino's sonnet ("Né si poteva, giunta a tanta altezza, / Vostra gloria più alzar senza il mortale / Colpo d'invidia, al fin di voi prigiona") with the relevant chapter of the humanist's lecture on envy (Varchi 1858–1859 [as in fn. 67], 2: p. 594): "Se bene tutti quegli che sono stati eccellenti in qual si voglia cosa, sono in tutte l'età e per tutti i luoghi stati invidiati […]. E la cagione è, perché quanto sono maggiori i beni, tanto sono maggiormente invidiati, e da più persone." Bronzino also expressed his solidarity with Varchi in a letter from May 6, 1546, whose contents partially overlap with those of the present sonnet. See the text in Bramanti 2012 (as in fn. 184), pp. 247–248: "Non può essere che per qualche tempo non si scuopra la verità et che sia stato in tutti i secoli et in tutti luoghi che sempre i migliori siano odiati et perseguitati, così non solo non vi dovete dolere, ma rallegrare di esser compagno di quanti chiarissimi huomini furono per la loro bontà et nobiltà d'animo malvoluti et danneggiati."

[192] For more on this sonnet, see *infra*.

[193] See esp. Maddelena Spagnolo, Ragionare e cicalare d'arte a Firenze nel Cinquecento: tracce di un dibattito fra artisti e letterati," in: Harald Hendrix and Paolo Procaccioli (eds.), *Officine del nuovo: sodalizi fra letterati, artisti ed editori nella cultura italiana fra Riforma e Controriforma*, Manziana 2008, pp. 105–128, pp. 112–114, which calls attention to Varchi's decision not to include Bandinelli among the artists whom he consulted for his "paragone poll" on the relative merits of painting and sculpture, as well as to his unusually abrasive comments on the *Her-*

tioners of the arts was remarkably extensive. At the time of the so-called *inchiesta* on the relative merits of sculpture and painting (1547),[194] other painters, sculptors, architects, and medalists were included in his *sodalitas*. Along with the names already mentioned and Michelangelo (the only artist asked to participate in the referendum from outside Florence), Giorgio Vasari and Jacopo Pontormo were also invited to write their opinions.[195] The respectful familiarity with which they answered the appeal can, in fact, be interpreted as proof that Pontormo's emphasis on Varchi's love of professionals of the arts was not merely a form of *captatio benevolentiae*.[196]

---

cules and Cacus in the context of the same academic lecture. Also relevant is Roberta Bartoli, Bandinelli contro tutti. L'artista negli occhi dei contemporanei, in: Detlef Heikamp and Beatrice Paolozzi Strozzi (eds.), *Baccio Bandinelli scultore e maestro (1493–1560)*, Florence 2014, pp. 36–59, pp. 49–50. The *Memoriale* ascribed to the sculptor provides further evidence of his difficult relationship with Varchi, for the work states that Baccio had even questioned the humanist's knowledge of Tacitus: "Contro al Varchi fu a·ccagione di un luogo di Tacito, il quale, ancora che fussi dotto, gli dissi in presenza del Duca che egli era più poeta che istorico" (quotation from Paola Barocchi, *Scritti d'arte del Cinquecento*, 3 vols., Milan 1971–1977, 2, p. 1384).

[194] The literature on both the lecture and the survey is impossible to cover here. Suffice it to mention the fundamental works by Mendelsohn 1982 (as in fn. 183); François Quiviger, Benedetto Varchi and the Visual Arts, in: *Journal of the Warburg and Courtauld Institutes* 50 (1987), pp. 219–224, and Marco Collareta, Le "arti sorelle": teoria e pratica del "paragone," in: Giuliano Briganti (ed.), *La pittura in Italia. Il Cinquecento*, 2 vols., Milan 1988, 2, pp. 569–580, along with the more recent studies of Oskar Bätschmann, The "Paragone" of Sculpture and Painting in Florence around 1550, in: Katja Burzer, Charles Davis, Sabine Feser, and Alessandro Nova (eds.), *Le Vite del Vasari: genesi, topoi, ricezione. Atti del convegno, 13–17 febbraio 2008, Firenze, Kunsthistorisches Institut, Max-Planck-Institut*, Venice 2010, pp. 85–96; Sefy Hendler, *La guerre des arts: le paragone peinture-sculpture en Italie XVᵉ–XVIIᵉ siècle*, Rome 2013, esp. pp. 53–69; Marco Collareta, Nouvelles études sur le paragone entre les arts, in: *Perspective* 1 (2015), pp. 153–160, and introduction to Varchi 2020 (as in fn. 64), pp. 1–90. For the sake of clarity, I am using such conventional definitions as "paragone" and "inchiesta" even though neither appears in Varchi's academic lecture (ibid., p. 36).

[195] On the occasion of the *inchiesta* on the paragone, it was probably Luca Martini who acted as intermediary between Varchi and the two artists: see Mendelsohn 1982, p. 290, n. 86. Martini (on which see *infra*) was probably also a liaison between Varchi and Michelangelo, inviting the latter to provide his opinion on the paragone debate: see Dubard de Gaillarbois' introduction to Varchi 2020 (as in fn. 64), p. 57. Varchi's acquaintance with Vasari probably dated back to the early 1530s, when the painter was in Rome: see the reference to a certain "messer Giorgio" in Annibal Caro's letter to Varchi of March 1, 1533 (text in Bramanti 2012 [as in fn. 184], p. 49); another mention of Vasari is to be found in Lorenzo Scala's letter to Varchi of February 1546 (see above, fn. 184). The survey on the paragone, on the other hand, seems to be the earliest written evidence of both Sangallo and Pontormo's acquaintance with Varchi. It is nonetheless likely that thanks to the good offices of Bronzino, Varchi might at that point have known Pontormo for several years. On March 26, 1555, Pontormo's so-called "diary" records that he received a sonnet from Varchi, which was certainly the one published later that year in the literato's first volume of the *Sonetti* (sonn. *Mentre io con penna oscura, e basso inchiostro*). Pontormo's account also informs us that in the 1550s, Varchi was among the friends who were admitted into the artist's house (Roberto Fedi, La cultura del Pontormo, in Roberto P. Ciardi and Antonio Natali [eds.], *Pontormo e Rosso*, Venice 1996, pp. 26–46, p. 30). In the *Ragionamento secondo* of his *Primo libro de' ragionamenti delle regole del disegno*, Alessandro Allori confirmed this familiarity by attributing to the character of his master, Bronzino, the following words: "E tu […] torna il più presto che puoi, ché credo verranno a cena con esso noi il nostro messer Benedetto Varchi e 'l cortesissimo Luca Martini, che credo che piglieranno piacer grandissimo nel sentire che cotesti signori hanno sì nobilissimo concetto dell'attendere al disegno, come già fecero essi nella gioventù loro, e sentirai forse trattare di alcuni passi sopra il nostro stupendissimo poeta Dante" (text from Barocchi 1971–1977 [as in fn. 193], 2, p. 1965; on this passage, see also Nelson 1995 [as in fn. 184], p. 283).

[196] See Pontormo's letter in Varchi and Borghini 1998 (as in fn. 80), pp. 69–70: "El diletto che io so che voi, magnifico M. Benedetto, pigliate di qualche bella pittura o scultura, e inoltre l'amore che voi agli uomini di dette

In truth, the *inchiesta* involving some of the most important sculptors and painters in Florence attests to how highly Varchi considered their opinion on a matter that could only be addressed – he insisted – by those with direct experience.[197] The unprecedented confidence that such a prominent figure of the humanistic elite placed in artists' intellectual capabilities thus intercepted and fostered that broad historical trend by which Italian artists, around the mid-Cinquecento, resorted increasingly to writing to intervene in questions that concerned them directly.[198] As Varchi wrote, the artists whose opinions he sought had not only demonstrated those specific professional skills that rendered them able to settle the dispute, but had also shown enough mastery of the pen to make their opinions no less worthwhile than pleasing:

> Et in vero ho cavato dell'oppennioni loro non meno utile che piacere, veggendoli non meno intendenti che ingegnosi, e che non solo lo scarpello o il pennello è bene adoperato da loro, ma ancora la penna, seguitando il Maestro loro nell'una arte e nell'altra; e confermatomi nella credenza mia che, chiunche è eccellentissimo in un'arte nobile, non sia del tutto privato di giudizio nell'altre.[199]

For the purposes of our analysis, this statement is of primary importance. It certifies how artists, with as much intellect as technical skill, were qualified to be fully recognized as citizens of the contemporary republic of letters. Their dual vocation for art and writing was likened to the supreme example of Michelangelo ("il Maestro loro"), whom Varchi celebrated as the individual who proved that mastery of one art of noble intellectual status was necessarily accompanied by adequate discernment in the others and whom he had praised, in his lecture on

---

professioni portate, mi fa credere ch'el sottilissimo intelletto vostro si muova a ricercare le nobiltà e ragioni di ciascuna di queste due arti."

[197] See ibid., p. 33: "Né penso ancora che alcuno mi creda tanto arrogante e presuntuoso che io osassi di muovere questa dubitazione e disputa per diciderla e risolverla, avendo pochissima cognizione dell'una e manco dell'altra; ma bene penso che come a filosofo, cioè a amatore del vero, mi sia lecito dire liberamente quel poco ch'io n'intendo, rimettendomi in tutto e per tutto al giudizio di chi è perfetto nell'una e nell'altra, cioè a Michelagnolo. E perché io non desidero altro che trovare puramente la verità, e sappiendo che a ciascuno si debba credere nell'arte sua, ho scritto et avuto i pareri e giudizii di quasi tutti gli scultori e pittori più eccellenti che oggi in Firenze si ritruovono; e se la brevità del tempo lo mi avesse concedutto, arei scritto ancora a tutti gli altri che io conosco fuora di qui." For more on this issue see Spagnolo 2008 (as in fn. 193), esp. pp. 115–117, to whose analysis my considerations here are indebted.

[198] Compare Dionisotti 1971 (as in fn. 17), p. 243: "I rapporti e scambi fra la letteratura e le altre discipline diventano in questo periodo [i. e. around the 1550s] molto più facili e frequenti. Così anche fra la letteratura e le arti. Non si ha più una aristocrazia letteraria che, dall'alto dell'enciclopedia umanistica allestita fra Quattro e Cinquecento, si guarda intorno e interviene e giudica in cose che direttamente non la riguardano."

[199] Varchi and Borghini 1998 (as in fn. 80), p. 33. Varchi argued that *giudizio* did not depend upon a traditional training in classics in a little-known letter to Carlo Strozzi (October 8, 1539): "Di quelli che studiano, perché molti di questi fanno peggio che gli altri, così come molti che di quelli che non istudiano fanno meglio. La forza tutta sta nella bontà et nel giuditio" (Varchi 2008 [as in fn. 183], p. 74). The humanist developed some related ideas in a famous passage of the *Hercolano*, where he distinguished the linguistic skills of those who did not know ancient languages but spoke their native tongue correctly, also in view of their literary interests and exchanges with men of letters, from those of both erudites and complete illiterates. Varchi labeled these culturally intermediate speakers, whom he regarded positively as authors of writings in the vernacular and amongst whom he assuredly included the majority of contemporary Florentine artists, as "non idioti." On this, see the considerations of Antonio Sorella in Varchi 1995 (as in fn. 186), pp. 14–15 and DXXXIII, and Paola Gambarota, *Irresistible Signs: The Genius of Language and Italian National Identity*, Toronto 2011, p. 38, with further references.

the sonnet *Non ha l'ottimo artista alcun concetto*, as the person who combined the perfection of poetry with that of the visual arts.[200]

Varchi's choice to seek the opinion of flesh-and-blood artists, as opposed to the fictional painters and sculptors who for decades had crowded the discussions of the most renowned literati whenever the conversation turned to art,[201] was therefore based on his appreciation of the dignity of their writings. Pausing a bit on the timeline helps to clarify how resolutely many Florentine intellectuals resisted Varchi's position: the lecture on the paragone, or *Lezzione nella quale si disputa della maggioranza delle arti*, was held on March 13, 1547, nine days after the approval of the reforms to the Accademia Fiorentina's bylaws that would lead, in August of that year, to the expulsion of every artist except Michelangelo.[202] In establishing that all academics had the duty to "legger publicamente, e privatamente, comporre opere in versi, o in prosa, e tradurre le scienzie," the stricter regulations set criteria for affiliation with the institute that practitioners of the arts were unlikely to be able to meet.[203] By stating for example that "una cosa piccola, come tre o quattro sonetti" was not sufficient for enrollment in the academy, these criteria set standards that might only be satisfied by a poet-artist of the caliber and literary ambitions of Bronzino, who was in any case readmitted only in 1566 by virtue of his submission of three long and elaborate "Canzoni sorelle" in praise of Cosimo de' Medici.[204]

---

[200] On the theme of the nobility of the arts, see the *Disputa prima* in the *Lezzione nella quale si disputa della maggioranza delle arti* (Varchi and Borghini 1998 [as in fn. 80], pp. 15–31). For Varchi's academic lecture on Michelangelo's poetic activity (March 6, 1547), see ch. 1 of this book.

[201] An early and relevant example is the section that Castiglione's *Libro del Cortegiano* devoted to the paragone debate (1.49–50), which sees the intervention of the character of the sculptor Gian Cristoforo Romano. On this, see Spagnolo 2008 (as in fn. 193), p. 120.

[202] The artists had submitted their letters to Varchi between the end of January and the first part of February 1547; the new constitutions for the Academy passed on March 4, 1547, but became effective only in the following summer: see Claudia Di Filippo Bareggi, In nota alla politica culturale di Cosimo I: l'Accademia Fiorentina, in: *Quaderni storici* 8 (1973), pp. 527–574, pp. 538 and 570–571. A full list of the academicians who were expelled from the institution on that occasion is in Plaisance 2004 (as in fn. 66), p. 186. Varchi complained about the reform in a letter of April 21, 1548 to Pietro Aretino, another prominent victim of the affair (text from Varchi 2008 [as in fn. 183], pp. 133–134): "Non potendo cavarne me o non volendo [...], ne cavarono tutti gli amici miei, come il molto reverendo, buono e dotto monsignore de' Lenzi, messer Benvenuto Cellini, scultore eccellentissimo, il Bronzino, pittore egregio, e molti altri." The 1547 expulsion from the Accademia Fiorentina led Bronzino to write many poems that commented on the event using allegorical imagery: see Geremicca 2013 (as in fn. 6), pp. 37–38.

[203] Quoted from Di Filippo Bareggi 1973 (as in fn. 202), p. 570. We should remember that, in September 1542, both Bronzino and Tribolo had been exempted, upon their requests, from giving academic lectures. See Plaisance 2004 (as in fn. 66), p. 131, and Firpo 1997 (as in fn. 159), p. 206, which argues that "Tribolo, figlio di un legnaiolo, [...] per due volte nel '42 dovette rinunciare a tenere le lezioni private del giovedì cui era stato designato, certo a causa della sua inadeguatezza a competere con personaggi come il Varchi, il Bartoli, il Giambullari nel commentare Dante e Petrarca."

[204] The quote is from the *Constituzione dell'obbligo degli Accademici* of March 4, 1547 (for the full text of the document, see Plaisance 2004 [as in fn. 66], pp. 232–233). It has been noted that the painter's engagement with lyrical poetry grew significantly after that year, probably as a consequence of his ambition to gain a new admission to the Academy, which took place on May 26, 1566: see Tanturli 2004 (as in fn. 6), p. 200, and Chiummo 2016 (as in fn. 6), pp. 258–260.

In short, Varchi's official endorsement of the writing of artists, in the dual realm of Michelangelo's poetry and the prose missives sent in response to the *inchiesta* on the paragone, arrived just as the academy was preparing to reverse its earlier acceptance of members of a different cultural background, including that of Florentine artist workshops.[205] While it is undoubtedly true that the 1547 reform was part of a process designed to have the academy better mirror Cosimo's cultural policy,[206] it also reflected to some degree that novel push toward closing off literary society that according to Dionisotti would triumph in Italy starting in the 1560s. Dionisotti himself emphasized how the unprecedented expansion of the community of vernacular writers which, in the decades preceding the Council of Trent, included artists among its central figures had led many of the peninsula's literati as early as the 1540s to try to regiment that growth through the sieve of the newborn academic institutions. These same intellectuals would have often sought to reassert a rigidly hierarchical, anti-pluralistic vision of the *res publica litterarum*, centered on the prestige of a classicistic language and culture.[207] Varchi's clear-cut position in favor of expanding contemporary literary society must therefore be understood in its relational dimension, as his choosing sides in a battle that for the moment would turn out to be lost.[208] With the Accademia Fiorentina's reform of 1547, what would instead temporarily prevail would be the position endorsed by humanists like Don Vincenzio Borghini, who often refused to credit visual artists with the proficiency needed to master the pen.[209]

---

[205] Dubard de Gaillarbois's introduction to Varchi 2020 (as in fn. 64), p. 34, convincingly suggests that the publication of Varchi's academic lectures might also have been intended as an indirect response to the expulsion of the artists from the Florentine Academy.

[206] On this, see Plaisance 2004 (as in fn. 66), pp. 123–234.

[207] See Dionisotti 1971 (as in fn. 17), pp. 236–237 (on the "disciplining function" of academic institutions: "Mi sembra innegabile una qualche corrispondenza fra l'ideale accademico che proprio intorno al 1540 si precisa e si impone alla cultura italiana, e la convocazione, di lì a pochi anni, della grande assemblea della Chiesa. La ragion d'essere di quell'ideale accademico è ovvia: la nuova società letteraria italiana doveva cercare, e però stentava a trovare, un assetto che accogliesse e al tempo stesso disciplinasse la folla degli associati. Era per l'appunto una folla come non s'era mai vista prima, per qualità e per numero, e ogni interpretazione della storia letteraria di quell'età deve partire dal riconoscimento, non di sforzi e avventure individuali, bensì di un'attività collettiva, esuberante e irrequieta"), and pp. 246–248, on literary society's return to a more rigid classicistic order in the 1560s.

[208] Compare the methodological indication of Pierre Bourdieu (*Distinction: A Social Critique of the Judgement of Taste*, trans. Richard Nice, Cambridge, MA 1984, p. 192) on the necessity for sociologists and scholars interested in the study of culture to consider "the field of struggles, the system of objective relations within which positions and postures are defined relationally and which governs even those struggles aimed at transforming it." For a discussion of the antielitist ideas of poetry and philosophy that underpinned Varchi's accreditation of the artists' literary activity, see the introduction to Varchi 2020 (as in fn. 64), p. 51.

[209] Consider, among other possible examples, Borghini's disdainful remarks on many of the letters in which painters and sculptors had responded to Varchi's *inchiesta* on the paragone (quoted from the *Selva di notizie* of 1564, in Varchi and Borghini 1998 [as in fn. 80], pp. 87–88): "Io mi sono un poco maravigliato di qualcuno di quegli uomini da bene che avendo alle mani un'arte nella quale e' vaglione assai assai, anzi pur sono eccellenti e se ne possono maravigliosamente onorare, egli abbino cercato gloria per un'altra nella quale egli hanno pochissima parte et hanno mal modo di onorarsene punto, hanno più presto dar cagione di ridere a chi legge quel che gli hanno scritto; e può parer maraviglia certo, da quelle stesse mani onde escono sì belle figure sieno usciti poi tali passerotti." On this passage, see Spagnolo 2008 (as in fn. 193), pp. 122–124, which also quotes an

Of pens, brushes, and hammers: the presence and dignity of the artists' poetry in Varchi's dialogues in verse

Against the backdrop of these struggles to redefine hierarchies and relative positions within an evolving literary field, the importance to Varchi's poetic output of his dialogues with painters, sculptors, architects, and goldsmiths is more readily understood. He was certainly not the only Florentine poet of the period who kept up a correspondence in verse with artists. A glance through Bronzino's canzoniere reveals his interactions, for example, with Anton Francesco Grazzini, Gherardo Spini, Tommaso Porcacchi, Laura Battiferri degli Ammannati, Jacopo Sellori, Antonio de' Bardi, and Piero della Stufa.[210] However, none of these authors pursued a dialogue with local artists with the same perseverance and consistency as Varchi. From this standpoint, the sixteenth-century editions of his *Sonetti* are of paramount importance. As Marco Collareta has observed, these collections document an "intense, ramified, long-lasting relationship" with the world of Florentine arts.[211] In *De sonetti di m. Benedetto Varchi. Parte prima* (published in Florence by Lorenzo Torrentino in June 1555), constituting the author's love canzoniere, artists are among the privileged recipients of Varchi's poems.[212] While that

---

excerpt from a speech that Borghini prepared for the artists of the Accademia del Disegno in 1564: "Voi havete a sapere che in tutte l'arte è differentia fra l'operare in quella et parlare o trattare di quella, et sta molto bene et quasi è il più delle volte che uno che operi eccellentemente non ne sappia parlar." On the latter text, most useful are Anthony Hughes, "An Academy for Doing." I: The Accademia Del Disegno, the Guilds and the Principiate in Sixteenth-Century Florence, in: *The Oxford Art Journal* 9, no. 1 (1986), pp. 3–10, and Eliana Carrara, Vincenzo Borghini, Lelio Torelli e l'Accademia del disegno di Firenze: alcune considerazioni, in: *Annali di critica d'arte* 2 (2006), pp. 545–568. We should keep in mind that Borghini's attacks did not extend to his close ally Giorgio Vasari, who had studied with the humanist Giovanni Lappoli, alias Pollastra.

[210] Compare the table of contents of the manuscript (BNCF, Fondo Nazionale II.IX.10) in Parker 2000 (as in fn. 6), pp. 174–184, and Tanturli 2004 (as in fn. 6), pp. 214–224. For many of the names of this literary circle, who often counted among Varchi's closest associates, see Victoria Kirkham in Battiferra 2006 (as in fn. 101), *ad indicem*, and Geremicca 2013 (as in fn. 6), *passim*.

[211] The quote is from Marco Collareta, Varchi e le arti figurative, in: Vanni Bramanti (ed.), *Benedetto Varchi, 1503–1565: Atti del convegno, Firenze, 16–17 dicembre 2003*, Rome 2007, pp. 173–184, p. 176 (my translation). On the relevance of Varchi's poetic corpus in the vernacular for an understanding of his relations with the contemporary Florentine arts, see also Geremicca 2017 (as in fn. 6), pp. 16–17, and Diletta Gamberini, I colloqui poetici degli artisti con Benedetto Varchi, in: *La Rivista. Études culturelles italiennes Sorbonne Universités* 5 (2017), pp. 61–69: https://etudesitaliennes.hypotheses.org/files/2017/05/4GamberiniFini-1.pdf (last accessed 31/01/2021).

[212] On the first edition of Varchi's sonnets (Benedetto Varchi, *De Sonetti di M. Benedetto Varchi parte prima*, Florence 1555), see esp. Bernhard Huß, "Cantai colmo di gioia, e senza inganni." Benedetto Varchis *Sonetti (parte prima)* im Kontext des italienischen Cinquecento-Petrarkismus, in: *Romanistisches Jahrbuch* 52 (2001), pp. 133–157; Giuliano Tanturli, Una gestazione e un parto gemellare: la prima e la seconda parte dei *Sonetti* di Benedetto Varchi, in: *Italique* 7 (2004), pp. 43–87; Laura Paolino, Il "geminato ardore" di Benedetto Varchi. Storia e costruzione di un canzoniere "ellittico," in: *Nuova rivista di letteratura italiana* 7 (2004), pp. 233–314; Domenico Chiodo, Varchi rimatore: modi e forme della poesia di corrispondenza, in: idem, *Più che le stelle in cielo: poeti nell'Italia del Cinquecento*, Manziana 2013 (essay first published in 2007), pp. 150–164; Giovanni Ferroni, "Si ricerca ancora dottrina non picciola." Varchi, la poesia pastorale e i *Sonetti* del 1555, in: *Italique* 20 (2017), pp. 211–259, and Selene Maria Vatteroni, I testi proemiali nei *Sonetti. Prima parte* di Benedetto Varchi, in: *La Rivista. Études culturelles italiennes Sorbonne Universités* 5 (2017), pp. 13–22 (https://etudesitaliennes.hypotheses.org/files/2017/05/2VatteroniFini-1.pdf, last accessed 31/01/2021).

editorial project deliberately excluded lyric poems by other authors, it contained a quantity of sonnets written to artists that has little comparison in the Italian Renaissance. In its exceptional breadth, the collection is enlightening, placing painters, sculptors, architects, goldsmiths, and medalists alongside goldbeaters, woodworkers, and embroiderers.[213] These are the recipients of sonnets on various topics, but centered primarily on the celebration of Varchi's love for that "laurel" that, along the lines of the Petrarchan model, represented both the symbol of poetry and the *senhal* of the poet's beloved: this time not the Laura of the *Rerum Vulgarium Fragmenta* but a new Lauro, Lorenzo Lenzi, whom Varchi depicts as the object of a sentiment devoid of passion, hence as a figure Platonically able to lift his devotee to heaven.[214] In the author's words, the 1555 volume was in fact fruit of the "volontà di celebrare […] non pure un lauro solo, di tutte le laudi degnissimo, anzi di qualunque loda per mio giudizio maggiore; ma eziandio buona parte di tutti coloro, i quali a me per qualunque cagione pareva, che di dovere essere celebrati meritassero." [215]

A manuscript note in which Varchi designated the *Sonetti* of the 1555 edition that were addressed to visual artists with the notation "Artefici nobili" confirms his view that artists were worthy of poetic celebration by virtue of the *nobilitas* of their profession, in keeping

---

[213] For the sake of clarity, the text and numbering of Varchi's published verse follow the nineteenth-century edition of the author's works (the numbering was absent in the sixteenth-century editions): see Varchi 1858–1859 (as in fn. 67), 2, pp. 832–1016. The sonnets to artists are nos. 9, 19, 25, 64, 65, 75, 153, 179, 239, 240, 242, 243, 353, 398, 486, 494, 512, 517, 518. The dedicatees are (in order of "fame") Michelangelo, Pontormo, Bronzino, Francesco Salviati, Alessandro Allori, Giulio Clovio, Leone Leoni, Raffaello da Montelupo, Giovambattista di Marco del Tasso, Galeazzo Alessi, Domenico Poggini, Ciano Compagni, Cesare da Bagno, Pietro Paolo Galeotti, Antonio Bachiacca, Alessandro Cesati or "il Grechetto," Giovanni di Francesco or "il Piloto," Antonio Crocini, and Francesco di Sandro. To these names we might add those of Niccolò Tribolo, Pierino da Vinci, and Benvenuto Cellini, who are not among the dedicatees of sonnets in the 1555 volume, but who are nonetheless the subjects of texts nos. 153 (a sonnet dedicated to Giovan Battista di Marco del Tasso on Tribolo's death), 155 (on Pierino's death), and 241 (a poem for Giovan Battista Ricasoli on Cellini's *Perseus*).

[214] On the strong (Neo)Platonic connotation of Varchi's love verse for Lenzi, see, among recent discussions, Huß 2001 (as in fn. 212), pp. 144–146; Tanturli 2004 (as in fn. 212), pp. 49–52; Paolino 2004 (as in fn. 212), pp. 254–256; Salvatore Lo Re, Gli amori omosessuali del Varchi: storia e leggenda, in: Elise Boillet and Chiara Lastraioli (eds.), *Extravagances amoureuses: l'amour au-delà de la norme à la Renaissance. Actes du colloque international du groupe de recherche "Cinquecento plurale," Tours, 18–20 septembre 2008* = *Stravaganze amorose: l'amore oltre la norma nel Rinascimento*, Paris 2010, pp. 279–295, pp. 280–282, and Ferroni 2017 (as in fn. 212), pp. 221–222; also relevant is Carlson 2014 (as in fn. 64), with reference to the kind of reading that Varchi offered of Michelangelo's poetry in his 1547 lecture at the Accademia Fiorentina. It should be highlighted that while Laura Paolino tends to interpret Varchi's use of such imagery as a sort of intellectual camouflage for a passion that would be anything but ethereal, Giovanni Ferroni stresses the "costruzione culturale nella quale egli inserì l'amore per altri maschi" and argues that the shaping Platonic and Ficinian component of the author's poems "in nessun caso può essere ridotto a scappatoia retorico-filosofica per coprire con un velo d'onestà e conformismo la propria passione per i giovinetti, amici e pupilli." For the wider argument that Platonic motifs, such as the paradigm of Socratic love, were deployed in the Italian Renaissance as a convenient concealment for homoerotic passions see Giovanni Dall'Orto, Socratic Love as a Disguise for Same-Sex Love in the Italian Renaissance, in: *Journal of Homosexuality* 16 (1989), pp. 33–66 (with a few references to Varchi). A basic portrait of Lorenzo Lenzi's historical and intellectual profiles can be found in Silvano Ferrone, Dialoghi poetici fra i Tasso e il Varchi, in: Michele Bandini and Federico G. Pericoli (eds.), *Scritti in memoria di Dino Pieraccioni*, Florence 1993, pp. 148–188, pp. 155 and 175–185, and Stefano Simoncini, Lenzi, Lorenzo, in: *DBI* 64, Rome 2005, pp. 387–392.

[215] Varchi 1858–1859 (as in fn. 67), 2, p. 831; the dedicatory letter was addressed to Francesco de' Medici.

with the premise of his lecture on the paragone.[216] Together with the notion that excellence in one intellectual discipline implied competence in the others, this designation explains why, in the subsequent collections of Varchi's writings, artists increasingly rise to the forefront as authors. In *De' sonetti di m. Benedetto Varchi colle risposte, e proposte di diversi parte seconda*, published by Lorenzo Torrentino in 1557 and conceived by the humanist as a sort of "poetic epistolary,"[217] the exchanges in verse with a painter like Bronzino and a sculptor like Francesco da Sangallo amount to ten poems. A more comprehensive picture emerges from the anthology of Varchi's *Sonetti spirituali*, published posthumously in Florence by Giunti in 1573, which contained his dialogues with Benvenuto Cellini, Agnolo Bronzino, Giorgio Vasari, Vincenzo Danti, Domenico Poggini, and the woodworker Antonio di Romolo Crocini.[218] A study of the papers left behind by Varchi, in particular the manuscript documents of the *Filze Rinuccini* at the Biblioteca Nazionale Centrale in Florence, demonstrates how such correspondence was paramount even in poetry collections and in uncollected compositions that were never published.[219] In the manuscript anthologies of sonnets Varchi compiled to commemorate the death of Luca Martini (January 9, 1561) and to praise Lorenzo Lenzi's expedition against the

---

[216] The manuscript note is preserved in BNCF, Filza Rinuccini 14, c. 357v and published in Tanturli 2004 (as in fn. 212), p. 50. Varchi offers an in-depth exploration of the theme of the nobility of arts in the *Disputa prima* of his lecture on the paragone (Varchi and Borghini 1998 [as in fn. 80], pp. 15–31).

[217] The definition comes from Tanturli 2004 (as in fn. 212), p. 46. On Varchi's wide network of poetic correspondents in Cinquecento Italy, of which the 1557 volume is the main testimony, see esp. Vanni Bramanti, Corrispondenza e corrispondenti nel secondo libro dei *Sonetti* di Benedetto Varchi, in: *Italique* 19 (2016), pp. 87–112.

[218] Most of these texts are the object of specific considerations below. While the other names on the list are well-known exponents of the contemporary artistic scene, little information is available on Antonio di Romolo, alias il Crocino, who nonetheless appears to have counted among Varchi's close acquaintances. This woodworker was not only the protagonist of a poetic dialogue with Varchi that was published in the context of the *Sonetti spirituali*, but also the dedicatee of sonnet 64 in the 1555 edition of Varchi's *Sonetti*. He also exchanged verse with Varchi on the occasion of Luca Martini's death (1561, see *infra*). As an artist, he collaborated on several occasions with his neighbor Benvenuto Cellini. For example, in January 1559 he prepared a wooden structure for the small model of the *Neptune* Fountain and, around 1562, the wooden case for the sculptor's marble *Crucifix*: see the commentary to Cellini 2014 (as in fn. 7), pp. 189 and 192, as well as Dario Trento, ed., *Benvenuto Cellini opere non esposte e documenti notarili*, Florence 1984, p. 76.

[219] On Varchi's manuscript materials in the Filze Rinuccini, see Anna Siekiera, Benedetto Varchi, in: Matteo Motolese, Paolo Procaccioli, and Emilio Russo (eds.), *Autografi dei letterati italiani. Il Cinquecento*, 3 vols., Rome 2009, 1, pp. 337–357, and now esp. the attentive study of Dario Brancato, I componimenti toscani di Benedetto Varchi nelle Filze Rinuccini della Biblioteca Nazionale Centrale di Firenze: genesi, riuso, varietà, in: *Schriften des Italienzentrums der Freien Universität Berlin*, 3 (2019, thematic issue *La cultura poetica di Benedetto Varchi*, eds. Bernhard Huß and Selene Maria Vatteroni: https://www.geisteswissenschaften.fu-berlin.de/italienzentrum/publikationen/schriften-italienzentrum/Schriften-Band-3/Schriften-des-Italienzentrums-Bd_-3.pdf, last accessed 31/01/2021), pp. 71–89, which sheds light on the articulation and chronological stratification of the poems preserved there. It is useful to recall that in the sixteenth century, more than 1200 vernacular poems by Varchi were published: the two Torrentino volumes of the *Sonetti* (1555 and 1557) and the Giunti edition of the *Sonetti spirituali* were followed by a small anthology of pastoral poetry (*Componimenti pastorali, di m. Benedetto Varchi. Nuovamente in quel modo stampati, che da lui medesimo furono poco anzi il fine della sua vita corretti*), published in Bologna by Giovan Battista and Cesare Salvetti in 1576 and republished in 1577 (see Paolino 2004 [as in fn. 212], pp. 235–236). Still, the posthumous thematic selections that resulted in the publication of the *Sonetti spirituali* and the *Componimenti pastorali* excluded the great majority of the poems that the humanist had composed between the publication of the second volume of his *Sonetti* (1557) and his death (1565).

Huguenots (1562), for example, painters, sculptors, architects, and goldsmiths were some of his preferred correspondents.[220]

Within this dense network of exchanges, we find much evidence of Varchi's appreciation of his artist friends' poetic vein. And while the *mare magnum* of his verse correspondence may leave the modern reader with the impression of a repetitive protocol of pleasantries and "salaams," a less superficial analysis shows how he was careful to adapt his praise to the intellectual countenance of his recipients.[221] Acting as a sort of "Prime Minister of the Republic of Letters, who gives more or less solemn praise, promises and favors and awards certificates of esteem,"[222] Varchi was most profuse in his accolades when corresponding with artist-writers. Considering the widespread resistance to granting artists citizenship in that same republic, such tributes no longer seem like anodyne celebratory clichés: rather, they outline an open, pluralistic conception of literature, partly by virtue of the principle of *ut pictura poesis*. To the author it was equally certain that "l'essere pittore giovi grandissimamente alla poesia" and that "la poesia giovi infinitamente a' pittori."[223] This helps explain his praise for individuals who, like Bronzino, possessed "la dotta penna al pennel dotto pari" (*Nuova casta Ciprigna e nuovo Marte*, Appendix, no. 14, l. 10), or who, like Giovann'Angelo Montorsoli, proved equal mastery of the instruments of sculpture and of writing (*Nunzio, e servo di Dio, che queste frali*: Appendix, no. 16, l. 6, with reference to the addressee's "glorious hands" as sculptor and poet; and *Spirto degno del Ciel, c'havendo a vile*: Appendix, no. 19, ll. 5–6).[224] Often modeled on the stylistic traits used to celebrate in Michelangelo the paradigm of the universal artist, the accolades hinge once again on the idea of a transitive property of talent in those arts that rely on the loftiest human faculties.

---

[220] Varchi had probably wanted to publish these two anthologies of poetry, but these projects were never accomplished. Giuseppe Aiazzi and Lelio Arbib reported having found an autograph note concerning this editorial plan among the humanist's papers: "Questi sonetti da un ricordo di mano del Varchi pare avesse idea di pubblicarli tutti insieme colla seguente indicazione e divisione: […] Ugonotti, quelli contro gli eretici di tal nome; Martini, quelli in vita ed in morte di Luca Martini suo amico e protettore" (Benedetto Varchi, *Lezioni sul Dante e prose varie di Benedetto Varchi, la maggior parte inedite […]*, eds. Giuseppe Aiazzi and Lelio Arbib, 2 vols., Florence 1841, 1, p. XXXIII). While this note has not been traced, further evidence of the project emerges from Ferrone 1993 (as in fn. 214), p. 148. For both these anthologies, see *infra*.

[221] The disparaging quote ("salamelecchi" in the original Italian), reflecting the bias which led to Varchi's poetic production remaining long neglected until recently, is from Umberto Pirotti, *Benedetto Varchi e la cultura del suo tempo*, Florence 1971, p. 188. Domenico Chiodo, on the other hand, has called attention to the individualizing features of Varchi's language of poetic praise (Chiodo 2013 [as in fn. 212], p. 153): "La forma del sonetto di corrispondenza qui descritta […] vede eccellere la penna del Varchi soprattutto in relazione al numero; sorprende insomma la sua capacità di interloquire in versi variando tra numerosi destinatari con appropriata sagacia uno schema comune incentrato sulla forma del sussigoso encomio, decorosamente cerimonioso. Per fare soltanto qualche esempio, si noti come il Molza, devoto cultore della classicità sia detto 'pien di quelle usanze antiche,' mentre di Trifon Gabriele sia soprattutto sottolineata l'"ineffabil bontate' e l'"umanità infinita,' che molti contemporanei gli riconobbero."

[222] Ibid., p. 157 (my translation).

[223] Varchi and Borghini 1998 (as in fn. 80), p. 56.

[224] For the genesis and analysis of the exchanges with both Bronzino and Montorsoli, see *infra*.

From this perspective, the forms of *diminutio sui* sprinkled through the response compositions of these painters and sculptors (as we read in Bronzino, *Quanto dal vero amor sovente parte*, Appendix, no. 15, l. 10, or Montorsoli, *Varchi gentil, che le mie poche, e frali*, Appendix, no. 17, ll. 1–6) are wholly consistent with those employed in replies to the paragone survey.[225] Faithful to the *topoi modestiae* typical of the period's poems of correspondence, these authors' insistence on the limitations of their poetic skills can also be seen as a veiled apology of their right to intervene in a field different from their chief profession. And we should not be misled by the fact that they often had their verses revised by Varchi, who sometimes radically changed their spelling, syntax, and vocabulary.[226] It was not only these "non-professional" poets, in fact, who submitted their poems for the humanist's scrutiny. Even writers of the caliber of Annibal Caro or a poet of the stature of Laura Battiferri sought the linguistic advice of the man considered to have the last word in Tuscan poetry.[227]

The main historical occasions for Varchi's dialogue in verse with artists

Inasmuch as Varchi's poetic output is a socialized literary form and a means of dialogue with a wide network of associates, rather than an introspective expression of a lyric ego folded in on itself, it is highly occasional in nature.[228] In pre-modern Italian poetry, for that matter, the

---

[225] See, for instance, the words of Vasari's letter (Varchi and Borghini 1998 [as in fn. 80], p. 61): "mi è parso vi siate fondato molto male a dimandar me di tal cosa; e Dio il volessi ch'io fussi abile a satisfarla," as well as those of Pontormo's (ibid., p. 70): "Non saperò o poterò forse con parole o enchiostro esprimere interamente le fatiche di chi opera." On the topoi of modesty used by the artist-writers in the 1547 *inchiesta* compare Dubard de Gaillarbois's introduction to Varchi 2020 (as in fn. 64), p. 30: "Les profils bas et les *declarationes modestiae* des artistes de l'anthologie ne relèvent donc pas que d'une *captatio benevolentiae*, mais d'un vrai complexe socio-culturel."

[226] It is possible to document the extent of such revisions by comparing, for example, the autograph versions of three sonnets by Benvenuto Cellini (*Benedetto quel dì che l'alma Varchi* in BNCF, Banco Rari 58, unnumbered folio) and Giorgio Vasari (*Varchi, io cognosco ben l'ingegno e l'arte* and *Com'a tristo nocchier governi e sarte* in BNCF, Filza Rinuccini 12, c. 60; see here Appendix, nos. 58 and 59) with the versions eventually published in the posthumous edition of Varchi's *Sonetti Spirituali*, which reflected many interventions made by Varchi. For more on this, see Vasari 2012 (as in fn. 7), pp. 78–80 (which nonetheless does not refer to the autograph versions of Vasari's poems), and Cellini 2014 (as in fn. 7), pp. 216–219.

[227] On Caro's request, see Richardson 2009 (as in fn. 18), p. 25; on Laura Battiferri's, see her letter (November 1557) to the humanist in: Bramanti 2012 (as in fn. 184), p. 364; for a broader treatment of Varchi's practices as a linguistic advisor, see Marco Biffi and Raffaella Setti, Varchi consulente linguistico, in: Bramanti 2007 (as in fn. 211), pp. 25–67. It should also be recalled that Benvenuto Cellini submitted the original manuscript of his autobiography to Benedetto Varchi (May 1559): having accepted the writer's response that the book's style did not need any intervention, the sculptor nonetheless solicited a substantial revision for the work's introductory sonnet (quoted ibid., p. 52: "Serbandovi il mio sonetto, ché quello ben desidero che senta un poco la pulizia della vostra meravigliosa lima").

[228] The dialogical and often occasional character of a great part of the poetic tradition of pre-modern Italy, with a special focus on the Middle Ages, is the focus of the enlightening study by Giunta 2002 (as in fn. 11). Only in recent years have scholars abandoned a long-standing aesthetic contempt for these defining features of the poetry by Varchi and many of his contemporaries. On this, see Tanturli 2004 (as in fn. 212), p. 71, which referred

fact that an author addressed a recipient in his social circle generally meant that the text was more strongly rooted in real circumstances outside of literature.[229] References to the political and cultural life of ducal Florence, and particularly to historical events of special significance to Varchi and his friends, are therefore very common in their correspondence poems. Against this backdrop, various occasions led Varchi to involve artists in a ritual of poetry writing: more than once the occasion was mourning, for example with the death of Jacopo Pontormo at the beginning of 1557.

This event is the focus of the largest cycle of thematically homogeneous texts in the poetic output of Bronzino, who in fourteen sonnets commemorated "l'amico e 'l fratello / anzi 'l padre e 'l maestro,"[230] and it is remarkable that in the manuscript of the painter's canzoniere, the fascicle containing the sonnets on the death of Pontormo begins with a poem by Varchi (*Bronzin, dove posso io fuggir, s'ancora*; Appendix, no. 20), followed by Bronzino's response (*Io sono, omai, sì di me stesso fuora*; Appendix, no. 21). Varchi's role is thus to set the themes on which the subsequent poems in the series are developed: specifically, the topical motif of a pain more suited to the living than the deceased who has ascended to heaven,[231] and the celebration of the supreme art and religious piety of the "gran pittor" (l. 5). The sonnet in question also has ties to other texts not included in Bronzino's canzoniere, which however cast light on the web of personal relationships and shared artistic, cultural, and literary options that underpin this poetic output. The homage to the *Christ in glory* at the center of the frescoes for the choir of San Lorenzo that Pontormo was working on when he died gives specificity, for example, to the more general praise that Varchi had showered on the painter's art and moral qualities in a sonnet of 1555.[232]

---

to a sort of "uso giornalistico del sonetto," and the insightful observations of Chiodo 2013 (as in fn. 212), pp. 108–109: "È indispensabile sgombrare preliminarmente il campo da due pregiudizi con i quali la modernità ha solitamente osservato le vicende cinquecentesche. Il primo di questi pregiudizi riguarda l'espressione 'poesia d'occasione,' che si usa abitualmente con tono dispregiativo, quasi contenesse una contraddizione in termini: ebbene, se vogliamo intendere e apprezzare la gran parte della poesia cinquecentesca [...] ci dobbiamo liberare dall'idea romantica dell'ispirazione sentimentale come unica possibile fonte di poesia. L'ispirazione poetica può essere mossa anche da un'occasione, da un'occasione della vita di corte, dalla capacità di farsi interpreti di un sentire collettivo, di ritrovare l'immagine o il concetto più efficace a esprimere la comune sensibilità, la diffusa affezione, ma anche la capacità di variare con fantasia [...] un sistema dato di ornamenti verbali." See also Richardson 2009 (as in fn. 18), p. 95, and, with reference to Laura Battiferri's *Il primo libro dell'opere toscane* (1560), Victoria Kirkham's introduction to Battiferra 2006 (as in fn. 101), pp. 36–37.
[229] Giunta 2002 (as in fn. 11), p. 117.
[230] Sonnet *Ben fu presagio di più grave danno*, ll. 12–13. On the text, see Parker 2000 (as in fn. 6), pp. 72–73, and Geremicca 2013 (as in fn. 6), p. 59 (also pp. 58–61 for a study of this sequence of compositions).
[231] Stefano Cremonini, Una topica petrarchesca: i versi in morte di amici, colleghi e mecenati, in: Loredana Chines (ed.), *Il petrarchismo: un modello di poesia per l'Europa*, 2 vols., Rome 2006, 2, pp. 329–347, p. 340. In the context of Petrarch's *Canzoniere*, the theme can be found, for instance, in sonnet 287, on the death of Sennuccio del Bene.
[232] By the time of his death, Pontormo had been working for twelve years on the ducal commission of the San Lorenzo frescoes (Philippe Costamagna, *Pontormo*, It. trans. Alberto Curotto, Milan 1994, p. 341). On the 1557 sonnet to Pontormo, see also Firpo 1997 (as in fn. 159), p. 214; a thorough critical reconstruction of the relationship between Varchi and Pontormo is provided in Lo Re 2008 (as in fn. 181), pp. 421–442. For the humanist's earlier composition to the painter, see Varchi 1858–1859 (as in fn. 67), 2, p. 905, sonnet 487 (*A messer Jacopo di*

At the center of the small amical circle united in mourning that the sonnet *Bronzin, dove posso io fuggir, s'ancora* delineates, Luca Martini emerges as an important liaison between Varchi and the Florentine artists.[233] These compositions therefore confirm and specify the information that we obtain from several other sources: in a sixteenth-century biography, Silvano Razzi described for instance how Varchi had developed extensive contacts with Medicean

---

Puntormo): "Mentre io con penna oscura e basso inchiostro / Tanti anni e tanti un vivo Lauro formo, / Voi con chiaro pennello, alto Puntormo, / Fate pari all'antico il secol nostro. // Anzi mentre io col volgo inerte dormo, / Voi nuovo pregio alla cerussa e all'ostro / Giugnete tal, che fuor del vile stormo, / A dito sete e per esempio mostro. // Felice voi che per secreto calle, / Ove orma ancor non è segnata, solo / Ven gite a gloria non più vista mai! // Onde la donna più veloce assai / Che strale o vento e ch'è sempre alle spalle, / Invan daravvi omai l'ultimo volo." On March 26, 1555, Varchi had sent the sonnet directly to the painter, who recorded the fact in his diary: see the introduction to Jacopo da Pontormo, *Diario, Codice Magliabechiano VIII 1490 della Biblioteca Nazionale Centrale di Firenze. Commentario al facsimile con edizione critica del testo*, ed. Roberto Fedi, Rome 1996, p. 18; Firpo 1997, p. 217; Salvatore Silvano Nigro, *L'orologio di Pontormo: invenzione di un pittore manierista*, Milan 1998, pp. 18–25; Lo Re 2008, p. 431; Cécile Beuzelin, Jacopo Pontormo: A Scholarly Craftsman, in: Damm, Thimann and Zittel 2013 (as in fn. 1), pp. 69–104, p. 81, and Geremicca 2017 (as in fn. 6), p. 22. Massimo Firpo, Salvatore Nigro, and Salvatore Lo Re have argued that with the reference to Pontormo's "secret path," Varchi was alluding to the heterodox religious message of the frescoes, which might have been rooted in the writings of Juan de Valdés. The argument of the "spiritual" iconography of the lost paintings is at the core of Firpo's detailed and deeply influential study. For alternative readings of the work's iconography, see, among others, Victor Stoichiță, La sigla del Pontormo: il programma iconografico della decorazione del Coro di San Lorenzo, in: *Storia dell'arte* 38–40 (1980), pp. 241–256, pp. 244–245; Carlo Falciani, *Pontormo*, Cinisello Balsamo 2014, pp. 308–312, and the forthcoming work by Elizabeth Pilliod, *Pontormo at San Lorenzo: The Making and Meaning of a Lost Renaissance Masterpiece*, Turnhout 2021. A recent assessment of the problem of the religious context of the frescoes is Chrysa Damianaki, Pontormo's Lost Frescoes in San Lorenzo, Florence: A Reappraisal of Their Religious Content, in: Abigail Brundin and Matthew Treherne (eds.), *Forms of Faith in Sixteenth-Century Italy*, Burlington, VT 2009, pp. 77–118.

[233] Varchi's poem on Pontormo's death lists the names of Bronzino and Luca Martini as the figures who had been most affected by the event. This small group of friends in part overlaps with the community that emerges from his compositions on the death of other artists dear to him; namely, Niccolò Tribolo (†1550) and Pierino da Vinci (†1553). See Varchi 1858–1859 (as in fn. 67), 2, p. 855, sonnet 153 (to Giovan Battista di Marco del Tasso, on Tribolo's death), ll. 9–14: "Increscemi di voi, duolmi del nostro / Luca e del Vinci, e 'l Marignolle ancora / Lasso! m'affligge, e 'l Puntormo e 'l Bronzino. // Pungemi il figlio, oimè, ferimi ogn'ora / La sconsolata sua consorte e 'l vostro / Davitte caro e 'l mio dolce Crocino." The circle of Varchi's acquaintances that the sonnet delineates includes, along with Tribolo's widow Elisabetta and son Raffaello, Luca Martini, Pierino Vinci, the plasterer Lorenzo Marignolli, the architect David di Raffaello Fortini (Tribolo's son in law), and the woodworker Antonio Crocini. On the poem, see Dario Trento, Pontormo e la corte di Cosimo I, in: Monika Cämmerer (ed.), *Kunst des Cinquecento in der Toskana*, Munich 1992, pp. 139–145, p. 140, which emphasizes how the group "non è una raccolta casuale di amici, è un gruppo influente nelle vicende culturali e artistiche dei primi anni del ducato di Cosimo I," and Cecchi 2001 (as in fn. 183), p. 33. See also Varchi 1858–1859 (as in fn. 67), 2, p. 855, sonnet 155, ll. 11–14 (on Pierino da Vinci's death): "Per far più ricco il cielo, e la scultura / Men bella, e col buon Martin dolente, / N'ha privi, o pietà! del secondo Vinci." In the Giuntina (Vasari 1967–1997 [as in fn. 74], 5, p. 236), Vasari included Varchi's sonnet at the end of the biography of Pierino Vinci, after recounting that "dolse a tutti gli amici la morte del Vinci et a Luca Martini eccessivamente, e dolse a tutti gli altri, i quali s'erano permesso di vedere dalla sua mano di quelle cose che rare volte si veggono, e messer Benedetto Varchi, amicissimo alle sue virtù et a quelle di ciascheduno, gli fece poi per memoria delle sue lode questo sonetto." For introductions to Martini's biography, see Franco Angiolini, Martini, Luca, in: *DBI* 71 (Rome 2008), pp. 234–238, on his artistic patronage, see esp. Nelson 1995 (as in fn. 184), and Detlef Heikamp, Luca Martini, i suoi amici artisti e Pierino da Vinci, in: Marco Cianchi (ed.), *Pierino da Vinci: Atti della giornata di studio, Vinci, Biblioteca leonardiana, 26 maggio 1990*, Florence 1995, pp. 67–71; for his friendship with Varchi, see Lo Re 2008 (as in fn. 181), pp. 257–294.

artists at Martini's residence in Pisa, where the ducal functionary was summoned in 1547 to oversee ditches, fortresses, and prisons. Razzi reported that Varchi, whenever he went to Pisa to see Duke Cosimo and read him new chapters of his *Storia Fiorentina*, "si stava in casa dell'amicissimo suo M. Luca Martini […] in compagnia di Pittori, Scultori, et altri sì fatti nobili artefici, de' quali havea quel buon gentil huomo sempre molti al suo servigio."[234] At his friend's home Varchi had probably had occasion to meet two sculptors who had trained in the workshop of Niccolò Tribolo, Pierino da Vinci and Stoldo Lorenzi, who for many years were guests of Martini, their most important patron and sponsor.[235] It was probably during Martini's stays in Florence, on the other hand, that he brought Varchi into Pontormo's circle, as we know from the dinner meetings Pontormo immortalized in his so-called *Diario* starting in 1555.[236]

With this web of relationships in mind, it's easy to understand why Luca Martini's death (January 9, 1561) was one of the events that most catalyzed poetry writing by the artists in Varchi's *sodalitas*. In compiling his own canzoniere, Bronzino for example dedicated to the commemoration of Martini almost all of the poems contained in the fascicle following his compositions on the death of Pontormo.[237] Along the lines of sonnet 296 in Petrarch's *Canzoniere*, which lamented the poet's desolation on the deaths of Laura and of his friend Giovanni Colonna, Bronzino coupled his two bereavements in various poems in this section: by 1561, for that matter, he had been close friends with Martini for decades, and had already painted a celebrated portrait of him and dedicated to him several poems.[238] In the poems written upon

---

[234] See Razzi's text in Benedetto Varchi, *Lezzioni di m. Benedetto Varchi Accademico Fiorentino, lette da lui publicamente nell'Accademia Fiorentina, sopra diverse materie, poetiche, e filosofiche, raccolte nuovamente, e la maggior parte non più date in luce, con due tavole, una delle materie, l'altra delle cose più notabili: con la vita dell'autore*, Florence 1590, unpaginated, also discussed in Nelson 1995 (as in fn. 184), p. 299.

[235] Relevant discussions of Martini's role as a patron of the two sculptors during their stay in Pisa are Hildegard Utz, Pierino da Vinci e Stoldo Lorenzi, in: *Paragone / Arte* 18 (1967), pp. 47–69; Roberto Paolo Ciardi, Claudio Casini, and Lucia Tongiorgi Tomasi, *Scultura a Pisa tra Quattro e Seicento*, Florence 1987, pp. 112–136; Alessandro Nesi, Le amichevoli sfide di Pierino da Vinci e Stoldo Lorenzi, per conto di Luca Martini, in: *Erba d'Arno*, 126–127 (2012), pp. 54–71, and esp. Oscar Schiavone, Luca Martini as an Art Consultant and Patron of Artists in Pisa (1547–1561), in: Antonio Geremicca and Hélène Miesse (eds.), *Essere uomini di "lettere": segretari e politica culturale nel Cinquecento*, Florence 2016, pp. 145–153.

[236] See, for instance, the annotation from December 10 in Pontormo 1996 (as in fn. 232), p. 69: "Martedì cenai in casa Daniello con messer Luca Martini e 'l Varchi."

[237] For a description of the fascicle, see Geremicca 2013 (as in fn. 6), pp. 61–65. This section of the manuscript includes eleven sonnets (four by other authors) and a sestina on the same subject, along with Bronzino's two sonnets on the death of Niccolò Tribolo, two sonnets that celebrate Michelangelo, and a few other exchange-texts by other authors, such as Laura Battiferri.

[238] On the portrait of Luca Martini now in the Galleria Palatina in Florence (ca. 1555) see the entry by Antonio Geremicca in: Falciani and Natali 2010 (as in fn. 6), p. 272, with further bibliography. Prior to 1561, Bronzino had dedicated to the engineer two burlesque capitoli, *Dei Romori* and *Contro a le campane*, for which see Frédérique Dubard de Gaillarbois, A proposito del *Capitolo in lode della prigione*, di un bernismo celliniano e di una scrittura materiale, in: *Studi italiani* 45 (2011), pp. 5–38, p. 22. To these compositions, we might add the lyrical sonnet *Sacra Minerva, ogni tuo studio, ed arte*, which in Bronzino's canzoniere opens the fascicle on Martini's death (Geremicca, *Agnolo Bronzino*, pp. 187–188). Martini was also mentioned in Bronzino's comical verse of the *Salterelli dell'Abbrucia* against Ludovico Castelvetro: see, for instance, Bronzino 1998 (as in fn. 6), p. 83.

his death he depicted the loss of his companion and patron, following the loss of Pontormo, as a "doppia morte" that had equally afflicted himself and his closest friends, Varchi first and foremost.[239] Bronzino's canzoniere therefore includes an exchange of sonnets with Varchi (the latter's *L'ultimo dì, ch'esser venuto omai*, followed by Bronzino's reply, *La dura pena che vince d'assai*: Appendix, nos. 22–23) on the same occasion: a circumstance that in the same series of poems also originated a lyrical dialogue with Benvenuto Cellini (*Deh, mirabil gran Varchi, e voi, Bronzino*, with Bronzino's reply *Non piange il divin Varchi, alto Cellino*: Appendix, nos. 24–25), in which the departed is mourned primarily as a most dear friend to both authors and as an irreplaceable officer in the Medici court.[240] An exchange with Stoldo Lorenzi is also part of the same poetic sequence, and while Lorenzi's *proposta* (*Tanto m'affligge, e mi tormenta il core*: Appendix, n. 26) assembles standard topoi of sixteenth-century funereal Petrarchism, Bronzino's *risposta* (*Che non piangiate in compagnia d'Amore*: Appendix, n. 27) is a revealing text that mourns Martini chiefly for his position at the forefront of private art patronage in Cosimo's time, honoring the memory of someone who had been the true "seat" of the Muses and the Arts and had – among other things – played a key role in promoting Lorenzi's career as a sculptor.[241]

While Bronzino was cultivating these dialogues in verse, Varchi was busy arranging an entire anthology – unpublished to this day – of *Cento sonetti sopra la morte di Luca Martini*, which called on a variety of practitioners of the arts of drawing to contribute to the poetic mourning.[242] What is immediately noteworthy is the sheer number of artists included in the collection: the first section of the anthology, covering the sonnets Varchi addressed to

---

[239] Quoted from the sonnet *Non che risalda, assai più larga, e cupa*, l. 13, in Geremicca 2013 (as in fn. 6), p. 246.

[240] For Cellini's friendship with Luca Martini, which dated back to at least the late 1530s, see Cellini 1996 (as in fn. 23), p. 313 (*Vita* 1.86, with a mention of "il mio carissimo amico Luca Martini"), Dubard de Gaillarbois 2011 (as in fn. 238), pp. 12–22, and Cellini 2014 (as in fn. 7), p. 190. In May 1556, Luca Martini had also provided the sculptor with the Carrara marble for his *Crucifix*: the document can be read in Trento 1984 (as in fn. 218), p. 78.

[241] In order to clarify Bronzino's reference to Martini's cult of the Muses, it is useful to recall that the deceased had also been a poet. Two of his capitoli, the *Capitolo a Visino Merciaio* and the *Capitolo in lode di Pegli*, were published in the Giunti anthology of Bernesque poetry *Secondo libro dell'Opere burlesche* (Florence 1555): see Dubard de Gaillarbois 2011 (as in fn. 238), p. 22. Bronzino's emphasis on the religious piety ("voler pio," l. 12) that had inspired some of the works that Lorenzi was supposed to create and that would honor Martini is perhaps an allusion to the role that the latter likely played in the allocation to Stoldo of a marble group of the *Annunciation* for the Pisan church of Santa Maria della Spina. The contract for the execution of this work was signed just a few days after Martini's death, on January 16, 1561: see Utz 1967 (as in fn. 235), p. 57. Vasari (1967–1997 [as in fn. 74], 6, p. 235 [1568]) records a similar pattern in the life of Bronzino, stating that "non partì di Pisa il Bronzino che gli fu allogata, per mezzo del Martini, da Raffaello del Setaiuolo, Operaio del Duomo, la tavola d'una delle cappelle del detto Duomo; nella quale fece Cristo ignudo con la croce."

[242] At least two manuscript testimonies of the poetic anthology survive. One can be found in BNCF, Filza Rinuccini 3 (unpaginated); the other, which is a clean copy in the hand of a copyist with minimal interventions from Varchi's hand, is cod. II. VIII. 140 from the same library. Quotations are taken from the latter. The collection was assembled soon after Martini's death: see its dedicatory letter, addressed to the ducal chamberlain Sforza Almeni (c. 3r): "Non mi sono peritato di mandarle alcuni sonetti composti da me subitamente sopra la morte di detto m. Luca, e a diversi comuni amici dell'uno, e dell'altro di Noi indiritti." Also in this anthology, as in Bronzino's canzoniere, the bereavement for Martini's death is linked to that for Pontormo's death: see, for instance, the text at c. 98r: "Sospirate il buon Martino / che, dopo il santo e buon padre Stradino, / col gran Puntormo e chiaro Tasso giace" (also quoted in Lo Re 2008 [as in fn. 181], p. 258).

others, sees Tiberio Calcagni, Bernardo Puccini, Giorgio Vasari, Domenico Poggini, Francesco Mosca alias il Moschino, Agnolo Bronzino,[243] Antonio Crocini, and Bartolomeo Ammannati among the dedicatees, while the second part, which includes his correspondents' submissions, comprises compositions by the architect and engineer Bernardo Puccini, as well as Vasari, Bronzino, and Stoldo Lorenzi (Appendix, nos. 28–38).[244] The fellowship gathered in poetic commemoration thus encompasses many of the painters and sculptors who had benefited from the patronage of the deceased, whose intellectual profile these authors are quick to capture and eulogize.[245] For instance, the high rate of Dantesque phrasing that we find in the exchange between Varchi and Stoldo Lorenzi (Appendix, nos. 37–38) seems to reflect the

---

[243] The exchange with Bronzino is the same that is preserved in the painter's canzoniere: see here, appendix, nos. 22–23.

[244] The full list of the dedicatees of the sonnets includes the names of Mario Colonna, Vincenzio Borghini, Giovan Girolamo Rossi bishop of Pavia, Monsignor Ricasoli bishop of Pistoia, Piero Stufa, Giovanni de' Pazzi, Don Antonio da Pisa, Don Silvano Razzi, Ser Benedetto d'Albizzo, Giovanni and Carlo Martini, Tiberio Calcagni, Achille Orsilago, Francesco Cattani da Diacceto, Giovanfrancesco Lottini, Giovambattista Concini, Tommaso Ferrini, Girolamo Tanini, Giovambattista Busini, Giovambattista Cini, Domenico Mellini, Bernardo Puccini, Giorgio Vasari, Moschino, Domenico and Tommaso Poggini, Antonfrancesco Grazzini, Lelio Bonsi, Laura Battiferri, Iacopo Aldobrandini, Tommaso Sertini, Bronzino, Giovambattista Santini, Antonio Crocini, Luca Mini, "Vicario di Firenze," Bartolomeo da Bagnacavallo, Piero Angelio, Bartolomeo Ammannati, Giulio Stufa, Baccio Valori, Lucantonio Ridolfi, Bernardo Vecchietti, Bernardo Davanzati, Emilio Vinta, Lorenzo Guidetti, Pierfrancesco Lapini, Francesco Cattani da Montevarchi, Baccio Baldini, Giovanni Campani, and Giulio de' Nobili. Starting from p. 54 of the codex, we read the sonnets by Varchi's interlocutors; that is, Mario Colonna, Giovan Girolamo de' Rossi, Piero Stufa, general of the Camaldulensians, Girolamo Tanini, Giovambattista Busini, Domenico Mellini, Bernardo Puccini, Giorgio Vasari, Antonfrancesco Grazzini, Lelio Bonsi, Laura Battiferra, Bronzino, Bartolomeo da Bagnacavallo, Laura Battiferra, Giulio Stufa, Lucantonio Ridolfi, Bernardo Vecchietti, Emilio Vinta, Lorenzo Guidetti, Pierfrancesco Lapini, Giulio de' Nobili, Piero Stufa, Baccio Nascimbene, Giovanbattista Adriani, Girolamo Tanini, Giulio Stufa, Stoldo Lorenzi, Felice Gualtieri, Bernardino Romena, and Lucio Oradini.

[245] The architect and sculptor Tiberio Calcagni was a friend of both Benedetto Varchi and Luca Martini, as documented by Annibal Caro's letter from Rome to Martini of May 25, 1560 (Caro, *Lettere familiari*, ed. Aulo Greco, 3 vols., Florence 1957–1961, 3, p. 26: "Messer Tiberio Calcagni m'ha resa la lettera di V. S., la quale mè stata gratissima con la nuova del vostro bene stare e del nostro Varchi"). No known document illustrates the relationships between Luca Martini, the goldsmith and sculptor Domenico Poggini, and the sculptor Francesco Mosca, but the latter had worked to a series of statues for the Pisa cathedral since 1558 (see Vasari 1967–1997 [as in fn. 74], 5, pp. 344–345 [1568]; Ciardi, Casini, and Tongiorgi Tomasi 1987 [as in fn. 235], pp. 189–225). It is plausible that during his work there he became acquainted with Martini and, given the proximity of his style to that of Martini's protégé Stoldo Lorenzi, it appears likely that Francesco too might have gravitated around the patronage of Duke Cosimo's administrator. The woodcarver Antonio Crocini is also mentioned in Benvenuto Cellini's sonnet on the death of Luca Martini as one of the engineer's closest friends. As for Ammannati, Victoria Kirkham in Battiferra 2006 (as in fn. 101), p. 434, stresses that the sculptor "seems to have hoped for support from him [Martini], either in form of direct patronage or courtly lobbying for a Medici commission." The florilegium on the death of Luca Martini confirms how the many poetic anthologies *in mortem* of the mid-Cinquecento lend themselves to "un'indagine in chiave di socialità letteraria […], a meglio individuare quell'aggregazione di intellettuali cui proprio la circostanza del collettivo compianto funebre *amicorum* dovette offrire l'occasione di 'autorappresentarsi' come compatta *sodalitas*" (Stefano Benedetti, Poesia funebre nella Roma leonina. Appunti sulle *Lacrimae* per Celso Mellini, in: Chines 2006 [as in fn. 231], 2, pp. 393–421, p. 394). On the fortune of the genre of funerary Petrarchism in sixteenth-century Italy see also the contribution by Cremonini 2006 (as in fn. 231).

scholarly discussions on the *Commedia* in which the pair participated at Martini's home in Pisa, and therefore the same intellectual climate in which Pierino da Vinci was commissioned to make his bronze relief depicting the death of Count Ugolino (*Inferno* 33).²⁴⁶

As often occurs in eulogies, the collective poetic mourning also served to disguise tensions that the deceased had fueled: a prime example is the exchange of sonnets between Varchi and Vasari (Appendix, nos. 35–36). In 1544, Martini had commissioned and obtained the famous group portrait of *Six Tuscan Poets* (Minneapolis Institute of Arts) from the painter, but the relationship between the two was not always idyllic:²⁴⁷ a 1552 missive by don Vincenzio Borghini, mentioned in both Varchi's *proposta* and Vasari's *risposta* as a good friend of the deceased, exposes for instance the rivalry that had pitted Vasari against Martini and his protégé sculptors, capturing a moment of bitter competition among artistic circles in Cosimo's Florence.²⁴⁸ Though Vasari emerged as the clear victor, he never really laid the matter to rest, if in the 1568 edition of the *Vite* he more or less openly criticized some of the painters and sculptors closest to Martini (Pontormo, Cellini, Giovan Battista del Tasso and even Bronzino to some degree) who had reigned over the Florence art scene of the 1540s and early 1550s, or gave them scant attention unbefitting of their stature.²⁴⁹

---

²⁴⁶ The second hemistich of the first line of Stoldo Lorenzi's sonnet *Varchi divin, che con sì dolci note* is modeled after Dante, *Purgatorio* 8.13 ("le uscìo di bocca e con sì dolci note"), while the designation of God as "Colui che tutto puote" in l. 4 is reminiscent of *Inferno* 3.95–96 ("vuolsi così colà dove si puote / ciò che si vuole, e più non dimandare"). The latter passage is even more explicitly echoed by Varchi in l. 4 ("dove ciò che si vuol tutto si puote"). On Martini's Dantean interests and philological works, see Enrico Garavelli, Riflessi polemici, difesa del fiorentino e culto di Dante in una lettera inedita di Luca Martini a Vincenzio Borghini, in: *Neuphilologische Mitteilungen* 108 (2007), pp. 709–727, and Oscar Schiavone, Luca Martini filologo dantesco: collazioni, annotazioni e committenze (1543–1551), in: Carlo Caruso and Emilio Russo (eds.), *La filologia in Italia nel Rinascimento*, Rome 2018, pp. 117–132, with further bibliography. On the genesis of Pierino's relief, see the account in Vasari 1967–1997 (as in fn. 74), 5, pp. 233–234 (1568): "Scriveva in questo tempo Luca Martini sopra la Commedia di Dante alcune cose, et avendo mostrata al Vinci la crudeltà descritta da Dante, la quale usorono i Pisani e l'arcivescovo Ruggieri contro al conte Ugolino della Gherardesca, facendo lui morire di fame con quattro suoi figliuoli […], porse occasione e pensiero al Vinci di nuova opera e di nuovo disegno […]. Non meno in questa opera mostrò il Vinci la virtù del disegno che Dante ne' suoi versi mostrasse il valore della poesia." On the bronze relief, which was the first to show "a single canto [from the *Commedia*] as the subject of an independent work of art," see also Nelson 1995 (as in fn. 184), p. 284; Nelson, Luca Martini, *dantista*, and Pierino da Vinci's relief of the Death of Count Ugolino della Gherardesca and His Sons, in: Cianchi 1995 (as in fn. 233), pp. 39–43, and Britta Kusch-Arnhold, *Pierino da Vinci*, Münster 2008, pp. 51–69.

²⁴⁷ See the entry on Vasari's portrait, by Novella Macola, in: Claudia Conforti, Francesca Funis, Francesca De Luca, and Cristina Acidini Luchinat (eds.), *Vasari, gli Uffizi e il duca*, Florence 2011, p. 138 (with further bibliography), as well as Deborah Parker, Vasari's 'Ritratto di sei poeti toscani': A Visible Literary History, in: *Modern Language Notes* 127, n. 1 (2012), pp. 204–215.

²⁴⁸ See Borghini's letter to Vasari of 20 August 1552 (Vasari 1923–1930 [as in fn. 76], 1, pp. 332–335), in which the writer exhorted Vasari to stay in Rome and thus far from the Florentine rumors that Martini, Tasso, and Cellini had been spreading about him: "Andate pur inanzi e fate buon animo e lasciate dire Tassi e Luchi Martini e Benvenuti; che il tempo e l'agio sarà optimo giudice d'ogni cosa e senza passione. E sopra tutto attenetevi pur costì, dove si fa a migliaia e' scudi; e lasciate abbaiar quaggiù, dove si ragiona di soldi." The letter is also briefly mentioned in Heikamp 1995 (as in fn. 233), p. 70.

²⁴⁹ On Vasari's biased depiction of his former adversaries in the *Vite*, see Elizabeth Pilliod, Representation, Misrepresentation, and Non-Representation: Vasari and His Competitors, in: Philip J. Jacks (ed.), *Vasari's Florence: Artists and Literati at the Medicean Court*, Cambridge 1998, pp. 30–52. On the rivalry between the two artistic

In drawing a detailed picture of Martini's patronage and artistic circles, the *Cento sonetti in morte di Luca Martini* are of remarkable significance to this book. No other passing, not even the death in quick succession of Duke Cosimo's wife and two of his children in December 1562, inspired Varchi to engage as many artists in this kind of collective ritual of poetry writing.[250] Painters and sculptors are, on the other hand, among the key names of a different kind of sylloge that Varchi assembled between the early summer and late fall of 1562.[251] With their hundred lyric poems, the *Sonetti contro gli Ugonotti* are a literary tribute to the victorious anti-Huguenot campaign in the Comtat Venaissin in Provence by Lorenzo Lenzi, then vice legate of Avignon for Pope Pius IV, and Fabrizio Serbelloni, head of the Papal Army.[252]

circles, compare also the insightful remarks of Trento 1992 (as in fn. 233), pp. 141–142: "L'ambiente che ruota attorno a Varchi e Martini […] costituisce una sorta di fluido partito che nei primi anni del potere di Cosimo porta l'operatività culturale e artistica fiorentina, intrisa ancora del costume e delle strutture dello stato repubblicano, a un rinnovamento linguistico profondo che tende all'unificazione e all'assimilazione delle innovazioni prodotte dalla cultura italiana nei primi tre decenni del secolo. Il gruppo che comprende Pontormo, Cellini, Tribolo, Tasso, Pierino da Vinci, Bronzino, Crocino, Martini, Varchi, a partire dalla metà degli anni Cinquanta, fu esautorato e sostituito da un gruppo di operatori meno autonomo e problematico nei rapporti col potere ducale, più efficiente e malleabile in rapporto alle sue esigenze, disposto anche a intrupparsi ufficialmente in una apposita istituzione statale, l'Accademia delle arti del disegno. Questo gruppo di artisti sarà egemonizzato da Vasari e Vincenzo Borghini." It should also be considered that many of the artists who had been close to Martini also counted among the protégés of the ducal maggiordomo Pier Francesco Riccio and that the two Medici bureaucrats seem to have been friendly. Elizabeth Pilliod, *Pontormo, Bronzino, Allori: A Genealogy of Florentine Art*, New Haven, CT 2001, p. 262, n. 71, for instance, quotes a letter from Martini to Riccio from January 1550, in which the engineer asked his interlocutor to extend greetings "al Tribolo, al Tasso e al Bronzino." This becomes relevant once we consider how Vasari, who never enjoyed Riccio's favor, provided a scathing account of his artistic networks, with a special vengefulness against Tasso: see Cecchi 1998 (as in fn. 184), pp. 118–124.

[250] Varchi exchanged many compositions with fellow poets of ducal Florence on the occasion of the sudden deaths of Garzia and Giovanni de' Medici, soon followed by that of Duchess Eleonora di Toledo. One of these sonnet exchanges (the greater part of which can be found in BNCF, Filza Rinuccini 5, cc. 147–210) was with an artist, Bronzino. To the humanist's *proposta*, *Esser morto più tosto che guarito*, the painter replied with the sonnet *Gran ventura havev'io se tanto ardito* (BNCF, Filza Rinuccini 5, cc. 180v and 210v; Bronzino's canzoniere, on the other hand, preserves a total of twelve compositions on such deaths: see Geremicca 2013 [as in fn. 6], pp. 82–83). Within the same collection, Varchi also addressed a sonnet to Bartolomeo Ammannati. The text (BNCF, Filze Rinuccini 5, c. 173v: *Quei verdi mirti, quegli allori stessi*, now discussed by Bruce Edelstein, *Eleonora di Toledo and the Creation of the Boboli Gardens*, forthcoming) commemorates the moral qualities of the deceased duchess while also celebrating Bartolomeo Ammannati's work toward the enlargement of Palazzo Pitti and new designs for the Boboli gardens as a great outcome of her artistic patronage. Varchi's composition is comparable to another that Gherardo Spini addressed to Ammannati on the same occasion: see the sonnet (preceded by the rubric "All'eccellente messer Bartolomeo Amannati, in materia del Palazzo de' Pitti, per la morte della Signora Duchessa") *Fidia, l'altero nido, emulo a quanti*, in Battiferra 2006 (as in fn. 101), p. 276.

[251] On the genesis of this anthology, see Firpo 1997 (as in fn. 159), pp. 250–252, and the meticulous historical reconstruction in Ferrone 1993 (as in fn. 214), pp. 175–180 (for the dating of the poetic collection, pp. 153–155). The collection is recorded by several manuscript testimonies that are now preserved in Florentine libraries (for the full list, see ibid., pp. 155–156). The basis for the present study is BNCF, Filza Rinuccini 5, cc. 2–89, which appears to preserve the last and most complete version of the collection.

[252] Lenzi and Serbelloni violently repressed the Huguenot insurrections that had seen some centers of the Venaissin fall into Protestant hands. Lenzi succeeded not only in defending the interests of the papacy in a moment of great instability in the political and religious history of France, but also in the delicate task of encouraging a rapprochement between the regent of France, Caterina de' Medici, and her cousin Duke Cosimo, who supported the military campaign with money and Tuscan military troops.

And as much as Varchi thanked the other poet contributors for having constructed with their verse something more lasting than artworks, according to the Horatian motif of poetry as a monument more enduring than bronze, the visual arts and those who practiced them have a central place in the anthology.[253] In addition to his poetic dialogues with Bronzino and Benvenuto Cellini, Varchi included two sonnets addressed to the painter Francesco Salviati and to the architect and sculptor Bartolomeo Ammannati. What all these poems have in common is their emphasis on the professional work of their addressees: as we will see, for example, the sonnets to Bronzino and Ammannati are ideally structured as "commission poems," in which the author invites the pair to dedicate a work of art to Lenzi and Serbelloni. In the poem *Caro Salviati mio, se l'empie e rie*, on the other hand, Varchi applauds Francesco Salviati's decision to temporarily leave Rome for Florence in late 1562, and praises his unspecified "honorate […] alte fatiche" as a painter.[254] The exchange in verse with Cellini also centers on his art: Varchi's *proposta* (*Valor, del gran Cellin l'alta opra visto*: Appendix, no. 39), addressed to Baccio Valori il Giovane, confines the reference to the war against the Huguenots to the final tercet, as a simple complement to the extensive praise for Cellini's marble crucifix. Varchi commends the sculpture, completed and signed that same year (1562), for its ability to overwhelm the viewer's emotions and presents it as an object of prayer that might favor the victorious outcome of Lenzi's expedition to Avignon. It is no surprise, then, that in his reply (*Honor d'Italia, che 'spresso hai, non visto*: Appendix, no. 40) Cellini evades the reference to such historical circumstances and instead concentrates on the glory bestowed on his art by Varchi's encomiastic sonnet.[255]

---

[253] See the sonnet that Varchi addresses *A tutti coloro, i quali hanno composto sopra gl'Ugonotti* (BNCF, Filza Rinuccini 5, c. 88v), ll. 1–4: "Incliti spirti, ch'al buon Lenzi havete / et al gran Serbellon con degni carmi / più salde assai, che di metalli e marmi / statue posto, et archi dritto, e mète […]." Compare Horace, *Odes* 3.30.1–5: "Exegi monumentum aere perennius / regalique situ pyramidum altius / quod non imber edax, non Aquilo impotens / possit diruere aut innumerabilis / annorum series et fuga temporum."

[254] The text is published in Geremicca 2013 (as in fn. 6), p. 313. For the chronology of Salviati's final stay in Florence, which must have taken place between the last months of 1562 and the early months of 1563, see Stefano Pierguidi, Francesco Salviati e il concorso per il sigillo per l'Accademia del Disegno, in: *Atti e memorie dell'Accademia Toscana di Scienze e Lettere "La Colombaria"* 80 (2015), pp. 191–203, p. 202. On the works that he completed there see Vasari 1967–1997 (as in fn. 74), 5, p. 531 (1568), which records a *Pietà* for Jacopo Salviati, the repainting of a "tondo d'arme" for the duke, and a book of drawings. Varchi was probably alluding to one of these works when mentioning the artist's "fatiche" (l. 7).

[255] In 1568, the sculptor included Varchi's sonnet within the selection of *Poesie toscane, et latine sopra il Perseo statua di bronzo, e il Crocifisso statua di marmo fatte da messer Benvenuto Cellini*, published at the conclusion of his *Treatises on Goldsmithing and Sculpture*: see Cellini, *Due trattati, uno intorno alle otto principali arti dell'oreficeria, l'altro in materia dell'arte della scultura* […], Florence 1568), c. Riir. For a more thorough analysis of the exchange, see Cellini 2014 (as in fn. 7), pp. 219–222.

Patron, broker, dedicatee: Varchi and the Florentine arts in light of his sonnet exchanges with artists

For many years, scholars analyzed Varchi's relationship with the arts of his time almost exclusively on the basis of his *Due lezzioni* of 1547. The theoretical scaffolding of these academic lectures, however, wound up obscuring the most concrete aspects of his ties to Florentine arts, such as the fact that at times he served as patron or iconographic advisor, at others as an intermediary between artists and the Medici power in the context of coveted ducal commissions, and at others still as the dedicatee or subject of an artistic creation. In Florence Varchi was thus at the center of a dense entanglement of personal relationships with artists, artwork commissions, and collaborative artistic endeavors that we can compare to the range of active art interests cultivated in the Venetian Republic by Pietro Bembo, his intellectual model of inspiration.[256] Of these dynamics, too, Varchi's vernacular poetry provides important testimonies that only in recent years have scholars begun to study closely.[257] There is still, however, no comprehensive critical overview of what verse tells us about his role in the artistic affairs of the time. The poetic models and the conventions followed by these texts remain to be revealed as well, and these are gaps that Varchi's exceptional literary learnedness – he owned one of the largest private libraries of Renaissance Italy[258] – demands be filled. To ignore the high level of

---

[256] In the funerary oration he made at the Accademia Fiorentina in the Venetian's honor (February 1547), Varchi celebrated Bembo's interest in the arts and provided an admiring testimony of his artistic collections (on which, see now Guido Beltramini, Howard Burns, and Davide Gasparotto [eds.], *Pietro Bembo e le arti*, Venice 2013; Guido Beltramini, Davide Gasparotto, and Adolfo Tura [eds.], *Pietro Bembo e l'invenzione del Rinascimento*, Venice 2013, as well as the insightful monograph by Susan Nalezyty, *Pietro Bembo and the Intellectual Pleasures of a Renaissance Writer and Art Collector*, New Haven, CT 2017). See especially the passage from the *Orazione* cited by Massimo Danzi, *La biblioteca del cardinal Pietro Bembo*, Geneva 2005, p. 37, regarding Bembo's *studiolo* in Padua, which Varchi had had the chance to visit after 1536: "Dilettavasi sommissimamente di tutte l'arti ingegnose, et sopra tutte dell'Architettura, della scultura et della pittura, et chiunque vide mai lo studio suo in Padova il mi crederà […] era di tante statue, et così perfette, di tante pitture et così nobili ricco et adorno, senza l'infinita moltitudine di diverse medaglie, vasi, pietre, gioie et altre varie cose preziosissime."

[257] Recent discussions of Varchi's vernacular poetry in relation to these questions include the pioneering essay by Collareta 2007 (as in fn. 211), as well as Diletta Gamberini, Benedetto Varchi, Giovann'Angelo Montorsoli e il Tempio dei "Pippi": un inedito dialogo in versi agli albori dell'Accademia Fiorentina del Disegno, in: *Mitteilungen des Kunsthistorischen Institutes in Florenz* 57.1 (2015), pp. 139–144; eadem 2016 (as in fn. 7); eadem 2017 (as in fn. 211); Geremicca 2017a (as in fn. 6); idem 2017b (as in fn. 121), pp. 87–113; idem 2019 (as in fn. 6). Varchi's extensive and still largely unpublished poetic output in Latin, which does not include any exchanges with artists and therefore falls outside the immediate scope of the present study, is another significant source for his active interests in the artistic life of the age. Among the few well-known examples of this corpus are some eulogistic poems on Bronzino's portrait of Eleonora di Toledo and a bronze statue of Philip II of Habsburg by Leone Leoni, the distichs composed to be inscribed on the pedestal of Benvenuto Cellini's bronze *Perseus and Medusa*, and a few compositions for Bartolomeo Ammannati's *Neptune* fountain, for which see Benedetto Varchi, *Liber carminum Benedicti Varchii*, ed. Aulo Greco, Rome 1969, and Silvano Ferrone, Materiali varchiani, in: *Paragone / Letteratura* 48–50 (2003), pp. 84–113.

[258] Varchi's book collections, whose remaining fragments are now to be found in different European libraries, included over 3200 items between manuscripts and editions: see Antonio Sorella's introduction to Varchi 1995 (as in fn. 186), pp. 93–94. Working from both inventory lists and the author's notes regarding his possessions, a few scholars have clarified many aspects of the formation and thematic concentrations of Varchi's library: on

conventionality of these poems and treat them like standard documentary materials is in fact a misleading practice, prompting uncritical acceptance of the literal level of texts in which the boundaries between adherence to thematic scores inherited from the poetic tradition and reference to real-life circumstances are often blurred.[259] It is therefore only by highlighting the relationship these poems establish with codified motifs typical of Renaissance poetry that we can try to understand what they might disclose not only about Varchi's participation in the artistic life of Florence in the mid-1500s, but also about artists' poetic and visual responses to the literary stimuli coming from the humanist's sophisticated verse.

Advice-to-a-painter poems

Such caveats are especially important when it comes to a rhetorically compact series of poems, in which Varchi urged individual artists to create works on a given subject. The better known examples are three sonnets (*Voi che nel fior della sua verde etate*; *Bronzino, ove sì dolce ombreggia e suona*; and *Nuova casta Ciprigna, e nuovo Marte*: Appendix, nos. 47, 49 and 14) that the poet addressed to Bronzino late in their friendship. We will come back to these lyrics later; it will suffice for the moment to note that they have recently been interpreted as means of commissioning art, though unusual ones given their poetic status: they have thus been read as sources that document ideas for artworks that Varchi intended to commission, and in some cases even saw to fruition.[260] According to this interpretation, in such instances the literato used the lyrical medium to ask Bronzino to paint Lorenzo Lenzi again after depicting him as a prepubescent, in the portrait now in the Castello Sforzesco in Milan, and to represent the divine virtues of Isabella de' Medici and Paolo Giordano Orsini, respectively daughter and son-in-law of Duke Cosimo.

What this kind of exegesis has overlooked, however, is the fact that these three compositions are wholly similar in terms of rhetorical-argumentative structures to other poems by Varchi. In the printed collection of *Sonetti* from 1555 we already find a piece very much like the so-called "commission poems" addressed to Bronzino, for the sonnet *Voi, che solo de i duo primi e maggiori* (Appendix, no. 41) invites the goldsmith and medalist Pietro Paolo Galeotti,

---

this, see Maria Prunai Falciani, Manoscritti e libri appartenuti al Varchi nella Biblioteca Riccardiana di Firenze, in: *Accademie e biblioteche d'Italia* 53 (1985), pp. 14–29, Piero Scapecchi, Ricerche sulla biblioteca di Varchi con una lista di volumi da lui posseduti, in: Bramanti 2007 (as in fn. 211), pp. 309–318, and Dario Brancato, Ancora sui libri di Benedetto Varchi. Notizie dalle biblioteche inglesi, in: Isabella Becherucci and Concetta Bianca (eds.), *Storia, tradizione e critica dei testi. Per Giuliano Tanturli*, 2 vols., Lecce and Rovato 2017, 1, pp. 47–60, with further bibliography.

[259] For a comparable warning against the use of poetic materials as an instrument for art historical *Quellenforschung*, see David Rijser, *Raphael's Poetics: Art and Poetry in High Renaissance Rome*, Amsterdam 2012, p. XXIII. Speaking of the Neo-Latin poetry on artistic subjects that was produced in High Renaissance Rome, he underscores that scholars should not be looking at poetry for the same genre of "evidence" that one can find in archives, adding that "the evidence may indeed be there, but must first be decoded."

[260] Compare Geremicca 2013 (as in fn. 6), p. 94, which discusses the poems as examples of "uso del sonetto come strumento di 'commissione.'"

whom Varchi praises along with Domenico Poggini for embodying the rebirth of the art of small bronzes, to dedicate one of his creations to the laurel motif.[261] As claimed by the author, giving artistic figuration to this image would in fact allow Galeotti to produce a work of incomparable beauty and to achieve the same eternal glory that Varchi enjoyed himself for his compositions in praise of Lenzi.

Of the same inclination is a sonnet to Bartolomeo Ammannati, *Poi ch'io non so con mie prose e miei carmi*, contained in the poet's anthology *Contra gli Ugonotti* (Appendix, no. 42). Varchi decries here his own inadequacy in celebrating the feats of Lenzi and Fabrizio Serbelloni during their anti-Huguenot campaign in the Comtat Venaissin, but while in other compositions from that collection, addressed to fellow poets like Annibal Caro and Lodovico Domenichi, a clichéd affectation of modesty systematically prefaced the request to honor with greater skill the two champions of the Catholic offensive in France,[262] in the sonnet to Ammannati this *topos modestiae* is functional to suggesting the creation of a visual work. By insisting that only the dedicatee, whom he addresses as a new Phidias and Myron, could suitably commemorate Lenzi and Serbelloni in "mille bronzi e 'n mille marmi" (l. 8), Varchi is issuing a general entreaty to dedicate sculptural works to the pair's deeds. In his view, such visual creations would eventually have found a worthy match in the poems that Laura Battiferri, Ammannati's wife, was urged to compose on the subject.

The focus of a final sonnet that replicates this structure is not Lorenzo Lenzi but the object of a new, avowedly Platonic love to which Varchi yielded towards the very end of his life, in December 1565. In the poem *Eccellente, e gentil pittore, c'havete* (Appendix, no. 43), the author exhorts Alessandro Allori to paint a portrait "del bello e buon caro Pallante" (l. 7). The reference is to the young scion of a noble Florentine family that was close to both Varchi and Allori, namely the prepubescent Palla Rucellai *iuniore*, whom Varchi introduced to the humanities and to whom he dedicated several unpublished poems.[263] Resuming a motif employed in his sonnet to Galeotti, in this composition Varchi argues that by painting Pallante,

---

[261] The poem to Galeotti was certainly composed after 1552, when the goldsmith and medallist returned to Florence from France: see Giuseppe Toderi and Fiorenza Vannel, *Le medaglie italiane del XVI secolo*, 3 vols., Florence 2000, 2, p. 505.

[262] Compare, for instance, the exhortation to sing Lenzi and Serbelloni that Varchi addresses to his fellow literato Annibal Caro (in BNCF, Filza Rinuccini 5, c. 17r, ll. 1–3 and 12–14): "Qual soggetto miglior, qual maggior tema / e più degno di voi, Caro, potrebbe / trovarsi mai? […] // Gran cose in picciol fascio abbraccio, e serro, / ma voi col vostro stil, c'hoggi ha l'impero, / aprite quel ch'io dentro ogn'hor riserro."

[263] On Varchi's connections to the Rucellai family and the young Pallante, see Lo Re 2008 (as in fn. 181), pp. 257, 295, 298, and *passim*. Varchi also addressed a consolatory sonnet to Alessandro Allori upon the death of Pallante's father Bernardo (†1565). Moreover, Allori's own *Ragionamenti delle regole del disegno* are imagined to have taken place in the gardens of one of the Rucellais's Florentine palaces, the Orti Oricellari, and see Cosimo Rucellai as a discussant, thereby confirming the close relationship between the artist and the Rucellais: see Geremicca 2017 (as in fn. 121), pp. 104–105. At about the same time when Varchi undertook the instruction of Pallante, Antonfrancesco Grazzini presented the child as an *enfant prodige* of Tuscan letters, writing that "Questo è un fanciullo, o più tosto bambino, / non avendo dieci anni ancor forniti, / ed ha giudizio ed ingegno sì divino, / che gli uomin fa restar muti e stupiti; / […] / e sol, mercé di lui detto Pallante, / vedrem nuovo Petrarca e nuovo Dante" (Antonfrancesco Grazzini, *Le rime burlesche edite e inedite di Antonfrancesco Grazzini detto il Lasca*, ed. Carlo Verzone, Florence 1882, p. 365). On the many unpublished pastoral texts that Varchi dedicated

Allori would not only be doing Varchi a welcome service but earning fame in the Florence art scene. He interweaves his inducement to depict the boy with a frequently recurring motif in Renaissance verse on portraits: the notion, of classical origins, that painting is the quintessential art for rendering its subjects' exterior features, but nearly always incapable of portraying their inner nature.[264] The sonnet's conclusion, in fact, is modeled on the famous *explicit* of Martial's epigram X 32 (ll. 5–6: "Ars utinam mores animumque effingere posset! / Pulchrior in terris nulla tabella foret"), with the author hoping Allori's portrait will ultimately manage to capture Pallante's inner world as much as his manifest beauty, thus making Allori the creator of an artwork superior to all others.[265]

Though in one case worded unusually as an exhortation to paint not Longi himself but his allegorical counterpart (i. e. the laurel), the rhetorical-argumentative scheme of these compositions was quite popular in the Romance poetic tradition of the early modern period. The structure of these texts identifies them with "advice-to-a-painter" poems, in which poets ask artists to portray individuals of exceptional qualities (sometimes a powerful protector, more often the author's beloved), usually with instructions on how to represent the subject. As we know from the most penetrating study of Italian Renaissance poetry on portraits, while on a literal plane this kind of verse would seem to imply the poet's resolute participation in the *inventio* of an artwork, in many cases such texts appear to constitute purely literary revisitations of classical models rather than catalysts of actual artistic creation.[266] This output, in fact, draws on a subgenre of ancient ekphrastic poetry whose origins lie in some pseudo-anacreontic poems, which during the period when Varchi was writing had been the object of one of the century's greatest editorial rediscoveries of Greek writings. The *editio princeps* of the *Anacreontis Teji Odae*, published by Henri Estienne in Paris in 1554, offered the strong textual paradigm of its fourth, sixteenth, and seventeenth odes. Addressed in one case to an artist specialized in metalworking and in two others to a painter, these compositions urged the addressees to leave aside other subjects and create works depicting the graces of the poet's beloved maiden or ephebos: exhortations that in *Anacreontea* 16 and 17 were combined with a description of the qualities the artist was asked to reproduce in his painting.[267]

---

to his pupil see Pirotti 1971 (as in fn. 221), pp. 52–53. For the letter of literary instruction that he wrote to Pallante in the summer of 1565 see Varchi 2008 (as in fn. 183), pp. 212–214.

[264] On this topos, see esp. Federica Pich, *I poeti davanti al ritratto: da Petrarca a Marino*, Lucca 2010, pp. 270–288.

[265] Compare ll. 11–14 of the sonnet *Eccellente e gentil pittor, c'havete*: "e se poteste, come il bel di fuore, / quel di dentro scolpir, pittura mai / non hebbe il mondo di sì gran valore." The verb *scolpir* here presumably means "to give depth to a painting" (for this sense of the word, see Salvatore Battaglia, ed., *Grande Dizionario della Lingua Italiana* [hereafter *GDLI*], Turin 1961–2004, now available online: http://www.gdli.it/, last accessed 31/01/2021, s. v. "scolpire" no. 2), with metaphorical reference to the capacity to provide a visual illustration of the subject's inner dimension. As is well known, Domenico Ghirlandaio's portrait of Giovanna Tornabuoni (Madrid, Museum Thyssen-Bornemisza) featured a *cartellino* with a slightly different version of these lines. On the inscription in the Ghirlandaio painting, see esp. Maria DePrano, "No Painting on Earth Would Be More Beautiful": An Analysis of Giovanna degli Albizzi's Portrait Inscription, in: *Renaissance Studies* 22 (2008), pp. 617–641.

[266] Pich 2010 (as in fn. 264), pp. 241–270, to which my considerations in this paragraph are indebted.

[267] On the ancient model of the "advice-to-a-painter-poem," see especially Patricia A. Rosenmeyer, *The Poetics of Imitation: Anacreon and the Anacreontic Tradition*, Cambridge 1992, pp. 88–89 and 181–182; Gérard Lambin,

In the ancient hypotexts of the genre, the invitations addressed to generic, unidentified practitioners of the arts exhibited a decidedly logocentric and probably fictive character. In other words, the rhetorical advice to an artist and the stylized ekphrasis of the beauties he was instructed to represent, which included aspects not depictable in the visual medium, served only to recreate the subject in the reader's mind.[268] Clearly, then, the revisitation of such models was apt to produce exhortations equally disconnected from concrete artistic translation. In this sense it is unsurprising that, like coeval Italian examples of the same subgenre of poetry,[269] these sonnets of Varchi's seem to refer to virtual artworks that are not reflected

---

Anacréon: Fragments et imitations, Rennes 2002, pp. 269–276, and Mario Baumann, "Come Now, Best of Painters, Paint My Lover": The Poetics of Ecphrasis in the Anacreontea, in: Manuel Baumbach and Nicola Dummler (eds.), *Imitate Anacreon! Mimesis, Poiesis and the Poetic Inspiration in the Carmina Anacreontea*, Berlin / Boston 2014, pp. 113–130. A classic study of later revisitations of this typology of poems, applied to the literary scene of early modern England, is Mary Tom Osborne, *Advice-to-a-Painter Poems, 1633–1856: An Annotated Finding List*, Austin, TX 1949. Also relevant is James A. W. Heffernan, *Museum of Words: The Poetics of Ekphrasis from Homer to Ashbery*, Chicago 1993, pp. 100–101. On the fortune of the genre in the French context see Roberto E. Campo, A Poem to a Painter: The *Élégie à Janet* and Ronsard's Dilemma of Ambivalence, in: *French Forum* 12 (1987), pp. 273–287. On the popularity of the genre among the poets of the Italian Renaissance, see especially Lina Bolzoni and Federica Pich, *Poesia e ritratto nel Rinascimento*, Rome 2008, pp. 16–19, 66–69, and *passim* (considering examples from such authors as Gaspara Stampa [1523–1554] and Niccolò da Correggio [1450–1508]), and Pich 2010 (as in fn. 264), pp. 256–270. These latter studies focus on the exemplarity of odes 16 and 17, but it is important to stress also the paradigmatic relevance of ode 4, on which see *infra*. Also useful, although the work does not explicitly discuss the format of the texts, is the essay by Francesca Pellegrino, Elaborazioni di alcuni principali *topoi* artistici nei *Coryciana*, in: Ulrich Pfisterer and Max Seidel (eds.), *Visuelle Topoi: Erfindung und tradiertes Wissen in den Künsten der italienischen Renaissance*, Munich 2003, pp. 217–262, pp. 230–235, which records several relevant examples in the poetry of Antonio Tebaldeo (1463–1537, e.g., the sonnet *Mondella mio, se ben m'acorgo*), Girolamo Angeriano (1470–1535, e.g., the carmen *Fingeret ut sculptor veros in marmore vultus*), and Pietro Bembo (1470–1547, e.g., the sonnet *Ben devria farvi onor d'eterno esempio*). Notably, such records demonstrate that the genre was known and imitated in Italy even before Henri Estienne's *editio princeps* of the Anacreontics (*Anacreontis Teji odae: Ab Henrico Stephano luce et Latinitate nunc primum donatae*, Paris 1554), which nonetheless turned the "advice-to-a-painter-poem" into an especially fashionable format among poets writing about art. The early fortune of this genre in Renaissance Italy can be explained once we consider that a shortened version of the pseudo-anacreontic ode 4, presenting "advice" to the smith Hephaestus, was also transmitted by the *Planudean Anthology* (the text corresponds to *Greek Anthology*, 11.48). It is well known that the collection, published for the first time in Florence in 1494, contained hundreds of Hellenic and Hellenistic texts on artworks which were immensely influential for the development of Renaissance poetry on artistic subjects (on this, see James Hutton, *The Greek Anthology in Italy to the Year 1800*, Ithaca, NY, 1935; John K. G. Shearman, *Only Connect…: Art and the Spectator in the Italian Renaissance*, Princeton, NJ 1992, pp. 113–114; Pich 2010 [as in fn. 264], pp. 21-28). Varchi himself was very familiar with the *Anthology* and translated many of its Greek epigrams into Latin: see Michele Feo, review of Benedetto Varchi, *Liber carminum Benedicti Varchii*, ed. Aulo Greco, Rome 1969, in: *Annali della Scuola Normale Superiore di Pisa. Classe di lettere e filosofia* 3 (1973), pp. 1193–1200, p. 1197, and now especially Giovanni Ferroni, *Carmina conversa*. Appunti su traduzioni e auto-traduzioni liriche di Benedetto Varchi, in: *L'Ellisse. Studi storici di letteratura italiana*, 13, no. 1 (2018), pp. 29–52.

[268] On the ancient models, see the considerations of Lambin 2002 (as in fn. 267), pp. 275–276. One particular characteristic that cannot be expressed through the pictorial medium is, for example, the exhortation to portray the scent of myrrh in the beloved's hair of *Anacreontea* 16.9.

[269] Consider Pich 2010 (as in fn. 264), p. 241. On introducing the characteristics of the genre as exemplified by compositions by Giuliano Gosellini (1525–1587), Giuseppe Leggiadro Galani (1516–1590), and Orazio Navazzotti (1560–1624), Pich maintains that the texts are "dedicati a effigi puramente immaginarie," in which the poet provides "improbabili istruzioni all'artista."

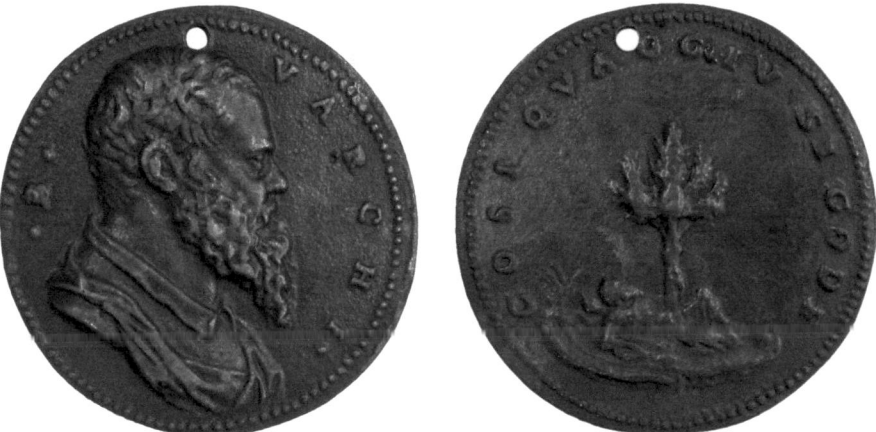

4+5 Domenico Poggini, portrait medal of Benedetto Varchi, cast bronze, ca. 1558–1562, obverse and reverse, Florence, Museo del Bargello.

in their recipients' output. Just as Galeotti does not seem to have devoted any of his creations to the laurel motif, we have no indication that Ammannati crafted a sculpture of Lenzi and Serbelloni, or that Allori ever immortalized the features of the young Pallante Rucellai. The fact that these lyrics follow the limited range of clichés typical of "advice-to-a-painter" poems would therefore appear to suggest that the portrayals solicited by Varchi only came to life in the reader's imagination. Still, the entirety of the literary and material evidence we have about Varchi's artistic interests serves to blur any such conclusion. Once viewed in the context of his relations with the contemporary art world, the compositions do show how even the most stereotyped, formulaic invitations could have repercussions on the creative choices of the painters, sculptors, and medalists in his inner circle. At the same time, we can understand from such contextualization how the genre of works these poems solicited was wholly consistent with Varchi's customary practice as a patron.

It is in this regard significant that while Galeotti probably declined Varchi's suggestion to celebrate the laurel in his work, the second medalist mentioned in that same sonnet from the 1555 collection did in fact respond.[270] Between 1558 and 1562, Domenico Poggini cast the famous portrait medal of Varchi, based on a design inspired by the figurative mythology of the tree sacred to Apollo. Reprising and expanding on the main descriptive elements of another of Varchi's *Sonetti* from 1555, the reverse of the medal thus shows the humanist reclining in the shadow of an unmistakable laurel tree (Figs. 4 and 5).[271] A poem Poggini addressed to

[270] It is useful to recall here that Poggini had also been the addressee of another sonnet from the same collection, *Voi, che seguendo del mio gran Cellino* (text in Varchi 1858–1859 [as in fn. 67], pp. 909–910, sonn. no. 518).
[271] The poem in question was addressed to another artist; namely, the Perugian architect Galeazzo Alessi (ibid., p. 841, sonn. no. 65; incipit: *Tal dentro il petto mio virtù rimane*). As Marco Collareta first recognized (Collareta 2007 [as in fn. 211], p. 183), the text's tercets describe a situation very close to the one we see depicted on the

him (*Varchi, chiaro splendor del secol nostro*; Appendix, no. 44) demonstrates that the artist presented him with this gift in homage to his merits; Varchi replied by showering praise on the medal itself and equally on its virtuous creator (*Poggino, il cui desio, le perle e l'ostro*; Appendix, no. 45).[272]

Some aspects of Wolfgang Iser's reception theory, and more specifically of his analysis of the reader's response to the prompts of a literary work, help provide a heuristic model for the way in which Poggini seems to have actualized the suggestion in Varchi's sonnet to Galeotti. According to this theory, the interaction between text and reader always entails the reader's completion of the indeterminations that the text contains in its rhetorical structure and that constitute the very condition for that exchange.[273] However detailed, a writer's descriptions always imply, for example, an irreducible margin of visual indeterminateness that can then be fleshed out and given consistency in the mental images such literary pieces elicit in the reader's imagination.[274] And if every historically determined reader relates to the text on the basis of his or her own experience, it is easier to comprehend how an artist-writer like Poggini could decide to translate into an artwork the mental images triggered by the mythology of the laurel at the center of Varchi's *Sonetti* of 1555, and in particular by the advice-to-a-painter poem to Galeotti. That vague suggestion to immortalize Apollo's sacred tree, addressed to Poggini's main colleague and local competitor in the production of medals, lent itself to a broad array of depictions. For the artists in Varchi's inner circle, in fact, it was in some sense a challenge to come up with the visual creation that best represented the cardinal role that subject played at the time in Varchi's poetry. For that matter, we know that the laurel tree had also been depicted by another Florentine sculptor friendly with Varchi, in a work that has not survived or remains to be identified: in a still unpublished sonnet (*Dal dì ch'io scorsi in alta sacra cima*: Appendix, no. 46), Varchi praised Francesco di Simone Mosca as an artist greater than Phidias and claimed that Mosca's piece showcasing the laurel motif had earned him the immortality already achieved by the poet himself.[275]

---

reverse of Poggini's medal and include a re-elaboration of the Petrarchan motto that is featured on the object (Cosí quaggiu si gode, a quotation from Petrarch, *Canzoniere* 128.111): "Ond'io, dove altro non si vede ed ode, / Che frondi, e venti ed onde, a piè d'un fonte / Vivo mi corco sotto l'ombra incerta // D'un verde alloro e verso il sol la fronte / Alzando dico: Così qui si gode, / E la strada del ciel si truova aperta."

[272] For a more detailed account of the contents of the poems, as well as of the genesis, chronology, context, and models of Domenico Poggini's portrait medal of Benedetto Varchi, see Gamberini 2016 (as in fn. 7).

[273] Wolfgang Iser, *The Act of Reading: A Theory of Aesthetic Response*, Baltimore 19977, pp. 170–231.

[274] Compare the general statement, ibid., p. 194: "The blanks transform themselves into stimuli for acts of ideation […]; what they suspend turns into a propellant for the reader's imagination, making him supply what has been withheld."

[275] It is not possible to date the sonnet on the grounds of codicological or internal evidence. In view of contextual considerations, it nevertheless appears plausible that the object representing "Lauro" to which Varchi refers might have been created around 1554. At that time, both Lenzi and Francesco Mosca were active in Orvieto: the former in his new capacity as city governor and the latter as the supervisor of a series of sculptural projects for the local cathedral (see Beatrice Franci, Le sculture di Simone e Francesco Mosca nel transetto del duomo di Orvieto, in: Laura Andreani and Alessandra Cannistrà [eds.], *Le cattedrali, segni delle radici cristiane in Europa*, Orvieto 2010, pp. 225–236, and Alberto Satolli, Una recente scoperta nell'attività orvietana di Francesco Mosca detto il Moschino [e qualche considerazione sui ritratti nel '500], ibid., pp. 255–274). Varchi might have seen

It is therefore likely that those poems we would be tempted to interpret as rhetorical constructions not reflecting the concrete art dynamics of the time actually provided significant creative suggestions to the artists in Varchi's circle. This is even more true in a setting where many of the painters, sculptors, and medalists solicited in Varchi's poems shared his practice of the pen, and more broadly a culture for which the topoi of vernacular poetry, far from being dead vestiges of the past, often guided the invention and reception of works of art.[276] Such an intersecting of highly codified formulae with aspects of real artistic invention is further confirmed if we consider the genre of creation that advice-to-a-painter poems implied. The fact that Varchi turned to artists in his circle for portrayals of the objects of his affections – following a pattern in which Lorenzo Lenzi or Pallante Rucellai *iuniore* were the Platonically correct reincarnations of the *hetaira* and the young boy whose portraits were sought in the pseudo-anacreontic odes – mirrored his actual inclinations as a patron. A few years before addressing a sonnet to Alessandro Allori requesting a portrait of Palla Rucellai, Varchi had already asked Allori to paint Giulio della Stufa, another subject of several of Varchi's compositions.[277] In this case as well, the artwork in question is now lost, or perhaps remains to be identified, but the commission is documented in a letter Giulio wrote to Varchi in March of

---

Francesco's sculptural portrait of Lenzi in the early months of 1555, when he spent a long period in Lenzi's house in Orvieto: see Simoncini 2005 (as in fn. 214). For the literary fortune of Phidias in medieval and Renaissance Italy as one of the paradigms of excellence in sculpture, see Ulrich Pfisterer, Phidias und Polyklet von Dante bis Vasari: Zu Nachruhm und künstlerischer Rezeption antiker Bildhauer in der Renaissance, in: *Marburger Jahrbuch für Kunstwissenschaft* 26 (1999), pp. 61–97.

[276] It is useful in this regard to recall the decisive role that the metaphors of love or canons of beauty crystallized by vernacular poetry, especially Petrarchist and Petrarchan poetry, played in so many portraits produced in Renaissance Italy. On this, see esp. Elizabeth Cropper, On Beautiful Women: Parmigianino, Petrarchismo, and the Vernacular Style, in: *The Art Bulletin* 58 (1976), pp. 374–394; Giovanni Pozzi, Il ritratto della donna nella poesia d'inizio Cinquecento e la pittura di Giorgione, in: Rodolfo Pallucchini (ed.), *Giorgione e l'umanesimo veneziano*, Florence 1981, 1, pp. 309–341; Marianne Koos, Petrarkistische Theorie oder künstlerische Praxis? Zur Malerei des Giorgionismo im Spiegel des lyrischen Männerporträts, in: Valeska Rosen, Klaus Krüger, and Rudolf Preimesberger (eds.), *Stumme Diskurs der Bilder: Reflexionsformen des Ästhetischen in der Kunst der Frühen Neuzeit*, Berlin 2003, pp. 53–84, and eadem, Amore dolce-amaro. Giorgione und das ideale Knabenbildnis der venezianischen Renaissancemalerei, in: *Marburger Jahrbuch für Kunstwissenschaft* 33 (2006), pp. 113–174; Stephen J. Campbell, Eros in the Flesh: Petrarchan Desire, the Embodied Eros, and Male Beauty in Italian Art, 1500–1540, in: *The Journal of Medieval and Early Modern Studies* 35 (2005), pp. 629–662. On the complex relationship between the use of recurrent literary conventions and the concreteness of specific artistic practices in Italian Renaissance poetry about art, see also the remarks by Pich 2010 (as in fn. 264), p. 9 ("L'abitudine a leggere i testi attraverso la lente della topica può fare passare sotto silenzio dati importanti, talvolta da prendere alla lettera; le metafore hanno uno spessore e un rapporto con la realtà e, sullo sfondo omogeneo della tradizione, bisogna riconoscere le zone dei testi in cui episodi e consuetudini materiali si riflettono conservando qualcosa della propria specificità e concretezza"), as well as the sophisticated critical assessment by eadem, La poesia e il ritratto, in: Gianluca Genovese and Andrea Torre (eds.), *Letteratura e arti visive nel Rinascimento*, Rome 2019, pp. 57–84.

[277] On Varchi's poetic compositions for Giulio della Stufa, see Paolino 2004 (as in fn. 212) and, with particular reference to poems in the pastoral mode, Ferroni 2017 (as in fn. 212), and Selene Maria Vatteroni, Le sezioni pastorali e la codifica del "doppio amore" nel canzoniere di Benedetto Varchi, in: *Italienisch* 40, no. 79 (2018), pp. 12–26.

1554.²⁷⁸ Evidence like this reveals a truth we cannot ignore when we speak of Varchi's advice-to-a-painter poems: the different objects of his amorous passion, the many "flames" his writings invoke with obsessive frequency, were indeed central to his patronly interests.²⁷⁹

And that's not all. Aside from being the preferred subjects of the artworks Varchi commissioned, his young beloveds were the main recipients of the gifts of paintings and medals in his possession.²⁸⁰ This is clear, for example, from the mostly unpublished Latin poems that Varchi addressed to Pallante Rucellai towards the end of his life. In addition to culinary gifts, inspired by the humble offerings in Martial's *Xenia*,²⁸¹ these very short poems tell us of several valuable creations sent to their dedicatee. Like Martial's *Apophoreta*, often presented as note cards for gifts like terracotta, marble or precious metal statues; paintings of mythological subjects; or small portraits of distinguished authors, Varchi's verses were meant to accompany gifts of small works of art. Varchi's letters confirm that this rhetoric of giving away art to his beloveds and accompanying these objects with poetry reflected a real habit of his.²⁸² Other examples include the hexameters *In effigiem Petri Bembi Cardinalis Pallanti Oricellario dono datam*, perhaps written to introduce Valerio Belli's portrait medal of Pietro Bembo, which surely passed through Varchi's hands.²⁸³ Just as revealing are the elegiac couplets that presented to Pallante

---

²⁷⁸ See the letter in Bramanti 2012 (as in fn. 184), pp. 313–315, alongside the careful discussion in Geremicca 2017 (as in fn. 121), pp. 90–92.

²⁷⁹ The study of the author's published and unpublished poetic corpora makes it clear that Varchi, in referring to the different "flames" that had inspired his love poetry, was alluding to his feelings for Lorenzo Lenzi, Giulio Stufa, Laura Battiferri, Cesare Ercolani, and Pallante Rucellai. On the definition of Laura Battiferri as the poet's "terza fiamma," for instance, see Tanturli 2011 (as in fn. 6), pp. 324–325.

²⁸⁰ Once again, such practices intersected with recurrent leitmotifs from Renaissance poetry on portraiture. Typical of this tradition were poems that commented on the effigy of the poet's beloved one or else addressed the theme of the poet donating his/her own portrait (whether a painting or a medal) to his beloved. For a historico-literary discussion of these tropes, see esp. Bolzoni and Pich 2008 (as in fn. 267), pp. 23–26 and 30–33.

²⁸¹ The *xenia* are the subject of book 13 of Martial's *Epigrams*. Relevant examples of Varchi's own *xenia* include some elegiac distichs in BNCF, Filza Rinuccini 15, c. 308r (incipit: *Cum tibi vel ficus, Pallas, vel persica mitto* and *Ficedulas alii dicunt se mittere*), on the gift of some fruits, and c. 315r (*Formosus non quo videare diebus*), on the gift of a hare. Exchanges of culinary gifts and short poetic compositions are also attested in the literary corpus of Michelangelo. On several occasions, the artist commented that the epigrams he wrote to Luigi del Riccio on the death of Cecchino Bracci (†1544) were compensation for the trouts, truffles, fennels, and turtle doves he had received from his correspondent: see Ernst Steinmann, *Michelangelo e Luigi del Riccio: con documenti inediti*, Florence 1932, p. 16, and Franz Voelker, I cinquanta componimenti funebri di Michelangelo per Luigi del Riccio, in: *Italique* 3 (2000), pp. 23–44.

²⁸² Relevant here is the letter that Varchi addressed to Palla Rucellai on August 31, 1565 (see Varchi 2008 [as in fn. 183], pp. 212–214). The text attests to the fact that the sender had enclosed some "glasses" with his message ("Egli mi sono stati mandati da Vinegia alcuni vetri de' quali io vi fo parte, ma poco e picciola, per la cagione che vi dirà il distico scritto di sotto"). The distich which he inserted at the bottom of the epistle ("Parva tibi nec multa damus chrystalla: etenim te / Tam puerum pauca et pocula parva decent," which is present in different manuscript redactions in the Filze Rinuccini: see Silvano Ferrone, Indice universale dei carmi latini di Benedetto Varchi, in: *Medioevo e Rinascimento* 8 [1997], pp. 125–195, p. 176) illustrates that the objects in question were small crystal drinking glasses. For ancient *Apophoreta* related to the gift of small artworks, see book 14 of Martial's *Epigrams*, esp. nos. 170–192.

²⁸³ See BNCF, Filza Rinuccini 15, c. 361r: "Ut nihil hoc maius, nil ut praestantius usquam / orbe fuit toto, sic te nil dignius illo: / hunc igitur dono, rerum carissime Pallas, / mitto tibi, ut primis talem mirere sub annis." I am grateful to Dario Brancato for helping with transcribing the poem. On Varchi's possession of at least one

an "excusam effigiem" of Varchi himself – likely the bronze portrait medal made by Poggini.[284] In this sense, these compositions help delineate patterns of artistic and literary production and circulation that – as Ulrich Pfisterer has shown with particular reference to the milieu of 1470s Rome – had long been typical of humanistic circles and of the kind of homosocial relationships, blurring the lines between male love and friendship, which were common in such classically educated coteries.[285]

The gift of small but valuable artworks therefore often crowned the gift of elegant little poems, and served an identical function: to strengthen the sentimental and intellectual ties between the aging humanist and those young boys, invariably aristocratic and handsome, who in the context of that discipleship began frequenting the muses. And it should come as no surprise that Varchi's rivals might condemn those ties as the reassertion not of a Platonic-Ficinian paradigm of Socratic love, but of the more earthly Greek pederastic model of the adult lover (*erastes*) and his prepubescent beloved (*eromenoi*). It is equally unsurprising that to that end, they would gossip about the gifts Varchi showered on his pupils: the literary critic Ludovico Castelvetro observed, for example, that Varchi often dedicated sonnets "per accattare la gratia et per acquistar[…] l'amore" of not a few "giovinetti, a' quali, poi che erano fatti huomini, ritoglieva senza rossore niuno quello che in altra età e forma haveva liberamente donato."[286]

---

version of Belli's portrait medal of Pietro Bembo see Gasparotto 1996 (as in fn. 187) and Gamberini 2016 (as in fn. 7), p. 382, with further bibliography.

[284] BNCF, Filza Rinuccini 15, c. 365v: "Qui tibi nos totos nuper donavimus ipsos, / nunc nostri excusam tradimus effigiem." The perfect participle *excusam* refers to a work forged in metal, typically in bronze (compare Virgil, *Aeneid* 6.847: "Excudent alii spirantia mollius aera"). This suggests that we should identify the effigy in question with the work of Poggini. We should also consider that in the Italian Renaissance, portrait medals were among the artistic objects most often exchanged as love or friendship gifts within humanistic circles; furthermore, these artifacts typically established a dense thread of allusions to the poems that often accompanied them: see Ulrich Pfisterer, *Lysippus und seine Freunde: Liebesgaben und Gedächtnis im Rom der Renaissance, oder, Das erste Jahrhundert der Medaille*, Berlin 2008, with the following note.

[285] By means of an analysis that partly draws on Marcell Mauss's anthropological theory of the gift, Pfisterer's book illuminates the phenomenon with special reference to the cultural world of the medalist Lysippus. While it focuses on this historical context, the book contains myriad references to later examples of comparable practices of gifting portrait medals and other artistic objects as signs of affection and devotion, often in the context of male relationships that – following ancient ideas – saw no clear divide between sentiments of *amor* and *amicitia*. Drawings too could perform a comparable function and could similarly be accompanied by lyrical compositions, as in the case of Michelangelo's refined presentation drawings for Tommaso dei Cavalieri, on which see especially ibid., pp. 377ff., Alexander Nagel, Gifts for Michelangelo and Vittoria Colonna, in: *The Art Bulletin* 79 (1997), pp. 647–668, and Marcella Marongiu, "…Perché egli imparassi a disegnare gli fece molte carte stupendissime…". I disegni di Michelangelo per Tommaso de' Cavalieri, in: *Horti Hesperidum. Studi di storia del collezionismo e della storiografia artistica* 4, no. 1 (2014), pp. 11–55.

[286] The quote is from Castelvetro's *Corretione d'alcune cose del "Dialogo delle lingue" di Benedetto Varchi*, as cited in Lo Re 2010 (as in fn. 214), p. 281. Lo Re's article is the best documented study of Varchi's contemporaries' reactions to the homoerotic dimension in his writings.

Varchi, Bronzino, and a revisitation of the advice-to-a-painter genre

The interferences and points of contact, as described above, between the rhetorical schemata typical of "advice-to-a-painter" poems and the references to concrete aspects of Varchi's relationship to the contemporary art scene illuminate one of the greatest challenges art historians face in interpreting such highly stereotypical poems. They demonstrate how adherence to the stylistic traits and motifs that were typical of certain literary genres does require the identification of similar elements, hence an interpretation that extends beyond a non-problematizing acceptance of the literal level of the text and its reading as a simple mirror of a historically determinable reality. At the same time, however, they show how these forms inherited from the code were adopted and manipulated depending on their congruence with material aspects of the author's life. And while Iser argued that allusions to the models inherited from the literary tradition typically satisfy the function of generalizing the references to the historical context to which all texts react, so that by introducing small variations "traditional schemata are rearranged to communicate a new picture,"[287] the considerations of method that Charles Segal inferred from the studies of the classicist Gian Biagio Conte are also pertinent to understanding this dynamic. What Segal emphasized was the role of mediation, rather than obliteration, that the thematic and formal conventions of every traditional genre play in depicting "real-life" elements external to literature:

> genre is the mediating term between the literary work and the various cultural discourses and social functions within which literature operates. Viewed from within the work, genre is the sign of an intention to invoke a certain set of readerly competences—codes, conventions, levels of style, situations, stereotypes, vocabulary, and so on. All of the markers that define the "form of the text" have a historical as well as a metaliterary dimension [...]. Thus while self-referentiality is a feature of all literature, a potential inherent in the nature of literary discourse, neither history nor referentiality is excluded. But whatever the work may have to say about external reality is said through the framework and constraints of its literary form [...]. The texts [...] do not simply create a fictitious world, or provide a mimetic image of a "real" one, but rather aim at creating their own world of formal design, where the elements taken from real life have been recomposed under the sign of the literary facticity of the genre. A literary work [...] is, therefore, located at the intersection of two axes, historicity and literariness. The relation between them is one of dynamic interaction and reciprocal modification each of the other.[288]

---

[287] See the considerations that the author drew from his analyses of such distant works as Edmund Spencer's *Eclogues* and James Joyce's *Ulysses* (Iser 1997 [as in fn. 273], pp. 80–81): "The literary text must comprise the [...] historical situation to which it is reacting. Now, the social and cultural norms that form this situation need to be organized in such a way that the reason for their selection can be conveyed to the reader, but since this cannot be conveyed explicitly (unless fiction is to be turned into documentary), there has to be a means of generalizing the repertoire, and herein lies the special function of the literary allusions. [...]. In this way, traditional schemata are rearranged to communicate a new picture [...]. The projection [of realistic references and literary allusions] is two-way, and so there follows a deformation of both elements [...]. Each element acts as an irritant upon the other." In these passages, Iser was relying on Maurice Merlau-Ponty's notion of the "coherent deformation" that every writer or artist's style imposes upon the "data of the world" (see Merlau-Ponty, *Signs*, trans. Richard C. McCleary, Evanston, IL 1964, pp. 54–55).

[288] Segal, introduction to Gian Biagio Conte, *Genres and Readers: Lucretius, Love Elegy, Pliny's Encyclopedia*, trans. Glenn W. Most, Baltimore 1994, p. IX. This approach to the interpretation of literary works, which is grounded in the study of Greek and Roman literature but provides fundamental insights for the study of Re-

Similar observations help us understand the exceptional density of some dialogues in verse between Varchi and Agnolo Bronzino.[289] Let us consider Varchi's *Voi che nel fior della sua verde etate* and Bronzino's reply *Tali e tante vid'io grazie adunate*, included in the *Sonetti contra gli Ugonotti* (Appendix, nos. 47–48). In the *proposta*, the exhortative, pseudo-anacreontic formula is suited to the intellectual status of a correspondent being asked to celebrate, as both painter and poet, Lorenzo Lenzi's triumph in the summer of 1562 against the Protestants who had besieged the Catholic stronghold of Avignon.[290] Once again, the "commission" implied by a literal reading of the text would seem to be entirely virtual, as we have no knowledge of any Bronzino work portraying "Lauro" at the time of his campaign against the Huguenots. Yet in this case too, the interweaving of a strong element of literary stereotype with the output of the artist to whom Varchi chose to write is more complex than a preliminary impression of abstractness would suggest. Varchi's sonnet is actually a highly significant document concerning a different work by Bronzino that is anything but imaginary. As Antonio Geremicca has pointed out, the first quatrain of the *proposta* dispels the long-standing doubts over the genesis of Bronzino's portrait of the pre-adolescent Lorenzo Lenzi (Fig. 6), now preserved at the Castello Sforzesco.[291] In these lines, Varchi states that Bronzino had produced "in [his] name" an extraordinary painting that illustrated Lenzi's beauty as he first blossomed into youth. This has rightly been interpreted as definitive confirmation of the theory Alessandro Cecchi first advanced that the painting was commissioned by Varchi, whose sonnet *Famose Frondi, de' cui santi honori* is shown alongside Petrarch's *O d'ardente vertute ornata e calda* (*Canzoniere* 146) in the book Lorenzo displays to the viewer.[292]

---

naissance texts, underpins also Gian Biagio Conte, *The Rhetoric of Imitation: Genre and Poetic Memory in Virgil and Other Latin Poets*, trans. Charles Segal, Ithaca, NY / London 1986. For a comparable discussion of the mediating function of poetic genres, see Giunta 2002 (as in fn. 11), pp. 321 and 356–360. In the latter passage, Giunta discusses some of the ways in which biographical reality is filtered in Italian medieval lyrical poetry in light of Philippe Lejeune's analysis of autobiographical writings (Lejeune, *Je est un autre: l'autobiographie de la littérature aux médias*, Paris 1980).

[289] The texts are the object of the fundamental considerations of Geremicca 2013 (as in fn. 6), pp. 89–96. Geremicca discusses them as examples of what he labels as "poesia di commissione."

[290] The references to the ungodly hordes that were besieging Avignon and to Lenzi's bloody victory against them (ll. 10–14) allow us to propose August 30, 1562 as a *terminus post quem*. On that day, Serbelloni, leader of the armed branch of Lenzi's campaign, achieved a victory that broke the siege of the city and reddened the Rodanus with the blood of many Huguenots: see Ferrone 1993 (as in fn. 214), p. 179.

[291] See the persuasive argument in Geremicca 2013 (as in fn. 6), pp. 86–90, following a hint in Firpo 1997 (as in fn. 159), pp. 206–207. Firpo was the first to identify the portrait mentioned in the first quatrain of the 1562 sonnet with the one now preserved in Milan.

[292] Compare Alessandro Cecchi, "Famose Frondi de cui santi honori…": un sonetto del Varchi e il ritratto di Lorenzo Lenzi dipinto dal Bronzino, in: *Artista* 2 (1990), pp. 8–19, p. 16: "[Varchi] l'aveva conosciuto [Lenzi], poco più che decenne, nell'estate di un anno ormai lontano, e il Bronzino gli aveva poco dopo fatto il ritratto, ancora fanciullo, forse, chissà, su richiesta dello stesso Varchi." Raffaele De Giorgi advanced the same hypothesis in his entry on the painting in: Falciani and Natali 2010 (as in fn. 6), p. 202. For the juxtaposition of the sonnet by Varchi, which celebrates Lenzi's beauty and virtue, with the one by Petrarch, which similarly addresses Laura's appearance as well as her moral incorruptibility, see ibid., as well as Geremicca 2013 (as in fn. 6), pp. 87–88, and Novella Macola, *Sguardi e scritture: figure con libro nella ritrattistica italiana della prima metà del Cinquecento*, Venice 2007, p. 69, which emphasizes how "i due sonetti […] scivolano l'uno nell'altro; i meriti di

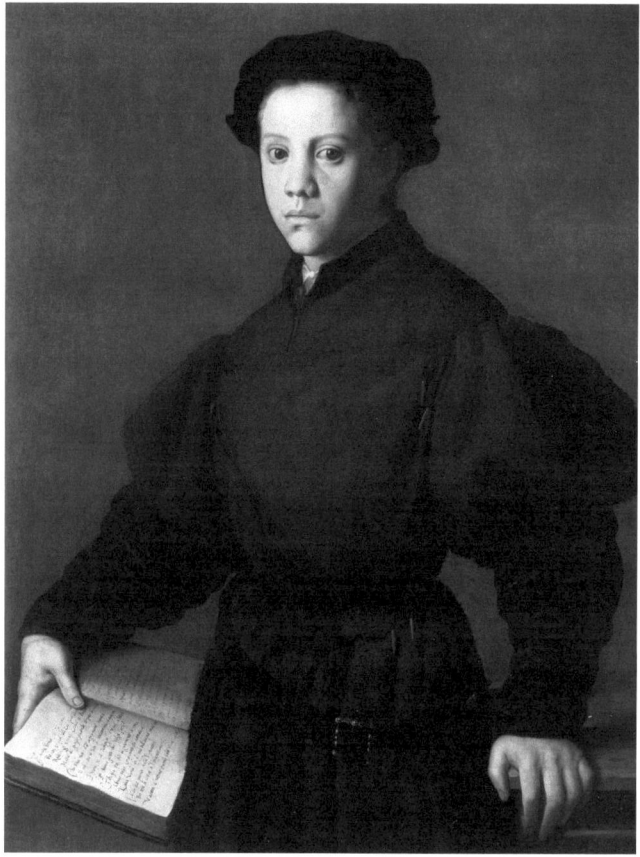

6: Agnolo Bronzino, *Portrait of Lorenzo Lenzi*, oil on panel, c. 1529, Milan, Pinacoteca del Castello Sforzesco.

What should be underscored is that Varchi's phrase "a nome mio" is reminiscent of a foundational text in the history of Italian poetry on portraiture. In praising Simone Martini's portrait of Laura, Petrarch had maintained that the inspiration for the work had given the painter the tool he needed to fulfill Petrarch's own mandate (*Canzoniere* 78.1–2: "Quando giunse a Simon l'alto concetto / ch'*a mio nome* gli pose in man lo stile").[293] By adopting the

---

Laura trascorrono in Lorenzo completandone il profilo morale affinché si stagli, sul fondo verde alle sue spalle, come 'torre in alto valor fondata e salda.'"

[293] My emphasis. Compare Giambattista Gelli, *Lezioni Petrarchesche di Giovan Battista Gelli [...]*, ed. Carlo Negroni, Bologna 1884 (Gelli's lectures at the Accademia Fiorentina were originally published in 1549), pp. 270–271: "A nome, cioè a cagione di M. F. Petrarca, fu quello il quale pose lo stile e il pennello in mano a Maestro Simone; cioè mosse la causa agente a ritrarre in carte Madonna Laura." Also useful is the commentary by Rosanna Bettarini in Petrarch, *Canzoniere*, ed. Rosanna Bettarini, 2 vols., Turin 2005, 1, pp. 398–399. For the fundamental place of this sonnet within the tradition of poetic commentaries on art, see Bolzoni and Pich 2008 (as in fn. 267), pp. 10–16 and 75–81, as well as Pich 2010 (as in fn. 264), pp. 54–65, with further references.

Petrarchan syntagma with minimal variation, Varchi was thus modeling his commissioning of Bronzino's portrait of the young Lenzi on the most renowned lyric paradigm of creative collaboration between an artist and a poet.[294] The choice of words suggests a web of analogies that run through Varchi's lyric and Bronzino's visual creation of over three decades earlier, according to a pattern that presents Lenzi, the humanist and the painter as the modern counterparts of Laura, Petrarch, and Simone Martini.

Yet the dialogue between Varchi and Bronzino that takes place in words and image differs from the relationship between their Trecento models to the extent that, as Massimiliano Rossi has noted regarding Bronzino's portrait of Laura Battiferri, the Cinquecento artist actively participates in poetic reflections on his own visual works.[295]

In response to Varchi's 1562 sonnet urging him to celebrate with pen and brush "Lauro's" feats in Avignon, Bronzino wrote a lyrical *recusatio* claiming that he was unable to adequately honor the subject. He argued that his earlier attempt to portray the exceptional charms of the young Lorenzo had already been rash, but at the time he was unable to refuse the assignment (Appendix, no. 48, l. 10). For that matter, the boy's extraordinary graces had made it impossible for the painter to set his gaze on him and produce an image faithful to that model.[296] Only Varchi, the sonnet concludes, could suitably laud the man who was now a modern-day Archangel Michael.

Building on the widespread poetic topos of the artist incapable of imitating the model's beauty, Bronzino's *recusatio* centered on a representational problem that the painting now at the Castello Sforzesco had brilliantly resolved. Similarly to what occurred, for example, in Domenico Ghirlandaio's portrait of Giovanna Tornabuoni, which aspired to be the visual response to the notion of painterly limits expressed in Martial's epigram X 32 displayed on the *cartellino* behind the young woman,[297] the likeness of Lenzi was originally intended as a dazzling visual reply to the challenge posed by Varchi's verse resting in the book in Lorenzo's hand. That sonnet, in fact, expressed the doubt that human art could ever fully capture the

---

[294] Varchi quoted the same lines of *Canzoniere* in his lecture on Michelangelo's sonnet *Non ha l'ottimo artista alcun concetto* (Varchi 1858–1859 [as in fn. 67], 2, pp. 616–617): "Onde il Petrarca favellando del Pittore, che ritrasse la sua Madonna Laura disse: 'Quando giunse a Simon l'alto concetto, / Ch'a mio nome gli pose in man lo stile.'" Also remarkable is Varchi's use of the Petrarchan word *stile* in his sonnet to Bronzino (l. 6). The noun indicates both the instrument of the painter, as in the Trecento model, and that of the writer, as in other sixteenth-century poets (see, for instance, Giovanni della Casa's use of the word in his sonnet *Ben veggio io, Tiziano, in forme nove*, discussed in Bolzoni and Pich 2008 [as in fn. 267], p. 96).
[295] The reference here is to the remarks of Rossi 2015 (as in fn. 9), p. 150, which discuss Bronzino's sonnets on the portrait of Laura Battiferri as an infraction of the Petrarchan model of *Canzoniere* 77 and 78, on the grounds that both the modern painter and the modern Laura possess a poetic voice.
[296] The motif of the artwork being unable to represent the subject's beauty is a common one in Renaissance poetry on art and dates back to Hellenic and Hellenistic epigrams on artistic subjects. See, among others, the epigrams by Rufinus and Paulus Silentiarius of *Greek Anthology* 5.15 and 16.77. In Quattro- and Cinquecento Italy, the motif was often inflected in terms of artists' inability to look directly at the subject of representation, for the excess of beauty would blind them: examples from Serafino Aquilano and Niccolò da Correggio are discussed in Bolzoni and Pich 2008 (as in fn. 267), pp. 34–36.
[297] See *supra*, fn. 265.

boy's beauty: "Qual sarà mai, che degnamente onori / Quel bello, onde ogni ben par che si mieta? / Che Giove irato e le tempeste acqueta, / e rende umili i più feroci cori?"[298]

At the core of the exchange we have just examined, Bronzino's dual status as artist and poet is also the focus of other advice-to-a-painter poems by Varchi. Another recommendation to paint Lorenzo Lenzi is the subject of *Bronzino, ove sì dolce ombreggia e suona*, to which Bronzino replied with two *recusatio* sonnets, *L'alma pianta, che Giove quando tuona* and *Ch'io cercarei dove più 'l Nil risuona* (Appendix, nos. 49–51).[299] In these lines, Varchi again asked Bronzino to commemorate Lenzi both in the poetic medium that ensured immortality to the subject and in the visual medium that could faithfully represent his physical features. Here, too, Bronzino declined his friend's invitation, claiming his inadequacy for such a lofty task, which in his view required the poetry-writing gifts of his correspondent.

In a pattern we have repeatedly seen in advice-to-a-painter poems, we have no evidence that the generic portrait urged by this exchange was ever realized. However, scholars do debate the possible visual translation of another such composition that Varchi addressed to Bronzino. Massimiliano Rossi has proposed the hypothesis that the sonnet in which Varchi asked his friend to celebrate both in painting and in poetry the 1558 marriage of Isabella de' Medici and Paolo Giordano Orsini (*Nuova casta Ciprigna, e nuovo Marte*: Appendix, no. 14) should be linked to a double portrait at the Musée des Beaux-Arts in Strasbourg (Fig. 7), traditionally ascribed to Bronzino (though the work has alternatively been attributed to Alessandro Allori or his workshop).[300] He disagrees with an earlier theory that identified the two subjects as Ludovico Capponi and his wife, Maddalena Vettori, and the painting with a work that was completed by Bronzino's workshop but for which the master himself appears to have received payments starting in 1559.[301] Rossi rejects that notion because of the poor resemblance between the man in the Strasbourg portrait and the young Ludovico, whom Bronzino had depicted around

---

[298] The text was also published in Varchi's *Sonetti* of 1555: see Varchi 1858–1859 (as in fn. 67), 2, p. 833, sonnet 7, ll. 5–8.

[299] For the hypothesis that these poetic exchanges refer to the execution of the portrait of the Castello Sforzesco, see Tanturli 2004 (as in fn. 6), p. 211, and Geremicca 2013 (as in fn. 6), p. 273. Still, in his sonnet, Varchi appears to adapt the eulogistic expressions he had first used in the sonnet *Ben vi devea bastar chiaro scultore*, which he had addressed to Michelangelo (see *supra*), to Bronzino. 1547 therefore seems to be a *terminus post quem* for the composition of these texts. Furthermore, Bronzino's sonnets imply a later chronology than the one that has traditionally been proposed by scholars. The compositions emphasize how the "laurel" Varchi should celebrate is no longer a shoot ("rampollo"), but rather a mature branch full of fruit (*L'alma pianta, che Giove quando tuona*, ll. 9–11), thus pointing to Lenzi's adult age.

[300] See Rossi 2010 (as in fn. 6), p. 177. Isabella de' Medici's engagement to Paolo Giordano Orsini took place in 1553, but their marriage was only celebrated in September 1558: see Caroline Murphy, *Isabella de' Medici: The Glorious Life and Tragic End of a Renaissance Princess*, London 2008, pp. 63–68, and Barbara Furlotti, *A Renaissance Baron and His Possessions: Paolo Giordano I Orsini, Duke of Bracciano (1541-1585)*, Turnhout 2012, pp. 7–8. Varchi paid homage to the latter event in many unpublished poems (for instance, in BNCF, Filza Rinuccini 3, cc. 392ff.; Filza Rinuccini 12, c. 450r; Filza Rinuccini 15, cc. 2ff. etc.). In 1562, he also dedicated the poetic anthology of the *Sonetti contro gli Ugonotti* to Paolo Giordano (the dedicatory letter is in BNCF, Filza Rinuccini 5, cc. 3–5.)

[301] See Beatrice Paolozzi Strozzi, Gli "Sposi" del Museo di Strasburgo: un'appendice al catalogo del Bronzino, in: Klaus Bergdolt and Giorgio Bonsanti (eds.), *Opere e giorni: studi su mille anni di arte europea dedicati a Max Seidel*, Venice 2001, pp. 505–512, which brings to light and discusses relevant archival documents on this com-

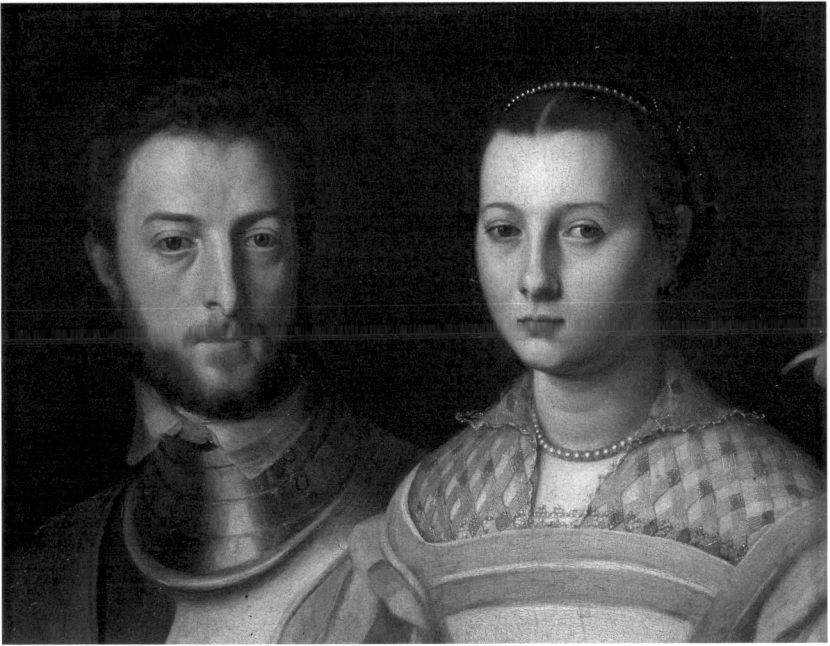

7 Agnolo Bronzino and workshop (or Alessandro Allori and workshop?), *Portrait of two spouses*, oil on panel, c. 1560, Strasbourg, Musée des Beaux-Arts.

1550–1555 in a painting now at the Frick Collection (Fig. 8).[302] (Antonio Geremicca is of a different opinion: while he considers it plausible that Bronzino really did paint Duke Cosimo's ill-fated third-born daughter and her husband, he agrees that Ludovico and Maddalena are the couple in the Strasbourg painting).[303] And as the woman in that portrait bears a certain resemblance to the effigy of Isabella de' Medici painted in Bronzino's workshop between 1552 and 1554 (Fig. 9), the man's sharp features are also somewhat consistent with the albeit heavier look that was attributed to Paolo Giordano Orsini in a 1565 engraving (Fig. 10).[304]

mission. The work is not mentioned in the partial list of the portraits by Bronzino that we read in the Giuntina edition of the *Vite*: see Vasari 1967–1997 (as in fn. 74), 6, pp. 231–232.

[302] In a forthcoming article ("'Ricco di tanto ardire.' A contextual study of Agnolo Bronzino's portrait of Lodovico Capponi [with a hypothesis for a portrait of Maddalena Vettori by Bronzino]"), Sanne Wellen follows Rossi in rejecting Paolozzi Strozzi's proposed identification of the subject of the Strasbourg painting. Although she does not specifically discuss the possibility that the pair portrayed in that work might be identifiable with Paolo Giordano Orsini and Isabella de' Medici, she stresses that the woman does not resemble another secure portrait of Maddalena Vettori, which is featured in Bernardino Poccetti's fresco cycle in the Florentine Palazzo Capponi-Vettori (1583–1586). I thank the author for letting me read the contribution before publication.

[303] Geremicca 2013 (as in fn. 6), pp. 94–95.

[304] Interestingly, the clothing of the male sitter in the Strasbourg double portrait characterizes him as a soldier: something we might easily relate to Varchi's definition of Paolo Giordano Orsini as a "nuovo Marte."

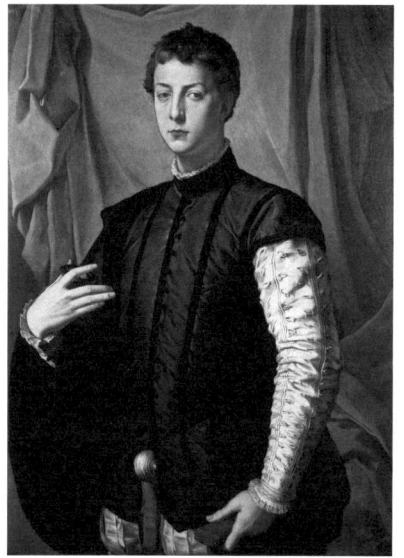 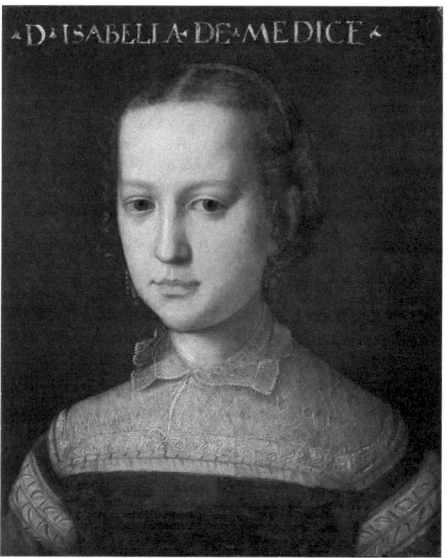

8 Agnolo Bronzino, *Portrait of Ludovico Capponi*, oil on panel, c. 1550–1555, New York, The Frick Collection.

9 Agnolo Bronzino's workshop, *Portrait of Isabella de' Medici*, oil on panel, 1552–1554, Stockholm, National Museum.

It may remain difficult to visually dispel doubts as to the identity of the couple in the Strasbourg portrait. From a textual perspective, it should be noted that Bronzino replied to Varchi's advice to paint Isabella and Paolo Giordano with a programmatic refusal or *recusatio* (*Quanto dal vero amor sovente parte*: Appendix, no. 15) that re-entrusted Varchi with the task of commemorating the noble couple's traits. Still, we cannot be certain from such a rejection that Bronzino never painted the effigy his friend desired, for among poets of the time a *recusatio* typically served to satisfy the mutual expectation of praising one's correspondent by claiming the inferiority of one's own expressive talents. A rhetorical trope gravitating within the semantic orbit of irony, it also undoubtedly assumed that it would be interpreted contrary to its letter: these declarations that so insist on the writer's inability to portray a given subject are in themselves a form of apophasis or *occultatio*, hence a feigned, virtuosic denial of that inability.[305] In this sense, they posed a challenge comparable to those poems emphasizing the insurmountable limitations of artistic portrayal. To a lyric in which the literato Gherardo

---

[305] Compare Pseudo-Cicero's definition of the trope in the *Rhetorica ad Herennium*, 4.27.37: "Occultatio est cum dicimus nos praeterire aut non scire aut nolle dicere id quod nunc maxime dicimus." Within the corpus of Varchi's poetic correspondence, typical examples of such preteritions come from the *Sonetti contro gli Ugonotti*. In many texts in the collection, the humanist exhorted some prominent fellow poets to write about Lenzi and Serbelloni's enterprises, and the addressees usually responded by claiming that they, unlike their interlocutor, were not up to the task. Relevant here are Varchi's lyrical exchanges with Annibal Caro, Lodovico Domenichi, Giovan Battista Adriani, and Bernardo Tasso in BNCF, Filza Rinuccini 5, *passim*.

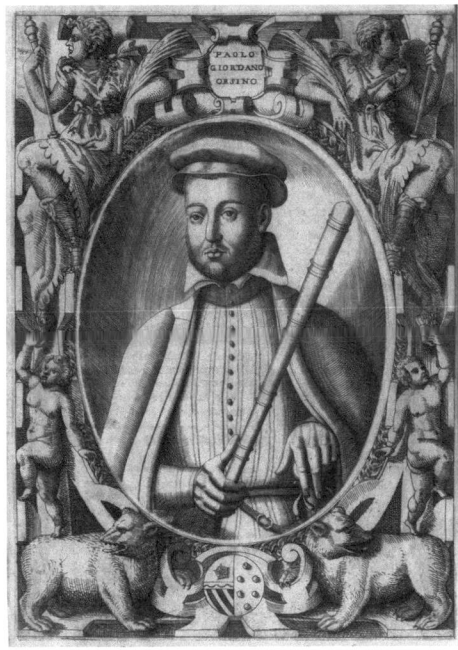

10 Attributed to Domenico Nicolini da Sabbio, *Paolo Giordano Orsini*, engraving, from Francesco Sansovino, *L'historia di casa Orsina* [...], Venice 1565, c. 90v.

Spini had urged him to honor as a poet the inner qualities of Laura Battiferri, whose "divina immagin viva" was supposedly impossible to replicate visually, even on the part of the addressee's "dotta man," Bronzino could for instance reply that he did not have the insane audacity to approach such a miraculous subject either in poetry or in painting.[306] In this case, however, the *recusatio* was accompanied by the execution of a portrait whose icy quality aimed to belie the artist's professed shortcomings.

Varchi as cultural broker

Within the domain of Varchi's output in verse, his advice-to-a-painter poems are excellent examples of the interferences that might occur between traditional poetic schemata and references to the historical/biographical context in which these compositions were situated. At any rate, the language of his sonnet exchanges with artists is not always informed by the same degree of literary stylization of historically identifiable occasions. The fact that the specific contours of some of those occasions were not easily cast in the rigid molds of genres inherited from the tradition, for example, helps explain why references to important pages of the city's

---

[306] See the exchange (Gherardo Spini's *Bronzin, quella divina imagin viva* and Bronzino's *Né l'uno né l'altro stil mio frale arriva*) in Carol Plazzotta, Bronzino's Laura, in: *The Burlington Magazine* 140 (1998), pp. 251–263, p. 262.

artistic life could sometimes be less oblique than those considered above. It is in this manner that Varchi's correspondence poetry may offer important clues to his role as a cultural broker in various Medici commissions in contemporary Florence.[307] These documents show how Varchi, a leading intellectual of that environment and official historiographer of the duchy, was the linchpin of an informal system of intermediation between the duke's authority and the artists gravitating around his court. In a competitive arts scene like Florence, where many qualified painters and especially sculptors vied for a limited number of ducal commissions, having someone influential to intercede with the court could after all be crucial to improving one's professional prospects.[308]

The poetic dialogue with Francesco da Sangallo evidenced in the second volume of Varchi's *Sonetti* (1557) is a telling example.[309] We can interpret Sangallo's opening sonnet (*Quei tre spirti del ciel pregiati e chiari*: Appendix, no. 12), written between 1546 and 1553, as a request that Varchi intervene with Duke Cosimo.[310] In these lines, Sangallo represented the spirits of Dante, Petrarch, and Boccaccio in the act of imploring recognition from "Flora," and asked his addressee to convince the Lord of Florence to make sure the three greats of Florentine

---

[307] This is obviously not to say that these compositions can be read as straightforward historical documents, for poetic language always maintains a specific level of "opaque depth" and "density" that makes it a "language divorced from the pure, uncomplicated function of communication" (Conte 1986 [as in fn. 288], p. 46). Still, references to historical circumstances play a pivotal role in a large part of Varchi's poetry, as well as that of many of his contemporaries, and this makes it impossible to fully understand and decode these poems without identifying the occasions from which they originated. On the concept of cultural brokerage as related to early modern patronage systems, see esp. Sharon Kettering, *Patrons, Brokers, and Clients in Seventeenth-Century France*, Oxford 1986, and, with reference to the Florentine and Roman networks of artistic and musical clientelism in the seventeenth century, Janie Cole, Cultural Clientelism and Brokerage Networks in Early Modern Florence and Rome: New Correspondence between the Barberini and Michelangelo Buonarroti the Younger, in: *Renaissance Quarterly* 60 (2007), pp. 729–788. On the role of cultural brokers for the careers of Medicean artists, see Anne E. Proctor, *Vincenzo Danti at the Medici Court: Constructing Professional Identity in Late Renaissance Florence*, PhD diss., University of Texas at Austin 2013 (https://repositories.lib.utexas.edu/bitstream/handle/2152/25889/PROCTOR-DISSERTATION-2013.pdf, last accessed 31/01/2021), pp. 7–9 and 43–44.

[308] On the high levels of competition in the Florentine artistic scene of the mid-Cinquecento, with a special reference to the roster of sculptors, see esp. Charles Davis, Benvenuto Cellini and the Scuola Fiorentina, in: *North Carolina Museum of Art Bulletin* 13.4 (1976), pp. 1–70, and Cole 2011 (as in fn. 98). For more on this, see also ch. 3 of this book.

[309] The most thorough and wide-ranging account of Francesco's artistic profile, his relationship to the glories of the Sangallo family and to the architectural languages of Quattrocento and Cinquecento Florence, and his cultural ambitions comes from Dario Donetti, *Francesco da Sangallo e l'identità dell'architettura toscana*, Milan 2020 (see particularly pp. 86–89 for a discussion of the artist's relationship with Varchi and of this poem, as well as of another sonnet that Francesco addressed to the man of letters and prelate Ludovico Beccadelli, bishop of Dubrovnik).

[310] The *terminus post quem* is provided by the clear allusion, in ll. 6–7 of the artist's poem, to Varchi's academic lecture on envy (March 1546). The *terminus ante quem* can be inferred on the basis of the presence of these two sonnets in the main preparatory manuscript for the 1557 edition, which was completed about four years before going to press: see Tanturli 2004 (as in fn. 212), p. 90. For a more detailed account of the context of the present exchange and of Sangallo's literary interests and devotion to Dante, see Diletta Gamberini, The Artist as a Dantista: Francesco da Sangallo's Dantism in Mid-Cinquecento Florence, in: *Dante Studies*, 135 (2017), pp. 169–191. Referencing a forthcoming publication by Alexander Röstel, Donetti 2020 (as in fn. 309) also records a few, previously unknown artworks of Dantean and Petrarchan subject that were present in Sangallo's Florentine house.

literature finally received a worthy tribute from their native land, in the form – we can infer from his reasoning – of a set of statues commemorating them. Sangallo's hope that he would be chosen to sculpt such a monument emerges from the final tercet. Here he argued that the prospective sculptures would exalt Cosimo and also Varchi, who as a historian would celebrate such an endeavor, but above all Sangallo himself, who could achieve immortal acclaim through such works.

In his response (*Francesco, se così pregiate e chiari*: Appendix, no. 13), Varchi agreed to support Sangallo's request and promised to ask Duke Cosimo to commission a visual tribute to the supreme glories of Tuscan literature. It does not appear, however, that any sculpture of the "Three Crowns" was produced during Cosimo's reign. Furthermore, there is no trace of statues dedicated to Dante, Petrarch, and Boccaccio in the catalog of Sangallo's works, and available documents shed no light on the plans mentioned in these sonnets. Before concluding that the hoped-for commission was a literary fiction, we should nevertheless consider that such a fiction could in no way be explained as following the thematic conventions of a given poetic genre. On the contrary, the allusions these lines contain are so clear-cut and irreducible to traditional poetic schemes that they seem likely to have been grounded in reality and associated with a project whose details are unknown to us.[311] We can also observe that soon thereafter, the city would implement a sculptural project similar to what the sonnets discuss: in the early 1560s, when construction began on the Uffizi, the plan was to fill the niches of the loggia with statues celebrating Florentines distinguished "nelle armi, nelle lettere e nei governi civili."[312] Inspired by the model of the Roman Forum, the propagandistic project was not completed at the time due to the deaths in quick succession of Grand Duke Cosimo and his architect Vasari (1574), and would not be realized until three centuries later.[313] In light of these circumstances, it is nonetheless plausible that the proposed sculpture cycle for the Uffizi loggia stemmed from a desire to honor the city's cultural triumphs that Cosimo had been nurturing for some time and that, years earlier, had whetted the ambitions as sculptor of Francesco da Sangallo.

The extent to which many of these dialogues in verse are informed by a marked referentiality to historical circumstances rather than patterned after predetermined topical models is also clear from another exchange, once again concerning an artistic project that was not completed at the time. Two of the four correspondence sonnets between Varchi and the sculptor and Servite friar Giovanni Angelo da Montorsoli illustrate the role Varchi played during a

---

[311] Compare the methodological suggestions that Giunta 2002 (as in fn. 11), p. 372, derives from the discussion of a medieval poem by Cino da Pistoia: "È […] difficile credere che allusioni così precise non abbiano un fondamento nella vita, nel reale comportamento di Cino."
[312] The quote is from Baccio Baldini's funeral oration for the Grand Duke (*Orazione fatta nella Accademia fiorentina in lode del serenissimo sig. Cosimo Medici gran duca di Toscana gloriosa memoria*, Florence 1574, unpaginated). On this artistic program, see Stefania Iacopozzi, "Il ciclo scultoreo degli Uffizi: genesi e sviluppo di un progetto non solo celebrativo," in: Magnolia Scudieri (ed.), *Gli uomini illustri del loggiato degli Uffizi: storia e restauro*, Florence 2001, pp. 15–33, and Claudia Conforti, Gli Uffizi e il Corridoio Vasariano nella rifondazione di Firenze ducale, in: Conforti, Funis, De Luca, and Acidini Luchinat 2011 (as in fn. 247), pp. 61–71, p. 65.
[313] Stefania Iacopozzi, *Le statue degli "illustri Toscani" nel loggiato degli Uffizi*, Florence 2000.

critical early phase of the Accademia del Disegno.[314] The final tercets of the two poems are especially instructive. In the *proposta* (*Nunzio, e servo di Dio, che queste frali*: Appendix, no. 16), Varchi recommended that Montorsoli, together with a certain "Giorgin," carry out Cosimo's plans for a temple to Pippo Spano. The artist replied that he and "buon Giorgio" were busy lobbying Cosimo about the shrine and the two "Pippi" (*Varchi gentil, che le mie poche e frali*; Appendix, no. 17): with the words "qual voi me fate" (l. 13), Montorsoli then acknowledged that this promotional effort was at Varchi's prompting.

These lines connect the poem exchange to the ambitious architectural project to complete the rotunda of Florence's Camaldolese monastery of Santa Maria degli Angeli, the building the Scolari family had commissioned from Filippo Brunelleschi through the bequest of Filippo Buondelmonti degli Scolari, alias Pippo Spano. Between the summer of 1562 and early 1563, Duke Cosimo granted the unfinished building to the artists of the newborn Accademia del Disegno, who were to complete, restore, and decorate with statues what was to be the seat of their institution. The sonnets therefore clarify how "Giorgin" Vasari and Montorsoli, the two artists who worked the hardest to establish the Accademia del Disegno, had acted in concert with Varchi to promote the completion of the fifteenth-century building. Although that plan was aborted within months, the poems show Varchi once again involved in an important public commission in Cosimo's Florence, as a sort of facilitator from behind the scenes of the campaign to have the duke complete Brunelleschi's project.

Disavowing art

The poetic exchanges discussed above document Varchi's broad, eclectic and active interests in the contemporary art scene. To conclude this chapter, it is now important to understand why a significant portion of the author's later poetry, namely the *Sonetti spirituali* published posthumously in Florence in 1573, is apparently disdainful of art. Though the poems printed in that volume were selected by Varchi's close friend Silvano Razzi from among the manuscripts of the deceased,[315] they do reflect some thematic nuclei found in the writer's original papers.

In the Filze Rinuccini, for example, almost all of the poetic dialogues with artists on religious themes are grouped together, forming a thematically and chronologically uniform series. Datable to the early 1560s, these texts exhibit the traits featured in the late writings of an

---

[314] For a more detailed study of the contents of these two texts and the historical circumstances behind them see Gamberini 2015 (as in fn. 257).
[315] For Razzi's responsibility for assembling the collection, see Lo Re 2008 (as in fn. 181), p. 114. A Camaldulense monk and a man of letters himself, Razzi was one of Varchi's closest friends in the last years of his life and was designated as the main heir of his books. On the presence and main characteristics of religious themes in Varchi's earlier collection of poetry, and particularly in the *Sonetti* of 1555, see Selene Maria Vatteroni, Dal *Beneficio di Cristo* ai *Sonetti. Parte prima*: tracce di Spiritualismo nel canzoniere di Benedetto Varchi, in: Huß and Vatteroni 2019 (as in fn. 219), pp. 90–111.

author who would take holy orders a few months before his death (Appendix, nos. 52–65).[316] Inspired as much by *Ecclesiastes*' meditation on the *vanitas* of all wordly goods as by Petrarch's sapiential verse, with its appeals to place no hope "in cosa mortale," the compositions lie within the framework of a contemporary flourishing of Italian religious poetry in line with the new Counter-Reformation sensibility.[317] In promoting the image of a poet now nearing his ultimate detachment from earthly cares, Varchi constantly urged his correspondents to embark on a similar conversion, abandoning all that might hinder their achievement of eternal salvation. In addressing painters and sculptors he specifically emphasized the supreme futility of artistic glory in an otherworldly perspective, following a famous Dantean model. His lines, in fact, echo the reflection contained in *Purgatorio* 11 79–96, which on comparable notes had stressed the vanity of professional ambition and of that "gran disio / de l'eccellenza" that motivated the greatest artists, while asserting that the only salvation from the pride of such worldly pursuits was a full conversion to God.[318] In Varchi's sonnets to Bronzino (*D'ogni cosa rendiam grazie al Signore*: Appendix, no. 55) and Vasari (*Quant'havete maggior l'ingegno e l'arte*: Appendix, no. 57), a similar refrain ties in with Pauline-like pleas to acknowledge God's grace as the sole provenance of his correspondents' artistic gifts.[319]

Yet, even these poems seemingly inspired by an ascetic disavowal of art are, on closer examination, dense with praise for their recipients' output, which in those years was often increasingly redirected towards religious and devotional subjects. Behind the emphasis on the

[316] See Pirotti 1971 (as in fn. 221), p. 42. For Pirotti, Varchi in the early 1560s "era occupato sempre più da pensieri di religione" and "non componeva sonetti che non fossero d'argomento 'spirituale,'" and see esp. pp. 194–195: "Ormai vecchio e stanco e scevro di giovanili illusioni, il Varchi vede la caducità, l'inanità delle cose terrestri a cui in altri tempi ha donato il cuore, e stretto dal rimorso per i peccati commessi, cerca e trova rifugio nella speranza della redenzione cristiana." Some internal elements help us clarify the chronology of some of these poems. For the exchange with Benvenuto Cellini, which can be dated to ca. 1562, see my discussion in Cellini 2014 (as in fn. 7), p. 216. The spiritual sonnet that Varchi addressed to Vasari has a *terminus post quem* of May 1561, when Bernardo di Francesco Puccini (the "Puccin" of l. 13) was designated *provveditore generale* of the Uffizi project and started overseeing the construction of the building (see the entry on the site by Antonio Godoli in: Conforti, Funis, De Luca, and Acidini Luchinat 2011 [as in fn. 247], p. 258, and Vasari 2012 [as in fn. 7], p. 79). The *terminus post quem* for Varchi's sonnet to Vincenzo Danti is most probably the end of 1562, when the sculptor's brother Egnazio (alluded to in l. 10) moved to Florence and entered the service of Duke Cosimo (see Francesco Paolo Fiore, Danti, Vincenzo, in: *DBI* 32, Rome 1986, pp. 667–673).

[317] See Petrarch, *Triumphus Mortis*, I 85–90: "Miser chi speme in cosa mortal pone / (ma chi non ve la pone?), e se si trova / a la fine ingannato è ben ragione. / O ciechi, el tanto affaticar che giova? / Tutti tornate a la gran madre antica, / e 'l vostro nome a pena si ritrova." On the Italian spiritual poetry of the age, see esp. Stefano Carrai, *L'usignolo di Bembo: un'idea della lirica italiana del Rinascimento*, Rome 2006, pp. 123–135.

[318] The reference here is to the passage of the canto in which Dante the pilgrim has an exchange with the miniaturist Oderisi da Gubbio: "'Oh!', diss'io lui, 'non se' tu Oderisi, / l'onor d'Agobbio e l'onor di quell'arte / ch'alluminar chiamata è in Parisi?'. // 'Frate,' diss'elli, 'più ridon le carte / che pennelleggia Franco Bolognese; / l'onore è tutto or suo, e mio in parte. // Ben non sare' io stato sì cortese / mentre ch'io vissi, per lo gran disio / de l'eccellenza ove mio core intese. // Di tal superbia qui si paga il fio; / e ancor non sarei qui, se non fosse / che, possendo peccar, mi volsi a Dio. // Oh vana gloria de l'umane posse! / com' poco verde in su la cima dura, / se non è giunta da l'etati grosse! // Credette Cimabue ne la pittura / tener lo campo, e ora ha Giotto il grido, / sì che la fama di colui è scura.'"

[319] For the source of this theme, see esp. *Corinthians* 1:12: "There are different kinds of gifts, but the same Spirit distributes them."

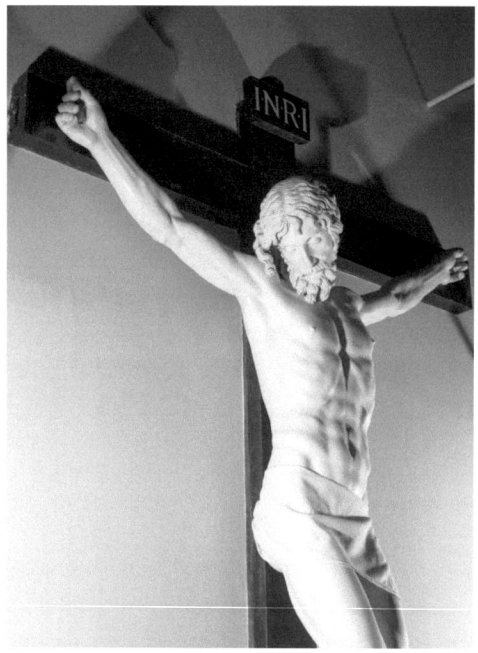

11 Benvenuto Cellini, *Crucifix*, marble, 1556–1562, Monasterio de San Lorenzo, El Escorial.

sacrifice of he who "'n tanti strazii e pene / il viver nostro al suo morir prepose" in his sonnet to Cellini (*Benvenuto, il tempo è che queste cose*: Appendix, no. 52, ll. 7–8) it is not difficult, for example, to detect a reference to the strongly Christocentric spiritual sensibility the artist had expressed in his marble crucifix of 1556–1562 (Fig. 11).[320] Meanwhile, the fact that Varchi never stopped having an active interest in the artistic life of the times is clear from the second quatrain of his sonnet to Bronzino, which alludes to a recent "bell'opera" in which Alessandro Allori had immortalized the humanist's features (l. 5): the work in question is a likeness of Varchi in Allori's fresco *Christ's Dispute with the Doctors* in the Montauto chapel of the Santissima Annunziata (1560–1564), which has just recently been identified (Table III).[321]

---

[320] A Christocentric sensibility also underpins many of the poems that the artist penned during his two terms of detention for assault and sodomy in the Florentine jail of the Stinche (1556 and 1557): see my commentary in Cellini 2014 (as in fn. 7), pp. 3–52.

[321] The hypothesis was first proposed by Pilliod 2001 (as in fn. 249), pp. 176–177. Pilliod writes that along with such prominent intellectuals and artists as Pier Vettori, Don Vincenzio Borghini, Bartolomeo Ammannati, Agnolo Bronzino, and Pontormo, "it seems likely that other prominent figures in mid-sixteenth-century Florence are present in the portrait gallery in Allori's Montauto *Christ among the Doctors*. One such individual would have been Benedetto Varchi." Still, Pilliod concluded that "comparison of several portraits of Varchi with the men in the painting produces no convincing candidate." In light of the painting's restoration (completed in 2010), which brought to light the inscription "Benedetto Va‹r›chi" on the cape of a figure standing next to the effigies of Don Vincenzio Borghini, Pier Vettori, and Isidoro Montauto in the left part of the fresco, Geremicca

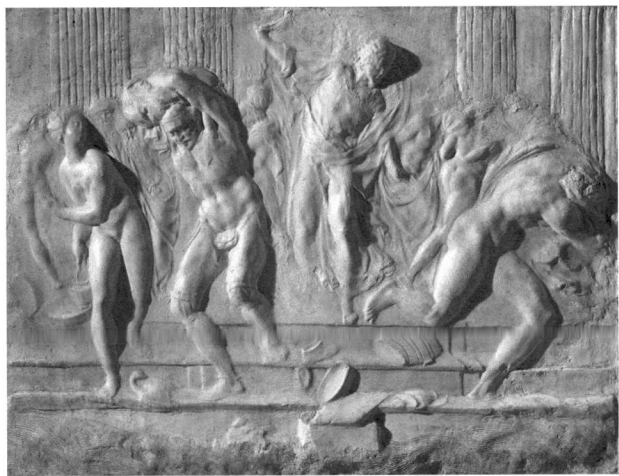

12 Vincenzo Danti, *Christ Expelling the Moneylenders from the Temple*, cast, c. 1555–1560, Perugia, Galleria Nazionale dell'Umbria.

Considering the many references in these poems to his correspondents' professional activity, it is also reasonable to interpret the sonnet to Vasari as a sort of crypto-celebration of the ducal commissions the artist was pursuing in the early 1560s: the mention of works of "squadra" and "pennel" that the were pleasing "chiaro Puccin" (ll. 12–13) is likely an allusion to Vasari's frescoes at Palazzo Vecchio and his plans for the Uffizi building – whose construction the architect and engineer Bernardo Puccini had been overseeing since May 1561.[322] It is more difficult to tell whether references to specific artistic creations hide behind the compositions penned for Bartolomeo Ammannati, Domenico Poggini, and Vincenzo Danti. In the sonnet to Danti (*Ben mi credea, dopo mie tali e tante*: Appendix, no. 62), however, it is probable that Varchi's exhortation to give thanks to God and to impart "potenza" and "fortezza" to "chi nacque per noi, visse e morio" (ll. 12–14) alludes to the motifs the sculptor was treating in works like his *Flagellation* (now at the Nelson-Atkins Museum in Kansas City) and *Descent from the Cross* (now at the National Gallery in Washington, DC) from 1559, or more probably in his lost relief with an energic *Christ Expelling the Moneylenders from the Temple*, of which only a cast is preserved (ca. 1555–1560; Fig. 12).[323]

2017 (as in fn. 121), pp. 98–99, has conclusively identified the humanist's portrait. For more on Allori's *Disputa*, see the following chapter.

[322] See *supra*, fn. 316.

[323] On these works, see David Summers, The Chronology of Vincenzo Danti's First Works in Florence, in: *Mitteilungen des Kunsthistorischen Institutes in Florenz* 16.2 (1972), pp. 185–198; Giovan Battista Fidanza, *Vincenzo Danti (1530–1576)*, Florence 1996, pp. 73 and 75–76; as well as the entries by Marco Campigli and the essay by Charles Davis, La 'Madonna del Monasterio degl'Angeli': Danti e l'ambiente intorno a Benedetto Varchi, tra la quiete fraterna e la stanza dei 'Sonetti spirituali', in: Charles Davis and Beatrice Paolozzi Strozzi (eds.), *I grandi bronzi del Battistero: l'arte di Vincenzo Danti, discepolo di Michelangelo*, Florence 2008, pp. 356–361 and 165–203, with further bibliography.

In these late sonnets, then, Varchi does not stop leaving traces of his ongoing interest in the Florentine arts scene, despite systematically exhorting detachment from the earthly prospect of artistic fame. It is in this regard interesting to note the different ways in which the artists he addressed declined to adopt the radically penitential tones that were typical of this genre of poetry. Only Bronzino echoed the disregard for human activity that permeated Varchi's *proposta* (*Ma ben nel farsi ogn'hor vile, e minore*: Appendix, no. 56): appealing to his friend as if to a spiritual guide, the painter emulated his rebuke of all efforts aimed at achieving earthly greatness, presenting such preoccupations as mistakes that could lead to perdition the very individuals who in engaging them had hoped to rise above,[324] and described himself and Alessandro Allori ("chi meco, ancor che 'n Dio, troppo accrescete": l. 11) as unworthy of esteem and in need of Varchi's moral assistance. While such an apparent disavowal of the rationale of art is an *unicum* among the artists' replies to Varchi's sonnets, Vincenzo Danti's response contains similar notes of contrition. In the sonnet *Beate colpe, che di tali e tante* (Appendix, no. 61), the sculptor presented himself as a sinner in want of prayer from the addressee, who had undergone a spiritual awakening from the slumber of sin, was fully in the grace of God and committed to producing devout writings.[325] Praise of Varchi the religious poet is instead the keystone of a partial reclamation of human endeavor in the poems of Benvenuto Cellini and Domenico Poggini. In the latter's *Ben so che la mondana e folta schiera* (Appendix, no. 63), in particular, Poggini's response to Varchi recognizes the existence of many snares on man's path to eternal salvation, and yet argues in favor of the value of mundane achievements. The notion that every incarnated soul is free, during its earthly existence, to act in a way that will determine its otherworldly destiny (ll. 5–8) is key to asserting the legitimacy of the terrestrial practice of virtue and of efforts to achieve fame and glory, viewed as endeavors dear to God and roads to the heaven.

In the context of this dialectic between the apparent disavowal of art and the assertion of its grand mission, Vasari's two replies to Varchi's *proposta* are especially significant. The first is a coherent argument for the supreme dignity of his work as a painter and architect (*Varchi, io cognosco ben l'ingegno e l'arte*: Appendix, no. 58). While in the quatrains Vasari acknowledged his debt to God for all of his artistic talent and claimed that he, with his poor spirit, aspired to nothing more than celestial glory, in the tercets he respectfully took his distance from Varchi's sonnet. He emphasized that pursuing a path of artistic refinement was an enterprise that could lead many people to eternal salvation, if the art produced was religious. Working at the time as an architect for the Uffizi construction site, he also argued that the creation of buildings using measures and squares was one of the noblest activities to which a man could strive, a pursuit that made it possible to both "ornare il mondo" and "al ciel far salita." A similar rationale underpins his second sonnet in response to Varchi (*Com'a tristo nocchier governi e sarte*: Ap-

---

[324] He also elaborated on similar notes of detachment in his burlesque production. Compare, for instance, the considerations of his *Capitolo dello starsi* (Bronzino 1988 [as in fn. 6], p. 378, ll. 175–177), which invokes the Creator while also "advocating withdrawal from the world" (Brock 2002 [as in fn. 6], p. 306): "Una vitetta quieta s'elegga, / cercando a chi ci fece, esser accetto: / questo si cerchi sol, questo si chiegga."

[325] For a more extensive treatment of Danti's exchange with Varchi see Proctor 2013 (as in fn. 307), pp. 201–204.

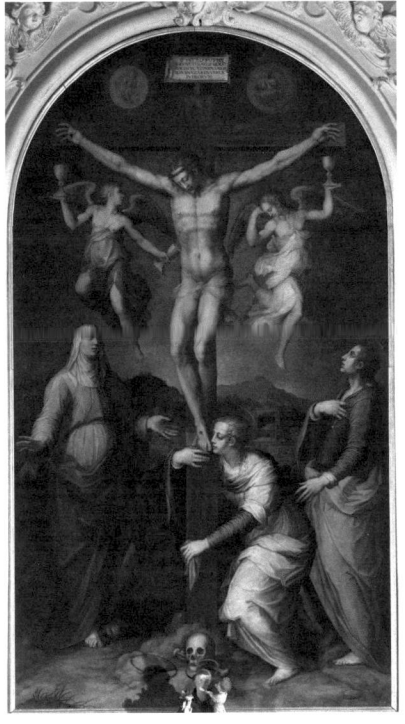

13 Giorgio Vasari, *Crucifixion*, oil on panel, 1562–1563, Florence, Santa Maria del Carmine, Chapel of the Crucifix.

pendix, no. 59). Here Vasari acknowledged that, in order to leave behind his mundane toils, he had emulated his spiritual guide Varchi in deciding to abandon pagan, mythological themes and to paint only Christ and his redeeming sacrifice on the cross (ll. 2–8). In some ways these words presage Bartolomeo Ammannati's mea culpa in his famous *Lettera agli Accademici del Disegno* (1582), where the sculptor would repudiate his earlier pagan-themed works,[326] and at the same time declare a change of direction in Vasari's visual output. While not entirely forsaking non-religious pictorial subjects, which he would use for example when decorating his Florentine house in Borgo Santa Croce, in his service for Cosimo and his private commissions alike Vasari became in this period one of the Florentine artists most representative of a new Counter-Reformation sensibility in painting. During the same period as these sonnets, for example (1562–1563), he painted the *Deposition of Christ with Mary, saints Cosma and Damiano, an angel and the symbols of the Passion*, commissioned by the duke for a chapel of the Medici villa at Poggio a Caiano, and a *Crucifixion*, commissioned by Matteo and Simone Botti for the Chapel of the Crucifix of Santa Maria del Carmine in Florence (Fig. 13). Similar

---

[326] In the letter, the sculptor famously condemned as immoral his past production of "statue ignude, Fauni e cose simili," as well as his *Neptune* fountain and the *Hercules* he had created for Marco Mantova Benavides in Padua (the "Gigante" and "Colosso" in the text, for which see Barocchi 1960–1962 [as in fn. 147], 3, pp. 119 and 122).

to the *Sonetti spirituali*, which combine an apparent *contemptus mundi* with ongoing interest in the earthly perspective of art, such devotional, pathos-infused images were obviously also informed by non-otherwordly aspirations.[327] Thus, when the final tercet of the sonnet *Com'à tristo nocchier governi e sarte* reveals that Vasari's decision to dedicate all his visual work to Christ ("fia mia disegno / Cristo": ll. 13–14) would be repaid with "gloria infinita," it is difficult to tell whether the phrase refers to celestial bliss or rather the mundane fame which (the *Vite* argued) was always tenaciously pursued by the finest professional artists.[328] For that matter, religious art and the refurbishment of several churches in Florence were increasingly the main opportunity for local artists of the 1560s and '70s to intercept commissions from the duke and the eminent families with ties to the Medici, and were therefore the terrain that most whetted the ambitions of those painters, sculptors, and architects.[329]

---

[327] On the paintings, see the entry by Matilde Simari in: Conforti, Funis, De Luca, and Acidini Luchinat 2011 (as in fn. 247), p. 172, and Daniele Rapino (ed.), *La* Crocifissione *di Giorgio Vasari nella chiesa di Santa Maria del Carmine a Firenze: studi e restauro*, Florence 2012, pp. 9–13. A different, less ascetic aesthetic sensibility characterizes Vasari's altarpiece for Alessandro Strozzi's altar in Santa Maria Novella. In the work, *Christ Crucified according to the Vision of Saint Anselm* (1567), "l'artista […] non sa resistere alla tentazione del virtuosismo e dell'artificio scenico, alla 'varietà' e alla 'fierezza,' alle scenografie spettacolari e altisonanti. In questo modo il pittore […] cercava di distinguersi dagli altri artisti, i quali invece indirizzavano il loro stile verso una narrazione più semplice, priva di astrazioni e artifici. Per Vasari un registro più sommesso e austero, quasi 'neopiagnone,' concentrato sul significato devozionale e teologico del tema rappresentato si confaceva a dipinti di formato più piccolo, destinati ad ambienti privati e circoscritti" (quotation from Elena Capretti's entry in: Cristina Acidini Luchinat and Giacomo Pierazzoli [eds.], *Ammannati e Vasari per la città dei Medici*, Florence 2011, p. 127).

[328] Compare, for instance, the author's words in the general *Proemio* of the Giuntina (Vasari 1967–1997 [as in fn. 74], 1, p. 9): "Soleano gli spiriti egregii in tutte le azzioni loro, per uno acceso desiderio di gloria, non perdonare ad alcuna fatica, quantunche gravissima, per condurre le opere loro a quella perfezzione che le rendesse stupende e maravigliose a tutto il mondo."

[329] For a broad-ranging assessment of new trends in Florentine artistic patronage after the Council of Trent, see Marcia B. Hall, *Renovation and Counter-Reformation: Vasari and Duke Cosimo in S.ta Maria Novella and S.ta Croce, 1565–1577*, Oxford 1979. The book takes Vasari's renovations of the churches of Santa Maria Novella and Santa Croce under the aegis of Duke Cosimo as the main focuses of its analysis, while also investigating (esp. pp. 29–30) how Vasari's prominent role within the recently founded Accademia del Disegno allowed him to have most commissions for new altar-pieces in the two churches allocated to younger academicians who were also his assistants, such as Giovanni Stradano, Giovan Battista Naldini, Girolamo Macchietti, Jacopo Coppi, and Alessandro del Barbiere. In the context of these works, which were largely executed between 1565 and 1577, Bronzino received the commission to paint the altarpiece for the Gaddi Chapel in Santa Maria Novella, while his associates Santi di Tito and Alessandro Allori "were excluded from early commissions" (ibid., p. 29.) On Vasari's interventions in the two churches, see also Claudia Conforti, *Vasari architetto*, Milan 1993, pp. 209–214.

Between Praise and Vituperation

The poetic triumph of the *Perseus*

In his autobiography, Benvenuto Cellini wrote a detailed, nostalgic account of the acclaim his *Perseus* (Fig. 14) received at its first public unveiling in the spring of 1554. He specified that it was Duke Cosimo who asked for the statue to be displayed, before the final polish was carried out, for the judgment of the Florentine public, who then expressed its enthusiasm for the sculpture in an unstoppable flow of laudatory poems. After mentioning the many sonnets and Greek and Latin compositions that the humanists of the Studium of Pisa affixed to the wooden structure that protected the work, Cellini reported that it was mostly the praise of other artists working in the ducal milieu that encouraged him in his struggles with the Florentine court and gave him hope that his relations with Cosimo would finally improve.[330] In what he described as a contest to come up with the highest praise, the accolades that stood out came from Jacopo Pontormo (possibly in the form of oral, improvised verse),[331] and above all from Bronzino. In addition to appending next to the bronze what Cellini claimed were "several"

---

[330] A selection of the Latin and vernacular compositions that humanists and artists wrote in praise of the *Perseus* was published as an appendix to the 1568 edition of Cellini's *Trattati* on goldsmithing and sculpture. More complete editions of this poetic production, preserved in the artist's manuscripts in the Biblioteca Riccardiana in Florence as well as in the original codex of the *Trattati* (Venice, Biblioteca Nazionale Marciana, ms. 5134), can be found in Benvenuto Cellini, *Vita di Benvenuto Cellini, orefice e scultore fiorentino*, ed. Francesco Tassi, 3 vols., Florence 1829, 3, pp. 455–493, and idem, *I trattati dell'oreficeria e della scultura novamente messi alle stampe secondo la originale dettatura del codice Marciano. Si aggiungono i discorsi e i ricordi intorno all'arte; le lettere e le suppliche; le poesie*, ed. Carlo Milanesi, Florence 1857, pp. 403–414. Against the backdrop of this lyrical triumph, two contemporary compositions criticizing the *Perseus* have come down to us: for the texts, which are the work of the satirical poet Alfonso de' Pazzi, see *infra*, fn. 449. For broad-ranging introductions to Renaissance encomiastic verse on artworks and their creators, see especially Arduino Colasanti, Gli artisti nella poesia del Rinascimento. Fonti poetiche per la storia dell'arte italiana, in: *Repertorium für Kunstwissenschaft* 27 (1904), pp. 193–220; Giovanni Agosti, Scrittori che parlano di artisti, tra Quattro e Cinquecento in Lombardia, in: Barbara Agosti, Giovanni Agosti, Carl Brandon Strehlke, and Marco Tanzi (ed.), *Quattro pezzi lombardi (per Maria Teresa Binaghi)*, Brescia 1998, pp. 39–93, and Luciano Patetta, La celebrazione degli artisti e degli architetti negli scritti poetici e letterari del Rinascimento, in: Luisa Secchi Tarugi (ed.), *Lettere e arti nel Rinascimento. Atti del X convegno internazionale (Chianciano-Pienza, 20–23 luglio 1998)*, Florence 2000, pp. 603–624.

[331] In the context of the passage quoted below, "diceva" might refer to extemporaneous performances of poems sung in the piazza (see *GDLI*, s.v. "dire"), as well as to the "message" of written compositions such as those by Bronzino, Poggini and other artists. On the importance of oral performance in the production and dissemination of Italian Renaissance poetry, see esp. Degl'Innocenti, Richardson, and Sbordoni 2016 (as in fn. 24).

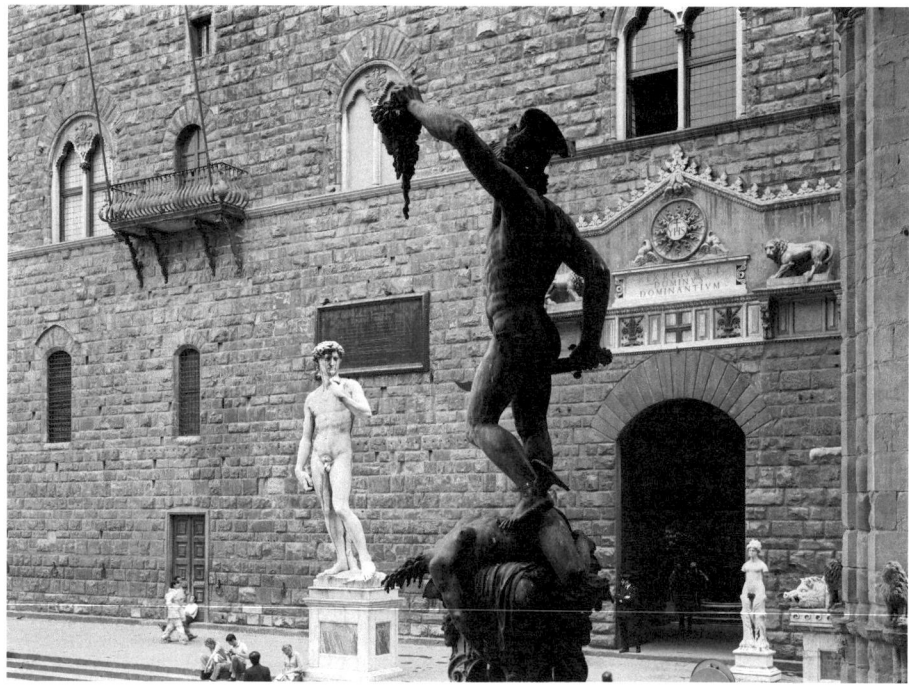

14 Benvenuto Cellini, *Perseus*, bronze, 1545–1554, Florence, Loggia dei Lanzi.

poems praising the work, Bronzino had the young Alessandro Allori deliver those lyrics to the sculptor's home:[332]

> Quando il Duca intese che tutta la mia opera del Perseo si poteva mostrare come finita, un giorno la venne a vedere, et mostrò […] che la gli sattisfaceva grandemente; et […] disse: 'Con tutto che questa opera ci paia molto bella, ell'ha anche a piacere ai popoli; sì che, Benvenuto mio, innanzi che tu gli dia la ultima sua fine io vorrei che per amor mio tu aprissi un poco questa parte dinanzi, per un mezzo giorno, alla mia Piazza, per vedere quel che ne dice 'l popolo; perché e' non è dubbio che da vederla a questo modo ristretta, al vederla a campo aperto, la mostrerrà un diverso modo […];' il giorno seguente io la scopersi. Or sì come piacque a·dDio, subito che la fu veduta, ei si levò un grido tanto 'smisurato in lode della detta opera, la qual cosa fu causa di consolarmi alquanto. Et non restavano i popoli continuamente di appicare alle spalle della porta […] inmentre che io le davo la sua fine. Io dico che 'l giorno medesimo che la si tenne parecchi ore scoperta, e' vi fu appiccati più di venti sonetti, tutti in lode smisuratissime della mia opera; dappoi che io la ricopersi, ogni dì mi v'era appicati quantità di sonetti, et di versi latini et versi greci; perché gli era vacanza allo Studio di Pisa, tutti quei eccellentissimi dotti e gli scolari facevano a·ggara. Ma quello che mi dava maggior contento con isperanza di maggior mia salute inverso 'l mio Duca, si era, che quegli dell'arte, cioè scultori et pittori, ancora loro facevano a·ggara a chi meglio diceva. Et infra gli altri, quale io stimavo più, si era il valente pittore Iacopo da

---

[332] Only two sonnets by Bronzino in praise of the *Perseus* are documented: for a discussion of the texts, see *infra*. The painter's choice to have his compositions also delivered to Cellini's house is consistent with a typical pattern of manuscript circulation of encomiastic verse in Renaissance Italy: see Richardson 2009 (as in fn. 18), p. 108.

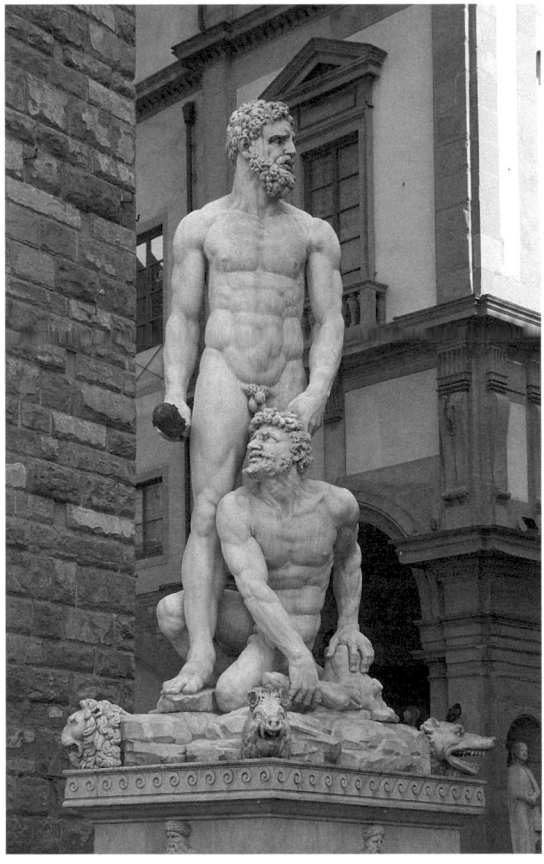

15 Baccio Bandinelli, *Hercules and Cacus*, marble, 1534, Florence, Piazza della Signoria.

Puntorno, et più di lui il suo eccellente Bronzino, pittore, che non gli bastò il farvene appiccare parecchi, che egli me ne mandò per il suo Sandrino insino a casa mia, i quali dicevano tanto bene, con quel suo bel modo, il quale è rarissimo, che questo fu causa di consolarmi alquanto.[333]

Next, Cellini described how Cosimo, despite these manifestations of enthusiasm, had maintained that the Florentines would surely find fault with the *Perseus* once the statue was completed. He claimed his patron was coached into saying so by Baccio Bandinelli, who had maliciously reminded the duke of the criticism the local public had hurled at Andrea del Verrocchio's *Incredulity of Saint Thomas* and even at Michelangelo's *David*, as well as the "in-

---

[333] Cellini 1996 (as in fn. 23), pp. 706–708 (*Vita* 2.90). While the author's account of the creation of the *Perseus* is among the best-known parts of his autobiography, the present passage has not received significant scholarly attention. Among the few exceptions to this general neglect are the studies of Ferrone 2003 (as in fn. 257), p. 100, which discusses the passage in the context of a broader study of Benedetto Varchi's compositions for contemporary Florentine artworks, and Maddalena Spagnolo, Poesie contro le opere d'arte: arguzia, biasimo e ironia nella critica d'arte del Cinquecento, in: Chrysa Damianaki, Paolo Procaccioli, and Angelo Romano (eds.), *Ex marmore: Pasquini, pasquinisti, pasquinate nell'Europa moderna*, Manziana 2006, pp. 321–354, p. 331.

finiti et vituperosi sonetti" that two decades earlier had greeted his own *Hercules and Cacus* (Fig. 15).³³⁴ After recounting the city's fresh acclaim upon the definitive unveiling of the sculpture, Cellini's reconstruction of an exchange with Cosimo gave him the opportunity to remark what a special honor it was for the *Perseus* to receive praise from the finest artists and, above all, laudatory poems like Bronzino's:

> Allora io dissi: "Signor mio, Vostra Eccellenzia illustrissima m'ha dato facultà che io ho fatto innella maggiore Scuola del mondo una grande et dificilissima opera, la quale mè stata lodata più che opera che mai si sia scoperta in questa divinissima Scuola; et quello che più mi fa baldanzoso sì è stato, che quegli eccellenti uomini, che conoscono et che sono dell'arte, comè 'l Bronzino pittore, questo uomo s'è affaticato et m'ha fatto quattro sonetti, dicendo le più iscelte et gloriose parole, che sia possibil di dire; et per questa causa, di questo mirabile uomo, forse s'è mossa tutta la città a così gran romore […].³³⁵

These passages from Cellini's autobiography are based on a single theme. Displayed to the audience of Florence in order to gauge its opinion, the *Perseus* had been met with universal acclaim. It had therefore managed to harvest that genre of poetic praise from literati that many Renaissance authors equated, along the lines of classical *auctoritates*, with the utmost consecration of an artwork – the blessing that would bestow immortal glory on the artist's perishable creations of painting or sculpture.³³⁶ But the *Perseus*, its creator argued, had achieved an even more difficult honor: the compliments and even the tribute in verse of "eccellenti uomini, che conoscono e che sono dell'arte," which he presented as the ultimate proof of his bronze's exceptional quality.

---

³³⁴ Cellini 1996 (as in fn. 23), p. 709 (*Vita* 2.91).
³³⁵ Ibid., pp. 724–725 (*Vita* 2.97).
³³⁶ Horace famously claimed (*Odes* 3.30.1) that his poetry was a more enduring monument than any commemorative work in bronze, while in the *Naturalis Historia* (34.57), Pliny the Elder argued that Myron owed his fame more to the many epigrams that had celebrated his bronze *Cow* than to his activity as a sculptor: "Myronem Eleutheris natum, Hageladae et ipsum discipulum, bucula maxime nobilitavit celebratis versibus laudae, quando alieno plerique ingenio magis quam suo commendatur." Along the same lines is the author's reasoning on Apelles's *Venus Anadyomene*. For Pliny, the painting became extraordinarily famous thanks to the Greek poems that praised it, even though these poems' quality was in itself superior to that of the artwork (ibid., 35.91–92): "Venerem exeuntem e mari […], quae anadyomene vocatur, versibus Graecis tali opere dum laudatur, victo sed inlustrato." For the diffusion of the motif of poetry as the ultimate medium for immortalizing its subject, as opposed to the more perishable products of the visual artists, see especially Shearman 1992 (as in fn. 267), pp. 115–116 (with a discussion of other relevant classical sources on the topic, such as *Greek Anthology* 16.125 and Martial, *Epigrams* 7.84) and Pich 2010 (as in fn. 264), pp. 103 and 131. In the Italian Renaissance, a most influential treatment of this theme was Ludovico Ariosto's "gallery" of the most famous painters and sculptors from antiquity (*Orlando Furioso* 33.1), whose creations only survived in the works of ancient writers; comparable reasoning is found in Pietro Bembo's *Prose della volgar lingua* (3.1), published in 1525, which asserted that both ancient and modern artists such as Myron, Vitruvius, and Leon Battista Alberti owed a great part of their fame to their own or someone else's writings. In several passages of both editions of the *Vite*, Vasari echoed such considerations, particularly when discussing the immortal renown that great poets (e. g., Petrarch, Ariosto, Pietro Bembo, and Giovanni della Casa) had bestowed on the painters they had commemorated in verse (respectively Simone Martini, Dosso Dossi, Giovanni Bellini, and Tiziano). For more extensive treatments of this motif, see Pozzi and Mattioda 2006 (as in fn. 80), pp. 331–335; Lina Bolzoni, Citazioni letterarie nella Giuntina: per una mappa delle loro funzioni, in: Alessandro Nova and Luigi Zangheri (eds.), *I mondi di Vasari: accademia, lingua, religione, storia, teatro*, Venice 2013, pp. 141–159, pp. 150–154; and Diletta Gamberini, Nel nome del fratello: Pietro Vasari e la memorializzazione poetica dell'arte nell'Italia di fine Cinquecento, in: *Italique* 22 (2019), pp. 81–104.

Although studies have not yet acknowledged this, the value Cellini places on this special category of encomiastic verse for his *Perseus* ties in with a long-running critical debate of the early modern period: namely, the discussion on what kind of audience was supremely qualified to judge art, and what specific competencies were possessed by the different types of beholders. Before examining the poems with which painters, sculptors, and medalists of Medicean Florence showered praise on the *Perseus*, it is therefore important to clarify the ideological assumptions on the basis of which they could rise to the function Cellini's autobiography assigns them, also because this will allow to point out the inconsistencies between the Renaissance theoretical debate on the legitimacy of aesthetic judgment and the reality of the judgment these compositions imparted.

General public, connoisseurs, and artists: categorizing the sculpture's audience

In Cellini's account, the *Perseus* had fully passed a kind of critical assessment that was very much alike to the one Leon Battista Alberti had recommended for new paintings in his *De Pictura*. The phrase the duke used to insist that the bronze be publicly displayed before receiving its finishing polish ("per vedere quel che ne dice 'l popolo"), for example, corresponds to Alberti's appeal to painters to submit their unfinished works for the judgment of the general public. In line with Pliny's example of Apelles, who would hide behind his paintings so he could hear the opinions of passersby,[337] Alberti urged painters not to fear the baseless invective of the envious and the overcritical, and instead to accept negative comments as a necessary means of identifying and correcting any defects in their creations. But an insistence on subjecting artworks to popular opinion was not the only common denominator between the *De Pictura* and the rhetorical construction of these passages from Cellini's autobiography: another factor they shared was the stated contrast between the opinions of a professionally indistinct audience and the judgment of those with specific qualifications in the visual arts. According to Alberti, this latter was the kind of appraisal the artist should most take to heart, because it was more apt to tell him how to improve his work. Here is how those recommendations sounded in the Italian translation by Lodovico Domenichi (Venice, 1547), which made the *De Pictura* accessible to a much wider audience than could have read it in the original Latin:[338]

---

[337] Compare Pliny, *Naturalis Historia* 35.84: "Idem perfecta opera proponebat in pergula transeuntibus atque, ipse post tabulam latens, vitia quae notarentur auscultabat, vulgum diligentiorem iudicem quam se praeferens." On the early modern textual fortune of the most famous anecdote related to this story, that of Apelles, who listens to a shoemaker's critique of one of his paintings, see Christiane J. Hessler, 'Ne supra crepidam sutor!' [Schuster, bleib bei deinem Leisten!]: Das Diktum des Apelles seit Petrarca bis zum Ende des Quattrocento, in: *Fifteenth-Century Studies* 33 (2008), pp. 133–150, and McHam 2013 (as in fn. 77), p. 323.

[338] Alberti's vernacular redaction of the *De Pictura*, preserved in three manuscripts from the fifteenth century, does not seem to have known any substantial circulation in the Renaissance: see Lucia Bertolini, Sulla precedenza della edizione volgare del *De Pictura* di Leon Battista Alberti, in: Marco Santagata and Alfredo Stussi (eds.), *Studi per Umberto Carpi: un saluto da allievi e colleghi pisani*, Pisa 2000, pp. 181–210, p. 181, as well as

mentre che si fa il lavoro s'ha da lasciare entrare et udire tutti quei che vogliono vedere, perché in questo modo l'opera del pittore sarà grata a la moltitudine. Non rifiuti dunque la censura, e 'l giudizio de la moltitudine, mentre ch'egli anchora può sodisfare a le opinioni. Dicono ch'Apelle era usato di stare ascoso dietro a una tavola, acciochè quei che vedevano più liberamente potessero dire, et egli più honestamente ascoltare i difetti de l'opera sua. Voglio dunque che i nostri pittori odano spesso, et domandino in palese a ogniuno quel che loro ne pare: perciochè questo giova a certe cose, et a guadagnare anchora la gratia al pittore […]. Et alhora non s'ha d'haver paura che il giudicio de i biasmatori, et de gli invidiosi possa alcuna cosa levare a le lode del pittore. Perciochè chiara et celeberrima è la lode del pittore, et l'opra istessa ben dipinta ha testimonio seco, che ragiona. Ascolti dunque ogniuno, et fra sé medesimo consideri egli prima, et emendi la cosa. Finalmente, quando havrà ascoltato ogniuno, ubbidisca a quei che più sanno.[339]

Such a hierarchy produced tensions that had existed even in ancient times regarding which viewers were fully entitled to judge the creations of painters, sculptors, and architects. As David Summers has noted, Alberti derived mainly from Cicero the notion that even amateurs had a natural ability to assess art.[340] In *De Oratore*, for example, Cicero had argued that the wide gap separating the expert from the ignorant in the capacity to produce, in music and other pursuits, was reduced to a tiny difference in the ability to judge the fruits of such production.[341] On the same basis, he argued in *De Officiis*, painters, sculptors, and poets chose to have their creations judged by a generic audience, which was still perfectly capable of pointing out deficiencies.[342]

Francesco Furlan, In familiæ patriæque absentia ossia d'illegittimità e sradicamento, in: Francesco Furlan, Gabriel Siemoneit, and Hartmut Wulfram (eds.), *Exil und Heimatferne in der Literatur des Humanismus von Petrarca bis zum Anfang des 16. Jahrhunderts: L'esilio e la lontananza dalla patria nella letteratura umanistica dal Petrarca all'inizio del Cinquecento*, Tübingen 2019, pp. 139–159, p. 147.

[339] Alberti 1547 (as in fn. 87), c. 20r (corresponding to Alberti 1972 [as in fn. 87], 3.62, pp. 104–105).

[340] See David Summers, *The Judgment of Sense: Renaissance Naturalism and the Rise of Aesthestics*, Cambridge 1987, pp. 129–134.

[341] Cicero, *De Oratore* 3.197: "Mirabile est, cum plurimum in faciendo intersit inter doctum et rudem, quam non multum differat in iudicando." In commenting on the passage as a fundamental source for the theory of *giudizio* that Alberti developed in both *De pictura* and *De architectura*, Summers 1987 (as in fn. 340), p. 134 also calls attention to a passage in Quintilian that runs along the same lines. In *Institutio oratoria* 9.4.116, the author argues that the expertise that is required for understanding the principles of rhetorical composition is not necessary in order to perceive the beauty of an oration: "docti rationem componendi intelligunt, etiam indocti voluptatem." Quintilian's reasoning, however, did encompass the idea that the most perfect judgment of every *ars* was that of the *artifices*: see *infra*, fn. 344.

[342] Cicero, *De Officiis* 1.147: "Ut enim pictores et ii, qui signa fabricantur, et vero etiam poetae suum quisque opus a vulgo considerari vult, ut, si quid reprehensum sit a pluribus, id corrigatur, iique et secum et ab aliis, quid in eo peccatum sit, exquirunt, sic aliorum iudicio permulta nobis et facienda et non facienda et mutanda et corrigenda sunt." Alberti's dependence upon this passage from *De Officiis* is discussed in Summers 1987 (as in fn. 340), p. 133. We might however add that a different passage of Cicero's work provided a less favorable representation of the generic audience's capacity of artistic *giudizio*, arguing that the *imperiti* are often unable to detect the specific deficiencies of a painting and are therefore prone to celebrating even shoddy artworks (*De Officiis* 3.15): "quod idem in poematis, in picturis usu venit in aliisque compluribus, ut delectentur imperiti laudentque ea, quae laudanda non sint, ob eam, credo, causam, quod insit in iis aliquid probi, quod capiat ignaros, qui quidem, quid in una quaque re vitii sit, nequeant iudicare; itaque, cum sunt docti a peritis, desistunt facile sententia."

The primacy the *De Pictura* attributed to the opinion of those "che più sanno" nevertheless tempered these Ciceronian positions with those of other ancient *auctoritates*.[343] Indeed, Alberti reinterpreted the idea of a universal capacity for artistic judgment without ignoring the viewpoint, condensed into aphorisms and maxims in various works of Quintilian, Pliny the Younger, and Saint Jerome, that only artists were entitled to judge art.[344] Some sections of Book 35 of Pliny the Elder's *Naturalis Historia* were also relevant in this regard, such as the passage that praised the painter Nicophanes for a certain accuracy, which only artists could appreciate.[345] Of similar tone was the Plinian anecdote of the famous dispute between Apelles and Protogenes over which of the two had drawn the finest line. Reporting how Protogenes, admitting defeat, had left to posterity the proof of Apelles's superiority, Pliny added that the painting astounded all who saw it, but artists most of all. The comment suggested that a professional audience was better able to understand Apelles's virtuosity – a concept Giorgio Vasari would develop in many anecdotal stories of his *Vite*.[346]

---

[343] Compare Alberti 1972 (as in fn. 87), 3.62, p. 104: "Deinde cum omnes audiverit, peritioribus pareat."

[344] Compare respectively Quintilian, *Institutio oratoria* 12.10.50: "at quod libris dedicatum in exemplum edatur, id tersum ac limatum et ad legem ac regulam conpositum esse oportere, quia veniat in manus doctorum et iudices artis habeat artifices," Pliny the Younger, *Epistulae* 1.10.4: "Quamquam ne nunc quidem satis intellego; ut enim de pictore sculptore fictore nisi artifex iudicare, ita sapiens non potest perspicere sapientem," and Jerome, *Praefatio commentarii in Isaiam* 16.1: "Felices essent artes, si de illis soli artifices iudicarent." For a classical treatment of the humanistic distinctions between informed and uninformed beholders see Michael Baxandall, *Giotto and the Orators: Humanist Observers of Painting in Italy and the Discovery of Pictorial Composition, 1350–1450*, Oxford 1971, pp. 59–62. On the relevance of Quintilian's statement for Quattrocento artist-writers such as Piero della Francesca, see Hessler 2014 (as in fn. 14), p. 453, which also devotes some attention to Petrarch's reworking of these ideas in *De remediis utriusque fortunae*. A brief introduction to sixteenth-century debates on the issue of the legitimacy of artistic judgment is provided by Ben Thomas, "Artefici" and "huomini intendenti:" Questions of Artistic Value in Sixteenth-Century Italy, in: Gabriele Neher and Rupert Shepherd (eds.), *Revaluing Renaissance Art*, Aldershot 2000, pp. 43–56, esp. pp. 42–46. Two more thorough treatments of the topic are the excellent works by Spagnolo 2008 (as in fn. 193), and Fabian Jonietz, *Das Buch zum Bild: Die "Stanze nuove" im Palazzo Vecchio, Giorgio Vasaris "Ragionamenti" und die Lesbarkeit der Kunst im Cinquecento*, Berlin 2017, pp. 236–240.

[345] Pliny the Elder, *Naturalis Historia* 35.137 ("diligentia, quam intellegant soli artifices"). In his will, Petrarch stated that he had decided to leave a *Madonna and Child* by Giotto that was in his possession to Francesco I da Carrara, emphasizing the painting's qualities with the following words: "Cuius pulchritudinem ignorantes non intelligunt, magistri autem artis stupent." On this note, see esp. Baxandall 1971 (as in fn. 344), p. 60; David Cast, *The Delight of Art: Giorgio Vasari and the Traditions of Humanistic Discourse*, University Park, PA 2009, p. 162, n. 40, and McHam 2013 (as in fn. 77), pp. 75–76 and 364, which highlights the significant circulation of Petrarch's will in Florentine humanistic circles.

[346] Pliny the Elder, *Naturalis Historia* 35.83: "At Protogenes victum se confessus in portum devolavit hospitem quaerens, placuitque sic ea tabulam posteris tradi omnium quidem, sed artificum praecipuo miraculo." The relevance of artists' judgments on the work of fellow painters or sculptors is the idea underpinning another anecdote by the same author. Pliny recounted (see ibid. 34.53) the competition among bronze sculptors working in the temple of Artemis in Ephesus, stressing how these artists cast their own votes in order to establish who had created the best statue of an Amazon: "Et in certamen laudatissimi, quamquam diversis aetatibus geniti, quoniam fecerant Amazonas, quae cum in templo Dianae Ephesiae dicarentur, placuit eligi probatissimam ipsorum artificum, qui praesentes erant, iudicio, cum apparuit eam esse, quam omnes secundam a sua quisque iudicassent." For the influence of these notions on the *Vite* compare Cast 2009 (as in fn. 345), p. 26: "Vasari had many comments about looking at art in different ways, some responses being recognized as better than

During the approximately 130 years separating Alberti's treatise from Cellini's autobiography, other artists had determined that there was an irremediable contradiction between the opinions of artists and those of nonspecialist beholders. Using the categories Pierre Bourdieu defined in analyzing the context in which Flaubert wrote his *Sentimental Education*, we could say in fact that these Renaissance painters and sculptors were well aware of the often conflicting nature of the two fundamental principles of hierarchy at work in every cultural field: the external hierarchization, which tends to equate the preeminence of an artist or writer with his or her success with a lay public, and the internal hierarchization, which attributes maximum consecration to professionals whose excellence is recognized by their peers, and who in fact derive part of their prestige from their refusal to meet the demands of the masses.[347]

At the turn of the sixteenth century, for example, Leonardo da Vinci had insisted on the irreconcilable discrepancy between the judgments of artists and of all other viewers. In one of the precepts of his *Libro di Pittura*, he remarked that painters wishing to please unqualified observers wound up producing works deficient in those very aspects (e.g. the capacity to foreshorten figures and to give them *rilievo*) that most distinguished an excellent painting. In Leonardo's view, the artist's goal was therefore to win the approval of his most capable colleagues, as only they could make an informed assessment of his creation.[348] In Francisco de

---

others, some more knowing, some more experienced. Always the praise of artists (another idea from Pliny) is taken to be the sign of truest worth." The centrality of the motif of "intra-artistic judgement" (the judgment that Renaissance painters, sculptors, and architects extended towards the works of their peers) in the framework of the *Vite*, as related to Vasari's own enterprise as a historiographer, is the object of a compelling analysis in Chiara Franceschini, Giudizi negativi e stime d'artista nel mondo di Vasari, forthcoming in: *Mitteilungen des Kunsthistorischen Institutes in Florenz* 63.1 (2021).

[347] Compare esp. Pierre Bourdieu, *The Rules of Art*, trans. Susan Emanuel, Stanford 1996, p. 217: "According to the principle of external hierarchization in force in the temporally dominant regions of the field of power (and also in the economic field) – that is, according to the criterion of temporal success measured by indices of commercial success (such as print runs, the number of performances of plays, etc.) or social notoriety (such as decorations, commissions, etc.) – pre-eminence belongs to artists (etc.) who are known and recognized by the 'general public.' On the other hand, the principle of internal hierarchization, that is, the degree of specific consecration, favours artists (etc.) who are known and recognized by their peers and only by them (at least in the initial phase of their enterprise) and who owe their prestige, at least negatively, to the fact that they make no concessions to the demand of the 'general public.'"

[348] Leonardo Da Vinci, *Libro di pittura: edizione in facsimile del Codice Urbinate Lat. 1270 nella Biblioteca Apostolica Vaticana*, ed. Carlo Pedretti, transcr. by Carlo Vecce, 2 vols., Florence 1995, 1, p. 174 (precept n. 59; ca. 1500–1505): "Se tu, pittore, te ingegnerai di piacer alli primi pittori, tu farai bene la tua pittura, perché sol quelli sono che con verità ti potran sindicare. Ma se tu vorrai piacere a quelli che non son maestri, le tue pitture aranno pochi scorti, e poco rilevo, o movimento pronto, e per questo mancarai in quella parte di che la pittura è tenuta arte eccellente, cioè del fare rilevare quel ch'è nulla in rilevo." On this passage, see, among others, the considerations of André Chastel, *Arte e umanesimo a Firenze al tempo di Lorenzo il Magnifico: studi sul Rinascimento e sull'umanesimo platonico*, It. trans. Renzo Federici, Turin 1964, p. 292; Ernst H. Gombrich, The Leaven of Criticism in Renaissance Art, in: Charles S. Singleton (ed.), *Art, Science, and History in the Renaissance*, Baltimore 1967, pp. 3–42, p. 20; Summers 1987 (as in fn. 340), p. 134; Pietro C. Marani, *La Vergine delle Rocce della National Gallery di Londra: maestro e bottega di fronte al modello. Quarantaduesima lettura vinciana*, Florence 2003, and Maddalena Spagnolo, Vasari e le 'difficultà dell'arte,' in: Maddalena Spagnolo and Paolo Torriti (eds.), *Percorsi vasariani tra le arti e le lettere*, Montepulciano 2004, pp. 89–108, p. 92.

Hollanda's account, Michelangelo similarly proclaimed "that a man cannot attain excellence if he satisfy the ignorant and not those of his own craft."[349] These instances of radical devaluation of the judgment of non-artists also found fierce advocates in Cosimo's Florence. In his response to Varchi's survey on the paragone, Francesco da Sangallo, for example, complained about the credibility afforded to the opinions of a public with no specific training in the arts, not to mention often morally compromised by malevolence and envy.[350] Nor was this position the sole prerogative of painters and sculptors wishing to claim for their own professional ranks a monopoly on the legitimate judgment of artworks, and more generally on all critical discussions of artistic matters. Two years after Varchi's poll, similar ideas would be voiced by Anton Francesco Doni, the versatile Florentine writer who had also developed some skill in the arts of drawing by keeping frequent company with the likes of Baccio Bandinelli and Giovann'Angelo Montorsoli.[351] Assuming the literato's *Due Lezzioni* as his implicit target of attack, Doni's book *Il Disegno* staged a dialogue in which Art and Nature reaffirmed the concept that only sculptors and painters were qualified to speak of sculpture and painting.[352]

---

[349] Francisco de Hollanda, *Diálogos em Roma (1538): Conversations on Art with Michelangelo Buonarroti*, ed. Grazia Dolores Folliero-Metz, Heidelberg 1998, p. 75. On this claim, see David Summers, *Michelangelo and the Language of Art*, Princeton, NJ 1981, p. 506, n. 4. The belief that an artist's willingness to "make concessions" to the aesthetics of non-experts would result in a shoddy work was already articulated in an ancient anecdote by Aelian (*Historical Miscellany*, ed. and transl. N. G. Wilson, Cambridge, MA 1997, p. 458 [14.8]): "Polyclitus made two sculptures of the same subject, one of which satisfied popular taste, and the other the rules of his art. He satisfied popular taste in this way: he made alterations and adjustments to suit each visitor, following all their suggestions. He then exhibited both pieces. One was universally praised, the other ridiculed. Polyclitus responded by saying: 'But you have made the one that you criticise, and I the one you admire.'"

[350] See the sculptor's letter in Varchi and Borghini 1998 (as in fn. 80), p. 76: "Che ce n'è pure assai che fanno professione d'intendere e lodano e biasimano, come se proprio de l'arte fussino, e per avere veduto quattro medagliucce e imparato qualche vocabolo de l'arte fanno tanto con varie adulazione." On these polemical accents, see the insightful considerations of Thomas 2000 (as in fn. 344), pp. 46–47; Spagnolo 2008 (as in fn. 193), p. 117; and Jonietz 2017 (as in fn. 344), p. 237. The painter and illuminator Giulio Clovio expressed a less disputatious but comparable view in the fourth part of de Hollanda 1998 (as in fn. 349), p. 122: "In Italy there is not a lord or gentleman who will not greatly praise and exalt a noble picture when he sees it, with a knowledge of all its parts equal to that of a painter himself; often I am astonished at the clear knowledge and understanding they reveal. But there are also gentlemen who presume to criticize painting foolishly and find fault with what they cannot understand."

[351] On Doni's artistic training and friendship with the two sculptors, see esp. Mario Pepe, Svolgimenti nella concezione del disegno in Anton Francesco Doni: dalla *Diceria* al Montorsoli del 1546 al trattato del 1549, in: Anna Forlani Tempesti and Simonetta Prosperi Valenti Rodinò (eds.), *Disegno e disegni: per Luigi Grassi*, Rimini 1998, pp. 123–132, and Carlo Alberto Girotto, Le accademie di Anton Francesco Doni, in: Carla Chiummo, Antonio Geremicca, and Patrizia Tosini (eds.), *Intrecci virtuosi: letterati, artisti e accademie tra Cinque e Seicento*, Rome 2017, pp. 27–37. On the genesis of his *Disegno* and the artistic ideals that the book endorses see Stefano Pierguidi, Il *Disegno* di Doni e la disputa sul "paragone": alle origini dell'Accademia del Disegno, in: Giovanna Rizzarelli (ed.), *Dissonanze concordi: temi, questioni e personaggi intorno ad Anton Francesco Doni*, Bologna 2013, pp. 199–213, with further references.

[352] Doni's line of reasoning in the *Disegno* partially overlaps with the attack that Alfonso de' Pazzi conducted against the academic lecture on the paragone by penning the sonnet *V.(archi), che v[u]oi tu dir della pittura*. In the text, one of the numerous vitriolic compositions that the author addressed to Varchi, the poet criticized Varchi's decision to discuss subjects of which he had neither direct knowledge nor experience. For insightful discussions of Doni's treatment of the problem of *giudizio*, see Thomas Frangenberg, *Der Betrachter: Studien*

Against the backdrop of these debates, the position Cellini adopted in his account of the reception of his *Perseus* was for once relatively moderate. While embracing Alberti's stance that expert and inexpert judgments of the artwork carried different weights, he distanced himself from the Cinquecento artists who had drastically downplayed the validity of artistic judgment by the general public. The issue the *De Pictura* did not address, however, was exactly how the opinions of those two categories of viewers were different. To borrow Cellini's phrasing, Alberti's work did not in other words clarify precisely where the viewpoint of "eccellenti uomini, che conoscono e che sono dell'arte" was superior to that of the ordinary citizens or educated humanists who had praised the *Perseus* in verse. A few years before Cellini penned his autobiography, another treatise had nonetheless provided an answer to that kind of question which other art theorists would later acknowledge and develop.

In Lodovico Dolce's *Dialogo della pittura* (1557), the characters of Pietro Aretino and Giovan Francesco Fabrini held a lengthy debate on the legitimacy of aesthetic judgment by the different categories of a painting's audience, triggered by Fabrini's wondering "se uno, che non sia pittore, è atto a far giudicio di pittura."[353] The character of Aretino argued for the validity of the artistic opinions of a general public, but especially of those literati whom the Torrentiniana had described as "intendenti" (connoisseurs) for their ability to deeply comprehend ("intendere") qualities such as the style, proportions, order, and *decorum* of artworks.[354] According to this view, the only discriminant separating the *giudizio* of these connoisseurs, trained in the study of antiquities and the creations of the best contemporary artists, from that of practicing painters was the "cognizione di certe minutezze, di che non avrà contezza un altro che pittore non sia."[355] In any case, Aretino continued, echoing the refrain inferred

---

zur florentinischen Kunstliteratur des 16. Jahrhunderts, Berlin 1990, pp. 68–69, and Spagnolo 2008 (as in fn. 193), pp. 118–119 (which also analyzes Pazzi's sonnet on the paragone debate). The paradox that these ideas were articulated in writing by a non-practitioner of the visual arts did not escape the author, who on the contrary ironically underscored it (see his letter to Paris Bordone in Anton Francesco Doni, *Disegno del Doni, partito in più ragionamenti* […], Venice 1549, c. 54v: "Che si dirà adunque havendo dato in publico quest'opera, che tratta della Scoltura et Pittura, che per mia fede non saprei fare un beveratoio da pulci con lo scarpello, né col pennello una testa […] di grillo; et pure […] n'ho cicalato non so quante carte"), and argued that his familiarity with many excellent artists gave him the right to write about artistic subjects.

[353] Dolce in Barocchi 1960–1962 (as in fn. 147), 1, p. 154.

[354] See ibid., 1, p. 156: "Ma io non intendo in generale della moltitudine, ma in particolare di alcuni belli ingegni, i quali, avendo affinato il giudicio con le lettere e con la pratica, possono sicuramente giudicar di varie cose, e massimamente della pittura." The term "intendenti" had already been used by Lorenzo Ghiberti's *Commentarii* (Ghiberti 1998, as in fn. 85, 3.3.2, p. 108: "[…] dagli intendenti fu tenuta maravigliosa opera") and by Lorenzo de' Medici in a 1498 letter to Giovanni Lanfredini, and it was adopted by Vasari in several passages from the *Vite* to designate connoisseurs (see, for the latter source, Cast 2009 [as in fn. 345], p. 57). One such example is the description of the reception of Giotto's mosaic of the *Navicella* in Saint Peter's Basilica, "la quale fu sì maravigliosa et in quel tempo di tal disegno, d'ordine e di perfezione, che le lode universalmente dàtele dagli artefici e da altri intendenti ingegni meritamente se le convengono" (Vasari 1967–1997 [as in fn. 74], 2, p. 106 [1550]).

[355] Dolce in Barocchi 1960–1962 (as in fn. 147), 1, p. 157. Among the classical *auctoritates* that had maintained that a divide separated the audience that was able to detect the most minute details of an artwork from the spectators who had a more generic understanding of it, Plutarch (*Moralia: On Love of Wealth. On Compliancy* […], transl. by Phillip H. De Lacy and Benedict Einarson, Cambridge, MA 1959, vol. 7, p. 373 [*De genio Socratis*,

from *De Oratore*, those specialized technical skills that were so vital to producing art were of marginal importance in judging it.[356]

At the time Cellini was writing about the reception of his *Perseus*, the prevailing opinion in Florence, too, was that the fundamental difference between artists and connoisseurs in their ability to evaluate painting and sculpture lay in a full understanding of technical details of its execution. Specifically, there was much emphasis on the fact that only practitioners could comprehend the material or manufacturing problem – the "difficultà," according to a critical category borrowed from Quintilian – that the artwork had managed to solve.[357] Unsurprisingly, however, different kinds of viewers would attribute a very different importance to this sort of understanding. For Cellini, the "bellissimi segreti e mirabili modi" of the goldsmith's and sculptor's arts were a dimension so fundamental as to inspire his ambitious technical-di-

1]) was particularly explicit: "[…] a painter once gave me, in the form of a comparison, no bad description of those who view pictures. Spectators who are laymen and without instruction in the art resemble, he said, those who greet a large company with a single salutation, whereas cultivated and artistic spectators resemble men who have a private word of welcome for everyone they meet; for the general impression that the first obtain of the performance is inaccurate and as it were a mere sketch; whereas the others use their critical judgement for a separate scrutiny of each detail, and thus allow nothing well or poorly executed to pass without a look or word of recognition."

[356] Dolce in Barocchi 1960–1962 (as in fn. 147), 1, p. 157: "Ma queste [the technical *minutezze* that only the painters know], se ben saranno importanti nell'operare, saranno elle poi di poco momento nel giudicare." On the relevance of these considerations in the context of Renaissance art theory, see Anthony Blunt, *Artistic Theory in Italy, 1450–1600*, Oxford 1956, p. 84: "One point is discussed explicitly in Dolce which had only been indirectly dealt with by earlier writers, namely, the right of the layman who does not himself paint to judge in questions of art. Earlier writers of the Renaissance seem to have assumed that the educated layman was competent to judge everything except the technical part of a painting, but Dolce expresses this opinion clearly. This view, based on the idea that painting is a learned pursuit and the sister of poetry, is again typical of Dolce's humanist outlook."

[357] For the relevance of processes of problem solving for conceptions of artistic evolution, see esp. Ernst H. Gombrich, The Renaissance Concept of Artistic Progress and Its Consequences, in: *Actes du XVIIme Congrès International d'histoire de l'art*, La Haye 1955, pp. 291–307, and idem 1967 (as in fn. 348). The idea that only the practitioners of the visual arts were able to appreciate an artwork's novelty and technical difficulty was addressed in Quintilian, *Institutio oratoria* 2.13.10, which also emphasized how such aspects represented paramount qualities of artistic creation: "quid tam distortum et elaboratum quam est ille discobolos Myronis? si quis tamen, ut parum rectum, improbet opus, nonne ab intellectu artis abfuerit, in qua vel praecipue laudabilis est illa novitas ac difficultas?" In his autobiography, Cellini explained the nature of the technical difficulty implied by the creation of the *Perseus*, a difficulty which a layman such as Duke Cosimo would not have been able to grasp. Recounting how his patron had voiced his doubts that Medusa's head could ever be realized in view of its elevated position above Perseus's body, the sculptor rehearsed his own explanatory response (Cellini 1996 [as in fn. 23], pp. 663–664 [*Vita* 2.74]): "'Or vedete, Signor mio, che se Vostra Eccellenzia illustrissima avessi quella cognizione dell'arte, che lei dice di avere, la non arebbe paura di quella bella testa che lei dice, che la non venissi; ma sì bene arebbe da aver paura di questo piè diritto, il quale si è quaggiù tanto discosto […] perché la natura del fuoco nonn-è l'andare all'ingiù, et per avervelo a spignere sei braccia in giù per forza d'arte, per questa viva ragione io dico a Vostra Eccellenzia illustrissima che gli è inposibile che quel piede venga; ma ei mi sarà facile a rifarlo." In the third dialogue of Doni's *Disegno*, the characters of Nature and Art discuss the difficulties in the casting of bronze statues (see esp. Doni 1549 [as in fn. 352], cc. 18v–19v), and Art observes: "Per mia fede che queste pratiche sono difficili a intendere ma molto più difficilissime a farle, che a ragionarne; come si può considerare da gl'infiniti accidenti, che da tanta vehemenza di fuoco; la quale è tanto spaventevole, che molti si perdono d'animo."

dascalic text *Due Trattati* (1565–1568) – an undertaking, he claimed, that was possible only for someone who practiced both arts first-hand.[358] Cellini then argued that possessing such skills was also the prerequisite for participating in debates like Varchi's paragone between painting and sculpture: in a bellicose sonnet he wrote when the dispute flared up again, triggered by the city's arrangements for Michelangelo's funeral in 1564, he declared for example that the only individuals entitled to express an opinion on the matter were the "dotti in tal arte." Those Cellini branded as "pedanti" and "filosofanti," who had acquired humanistic knowledge from books, would not understand the specific value of the practice of sculpture, which he linked to direct familiarity with the materials and tools of the trade.[359] In this case his target was the lieutenant of the Accademia del Disegno, don Vincenzio Borghini, who with Vasari had conceived of the iconographic program for Michelangelo's exequies that symbolically affirmed the primacy of painting over sculpture. For his part, in the *Selva di Notizie* (1564), Borghini argued that connoisseurs were in fact the only individuals culturally qualified to express opinions in artistic debates, except for discussions "delle particularità del'arte, di certe dificultà e particulari intelligenzie de l'arti" pertaining to the direct practice of painting and sculpting.[360] He recognized painters and sculptors as exclusively entitled to discuss such matters, which he nonetheless brushed off as almost insignificant "sottigliezze."[361]

---

[358] See the author's introduction to the manuscript of the *Trattati* (Benvenuto Cellini, *Opere*, ed. Giuseppe Guido Ferrero, Turin 1980, p. 593; the passage was not included in the 1568 edition, the result of Gherardo Spini's radical revision and ideological censorship of the original text): "Veduto come mai nessuno si sia messo a scrivere i bellissimi segreti e mirabili modi che sono in nella grand'arte della oreficeria, i quali non stava bene a scriverli né a filosafi, né ad altre sorte di uomini, se non a quegli che sono della stessa professione: e perché una tal cosa non abbia mai mosso nessun altro uomo, forse la causa è stata che quegli non essere stati tanto animosi al ben dire sì come e' sono stati al ben fare pronti. Avendo io considerato un tale errore di tali uomini; ed io, per non stare in cotal peccato, mi sono messo arditamente a una cotale bella impresa."

[359] See Cellini 2014 (as in fn. 7), p. 258 (sonnet 89, ll. 1–6): "Nessun può dar iuditio, se non quelli / che son dotti in tal arte e non pedanti; / se fussin bene anchor saper il valor delli scarpelli, // squadre, trapani, mazzuoli, e ceselli, / e cera, e terra, archipenzol, quadranti" (the edition [ibid., pp. 258–260] offers a detailed discussion of these lines). This poetic celebration of the tools of the artist's trade found a visual correspondence in the ideographic alphabet, each letter of which corresponds to objects such as a compass, a chisel, and so on, that he drew in two of his proposals for a new seal of the Accademia del Disegno. In the letter containing one of these proposals (formerly in the private collection of Piero Calamandrei; see Charles Avery and Susanna Barbaglia, *L'opera completa del Cellini*, Milan 1981, pp. 99–100, as well as Victoria von Flemming, Gezähmte Phantasie. Cellinis Entwürfe für das Akademie-Siegel, in: Nova and Schreurs 2003 [as in fn. 53], pp. 59–98, p. 63), he suggested that the institution should adopt the new alphabet in its communications as a sign of "quei propii strumenti con che noi hoperiamo queste gentile et tanto necessarie arte."

[360] Quoted from Varchi and Borghini 1998 (as in fn. 80), p. 101. Borghini's lengthy and polemical argument regarding the literati's right to discuss painting and sculpture seems to be reminiscent, among other sources, of Dionysius of Halicarnassus (*On Thucydides*, transl. W. Kendrick Pritchett, Berkeley / Los Angeles / London 1975, p. 3): "For men who do not possess the same skill as Apelles, Zeuxis, Protogenes, and other famous artists, are not thereby prevented from judging the art of these men."

[361] Borghini in Varchi and Borghini 1998 (as in fn. 80), p. 101. On this passage, see the enlightening considerations of Frangenberg 1990 (as in fn. 352), pp. 47–58 (esp. 54), and Eliana Carrara, Vasari e Borghini sul ritratto: gli appunti pliniani della *Selva di notizie*; ms. K 783.16 del Kunsthistorischen Institut di Firenze, in: *Mitteilungen des Kunsthistorischen Institutes in Florenz* 44 (2000, but: 2001), pp. 243–291, p. 281, n. 37.

Though they disagreed about the importance of knowing the technical details of the artworks' execution, Cellini and Borghini did share the conviction that this type of discernment was the artist's prerogative. Considering how these theoretical coordinates guide the sculptor's narration of the triumphal reception with which the lay audience and artists alike had greeted his *Perseus*, it would be reasonable to expect the poems celebrating that work to reflect their authors' specific level of hands-on competence. To put it differently, we could expect the lyrics composed by painters and sculptors active in the Medicean scene to express that sort of technically astute judgment founded in direct artistic practice that Cellini viewed as the supreme recognition of his sculpture's quality. As we will see, the type of praise these texts offered only touched on such aspects tangentially, through references mediated by their codified literary form. Still, in several cases the encomium did not fail to mention the common professional extraction of acclaimer and acclaimed, or more generally to develop motifs at least partially irreducible to the topoi at the basis of the celebratory poems by humanists and other viewers not practiced in the arts of drawing.

Artists' poems in praise of the *Perseus*

Of the compositions celebrating Cellini's most famous bronze, four or five by artists active in the Medicean scene have survived.[362] In addition to two sonnets by Bronzino, which according to Cellini were part of a more extensive set of encomiastic lyrics by the painter, we have poems by the goldsmiths, medalists, and sculptors Domenico Poggini and Cesare da Bagno. The unveiling of the *Perseus* was also most likely the occasion behind the sonnet by the bronze-caster and sculptor Zanobi Lastricati, who does not mention the statue explicitly but echoes the celebratory tones with which other Florentine poet-artists praised it.[363] Because these compositions were written by artists who in many cases had been Cellini's students or

---

[362] The poems under consideration are preserved in the main manuscript testimonies of Cellini's poetic corpus, codices Riccardiano 2353 and 2728 of the Biblioteca Riccardiana in Florence. Cellini also included three of them – the two sonnets by Bronzino and the one by Domenico Poggini – in the anthology of the *Poesie toscane et latine sopra il Perseo statua di bronzo, e il Crocifisso statua di marmo fatte da messer Benvenuto Cellini* that was published as an appendix to the first edition of the *Due trattati*: Cellini 1568 (as in fn. 255), cc. Riiiv, Rivr, Siv.

[363] The earliest sculptural work that can be attributed to Zanobi Lastricati is a bronze *Venus Anadyomene* (ca. 1543), now in the Jardìn de la Isla of Aranjuez, not far from Madrid. Between 1555 and 1560, Zanobi realized his first marble sculpture, a *Hunter* now in the Boboli Garden: on his artistic career, see esp. Marco Spallanzani, The Courtyard of Palazzo Tornabuoni-Ridolfi and Zanobi Lastricati's Bronze Mercury, in: *Journal of the Walters Art Gallery* 37 (1978), pp. 6–21; Gino Corti, Il testamento di Zanobi Lastricati, scultore fiorentino del Cinquecento, in: *Mitteilungen des Kunsthistorischen Institutes in Florenz* 32 (1988), pp. 580–581; Antonia Boström, A New Addition to Zanobi Lastricati. *Fiorenza* or the *Venus Anadyomene*: The Fluidity of Iconography, in: *The Sculpture Journal* 1 (1997), pp. 1–6; Alessandro Nesi, Tra classicismo e modernità: un'identificazione e una proposta per gli esordi di Zanobi Lastricati, in: *Bollettino d'arte* 114 (2000), pp. 79–86; idem, Zanobi Lastricati tra i cantieri medicei fiorentini e la cattedrale di Pistoia, in: Nicoletta Lepri, Simona Esseni, and Maria Camilla Pagnini (eds.), *Giorgio Vasari: tra capitale medicea e città del dominio*, Florence 2012, pp. 69–78, and idem, Piero Frizzi, and Chiara Piani (eds.), *Il Cacciatore di Zanobi Lastricati nel Giardino di Boboli: storia e restauro*, Florence 2013.

assistants, or who, like Bronzino, were bound to him by a commonality of aesthetic ideals, they satisfied first and foremost one of the main purposes of the texts that circulated in manuscript form in the early modern period: the function "of bonding groups of like-minded individuals into a community, sect or political faction, with the exchange of texts [...] serving to nourish a shared set of values and to enrich personal allegiances."[364] Through poetic praise of the *Perseus,* in other words, these poems delineated fellowships of artistic taste and practice, affirming their authors' observance of the kind of figurative language the sculpture embodied.

The form of that observance, however, differed from author to author. Let us first consider Cesare da Bagno's epigram *Dovea ben porsi di Perseo il segno* (Appendix, no. 66). Unique among the compositions praising Cellini's bronze, it is the Italian version of a Latin poem composed for the work's unveiling, the elegiac couplets *Debuerat Persei signum coelestia poni* by the now nearly unknown Andrea Anguli.[365] Descendent of a wealthy family that had populated its native Bagni di Santa Maria (a small village in the Apennines) with doctors and notaries, Cesare was making use of his linguistic skill as a translator from humanistic Latin that was not common among the period's artists.[366] What is especially noteworthy, however, is the genre of poetry he chose to translate into the vernacular: Anguli's text, whose opening lines interpreted the sculpture as the earthly transposition of the constellation the hero Perseus became upon his death, was more complimentary of Cosimo than of Cellini. Anguli did note that Florence was indebted to the sculptor for a work that opened the veil of heavens and revealed the forms inscribed in the sky, but only after emphasizing that the city was even more beholden to the ruler who with his generous patronage ("con l'oro") had made the bronze *Perseus* possible.

---

[364] The quote is from Harold Love's study of scribal communities in early modern England (Love, *The Culture and Commerce of Texts: Scribal Publication in Seventeenth-Century England*, Amherst, MA 1998, p. 177), which did not specifically refer to the role of manuscript circulation of poetry in building communities of the "like-minded." The most illuminating analysis of the latter phenomenon in Renaissance Italy is provided by Richardson 2009 (as in fn. 18), pp. 95–152; fundamental insights also come from the wide-ranging analysis in Giunta 2002 (as in fn. 11), even though this book is mostly dedicated to medieval Italian poetry. For the commonality of aesthetic ideals between Cellini and Bronzino, consider the expressions of praise with which the sculptor always referred to the painter; for instance, in his letter in response to Varchi's poll on the paragone debate: "Oggi si vede Michelagnolo essere il maggior pittore che mai ci sia stato notizia [...], solo perché tutto quello ch fa di pittura lo cava dagli studiatissimi modegli fatti di scultura; né so cognoscere chi più s'apressi oggi a tale verità d'arte, che il virtuoso Bronzino. Veggio gli altri immergersi infra fioralisi e dividerli con molte composizione di vari colori, qual sono uno ingannacontadini" (Varchi and Borghini 1998 [as in fn. 80], p. 82).
[365] Anguli must have been in contact with prominent humanists of the age, since he was the author of a Latin epitaph published in Paolo Giovio, *Elogia virorum [bellica virt]ute illustrium [...]*, Florence 1551, p. 171.
[366] On the biography and artistic activity of Cesare da Bagno, alias Cesare di Niccolò di Mariano Federighi, see Toderi and Vannel 2000 (as in fn. 261), 2, p. 539; Philip Attwood, *Italian Medals c. 1530–1600 in British Public Collections*, 2 vols., London 2003, 1, pp. 141–142; and esp. Martha McCrory, Cesare Federighi Da Bagno: Medalist, Gem Engraver and Sculptor in the Workshop of Cellini, in: Lars R. Jones and Louisa C. Matthew (eds.), *Coming About... A Festschrift for John Shearman*, Cambridge, MA 2001, pp. 227–234. In her study of Pontormo's cultural profile, Cécile Beuzelin has argued that "a large number of artists and craftsmen didn't know Latin or only had an empirical knowledge of it" (Beuzelin 2013 [as in fn. 232], p. 74), as demonstrated by such authors as Lorenzo Ghiberti and Leonardo.

Glorification of the magnanimous commissioning of a painting or sculpture is a well-established motif in Renaissance poetry on art,[367] but the fact that Cesare da Bagno chose to translate a poem centered on this theme may at least in part indicate an attempt to win Cosimo's favor through a medium different from his usual profession. The artist's local standing, at the time, was in fact quite precarious. After training in Tribolo's workshop and winning some ducal commissions to complete works left unfinished upon the master's death (1550), Cesare had worked as a salaried assistant of Cellini just as the *Perseus* was nearing completion: from February to April of 1554 he was thus paid as a sculptor for his work on the *Liberation of Andromeda* relief.[368] Once he completed that assignment, however, he was left without professional prospects and eager to join the already crowded roster of sculptors, medalists, and goldsmiths in Cosimo's service. As he himself would recall years later, writing a heartfelt letter to the duke beseeching re-employment, no manifestation of his loyalty to the Medicis or of his many talents – including, evidently, as translator of Anguli's verse panegyric – earned him Cosimo's interest or favor. The lack of ducal commissions, Cesare stressed, had forced him to leave Florence and eventually settle in Milan:[369] and from there he was never to return, falling victim to a rival's ambush in 1564.

While Cesare da Bagno with his translation aimed to seek the favor of the *Perseus*'s patron, Agnolo Bronzino's two sonnets were more directly focused on celebrating the sculpture

---

[367] Panegyrical texts that praise the sculpture's patron rather than its creator are recurrent in one of the age's earliest and most influential collections of poems on artworks: namely, the anthology of the *Coryciana*. First published in 1524, the work collected many Latin compositions in praise of Andrea Sansovino's statue of *St. Anne with the Madonna and Child* or (to a small extent) of Raphael's fresco of the *Prophet Isaiah*, the two artworks that adorned the humanist Johann Goritz's pillar altar for the Roman church of Sant'Agostino, along with others that focused rather on the artistic ensemble's patron. On this, see Pellegrino 2003 (as in fn. 267), pp. 219, 227, and *passim*; on the poetic collection, see the critical edition by Jozef Ijsewijn, *Coryciana*, Rome 1997, as well as Phyllis Pray Bober, The *Coryciana* and the Nymph Corycia, in: *Journal of the Warburg and Courtauld Institutes* 40 (1977), pp. 223–239; Rosanna Alhaique Pettinelli, Punti di vista sull'arte nei poeti dei *Coryciana*, in: *Rassegna della letteratura italiana* 90 (1986), pp. 41–54; Giovanna Perini Folesani, Carmi inediti su Raffaello e sull'arte della prima metà del Cinquecento a Roma e Ferrara e il mondo dei *Coryciana*, in: *Römisches Jahrbuch der Bibliotheca Hertziana* 32 (1997/98, but 2002), pp. 367–407, and David Rijser, The Sculptor as Philologist: Interaction between Scholarship and the Arts in the Goritz Chapel and the *Coryciana*, Rome 1512–1527, in: Hendrix and Procaccioli 2008 (as in fn. 193), pp. 257–265. If we consider the collection of compositions on Cellini's bronze, we can see that a few Florentine poets celebrated the *Perseus* as the most splendid fruit of Duke Cosimo's patronage. For their Latin texts (Andrea Martelli's *Descendens olim superis Cellinus ab astris* and Giulio della Stufa's *Hoc quodcunque vides, Persei memorabile signum*), see Cellini 1829 (as in fn. 330), 3, pp. 483 and 485.

[368] See McCrory 2001 (as in fn. 366), p. 227. In his autobiography (2.94), Cellini recounts travelling with Cesare to Santa Maria in Bagno right after the final unveiling of the *Perseus* and meeting the Federici family there.

[369] Consider the following passage from Cesare's letter to the Duke, dated October 28, 1562 (text from McCrory 2001 [as in fn. 366], p. 233): "Servi' a Benvenuto sino al fine nell'opera del Perseo. Ma perché mai non hebbi sorte, che in quel tempo alcuno mi volesse fare un minimo favore apresso di V. Ecc.a; anchorché per me stesso usai ogni modesto modo farmi cognoscer a Quella, et all'Ill.mo Principe; con tutti gli altri suoi Ill.mi Figliuoli, con ogni opera buona, fatica, et servitù che sempre io feci, né mai imperò mi valse […]. Al fine, di poco et nulla da la buona sorte favorito, mi levai meno contento di quelle parti; racomandandomi a Dio, et all'arbirio di Fortuna, per trovare qualche altra aventura. Et così sempre assai ho travagliato la vita, sino ad hora, con bene et virtuosamente operare. Et già duoi anni sono, che pervenni qui in Milano."

itself (Appendix, nos. 67–68).³⁷⁰ The painter was, in fact, the sole poet on that occasion to whom Cellini responded in kind, as evidence of the sculptor's esteem for his fellow artist.³⁷¹ The defining features of Bronzino's second lyric (*Ardea Venere bella, e lui che 'n pioggia*), such as its particularly mannered phrasing and the fact that it proposes an alternative mythological etiology for the subject of Cellini's work, have been studied in depth,³⁷² and therefore need not be discussed in detail. Conversely, scholarship has thus far overlooked the critical categories underlying Bronzino's acclaim in the first of his poems, a sonnet (*Giovine alter, ch'a Giove in aurea pioggia*) that begins by affirming how the glory Perseus achieved through his deeds had been intensified by the statue now adorning the banks of the Arno and a setting like the Loggia della Signoria, already abounding in artistic excellence.³⁷³ Given new life by Cellini's bronze – the poet continued – the ancient slayer of monsters now exhibited valor as well as grace and beauty. In his closing lines, Bronzino directly addressed the hero with an appeal to obscure the petrifying gaze of the bewitching Medusa.

While praising a work's aesthetic value and especially its characterization as "più che mai vivo" (l. 9) are two of the most topical motifs in Renaissance poetry on art,³⁷⁴ less current is the third conceptual focus of Bronzino's encomium of the *Perseus*: his emphasis that the proud youth immortalized by Cellini displayed all of the battlefield *virtus* that Zeus's son had demonstrated in his many "alti, e gloriosi […] gesti" (ll. 3–4.) Such a constellation of ideas is noteworthy because it largely overlaps with the kind of praise the Torrentiniana reserved to Donatello to celebrate a work presented as the pinnacle of Quattrocento marble statuary. Vasari, in fact, had applauded the *Saint George* that the sculptor created for a niche in the Florentine church of Orsanmichele as a "figura […] vivissima e fierissima, nella testa della quale

---

³⁷⁰ For general introductions to Bronzino's compositions in praise of the *Perseus*, see Parker 2000 (as in fn. 6), pp. 88–91, and Geremicca 2013 (as in fn. 6), pp. 67–68.

³⁷¹ See the text and commentary of the sculptor's sonnet in Cellini 2014 (as in fn. 7), pp. 70–73.

³⁷² See Michael W. Cole, Cellini's Blood, in: *The Art Bulletin* 81 (1999), pp. 215–235, pp. 223–224. Cole emphasizes how Bronzino's sonnet calls attention to the bronze statuettes in the niches of the pedestal for the *Perseus*, while also identifying the figures of Danae and little Perseus as Venus and Cupid: "The child is thus both the desire that causes Jupiter's transformation and the warm result of Danae's fulfillment, the actual burning within her breast and the child from it, now at her side." His contribution also persuasively suggests that the second quatrain of the sonnet, which depicts Jupiter filling Danae's breast as a gold shower, might be intended to specifically evoke "Cellini's heated filling of the body with his own golden metal."

³⁷³ When the *Perseus* was unveiled, Donatello's *Judith and Holofernes* was standing in the west part of the Loggia dei Signori. Scholars have rightly emphasized how the statue was the major term of comparison for Cellini's bronze and how many contemporary poems in praise of the latter artwork addressed this comparative relationship. On this, see esp. Shearman 1992 (as in fn. 267), pp. 50–57.

³⁷⁴ Thorough discussions of the most common topoi in Renaissance poetry on art and of their grounding in ancient textual models include Marianne Albrecht-Bott, *Die bildende Kunst in der italienischen Lyrik der Renaissance und des Barock: Studie zur Beschreibung von Portraits und anderen Bildwerken unter besonderer Berücksichtigung von G. B. Marinos Galleria*, Wiesbaden 1976; Norman E. Land, *The Viewer as Poet: The Renaissance Response to Art*, University Park, PA 1994; Rebekah Jane Smick-McIntire, Vivid Thinking: Word and Image in Descriptive Techniques of the Renaissance, in: Payne, Kuttner, and Smick 2000 (as in fn. 141), pp. 159–173; Francesca Pellegrino, *La poesia sull'arte: il caso di Giovan Battista Marino nella tradizione della poesia sulle arti figurative*, PhD diss., Università degli Studi di Salerno 2003, eadem 2003b (as in fn. 267), and Pich 2010 (as in fn. 264).

si conosce la bellezza nella gioventù, l'animo et il valore nelle armi, una vivacità fieramente terribile."³⁷⁵ In echoing the aesthetic categories Vasari had used to praise Donatello's heroic statue, Bronzino's poem was also anticipating the directions Francesco Bocchi would take in developing the most detailed critique of a sculpture that Cinquecento Florence would produce. In his treatise *Eccellenza della statua del San Giorgio di Donatello Scultore Fiorentino*, completed in 1571 (though not published until 1584), Bocchi would indicate possession of the three qualities of "vivacità," "bellezza," and "costume" as the condition for considering a statue to be perfect – a perfection that in his view only Donatello and Michelangelo had truly attained.³⁷⁶ Bocchi would provide a thorough Aristotelian disquisition on these three critical categories, which he identified, respectively, as a form of vivacious movement and ability to render force and dynamism of action; as the graceful, harmonious union of parts in the human body and in its portrayal; and as the capacity to represent in exterior traits the permanent disposition of the subject's soul and not just his fleeting state of mind.³⁷⁷ The fact that Bronzino structured his homage to the *Perseus* along the same lines as Vasari's praise of the *Saint George*, according to a triad of concepts to which Bocchi's treatise would give systematicity and breadth of theoretical references, is instructive of the often profound osmosis in the second half of the Cinquecento between the languages of art criticism and of the poetry that chose paintings or sculptures as its subject. And if scholars have remarked that the celebratory *ekphraseis* of Vasari's *Vite* often drew on topoi that were very frequent in ancient and Renaissance poetic compositions

---

³⁷⁵ Vasari 1967–1997 (as in fn. 74), 3, p. 208. The author observed at the end of his *ekphrasis*: "E certo nelle figure moderne non s'è veduta ancora tanta vivacità né tanto spirito in marmo quanto la natura e l'arte operò con la mano di Donato in questo." On this description, compare Rubin 1995 (as in fn. 61), p. 324, which argues that Vasari particularly appreciated "the valiant stance" in Donatello's *St. George* and that one of those poses "also embodied meaning and character and therefore brought the material to life."

³⁷⁶ Consider Bocchi in Barocchi 1960–1962 (as in fn. 147), 3, pp. 132–133: "E comecché molti siano divenuti sommi et eccellenti, due tuttavia ce ne ha che nella scultura più degli altri si conoscono singulari, io dico Michelagnolo Buonarroti e Donatello […]. Bene fu agevole al grande intelletto di questo nobile artefice [Donatello] e contemplare nella sua mente et isprimere poi nel marmo con felice artifizio pensieri eroichi e gentili, e far quasi vivo quello che non ha vita, dar moto ove è fermezza e ridurre in colmo la virtù della scultura […]. Ma perché noi sì fatta conoscere la possiamo, innanzi che più adentro si proceda, consideriamo primamente che cose siano quelle, le quali a constituire una somma eccellenza concorrono e creano negli animi nostri non solo diletto, ma maraviglia oltre a ciò. Sono adunque tre senza più (secondo che io avviso), che una tale perfezzione deono partorire: il costume, la vivacità e la bellezza." On the aesthetic ideals that Bocchi developed in his treatise, as well as the classical models underpinning these ideals, see Moshe Barasch, Character and Physiognomy: Bocchi on Donatello's *St. George*, a Renaissance Text on Expression in Art, in: *Journal of the History of Ideas* 36 (1975), pp. 413–430; Marek Komorowski, Donatello's *St. George* in a Sixteenth-Century Commentary by Francesco Bocchi: Some Problems of the Renaissance Theory of Expression in Art, in: Juliusz A. Chrościcki (ed.), *Ars auro prior: Studia Ioanni Białostocki sexagenario dicata*, Warsaw 1981, pp. 61–66; Thomas Frangenberg, The Art of Talking about Sculpture: Vasari, Borghini and Bocchi, in: *Journal of the Warburg and Courtauld Institutes* 58 (1995), pp. 115–131; Arjan de Koomen, Aristotle's *Poetics* into Art Criticism: Francesco Bocchi in Praise of Donatello's *Saint George*, in: Hendrix and Procaccioli 2008 (as in fn. 193), pp. 89–103; Robert Williams, *Art, Theory, and Culture in Sixteenth-Century Italy: From Techne to Metatechne*, Cambridge 2010, pp. 201–212, and Lex Hermans, Going Local: Three Sixteenth-Century Florentine Views on Donatello's *St. George*, in: Joost Keizer and Todd M. Richardson (eds.), *Transformation of Vernacular Expression in Early Modern Arts*, Leiden / Boston 2012, pp. 99–122.

³⁷⁷ For these definitions, see respectively Bocchi in Barocchi 1960–1962 (as in fn. 147), 3, pp. 153, 180 and 134–135.

on art,[378] it is perhaps just as true that the exchange between the language of poetry and prose might be two-way. By borrowing Vasari's conceptual scheme, Bronzino was also able to suggest, as did other poets who wrote about the *Perseus*, that the bronze withstood the difficult comparison with the supreme art of Donatello, but implicitly shifting the axis of comparison from the *Judith and Holofernes* of Piazza della Signoria to the *Saint George* of Orsanmichele.[379]

The taste for laborious, affected phrasing that characterizes Bronzino's sonnets on the *Perseus* and that earned his recipient's admiration for those lines that "dicevano tanto bene, con quel […] bel modo, il quale è rarissimo"[380] also informs the lyric that Domenico Poggini composed for the same occasion. The syntactical and conceptual density of his sonnet *Sì come 'l ciel di vaghe stelle adorno* is, in truth, difficult to penetrate (Appendix, no. 69). Over the course of one sentence that runs for fourteen lines, Poggini set up an analogy between Cellini's act of creation and the emanative process with which – according to a neoplatonic vision of the cosmos popular since the Middle Ages – the heavens bestow their virtues onto nascent creatures. Starting with the observation that this irradiance involved all natural entities to varying degrees, he argued that the men who were more lavishly endowed with it could achieve immortality and ascend to the brightest parts of the firmament, referencing the classical myths of catasterism or the transformation of heroes like Perseus into stars (ll. 1–8). Likewise, Poggini continued, Cellini had proven the extraordinary power possessed by the star that presided over his birth, which the sculptor manifested with the outward signs ("rai") of his virtue, as well as by art and nature (ll. 9–11). Cellini had managed to do so by creating a "grande," "bella," and "leggiadra" bronze statue,[381] which Poggini praised in closing as a work that God had wished to reserve to modernity and that would earn its maker a glorious place in Heaven.

Of particular note is the distance Poggini's sonnet maintains from the limited repertoire of concepts, expressed with varying degrees of inventiveness, that are typically at the center of Renaissance poetry on art: e. g. the artwork that outdoes nature, the senses deceived by the

---

[378] See, for instance, Alpers 1960 (as in fn. 166) and Land 1994 (as in fn. 374), pp. 158–181.
[379] The motif of the paragone between Donatello and Cellini's bronzes underpins Niccolò Mochi's sonnet *Non bisogna, Cellin, che più t'industri*, which extends the paragone to all the other sculptures then in the piazza, Michelangelo's *David* and Bandinelli's *Hercules and Caccus* (Cellini 1857 [as in fn. 330], p. 410, ll. 12–14): "Te sol conosco non aver rivali, / E sei qual sole in mezzo a queste stelle / Di Michel, di Donato e Bandinello." Along comparable lines, both Paolo Mini's sonnet *Nuovo Miron, che con la dotta mano* and Benedetto Varchi's *Tu che vai, ferma 'l passo: e ben pon mente* imagine Donatello's *Judith* rejoicing in the excellence of the new statue that had been unveiled next to her (see, in order, ibid., p. 406, ll. 11–14: "Ma così bei vicin Judit ammira, // E dice: poi che 'n bronzo ancor l'un spira / Valor, e l'altra a crudeltà par desta, / Ben venut'è dal ciel chi questi feo," and p. 403, ll. 12–14: "E quella casta, che tra l'empio stuolo / L'orribil teschio al fier busto precise, / D'aver degno vicin s'allegra e vanta"). On these poems, see Shearman 1992 (as in fn. 267), pp. 53–58; on Cellini's ambition to rival Donatello's bronze, see also the passage of his *Discorso dell'architettura*, quoted *infra*.
[380] Cellini 1996 (as in fn. 23), p. 708.
[381] Poggini (l. 12) uses the verb "statuar," which specifically designates the art of bronze-casting. Compare the distinction that Varchi draws in his lecture on the paragone, based on the terminology that Pliny had used in the *Naturalis Historia* (36.15): "Plinio […] dice che l'arte della scultura, che i Latini chiamano marmoraria, fu molto innanzi della pittura e della statuaria, cioè del gittare le statue di bronzo" (Varchi and Borghini 1998 [as in fn. 80], p. 39). In the letter with which he answered to Varchi's poll on the pre-eminence of painting or sculpture, Cellini used the verb "statuare" in the same sense (ibid., p. 83).

illusionism of artistic creation, or the supremacy of the modern artists over the ancients.[382] Nor does Poggini resort to the usual tropes of the "Medusa effect." That is, his verse avoids the conceits that John Shearman identified as the most frequently used in poems about the *Perseus*, those of Medusa's petrifying gaze that would have turned into stone Michelangelo's *David* and Bandinelli's *Hercules and Cacus*, which likewise adorned the piazza.[383] Poggini instead followed a model that, in reworking various emanatist doctrines, drew a parallel between the act of artistic creation and the process of irradiance and transmission of virtues from the heavens to earthly beings. In the central section of canto 13 of Dante's *Paradiso*, Saint Thomas had illustrated the theory by which the astral influences, under divine impulse, transmit diverse qualities to creatures about to come into existence on Earth.[384] He described how the raw material of which those generated things were composed, similar to malleable wax, absorbed such influences to a greater or lesser degree and how this explained why men were born with different talents. Commonly, Dante's passage continued, the disposition of the heavens and the substance of the things created were not at the peak of perfection, thus preventing the full manifestation of the divine light that stamped at the origin that molding principle, as a sort of ideal seal. It was in this context, rich in metaphors borrowed from the art of wax modeling and sculpture, that Dante made an explicit comparison with the act of artistic creation: the creatural essence, he stated, was a kind of obstacle to achieving perfection similar to that faced by the artist, who fails to fully convey the image his mind has conceived. Even with the skill attained through years of practice, the artist described in Dante's verse has a hand that trembles when he sets out to create his work.[385]

In his sonnet, Domenico Poggini echoes not only the artistic analogy developed in Dante's dense cosmological reasoning, but all of its key syntagmas as well: the "ciel" that "discende" ("irradiates," "bestows") its virtues on creatures, and the two poles of "natura" and "arte." But how can we explain a hypotext of this kind, so uncustomary in Renaissance poetry in praise of artworks? Almost surely, the author was here following Michelangelo. In his lecture on the sonnet *Non ha l'ottimo artista alcun concetto*, Varchi had identified canto 13 of *Paradiso* as the fundamental model behind Michelangelo's reflection on the excellent sculptor.[386] The very fact that Poggini reformulated Dante's analogy between the celestial irradiating of virtues and the

---

[382] On these topoi, see esp. Pellegrino 2003 (as in fn. 267).
[383] Shearman 1992 (as in fn. 267), pp. 55–58.
[384] Dante, *Paradiso* 13.61–78: "Quindi discende a l'ultime potenze / giù d'atto in atto, tanto divenendo, / che più non fa che brevi contingenze; // e queste contingenze essere intendo / le cose generate [...]. // La cera di costoro e chi la duce / non sta d'un modo; e però sotto 'l segno / idëale poi più e men traluce. // Ond' elli avvien ch'un medesimo legno, / secondo specie, meglio e peggio frutta; / e voi nascete con diverso ingegno. // Se fosse a punto la cera dedutta / e fosse il cielo in sua virtù suprema, / la luce del suggel parrebbe tutta; // ma la natura la dà sempre scema, / similemente operando a l'artista / ch'a l'abito de l'arte ha man che trema."
[385] Consider how Vellutello illustrated *Paradiso* 13.76–78 in his *Nova espositione* of the *Commedia* (Dante, *La comedia* [...], commentary by Alessandro Vellutello, Venice 1544, unpaginated): "Ma la natura, la qual è ministra tra la virtù de l'influentia e l'individuo, *dà* essa virtù *sempre scema*, sempre imperfetta e difettiva, secondo le non buone congiuntioni de le stelle, da le quali nasce tal imperfettione, a similitudine de l'artefice, il qual avenga c'habbia *l'habito de l'arte*, nondimeno, perché li *trema la mano*, non può perfettamente operare."
[386] Commenting on Michelangelo's use of the word "artista," the humanist evoked several possible literary precedents and then stated (Varchi 1858–1859 [as in fn. 67], 2, p. 616): "E più chiaramente ancora, donde potemo cre-

process of artistic creation in a manner suited to extolling the thorough perfection of the *Perseus* indicates that he was reinterpreting that example through Michelangelo. Dante had used the parallel to emphasize the existence of an unbridgeable gap between the idea the artist seeks to realize and the imperfection of his creations, which necessarily reveal the limits of his human hand.[387] Conversely, Michelangelo's sonnet was based on the assumption – which Poggini then adopted as his own – that an excellent sculptor could bridge that ontological distance.[388]

When Domenico, who had trained as a goldsmith in Cellini's workshop, was writing his verses of praise to the *Perseus*, he was also completing his first large sculpture: the marble *Bacchus* now at the Metropolitan Museum of Art in New York (Fig. 16).[389] The work inaugurated what Varchi, in a sonnet published in 1555, described as Poggini's conscious decision to follow Cellini's example and abandon goldsmithing in the name of the more noble pursuit of sculpture.[390] In this sense, we can describe the sonnet *Sì come'l ciel di vaghe stelle adorno* as the tribute an emulator paid to one of his masters and most important standards of reference.

---

dere che lo cavasse il Poeta, nel tredicesimo [i.e canto of the *Paradiso*]: 'Ma la natura la dà sempre scema [...]'." On the choice of the word, see the commentary by Corsaro and Masi in Michelangelo 2016 (as in fn. 4), p. 992, n. 1.

[387] See the discussion of Dante's ideas in Giovanni Barberi Squarotti, Il modello lontano. Arte umana e arte di Dio in alcune immagini del *Paradiso*, in: Giorgio Barberi Squarotti and Valter Boggione (eds.), *Pitture di parole: per Barbara Zandrino*, Avellino 2012, pp. 73–91, esp. p. 79: "Questo spiega come mai l'arte umana evocata come termine di confronto per la creazione divina – emanazione nei vari gradi della materia, attraverso le gerarchie angeliche che governano i cieli [...] – appaia in esse [the poetic images of comparisons between the two arts] tendenzialmente pregiudicata da un limite o da un difetto [...]. Il confronto insomma mette in luce più che altro le ragioni di una profonda dissimilitudine".

[388] The relevant lines of Buonarroti's sonnet are examined by Erwin Panofsky, *Idea: contributo alla storia dell'estetica*, It. trans. Edmondo Cione, Florence 1952, pp. 91–92. Other poems by Michelangelo complicate the idea that the sculptor's manual skills might ever equate and fully express his *concetto*: for a discussion of the relevant texts, see Peter Armour, "A ciascun artista l'ultimo suo": Dante and Michelangelo, in: *Lectura Dantis* 22/23 (1998), pp. 141–180, pp. 165–166.

[389] On Poggini's biography, see Fabian Jonietz, Poggini, Domenico, in: *DBI* 84, Rome 2015, only available in digital edition: https://www.treccani.it/enciclopedia/domenico-poggini_%28Dizionario-Biografico%29/ (last accessed 31/01/2021). The earliest testimonies of his artistic activity date from 1545, when Cellini records having given Domenico and his brother Giovan Paolo a golden vase for finishing. On the *Bacchus*, see Hildegard Utz, Sculptures by Domenico Poggini, in: *Metropolitan Museum Journal* 101 (1976), pp. 63–78.

[390] In his sonnet, Varchi presented Poggini's alleged intention to renounce the practice of goldsmithing and become a sculptor in bronze, marble, and clay as the result of an aspiration to pursue the arduous and honorable path opened by Cellini (ll. 1–4 of sonnet 518 from the *Sonetti* of 1555, in Varchi 1858–1859 [as in fn. 67], 2, pp. 909–910): "Voi, che seguendo del mio gran Cellino / Per sì stretto sentier l'orme onorate, / Ori ed argenti e gemme altrui lasciate / Per bronzi e marmi e creta, alto Poggino." It is important to highlight that until his death, Poggini continued to work as a medalist and goldsmith. Furthermore, in 1554, the artist signed his marble *Bacchus* as an "aurifex" and his sonnet for Cellini's *Perseus* as "D. P. O.", i. e. "Domenico Poggini Orefice" (Florence, Biblioteca Riccardiana, ms. Ricc. 2728, c. 32r). A comparable signature is featured in his marble group of *Apollo and Capricorn*, now in the Kaffeehaus of the Boboli Garden (1559; see *infra*): "[D]ominicus Pogginus Flor[entinus] Aurifex F[ecit]." Still, the artist's aspirations to obtain recognition solely as a sculptor increased from the early 1560s, and in 1564 he gained admission into the Accademia del Disegno "per aver fatto di scultura più cose di marmo e non s'esercitando più a l'orafo." For more on this, see Jonietz 2015 (as in fn. 389), and Gamberini 2016 (as in fn. 7), with further references. For the devaluation and marginalization that the art of goldsmithery underwent in the statutes and practices of the Accademia del Disegno, see esp. Collareta 2003 (as in fn. 53), and idem, Vincenzo Danti e l'oreficeria, in: Davis and Paolozzi Strozzi 2008 (as in fn. 323), pp. 77–85.

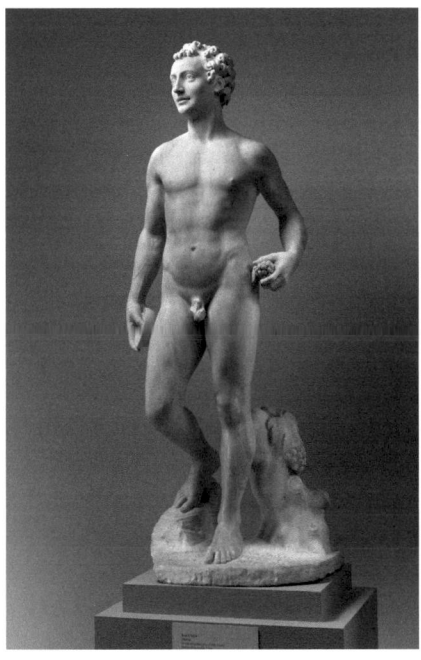

16 Domenico Poggini, *Bacchus*, marble, 1554, New York, The Metropolitan Museum of Art.

The motif of imitation, merely implicit in Poggini's poem, becomes explicit and entirely central in a sonnet by another of Cellini's former assistants, most likely penned for the same occasion of the *Perseus* unveiling. The poem's author is Zanobi Lastricati, who with his brother Alessandro had helped cast the head of Medusa for Cellini's statue (1548), and who from that time onward proved to be a perceptive imitator of the slightly older artist's sculptoreal language.[391] Like Domenico Poggini's verse, the complex sonnet he composed (*Quello splendor che 'n voi chiaro riluce*: Appendix, no. 70) underscored how the light of virtue shone with singular brightness in Cellini. In the author's words, that brightness was such that not even the darkness of night could obscure it, and his own spirit – already reduced to "freddo smalto" and nearly turned to stone[392] – was flooded with elation in its presence (ll. 1–8). What's more,

---

[391] Cellini's *Giornale di ricordi* reveals that Zanobi and Alessandro Lastricati took part in the casting of the head of Medusa on July 3, 1548: see Maurizia Cicconi, Lastricati, Zanobi, in: *DBI* 63, Rome 2004, pp. 814–816, with further references. Alessandro Nesi, Il "Cacciatore" di Zanobi Lastricati nel Giardino di Boboli, in: Nesi, Frizzi, and Piani 2013 (as in fn. 363), pp. 5–6, claims that only Alessandro Lastricati and the bronze founder Zanobi di Pagno Portigiani assisted Cellini in the casting of the *Perseus*, but an autograph note by Cellini (BNCF, *Autografi Palatini*, Cellini I.2) confirms that both the Lastricati brothers took part in the process: "A m. Alessandro e Zanobi suo fratello che m'aiutorno a conciare la fornacie e fondere lire 22 soldi 10. A Nicolò loro lavorante che m'aiutò lire 2." With reference to Zanobi's imitation of Cellini, Alessandro Nesi (ibid.) particularly highlights the formal similarities between Lastricati's marble *Hunter* (ca. 1555–1560) and Cellini's *Narcissus* (ca. 1548).

[392] Lastricati's reference to the "smalto," a term that could designate not just enamel but every other substance with a hard surface, was probably an allusion to Medusa's petrifying power. The trope was rather common in

Lastricati continued with an homage to Cellini's artistic exemplarity, the same light illuminated the paths that made it possible to imitate him ("le vie del seguir voi": l. 11). In closing, he noted that in descending to the inferior realms of creation, the essence of a superior substance like Cellini's supernatural luminosity lost only a minimal part of its power: referencing a common idea in the emanatist doctrines of the ancient and early modern periods, Lastricati maintained that the greater portion of that good stayed close to the source from which it received its light.[393]

This survey of poems highlights a basic contradiction with respect to the conceptual framework described at the beginning of this chapter. Underlying Cellini's reconstruction of the poetic triumph celebrated in the Loggia dei Signori in the spring of 1554, and his emphasis on the special role that other artists' compositions had played on that occasion, was the critical assumption that only the practitioners of the arts of drawing had the necessary knowledge to fully understand the kind of technical difficulties the *Perseus* had solved. Despite this theoretical premise, we can easily note that although Florentine artists probably discussed these matters aloud in the presence of Cellini's bronze, they did not tackle them in their poems.[394] While free of the most oft-exploited topoi of the genre, their compositions did not differ in this from the average contemporary verse in praise of artworks. That output in fact tended to avoid all straightforward reference to *techne*, based on a principle of abstraction that lent the painting or sculpture in question a largely generic character: faithful to the epideictic manners of praise typical of many classical epigrams on artworks, these compositions shared their propensity to laud visual creations not for their material specificity but as universal paradigms of artistic excellence. This sublimating tendency was, for that matter, consistent with the general refusal to linger on the concrete aspects of reality that characterizes the aulic poetic registers of the Italian pre-modern literary tradition.[395] During the period when Cellini was dictating

Tuscan poetry; compare, for instance, Dante, *Inferno* 9.52: "Vegna Medusa: sì 'l farem di smalto," and Petrarch, *Canzoniere* 213.9: "Et que' belli occhi che i cor' fanno smalti."

[393] To name just one example, this idea played a fundamental role in the metaphysics of an influential Neoplatonist thinker of the Middle Ages, the Andalusian Jewish poet-savant Salomon ibn Gabirol (eleventh century), alias Avicébron. See Fernand Brunner, La doctrine de la matière chez Avicébron, in: *Revue de théologie et de philosophie*, n. s. 6 (1956), pp. 261–279. Notably, such emanatist theories were grounded, like Lastricati's reasoning, in the comparison between the superior substances descending from the skies and the nature of light.

[394] In the texts under consideration, the few references to these aspects of the creation of the *Perseus* are typically transfigured by means of highly figurative or mythographic language, as is the case with the parallel between the act of casting bronze and Zeus's shower of gold pouring down into Danae's lap in Bronzino's *Ardea Venere bella e lui che 'n pioggia*. Indeed, the only explicit reference to the materiality of Cellini's statue is the technical verb "statuar" in Domenico Poggini's poem.

[395] Many have noted that the tendency towards abstraction was typical of the tradition of ancient ekphrastic poetry. Consider, for instance, the dismissive remarks by Goethe on the thirty-six epigrams celebrating Myron's *Cow* in the *Greek Anthology*: "Although considerable information concerning this statue has come down to us, none of it is much help in forming a clear idea of the original. Even more surprising is the fact that some thirty-six epigrams on the subject are not more useful in this respect [...]. These epigrams are monotonous and dull and neither descriptive nor informative: for this reason they tend to be more misleading than helpful when used as a basis for visualising and defining the lost bronze" (quotation from Michael Squire, Making Myron's Cow Moo? Ecphrastic Epigram and the Poetics of Simulation, in: *The American Journal of Philology* 131 [2010],

his autobiography, it was a different poetic genre that took on the task of judging art for its concrete qualities, including the technical and material aspects excluded from the sphere of what "high" poetry deigned to express. These were the comical poems written to vituperate artworks[396] – a genre that was wholly familiar to Cellini due to its popularity in Cinquecento Florence and the fact that he and other artists in that milieu were among its authors.

"sì come s'usa nelle grandi scuole"

As demonstrated by his reconstruction of a famous squabble the author had had with Bandinelli in Duke Cosimo's presence, in the *Vita* Cellini deliberately constructed his account of the poetic triumph of his *Perseus* as a reception that both replicated the lyrical ovation that had greeted the unveiling of Michelangelo's statues in the New Sacristy of San Lorenzo (1546) and served as the perfect antithesis to the deluge of "vituperosi sonetti" that assailed his rival's *Hercules and Cacus* (1534).[397] Less well known than the autobiography is the passage from the

pp. 589–634, p. 589, which subsequently provides an illuminating analysis of the poetic series according to its own literary terms). For a different approach to such a distinguishing feature of Hellenistic ekphrastic epigrams, see esp. Simon Goldhill, The Naïve and Knowing Eye: Ecphrasis and the Culture of Viewing in the Hellenistic World, in: Simon Goldhill and Robin Osborne (eds.), *Art and Text in Ancient Greek Culture*, Cambridge 1994, pp. 197–223, p. 223, which observes how these texts "do not merely describe works of art – and they often offer no physical description at all – but play a role in the production of a cultural milieu that aims to create and enforce and explore particular ways of seeing meaning." For examples of the general disregard of Italian ekphrastic poetry towards the formal and technical qualities of the artistic object, see Gombrich 1967 (as in fn. 348), p. 3 (according to which "in their poetic tributes they [i. e., the humanists] were generally satisfied to ring the changes on the conventions evolved by the ancient writers of epigrams which praise the lifelikeness of a figure that 'only lacks the voice'"), and Land 1994 (as in fn. 374), p. 56 and *passim*, which highlights how such a production typically favored a focus on the subject matter of the artwork and on its emotional effects upon the beholder. With regard to the sub-genre of Italian poetry on portraits, see esp. Bolzoni and Pich 2008 (as in fn. 267), pp. 10–11 and 26, with the observation that "del ritratto vero e proprio i nostri testi […] non ci dicono in genere quasi nulla." On the general tendency towards sublimation and abstraction of medieval and early modern Italian poetry of the aulic register, see Giunta 2002 (as in fn. 11), p. 271, with further references.

[396] On this, see Spagnolo 2006 (as in fn. 333). Spagnolo convincingly establishes a connection between these poems' attention to the concrete reality of the criticized artwork and the kind of material dissemination and fruition they envisioned. These compositions were typically appended to, or in the immediate proximity of, the artistic object, also because this allowed readers to fully appreciate the precise referentiality of the critiques. See esp. p. 332: "Quel tratto tipico delle poesie in biasimo di aderenza e pertinenza alla realtà concreta dell'opera d'arte sottintendeva una lettura del testo davanti all'opera stessa: solo con un'osservazione attenta, preferibilmente in loco, era possibile comprendere il senso delle critiche – che spesso si appuntavano su singoli, anche minimi, dettagli stilistici o iconografici – ed apprezzarne appieno la vis comica." For more on this, see also *infra*. To Spagnolo's remarks, we might add the broader consideration that in the literary tradition of pre-modern Italy (and Europe at large), attention to the more material aspects of life was typical of comic poetry: see Giunta 2002 (as in fn. 11), p. 171.

[397] See Cellini 1996 (as in fn. 23), p. 652 (*Vita* 2.70): "Così il detto Bandinello cominciò a favellare et disse: 'Signore, quando io scopersi il mio Ercole e Cacco, certo che io credo che più di cento sonettacci ei mi fu fatti, i quali dicevano il peggio che immaginar si possa al mondo da questo popolaccio.' Io allora risposi e dissi: 'Signore, quando il nostro Michelagnolo Buonarroti scoperse la sua Sacrestia, dove ei si vidde tante belle figure, questa mirabile et virtuosa Scuola, amica della verità et del bene, gli fece più di cento sonetti, a gara l'un l'altro a

Discorso della Architettura in which Cellini explained the meaning of the contrast between the poems that had panned Bandinelli's sculpture and those in praise of his own.[398] The author based his reasoning on the assumption that the Florentine public had a ruthless critical sense when it came to art and that such intransigence only spared truly perfect works, the sole creations that could achieve unanimous acclaim in that contentious setting. Because the local audience was so eager to draw attention to even the slightest shortcoming, Cellini argued, it was natural for him to expect some jabs for his unfinished *Perseus*, especially since it would be compared in the arena of Piazza della Signoria with the great mastery of Donatello's *Judith and Holofernes* and Michelangelo's *David*. The unanimous praise of the poems with which humanists and especially other artists had received the new bronze of the Piazza thus confirmed, Cellini asserted, its supreme excellence:

> il maggior desiderio che io avessi al mondo, e il più glorioso premio che io ne desideravo, si era il piacere più che per me si poteva alla maravigliosa scuola fiorentina, e, trovando l'opera mia messa in mezzo di quel mirabil Donatello e di quel maraviglioso Michelagnolo Buonaroti; conosciuto le grandissime lor virtù, non già che io aspettassi che la detta scuola mi sgraffiassi il viso tanto quanto l'aveva fatto all'Ercole e al Cacco del Bandinello, ma sì bene aspettavo qualche punzecchiata, sì come s'usa nelle grandi scuole: se bene un'opera s'accosta al meglio, alla scuola non manca mai che dire. Imperò a me avvenne tutto il contrario, perché non tanto i valorosi e dotti poeti m'empierono la basa di versi latini e vulgari, che ancora quei più eccellenti di mia proffesione scultori e pittori scrissono tanto onoratamente in lode della detta opera che io mi domandai satisfattissimo lo averne ritratto il maggior premio che io desideravo.[399]

Cellini was here expressing ideas that were current in contemporary art criticism. In Vasari's *Vite* of 1550, for example, the conviction that the Florentine public was especially inclined to disparage every less-than-perfect artwork, and that this penchant was in fact one of the reasons for the city's primacy over other Italian art centers, was the focus of some key passages in the biography of Pietro Perugino.[400] What Vincenzio Borghini would define as the local

---

chi ne poteva dir meglio: et così come quella del Bandinello meritava quel tanto male che lui dice che della sua si disse, così meritava quel tanto bene quella del Buonaroti, che di lei si disse.'" On the texts that were written to criticize Bandinelli's marble, see especially, along with the contemporary testimony of Vasari that is discussed *infra*, Detlef Heikamp, Poesie in vituperio del Bandinelli, in: *Paragone / Arte* 15 (1964), pp. 59–68; Davis 1976 (as in fn. 308), p. 20; Louis Alexander Waldman, 'Miracol' Novo et Raro': Two Unpublished Contemporary Satires on Bandinelli's *Hercules*, in: *Mitteilungen des Kunsthistorischen Institutes in Florenz* 38 (1994), pp. 419–427; Giorgio Masi, Le statue parlanti del cavaliere e altri prodigi pasquineschi fiorentini (Bandinelli, Cellini, Michelangelo), in: Damianaki, Procaccioli, and Romano 2006 (as in fn. 333), pp. 221–274; idem, Un sonetto inedito sull'*Ercole e Caco* di Baccio Bandinelli, con ipotesi attributive (e il topos burlesco del dimissionario), in: *Italique* 16 (2013), pp. 79–109; Spagnolo 2006 (as in fn. 333), pp. 335–341, and Jonathan Schiesaro, *Contra Baccium*. Sonetti, sonettesse ed epigrammi in scherno del Bandinelli, in: *Theory and Criticisim of Literature & Arts* 5.1 (2021), pp. 50–103. Other contemporary testimonies of the "bad reception" of Baccio's works are analyzed in Bartoli 2014 (as in fn. 193), pp. 37–59, with bibliography. On the reactions of the Florentine artistic community to the unveiling of Michelangelo's statues for the *New Sacristy*, see Lazzaro 2016 (as in fn. 97).

[398] Only Masi 2006 (as in fn. 397), p. 228, n. 21, briefly discusses the text in the context of an analysis of the poetic reception of Bandinelli's work.

[399] Cellini 1980 (as in fn. 358), pp. 820–821.

[400] The passage purportedly reported the opinion of Perugino's master, who thus explained to his pupil why artists became excellent in Florence (Vasari 1967–1997 [as in fn. 74], 3, p. 597): "In Firenze più che altrove venivano gli uomini perfetti in tutte l'arti e specialmente nella pittura, attesoché in quella città sono spronati gli uomini

audience's "buon occhio" and "cattiva lingua" were also traits that Francesco Bocchi would insist on at length, when he analyzed the reception of public statuary in his treatise on Donatello's *Saint George*.[401] With the exception of Bocchi, these authors did not fail to emphasize how it was mainly the artists themselves who relished this kind of virulent criticism. In the Torrentiniana, Vasari had for instance noted that some exponents of the Florentine art scene pitilessly ridiculed the manner in which Perugino had completed the *Annunziata Polyptych* (1504–1507), begun by Filippino Lippi and left unfinished on his death. Pioneers of a more modern visual language, these unnamed artists apparently berated Perugino "aspramente con sonetti e publiche villanie" for the crime of having produced an irremediably repetitive, outmoded work.[402] Writing about a stay in Florence by his contemporary Perino del Vaga, Vasari also wrote that the painter had the occasion to participate in those discussions in

da tre cose: l'una dal biasimare che fanno molti e molto, per far quell'aria gli ingegni liberi di natura e non contentarsi universalmente dell'opere pur mediocri, ma sempre più ad onore del buono e del bello che a rispetto del facitore considerarle." On Vasari's interpretation of Florentine criticism as a spur towards artistic perfection, see Gombrich 1967 (as in fn. 348), pp. 18–20, and Pozzi and Mattioda 2006 (as in fn. 80), pp. 401–403.

[401] Compare Bocchi in Barocchi 1960–1962 (as in fn. 147), 3, pp. 167 168: "Assai è cosa chiara che a tanta perfezione gli artifizii sono divenuti, et i giudizi umani cotanto in simili opere la vista hanno assottigliato, e qui in Firenze particolarmente, che, sì come di Roscio si scrive che e' non avea in Roma alcuno istrione che da lui, movendosi, e' non fosse di presente ne' gesti, dove e' fallasse, conosciuto, così né più né meno nelle pitture e nelle statue avviene, le quali, tuttoché appariscano singolari, nondimeno elle non prima ne' luoghi publici sono collocate, che tantosto le lingue a biasimarle e lacerarle sono preste. Ma nel San Giorgio, perocché gli avvedimenti di Donatello sono stati singolari, non ha luogo alcuno errore, e perciò chi lo guarda altro fare non puote che magnificarlo e sommamente aggradirlo." See also ibid., p. 186: "E comecché le due bellezze nel San Giorgio appariscano, una nondimeno vi si conosce con sì grande unione di tutte le parti, che maggiore bramare non si potrebbe. Quanto elle siano verso di sé convenevoli e congiunte ottimamente insieme, bene lo sanno gli ingegni fiorentini, per avventura troppo più acuti nel giudicare e troppo più severi che queste simili cose non richieggono. Ma poiché la compiuta bellezza ha tolto via, non che altro, il sospicarvi un picciolo segno di errore, tutte le lingue, qualunque volta ella è veduta, sono a celebrarla et a magnificarla invitate." On this set of ideas, see Thomas Frangenberg, The Notion of Beauty in Francesco Bocchi's *Bellezze Della Città Di Fiorenza*, in: Francis Ames-Lewis and Mary Rogers (eds.), *Concepts of Beauty in Renaissance Art*, Aldershot 1997, pp. 191–198, p. 194: "The notion that artistic perfection is as much the fruit of the artist's labour as the result of the consensus reached in a society with a sophisticated visual culture is very close to the emphasis on laymen's judgment of art works found in Vincenzo Borghini's *Selva di notizie*."

[402] Compare Vasari 1967–1997 (as in fn. 74), 3, pp. 609–610 (1550): "Dicesi che quando detta opera si scoperse, poi fu da tutti i nuovi artefici assai biasimata. Erasi Pietro servito di quelle figure ch'altre volte era usato mettere in opera: dove tentandolo gli amici suoi, dicevano che affaticato non s'era, e che aveva tralasciato il buon modo dell'operare, e per avarizia o per non perder tempo era incorso in tale errore. Ai quali Pietro rispondeva: 'Io ho messo in opera le figure altre volte lodate da loro, e songli infinitamente piacciute: se ora gli dispiacciono e non le lodano, che ne posso io?'. Ma coloro aspramente con sonetti e publiche villanie lo saettavano." On the *Annunziata Polyptych* and its contested reception, see Jonathan K. Nelson, The High Altar-Piece of SS. Annunziata in Florence: History, Form, and Function, in: *The Burlington Magazine* 139 (1997), pp. 84–94, and Franca Falletti and Jonathan K. Nelson, *Filippino Lippi e Pietro Perugino: la Deposizione della Santissima Annunziata e il suo restauro*, Livorno 2004. On Vasari's account, see the considerations of Gombrich 1967 (as in fn. 348), p. 20: "Vasari also tells us […] who the people were who raised this criticism. It was the 'new artists,' critics in other words, who […] had a professional interest in problem solutions. Artists, we may supplement Vasari's account, did see many of Perugino's works, if not side by side at least in succession, because they were interested in art. Hence their dissatisfaction with a master who repeated himself. He had begun to bore them. But if we can believe Vasari's simplified model situation, the new artists also carried the public with them. They had fresh

front of artworks that "secondo il costume antico" involved "molti artefici, pittori, scultori, architetti, orefici et intagliatori di marmi e di legnami," who would meet "per udire i biasimi e le lode che sogliono spesso dire gli artefici l'un de l'altro."[403] Borghini, too, remarked more than once that it was primarily artists who embodied the city's argumentative nature when it came to artworks, for example in a letter warning Vasari about the criticism he might face for his paintings in the Salone dei Cinquecento at Palazzo Vecchio.[404] And it was mainly the same professional community that Cellini himself had in mind when he attributed the poems praising Michelangelo's New Sacristy sculptures and those panning Bandinelli's *Hercules and Cacus* to the revered "Scuola Fiorentina," for the expression designated first and foremost those Florentine practitioners of the arts of drawing whose collective identity was rooted in their devotion to the city's glorious artistic tradition.[405]

Both Vasari and Cellini, then, reported that painters and sculptors active in Florence had made poetry one of their primary tools for criticizing art they found less than outstanding. It should in this regard be noted that although the lack of documentation of poems disparaging Perugino has led some scholars to suspect that Vasari was incorrectly attributing to the past a custom typical of the period in which he was writing,[406] there is evidence of poetic *querelles*

---

and more convincing solutions to offer which made the earlier ones suddenly look inadequate." Also relevant is Franceschini 2021 (as in fn. 346), with further references.

[403] Vasari 1967–1997 (as in fn. 74), 5, p. 125 (1550). In the author's account, such exchanges would have taken place in front of "opere e vecchie e moderne per le chiese," and the narration subsequently concentrates on the debates in front of Masaccio's frescoes for the Brancacci Chapel. On Vasari's own rhetoric of praise and blame on the works of fellow artists, see Rubin 1995 (as in fn. 61), pp. 231–234.

[404] Borghini's allusion to the malice of Florentine artists is to be found in his letter to Vasari of December 4, 1568 (Vasari 1923–1930 [as in fn. 76], 2, pp. 411–412): "L'opera della sala è grande et ha bisogno […] di uno assiduo, lungo e consideratissimo studio, a voler fare onore a voi e satisfare non solo a loro Eccellenze Illustrissime, a' quali principalmente si deve satisfare, e non solo agli artefici vostri, la natura de' quali voi ben conoscete, ma ancora a una città tanto oculata, tanto apunto, quanto è questa, e che ha l'umore suo come sapete in questa parte."

[405] See the observations of Davis 1976 (as in fn. 308), pp. 18–19: "Cellini's awareness of the separate identity of the local school of artists – he terms it the Scuola Fiorentina – was no doubt sharpened by his long experience outside the city, and even outside Italy […]. Thus he had experienced directly the enviable reputation Florentine artists enjoyed far and wide, and so he writes of *questa mirabile e virtuosa Scuola. Nobilissima*, he calls her, *divinissima, eccellentissima, amica della verità e del bene*! He writes often of the Florentine school, and with pride, but also with […] a sense for its chorporate character. What Cellini has in mind when he speaks of the Scuola Fiorentina is, however, something quite independent of the formally organized Florentine Accademia del Disegno. Cellini regarded the latter group with suspicion […]. In the broadest sense, the school included not only artists, but informed literati and amateurs of art as well. The critical judgments of both are preserved in sonnets composed when important works of art were first exposed to public view." On the participation of artists in poetic commentaries on art, see also Detlef Heikamp, Rapporti fra accademici ed artisti nella Firenze del '500 da memorie e rime dell'epoca, in: *Il Vasari* n. s. 1, 15 (1957), pp. 139–163, p. 147, and Margaret A. Gallucci, *Benvenuto Cellini: Sexuality, Masculinity, and Artistic Identity in Renaissance Italy*, New York 2003, pp. 49–50: "For artists in particular, the sonnet was a forum for aesthetic judgments in artistic matters in Florence. When Cellini's *Perseus* was unveiled in 1554, artists and men of letters attached encomiastic sonnets to its base […]. The sonnet was a forum not only for praise, but also for censure. When Bandinelli's marble group of *Hercules and Cacus* was displayed, numerous artists and writers heaped vituperative abuse upon Bandinelli."

[406] The hypothesis was suggested by Gombrich 1967 (as in fn. 348), p. 19, and reported by Spagnolo 2006 (as in fn. 333), p. 322.

among artists in Florence already dating to the first half of the Quattrocento. According to Antonio Manetti, for example, Filippo Brunelleschi had responded to the calumnious attacks of his old friend Donatello by composing sonnets that criticized Donatello's work, in particular his doors for the Old Sacristy of San Lorenzo.[407] Feuds such as this were also a little-known form of rebirth of a classical custom: many painters and sculptors active in the Florentine milieu, with its high rate of intellectual osmosis with the world of literati, knew that their ancient predecessors had debated professional matters amongst themselves in verse of a markedly polemical tone. For example, a poetic skirmish that Pliny recounts in Book 35 of *Naturalis Historia* is emblematic of the competitive atmosphere that so often emerges from his anecdotes on artists. As the story goes, Apollodorus penned an epigram accusing Zeuxis of having stolen his prized technical invention, the *skiagraphia* or ability to modulate light and shade in painting.[408] Zeuxis then responded to such attacks through the same poetic medium: beneath his own depiction of an athlete, he wrote a line asserting that it would be easier to find fault with his work than to imitate it.[409]

To theorize that an ancient model influenced the custom of many Renaissance Florentine painters and sculptors to hold poetic confrontations on matters of art is not necessarily to engage in the fallacy of *post hoc ergo propter hoc*.[410] In taking part in those *querelles*, as either apologists or faultfinders, it was sometimes the artists themselves who alluded to Pliny's exemplary anecdotes. With criticism and vituperative sonnets raining down on him upon completion of the innovative Palazzo Bartolini-Salimbeni (1523), for example, Baccio d'Agnolo

---

[407] For Manetti's testimony on Brunelleschi's poetic activity and the scholarly debate on its reliability, see here, introduction, pp. 23–24 and fnn. 38–39.

[408] See Pliny, *Naturalis Historia* 35.62: "In eum [scilicet Zeusis] Apollodorus supra scriptus versum fecit, artem ipsi[s] ablatam Zeuxim ferre secum." The text follows the emendation (*ipsis* → *ipsi*) that has been convincingly proposed by Salvatore Settis, Luci e ombre di Zeusi (Plin. nat. 35,62), in: *Materiali e discussioni per l'analisi dei testi classici* 60 (2008), pp. 201–204, which identifies the victim of Zeuxis's "artistic theft" as Apollodorus himself (rather than as Zeuxis's masters). The composition is also mentioned in Maddalena Spagnolo, Effimere saette: sfide e limiti di una Kunstliteratur satirico-burlesca, forthcoming in: *Mitteilungen des Kunsthistorischen Institutes in Florenz* 63.1 (2021), as a relevant classical antecedent for the early modern development of vituperative poems on art.

[409] See Pliny, *Naturalis Historia* 35.63: "Fecit […] et athletam adeoque in illo sibi placuit, ut versum subscriberet celebrem ex eo, invisurum aliquem facilius quam imitaturum." According to Pliny, Parrhasius was the author of comparable self-celebratory short poetic compositions, in which he arrogantly claimed his own primacy in the realm of painting. See ibid., 35.71: "Fecundus artifex, sed quo nemo insolentius usus sit gloria artis, namque et cognomina usurpavit habrodiaetum se appellando aliisque versibus principem artis et eam ab se consummatam." For other ancient sources on Parrhasius's verse (e. g. Athenaeus's *Deipnosophists*) see Fabio Guidetti, "Quo nemo insolentius." La 'superbia' di Parrasio e l'autoaffermazione dell'artista nella Grecia classica, in: *Opera Nomina Historiae* 1 (2009), pp. 1–50, 4–8.

[410] On the exemplarity of Plinian anecdotes for the intellectual and artistic practices of Renaissance artists, see especially the wide-ranging accounts of McHam 2013 (as in fn. 77), and Peter Fane-Saunders, *Pliny the Elder and the Emergence of Renaissance Architecture*, Cambridge 2016. On the fortune of the books of Pliny's work dedicated to art historical matters among sixteenth-century Florentine art theorists, see Eliana Carrara, Plinio e l'arte degli Antichi e dei Moderni: ricezione e fortuna dei libri XXXIV–XXXVI della *Naturalis historia* nella Firenze del XVI secolo (dall'Anonimo Magliabechiano a Vasari), in: *Archives internationales d'histoire des sciences* 61 (2011), pp. 367–381.

came up with a reply in the manner of Zeuxis.⁴¹¹ Most likely in concert with his patron,⁴¹² he had the Latin Alcaic decasyllable CARPERE PROMPTIUS QUAM IMITARI ("[it is] easier to criticize than to imitate") inscribed over the palazzo door. With that manifest reference to Pliny's version of the phrase Zeuxis appended to his masterpiece ("invisurum aliquem facilius quam imitaturum"), Baccio intended to respond to the attacks and reassert his pride as the creator of Giovanni Bartolini's new residence in Florence.

An example of a poetic offensive modeled on Pliny comes from the pen of Benvenuto Cellini. He has been convincingly credited with the sonettessa *Io son quel nominato Cavaliero*, an attack on the marble *Dead Christ with an Angel* that Baccio Bandinelli revealed to the city in the summer of 1552 (Fig. 17).⁴¹³ In the poem the main subject of the sculpture speaks, revealing that he is not Christ but Baccio himself, his weight supported by a young apprentice – a paradoxical interpretation targeted at what Cellini viewed as the iconographic indecipherability of a work in which, for example, the angel was without customary wings. The passage of greatest interest, however, which has thus far been neglected in critical discussions of the text, lies in the first quatrain:

> Io son quel nominato Cavaliero,
>   Baccio scalpellator de' Bandinelli,
>   qui posto ad ascoltar questi cervelli
>   s'alcun nel lacerarmi dice il vero.⁴¹⁴

This self-introduction by the sculpture, eager to listen in on observers' critiques, is a humorous take on Pliny's anecdote about Apelles, who would hide behind his own paintings to intercept the revealing comments of passersby.⁴¹⁵ If we believe Vasari's account of the unveiling of the

---

⁴¹¹ See Vasari 1967–1997 (as in fn. 74), 4, p. 611 (1568): "Fece in sulla piazza di Santa Trinita un palazzo a Giovanni Bartolini […]. E perché fu il primo edifizio […] che fusse fatto con ornamento di finestre quadre con frontispizii e con porta, le cui colonne reggessino architrave, fregio e cornice, furono queste cose tanto biasimate dai Fiorentini con parole, con sonetti e con appiccarvi filze di frasche, come si fa alle chiese per le feste, dicendosi che aveva più forma di facciata di tempio che di palazzo, che Baccio fu per uscir di cervello: tuttavia, sapendo egli che aveva imitato il buono e che l'opera stava bene, se ne passò. Vero è che la cornice di tutto il palazzo riuscì […] troppo grande: tuttavia l'opera è stata per altro sempre molto lodata." According to Maddalena Spagnolo (Filze di frasche e fogli volanti su Palazzo Bartolini Salimbeni, in: Novella Barbolani di Montauto, Gerardo de Simone, Tomaso Montanari, Chiara Savettieri, and Maddalena Spagnolo [eds.], *Arte e politica: studi per Antonio Pinelli*, Florence 2013, pp. 49–52), many contemporary critiques of Baccio's work were politically motivated and expressed anti-Medicean feelings. Following this hypothesis, the satires would have been a way of indirectly attacking Giovanni Bartolini's close allegiance with Pope Leo X, alias Giovanni de' Medici.

⁴¹² Compare ibid., p. 51 (without references to Zeuxis's verse): "Occorre sottolineare che, per quanto si sa della posizione sociale degli artisti, è difficile credere che si permettesse a un architetto di 'regolare i suoi conti' sulla facciata principale di un palazzo nobiliare tanto in vista. Qualora si volesse ricondurre a Baccio un'idea tanto audace, dovremmo perciò convenire che […] artista e committente agissero in stretta collaborazione, il primo nulla potendo senza la legittimazione del secondo."

⁴¹³ For more thorough discussions of the poem, first published in Heikamp 1964 (as in fn. 397), see Masi 2006 (as in fn. 333), pp. 238–245, which first attributed the text to Cellini, as well as my own commentary in Cellini 2014 (as in fn. 7), pp. 343–347.

⁴¹⁴ Ibid., p. 345.

⁴¹⁵ See *supra*, fn. 337.

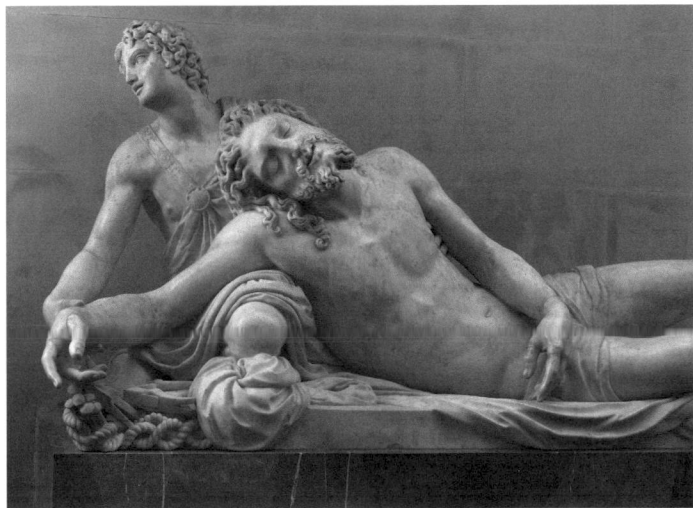

17 Baccio Bandinelli, *Dead Christ with an Angel*, marble, 1552, Florence, Santa Croce, Famedio (formerly in Santa Maria del Fiore).

Hercules and Cacus, Bandinelli used to send members of his entourage to record the public's reactions to his works, and would then be deeply tormented by how invariably disapproving they were.[416] Perhaps inspired by that episode in his rival's past and filtering it through Pliny's story of Apelles, Cellini imagined in these lines that Baccio himself was listening in on his viewers in the choir of Florence Cathedral. Transformed by a spell into his own marble work, thus (unlike Apelles) unable to escape the public's comments, in the sonettessa Bandinelli had to endure the agony of eternally hearing those viewers tear his art to shreds.

The history of vituperative poems by artists and the example of Cellini

The poems cited above demonstrate that Florentine Renaissance artists could equally take the offensive or the defensive position when they engaged in verse challenges on matters of art. And although this kind of skirmish became a recurrent phenomenon when the genre of poetic

---

[416] Vasari 1967–1997 (as in fn. 74), 5, pp. 254–255 (1568): "Desiderando lui di sapere ciò che dell'opera sua si diceva, mandò in piazza un pedante, il quale teneva in casa, dicendogli che non mancasse di riferirgli il vero di ciò che udiva dire. Il pedante non udendo altro che male, tornato malinconoso a casa, e domandato da Baccio, rispose che tutti per una voce biasimano i giganti e che e' non piacciono loro […]. Dissimulava Baccio il suo dolore, e così sempre ebbe per costume di fare, mostrando di non curare del biasimo che l'uomo alle sue cose desse. Nondimeno egli è verisimile che grande fusse il suo dispiacere, perché coloro che s'affaticano per l'onore e dipoi ne riportano biasimo, è da credere, ancorché indegno sia il biasimo et a torto, che ciò nel cuor segretamente gli affligga e di continuo gli tormenti."

vituperia reached its heyday in the Florentine scene of the later Cinquecento,[417] our knowledge of such disputes is sharply limited by an incomplete textual history.

As Maddalena Spagnolo has shown, sixteenth-century compositions criticizing works of art were usually anonymous and only available to the audience through loose sheets of paper, which were affixed in the immediate proximity of the object of their critique. For while the laudatory poems that were sometimes appended next to paintings and sculptures often found their way into printed collections like the sylloge included at the end of Cellini's *Trattati*,[418] those that criticized art were virtually impossible to publish. Like Roman pasquinades and other lampoons that Renaissance authors displayed in highly visible locations in order to mock public figures, these poems were posted in the open semi-covertly and were generally short-lived,[419] also because the same prominent clients who had commissioned the work would sometimes nip the invective in the bud. This is how Vasari, for example, justified the fate of some imprudent Florentine rhymesters who had believed they could openly satirize Bandinelli's *Hercules and Cacus*, the muscular symbol of Alessandro de' Medici's autocratic power:

> Non sarebbe facile a dire il concorso e la moltitudine che per due giorni tenne occupata tutta la piazza, venendo a vedere il gigante tosto che fu scoperto; dove si sentivano diversi ragionamenti e pareri d'ogni sorte d'uomini, e tutti in biasimo dell'opera e del maestro. Furono appiccati ancora intorno alla basa molti versi latini e toscani, ne' quali era piacevole a vedere gl'ingegni de' componitori e l'invenzioni et i detti acuti. Ma trapassandosi col dir male e con le poesie satiriche e mordaci ogni convenevole segno, il duca Alessandro, parendogli sua indegnità per essere l'opera pubblica, fu forzato a far mettere in prigione alcuni, i quali senza rispetto apertamente andavano appiccando sonetti: la qual cosa chiuse tosto le bocche de' maldicenti.[420]

---

[417] On the fortune of the genre in the Florentine scene, see Heikamp 1957 (as in fn. 405), pp. 146–148, and Zygmunt Waźbiński, Artisti e pubblico nella Firenze del Cinquecento: a proposito del topos 'cane abbaiante,' in: *Paragone / Arte* 28 (1977), pp. 3–24. Spagnolo 2006 (as in fn. 333), pp. 324–327, rightly observes that Florence was certainly not the only Renaissance city where many mocking poems were composed against artworks. The essay thus calls attention to the example of the Venetian poet Andrea Michieli, alias lo Squarzola (or Strazzola, †1510), who wrote a number of compositions criticizing the work of contemporary painters such as Gentile Bellini, Vittore Carpaccio, and Ombrone da Fossombrone. For two excellent analyses of poetic vituperations of art that were produced in seventeenth-century Rome, see Steven F. Ostrow, The Discourse of Failure in Seventeenth-Century Rome: Prospero Bresciano's *Moses*, in: *The Art Bulletin* 88.2 (2006), pp. 267–291, and Maddalena Spagnolo, Barn-Owl Painters in St. Peter's in the Vatican, 1604: Three Mocking Poems for Roncalli, Vanni and Passignano (and a Note on the Breeches-Maker), in: *Journal of the Warburg and Courtauld Institutes* 73 (2010), pp. 257–296.

[418] In the Italian Renaissance, one early and most influential example of laudatory poems that were appended next to the artworks on which they were commenting is that of the *Coryciana* (for bibliography, see *supra*, fn. 367). Most of the compositions that were published in 1524 had first been transcribed on *tabulae* hanging from Goritz's pillar altar in the Roman church of Sant'Agostino.

[419] For a more thorough discussion of the Renaissance fruition and circulation of vituperative poetry on art and its genetic relations to the genre of the *pasquinate*, see Spagnolo 2006 (as in fn. 333), pp. 331–333 and 348, as well as eadem, *Pasquino in piazza: una statua a Roma tra arte e vituperio*, Rome 2019. For a treatment of the manuscript dissemination of sixteenth- and seventeenth-century pasquinades through *cedolae* and *Flugblätter* and how such practices were intertwined with oral performances of these compositions, see eadem, "Pasquino" al bivio: la statua, la piazza e il suo pubblico nel Cinquecento, in: Alessandro Nova and Stephanie Hanke (eds.), *Skulptur und Platz: Raumbesetzung, Raumüberwindung, Interaktion*, Munich 2014, pp. 253–281, pp. 270–274.

[420] Vasari 1967–1997 (as in fn. 74), 5, p. 254 (1568). On the account, see also Nicole Hegener, *Divi Iacobi Eqves: Selbstdarstellung im Werk des Florentiner Bildhauers Baccio Bandinelli*, Munich 2008, p. 510.

We do not know whether Cosimo and Francesco de' Medici also took specific measures against the public posting of these texts. What we do know is that from the mid-Cinquecento, ecclesiastical and political censorship of written injury against a person's honor became stricter throughout Italy, and this legal clampdown almost surely affected the poetic *vituperia* attached to artworks, with the result that most of them have been lost.[421] It is therefore extremely likely that in the period of most interest here, the Florentine authorities promptly destroyed the poetic jeers affixed to some of the most important works the local rulers had commissioned.[422] This would explain, for instance, why we only have a tiny portion of the many compositions we know were written to mock not only Bandinelli's *Hercules and Cacus* but also Giorgio Vasari and Federico Zuccari's *Last Judgment* for the cupola of Florence Cathedral (1572–1579).[423] Saved from oblivion were the few poems that contemporaries managed to transcribe from the loose sheets affixed near the contested painting or sculpture, and those whose authors preserved a copy among their manuscripts. Alongside the evidence of that genre left by prolific authors such as Anton Francesco Grazzini, alias "il Lasca," and Alfonso de' Pazzi, or "l'Etrusco,"[424] we therefore have some poetic *vituperia* that Cellini stored among his papers starting in the 1550s – the sole, non-anonymous trace of the insults that painters and sculptors in that setting would hurl at one another through the poetic medium.

Odium figulinum, that form of exacerbated, malicious professional rivalry that according to Vasari thrived like a sickness among the ranks of Renaissance artists,[425] does inform a signif-

---

[421] Compare Spagnolo 2010 (as in fn. 417), p. 283: "Poems mocking works of art were probably considered as illegal as any other text which undermined someone's honour. Pasquinades were condemned both in the Indices of the Inquisition and in the bandi of the Roman governors from the mid-sixteenth century onwards." Spagnolo 2021 (as in fn. 408) also discusses early seventeenth-century Roman archival documents that demonstrate how vituperative poems on art often enjoyed an oral circulation, which allowed these texts to bypass the restrictions and censures on written compositions. On the latter aspect, see Gigliola Fragnito, Censura ecclesiastica e pasquinate, in: Damianaki, Procaccioli, and Romano 2006 (as in fn. 333), pp. 181–186.

[422] We can observe how the new set of rules of the Florentine Academy that was promoted by the ducal power in 1547 prescribed the material destruction of vituperative compositions. According to the reformed *Capitoli* of the institutions, the censors of the Academy had to "abbruciare, e stracciare senza farne parte a persona" any form of "compositioni disoneste, o maledìche": see Di Filippo Bareggi 1973 (as in fn. 202), p. 541.

[423] On the loss of many of the compositions that were written in criticism of Bandinelli's marble, compare Waldman 1994 (as in fn. 397), p. 419: "In view of the lasting resonance of the statue's fatal reception in the historiography of art, it is unfortunate that nearly all of these colorful verse-documents have perished." For the hypothesis that Grand Duke Francesco I might have taken dispositions to prohibit the circulation and preservation of the many derisive poems that were written on the *Last Judgment* for the Cupola of Santa Maria del Fiore, see Detlef Heikamp, Federico Zuccari e la cupola di Santa Maria del Fiore: la fortuna critica dei suoi affreschi, in: Bonita Cleri (ed.), *Federico Zuccari: le idee, gli scritti*, Milan 1997, pp. 139–157, p. 145, and idem, Federico scandalista, in: Cristina Acidini and Elena Capretti (eds.), *Innocente e calunniato: Federico Zuccari (1539/40–1609) e le vendette d'artista*, Florence 2009, pp. 46–77, p. 68.

[424] For useful introductions to these authors' poems on art see Silvia Vantaggiato, "Non fate enigmi o poesie storpiate": alcune osservazioni di Antonfrancesco Grazzini sul "parlar fiorentino," in: *Annali di critica d'arte. Nuova serie* 1 (2017), pp. 123–143, and Masi 2007 (as in fn. 91).

[425] Compare Vasari 1967–1997 (as in fn. 74), 5, p. 268 (from the Giuntina's biography of Bandinelli): "Ma come avviene che il figulo ['the potter'] sempre invidia e noia il figulo, e lo scultore l'altro scultore, non potette Baccio sopportare i favori varii fatti a Benvenuto." The definition of *odium figulinum*, designating a professional rivalry spurred by envy and a malicious form of emulation, was first used by Friedrich Nietzsche with reference to

icant portion of Cellini's poems. In his verse artistic criticism, often mocking his rivals' technical inadequacy or lack of professional ethics, goes hand in hand with taunts that do not shy away from the scatological register nor, for example, from unflattering gossip about their sex lives.[426] In short, his poems combine arguments more specifically pertinent to judging art with the kind of base insults that in Tuscany had fueled a rich tradition of comical poetry dating to at least the thirteenth-century Rustico Filippi, and that underlay the foul language of many Renaissance pasquinades and "libelli famosi."[427] In following the codes of the *vituperium ad personam*, Cellini's poems attacking other artists of ducal Florence were thus perfect representations of the genre of libelous, malicious, and sometimes indecent writing that don Vincenzio Borghini decried as the fruit of "animi ignobili e villani" in his discourse *Dello scrivere contro ad alcuno*.[428] Cellini's polemical compositions were also a sign of the Florentine artists' habit of sectarianism and venomous professional criticism that, under the hand of its lieutenant Borghini, the Accademia del Disegno tried to contain: aimed at discouraging all conduct that

---

Hesiod (Hesiod, *Works and Days*, ed. Martin Litchfield West, Oxford 1978, p. 147, ll. 25–26: "And the potter bears ill will towards the potter and the carpenter to the carpenter, and the beggar envies the beggar and the singer, the singer"). For the Renaissance afterlife of this idea, see Pigman 1980 (as in fn. 131), pp. 16–17; David Cast, *The Calumny of Apelles: A Study in the Humanist Tradition*, New Haven, CT 1981, pp. 141–148, and, with reference to Vasari's discussion, Cast 2009 (as in fn. 345), p. 186, n. 37. For the central place of envy in Vasari's descriptions of artistic rivalries, see Goffen 2002 (as in fn. 145), p. 71 and *passim*, as well as Jana Graul, "Particolare Vizio de' Professori di Queste Nostre Arti": On the Concept of Envy in Vasari's *Vite*, in: *I Tatti Studies in the Italian Renaissance* 18 (2015), pp. 113–146.

[426] Compare, for example, the author's poetic attack on Giorgio Vasari in the sonettessa *Veduto Giove poi sciolto 'l Furore* (Cellini 2014 [as in fn. 7], p. 111, ll. 17–20: "Ogni cosa enterrà 'n culo a Giorgietto: / se' non à più diletto / sel torrà in culo la sua pulita moglie, / che può cavarsi tutte le sue voglie"), which describes the painter as someone who had long practiced sodomy and claims that his wife was suffering from the ills of marital neglect. On this use of sodomy as a mode of attack, see Gallucci 2003 (as in fn. 405), p. 63. Also relevant is the scatological four-verse stanza that Cellini's autobiography records him having written against the rival goldsmith Bernardone Baldini, whom he depicted as a man incapable of controlling his corporeal functions (see Cellini 1996 [as in fn. 23], p. 705 [*Vita* 2.89], incipit: *Qui giace Bernardone, asin, porcaccio*; on which see Gallucci 2003, p. 64).

[427] On the "poetics of insult" in medieval Italian poetry, see most recently Fabian Alfie, *Rustico Filippi, "The Art of Insult,"* Cambridge 2014, and idem, *Dante's Tenzone with Forese Donati: The Reprehension of Vice*, Toronto 2011 (Dante's *tenzone* with Forese Donati was an exchange in which Dante notoriously alluded to how Forese's wife was suffering from marital neglect). On the early modern genre of the *libello famoso*, which Giovan Battista De Luca described in the second half of the seventeenth century as "quella scrittura, la quale in forma di cartello o di epitafio s'affigga pubblicamente per infamare e per ingiuriare qualche persona, descrivendovi alcuni suoi delitti o mancamenti; overamente sia quella scrittura in folio la quale come una specie di manifesto si manda in giro, o sia scrittura in prosa, o sia in verso," see Ottavia Niccoli, Anticlericalismo italiano e rituali dell'infamia da Alessandro VI a Pio V, in: *Studi storici* 43 (2002), pp. 921–965 (De Luca's quote is on p. 928). Notably, according to the sculptor's autobiography (Cellini 1996 [as in fn. 23], p. 705 [*Vita* 2.89]), Cellini appended his poem against Bernardone Baldini to a corner of the church of San Piero Scheraggio that Florentines used as a latrine. This is consistent with what was then the typical mode of publicizing the *libelli famosi*, which were hung in prominent places that bore some symbolic association with the object of the attack: see Spagnolo 2014 (as in fn. 419), p. 271.

[428] See Vincenzo Borghini, *Dello scrivere contro ad alcuno, discorso inedito*, ed. Giuseppe Aiazzi, Florence 1841, p. 2. On Borghini's condemnation of *ad personam* attacks, see also Waźbiński 1977 (as in fn. 417), pp. 12–13.

might undermine the institution's internal unity, the academic *Capitoli* of July 1563, for example, went so far as to demand that all of the Academy's members love each other like brothers.[429]

While it is reasonable to doubt that the artists of ducal Florence were ever persuaded to embrace such ideals of fraternal love, some of them did choose to conduct their artistic diatribes within limits of decorum not far from the boundaries that Borghini called for. In this sense we can compare the virulence, derisive tone, and frequent vulgarity of Cellini's poems attacking his Florentine rivals with the allusions Bronzino employed to criticize the stylistic tendencies advocated by certain unnamed contemporary painters and architects in his capitolo *Secondo delle Scuse*.[430] Avoiding *ad hominem* attacks was an expressive choice suited to an individual from whom his contemporaries considered it difficult to "cavar[...] l'opininion," being "modesto" and unwilling to talk about others "se non bene,"[431] but above all it was a deliberate choice Bronzino stated in those very lines. Heeding Martial's vow to spare people and speak of vices ("parcere personis, dicere de vitiis:" *Epigrams* 10.33.10) and adopting a satirical voice reminiscent of Horace in its tendency to avoid the harshness of personal insult and concentrate on the instructive, philosophical value of criticism, he wrote:

> Io pur so ch'avvertito e a rilento
>   andar m'ingegno e far danno o dir male
>   a uom del mondo non cerco o consento.
> Ben veggio il segno e vi saprei lo strale
>   voltar, ma no 'l farei, che ben intende
>   a chi tocca, un che parli in generale.[432]

Bronzino would return to the theme of the constructive utility of criticism for those who accepted it intelligently in lengthy passages of his burlesque capitolo *Del biasimo*. Here, in

---

[429] For the relevant precept of the *Accademia del Disegno*, see the *Capitolo Primo* of July 1563, under the rubric *Dell'Amor d'Iddio e charità verso il Prossimo* (text in Waźbiński 1987 [as in fn. 149], 1, p. 437): "Siamo poscia tenuti d'amarci scambievolmente tutti l'un l'altro a guisa de Fratelli, di vero e perfetto Amore, e d'aiutarci, e consigliarci insieme sinceramente, e con fede pura." We might compare this precept with one of the laws that regulated the Roman artistic Academy of Saint Luke, which specifically targeted artists who had written vituperative compositions against fellow painters and sculptors (see ibid., p. 514, among the *Ordini dell'Accademia de' Pittori et Scultori di Roma* of 1609): "Nissun Academico possa porre, o far porre [...] Sonetti [...] nell'Academia, senza licenza del Prencipe Academico, & Congregatione secreta [...]. Che non si possa ammetter, ne ricever per Academico alcuno, che havesse scritto, ò fatto scrivere contra la reputatione di questi professori ò in stampa, ò à mano scrittura contra la reputatione di questi professori Academici, se non in caso, che quel tale si disdicesse in publico dell'errore commesso e ne domandasse perdono, & si sottomettesse alla coretione da farsegli." On the latter document, see Spagnolo 2010 (as in fn. 417), p. 283.
[430] On the poem, see esp. Brock 2002 (as in fn. 6), pp. 312–313, and Parker 2004 (as in fn. 6), as well as the considerations in ch. 1.
[431] The quote is from Vincenzio Borghini's letter to Giorgio Vasari, August 15, 1564 (Vasari 1923–1930 [as in fn. 76], 2, pp. 104–105). Compare also Vasari's depiction of his colleague's good nature in the Giuntina: "è stato di natura quieto e non ha mai fatto ingiuria a niuno, et ha sempre amato tutti i valent'uomini della sua professione" (Vasari 1967–1997 [as in fn. 74], 6, p. 238).
[432] Bronzino 1988 (as in fn. 6), p. 193, ll. 27–32. For a discussion of the characteristics of Horace's satirical voice, see J.C. Bramble, *Persius and the Programmatic Satire: A Study in Form and Imagery*, Cambridge 1974, pp. 190–204.

addition to denouncing the inordinate appetite for backbiting of the many who "Hanno nel biasimar […] un diletto, / ch'e' non n'hanno tanto [i.e. altrettanto] a tavola e nel letto," he criticized the exaggerated sense of self of those who responded to caustic comments with a wish to silence their rivals. What's more, Bronzino stated that fighting scorn with scorn wasted the valuable opportunity to improve oneself and one's work in light of the criticism received. Fusing Alberti's and Vasari's points of view, he noted that this was all the more true for good painters, who by simply hearing their creations critiqued would be motivated to refine their art, even if the rebukes were unwarranted:

> Un dipintor, quando l'opere sue
>   sente lodar, poco n'avanza e parli
>   esser qualcosa almanco delle due;
> ma quand'egl'ode ch'uno o più ne parli
>   con biasimarlo o sia vero o bugia,
>   s'egli è da ben, non può se non giovarli.[433]

While in Bronzino's poetry both the theory and the practice of artistic critique were on a higher plane than the low blows of *ad hominem* attacks, as noted earlier such attacks were the mainstay of the many poems Cellini addressed to other artists in Medici Florence. Several events in the city's arts scene served as catalysts for his *vis polemica*. The most notable of these was the contest among sculptors to win the ducal commission to build the *Fountain of Neptune* in the Piazza della Signoria, which led Cellini to aim his barbs first at the despised Baccio and later, after Baccio's death, at Ammannati, whom Cosimo selected to realize the work.[434] And Cellini was given plenty to ridicule when in 1557 the young Vincenzo Danti, who had recently moved to Florence from his native Perugia hoping to become a successful sculptor in the service of Duke Cosimo, failed three times at casting the bronze *Hercules and Antaeus* for the fountain at the Medici Villa of Castello.[435] Sometimes the target of his poetic invective

---

[433] For the relevant considerations in Alberti's *De pictura* (in Domenichi's Italian version from 1547), see *supra*, p. 124. Compare also Vasari's remarks in the 1550 biography of Donatello on the necessity that artists be exposed to pungent criticism to improve themselves, as well as on the fact that excessive praise is counterproductive. This reasoning justified Donatello's decision to leave behind the encomia he received in Padua and return to the harsh criticism of the Florentine audience (Vasari 1967–1997 [as in fn. 74], 3, p. 215): "Onde essendo per miracolo quivi tenuto e da ogni intelligente lodato, si deliberò di voler tornare a Fiorenza, dicendo che se più stato vi fosse, tutto quello che sapeva dimenticato s'averebbe, essendovi tanto lodato da ognuno, e che volentieri nella sua patria tornava per esser poi colà di continuo biasimato: il quale biasmo gli dava cagione di studio, e consequentemente di gloria maggiore."

[434] See, for instance, the sonnet *Cavalier, se voi fussi anche poeta* (Cellini 2014 [as in fn. 7], no. 46) and the fragment *io fo modegli, altrui à l'opre e 'l vanto* (ibid., no. 62), as well as the prosimeters *Sogno di Benvenuto Cellini* and *Sognio fatto innel sonnellin dell'oro* (nos. 49–50). The vituperative poems that the author penned against other artists, whose salient characteristics are here discussed, are the object of an extensive contextualization and a detailed commentary in ibid. For this reason, I refer to that work for the critical edition and in-depth analysis of these compositions.

[435] See ibid., the commentary on the sonnets *E' suol la gioventù gittar pur bene* (no. 43) and *Hercol sospese, uccise Anteo et poi* (no. 55), as well as on the fragment *Hercol sospese Anteo poi 'l gittò via* (no. 44), with further references. It is noteworthy that just a few years after the failure of the casting of the *Hercules and Antaeus*, the victim of these poetic attacks wrote a highly encomiastic sonnet for Cellini's marble *Crucifix* (completed in

was not specific commissions or artworks by his rivals, but a position they had taken on a question of artistic theory or practice: this is the case of the composition Cellini addressed to Vasari during the debate over the iconographic program for Michelangelo's funeral in Florence, contesting Vasari's stance that the allegory of painting should take visual prominence over that of sculpture.[436] Equally instructive is the sonnet in which the author accused the sculptors Bartolomeo Ammannati and Vincenzo de' Rossi of having chosen to follow the model of Baccio Bandinelli rather than the incomparably superior example of Buonarroti, the emblem of pure *Fiorentinità* in art.[437]

This survey at the artistic debates Cellini conducted through the poetic medium is sufficient to suggest that his *Rime*, in all probability, are the most explicit evidence of the highly rivalrous environment of the Florentine sculpture in the second half of the Cinquecento. The *odium figulinum* that runs through these compositions offers, in fact, an instructive and less than edifying counterpoint to Cosimo Bartoli's description of competition as the driving force of the city's contemporary sculptoreal scene in his *Ragionamenti Accademici*. Praising the exceptional achievements of local sculptors, Bartoli reported that masters of the caliber of Bandinelli and Cellini himself had to compete with a constant influx of brilliant, cutthroat new rivals for the few available ducal commissions, and that such an antagonism was all the fiercer due to the decrease in private commissions, which had forced many other Florentine artists into a kind of diaspora in search of better prospects than those offered by the duchy.[438] Within this scenario, writing poetry against someone of the likes of Ammannati or Danti, having presented artists' verse as the ultimate bar of judgment on art, became one of Cellini's methods of waging the "struggles for the monopoly of the definition of the mode of legitimate

---

1562), as well as a second celebratory poem for the older sculptor-writer, most probably in the attempt to win his former critic's allegiance (for a discussion of the compositions, *Voi Ben dal ciel, voi Ben venuto siete*, and *Non vogliate, Signor, prendere a sdegno*, see Proctor 2013 [as in fn. 307], pp. 193–201 and 229–230). The poems, whose manuscript versions are preserved among Cellini's papers in the Biblioteca Riccardiana in Florence, seem to have accomplished this mission. In the first version of his *Trattati dell'Oreficeria e della Scultura* (1565–1567), Cellini was far more generous towards Danti, whom he designated as a "valent[e] giovan[e]," and justified his aborted project of the *Hercules and Antaeus* by attributing it to the peculiar characteristics of Florentine plasters for bronze casting (on this, see Cellini 2014 [as in fn. 7], commentary to no. 43, p. 118).

[436] Consider, for example, the poems *Crocino, io spendo in Dïo tutte l'ore* (ibid., no. 110) and *Gli à dato la sentenzia giusta et pura* (no. 125).

[437] See ibid., no. 66, sonnet *Fiesol et Settignian Pinzedimonte*.

[438] As Charles Davis observed (Davis 1976 [as in fn. 308], p. 26, but see also pp. 27–37 for an insightful analysis of the text under consideration), Bartoli's *Ragionamenti* were published in Venice in 1567, but had been written in Florence in ca. 1550. The relevant passage, which explains how the commissions from the duke or being forced to leave Florence were the only means for Florentine sculptors to avoid poverty, is Bartoli 1567 (as in fn. 138), c. 19v: "So bene che, oltre al Cavalier Bandinello et Benvenuto Cellini, che sono di età, che egli ci è una sorte di giovani fiorentini che sono talmente esercitati in questi tempi in questa arte, che s'eglino havessero per oggetto quelle ricchezze et quegli huomini che havevano in quel tempo gli statuarii romani, che noi vedremmo in breve tempo cose eccellentissime et grandi, che darebbero forse non meno fama a Firenze che si facessero le cose antiche a Roma. Ma noi non siamo tali che possiamo, ancor che questa arte ci diletti, trattenere così fatti maestri, et che ciò sia il vero, vedete che nostri scultori ne sono oggi per tutto il mondo, et particularmente guadagnano assai per tutta Italia, dove qui in Firenze non hanno chi gli possa trattenere, sadvo però quegli che lavorano per sua Eccellenzia."

cultural production" which, Bourdieu wrote, are the fundamental dynamic forces of change in the fields of artistic and literary production of every age.[439] To put it differently, these compositions that decried (for example) a sculptor's betrayal of Michelangelo's teachings were for their author a form of *extension du domaine de la lutte* which pointed out, for a lay audience, all the errors and shortcomings of his competitors. We can also assume that he found nothing reprehensible in that ferocious mode of criticism within the artistic community. Like Alberti before him, Cellini believed that this kind of censure would never afflict works of manifest excellence, which would manage to impress even the envious and overcritical – a faith he had seen confirmed, for example, when the abhorred Baccio Bandinelli had given Duke Cosimo an astronomical estimate of the *Perseus*.[440] But these critical poems were not merely instrumental to conducting a theoretical dispute over the proper way to make art, to the detriment of competing aesthetic preferences embodied by other artists then working in Florence. Cellini also theorized that such compositions should play a key role in influencing the assignment of the most coveted ducal commissions, and therefore have a concrete impact – in Bourdieu's terms – on economic capital.[441] He left an instructive example in his autobiography when he described

---

[439] Bourdieu 1996 (as in fn. 347), pp. 227ff.
[440] Compare Cellini 1996 (as in fn. 23), pp. 726–727 (*Vita* 2.97): "Giunto che Sua Eccellenzia fu a Palazzo, ei chiamò il vescovo de' Bartolini […] et […] misser Pandolfo della Stufa, et disse loro che dicessino a Baccio Bandinelli da sua parte, che considerassi bene quella mia opera del Perseo, et che la stimassi, perché el Duca me la voleva pagare el giusto prezzo […]. Il detto rispose che l'aveva benissimo considerata […] et che quella opera era riuscita molto ricca et bella, di modo che gli pareva che la meritassi sedicimila scudi d'oro et da vantaggio. Subito i buoni gentili uomini lo riferirno al Duca, il quale si adirò malamente." It is evident from this passage how the idea that artists would express the most knowledgeable *giudizio* (whether orally or by means of written compositions) about the works of colleagues relied on the same assumptions as the long-established practice of having painters or sculptors as the most qualified consultants for the assessment of an artwork's monetary value, especially in the case of a disagreement between an artist and his patron. Focusing on the case of Vasari's *Vite*, Franceschini 2021 (as in fn. 346) examines comparable interferences between the practice of an artist who wrote evaluations of the works of his predecessors or contemporary colleagues and the historical phenomenon of Renaissance painters and sculptors taking part in processes of economic assessments of artworks such as the *stime*, *lodi*, and *arbitrati*. It is useful to recall that in Florence, such processes were already codified for painters in the *Statuti dell'Arte dei Medici e Speziali* from 1349 (see the norm *Delle questioni che vengono per la dipintura de' dipintori* in Waźbiński 1987 [as in fn. 149], 2, pp. 415–416), and were revitalized after the foundation of the Accademia del Disegno (see, for instance, ibid., pp. 434–435, *capitolo* no. 40 of the newly founded institution, from January 1563). It is also useful to observe that in the final months of the artist's life, the artworks that Cellini had created for Cosimo underwent one such assessment by his peers. When, in September 1570, Cellini appealed to the Florentine magistrature of the Soprassindaci, requesting over 2400 *scudi* from the grand duke as a settlement for several payments due for his marbles of *Ganymede* and the *Crucifix*, as well as for his bronze bust of Cosimo and a gold chalice representing the theological virtues, the magistrates summoned two sculptors and one goldsmith to provide a new estimate for these artworks. It was probably not an accident that the Soprassindaci chose two of the sculptors that Cellini most despised and whom he had most vehemently attacked in his writings – namely, Bartolomeo Ammannati and Vincenzo de' Rossi – along with the goldsmith Niccolò di Francesco Santini. Perhaps the fact that these artists provided a total estimate of just 1030 *scudi* for their peer's creations eventually crushed Cellini's belief that artistic excellence would always overcome professional rivalries: see the documents in Cellini 1829 (as in fn. 330), 3, pp. 192–202.
[441] The reference here is to Bourdieu's influential classification of the three main types of capital (economic, social, and cultural) in: John G. Richardson, *Handbook of Theory and Research for the Sociology of Education*, Westport, CT 1986, pp. 46–58.

the artistic competition for the block of marble destined to become the *Fountain of Neptune*. In recounting his attempt to convince Duke Cosimo to reassign the work previously given to Bandinelli only after holding a public competition among the court's sculptors, he wrote:

> Fate, Signor mio, che ogniuno che vuole faccia un modello e dipoi tutti si scuoprano alla Scuola, e Vostra Eccellenzia con quel suo buon iudizio saprà scerre il meglio, et in questo modo voi non gitterete via i vostri dinari, né manco torrete l'animo virtuoso a una tanto mirabile Scuola, la quale si è oggi unica al mondo: ch'è tutt'a gloria di Vostra Eccellenzia illustrissima.[442]

According to Cellini, then, Cosimo had to decide who deserved the commission only after considering the ultimate arbiter of the sculptors' work: the reactions of the Florentine artistic community to the competing models, which would presumably be expressed to some extent in verse. In this way, a creation fiercely criticized by the Scuola Fiorentina could properly orient the duke's "buon iudizio" and dissuade him from investing money on an artist not up to the task.

Self-defense poems

In an art scene rife with critical turbulence like Florence in the second half of the Cinquecento, painters, sculptors, and architects targeted by poems berating their work responded in a variety of ways to such attacks. Sometimes, despite their full mastery of the pen, they mounted a vigorous self-defense of themselves and their art through the visual medium rather than writing. This is the case of the Marchigian painter Federico Zuccari, selected by Grand Duke Francesco to complete the *Last Judgment* for the cupola of Santa Maria del Fiore that had been left unfinished upon Giorgio Vasari's death in 1574. To the many "sonetti, canzone et madrigali in biasimo dell'opra" that the Florentines had begun to compose even before the painted cycle was unveiled (August 19, 1579), Zuccari responded by commissioning a medal from Pastorino de' Pastorini celebrating his work in the Cathedral.[443] The contentious tone

---

[442] Cellini 1996 (as in fn. 23), p. 735 (*Vita* 2.99). On the presence of the idea that artistic competition is the catalyst for the best creative energies in Cellini's writings, which had been expressed several times in Vasari's Torrentiniana, see esp. Patricia L. Reilly, Drawing the Line: Benvenuto Cellini's "On the Principles and Method of Learning the Art of Drawing" and the Question of Amateur Drawing Education, in: Gallucci and Rossi 2004 (as in fn. 119), pp. 26–50, pp. 39–43; Victoria C. Gardner Coates, "Sculpsit Cellinius Neptunam": The Biography of the *Neptune* Fountain in Cellini's *Vita*, in: *Renaissance Studies* 19 (2005), pp. 604–618, pp. 612–613; Stimato 2008 (as in fn. 8), pp. 175–178, and my own commentary in Cellini 2014 (as in fn. 7), pp. 142–143.

[443] With these words of 1581, Zuccari indicated a blizzard of vituperative compositions criticizing the *Last Judgment*, which were in part an expression of the Florentine audience's campanilistic hostility towards the Marchigian painter: see Vincenzo Lanciarini, *Dei pittori Taddeo e Federigo Zuccari di S. Angelo in Vado*, Jesi 1893, pp. 125–126; on the process, see Elena Capretti, Firenze 1575–1579: l'impresa del *Giudizio Universale*, le polemiche, la casa di via del Mandorlo, in: Acidini Luchinat and Capretti 2009 (as in fn. 423), pp. 122–127. On Pastorino's medal, see, most recently, the entry of Capretti, ibid., pp. 150–151. For a discussion of the only remaining poem mocking Zuccari's work for the Cupola, see Diletta Gamberini, La "concucia nana" di Federico Zuccari: critica d'arte in versi all'ombra del *Giudizio Universale* per la cupola di Santa Maria del Fiore, in: *Mitteilungen des Kunsthistorischen Institutes in Florenz* 59, no. 3 (2017), pp. 362–387.

of Zuccari's self-defense would become even more explicit in the invention he developed for Cornelis Cort's engraving *The Painter of True Intelligence* or *Lament of Painting*, a complex allegory portraying a noble artist at work in his studio surrounded by Envy, the Furies, and rabid dogs that has usually been interpreted as a response to criticism of the Cathedral's *Judgment*.[444]

Unlike Zuccari, other artists might have chosen the poetic medium in response to the poems Florentine authors had composed to mock their works: this appears to be the case for two sonettesse that read like justifications of artworks targeted by such attacks. Attribution is in this case a slippery issue because the compositions have come down to us in anonymous and non-autograph manuscript form, which leaves some doubt as to their paternity – all the more so because some of the principal burlesque poets of ducal Florence would sometimes write and circulate their caustic verse under other names.[445] Necessary caution in attributing these poems does not, however, negate the well-founded suspicion that they were penned by the two painters criticized in verse. In any case, a look at the exchanges in which these compositions are situated will allow us, in conclusion, to tie together the threads discussed in this chapter.

The first of these confrontations was prompted by the allegorical frescoes outside the home of the Perugian Sforza Almeni, Duke Cosimo's cupbearer and private chamberlain. The story of those lost paintings is well known: when Almeni asked him to propose a decorative scheme for the Via de' Servi façade of his Florentine palazzo, Giorgio Vasari responded by developing some inventions by Cosimo Bartoli into an iconographic program as ambitious as it was complex. Described in its innermost details and meanings in letters Vasari sent to his patron from Rome in the fall of 1553, the program, "che conteneva, per dirlo brevemente, tutta la vita dell'uomo dalla nascita per infino alla morte," was mostly executed by the painter Cristofano Gherardi.[446] Upon its completion in September 1555, the dense forest of person-

---

[444] See esp. Ważbiński 1977 (as in fn. 417), and idem, Lo studio: la scuola fiorentina di Federico Zuccari, in: *Mitteilungen des Kunsthistorischen Institutes in Florenz* 29, no. 2/3 (1985), pp. 275–346; Heikamp 1997 (as in fn. 423), p. 145, as well as the entry by Giorgio Marini in: Acidini and Capretti 2009 (as in fn. 423), pp. 154–157. For a different interpretation of the allegorical print see Wendy Thompson, Federico Zuccaro's Love Affair with Florence: Two Allegorical Designs, in: *Metropolitan Museum Journal* 43 (2008), pp. 75–97.

[445] The practice of composing burlesque poems with false attributions is well attested in the literary output of Antonfrancesco Grazzini, alias il Lasca, who on different occasions penned his texts "in nome di" someone else: to name just a few examples, see the sonettesse *Al Signor Diego Spagnuolo in nome di messer Goro della Pieve*, *A Michel da Prato in nome del Margolla* ("Margolla" being the nickname of Francesco da Sangallo), and the capitolo *A M. Bernardino Grazzini in nome di Lorenzo degli Organi* (see Grazzini 1882 [as in fn. 263], pp. 64, 108, and 596). One famous and earlier example of the diffusion of pseudepigraphic comic poems is the capitolo *Com'io ebbi la vostra, signor mio*, which Michelangelo addressed to Francesco Berni in the name of their common friend Sebastiano del Piombo. We should note, however, that in Grazzini's poetic corpus these compositions bore an indication of their pseudepigraphic character in the rubric.

[446] The quote is from Vasari's biography of Cristofano Gherardi in the Giuntina (Vasari 1967–1997 [as in fn. 74], 5, p. 295), which described at length the iconographical program for the façade. On the program see also the letters that the Aretine addressed to Almeni in the fall of 1553 (Vasari 1923–1930 [as in fn. 76], 1, pp. 368–388). Fundamental studies of the frescoes include Hans-Werner Schmidt, Vasaris Fassadenmalerei am Palazzo Almeni, in: Franz Graf, Wolff Metternich, Leo Bruhns, and Ludwig Schudt (eds.), *Miscellanea Bibliothecae Hertzianae*, Munich 1961, pp. 271–274; Charles Davis, Frescoes by Vasari for Sforza Almeni, "Coppiere" to Duke Cosimo I, in: *Mitteilungen des Kunsthistorischen Institutes in Florenz* 24, no. 2 (1980), pp. 127–202; Antonella Fenech Kroke,

ifications and allegorical scenes painted on the façade of Palazzo Almeni became a topic of fierce debate for those sonnetists most attuned to the city's artistic affairs. While Antonfrancesco Grazzini sent Almeni a poem praising Vasari for the "giudizio" and "pennel" he had demonstrated in the "miracol" of that decorative program, the city's other great specialist in vituperative poems of artworks took a decidedly different stance.[447] In his sonnet *L'Etrusco non ne dice ben né male* (Appendix, no. 71), Alfonso de' Pazzi began by claiming that he wished neither to compliment nor criticize the work, then essentially demolished the "nuova bizzarra e gran facciata."[448] His critique was an explicit counterpoint to the frescoes' popularity with a certain "brigata," almost certainly meaning the cadre of literati and artists who gravitated around Benedetto Varchi and whose taste in the visual arts Pazzi had already ridiculed in a poem mocking Cellini's *Perseus*.[449]

Pazzi aimed his barbs at the entire allegorical program of Palazzo Almeni (Fig. 18). Alleging their violation of the principle of expediency and decorum, he critiqued many of Vasari's subjects: the liberal arts, which "l'Etrusco" complained were positioned too far down the wall; the ages of man; the planets, noted with irony for their position outside the palazzo's kitchen; the theological and cardinal virtues; the personifications of Perugia and Florence; the incongruous painted architecture allegedly recalling a triumphal arch or a "prospettiva," that is, a theater scenography; and above all, the final resurrection ("surretione") of the dead that

---

Giorgio Vasari: la fabrique de l'allégorie. Culture et fonction de la personification au Cinquecento, Florence 2011, pp. 246–257, and Ruffini 2011 (as in fn. 135), pp. 49–53. For the exact chronology of the decoration, see the note in Vasari's *Ricordanze* in Vasari 1923–1930, 2, p. 871.

[447] See the sonnet *Alto signor, che 'n questa bassa e frale* (Antonfrancesco Grazzini, *Rime di Antonfrancesco Grazzini detto Il Lasca* […], eds. Antonio Maria Biscioni and Francesco Moücke, 2 vols., Florence 1741–1742, 1, p. 26), ll. 9–14: "Oggi il grande Aretin, vostra mercede, / Ha col giudizio e col pennel dimostro, / Quanto far possa la Natura e l'Arte; // Che chi mira di fuor l'albergo vostro, / Miracol tale, e così fatto vede, / Ch'attonito e stupito indi si parte."

[448] First examined from the point of view of its art historical implications by Heikamp 1957 (as in fn. 405), pp. 161–62 (154–155 for the edition of the text), Pazzi's composition has recently been the object of two most useful critical discussions: Jonietz 2017 (as in fn. 344), pp. 303–305, considers the poem's attack on the most distinguishing visual features of the iconography of the frescoes, while Paolo Celi, "Che non l'arebbe fat'a pena Cuio". Porte, apparati e facciate fiorentine in tre testi pasquineschi dello Zoppo carrozziere e dell'Etrusco, forthcoming in: *Mitteilungen des Kunsthistorischen Institutes in Florenz* 63.1 (2021), provides a new critical edition of the poem.

[449] According to Pazzi, the painted façade of Palazzo Almeni "molto contenta la brigata" (l. 3). Compare what the author had written in a sonnet that he had penned before the final unveiling of the *Perseus*, in which he mockingly anticipated that Benedetto Varchi and his friends would lavish much undue praise on Cellini's statue: "Un gran vedere ha il nostro Benvenuto / da tener la sua opera turata: / ed a più cautela ei l'ha murata, / acciò che 'l suo Perseo non sia veduto. // E così buono e bel sarà tenuto / da 'l Varchi nostro e da l'orba brigata; / ma, come la fia ritta ed isvelata, / conseguirà il guidardon dovuto. // Selvaggio fu, più daga che dottore, / al colpo marziale; e se Medusa / sodisfar sapea di Perseo 'l furore, // e non dava le rene, come già usa, / in preda non saria di uno scultore, / e manco 'l Varchi e lui della mia Musa" (text from Heikamp 1957 [as in fn. 405], pp. 152–153, and see also ibid., pp. 148–149). After Cellini's bronze statue was unveiled, Pazzi penned a new, mocking poem against it (see Cellini 1857 [as in fn. 330], p. 228): "Corpo di vecchio e gambe di fanciulla / Ha il nuovo Perseo; e, tutto insieme, / Ci può bello parer, ma non val nulla."

clashed with the profane character of the other scenes.[450] The point of this rundown was to ridicule the iconography's confused, cumbersome nature, which Pazzi argued was akin to the jumble of disparate arguments typical of Varchi's academic lectures. Hostile to the allegories' alleged pretentiousness, he also denounced what he saw as their improper educational mission: he thus derided Vasari's choice to include an abundance of explanatory inscriptions, in an attempt to communicate even to "contadini" the frescoes' arcane philosophical meanings and therefore "insegnar le scienze con le mure."[451] In Pazzi's view, Architecture herself would have objected that these supposed explanations merely obscured further the already cryptic content they were meant to illuminate.

Pazzi's biting text was met by an equally pugnacious reply by an anonymous poet (*Certo, Etrusco, tu sei un huom bestiale*: Appendix, no. 72), and there is reason to suspect that it was Vasari who composed this sonettessa, for the *vox auctoris* identifies himself as responsible for the iconographic program of the disputed façade (ll. 11–14).[452] The kind of *ad personam* attack in which the text engages also suggests that the criticism of the Palazzo Almeni paintings had struck a nerve in the person who wrote it: the author berates Pazzi with insult upon insult, accusing him of bestiality, insanity, poor intellect, and a complete lack of moral integrity, not to mention the most contemptible inclination for malicious gossip. In siding with Varchi and his *sodalitas*, targeted by Pazzi's disapproval, he then chooses not to address the specific complaints concerning the supposed shortcomings of the façade. Instead, he brings the dispute to the moral plane, in an attempt to discredit his rival's artistic critique as the expression of a "peste venuta al mondo per dir male," following a strategy of thoroughly delegitimizing an unfavorable aesthetic judgment which for that matter finds several echoes in Vasari's *Vite*.[453]

---

[450] All these elements find exact correspondences in Vasari's lengthy description of the painted façade in the Giuntina biography of Gherardi (Vasari 1967-1997 [as in fn. 74], 5, pp. 297–300; my emphasis): "A canto dunque alla cornice del tetto è in prospettiva un cornicione con mensole [...]. Finita questa fregiatura, in fra i vani delle dette finestre di sopra [...] si fecioro i *7 pianeti* con i 7 segni celesti [...]. Sotto il davanzale di queste finestre, nel parapetto, è una fregiatura di *Virtù* che a due a due tengono sette ovati grandi; dentro ai quali ovati sono distinte *le sette età dell'uomo* [...]. Fra le finestre inginocchiate poi è la Vita attiva e la contemplativa, con istorie e statue per insino alla morte, inferno et *ultima resurrezione nostra* [...]. Fra gli spazii delle finestre di sotto, sono *le tre Virtù teologiche e le quattro morali*; e sotto [...] sono *le sette Arti liberali* [...]. Fra questa storia et il fregio, dove sono l'Arti liberali [...] è *Perugia in una figura ignuda*: avendo un cane in mano, lo mostra a una *Fiorenza* ch'è dall'altra banda."

[451] On this, see esp. Jonietz 2017 (as in fn. 344), pp. 304–305.

[452] An aggressively burlesque text would not be an unicum in Vasari's poetic output: one relevant example is the composition in ottave criticizing Pietro Aretino in Vasari 2012 (as in fn. 7), pp. 32–38. Contrary to what has happened with Pazzi's vituperative poem, the poem in defence of the painted façade of Palazzo Almeni (first published in Heikamp 1957 [as in fn. 405], pp. 155–156) has not attracted any scholarly attention, nor has it ever been suggested that it might be by Vasari himself.

[453] We might compare the moralistic arguments that our sonettessa directs at Pazzi with those that Vasari used in the Giuntina biography of Jacone, on which see Antonio Pinelli, Vivere "alla filosofica" o vestire di velluto? Storia di Jacone fiorentino e della sua "masnada" antivasariana, in: *Ricerche di storia dell'arte* 34 (1988), pp. 5–34; Charles Davis, Michelangelo, Jacone and the Confraternity of the Virgin Annunciate Called "Dell'Orciuolo," in: *Apollo* 156 (2002), pp. 22–29; Karen Hope Goodchild, Bizarre Painters and Bohemian Poets: Poetic Imitation and Artistic Rivalry in Vasari's Biography of Piero di Cosimo, in: Cast 2014 (as in fn. 86), pp. 129–144, pp. 143–144. Vasari evoked, without ever specifying its contents, the criticism that Jacone and his friends had

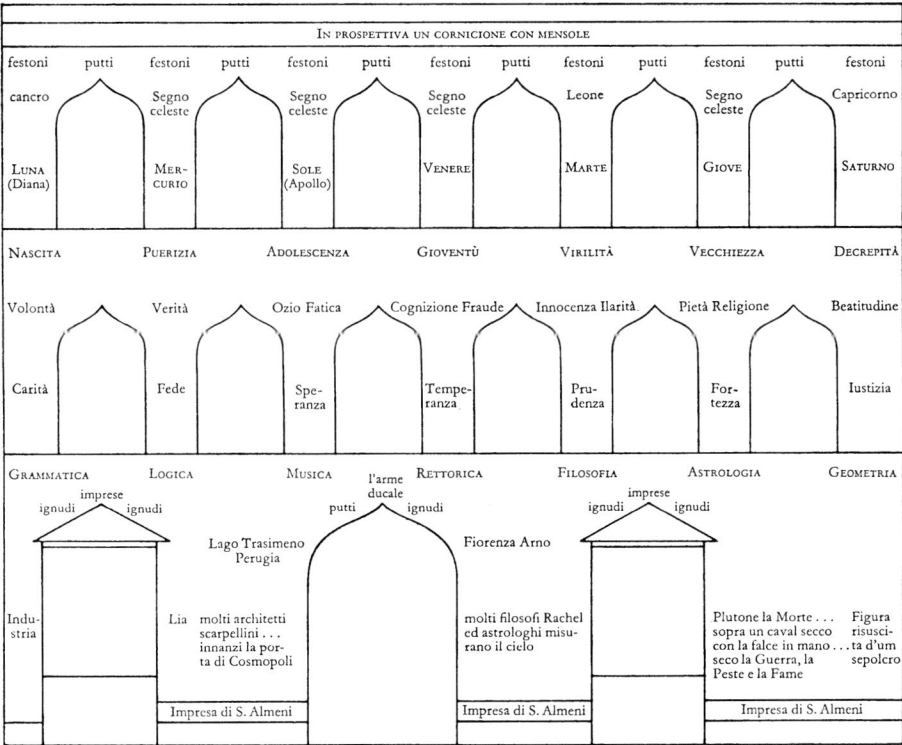

18 Scheme of Giorgio Vasari's allegorical program for the painted façade of Palazzo Almeni.

Indeed, the author rebuts just one of Pazzi's comments about the decorative program of Palazzo Almeni; even this, however, is a means of denouncing the immorality of he who dared criticize the work. Recalling Pazzi's use of the term, our poet argues that it was not his intention to depict a "prospettiva" (l. 12) and that if he had wished to do so, he would have chosen to paint Pazzi himself: this is probably a play on the phrase "essere di prospettiva," which at the time signified a liar and cheat.[454] The sonnet's conclusion continues to berate Pazzi as the essence of all vice, without rebutting the merits of his aesthetic opinions.[455]

leveled against some of his works, while also depicting this criticism as the fruit of malevolence and moral corruption: "Iacone spese il miglior tempo di sua vita in baie, andandosene in considerazioni et in dire male di questo e di quello, essendo in que' tempi ridotta in Fiorenza l'arte del disegno in una compagnia di persone che più attendavano a far baie et a godere che a lavorare, e lo studio de' quali era ragunarsi per le botteghe et in altri luoghi, e quivi malignamente e con loro gerghi attendere a biasimare l'opere d'alcuni che erano eccellenti e vivevano civilmente e come uomini onorati."

[454] See *GDLI*, s.v. "prospettiva," no. 8.

[455] The meaning of the final three lines of the poem, with their reference to "contraries" that would have "embraced" Pazzi, escapes me. It is, however, possible that the text might be corrupted here due to problems in the manuscript transmission.

Less than a decade after the Palazzo Almeni altercation, Florence witnessed another poetic duel over a work of art. This time, the object of contention were Alessandro Allori's paintings for the Montauto chapel of the Santissima Annunziata (1561–1564).⁴⁵⁶ The year Allori completed this important cycle, which along with the *Last Judgment* altarpiece and a lost canvas of the *Saint Ezekiel's Vision* includes the frescoes *Christ Expelling the Moneylenders from the Temple* and *Christ's Dispute with the Doctors*, Grazzini penned the sonettessa that begins *Hor se ne va, Cellino, la Tarsia*, and an anonymous author replied with the homometrical *Vogliomi, Benvenuto, disperare* (Appendix, nos. 73–74). Michael Cole, who discovered the poems, has convincingly associated their genesis with the revived debate over the paragone between painting and sculpture prompted by Michelangelo's funeral in Florence.⁴⁵⁷ His detailed critical contextualization has highlighted all the significance of the many linguistic and argumentative ties those compositions have with the poems Benvenuto Cellini composed during that dispute, while also noting how the sculptor, who had emerged in that context as leader of the losing party that championed sculpture but also as a proponent of the idea that only artists were entitled to express an opinion on the paragone, had become the *auctoritas* to whom both poets turned to give credit to their opposing arguments.

According to Cole, the primary target of Grazzini's satire would be the profusion of Michelangelesque citations in Allori's *Last Judgment* (fig. 1), that "giuditio del nostro gran Messia" probably referenced in the closing line of the second quatrain. The tercets would then take a second jab at the portrait gallery of prominent Florentines that contemporary spectators could find in the onlooking *Christ's Dispute with the Doctors* (Table IV): the likely mark of the lines mocking certain "visi sbigottiti tanto / ch'usciti sembran della sepultura."⁴⁵⁸ If we pursue this latter hypothesis and bear in mind how the comic gist of this kind of poem derived from the reader's ability to see *de visu* the pertinence of its observations, we can further argue that Grazzini's sole target was the *Dispute* fresco. A minute referentiality to the details of the iconography and of the *dispositio* of that crowded pictorial space could in fact explain some parts of the poem that are otherwise unintelligible. Pointing out such referentiality can also illustrate how this type of Renaissance poetry, whose meaning can only be fully grasped through a simultaneous reading of the artwork, functioned as a sort of corrosive, cannibalizing iconotext that ridiculed the artistic object by way of a dense web of references to its specific "syntax of the visible."⁴⁵⁹

---

⁴⁵⁶ On Allori's paintings for the Cappella Montauto, see esp. Lecchini Giovannoni 1991 (as in fn. 178), pp. 218–219; Pilliod 2001 (as in fn. 249), pp. 148–163 and 168–182; eadem 2003 (as in fn. 97), pp. 37–39; Ruffini 2011 (as in fn. 135), pp. 59–62, and Geremicca 2017 (as in fn. 121), pp. 96–99.

⁴⁵⁷ See Michael W. Cole, Grazzini, Allori and Judgment in the Montauti Chapel, in: *Mitteilungen des Kunsthistorischen Institutes in Florenz* 45 (2001), pp. 302–312.

⁴⁵⁸ Ibid., p. 307. For thorough discussions of the portraits of prominent Florentines that can be found in the *Disputa*, see esp. Pilliod 2001 (as in fn. 249), pp. 170ff., and Geremicca 2017 (as in fn. 121), pp. 98–99.

⁴⁵⁹ For the notion of iconotext, see esp. Liliane Louvel, *Poetics of the Iconotext*, ed. Karen Jacobs, trans. Laurence Petit, Farnham 2011; for the concept of the "syntax of the visible," see Jean Paris, *Lisible/visible: Six essais de critique générative*, Paris 1978. For the extent to which vituperative poems about art relied on a concurrent and integrated reading of words and images, see esp. Spagnolo 2021 (as in fn. 408): "L'affissione permetteva inoltre di condurre una critica puntuale deridendo dettagli (stilistici, tecnici e iconografici) che solo di fronte all'opera si

In his opening lines, Grazzini addressed Cellini to declare that he, Giovan Maria Tarsia, don Vincenzio Borghini ("la Badia"), and some other members of the Accademia del Disegno ("l'altra scuola"), that is, the main Florentine advocates of the superiority of painting during the dispute over Michelangelo's funeral, were leaving the battlefield after the unveiling of Allori's fresco. The work, in fact, demonstrated how what is true ("ver") had to take precedence over specious, philosophy-laden reasoning, which like a cloud could only be dispersed by the light of truth (ll. 4–6). The poet continued by asserting that the aforementioned champions of the primacy of painting were without valid arguments and silenced by the "giuditio del nostro gran Messia." The enigmatic language and the obscurity of the accumulated references dissolve, at this point, with a glance at the twelve-year-old Christ at the center of the *Dispute*: condensing the opposing gestures of Plato and Aristotle from Raphael's *School of Athens*, Allori represents the young Jesus pointing with his left hand toward the heavens and with his right hand toward the ground.[460] In Grazzini's telling, however, what the Messiah meant to indicate in this way was the fact that the "madre scultura" was on high, as the art of truth, while the supporters of painting – the dimension of shadow and of a deceitful appearance of truth – were necessarily down below.[461] His ironic exegesis thus re-signified the body language of Christ, who with his left hand seems to point to the allegorical statue of the *Old Law* painted at the fresco's summit,[462] as an incontrovertible Messianic judgment on the much-debated question of where to position the effigies of Painting and Sculpture on Michelangelo's catafalque. According to this *witz*, the divine verdict was addressed to "frati" and "pittor" (l. 10), that is, don Vincenzio Borghini, Bronzino, Maso da San Friano, Giovanni Maria Butteri, and perhaps other painters whose portraits Allori had included among the doctors surrounding Jesus.[463] This is why, the sonetessa concluded with a jab at the quality of Allori's portraiture,

---

potevano apprezzare: resi pubblici contestualmente alla prima apparizione dell'opera, i testi avevano il potere di condizionare fin da subito la ricezione. È difficile sottostimare l'importanza di questo aspetto a fronte di una *Kunstliteratur* a stampa che, nel Cinque e Seicento, raramente era contestuale all'esecuzione di opere d'arte e quasi mai era accompagnata da riproduzioni delle stesse. Il suo pubblico di lettori (e quindi il suo impatto) restava circoscritto a quei pochi che avessero una memoria visiva delle opere o potessero recarsi a vederle testo alla mano."

[460] For these Raphaelesque quotations see Pilliod 2001 (as in fn. 249), p. 162.

[461] Grazzini here condenses arguments that were recurrent in the letters of sculptors in response to Varchi's *inchiesta* on the paragone – arguments based on the idea that sculpture is a tridimensional representation of tridimensional subjects, whereas painting provides only an illusion of depth. Compare, for instance, the words of Niccolò Tribolo (in Varchi and Borghini 98 [as in fn. 80], pp. 80–81): "questo mi pare a me, che la scultura sia [...] dimostrare manualmente quello ch'è el vero [...]; e a l'incontro, fussi la pittura [...] bugia, perché è cosa falsa mostrare quello che non fa el vero." See also Cellini's declaration (ibid., p. 83) that the difference between painting and sculpture "è tanta quanto è dalla ombra e la cosa che fa l'ombra."

[462] The iconography of the feminine effigy, which stands on a pedestal and holds two tables in her hand, is very close to that of Domenico Poggini's statue of the *Old Law* (1579), the personification of the precepts of the Old Testament, which is now preserved in Palazzo Medici Riccardi.

[463] For the presence of these figures (sometimes indicated by identifying inscriptions) in the portrait gallery of the *Disputa*, see Pilliod 2001 (as in fn. 249), pp. 170–173. By comparing one of the likenesses in the fresco with an engraved portrait of the poet based on a lost sixteenth-century painting by Bronzino or Allori, Pilliod also convincingly argues that Lasca himself was represented among the Doctors (p. 177).

these characters appeared to be speechless and nearly cadaverous in the fresco: guilty of ignoring that painting is merely the shadow of sculpture and that sculpture is the only truth, when faced with the irrefutable judgment of Christ they now looked like criminals who have just heard a verdict against them (ll. 12–20).

Cole has noted how the sonettessa is a palinode for the author with respect to the position he had argued just a few months prior, when the debate over the paragone flared up in 1564. After advocating the primacy of painting and disputing the matter in verse with Cellini, in this text Grazzini gladly disavowed his own recent militancy to embrace the arguments of Cellini and his fellow supporters of sculpture.[464] The retraction is so conspicuous, in fact, that in recent years there has been an attempt to refute it, against the inarguable evidence of the text.[465] We should however keep in mind that several Cinquecento burlesque poets, and Lasca among them, wrote verse both for and against a given subject, in literary exercises steeped as much in rhetorical virtuosity as in a taste for paradox.[466]

This inclination for ironically arguing both sides and wearing opposing authorial masks with sophistic nonchalance makes it especially treacherous to assign paternity to the anonymous sonettessa written in response to the attack on Allori's *Dispute*, as there is no way to categorically rule out that its author was Grazzini himself. In the polemical climate of contemporary Florence, however, it seems more plausible that the counterattack in verse expressed a real disagreement with the criticism of the Santissima Annunziata fresco than the intellectual display of a *disputatio in utramque partem*. Important, in this sense, are the considerations with which Cole has called attention to the arguments the unnamed poet used to emphasize Lasca's unfitness to state an opinion on the paragone. The keystone of this reasoning was the complaint that Grazzini was not qualified to support a rationally argued, unchanging position on the matter: alien to the world of painters' and sculptors' workshops, he could not know whether the colors "reggano al martello," with a play on words designating two tools of the arts at the center of the dispute as well as the ability to understand their relative place in the ultimate light of experience.[467] It is this appeal to the irreplaceable heuristic value of the direct practice of art, sustained by specific references to the arguments with which Cellini had contested Grazzini's claim to have a valid opinion on the paragone, that lends full credibility

---

[464] See Cole 2001 (as in fn. 457), pp. 302–303.
[465] This is the position of Pilliod 2001 (as in fn. 249), p. 269, n. 143.
[466] Compare Silvia Longhi, *Lusus: il capitolo burlesco nel Cinquecento*, Padua 1983, pp. 172–176, with reference to the genre of paradoxical *encomia*: "i poeti burleschi praticano volentieri l'elogio e il biasimo di una stessa cosa, in un gioco di dire e disdire, di proclamazioni e smentite a sorpresa [...]. Quel che conta, naturalmente, è l'idea della palinodia; cioè della disponibilità indifferenziata alla celebrazione e al biasimo di una stessa cosa. La radice remota di questo atteggiamento sprofonda fino al terreno della sofistica greca, cioè allo stesso ambito ideologico in cui è nato il genere dell'encomio paradossale." Among other relevant examples from the author's burlesque verse, it is useful to recall that Grazzini penned two *capitoli In lode della Caccia* and one *capitolo In disonor della Caccia* (Grazzini 1882 [as in fn. 263], pp. 544–556).
[467] The *GDLI*, s. v. "martello," no. 25, testifies to the early modern currency of the metaphorical expression "reggere al martello" to indicate the persuasiveness of an argument. In the literal sense, the phrase technically designated the capacity of certain materials to be worked with hammer blows without breaking.

to the hypothesis that these lines were penned by Alessandro Allori himself.[468] And while in the absence of incontrovertible manuscript evidence the painter-poet is only the main suspect of having authored the poem, the composition is still of great paradigmatic significance.[469] It illuminates how in later sixteenth-century Florence, poetic skirmishes were one of the privileged arenas in which to debate not only art but the controversial question of the legitimacy of aesthetic judgment.

---

[468] Compare Cole 2001 (as in fn. 263), p. 308: "The most plausible conjecture is that a […] new speaker has entered the exchange [between Grazzini and Cellini]. There is reason to speculate that this speaker is the person who, in Grazzini's attack, had the most to lose – Alessandro Allori. What speaks most for the painter's authorship is the tactic of the response. Had this poem been conceived within the debate over the Michelangelo catafalque, its reply would inevitably have involved a counter-attack on sculpture. The absence of such a move is striking […]. Most suggestive […] is the broader appeal to professional camaraderie. The author implies that he, like Cellini, is a practicing artist, and that only through this practice can there be knowledge. The general topos is an old one […]. But it is also the very argument that Cellini used at length when constructing his own replies to Grazzini."

[469] Raffaello Borghini testifies to Allori's activity as a poet. Speaking of Bronzino's death in 1572, he writes (Raffaello Borghini, *Il Riposo, in cui della pittura, e della scultura si favella* […], Florence 1584, p. 532): "Nell'Accademia del Disegno fu da Alessandro Allori suo discepolo (non meno nell'eccellenza della pittura imitatore del maestro, che nella poesia e nell'altre virtù) fu sopra la sua morte recitata una bellissima oratione composta da lui, e poscia fattoli questo epitaffio. 'Non muor chi vive come il Bronzino visse, / L'Alm'è in ciel, qui son l'ossa, è 'l nome in terra / Illustre, ov'ei cantò, dipinse, e scrisse.'" No handwritten evidence of Allori's poetry has emerged so far: see Marco Nava, Note in corso d'opera sugli autografi di Alessandro Allori, in: *Theory and Criticisim of Literature & Arts* 5.1 (2021), pp. 115–128, 116–118. It is also worth mentioning that Allori inherited all the original manuscripts of Bronzino's verse: see Carla Rossi, Nuove indagini attorno ai due maggiori codici latori delle rime burlesche del Bronzino, ivi, pp. 104–114, 113.

The Problem of Patronage

The gray areas of propaganda

Sitting on the marble steps of Santa Maria del Fiore that give the work its title, two characters of Anton Francesco Doni's *I marmi* (1552–1553) discuss the golden age that both Florence and Venice are apparently experiencing. Comparing the respective state of affairs in the capitals of the Duchy and of the Serenissima Repubblica are the Florentine Alfonso de' Pazzi and Count Fortunato Martinengo of Brescia, an intellectual of complex learning and sophisticated artistic interests who appears several times in the book.[470] Urged by Martinengo, who in the author's telling has recently arrived in the city and wishes to learn how Florentines are faring under their young prince, Pazzi replies with a panegyric of Duke Cosimo that immediately emphasizes his patronage and the generous, sometimes even excessive, sums he would pay to talented artists and literati:

> Divinamente: egli è uno de' mirabilissimi uomini che sieno al mondo. Egli ci dà la libertà, egli ci lascia godere il nostro, ce lo conserva, ce lo aumenta; fa che per l'essempio suo conosciamo la virtù, perché la sua Eccellenza ama i virtuosi sopra tutte le cose. Lui premia la virtù, riprende i mal costumati, e gastiga gli ostinati nel mal fare. Vedeci tutti con occhio netto d'odio o d'ambizione, anzi ci tien tutti tutti, dal minimo al maggiore, per frategli e amaci da figliuoli; dalla sua illustrissima persona non s'impara se non ottimi amaestramenti e santi costumi […]. Qua s'attende alle lettere greche, latine e volgari, come dovete sapere, all'arte per il vivere e non vivere oziosi […]. Dove sono premiati i litterati così bene? Dove possono vivere i virtuosi meglio? Qua ci sono scultori da sua Eccellenza acarezzati e strapagati […], qua pittori in supremo grado, qui architetti.[471]

Pazzi's *laudatio*, which goes on to flaunt other cultural merits and moral qualities of the Lord of Florence, leads Martinengo to exclaim that "Cosmo" must be a "mondo pieno di fede, di carità e d'amore," matching the propagandistic image of the duke as a microcosm of all virtues that we find so frequently in Florentine art and literature of the time.[472] As a matter of fact, Martinengo makes

---

[470] On this dialogue from *I marmi*, see Carmen Menchini, Sguardi incrociati. Rappresentazioni di Firenze e Venezia all'epoca di Anton Francesco Doni, in: Giovanna Rizzarelli (ed.), *"I marmi" di Anton Francesco Doni: la storia, i generi e le arti*, Florence 2012, pp. 3–26. On Alfonso de' Pazzi, see *supra*, particularly fn. 91; on Fortunato Martinengo, who was probably the subject of a famous portrait by il Moretto that is now preserved in the National Gallery of London, see Marco Bizzarini and Elisabetta Selmi, eds., *Fortunato Martinengo: un gentiluomo del Rinascimento fra arti, lettere e musica*, Brescia 2018, with further references.

[471] Anton Francesco Doni, *I marmi*, eds. Carlo Alberto Girotto and Giovanna Rizzarelli, 2 vols., Florence 2017, 2, pp. 93–94.

[472] For the encomiastic character and recurrence of the "cosmic" motif in Florentine cultural production of the age, see esp. Janet Cox-Rearick, *Dynasty and Destiny in Medici Art: Pontormo, Leo X, and the Two Cosimos*,

explicit reference to contemporary representations of Cosimo's power by asserting that the duke's infinite qualities have been fully confirmed in "tutto quello che la fama spande della sua illustrissima eccellenza."[473] But in Doni's polymorphic book, in which irreconcilable points of view are equally supported,[474] the image of the ideal working conditions that Florence was said to provide to its most talented artists and literati irreparably cracks a few dialogues later. Inspired by the author's disillusionment over having to leave his native city in 1548 when his printworks went out of business due to a lack of ducal subsidies,[475] this famous conversation takes place before Michelangelo's sculpture of *Dawn* in the New Sacristy of the Basilica of San Lorenzo. Under questioning by another visitor from out of town, a nameless member of the fictional Accademia Peregrina of Venice, the situation of artists and literati active in the Medicean scene loses its idyllic sheen and appears more like an arena in which the best of them are frequent targets of the envy and malice of a city that has always been stingy in honoring its most gifted sons. As evidence, the visitor recalls Michelangelo's nearly twenty-year absence from Florence and the biographical arcs of several other excellent painters and sculptors, forced to seek work and recognition far from home – a situation similar to what Cosimo Bartoli would portray in his *Ragionamenti Accademici*, with particular reference to the dynamics governing the Florentine sculptural milieu.[476] In Doni's text, the visiting academician later tempers this bleak view of the city's cultural life by observing that only the duke's paternalistic patronage allowed some of the best living artists and writers to continue working in such a hostile environment:

> Perché non si dava egli grado […] e stato, e ricchezze, e palazzi, e possessioni a un tanto uomo, e che tutto il bello che egli ha fatto a Roma fosse stato fatto qua in questa città fior del mondo? Voi avete pure gli animi feroci in verso i vostri sapienti, inverso i vostri compatrioti mirabili! Mentre che son vivi, voi gli sprezzate, offendete e perseguitate: onde quel che fanno, lo fanno con un animo carico di mille fastidii; che se potessino godere la patria con quiete e fossero riconosciuti, meglio assai opererebbono […]. Leggete la vita di Filippo di ser Brunellesco scritta da messer Giorgio Vasari, e vedrete quanta fatica egli durò a mostrar la sua virtù a dispetto de gli invidiosi vostri. Qual maggior pittore arete voi mai d'Andrea del Sarto? Dove diaciono le sue ossa? Il vostro gran Rosso perché non lo aver mantenuto qua? Perin del Vaga? O Dio, che voi abbiate sì fatta dote dal cielo e l'uno e l'altro ve la conculchiate e cerchiate di ficcarla sotto terra! […] Quanti anni è stato il vostro Bandinello fuori? Quanti Benvenuto? Dove è Francesco Salviati? Dove Giovann'Angelo? Dove Michel Angelo? […] Se Fiorenza godesse i suoi figliuoli, qual sarebbe più felice patria? Il difetto non vien da' governi, ma dalla malignità di molti, che tutti s'uniscano a porre a terra un bello intelletto […]. Con quale animo volete voi che la gioventù si metta a opere egregie, all'imprese immortali, a i fatti eterni? Io stupisco che alcuni eccellenti stieno e sieno stati tanto: il Tribolo, il Pontormo, il Bronzino, il Vittori, il Bandinello, Benvenuto, il Varchi; ma questo viene dalla nobiltà del Principe, che gli ha per figliuoli.[477]

Princeton, NJ 1984, pp. 281–282; Roger J. Crum, 'Cosmos, the World of Cosimo': The Iconography of the Uffizi Façade, in: *The Art Bulletin* 71 (1989), pp. 237–253, and Mark S. Rosen, *The Cosmos in the Palace: The Palazzo Vecchio Guardaroba and the Culture of Cartography in Early Modern Florence, 1563–1589,* PhD diss., University of California Berkeley 2004.

[473] Doni 2017 (as in fn. 471), 2, p. 95.
[474] On the ideological inconsistencies and dissonances that characterize the dialogues of the book see the considerations of Giovanna Rizzarelli and Carlo Alberto Girotto ibid., 1, pp. XIII–XIX.
[475] The impact that these biographical circumstances had on the *Marmi* are discussed ibid., pp. XI and XIX.
[476] On Bartoli's argument in the *Ragionamenti*, see *supra*, p. 153.
[477] Doni 2017 (as in fn. 471), 2, pp. 403–406.

In light of the bitter tone of rejection from his homeland that runs through many of Doni's works, it is reasonable to suspect that even this conclusive praise of Cosimo's noble character was streaked with a certain skepticism. That suspicion becomes a near certainty when, in a subsequent dialogue of *I marmi*, the reader encounters another member of the Accademia Peregrina and his ironic historico-etymological digression on the origin of the professional class of *medici* (physicians). His description of the genesis of this group of usurpers, who had originally called themselves "Mendici [i. e. beggars], conciosia che andavan mendicando" but later, once they had grown rich, "si son fatti, per forza di soldi, chiamar Medici," reveals a wholly irreverent attitude toward one of the favorite metaphors of the panegyrists of ducal power, who glorified Cosimo as the "Medico" who had providentially healed the wounds of the Florentine body politic.[478]

These passages from Doni's dialogues are noteworthy because they problematize the image of Cosimo's patronage that nearly five centuries later is still mainstream among the scholars who study the city's cultural history. It has for instance been observed that the sometimes candid enthusiasm with which recent exhibitions have celebrated the "magnificence" and "splendors" of the Medici tends to obscure the brutal side of their reign, as when Cosimo had his political opponents slaughtered after the victory of Montemurlo in 1537.[479] And while posthumous indictments of Cosimo's power carry the opposite risk of a naively moralistic reading of the past and of a loss of what Eric Auerbach labelled as the greatest progress in the historical arts of the past two centuries, namely the "perspectival formation of judgment, which makes it possible to accord the various epochs and cultures their own presuppositions and views,"[480] the admonition reminds us that no scholarly discussion of Medici patronage in the second half of the Cinquecento should ignore the documents from those years that diverge from the arguments of ducal propaganda. In this sense, the poetic output of the artists working in and around Cosimo's court highlights the cracks in the narrative of an exceptionally generous patronage ensuring that local practitioners of the arts could prosper under the best possible working conditions. Such cracks, in fact, transpire frequently in the writings of Florentine painters and sculptors. Bringing these aspects to the fore, then, will clarify how encomia for the duke's patronage often performed a conative function as opposed to a descriptive one.

---

[478] The passage can be read ibid., 2, pp. 548–549. The hypothesis that the discussion was intended to construct a sarcastic paraetimology of Duke Cosimo's family name is put forward by Rizzarelli and Girotto ibid., 1, p. XVIII. For a more extensive treatment of the subtle ways in which Doni articulated his criticism of the Medici power see esp. Salvatore Lo Re, Varchi, Doni e l'Accademia Fiorentina, in: Giovanna Rizzarelli (ed.), *Dissonanze concordi: temi, questioni e personaggi intorno ad Anton Francesco Doni*, Bologna 2013, pp. 171–197, pp. 178–186.

[479] See, for instance, Cole 2011 (as in fn. 98), pp. 11–12. A few contemporaries of Duke Cosimo did not miss the link between his use of brutal force against his enemies and his shrewd cultural patronage. Consider, for instance, the observations in the *Relazione di Firenze* by the Venetian ambassador Lorenzo Priuli from 1566: "È principe molto altiero, vendicativo e severissimo, la qual severità gli è però tornata a bene, usandola verso quelli che gli macchinavano contra nello stato […]. Ama i letterati e li ajuta, e così fa di ogni sorte di artefici più eccellenti, massime della scultura e pittura" (Eugenio Albèri [ed.], *Relazioni degli ambasciatori veneti al Senato […]. Serie 2, Volume 2*, Florence 1841, pp. 76 and 78).

[480] Erich Auerbach, Epilegomena to *Mimesis*, in: idem, *Mimesis: The Representation of Reality in Western Literature*, trans. Willard R. Trask, introduction by Edward W. Said, Princeton, NJ 1953, pp. 559–574, 573.

Consistently with classical notions of the didactic value of praising virtue,[481] their purpose – in other words – was more to suggest to Cosimo a model of conduct than to express the historical reality. It will also be possible to gauge how much truth there was to the idea that writing poetry was so culturally prestigious that it would *always* raise an artist's standing with his patrons – a motif we find for example in the *Memoriale* traditionally ascribed to Baccio Bandinelli.[482]

When art and poetry do not suffice: the case of Pilucca

A coveted ducal patronage is the motif that runs through much of the poetry of an author whose own life story demonstrates the concrete difficulties an artist active in the Medici scene might experience. The artist in question has been almost completely forgotten today but played a fairly important role in the Florentine cultural milieu of the 1530s: member of a family that in the Quattrocento had produced the sculptor Desiderio da Settignano, Paolo Geri (alias "il Pilucca") trained in Tribolo's workshop and in 1535 was registered as a "schultore" in the ranks of the Compagnia di San Luca, forerunner of the Accademia delle Arti del Disegno;[483] around that time he also served as *capomastro dell'Opera del Duomo*, as Antonfrancesco Grazzini recorded in his *Cene*.[484] With no mention of Pilucca in Vasari's *Vite*, Grazzini's novellas are

---

[481] A thorough treatment of classical and early modern ideas about the functions of literary praise is O. B. Hardison, *The Enduring Monument: A Study of the Idea of Praise in Renaissance Literary Theory and Practice*, Chapel Hill 1962. We might note that while single encomiastic compositions addressed to Duke Cosimo and his family are often mentioned in the ever-growing bibliography on the cultural world of Medici Florence, no comprehensive study of the most recurring motifs of the genre exists. Useful indications come from the works devoted to other literary genres that centered on the praise of the lord of Florence – for instance, funeral orations, on which see Luisella Giachino, *Al carbon vivo del desio di gloria: retorica e poesia celebrativa nel Cinquecento*, Alessandria 2008, pp. 1–72.

[482] Here, the compiler of the work had Bandinelli attribute his allegedly vast and elaborate poetic ouevre, including a *Trionfo* on Duke Cosimo's conquest of Siena, to his position as sculptor-courtier, who "havendo avuto a trattare co' principi […], dove continovamente asistono grandi personaggi," found a way to "comparire" thanks to the pen (Barocchi 1971–1977 [as in fn. 9], 3, p. 1382). For doubts about the paternity of the work, see fn. 48. No trace of the poetic output that the memoir ascribes to the sculptor appears to have come down to us. Also notable is the fact that the words from the *Memoriale* take the more general motif of the artist who, thanks to his literary education, not only obtains access to the city's most exclusive intellectual and social circles, but is also able to win his patrons' favor, and apply it to a direct engagement with poetry. Compare, for instance, the remarks in the Torrentiniana biography of Ambrogio Lorenzetti (Vasari 1967–1997 [as in fn. 74], 2, pp. 181–182): "Fu grandemente stimato Ambruogio nella sua patria non tanto per esser persona nella pittura valente, quanto per avere dato opera agli studî delle lettere umane nella sua giovanezza. Le quali gli furono tanto ornamento nella vita, in compagnia della pittura, che praticando sempre con lit[t]erati e studiosi, fu da quegli con titolo d'ingegnoso ricevuto e del continuo ben visto, e fu messo in opera dalla Republica ne' governi publici molte volte e con buon grado e con buona venerazione."

[483] Information on the artist's biography is based on the research and archival discoveries of Fabrizio Corrado and Paolo San Martino, Un Buffalmacco del Cinquecento: Paolo Geri detto Pilucca, in: *Critica d'arte*, 8th ser., vol. 74, nos. 51/52 (2012), pp. 113–120, with further bibliography.

[484] Giannotti 2007 (as in fn. 183), p. 108, mentions Paolo Geri in the context of a wider discussion of Tribolo's association with the world of the Florentine literati. Three different stories by "il Lasca" feature the artist as one of the main characters – namely, the third *novella* of the first *Cena* and the fourth and sixth *novella* of the sec-

indeed the most important source of information on the artist's years in Florence: while generally portraying his character as a sort of spiritual heir of Buffalmacco, the Trecento literary prototype of the artist who was as little inclined toward hard work as he was intent on thinking up pranks with friends,[485] the author does report that Pilucca's sculpture enjoyed a good reputation among his contemporaries. Il Lasca thus writes that Paolo and his main accomplice, the goldsmith Scheggia, were "uomini di buon tempo, e dell'arte loro ragionevoli maestri […], e ben che fussero anzi che no poveri, erano nemici cordiali della fatica: facendo la miglior cera del mondo e non si dando pensiero di cosa niuna, allegramente vivevano."[486] Grazzini, who was on good personal terms with Pilucca,[487] is silent on the artist's intellectual aspirations and familiarity with the Florentine literati, yet such ambitions and social ties must have played a decisive role in making Geri the first Italian Renaissance artist to be officially enrolled in a literary academy. Less than three weeks after the Accademia degli Humidi was founded in Florence on November 1, 1540, Luca Martini could thus record that the institution "comincia a crescer che di nuovo vi haveano messo il Pilucca che stava col Tribolo allo scultore."[488] Added to the academy's list of founders, who included such poets and devotees of the Tuscan literary tradition as Grazzini himself and Nicolò Martelli, Geri assumed the nickname "Lo Scoglio" and took an active part in academic life.[489]

Unlike many of the painters and sculptors who would enroll in the Accademia Fiorentina – the state cultural institution born from the radical reform of the Accademia degli Humidi – and who maintained a low profile when it came to the institution's official activities,[490] Pilucca became a prominent voice within the ranks of the academy. Many of his poems are thus recorded as examples of the group's most commendable literary undertakings in the manuscript

---

ond *Cena*: see Anton Francesco Grazzini, *Le cene*, ed. Riccardo Bruscagli, Rome 1976, pp. 38–49, 200–232, and 254–270; the texts are discussed at some length in Fabrizio Corrado and Paolo San Martino, *Scherzi d'artista*, Turin 2008, pp. 151–162.

[485] On Grazzini's literary representation of artists as witty and often cruel pranksters, which informs many *novelle* in the *Cene* and is rooted in the models of Boccaccio's *Decameron* and Franco Sacchetti's *Trecentonovelle*, see Laura Riccò, Tipologia novellistica degli artisti vasariani, in: Giancarlo Garfagnini (ed.), *Giorgio Vasari tra decorazione ambientale e storiografia artistica*, Florence 1985, pp. 95–115, pp. 102–103; Adriana Mauriello, Artisti e beffe in alcune novelle del '500 (Lasca, Doni, Fortini), in: *Letteratura e arte* 3 (2005), pp. 81–91, and Frédérique Dubard de Gaillarbois, De la "beffa" comme l'un des beaux-arts ou l'inquiétante esthétique de Lasca, in: *La Rivista. Études culturelles italiennes Sorbonne Universités* 0 (2013), pp. 109–123 (https://etudesitaliennes.hypotheses.org/files/2016/02/Dubard-.pdf: last accessed 31/01/2021).

[486] Grazzini 1976 (as in fn. 484), p. 201 (*Cene* 2.4).

[487] See Plaisance 2004 (as in fn. 66), p. 39.

[488] The letter, dated November 20, 1540 and addressed to Carlo Strozzi, is transcribed ibid., pp. 119–121 (the quote is on p. 121). The Accademia had been founded on November 1, 1540, and had taken the name of "Humydi" on November 14 (see ibid., p. 57).

[489] In manuscript BNCF, Fondo Nazionale II.iv.1, which contains the *Capitoli, Compositioni, et Leggi della Accademia degli Humydi di Firenze*, "Il Pilucca scultore / Paulo Geri Lo Scoglio" is listed in a scheme with the identities of the twelve *Primi Fondatori della Academia Humyda* (c.viv). This makes it clear that although he was enrolled slightly later than the other eleven names on the list, the artist was indeed considered one of the founding members of the institution. Plaisance 2004 (as in fn. 66), p. 186, records that Geri was also one of the academicians who were expelled from the institution in 1547.

[490] For instance see above, fn. 203.

containing the *Capitoli, Compositioni, et Leggi della Accademia degli Humydi di Firenze*, and it is also quite possible that he made some of the pen drawings that illustrate the opening pages of the codex (Tables V and VI). Among the texts recorded here are three short compositions in praise of Dante, Petrarch, and Boccaccio that Pilucca wrote as part of an academic ritual in which members would collectively celebrate the greats of Florentine literature in verse.[491] Far more numerous, however, are the poems, many of them in the pastoral mode, that Geri composed for another kind of choral poetic exercise by the academy – which the codex introduces (c. 17r) under the title *Allo illustrissimo et eccellentissimo signor Duca Cosimo Medici per impetrar favor da sua eccellenza*. As Michel Plaisance has pointed out, during the academy's earliest months its literati tried in fact to win Cosimo's protection by way of conceit-filled poems of a hortative-celebratory nature.[492]

These compositions flattered the young duke for his virtues while simultaneously urging him to support the new academy, often through the self-serving argument that the poems its members wrote in his praise would ensure Cosimo everlasting fame, while its program of promoting the Tuscan language and literary tradition would bring the city he governed a renown even greater than that of the cultural centers of the ancient world. The *concettismo* of these poems is most evident in the many allegorical passages that liken Cosimo to a sun whose rays warm the "humori" of the earth – an etymological reference to the group's self-characterization as "humidi" or rich in humors – and in so doing generates life. Within this corpus, Geri's poems stand out for their particularly insistent solicitations of Duke Cosimo's favor, as well as for their high rate of contamination between the allegorizing lexicon of political encomium and the Petrarchan language of love poetry.[493] For example, the manner in which Pilucca – trying his hand at the more mannered verse form of the romance tradition, the sestina – declared himself afflicted because his sun eluded him (*Per campagne, per boschi, piagge et monti*: Appendix, no. 75) closely echoes some erotic tropes of the time relating a lover's discouragement over his beloved's indifference.[494]

---

[491] The poems can be read in BNCF, Fondo Nazionale II.iv.1, cc. 8v (on Dante; incipit: *Col pensar giunsi al loco de' dannati*), 10v (on Petrarch; incipit: *Tutti i miei giorni in dar lode a colei*), and 14v (on Boccaccio; incipit: *Felici marmi, ch'in voi ascondete*.)

[492] Plaisance 2004 (as in fn. 66), pp. 71–75, which examines some of the poems for the duke and the most recurrent tropes within this set of compositions.

[493] For the remark on Pilucca's especially insistent addresses to Cosimo, see ibid., p. 73. Developing motifs present in the poetry of such ancient authors as Martial and Ovid, several Quattrocento humanists had experimented with the systemic cross-fertilization between the poetic discourses of the praise of the beloved and that of the patron: a relevant case is that of Giannantonio Campano's use of elegiac love motifs in his poetry for Cardinal Giacomo degli Ammannati, which is discussed in Susanna de Beer, *The Poetics of Patronage: Poetry as Self-Advancement in Giannantonio Campano*, Turnhout 2013, pp. 120–128.

[494] The solar metaphor for the beloved woman – present in several passages of Petrarch's *Canzoniere* (e.g., 135.55 and 141.5) – is, for instance, the overarching refrain of the Petrarchist canzoniere *La gelosia del sole* (1519) by the Lucan poet Girolamo Britonio. In some of his compositions, references to the obscurity produced by the "sun" in the author's spirit designate the effects of the woman's indifference towards him: see Britonio, *Gelosia del Sole: edizione critica e commento*, ed. Mauro Marrocco, Rome 2016, p. 480 (sonnet 387).

Put differently, Pilucca presented his coveted conquest of the duke's favor in the same allegorical disguise and with the same formulaic repertoire (the lament for his own suffering, the apostrophe in absentia addressed to someone the author wished to draw into reciprocating his feelings) with which early modern lyric poems described the efforts to win the affections of perennially inaccessible women. In such a repurposing of the emblematic story of unhappy love typical of contemporary erotic poetry (see especially the sonnet *Vattene stanco cor, da quel bel sole*: Appendix, no. 76) lies the transfiguration of the biographical travails of an author who, through his verse, strove to win over the duke's impervious stance. Transfiguration is an apt term here because what Geri expressed in his compositions is an "I" stripped of identified (or, to borrow an adjective used by the literary critic Leo Spitzer in his work on medieval lyric poetry, "empirical") characteristics,[495] a poetic voice in which the recognizable biographical traits of the author himself – above all, his identity as an artist – are replaced by a typified representation of the poet as an unrequited lover. This degree of sublimation of real experience is characteristic of what scholars have termed the "transcendental autobiographism" of Petrarch's poetry and of part of the poetic tradition that was built on that model,[496] including the Humidi group's socialized Petrarchism. For Geri, it was also a rhetorical means of filtering through highly stereotyped forms the biographical substance of a difficulty in his relationship with the duke, and thus a way of defusing the criticism that would have been inherent in an explicit protest against Cosimo's indifference (by contrast, Cellini often complained of the duke's unfair treatment of him, in heartfelt poems with transparent, detailed autobiographical references that do not seem to have left his private desk or his innermost circle of friends).[497] Although tending to read Geri's expressions as simple, direct requests for material assistance, those scholars who have interpreted his entreaties to the sun (consider particularly his sonnet *Lieti pastor, che in sulla riva tosca*: Appendix, no. 77) as appeals for ducal patronage that would benefit not just the Accademia degli Humidi but primarily Geri himself are therefore not far from the truth.[498]

As a front-line participant in the concerted poetic effort with which the Humidi tried to win Cosimo's patronage, Geri thus sought a way to carve out a privileged personal audience with the duke. Though we know nothing of his sculptural work in those months, the fact that he devoted so much energy to writing amorous laments for Cosimo raises the suspicion that he was apprehensive about his professional prospects in the Florentine scene. Those prospects must certainly have become more precarious when he left the workshop of his former master

---

[495] Leo Spitzer, Note on the Poetic and the Empirical "I" in Medieval Authors, in: *Traditio* 4 (1946), pp. 414–422.
[496] Gianfranco Contini was the first scholar to use the label of "autobiografismo trascendentale" for the kind of autobiographical experience that is at the core of Petrarch's *Canzoniere*: see Contini, *Varianti e altra linguistica: una raccolta di saggi (1938–1968)*, Turin 1970, p. 178. For an illuminating analysis of the distinguishing features of this poetic mode of expression and its pervasive presence in the pre-modern lyrical genre, see Mazzoni 2005 (as in fn. 10), p. 112.
[497] Consider, among other possible examples, sonnets 34, ll. 12–14, and 37, extensively discussed in Cellini 2014 (as in fn. 7), pp. 92–94 and 100–101.
[498] Such is the interpretation of Corrado and San Martino 2012 (as in fn. 483), p. 114: "Degli anni dell'Accademia degli Umidi restano di Geri prove poetiche concettose nelle quali Cosimo I, nuovo duca dei toscani, è assimilato a un sole fruttifero colmo di più tangibili aurei doni."

Tribolo, who since the late 1530s had been receiving ever more valuable, numerous, and prestigious ducal commissions, such as the *Victory* of Fort Belvedere and the ephemeral *apparati* for the wedding of Cosimo and Eleonora de' Medici in 1539.[499] But wagering on poetry to earn him the duke's interest and patronage was a losing proposition for Geri: Plaisance has emphasized that the advances Pilucca and other Humidi made towards the duke clashed with the disposition of a ruler who was quite impervious to the sirens of lyric adulation, and even less inclined to lavish money on projects without an obvious utilitarian reward.[500]

As a matter of fact, more talented literati encountered the same brick wall as the young academicians. In 1539, for example, the Florentine *poligrafo* Gabriele Simeoni, who spent his life between France and Italy always in search for patrons who would richly reward his many talents, sent the duke a manuscript of poems from Provence; seven years later he followed this tribute with the dedication of other poems and of the printed collection of prose and poetry *Le tre parti del campo dei primi studii*, through which he tried in vain to enter Cosimo's graces and obtain a stable position as his cultural advisor.[501] The duke's snub of Pietro Aretino must have carried an even sharper sting. At the height of his fame, the "Scourge of Princes" was under the illusion that the son of his old protector, the condottiero Giovanni dalle Bande Nere, would be as willing as other rulers to respond with generous financial compensation to promises of praise or threats of rebuke from his pen. As we know from his epistles, however, in the end he had to acknowledge Cosimo's indifference to his repeated declarations that he was ready to leave Venice and become the duke's subject, were he to receive any sign of interest. He then complained that Cosimo was far more generous with the authors of translations from the classical languages into Florentine vernacular than with Aretino himself, who dedicated original poems and plays to the young duke.[502] The Scourge of Princes evidently struggled to understand how the object of his adulation viewed translations as the main literary vehicle for the duchy's cultural affirmation, despite the fact that for years Cosimo had invested the Accademia Fiorentina with the primary function of writing texts that delivered "da ogni altra Lingua, ogni bella Scienza in questa nostra," thereby making a wealth of philosophical, technical, and scientific texts in Latin and Greek accessible to a wide audience of artisans and merchants.[503]

---

[499] Alessandra Giannotti, Pericoli, Niccolò, detto il Tribolo, in: *DBI* 82, Rome 2015, pp. 379–386.

[500] Plaisance 2004 (as in fn. 66), p. 74: "Les avances faites par les Humidi à Côme ne rencontrent aucun écho [ ] D'apres ce que l'on sait, Côme était peu sensible à la flatterie et assez peu prodigue de son argent." On the duke's lack of interest in literary adulation, see also Eric W. Cochrane, *Florence in the Forgotten Centuries, 1527–1800: A History of Florence and the Florentines in the Age of the Grand Dukes*, Chicago 1973, p. 86: "Too many writers were being tempted to let flattery take the place of work, in spite of Cosimo's efforts to resist the flattery."

[501] Alexandre Parnotte, Simeoni, Gabriele, in: *DBI* 92, Rome 2018, pp. 686–689.

[502] On Aretino's relationship with Duke Cosimo see Luisa Mulas, L'Aretino e i Medici, in: *Pietro Aretino nel cinquecentenario della nascita*, 2 vols., Rome 1995, 2, pp. 535–572, pp. 567–568.

[503] The quote is from the duke's deliberation that officially founded the Accademia Fiorentina (February 23, 1541): for the whole text, see Jacopo Rilli, *Notizie letterarie ed istoriche intorno agli uomini illustri dell'Accademia Fiorentina*, Florence 1700, pp. XXI–XXII. For the centrality of translations in the cultural politics of the institution, see the considerations of Antonio Ricci, Lorenzo Torrentino and the Cultural Programme of Cosimo I de' Medici, in: Konrad Eisenbichler (ed.), *The Cultural Politics of Duke Cosimo I de' Medici*, Aldershot 2001, pp. 103–119, p. 113, with reference to the volumes that were printed by the ducal impressor Lorenzo Torrentino in the

Pilucca was therefore one of the many writers unable to comprehend how the new lord of Florence could have so little interest in compositions about himself. Anchored to a manner of understanding the relationship between literature and power that had been common in the age of Humanism, by which leaders would richly reward the eternal fame that only poets could bestow on them,[504] these figures were bewildered by Cosimo's chilly attitude toward their verse. Arising from a different concept of how literati were beneficial to the state, this attitude may also have been fueled by the suspicion that the extraordinary expansion of the ranks of contemporary vernacular poets had somehow reduced – to use once more Bourdieu's terms – the "quarters of cultural nobility" and level of "distinction" the category had once enjoyed.[505] In this sense, Geri's biography beyond his years in Florence shines a light on some salient characteristics of Cosimo's duchy. If political power can be understood as the interweaving of force and power of persuasion, it is noteworthy that a figure who had not

1540s: "The preponderance of vernacular titles reflects […] his specific function within the cultural machinery that revolved around the Accademia Fiorentina, the institution designed to organize Florentine intellectuals and the best expression of Cosimo's cultural politics. The purpose of the Academy, defined gradually but explicitly in a series of reforms enshrined in its statutes, was to promote and publicize the virtues of the Florentine language and its literature. In pursuit of their mission, the academicians gave lectures, most often on Dante and Petrarch, composed works in the vernacular, and translated classical texts into Tuscan […]. The translation of works into the vernacular, for example, linked it to a characteristic feature of Florentine culture under Cosimo, the 'emphasis on the dissemination and popularization of learning' [Cochrane 1973 (as in fn. 500), p. 85] that sought to make learning available to a wider public which included artisans and other laymen traditionally excluded by their lack of Latin and Greek. Its promotion of the vernacular rendered the academy a political instrument, for the glory of the Tuscan language and its literature, and the cultural hegemony that had accrued to them, favoured the prestige and authority of the duke and his house." On Cosimo's project of establishing linguistic prominence for Florence see also Sergio Bertelli, Egemonia linguistica come egemonia culturale e politica nella Firenze cosimiana, in: *Bibliothèque d'Humanisme et Renaissance* 38 (1976), pp. 249–283.

[504] On the humanistic idea that poetry is the most effective medium for granting eternal fame to both human beings and their endeavors or creations, see Stephen Murphy, *The Gift of Immortality: Myths of Power and Humanist Poetics*, Madison 1997. De Beer 2013 (as in fn. 493), pp. 4–11, takes Giannantonio Campano, who served some of the most prominent patrons of Quattrocento Italy, as a representative case study for how this argument drove the development of a thriving system of literary patronage in Renaissance Italy. Also adopting the categories laid out by Pierre Bourdieu (*Outline of a Theory of Practice*, trans. Richard Nice, Cambridge 1977), she examines how the idea provided poets with a level of cultural capital that was a valuable currency of exchange with patrons, who would reward the poetic celebrations they received by drawing on their own economic and social capital.

[505] Bourdieu 1984 (as in fn. 208), esp. chapters 1 and 2 (pp. 9–256). The idea that contemporary poetry had seen a lowering of its average standards of quality and a reputational loss because of the ever-growing number of its practitioners underpins the works of several Florentine writers of the mid-sixteenth century. Relevant in this sense are the letter of Nicolò Martelli to Selvaggio Ghettini of November 1, 1545 (Martelli, *Il primo libro delle lettere di Nicolo Martelli*, Florence 1546, cc. 65v–66v) and several dialogues from Doni's *Marmi*. See esp. Doni 2017 (as in fn. 471), 1, pp. 336–337 (*Ragionamento della poesia* between Baccio del Sevaiuolo and Giuseppe Betussi, which deplores the abundance of maladroit rhymesters at the time) and 2, pp. 549–551 (an exchange among the characters of Savio, Pazzo, Viandante and Spedato), in which Pazzo ironically argues that contemporary patrons no longer appreciated the praise coming from poets: "Così son disprezzati i poeti ancor per questo da' loro signori, perché […] lor donano un libro a qualche bacalare 'eccellentissimo' o 'reverendissimo' o 'illustrissimo' o 'magnifico' o 'ricco;' subito colui che è donato legge la pistola e, quando che egli vi trova dentro 'liberale, cortese, stupendo, virtuoso,' o 'eccellente, nobile, gentile, reale, splendido, benefattor de' virtuosi, raro d'intelletto' […], subito egli dice: 'Costui mente per la gola; perché, da i beni che mi son dati dalla fortuna in fuori, io sono un asino' […]. Si trovano pochi poeti […] buoni, et assai cattivi: […] ciascun vuol poetare.'"

succeeded in intercepting the duke's interest by offering his services as an artist and poet, in two spheres pertaining to consensus building and the development of symbolic languages, did finally win Cosimo's favor with services benefitting his military domain. At a time when he was defending and fortifying the duchy on several fronts, starting especially with his campaign to vanquish Siena (1552–1559), Cosimo also had a policy of reduced spending on culture, which left little hope of ducal employment for middle-rank artists who couldn't offer such services.[506] Pilucca's professional history has much in common here with that of the architect, engineer, and scholar Girolamo Maggi of Anghiari, who included several octaves celebrating the duke of Florence in his epic poem *Cinque primi canti della guerra di Fiandra* (published in Venice in 1551), but only succeeded in entering the duke's service after dedicating to him, in 1552, a manuscript treatise on artillery entitled *Ingegni et invenzioni militari*.[507]

Thanks to Pietro Aretino's letters, we know that Geri, who moved to the Veneto a few years after his experience at the Accademia degli Humidi, continued for some time and with little success to try to make a name for himself as a sculptor and poet. In the first of his missives to Pilucca, dated November 1545, Aretino for instance had to reassure him that the criticism some of his poems had received was merely due to widespread envy of his poetic talent.[508] Just a couple of years later, however, Aretino noted a shift in Geri's ambitions, as he had evidently learned the hard way that not all sculptors who were forced to leave Florence because of a lack of ducal commissions achieved elsewhere the spectacular successes Cosimo Bartoli described in his *Ragionamenti*. Because sculpture was earning him neither wealth nor the "laude dell'artificio," while his poetry continued to evoke the mock bewilderment of several contemporaries, Pilucca had begun – Aretino wrote – to practice increasingly "le faccende de gli avvocati."[509] In 1553 the Scourge of Princes sent Pilucca another letter professing full esteem for his having recently demonstrated a rare talent not only for sculpture and poetry but

---

[506] Several contemporary sources testify to this trend. Particularly relevant is the testimony of a writer as favorable to Cosimo as Vasari, who several times in the *Vite* recorded the negative effect of his military campaigns on his artistic patronage. In the Giuntina biography dedicated to the Della Robbia family, for instance, he recorded in the following terms the destiny of the last exponent of the dynasty, Girolamo (Vasari 1967–1997 [as in fn. 74], 3, p. 58): "risolutosi di tornare a godersi nella patria le ricchezze che si aveva con fatica e sudore guadagnate, et anco lasciare in quella qualche memoria, si acconciava a vivere in Fiorenza l'anno 1553, quando fu quasi forzato mutar pensiero; perché vedendo il duca Cosimo, dal quale sperava dovere essere con onor adoperato, occupato nella guerra di Siena, se ne tornò a morire in Francia." On Cosimo's wars, see now the assessment of Giulio Talini, *Le guerre di Cosimo I de' Medici, granduca di Toscana*, Florence 2019 (pp. 67–161 for the war with Siena).
[507] Venezia, Biblioteca Nazionale Marciana, Mss. It., cl. IV.42 (= 5364). On the manuscript and its author's adventurous biography, see Lorenzo Carpané, Maggi, Girolamo, in: *DBI* 67, Rome 2006, pp. 347–50.
[508] See Aretino 1957–1960 (as in fn. 25), 2, p. 114: "Le stanze uscite de lo ingegno di voi, messer Paolo scultore, sono degne di chi si voglia ispirito famoso di poesia. E se fino a i vostri amici ci torcono il ciglio, non vi paia strano: imperoché anco i figliuoli invidiano i padri, quando da loro sono avanzati di laude." Corrado and San Martino 2012 (as in fn. 483), pp. 116–117, give an in-depth discussion of Aretino's letters to the artist.
[509] The reference to Pilucca can be read in the author's letter of January 1548 to Gianfrancesco Franchini (Aretino 1957–1960 [as in fn. 25], 2, p. 192): "Egli che di poeta et di scultore faceva professione, avedutosi che ne l'andar drieto ai marmi e dinanzi agli inchiostri, da questi ritraeva un poco di pane senza laude dell'artificio, e da questi non sò che udienza circa l'ingegno ridicula; ne le faccende de gli avvocati si essercita, con sopportatione del Petrarca e di Fidia."

also for handling "gli interessi de i maneggi Ducali." And while a decade earlier, in response to Danese Cataneo who wondered whether he should follow his inclination to devote himself entirely to poetry or else continue practicing the more profitable art of sculpture, Aretino had advised cultivating the more remunerative profession without abandoning the noble exercise of poetry,[510] now his recommendation to a correspondent who was having difficulty emerging in both art and writing was even more openly utilitarian. In his letter to Geri, Aretino urged him to stay with the profession that was more advantageous, implying that this consisted of his services for the duke, and in closing took the occasion to reassert himself as servant of the master Pilucca now obeyed and ask him to put in a good word with "Signor Pero."[511]

What "maneggi" Aretino intended is clear from the correspondence Pilucca exchanged in those years with the "Signor Pero" whose good graces Aretino sought, that is, the resident Florentine secretary in the Venetian Republic, Piero Gelido.[512] These letters show that Pilucca was now engaged primarily in working for Duke Cosimo as an informer and military spy in the conflicts between the French and imperial forces that took place in Italy before the Peace of Cateau-Cambrésis (1559). Although ongoing sculptural work led him to Venice, Padua (where in 1554 he received the never-completed commission to sculpt one of the reliefs for the Cappella dell'Arca at the Basilica of Saint Anthony), and Brescia (where his three marble water spout figures for a balustrade of the city's Palazzo della Loggia, which he began in 1553, still stand although much ruined by the elements),[513] Geri used that profession mainly for access to the information he would pass on to Gelido. First-hand news of troop movements in Veneto and Lombardy, gathered thanks to the mobility his work entailed, made Pilucca a valuable pawn in the extensive intelligence network that Duke Cosimo began to use in the late 1540s to strengthen his control over the state and secure its borders.[514] And Geri's awareness that Cosimo was more appreciative of his services in helping to fortify the Medici domain than of those he had previously offered as a sculptor and poet informed the letter he wrote to the lord of Florence in 1554. Introducing a technical report on how to quickly build safe lodgings for Cosimo's troops, he wrote that his own expertise on military art finally allowed him to settle part of his debt of servitude with the duke – a result he had already pursued in vain "con qualche dolce et amoroso fingimento."[515]

---

[510] Ibid., 1, pp. 216–217 (July 1542). For a discussion of the document and its implications of the professional parable of Cattaneo, see Rossi 1995 (as in fn. 5), pp. 7 and 44–45.
[511] Aretino 1957–1960 (as in fn. 25), 2, pp. 422–423: "Io credevo, caro messer Paolo, che [...] vi bastasse la vertù che vi fa raro ne la scoltura e in la poesia, qual si legge e si vede ne le carte e nei marmi: ma che passate con lo ingegno più oltre mi sforza a confessarlo lo essercitarvi negli interessi dei maneggi ducali [...]. Del che mi rallegro, sì perché vi amo, sì perché del padron che ubidite son servo. Sì che attendete a operarvi in quello che più vi risulta di beneficio e di laude. Intanto conservatevi sano, e del signor Pero, me conservando in la grazia."
[512] The most important passages from this body of letters, which remains largely unpublished in the Archivio di Stato of Florence, are quoted or synthetized in Corrado and San Martino 2012 (as in fn. 483), pp. 117–120.
[513] On these commissions, see ibid., pp. 114–116.
[514] For Cosimo's reliance on an extensive network of spies in his foreign policy, see Ioanna Iordanou, *Venice's Secret Service: Organizing Intelligence in the Renaissance*, Oxford 2019, p. 40, with further references.
[515] See the artist's letter to the duke of July 7, 1554 (first published in Gaye 1839–1840 [as in fn. 111], pp. 399–400, but newly transcribed from the digital reproduction of the document in the database EpistolART: http://ci-

Polemical streaks in Bronzino's reflection on Cosimo's patronage

From Pilucca's experience one should not assume that veiled protests against Cosimo only informed the poetry of figures who were struggling for recognition in the hyper-competitive Florentine artistic scene. Even without considering Benvenuto Cellini, whose poems are notoriously dense with critical barbs against the duke,[516] reflections not entirely in line with the myth of the golden age of the arts that flourished under Cosimo's patronage emerge from the compositions of some of the most successful artists of the Medici court. These motifs are not uncommon, in particular, in the compositions of Agnolo Bronzino, and paint a somewhat different portrait of the author than the image that prevails in studies of his poetry. Scholars in fact have typically remarked that many recurrent encomiastic motifs of literary and visual ducal propaganda are present in Bronzino's lyric output. They have for instance focused on his poems expressing support at critical junctures in the history of the House of Medici, such as the funeral compositions for the deaths in quick succession of Giovanni de' Medici, his brother Garzia, and their mother, Eleonora di Toledo, in late 1562. Other relevant objects of attention include the sonnets *Nell'infermità dell'illustrissimo et eccellentissimo signore il signor duca di Fiorenza e Siena*, which Bronzino penned following a code of conduct that required poets working at court to write about the major dynastic events of the reigning family (under the same code, for example, in 1579 Accursio Baldi would write the sonnet *Nelle felicissime nozze del Serenissimo Gran Duca di Toscana e della Serenissima Signora Bianca Cappello*: Appendix, no. 78, a literary tribute supplementing his prints for the booklet that described the festive *apparati* for Francesco de' Medici's second marriage).[517] But scholars have focused especially on the three lengthy and ambitious "canzoni sorelle" in Cosimo's honor which earned Bronzino readmission to the Accademia Fiorentina nearly twenty years after his expulsion (1566).[518] The indispensable emphasis on the importance of

---

pl-loud09.segi.ulg.ac.be/epistolart2017/requetes_internet/DBResultfound_details_2cols.aspx?id=427, last accessed 31/01/2021): "Signor Duca […], là ove io mi speravo con qualche dolce et amoroso fingimento cerchare in parte satisfare a quella debita servitù, che come fedel subdito io debbo a l'eccelsa vossignoria, al presente in lor vece mi sia stato forza rivolger l'animo et la mente a l'arte militare, per ritrovar difensivi et bellici strumenti, sì come al presente potrà comprendere l'alteza vostra per questo disegno, che io le mando […]. Anchora, ò giudicato conveniente cosa il mandarle il modo del formar questo sicurissimo alloggiamento […]. Di Vostra Eccellenza e per natura sudito e per volontà buon servitore Paolo Geri, detto il Pilucca, sculptore."

[516] See the detailed commentary to Cellini 2014 (as in fn. 7), poems nos. 13, 25, 34, 37, 50, 62, 113, 116, 118, 124.

[517] For discussions of the volume by Raffaello Gualterotti, *Feste nelle nozze del Serenissimo Don Francesco Medici Gran Duca di Toscana; et della Serenissima Sua Consorte la Signora Bianca Cappello*, Florence 1579, which contained a description of the festivities by Raffaello Gualterotti and sixteen engravings by Accursio Baldi and Sebastiano Marsili, see the entry by Jacqueline Marie Musacchio in: Andrea Bayer (ed.), *Art and Love in Renaissance Italy*, New York 2008, pp. 272–274, and Annamaria Testaverde, L'editoria fiorentina della festa e la memoria storica preventiva, in: Jean-Philippe Genet (ed.), *La Vérité. Vérité et crédibilité: Construire la vérité dans le système de communication de l'Occident (XIIIe–XVIIe siècle)*, Paris / Rome 2015: https://books.openedition.org/psorbonne/6691?lang=de, unnumbered pages, last accessed 31/01/2021.

[518] On Bronzino's verse panegyrics for the Medici and their adherence to the genre conventions of poetic praise, see Pasti 2010 (as in fn. 6), p. 228: "Non si deve però credere che si tratti solo di piaggeria cortigiana […]: si tratta anche qui, piuttosto, di un genere letterario che ha tradizioni antiche, che a sua volta il poeta deve dimostrare di

such motifs in Bronzino's poetic oeuvre, as epitomized in the sonnet *Se ben di mille palme, e mille accese* that lauded Duke Cosimo as the originator of a modern renaissance of arts and letters (Appendix, no. 79),[519] needs to be supplemented therefore with research giving due weight to his writings that problematize that theme.

Never failing to profess his devotion to a "padron" who had always guaranteed his livelihood, as he declared in his *Capitolo in lode del dappoco*, and expressing himself through a poetic "I" closely reminiscent of the models of human wisdom provided by Horace's *Epistles* and Ariosto's *Satires*,[520] Bronzino remarked several times in his poems on the difficulties faced by artists who served a *signore*. Often such comments are presented as general maxims, fueled by an Ariostesque skepticism over the immoderate ambitions that found their natural outlet in the court. However, in several passages Bronzino explicitly anchors these observations to Florence, enriching them with more or less veiled allusions to his own professional circumstances. For that matter, ancient models like Horace's *Epistles* to Maecenas or Martial's epigrams for Domitian had provided Renaissance poets with authoritative examples that it was possible for them to address their powerful *patroni* with compositions that were respectful but not entirely positive: that tradition actually encouraged authors to balance panegyrics with other types of poetry, based on the idea that untempered adulation would have the opposite of the intended effect and would be read as ironic criticism of the recipient.[521] Forming an illuminating case

---

conoscere. Le tre canzoni che gli valgono la riammissione all'Accademia Fiorentina nel 1566 sono un modello di genere, in cui tutti i topoi dell'encomio letterario vengono sfruttati e montati con estrema abilità, dai paragoni biblici a quelli mitologici, dai Medici veri medici di Firenze di cui curano tutte le piaghe, al sorgere del nuovo Sole e della nuova Età dell'oro, dalla benedizione del popolo di Firenze alla rinascita delle arti." On these texts, see also Geremicca 2013 (as in fn. 6), pp. 50–58 and 69–72; and Chiummo 2016 (as in fn. 6), pp. 266–268. The fundamental work on the topic is, however, Parker 2003 (as in fn. 6), which takes the *Canzoni sorelle* as a point of departure for a wider discussion of the author's so-called "poetry of patronage." One fundamental exception to this scholarly trend, which has generally focused on the painter's encomiastic dimension, is eadem 2000 (as in fn. 6), pp. 109–112, which discusses the most critical passages on the strains of court life in the artist's *Capitolo in lode del dappoco*. Commenting on the poem, Parker (p. 111) thus observes: "Although he is grateful for the patronage of the Medici, the painter is hard-pressed to meet all their demands. The court artist must produce – and quickly – or trust the vagaries of inept apprentices." For more on the *Capitolo*, see *infra*.

[519] For the fortune of the encomiastic motif of the "golden age" in the arts and literature sponsored by the Medici, see Cox-Rearick 1984 (as in fn. 472).

[520] Compare Bronzino 1988 (as in fn. 6), pp. 149–150, *Capitolo in lode del dappoco*, ll. 193–195: "E del mio esser lo lodo e ringrazio / el mio padron, che fa ch'io mi mantenga / con tanto pan, ch'ogni giorno mi sazio?" Bronzino's overarching imitative stance towards the models of Horace and Ariosto in his *Rime in burla* clearly emerges from the thorough and illuminating exegetical work of Latini 2015 (as in fn. 6). With reference to the author's *Capitolo del dappoco*, this quality is also underlined by Chiummo 2016 (as in fn. 6), p. 261.

[521] Compare, for instance, Quintilian, *Institutio Oratoria*, 8.6.53–55: "in eo vero genere quo contraria ostenduntur, ironia est [...]. quae aut pronuntiatione intelligitur aut persona aut rei natura; nam, si qua earum verbis dissentit, apparet diversam esse orationi voluntatem. quanquam in plurimis id tropis accidit, ut intersit, quid de quoque dicatur, quia quod dicitur alibi verum est. Et laudis adsimulatione detrahere et vituperationis laudare concessum est." On the place that these arguments had in the development of Renaissance poetry on patronage, see De Beer 2013 (as in fn. 493), pp. 176–183; on the underlying assumption that didactic and exhortative texts should balance praise and blame, see Hardison 1962 (as in fn. 481), pp. 30–31. For an analysis of the trend in the literature of classical antiquity, see Frederick Ahl, The Art of Safe Criticism in Greece and Rome, in: *The American Journal of Philology* 105 (1984), pp. 174–208. Vasari articulated related ideas in his 1568 biography of

study here is Bronzino's poem *Hor che voi siete, o mio signore, andato* (Appendix, no. 80), which has thus far remained on the sidelines of research on his corpus.[522]

Form and content of Bronzino's verse-letter to the duke

Hor che voi siete, o mio signore, andato is striking first for a metric anomaly: it is the only *capitolo in terza rima* to appear in Bronzino's lyrical canzoniere instead of his burlesque corpus. The unusual feature, however, is explained once we note that the poem is actually a long missive to the duke, for the Renaissance literary tradition had sanctioned this rhyme scheme as a possible vehicle for para-epistolary communication.[523] Because compositions of this genre were nearly always delivered to the dedicatee,[524] it is reasonable to suspect that the mode of address of Bronzino's text was not just a poetic pretense.

The event that occasioned the letter must have been Cosimo's visit to Pietrasanta (paraphrased in the opening lines as "la Pietra, che ben oggi / si può dir Santa al suo signore a lato"), which the duke undertook to bolster his spirits over governing a large territory (ll. 17–21) but probably also to oversee the attempts to mine the gold and silver thought to exist in that region (l. 4). Unfortunately, these notations provide no more than a vague indication of the poem's chronology, nor is this aspect clarified by the concluding lines in which Bronzino – following the typical epistolographic formula of the time – called for divine protection of his correspondent and the duke's wife and children. Cross-referencing this information only allows us to place the composition within a twenty-year period between the early 1540s, when Cosimo made the first of many visits to the Pietrasanta mines he had ordered reopened in 1539,[525]

Bandinelli (Vasari 1967–1997 [as in fn. 74], 5, p. 257), after criticizing the sculptor's bombastically celebratory program for the tombs of Popes Leo X and Clement VII: "Mostrò in questa fabbrica Baccio o poca religione o troppa adulazione, o l'uno e l'altro insieme […]; volendo lodare et onorare qualunche persona, giudico che bisogni raffrenarsi e temperarsi, e talmente dentro a certi termini contenersi, che la lode e l'onore non diventi un'altra cosa, dico imprudenza et adulazione, la quale prima il lodatore vituperi, e poi al lodato, se egli ha sentimento, non piaccia tutta il contrario." For Barbara Irene Mitchell, *The Patron of Art in Giorgio Vasari's "Lives"*, PhD diss., Indiana University 1975, p. 162, these words demonstrate that the author "was convinced that a just historian must not give a one-sided view of even the greatest men" and that his general mode of representing the Medici in the *Vite* would be informed by such a belief: "Direct expressions of praise are surprisingly limited; instead, the reader is shown the Medici patron in action and allowed to come to a favourable conclusion himself."
[522] Concise discussions of the poem can be read in Tanturli 2004 (as in fn. 6), p. 209, and Geremicca 2013 (as in fn. 6), p. 72.
[523] Along with several letters in *terzine* or "lettere in capitoli" by Berni and his imitators (on which see Longhi 1983 [as in fn. 466], p. 182), relevant examples of the genre include Vittoria Colonna's letter to her husband Ferrante d'Avalos, who was at that time (1512) being held captive, *Eccelso mio Signor questa te scrivo*, and Antonio Tebaldeo's *Non aspettò già mai cum tal desio* (first published in 1520).
[524] Longhi 1983 (as in fn. 466), pp. 182–185.
[525] On Cosimo's trips to Pietrasanta in the early 1540s, see Elena Fasano Guarini, Cosimo I de' Medici, duca di Firenze, granduca di Toscana, in: *DBI* 30, Rome 1984, pp. 30–48, p. 36. On his initiatives to restore the minerallurgic activities of the local mines specializing in the extraction of iron and silver, see Giovanni Targioni Tozzetti, *Relazioni di alcuni viaggi fatti in diverse parti della Toscana per osservare le produzioni naturali e gli antichi monumenti di essa (etc.)*, Florence 1752, pp. 218–219; Magda Fabretti and Anna Guidarelli, Ricerche sulle iniziative dei Medici nel campo minerario da Cosimo I a Ferdinando I, in: Giorgio Spini (ed.), *Potere centrale*

and late 1562, when he was widowed. The difficulty of establishing when the poem was written also prevents us from determining the historical events underlying the panegyric allusions that Bronzino weaves into the first half of his letter in verse. Beyond general praise for the duke's restorative actions in the wake of the bloody struggles that had afflicted Florence (ll. 31–39) and for his countless moral and administrative virtues as a leader (ll. 28–30, 40–54), it has therefore not been possible to understand, for example, who the poor, hungry exiles were who had been chased from their city and found generous refuge in the duchy's capital – an event Bronzino celebrated at length as a supreme example of Cosimo's charity (ll. 55–108).

These problems of contextualization, however, do not prevent us from grasping the letter's notable rhetorical structure, which follows lengthy praise of the recipient with words he might have found disagreeable. Bronzino himself acknowledged the risk that the second part of the letter might displease Cosimo, by expressing the hope that he would appreciate the "spirto vero" and the devotion that inspired the poem (ll. 22–27). And this potentially problematic part of the lyric was the real crux of the matter: Bronzino explained that the main reason he had put pen to paper was to speak humbly of himself to his lord, and that the albeit inadequate praise of the duke in which he had indulged was a digression from that goal. Not until the letter's conclusion does it become clear that the purpose of the missive was to solicit the grace, once again ("pensai […] ricordarvi / per la vostra bontà cortese, e pia, / quel ch'altra volta m'indusse a pregarvi": ll. 116–120), of Cosimo's material aid. Before arriving at this request, Bronzino shared some programmatic considerations on art theory that closely resonate with thoughts we find, as we will see, in several of his burlesque capitoli. He thus advocated for the meticulous execution of visual works and flawless attention to detail, while implying that such ideals of study and technical diligence were becoming unfashionable among his peers. The awareness that these principles were outdated informs for instance the lines in which Bronzino, noting that he had long passed the Dantean milestone of the midpoint of human existence (i. e. the age of 35 years, which he had hit in 1538), claimed that his own "giusto, santo, e lodevole amore" for painting had become reason for both happiness and distress (ll. 123–126). If joy was for him the chance to devote himself to "quelle diligenzie, e quelli studi" necessary for that noble pursuit, the artist argued that great suffering was caused by his current circumstances of absolute hardship; he then complained that the specter of poverty would soon force him to follow the undignified, coarse, and increasingly trodden ("trita") path taken by those who painted illusory works with no basis ("opre da sogno"), as the natural instinct for self-preservation would drive him to abandon all devotion to artistic honor (ll. 127–138).

Further to these thoughts, the author insisted he was immune from the avarice that corrupts mindsets and art: arguing that no "retto giudizio" could ever condemn he who sought what was necessary to escape poverty, and to conserve the life, friendships and social status ("grado") he had acquired, the poet made his request for some kind of subsidy or fixed income that would ensure him such basic security until the end of his days ("ond'io chieggio, signor,

---

e strutture periferiche nella Toscana del '500, Florence 1980, pp. 139–217; Clara Baracchini and Severina Russo, *Arte sacra nella Versilia medicea: il culto e gli arredi*, Florence 1995, p. 14.

tanto, ond'io prenda / mentre ch'io vivo al mio viver tal frutto, / che da necessità sol mi difenda": ll. 157–159). If Cosimo agreed – the entreaty continued – Bronzino would serve him for the rest of his life: his cares forgotten, he would consider himself rich as the legendary King Croesus, and would immediately return to shouldering the burdens of art, thus making up for "qualche tempo inutilmente speso" (ll. 160–171). After hoping the duke would soon commission him for "qualch'opra non vile," which would reflect glory on Cosimo as both patron and benefactor, Bronzino stated that he had always been forced to disturb him solely out of absolute need (ll. 175–178). The final tercets then emphasized that his words were not inspired by arrogance, but by "reverenza," "fede," and "rispetto," and that he would submit, obedient and devoted, to any decision the lord of Florence chose to make. In closing, Bronzino urged the duke not to take umbrage over his message, invoking God's protection of the House of Medici and declaring he would be awaiting "un sì" of reassurance.

The painter's poverty

Philip Sohm has observed how, in the early modern period, "most painters did not have the inclination, education, or luxury of time to philosophise about 'value', an elitist idea like 'art' itself, which elevates intangible qualities such as beauty, creativity, and expression over the material and tangible."[526] This makes Bronzino's missive in verse a pivotal text for two orders of reason. First, it is one of the writings in which he most explicitly theorized about the ideals that inspired his painting, while reflecting on the nexus between his economic conditions and the quality of the art he created. Second, the composition – alone among the author's poems – develops these themes in a serious register and in a message addressed to the very patron on whom his professional fortunes primarily depended.

Sohm in fact has remarked that starting in the mid-Cinquecento, the motif of the connection between economic and artistic value assumed an unprecedented centrality among theorists of art. Often by virtue of their own practice of art, these authors had experienced the transformation of the conditions under which painting and sculpture were typically produced, and variously addressed the issues of the ever more pervasive application of the laws of the market to the sphere of artistic creativity.[527] To highlight the significance of Bronzino's lyric in the context of that historical process, it is therefore useful to examine its dialectical relationship not only with his other writings, but also with the theoretical reflections of contemporary authors.

The lament of a painter who declared himself so distressed by poverty that he was forced to contemplate slashing both production time and the quality of his output addressed first and foremost the theme of the incompatibility of hardship with excellence in art. Disregarding the question of just how poor Bronzino was when he wrote this letter, considering that from

---

[526] Philip Sohm, Introduction, in: Richard E. Spear and Philip L. Sohm, eds., *Painting for Profit: The Economic Lives of Seventeenth-Century Italian Painters*, New Haven, CT 2010, pp. 1–32, 2.
[527] Ibid.

1540 to 1564 he had a regular ducal salary and the fact that avowals of penury are one of the main leitmotifs of the hundreds of petitions Cosimo received from painters and sculptors in his service,[528] the document hits on a fundamental question. Contrary to certain idealistic notions of the artist as wholly indifferent to money and devoted exclusively to producing the finest work, according to the ancient and semi-legendary model of the indigent Protogenes,[529] Bronzino's pragmatic premise was that the need to earn enough to live on and to enjoy some material comforts was a valid motive for exercising the arts of drawing. This is a theme we encounter frequently in his burlesque poems. In his two capitoli *Del bisogno*, for example, he praised the effects of need by arguing that all human activism is inspired by it, that is, by the privation of what one needs not so much to survive as to lead a more comfortable life. Modeling his argument on the theodicy of work from Virgil's *Georgics* (1.118–146),[530] Bronzino wrote that only in the golden age could men choose to devote themselves to lives of leisure, which for that matter meant neglecting all artistic practice ("[…] e la scuola e la bottega / ancor non erano in rerum naturae. / Non il martel, non l'ago e non la sega, / non il pennello o la squadra o 'l mazzuolo").[531] Once Jupiter had determined that humans need to be prodded out of their state of inertia, however, need had become the authentic foundation of human existence, and the author recognized the importance of such a stimulus for his own work as a painter. Not

---

[528] Information on the payments that Bronzino received as a salaried painter to the duke can be found in Elena Fumagalli, On the Medici Payroll: At Court from Cosimo I to Ferdinando II (1540–1670), in: Elena Fumagalli and Raffaella Morselli (eds.), *The Court Artist in Seventeenth-Century Italy*, Rome 2014, pp. 95–136. Fumagalli documents (p. 97) that the artist's salary was initially 6 scudi per month, and that the sum was raised to 11 scudi in 1543 and to 12.5 scudi in 1547. While she maintains that "this remained his salary for the rest of his life," evidence has come down to us that for at least some months in 1564, the painter found himself excluded from the Medici payrolls. On April 15 of that year, the painter wrote a deferential letter to Cosimo, in which he warmly thanked him "dell'havermi fatto pagare li danari di quel salario, che la bontà e amorevolezza vostra più tempo fa mi hordinò, del quale sono stato al tutto pagato, cagione che per la di vostra grazia e magnificenzia, io doverrò per al presente por fine a tutti li miei affanni." The document then goes on to state that the artist had been informed by Tommaso de' Medici "che tal salario non mi corre più," and then humbly solicits Cosimo to find occasions to re-employ him. For the full text of the letter, see Gaye 1839–1840 (as in fn. 111), 3, pp. 134–135 (another transcription in Cox-Rearick 1993 [as in fn. 122], p. 342); for a discussion of this source, see Parker 2003 (as in fn. 6), pp. 230–231. The collection of letters put together by Gaye amply demonstrates just how common similar professions of poverty were among the artists who served Duke Cosimo: consider, among others, Cristofano dell'Altissimo's letters to the duke from 1553 and 1554 in Gaye 1839–1840, 3, pp. 389–392 and 401–402. On the problematic trustworthiness of similar complaints, which appear to have been rather common throughout early modern Europe, see the considerations of Wittkower and Wittkower 1963 (as in fn. 1), pp. 255–256: "Perhaps the least reliable basis for assessing their earnings are the artists' own declarations […]. It can scarcely be doubted that many a petitionary letter was written with the sole purpose of moving the recipient's heart and opening his purse."

[529] Early modern sources transformed the ancient painter into the paradigm of the frugal and perfectionist artist who is indifferent to money: see Sohm 2010 (as in fn. 526), p. 5.

[530] Bronzino's reasoning closely follows that of the Latin poet, who had presented *egestas* ("bisogno") as the most effective civilizing power in human history and the greatest spur to human activity. Virgil's main literary model for the first *Georgic*, Hesiod's *Works and Days* (esp. ll. 112–119), had instead lamented how the end of the golden age had forced men to undergo the fatigue of work, which was depicted in a deeply negative way.

[531] Bronzino 1988 (as in fn. 6), p. 282, *Del bisogno capitolo primo*, ll. 69–72.

unlike Vasari when he argued that Sebastiano del Piombo's position as sealer of papal briefs had destroyed his motivation to paint when he was showered with riches unassociated with art,[532] Bronzino implied that if "bisogno" were eliminated he might have stopped creating art altogether:

> Qui nasce un dubbio e no 'l risolvo io stesso,
>   che pensando dipinger senza lui,
>   meco di me mi maraviglio spesso,
> ché se ben fu 'l piacer più volte cui
>   mi trasse a lavorar, non però senza
>   bisogno sono o spero essere o fui.
> Onde, volendo farne esperienza,
>   bisognerebbe il bisogno levarmi,
>   liberando in me l'atto e la potenza,
> e veder poi se la virtù tirarmi
>   potesse a lavorare e 'l piacer solo
>   o pur mi risolvessi in tutto a starmi.[533]

While Bronzino acknowledged that the motivation to improve one's living conditions had a positive effect on art, he took quite a different tone when it was not material comfort but a painter's own survival under threat. He saw poverty as a pressing material care that would lead an artist to worry more about how to avoid starving to death than about the quality of his creations. From this point of view as well, then, Bronzino's letter is consistent with several of Vasari's reflections. In the preface to the third section of the 1550 edition of the *Vite*, Vasari argued for example that only "rarissimi ingegni" in the throes of material hardship could achieve excellence in art. And while the ancients had produced their artistic masterpieces "provocati con sì eccessivi premii e con tanta felicità," Vasari was certain that the moderns could attain even better results, if only their patrons would lift them from penury by properly compensating them for their work:

---

[532] Compare Vasari 1967–1997 (as in fn. 74), 5, pp. 95–96 (1568, though the text was almost identical in the 1550 edition): "Il Papa […], perché così la virtù di Sebastiano meritava, ordinò che esso Bastiano avesse l'ufizio […]. Laonde Sebastiano prese l'abito del frate, e sùbito per quello si sentì variare l'animo: perché vedendosi avere il modo di potere sodisfare alle sue voglie, senza colpo di pennello se ne stava riposando, e le male notti et i giorni affaticati ristorava con gli agi e con l'entrate, e quando pure aveva a fare una cosa, si riduceva al lavoro con una passione che pareva andasse alla morte." Remarkably, Benvenuto Cellini offered an antithetical interpretation of the wealth that such offices could bestow on Renaissance artists. In his autobiography (Cellini 1996 [as in fn. 23], *Vita* 1.56, p. 206), the author recounts having requested Pope Clement VII one "ufizio del Piombo," and in this way records the witty exchange that ensued with his patron: "Al […] Papa non sovvenendo più di quella ismania […] mi disse: 'L'ufizio del Piombo rende più di ottocento scudi, di modo che se io te lo dessi, tu ti attenderesti a grattare il corpo, e quella bell'arte che tu hai alle mane si perderebbe, et io ne arei biasimo.' Subito risposi che le gatte di buona sorte meglio uccellano per grassezza che per fame: 'Così quella sorte degli uomini dabbene che sono inclinati alle virtù, molto meglio le mettono in opera quando egli hanno abundantissimamente da vivere; di modo che quei prìncipi che tengono abundantissimi questi cotali uomini, sappi Vostra Santità che eglino annaffiano le virtù: così per il contrario le virtù nascono ismunte et rognose.'"

[533] Bronzino 1988 (as in fn. 6), p. 290, *Del bisogno capitolo secondo*, ll. 79–90. The passage is briefly discussed in Chiummo 2017 (as in fn. 6), p. 232.

> […] se in questo nostro secolo fusse la giusta remunerazione, si farebbono senza dubbio cose più grandi e molto migliori che non fecero mai gli antichi. Ma lo avere a combattere più con la fame che con la fama tien sotterrati i miseri ingegni, né gli lascia (colpa e vergogna di chi sollevare gli potrebbe e non se ne cura) farsi conoscere.[534]

After Vasari, the theory that artists needed some sort of basic economic security to create exceptional works would resurface several times in the century's art treatises. In an exchange from Gregorio Comanini's *Il Figino* (1591), for instance, the title character and painter Ambrogio Figino claimed proudly that he did not need to struggle to escape hunger, and was therefore not "costretto dalla necessità d'avilir l'arte."[535] The ideological consistency of these sources extends to the acknowledgment that to avoid misery, many sixteenth-century artists had given up basing their practice on the ideals of diligence and quality in order to radically increase their productivity: indulging their patrons' desire to see works completed quickly, they had realized they could not only earn enough to survive but increasingly improve their position in the artistic scene, pushing past colleagues less capable of "prestezza" in the fight for commissions.[536]

Most of the authors who discussed this trend were critical of the pressure on visual artists, especially painters, to work at an ever more hurried tempo. They labeled such pressure as an undue extension to the artistic sphere of the laws governing mechanical labor, which tied workers' pay solely to the quantities they were able to produce. Already in the 1550 edition of the *Vite*, Vasari condemned the fact that at the dawn of his career, Perino del Vaga was forced by his own "infinita bassezza e povertà" to "lavorare a opere per quelle botteghe oggi con uno dipintore e domane con un altro, nella maniera che fanno i zappatori a giornate."[537]

---

[534] Vasari 1967–1997 (as in fn. 74), 4, p. 12.

[535] Barocchi 1960–1962 (as in fn. 147), 3, p. 377. Commenting on the passage, Sohm 2010 (as in fn. 526), p. 5 speaks of an acknowledgment of "the realities of poverty without glamorizing its benefits," as well as of the reality that "money liberates artists from the tyranny of production at the expense of quality."

[536] In discussing how the seventeenth-century "entrepreneurial society where painters engaged in business was etched with psychological complexities," Sohm (ibid., p. 3) cites a testimony from Baldinucci's biography of Carlo Dolci in his *Notizie de' professori del disegno*. A significant portion of the text (Filippo Baldinucci, *Notizie de' professori del disegno da Cimabue in qua […] Secolo V. Dal 1610 al 1670 […]*, Florence 1728, pp. 507–508) revolves around the abysmal crisis of self-doubt that would have affected the slow and meticulous Carlo after Luca Giordano had ironically remarked that his diligence would have led him to starve to death – a crisis that only grew worse when Dolci admired a dazzling painting that his Neapolitan colleague had completed in just a handful of days.

[537] These and the following quotes are from Vasari 1967–1997 (as in fn. 74), 5, p. 111 (1550). Relevant is here the comparison with a passage from the Giuntina's biography of Francesco Rustici (ibid., p. 475), where the author claimed that those artists "che hanno per ultimo e principale fine il guadagno e l'utile […] rade volte […] riescono eccellentissimi," adding that "il fare […] per bisogno dalla mattina alla sera, è cosa non da uomini che abbiano per fine la gloria e l'onore, ma da opere, come si dice, e da manovali." On the thematic focuses of Perino's biography, see Elena Parma Armani, *Perin del Vaga: l'anello mancante. Studi sul Manierismo*, Genoa 1986, pp. 237–243; Rubin 1995 (as in fn. 61), pp. 33, 75, 93, 109, and 120–122; and esp. Giovanna Sapori, Lo specchio di Perino. La biografia di Perino del Vaga nell'edizione delle *Vite* di Vasari del 1550, in: Barbara Agosti, Silvia Ginzburg Carignani, and Alessandro Nova (eds.), *Giorgio Vasari e il cantiere delle* Vite *del 1550*, Venice 2013, pp. 75–89.

According to Vasari, Perino at first managed to achieve excellence in art by choosing to halve the time he spent in that ignoble activity, entirely "disconveniente allo studio," and devote the remaining hours to the practice of drawing. Toward the end of his career, however, the thirst for money would prevail over the quest for outstanding achievement. The author was thus critical of how Perino hired a bevy of assistants to prepare his cartoons for family chapels in Rome, observing that this way of delegating the execution of frescoes did manage to "piacere ai principi per dar loro l'opere presto," but was ruinous for the quality of the paintings, since no collaborator could ever care about another's work as much as he loved his own.[538] As support for this argument, Vasari described an episode in his own artistic career that would eventually become notorious. Persuaded to have others translate into frescoes his cartoons for the Sala della Cancelleria of the Palazzo di San Giorgio in Rome, "per aversi [the paintings] a fare con gran prestezza in cento dì," he wrote of his pain upon realizing that the quality of his drawings had been betrayed in the execution phase and claimed, though untruthfully, that he would never again delegate his work.[539]

Vasari's frequent and well-known appreciation for the typical virtue of the "maniera moderna" of "prestezza," which in the Giuntina had him state admiringly that while "prima da que' nostri maestri si faceva una tavola in sei anni, oggi in un anno questi maestri fanno sei,"[540] thus coexisted with his episodic acknowledgment of the risks of emphasizing the value of speed of execution above all else. According to Renzo Bragantini, on the theoretical-prescriptive plane the *Vite* struck some kind of balance between the ideals of "prestezza" and "facilità" on the one hand and "diligenza" and "perfezzione" on the other, the latter being the foundations of an aesthetic that echoed Horace in urging a patient *labor limae* for literary as well as visual creations.[541] There is no need to stress the discrepancy between the theory and what we know

---

[538] These and the following quotes are from Vasari 1967–1997 (as in fn. 74), 5, p. 155 (1550).

[539] On Vasari's paintings in the Sala dei Cento Giorni and his self-criticism in the two editions of the *Vite*, see especially the recent works of Liana De Girolami Cheney, *Giorgio Vasari: Artistic and Emblematic Manifestations*, Washington, DC 2012, pp. 234–235; Barbara Agosti, *Giorgio Vasari: luoghi e tempi delle* Vite, Milan 2013, pp. 68–72; Philip L. Sohm, Giving Vasari the Giorgio Treatment, in: *I Tatti Studies in the Italian Renaissance* 18 (2015), pp. 61–111, pp. 107–108; Robert Williams, *Raphael and the Redefinition of Art in Renaissance Italy*, Cambridge 2017, pp. 200–201; Douglas Biow, *Vasari's Words: The* Lives of the Artists *as a History of Ideas in the Italian Renaissance*, Cambridge 2018, pp. 85–88, and Franceschini 2021 (as in fn. 346), with further bibliography on the topic.

[540] Quoted from the *Proemio* to the third age of the arts in Vasari 1967–1997 (as in fn. 74), 4, p. 10.

[541] See the nuanced treatment of the topic in Renzo Bragantini, Figure e topoi della prestezza, in: Chiara Cassiani and Maria Cristina Figorilli (eds.), *Festina lente: il tempo della scrittura nella letteratura del Cinquecento*, Rome 2014, pp. 15–30, pp. 17–20, as well as Pozzi and Mattioda 2006 (as in fn. 80), pp. 215–219 (particularly 219: "Vasari teorico insomma mantiene un saldo equilibrio: non loda la prestezza eccessiva, non dovuta a piena assimilazione del disegno"). One early and influential treatment of the theme of *prestezza* in Vasari's *Vite* is that of Giovanni Previtali, *La fortuna dei primitivi dal Vasari ai neoclassici*, Turin 1964, pp. 21–27, which strongly emphasizes the positive connotations of the idea in the work. The important discussion by Angela Cerasuolo, *Literature and Artistic Practice in Sixteenth-Century Italy*, trans. Helen Glanville, Leiden 2017, pp. 101–114, similarly underlines how the idea is presented in the most favorable light, as an "all-positive value" (p. 101) within the *Vite*. On the other hand, Biow 2018 (as in fn. 539), pp. 80–108, pp. 88–89, stresses the ambivalence inherent in Vasari's prevailingly positive discussions of *prestezza* in the following terms: "Two views about *prestezza*, then,

of Vasari's practice as an artist. Many studies have recognized that his success in Cosimo's Florence was strictly related to his astonishing production capacity, which allowed him to lower costs for his patrons while meeting the agreed-upon deadlines, though this often happened at the expense of quality. Scholars have also noted that his prolific output owed both to the rapidity with which he worked individually and to his shrewd management of the army of assistants under his supervision in large-scale decorative projects, such as the interiors of Palazzo Vecchio.[542]

Bronzino's stance on these matters was far clearer and more consistent. He advocated the idea, as Plutarch wrote about the slow and meticulous painting of Zeuxis, that "deftness and speed in working do not impart to the work an abiding weight of influence nor an exactness of beauty" and that "the time which is put out to loan in laboriously creating, pays a large and generous interest in the preservation of the creation."[543] A similar credo informed both his practice, which Vasari in private letters described as exasperatingly slow,[544] and his writings. It is noteworthy, in fact, that in his poetry Bronzino never explicitly theorizes about the need to avoid excessive diligence. The absence is instructive because this kind of warning, rooted in a different set of ancient anecdotes that viewed perfectionism as an obstacle to excellence in painting and sculpture, was scattered through other sixteenth-century writings even if they criticized the way rapidity had become the supreme rule of creating art, from Paolo Pino's *Libro di pittura* (1548) to Giovan Battista Armenini's *De' veri precetti della pittura* (1587).[545]

---

each with a clear upside and downside, are set before us throughout the *Lives* […]. On the upside, *prestezza* can signal effortless facility and virtuosity coupled with a remarkable ability to get things done in a timely and businesslike manner […]; *prestezza*, on the downside, can all too easily lead to shoddy workmanship, no matter how excellent the underlying *disegno* is or how dexterous and competent the supervising master is." On Vasari's critiques of artists who worked slowly in the *Vite*, see Parker 2004 (as in fn. 6), p. 166.

[542] See, among others, the remarks of Sohm 2010 (as in fn. 526), p. 5, arguing that, for Vasari, economic considerations inspired "an awesome rate of production, but not a concordant quality of art," and that such an astonishing productivity was made possible by the artist's capitalization "on a technique, studio organization, and societal network that enabled him to become conspicuously rich." On the role that these factors, which "the economy of late Renaissance Italy with its booming court culture, its keen investment in nascent state building, and its equally keen appetite for conspicuous consumption," played in the Aretine's career, see also Biow 2018 (as in fn. 539), p. 89. Cerasuolo 2017 (as in fn. 541), pp. 110–111, underlines how the *Vite* document over and over again that throughout his career, Vasari made a "massive use of assistants" and explains the contradiction between this practice and the arguments he presents in the biography of Perino in the following terms: "This contradiction can be explained by the fact that Perino's *Vita*, already present in the Torrentiniana edition, was written soon after the execution of the paintings in the Cancelleria (1546), and in a certain sense Vasari in the heat of the moment declares himself dissatisfied with the result […]. In order therefore in part to preserve his dignity, and maybe also driven by a genuine desire to redeem himself, Vasari probably chose Perino's *Vita* as an opportunity for self-criticism, while putting forward all possible arguments to excuse himself."

[543] Plutarch, *Lives*, with an English Translation by Bernadotte Perrin, 10 vols. London /New York 1932, 3, p. 141 (*Life of Pericles* 159.2).

[544] Giorgio Vasari, letter to Vincenzio Borghini of September 22, 1565, on the preparation of the ephemeral apparati for the wedding of Francesco I de' Medici and Joanna of Austria: "Bronzino va piano al solito" (Vasari 1923–1930 [as in fn. 76], 2, p. 210, quoted and discussed in Emiliani 1960 [as in fn. 125], p. 89; Pilliod 2001 [as in fn. 249], p. 234; Parker 2004 [as in fn. 6], p. 169).

[545] A most typical and influential ancient anecdote is that of Apelles, who according to Pliny's *Naturalis Historia* (35.80) would have criticized the excessive diligence of Protogenes. As the story goes, even though Apelles ad-

Asserting that art no longer grounded in the slow pace of "diligenzie" and "studi" was inevitably destined for ruin, Bronzino's letter in verse to Cosimo de' Medici condensed a number of motifs he also developed in his *Rime in burla*. As close terms of reference we have those passages of the aforementioned *Secondo capitolo delle scuse* in which the author targeted the most common excuses painters used to justify the debatable quality of their work. As Deborah Parker has pointed out, this text included a lengthy tirade against painters led by greed into working speedily, who were in fact so used to making mistakes that they were no longer able to produce good work even when they painted "adagio." In this sense, the motif was closely entwined with the poet's insistence that painting should be based on careful study and resolute imitation of Michelangelo.[546] Unlike contemporaries who emphasized how the "Divine" would sometimes paint or sculpt with astonishing speed,[547] Bronzino evidently associated that model with the practice of an art conducted without haste. His ideas were therefore consistent with what Giovan Battista Giraldi Cinzio most elaborately expressed in a novella of his *Hecatommithi* (1565), which treated Michelangelo as the supreme example of an artist who worked "con gran tempo […], con gran studio," and with the "molta diligenza" necessary for bringing his works to perfection:[548]

---

mired his colleague, he asserted that he had overcome him in just one quality: namely, the ability to understand when to take his hand away from a painting. Quoted or indirectly alluded to in numerous art historical writings of the early modern period, the anecdote was also evoked in one of the most pivotal passages of Castiglione's *Libro del Cortegiano* (1.28): in discussing the necessity for the courtier to avoid *affettazione* and to always practice *sprezzatura*, the character of Count Ludovico da Canossa linked the former vice with Apelles's critique of Protogenes's excessive diligence. For more on this, see Valeska von Rosen, "Celare artem." Die Ästhetisierung eines rhetorischen Topos in der Malerei mit sichtbarer Pinselschrift, in: Pfisterer and Seidel 2003 (as in fn. 267), pp. 323–350, and Emison 2004 (as in fn. 77), pp. 41–44, while Cerasuolo 2017 (as in fn. 541), p. 100, n. 45, discusses some other Plinian anecdotes of artists who were excessively diligent (e. g. Callimachus), or, conversely, who could complete their works in the swiftest possible way (e. g. Nicomachus of Tebes). Cerasuolo (pp. 100–101) also emphasizes that "both Pino and Dolce in their writings censure an exaggerated diligence, the former inviting the artist to 'moderate diligence,' and the latter to beware of 'excessive diligence'; at the same time, however, excessive speed is denounced as an 'imperfection,'" and subsequently discusses (pp. 102–114, at 102) Armenini's generally negative view of "prestezza," which is nonetheless balanced in a few passages by a focus on its capacity to foster "immediacy, freshness in colouring, manifest virtuosity."

[546] Parker 2004 (as in fn. 6), p. 162.

[547] For contemporary accounts on Michelangelo's *prestezza* in working marble, the most explicit of which is a text by the French humanist Blaise de Vigenère, see Robert J. Clements, Michelangelo on Effort and Rapidity in Art, in: *Journal of the Warburg and Courtauld Institutes* 17 (1954), pp. 301–310, p. 304. The article as a whole is an important assessment of the artist's mixed and evolving approach to matters of speed in the process of artistic creation, which could entail a slow and deliberate work in the composition stage as well as a hasty realization.

[548] This *novella* (Giovan Battista Giraldi, *Gli Ecatommiti ovvero centro novelle*, Florence 1833, 7.10, pp. 2083–2086, p. 2084) recounts the story of an alleged young Greek pupil of Buonarroti, Alazone, who presumed to surpass his master by virtue of his capacity to paint hastily and who eventually had to learn from Michelangelo that perfect art requires a long gestation, much study, and the utmost diligence. Among the few scholarly works that discuss the *novella*'s important implications in matters of aesthetics are the studies of Clements 1954 (as in fn. 547), pp. 306–307; Bragantini 2014 (as in fn. 541), p. 25, and Corinne Lucas Fiorato, Appunti sulle immagini negli scritti di Giraldi Cinthio, in: *Studi giraldiani. Letteratura e teatro* 5 (2019), pp. 265–294, pp. 282–283.

> Naturalmente certi pe non poco
> in su l'opere lor, per più danari
> tirare a sé, che piace lor quel gioco.
> E sonsi avvezzi per modo, i compari,
> che, quand'e' voglion far adagio, fanno
> peggio che tosto e non son mica rari.
> Lavoran lieti e non piglionsi affanno
> d'altro, che venir presto alla vernice,
> che solo il guadagnar per iscopo hanno.
> Costor le scuse in sin dalla radice
> sbarbon, con dimostrar ch'a chi fa tosto,
> qualch'error comportar non si disdice [...].[549]

Several passages of the *Capitolo del Bronzino pittore in lode del dappoco* are equally important, as they cast light on the probable theoretical foundations of the painter's claims in his letter in verse to Duke Cosimo. In presenting a life model inspired by the Horatian-Ariostean ideals of the golden mean and of a frugal life, he aimed his satire in particular at the greediness that led many people at court to work themselves to the bone – figures who deserved, in his estimation, to have Circe transform them "in asini o 'n cavagli."[550] That his criticism also targeted a way of painting alien to his own inclinations became clear when Bronzino disparaged the times he found himself working "a marcia forza," driven by the need to put food on his table.[551] Also revealing was the passage in which he justified his unwillingness to devote more time than necessary to the rituals of court life, as that time would be robbed from the artistic thought that constantly "affatica l'anima e 'l cervello" of all painters while also undermining the need for "qualche ristoro" that this incessant motion of the mind imposed. Encouraging a painter's creative process and hence his need for rest – the text continued in a vein recalling Vasari's diatribe against the use of assistants, but far more reflective of Bronzino's own artistic practice – would also prevent him from having to resort to "fattori, / che soglion far mille abborracciamenti [i. e. botches]" to complete his creations.[552] In concluding the most strictly

---

[549] Bronzino 1988 (as in fn. 6), p. 195, *Delle scuse capitolo secondo*, ll. 106–117, on which see Parker 2004 (as in fn. 6), p. 162.

[550] Bronzino 1988 (as in fn. 6), p. 146, *Capitolo del Bronzino pittore in lode del dappoco*, ll. 67–72: "Chi è dappoco, oltr'allo stare in agio, / scampa mille pericoli e travagli, / che soglion dar la bottega e 'l palagio; / lavoran dì e notte – dagli, dagli! – / certi, che Circe arebbe fatto bene a trasformarli in asini o 'n cavagli."

[551] Ibid., p. 147, ll. 97–105: "Ben lo sai tu che tal volte con ira / mi vedi porre a lavorare e follo / per marcia forza e perch'el pan s'adira. / Ma s'io potessi, senza lui, satollo / la sera andare a lletto e riposarmi, / scoterei volentier dal giogo il collo. / E se bene in cert'opre affaticarmi / vedi ch'io ho'n fastidio, pel bisogno / lo fo, ti dico: i' non voglio scusarmi." On this passage, see Parker 2000 (as in fn. 6), p. 109, which observes: "The admission that economic necessity obliges him to work on irksome projects underscores Bronzino's pragmatism."

[552] Bronzino 1988 (as in fn. 6), p. 149, ll. 160–176: "I proprii cortigian tanto conforto / posson pigliar quant'egli avanza loro / di tempo e tutto spenderlo in diporto, / ma noi, che sempre abbiàn qualche lavoro, / che ci affatica l'anima e 'l cervello / – e pur bisogna aver qualche ristoro – / sappiam che quanto tempo dassi a quello, / che forse invan si perde, se ne toglie / alle nostre opre [...] /. Così, tardi o non mai, fornir convienti / l'opere o farle condurre a fattori, / che soglion far mille abborracciamenti." Commenting on these lines, Parker 2000 (as in fn. 6), pp. 111–112 mentions some passages from a letter that the painter addressed to Duke Cosimo to request an increase in his stipend up to the sum of 20 scudi per month – a request that he justified with his necessity to hire "uno et alle volte più garzoni che lo aiutino, et massime che oltre all'impresa delle *Storie* [the cartoons

art-related passage of the capitolo, Bronzino did however acknowledge, once again, how such a *modus operandi* had become unpopular and unprofitable – as the poet's haggard appearance clearly evidenced.[553]

This rejection of a degrading workhorse ethic in painting appears to closely echo some fundamental theoretical reflections of artist-writers from earlier generations. While urging painters to "lavorare la istoria" with "prestezza di fare, congiunta con diligenza, quale [...] non dia fastidio o tedio lavorando," Leon Battista Alberti had for example maintained that artists should not let themselves be overwhelmed by such "cupidità di finire le cose quale [...] facci abborracciare il lavoro," and stressed that they also had to "qualche volta [...] interlassare la fatica del lavorare ricreando l'animo."[554] Like Alberti, Leonardo would similarly exhort painters to "spesso levarsi e pigliare un poco d'altro sollazzo," based on the assumption that such interruptions would clarify their "giudizio" of the artwork.[555] And while a pace of work adhering so closely to the ebb and flow of inspiration that it could seem erratic was part of the painter's literary persona at least since Franco Sacchetti's depiction of Buffalmacco in the *Trecentonovelle*, in the Cinquecento it became a characteristic associated with several of the

---

for the tapestries of the *Stories of Joseph*] se li aggiunge quella di tutti i fregi" (the original document was published in O. C. Tosi, Una lettera inedita del Bronzino, in: *Arte e storia* 27, nos. 1–2 [1907], pp. 8–9, and dated and discussed in Cox-Rearick 1993 [as in fn. 122], p. 156). In examining Bronzino's work on the cartoons for the tapestries, Cox-Rearick also quoted a set of other contemporary letters (pp. 46–47) that document the painter's use of a limited number of assistants when he was working on the cartoons. Particularly relevant is the letter (transcribed and examined on pp. 289–291) that he addressed to Duke Cosimo on April 30, 1548, in which he requested the permission to hire Raffaello dal Borgo (i. e. Raffaellino dal Colle) to help him work on the project of the tapestries, "per essermi dattorno tutti questi maestri de / panni con pregarmi, ch'io solleciti." Cox Rearick also specified (p. 47) that Bronzino's collaborators generally played a limited role in the execution of the task: "while the cartoons were painted with the help of assistants, the preliminary design drawings for the tapestries [...] are all attributable to Bronzino himself."

[553] Bronzino 1988 (as in fn. 6), p. 149, *Capitolo del Bronzino pittore in lode del dappoco*, ll. 178–183: "Pare a qualcun ch'i' danari e' favori / non vadan dietro a chi fa come noi / e par ch'il volgo assai manco l'onori; / e tu per prova conoscer lo puoi, / che spesso hai visto la cappa e 'l saione / ir balzellando o negli sciugatoi."

[554] Quoted here from the vernacular version of *De pictura* (Leon Battista Alberti, *De pictura: redazione volgare*, ed. Lucia Bertolini, Florence 2011, p. 318 [3.240]). Manuscripts of this text do not seem to have circulated in the fifteenth and sixteenth centuries, which explains why Lodovico Domenichi chose to provide the first Italian translation of the Latin version in 1547. For this reason, the strikingly similar usage of then rare words such as "abborracciamenti" and "abborracciare" in Bronzino and Alberti's writings is probably not the result of a textual memory in the later poem. Domenichi's translation of the passage, on the other hand, runs as follows (Alberti 1547 [as in fn. 87], c. 42v): "In fornire l'opra vi metteremo quella diligentia, la quale sia congiunta a la prestezza del fare, la quale il fastidio non spaventi da proseguirla; né 'l desiderio di fornire la precipiti." On Alberti's prescription to the painter to temper *prestezza* with *diligenzia*, see especially the commentary of Barocchi 1960–1962 (as in fn. 147), 1, p. 416, which quotes these words in relation to Paolo Pino's discussion of the risks of *prestezza* and links it to Leonardo's negative view of hastened work; the same scholar's commentary on Vasari's biography of Michelangelo (Vasari 1962 [as in fn. 73], 2, pp. 184–186), which traces its influence on a number of other sixteenth-century sources; and Sonia Maffei's commentary on Giovio 1999 (as in fn. 82), p. 255, with reference to Alberti's re-use of Plinian motifs. On the longue durée and extra-Italian ramifications of the debate about the opposite artistic values of *prestezza* and *diligenzia*, see Nicola Suthor, *Bravura: Virtuosität und Mutwilligkeit in der Malerei der Frühen Neuzeit*, Munich 2010, pp. 113–163.

[555] Quotation from the *Libro di pittura*: Leonardo 1995 (as in fn. 348), 2, pp. 301–302 (no. 407: *Del giudicare il pittore la sua pittura*).

greatest names in the century's pantheon of artists.[556] In contemporary sources, however, it grew into a distinctive trait of the manner in which Leonardo worked.[557] The fact that in one of these sources – a famous novella by Matteo Bandello (1554) – Leonardo argued that patrons had to learn to treat painters "d'ingegni rari e sublimi" as "forme celestiali e non asini da vettura"[558] confirms that Bronzino's hostility toward the expectation that artists should toil like beasts of burden was rooted in the most esteemed Florentine artistic tradition, and in its belief that the intellectual aspect of the painter's work prevailed over manual drudgery.

The patron's response?

The epistle in verse that Bronzino addressed to Cosimo, then, condenses themes of artistic theory that are of capital importance in the author's poetic output, and that tie in closely with issues to which artists and art theorists active in the Quattrocento and Cinquecento had devoted ample attention. Since he developed these motifs in a composition with an explicitly conative function, hoping to convince the duke to agree to economic conditions he was perhaps not overly disposed to grant, it is worth investigating how Cosimo reacted to the arguments and requests set forth in the poem.

In this regard it is interesting to note the points of contact between the lyric and a patent letter in which the duke accorded Bronzino some properties. With the patent, dated October 1551 and issued in response to requests the artist had addressed to his patron the previous April, the duke granted Bronzino the benefit of two properties in the vicinity of Florence

---

[556] Novella 169 of Sacchetti's *Trecentonovelle*, for instance, recounted the visual prank that Buffalmacco had devised to punish the inhabitants of Perugia, who "eight or ten days" after the beginning of the work had started pestering him to finish the painting they had commissioned of their patron, St. Ercolano. Also relevant is novella 199, in which the painter devises a prank against his industrious master Tafo, who requested him to paint day and night: on these stories see Marcello Ciccuto, *L'immagine del testo: episodi di cultura figurativa nella letteratura italiana*, Rome 1990, pp. 113–155, pp. 137–139; Anita Simon, Letteratura e arte figurativa: Franco Sacchetti, un testimone d'eccezione?, in: *Mélanges de l'école française de Rome* 105 (1993), pp. 443–479, pp. 459 and 476–478; Michelangelo Zaccarello, Ingegno naturale e cultura materiale: i motti degli artisti nelle Trecento Novelle di Franco Sacchetti, in: *Italianistica* 38, no. 2 (2009), pp. 129–140, pp. 135–137; Paul Barolsky, *Why Mona Lisa Smiles and Other Tales by Vasari*, University Park, PA 2010, pp. 18–23. For a number of other anecdotes on the "creative idleness" of early modern artists, see Wittkower and Wittkower 1963 (as in fn. 1), pp. 59–63. For the discussion of a mid-sixteenth-century medical treatise that thematized the motif of the oscillations in the desire to work, with reference to the working practices of several artists, see Ulrich Pfisterer, Subject to Mood Swings: Michelangelo, Titian and Adrian Willaert on Creativity, in: Henri de Riedmatten, Nicolas Galley, Jean-François Corpataux, and Valentin Nussbaum (eds.), *Senses of Sight: Towards a Multisensorial Approach of the Image. Essays in Honor of Victor I. Stoichita*, Rome 2015, pp. 151–166.

[557] Ibid., p. 161.

[558] Matteo Bandello, *Tutte le opere di Matteo Bandello*, ed. Francesco Flora, 2 vols., Milan 1934–1943, 1, p. 649, novella I.58. On the story see Norman E. Land, Leonardo Da Vinci in a Tale by Matteo Bandello, in: *Discoveries* 23 (2006), pp. 9–17; Pietro De Marchi, Leonardo da Vinci narratore, o la libertà dell'artista. Su una novella di Matteo Bandello (I, 58), in: *Strumenti critici* 114 (2007), pp. 177–191, and Ismène Cotensin, De Vasari à Bandello: la nouvelle de Filippo Lippi (I, 58) et la représentation des artistes. "Forme celestiali e non asini da vettura", in: *La Rivista. Études culturelles italiennes Sorbonne Universités* 0 (2013), pp. 39–48 (https://etudesitaliennes.hypotheses.org/files/2016/02/Cotensin.pdf: last accessed 31/01/2021).

that had belonged to Matteo delle Macchie, a Medici official recently executed for embezzlement.[559] From the very first lines, he presented his granting of the privilege as a sign of gratitude for the quality of the art ("picturae artificium") with which the recipient had long served Cosimo and his family. The lord of Florence also referred to Bronzino as "pictori ac ministro nostro," showing that he tended to equate the services rendered by an eminent court artist with those provided by functionaries in key roles within the duchy. This is confirmed by the fact that we find similar phrasing in official documents from around the same time with which Cosimo assigned material assets as remuneration for the good work of individuals such as the first tax officer Jacopo Polverini: using the same syntagma ("exactissimaque cum diligentia") with which the duke praised Polverini's unyielding assiduity in collecting taxes, he would for instance compliment the attention to detail Bronzino demonstrated as court painter.[560] Pro-

---

[559] Given the text's significance, I provide here a new, full transcription of the document, based on the original in the State Archive of Florence (*Auditore delle Riformagioni*, I, cc. 28r–29r; a copy of the same text is at cc. 43r–v; the document was first published by Leopoldo Tanfani Centofanti, *Notizie di artisti tratte dai documenti pisani*, Pisa 1897, pp. 3–4, which however based its transcription on a copy of the source in Pisa; it was then re-published, but with several misreadings due to the difficult handwriting of the Florentine source, in Pilliod 2001 [as in fn. 249], p. 219): "Cosmus Medices Dei gratia Florentie Dux secundus. Angelo Cosmae, alias Bronzino, pictori ac ministro nostro nobis dilectissimo, salutem et omne bonum. Gratum tue picture artificium, in quo diu appud nos ac in beneficium nostrum nostraeque Medices domus in diversis occasionibus, et tam intus quam foris, assidue te exercuisse ac summa cum affectione exactissimaque cum diligentia exercere non desinis, plurimave obsequia quae nobis cum exuberanti fide praestitisti atque hodie prestas, in causa sunt ut tibi reddamur ad gratiam liberales. Cum itaque nonnulla immobilia bona que Mattias olim de Macchis exactor quondam decimarum ecclesiasticarum acquisieret a monasterio, capitulo et conventu fratrum Sancti Pancratii, vel quo ad directum, vel saltem quo ad utile dominium, in populo sanctae Mariae de Peretola comitatus nostre ducalis civitatis Florentie, et quedam alia bona que ipsemet Mattias prefatus per successionem acquisierat in populo Sancti Blasii de Petriolo comitatus predicti inter cetera pervenerint, quo ad iura quae ipse Mattias in illis habebat, in fischum nostrum nostramque cameram ducalem ex generali confiscatione bonorum que de patrimonio suo facta fuit per capitalem sententiam que ob nonnulla enormia per eum crimina commissa in ipsum per illius sindicos dicta est; cumque nos animadvertamus ad debilem patrimonium tuum, et ad pondus tuae rei domestice quod quotidie sustines, et quod, ni tibi a nobis succurratur, semper in paupertate viveres et post mortem tuam parum vel nihil posteris tuis relinquerest, et nostre intentionis semper fuerit et sit hodie quam maxime illos remunerare [qui] virtute sua et operibus bene meritos se exhibuerunt. Hinc est quod dictis de causis moti, et a prenarratis meritis tuis excitati, tibi omnia iura que quomodlibet in prenarratis bonis habemus, et que nobis, seu camere nostre ducali in illis quomodlibet competierunt atque hodie competunt vigore iam dicte confiscationis bonorum, et pariter ipsa bona, quo ad iura prefata, motu proprio ac ex certa scientia et de plenitudine nostre ducalis potestatis in remunerationem prefatorum tuorum meritorum ilari fronte animoque prompto inrevocabiliter et inter vivos donamus ex titulo et causa inrevocabilis donationis inter vivos, in te tuosque heredes et successores transferimus et translata esse volumus atqe mandamus, ita quod effectus sit ut de dictis iuribus et quo ad dicta iura de prelibatis bonis disponere possis et valeas ad libitum tue voluntatis. Accipe igitur, Bronzine noster, munus Principis tui, et spes te certissima foveat, maiora a nobis te esse consequturum, si in operibus tuis, virtute preditis perseverabis, sicuti iam incepisti. In quorum fidem has nostras patentes litteras, nostra manu firmatas, exarari fecimus per infrascriptum secretarium nostrum iussimusque nostri soliti sigilli plumbei appensione muniri. Datum Florentie in ducali palatio nostro. Die 6 ottobris anni Domini 1551 et ducatus nostri anno XV." On Matteo delle Macchie's execution, see Bernardo Segni, *Storie fiorentine di messer Bernardo Segni gentiluomo fiorentino [...]*, 3 vols., Milan 1805, 2, p. 338.

[560] The full text of the Ducal patent for Jacopo Polverini (April 1548), which was probably issued in response to a plea in which the bureaucrat had lamented his dire financial condition, is preserved in the same archival folder (Archivio di Stato di Firenze, *Auditore delle Riformagioni*, I, cc. 124r–125r). In the document, Cosimo addressed

fessionals who apparently had little in common were thus grouped together by virtue of their being useful to the duke, in different ways but with the same work ethic – in which diligence was framed as one of the most highly regarded qualities of those who were in Cosimo's service.

Among Bronzino's merits, the patent cited the devotion he had demonstrated in his many tributes to the duke ("plurimave obsequia quae nobis cum exuberanti fide praestitisti atque hodie prestas in causa sunt ut tibi reddamur ad gratiam liberales") and its terminology suggests that the document was in reply specifically to the painter's written respects (letters, or perhaps also poems). Consistent with the content of Bronzino's entreaty in verse, for that matter, is the fact that the duke was explicitly conceding the two properties in order to help a talented person in a precarious economic situation, who could hope to escape poverty only with Cosimo's help. The document ended by urging the painter to accept the gift and to trust that the duke would certainly bestow other, greater ones on him if he continued to work with perseverance.

Although the difficulty of dating Bronzino's composition makes it impossible to securely establish the relative chronology of the two documents, the parallels suggest the hypothesis that they might be somehow genetically related. The most optimistic conjecture is that the painter's missive is one of the factors behind the granting of the ducal patent and that he was therefore successful in convincing his chief patron to respond generously to his entreaties. Yet a less uplifting explanation is equally compatible with what we know from the texts. It is possible that Bronzino penned his composition after Cosimo had granted the patent, perhaps when he was having difficulty using the properties he had been assigned, or when – in the early 1560s – he was forced to repeatedly ask for payment for some paintings he had produced for the duke.[561] If this were the case, he might have echoed some of the expressions contained in the patent to remind Cosimo indirectly of his past promises of generosity, and with these, his moral obligation to provide economic support to the painter in need. In other words, the artist might have used the poetic medium to advocate for the reciprocity of service or assistance, which according to a moral code that the world of Renaissance courts had borrowed from the Latins, bound the good *patronus* and his faithful *cliens*.[562]

---

his servant as "dilectissimo," and awarded him some properties formerly in the possession of Alessandro di Giovanni Rondinelli, who was among those Florentine patricians who had been beheaded for their opposition to the new duke in 1537. Similarly to the one addressed to Bronzino, the patent singled out the qualities that Cosimo intended to reward, praising how Polverini had served him "diu et assidue [...], cum incomparabili affectione, solertia non mediocri, ingenti fede, constantia summa ac exuberanti studio, reverenter," and how he continued to work "exactissima cum diligentia." From other documents preserved in the same folder, it appears that during the late 1540s and early 1550s, the duke issued a number of such letters for other courtiers and high officials of his state, including one to Sforza Almeni, who was rewarded with gifts of property for his faithful and dutiful service, as well as for the "diligentia" he had demonstrated in his role of *cameriere segreto* (ibid., cc. 126r–127v).

[561] On these circumstances, see Emiliani 1960 (as in fn. 125), pp. 85–86, and Maurizia Tazartes, *Bronzino*, Milan 2003, p. 67.

[562] A useful discussion of how Renaissance writers and intellectuals modeled their ideas of patronage after those that were elaborated in Roman antiquity is in De Beer 2013 (as in fn. 493), pp. 1–22, with further bibliography.

Between courtly panegyric and artistic self-exegesis

Among the poems that artists working in the Florentine court wrote in praise of their principal patron, Domenico Poggini's sonnet *Ben fu grande, e pregiato il tuo valore* stands out for the unusual form in which the author makes his tribute (Appendix, no. 81). Introduced as a composition "molto più da leggiadro Poeta, che da Scultore," the text was first published at the end of the chapter on Cosimo de' Medici in Girolamo Ruscelli's book *Le imprese illustri con espositioni, et discorsi* (1566). Ruscelli declared that Poggini had composed the poem "a lode del duca" taking as object one of his own artistic creations,[563] namely, the portrait medal of Cosimo with Apollo crowning Capricorn on the reverse (Figs. 19 and 20). In recent decades, scholars have therefore referenced the poem to illustrate the constituent elements of the medal, whose stucco model Lodovico Domenichi had already described in his *Ragionamento* on *imprese* (1556), which furthermore praised the Horatian motto that framed the figuration ("Integer vite scelerisque purus," i. e. "upright of life and clean from crimes," a citation from *Odes* 1.22.1) as "conveniente molto alle ottime qualità di così virtuoso principe."[564] Art historians have also often referred to the sonnet to clarify the iconography of the marble sculpture, for centuries on display in the Boboli Gardens, which Poggini completed in 1559 from an invention very similar to the medal's (but, among other small differences, Apollo is no longer holding a lyre and the monstrous serpent at his feet has been replaced with a plinth; Table VII).[565]

---

[563] See the text that introduces the sonnet in Girolamo Ruscelli, *Le imprese illustri con espositioni, et discorsi* [...], Venice 1566, p. 172: "L'impresa del Capricorno si vede scolpita in molte medaglie di questo duca, et alcune se ne veggon bellissime con un'altra impresa d'un Apollo, fatta per mano di Domenico Poggini, scultore et antiquario rarissimo [...], sopra la qual egli stesso a lode del duca, suo signore, fece questo sonetto, molto più da leggiadro poeta che da scultore." We might compare Poggini's choice to use the poetic medium to comment on some of his medallic creations, such as the portrait medals for Cosimo I de' Medici and Benedetto Varchi, with a number of significant antecedents in other cultural contexts. The case of the Dutch sculptor, medalist, and poet Johannes Secundus (Johann Nico Everaerts, 1511–1536) is particularly interesting in this regard, as the artist commented on several of his approximately 35 medals in Neo-Latin poetic compositions: see Pfisterer 2008 (as in fn. 284), pp. 108–109.

[564] See Paolo Giovio and Lodovico Domenichi, *Dialogo dell'imprese militari et amorose, di monsignor Giovio vescovo di Nocera. Con un Ragionamento di messer Lodovico Domenichi, nel medesimo soggetto*, Venice 1556, pp. 120–121: "Et io m'era scordato dirvi di due belle imprese del signor duca Cosmo formate amendue dal mio carissimo amico, et eccellentissimo artefice et maestro di zecca di Sua Eccellenza, Domenico Poggini; l'una in acciaio et l'altra di stucco [...]. La seconda ha per rovescio uno Apollo, il quale mette la mano in capo al Capricorno, felicissimo ascendente di Sua Eccellenza e un piede sopra il serpente Fitone [sic] con l'arco e 'l turcasso. Il motto è quel verso d'Horatio, conveniente molto alle ottime qualità di così virtuoso principe: Integer vitae scelerisque purus." Scholarly works that have mentioned or quoted the sonnet in their discussion of the iconography of the medal include Friedrich Kriegbaum and Ulrich Middeldorf, Forgotten Sculpture by Domenico Poggini, in: *The Burlington Magazine* 53 (1928), pp. 9–17, p. 11; Toderi and Vannel 2000 (as in fn. 261), 2, pp. 737–738; Attwood 2003 (as in fn. 366), 1, p. 339; Eike Schmidt's entry in: Gabriella Capecchi, Amelio Fara, and Detlef Heikamp (eds.), *Palazzo Pitti: la reggia rivelata*, Florence 2003, p. 516, and Claudia Rousseau, Astrological Imagery and Rulership Propaganda in the Art of Cosimo I de' Medici, in: Nicholas Campion and Jennifer Zahrt (eds.), *Astrology as Art: Representation and Practice*, Ceredigion 2018, pp. 63–85.

[565] The head of a wolf appears to be carved on the plinth. For the iconographical differences between the two works, see Schmidt 2003 (as in fn. 564). Among the main discussions of the iconography of the marble as related to the sonnet are Kriegbaum and Middeldorf 1928 (as in fn. 564), p. 11; Utz 1976 (as in fn. 389), p. 68; Hendrik

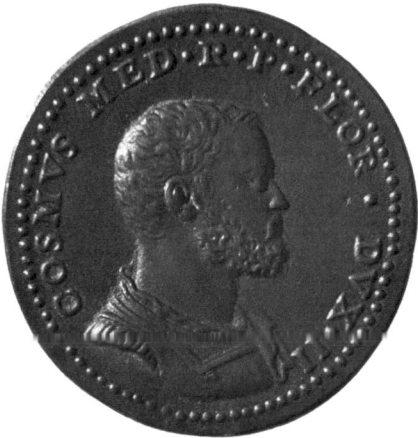 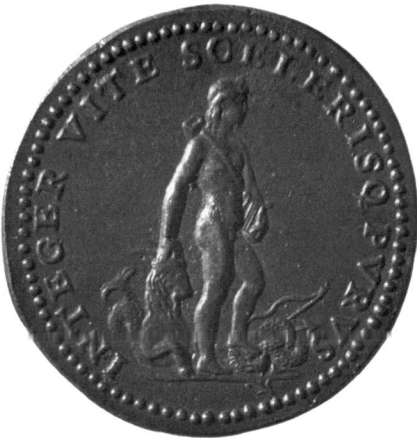

19+20 Domenico Poggini, portrait medal of Cosimo I de' Medici with Capricorn and Apollo, cast bronze, c. 1556, obverse and reverse, Florence, Museo del Bargello.

Contrary to what Ruscelli's words suggested, Poggini's sonnet does not read like open praise of Cosimo, nor does it explicitly mention the existence of a visual creation. If read independently of viewing the medal, the poem nonetheless becomes nearly incomprehensible, and this means that the medalist conceived it to materially accompany the object to which it referred, perhaps as a new *xenion* or poetic note to be delivered to the duke along with the artwork.[566] It is moreover certain that the deity who is object of the laudatory apostrophe that opens the composition and is depicted on the back of the medal, the Pythian Apollo, was one of the many pagan divinities with whose image Cosimo, like Augustus and other Roman emperors before him, aspired to be identified.[567] Poggini knew the story of Apollo's victory over the serpent Python through Ovid's *Metamorphoses* (1.434–451), perhaps by way of Lodovico Dolce's successful Italian translation, *Le Trasformationi* (1553), and in the sonnet he made reference to it in order to explain the imagery on the reverse of his portrait medal of the duke.

Thijs Van Veen, *Cosimo I De' Medici and His Self-Representation in Florentine Art and Culture*, Cambridge 2006, p. 31, and Rousseau 2018 (as in fn. 564). On the statue see also Bruce Edelstein, Le sculture nel Giardino di Boboli ai tempi di Cosimo I. Una passeggiata con il Principe, in: Alessandra Griffo (ed.), *La prima statua per Boboli. Il Villano restaurato*, Livorno 2019, pp. 77–87, p. 83.

[566] The sonnet that Poggini composed over his portrait medal of Benedetto Varchi undoubtedly functioned as a *xenion*: see *supra*, p. 98, with further references.

[567] Paul William Richelson, *Studies in the Personal Imagery of Cosimo I de' Medici, Duke of Florence*, New York 1978, pp. 36–38, examines how the two works by Poggini fit into Cosimo's visual propaganda, which extensively drew on a number of Augustan iconographies. The study also lists some of the ancient monuments (e. g., the Palatine Temple of Apollo in Rome) that promoted an association between Augustus and the solar god. See also Jonietz 2017 (as in fn. 344), p. 174, which considers the case of Poggini's marble within the framework of the wider reception of the *Apollo Pythius* motif among sculptors who were active in sixteenth-century Florence (e. g., Giovan Francesco Rustici, Vincenzo Danti, and Pietro Francavilla).

Functioning as an exegetic support for one of the "argutissime inventioni et significationi" that Domenichi deemed typical of Poggini's medals,[568] the composition thus dispels possible doubts as to the identity of both the young male nude at the center of the image and of the serpent coiled around his left foot. The text clarifies that the quiver we see on Apollo's back and the bow lying on the ground were the instruments he used to claim his first victory, and what follows is likewise explanatory in nature. The reference to Eros's "dorato stral" that had struck the god's chest, igniting his unrequited love for Daphne, ascribes a dual meaning to the arrow around which Python is wrapped on the reverse of the medal, reading it as a sign not only of the thousand darts Apollo used – in Ovid's telling (*Metamorphoses* 1.443) – to pierce the monstrous serpent, but also of the god's most famous infatuation (*ibid.*, 452–567). Discussing in linear sequence those parts of an image that the beholder takes in almost instantaneously with a glance at the artwork,[569] the sonnet finally concentrates on the left-hand side of the medal, focusing on the gesture with which Apollo has just laid a crown "d'oro e di gemme" on the head of Capricorn lying behind him. With a play on words on the nature of the reverse of the medal, which in the Renaissance was typically intended as an impresa or device of the individual portrayed and therefore as a symbolic figuration of a personal deed or line of conduct through the dual means of word and image,[570] Poggini presents the coronation as a modern, noble "impresa" or heroic action by Apollo. According to the poet, with this deed the god demonstrated a valor greater than ever before, by returning "oltraggio, e scorno" to certain unnamed adversaries of Capricorn (ll. 9–14).

An example of a poem that an artist likely conceived to illustrate one of his visual works, the sonnet addresses as primary audience the lord whose idealizing portrait is featured on the medal: his physical profile immortalized on the obverse, and his political-spiritual likeness on the allegorical reverse, in which the Horatian motto emphasized Cosimo's immaculate integrity.[571] Though on a much smaller scale, the composition thus served a comparable purpose as

---

[568] Giovio and Domenichi 1556 (as in fn. 564), p. 122: "Vi potrei ragionare d'infinite altre medaglie fatte dal Poggino, con argutissime inventioni et significati."

[569] On this distinguishing feature of ecphrastic texts, see esp. Michael Baxandall, *Words for Pictures: Seven Papers on Renaissance Art and Criticism*, New Haven, CT 2003, pp. 112–113.

[570] See esp. Ulrich Pfisterer, "Soweit die Flügel meines Auges tragen." Leon Battista Albertis Imprese und Selbstbildnis, in: *Mitteilungen des Kunsthistorischen Institutes in Florenz* 42 (1998), pp. 205–251, and Kristen Lippincott, "Un gran pelago": The Impresa and the Medal Reverse in Fifteenth-Century Italy, in: Steven K. Scher (ed.), *Perspectives on the Renaissance Medal*, New York 2000, pp. 75–96, for two discussions of the central role of imprese in fifteenth-century medals. Attwood 2003 (as in fn. 366), 1, pp. 35–36 (with further references) offers a concise assessment of the role of devices in sixteenth-century medallic production, while Andrea Torre, *Vedere versi: un manoscritto di emblemi petrarcheschi (Baltimore, Walters Art Museum, ms. W476)*, Naples 2012, pp. 35–40, discusses some of the most relevant Cinquecento writings that examined this association. In addition, Alessandro Benassi, La teoria e la prassi dell'emblema e dell'impresa, in: Genovese and Torre 2019 (as in fn. 276), pp. 113–146, provides a useful synthetic overview of the burgeoning scholarly literature that in recent decades has focused on emblems and imprese, along with a summary of some of the most influential early modern writings on these genres.

[571] On the sub-genre of princely devices in the Italian Renaissance, its propagandistic functions, and its most typical features, see Guido Arbizzoni, Le imprese come ritratto interiore del principe, in: Lucia Bertolini, Arturo Calzona, Glauco Maria Cantarella, and Stefano Caroti (eds.), *Il principe invisibile: Atti del convegno internazio-*

Giorgio Vasari's *Ragionamenti* (begun in 1558 but left unfinished on the painter's death),[572] in which the author imagined accompanying the young prince Francesco de' Medici through the forest of mythological allegories he had painted in the Palazzo Vecchio, missing no opportunity to explain how his frescoes paid tribute to Medici power. The *Ragionamenti*, in fact, are the epitome of a certain tendency of Florentine artists of the later Cinquecento to commit to the written word their interpretation of the complex iconographies they developed in their own artworks, but this kind of artistic self-commentary was usually in prose form: beyond Vasari's dialogue we also find it, for example, in various passages of Benvenuto Cellini's autobiography and of his *Trattati*.[573] In the Medicean context of those years, Poggini's use of verse to explain one of his visual creations is therefore somewhat anomalous, though it may have embodied a more widespread aspiration among Renaissance artists to experiment with this kind of use of the poetic medium. It is in this respect noteworthy that, in one of the sonnets of his *Rime* (1587), Giovan Paolo Lomazzo acknowledged the chance to use poetry for this purpose as the main advantage an artist could draw from possessing full mastery of the pen. After summarizing Leonardo's theories regarding painting's greater representative power with respect to poetry, Lomazzo concluded his poem by declaring that only those who mastered both arts held the key to the apex of glory, as this dual expertise would allow a painter to describe the subject and meaning of his own visual creations.[574] The ability to use verse as an exegesis of art thus crowned an ideal paradigm of communication, stemming from Vitruvius's *De Architectura* and widespread in Renaissance sources, between a savvy artist and an audience wishing to understand from him the reasons for his erudite figurations.[575]

---

nale di studi (Mantova 27–30 novembre 2013), Turnhout 2015, pp. 373–399, and Fabrizio Bondi, *Il principe per emblemi: letteratura e immagini del politico tra Cinquecento e Seicento*, Bologna 2016.

[572] On the book see Paola Tinagli, The Identity of the Prince: Cosimo de' Medici, Giorgio Vasari and the *Ragionamenti*, in Rogers 2000 (as in fn. 47), pp. 189–196; Émilie Passignat, The Order, the Itinerary, the Beholder. Considerations on Some Aspects of the *Ragionamenti del Sig. Cavalier Giorgio Vasari*, in: Maia Wellington Gahtan (ed.), *Giorgio Vasari and the Birth of the Museum*, Burlington, VT 2014, pp. 151–162, and the dense monograph by Jonietz 2017 (as in fn. 344).

[573] Two cases in point are the author's detailed illustrations for the iconography he had devised for his *Saltcellar* (1540–1543), now preserved in the Kunsthistorisches Museum Wien, in both his autobiography (2.2) and his treatise on goldsmithery (ch. 12). In the *Descrizione dell'opere di Giorgio Vasari pittore e architetto aretino*, which is the second-to-last section of the Giuntina, Vasari similarly inserted several iconographic analyses of his own works, such as the elaborate *Allegory of the Immaculate Conception* (1540) that he had painted for the family chapel of Bindo Altoviti in the Florentine church of Santissimi Apostoli: Vasari 1967–1997 (as in fn. 74), 6, pp. 380–381.

[574] See Lomazzo 2006 (as in fn. 27), p. 138 (sonnet 2.82, *Paragon de la pittura con la poesia*, my emphasis): "Quel che rappresentar pônno i pennelli, / Chè tutto ciò che qui contempla e mira / L'occhio mortal, la penna poi sospira, / Che formar non lo puote al par di quelli. // La Poesia e suoi versi ornati belli / Si senton soli; e l'altra a veder gira, / Sì come a principal: onde con ira / Van contro lei tutti i poeti snelli. // Non è di pareggiar il dir al fare, / Perché è come ombra al corpo, il qual si vede / Pur ch'uomo sappi l'invenzion trovare, // *Ma chi la penna co'l pennel possiede, / E ciò che pinge sa co'l dir spiegare, / A questo ognun la gloria e 'l vanto cede*.") The sonnet's main gist seems to imply a necessary unity of poetic and pictorial ispirazion, which the author developed in the sixth book of the *Trattato dell'arte della pittura* (Lomazzo 1973–1975 [as in fn. 28], 2, pp. 244–245).

[575] Compare the passage in which the ancient theorist recommended that an architect should have extensive historical knowledge in order to answer the beholders' questions on the subjects of the decorative elements of

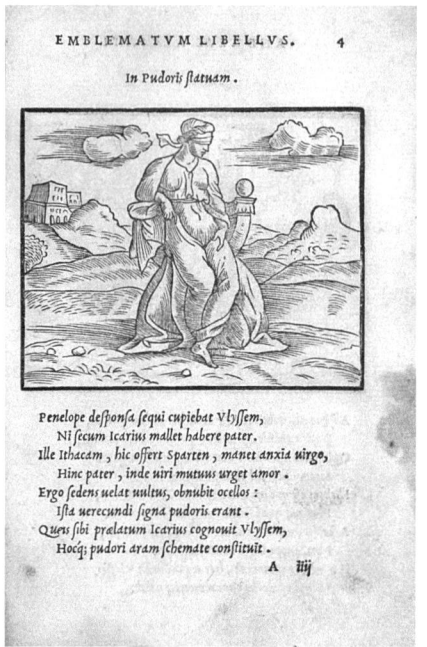

21 Andrea Alciato, Emblematum Libellus, Venice 1546, c. Aiiiir.

It is also plausible that Poggini's decision to compose a sonnet on the impresa featured in the portrait medal of Duke Cosimo was favored by another symbolic form based on the interaction of verbal and iconic codes: the emblem, which became particularly popular in Italy after the publication in Venice of Andrea Alciato's *Emblematum libellus* (1546). In fact, whereas most sixteenth-century writings on the impresa genre insisted on a bipartite structure of visual image and motto, the emblem had taken hold as a tripartite device that normally consisted of a witty epigrammatic poem (*subscriptio*) underlying an image (*pictura*) topped by a motto (*inscriptio*)

his buildings (Vitruvius, *De Architectura* 1.1.5): "Historias autem plures novisse oportet, quod multa ornamenta saepe in operibus architecti designant, de quibus argumentis rationem cur fecerint quaerentibus reddere debent. Quemadmodum si quis statuas marmoreas muliebres stolatas, quae caryatides dicuntur, pro columnis in opere statuerit et insuper mutulos et coronas conlocaverit, percotantibus ita reddet rationem." Vitruvius's recommendations underpin, among others, an important passage in Gauricus's *De sculptura* (1504), in which the author stated that being a sculptor required extensive antiquarian knowledge (Gauricus 1999 [as in fn. 84], 1.7, p. 136): "Ac mille eiusmodi, quorum omnium causas, sculptor tenere debebit, ut quum quaeratur, quid sibi velit ille in Thessalia tres oculos habet Iuppiter, respondeat sic." The motif of the *doctus artifex* who can enlighten an inquisitive audience on the iconographical choices underpinning his savvy visual creations is well attested across a variety of literary genres in medieval and early modern Italy. One relevant example is an anecdote about Giotto that we read in Anonimo Fiorentino's commentary on Dante's *Commedia* (late fourteenth/early fifteenth century). As the story goes, the painter was able to give a witty answer to a cardinal who asked him to account for the way in which he had represented some bishops in a chapel in Bologna, while also ridiculing the clergy's ignorance of the holy writs (see Enid T. Falaschi, Giotto: The Literary Legend, in: *Italian Studies* 27 [1972], pp. 1–27, p. 13, and Baldassarri 1997 [as in fn. 31], pp. 385–386).

(Fig. 21).⁵⁷⁶ Yet Poggini's sonnet remains closer to the rhetoric of the impresa for its deliberately enigmatic tone, giving the reader the key to identify the picture's constituents but no clue about their innermost meaning. The variety of scholars' theories as to the specific encomiastic message that the medal, and the marble derived from it, intended to send is telling from this perspective.

While all modern exegeses have followed Domenichi in identifying Capricorn as the duke's astrological impresa, linking Poggini's work to the creature's ubiquity in Florentine art of the mid-Cinquecento and its propagandistic role in associating Cosimo's power with that of Augustus and Holy Roman Emperor Charles V,⁵⁷⁷ some have insisted on the fundamentally polysemic nature of the symbol. Referencing a letter Poggini wrote to the consuls of the Accademia del Disegno to propose his design for the institutional seal (1563), Hildegard Utz interpreted Capricorn as a symbol of the three arts of drawing, but also of the ducal patronage that had allowed them to flourish in Florence.⁵⁷⁸ Interpretations of the medal's other elements

---

⁵⁷⁶ For these sixteenth-century theoretical writings on *imprese*, which included the aforementioned treatises by Domenichi and Ruscelli, see, among others, Guido Arbizzoni, *Un nodo di parole e di cose: storia e fortuna delle imprese*, Rome 2002, pp. 11–36; idem, Giovio, Domenichi e le imprese, in: *Bollettino storico piacentino* 110 (2015), pp. 9–23; Dorigen Sophie Caldwell, *The Sixteenth-Century Italian Impresa in Theory and Practice*, New York 2004, pp. 3–42; Gennaro Savarese, *Indagini sulle arti sorelle: studi su letteratura delle immagini e ut pictura poesis negli scrittori italiani*, eds. Stefano Benedetti and Gian Piero Maragoni, Manziana 2006, pp. 3–48. On the typical tripartition of emblems see Peter M. Daly, *Literature in the Light of the Emblem: Structural Parallels Between the Emblem and Literature in the Sixteenth and Seventeenth Centuries*, Toronto 1998², p. 7, as well as idem, *The Emblem in Early Modern Europe: Contributions to the Theory of the Emblem*, Farnham 2014, pp. 3–6. Among the not always clear-cut differences between emblems and *imprese*, Caldwell 2004, p. XII, underscores that while emblems "convey a universal moral message […], imprese were seen as expressing ideas in the mind of the individual. The emphasis on imprese as personal statements of thought or sentiment was absolutely central to the way in which they were defined and served to distinguish them from other badges of identity, such as familial coat of arms." On this difference between imprese and emblems, see also the introductory remarks by Lina Bolzoni to: Lina Bolzoni, Barbara Allegranti, Arianna Andrei, Giovanna Bosco et alii (eds.), *"Con parola brieve e con figura". Libri antichi di imprese e emblemi*, Lucca 2004, pp. 1–10, emphasizing how the devices were meant to visualize their bearer's intention and how, on different levels, they sometimes tended to partially overlap with emblems. On the blurred boundaries between the earliest prototypes of *imprese* and other visual or textual products of the fifteenth century, see Pfisterer 2008 (as in fn. 284), p. 117.
⁵⁷⁷ Kriegbaum and Middeldorf 1928 (as in fn. 564), p. 11; Richelson 1978 (as in fn. 97), pp. 36–38; Toderi and Vannel 2000 (as in fn. 261), 2, pp. 737–738; Attwood 2003 (as in fn. 366), 1, p. 339; Van Veen 2006 (as in fn. 565), p. 31; Schmidt 2003 (as in fn. 564), and Rousseau 2018 (as in fn. 564).
⁵⁷⁸ See Utz 1976 (as in fn. 389), p. 69 ("Hence the Capricorn symbolized, in Poggini's iconology, the Disegno as the generator of the three arts: Architecture, Sculpture, and Painting […]. In addition it symbolized Duke Cosimo I, respectively his virtue, force, and force, and patronage of the fine arts"), after quoting the following letter (text from Bottari and Ticozzi 1822 [as in fn. 184], 1, pp. 265–266): "Avendosi a fare il Sigillo per questa onoratissima Accademia del Disegno, e considerando quanta e quale sia la cortesia e benignità dell'Ill. et Ecc. sig. Duca, unico signore e padron nostro, e come egli ne sia fautore a benefattore, mi pare a proposito, seconde il mio debol giudizio, trovare una invenzione, la quale esprima che queste tre arti sono sostenute, favorite e difese da S. E. Illustrissima. Però ho finto che Minerva, Dea delle scienze, abbracci queste tre Arti, le quali, benchè il Disegno sia un solo nome, è però necessario sprimerle e significarle con tre modi e nomi. E perchè tutte e tre si partono da un solo gambo e da una sola scienza, figuro ch'ella si riposi e regga sul Capricorno, come virtù di S. E. Ill.; e nello scudo, che Minerva tiene nel braccio sinistro, formo l'arme di S. E. Ill., col quale scudo ella si difende, e guarda da chi volesse offenderla, siccome questa compagnia si regge, si guarda e si difende con la virtù, forza e favore di S. E. Ill. Questo è, quanto al suggetto, che a me pare che sia a proposito, rimettendomi però al molto giudizio, che in ciascuno de' vostri eccellentissimi ingegni si trova. E quello, ch'è finto a modo di vaso

vary widely: the object Apollo is setting on the animal's head has for instance been read as a reference to the ducal diadem ("mazzocchio") or to the constellation of Ariadne's crown.[579] Similarly, the representation of Apollo as the killer of Python has been interpreted as a panegyristic allusion to the prophetic gifts Cosimo supposedly demonstrated on the occasion of the victorious siege of Siena (1554–1555) or, with stricter references to texts and other visual objects produced in the same context as the medal, to the reclamation of the swamps around Pisa that he had promoted since the late 1540s.[580]

More or less convincingly tied to the intellectual horizon within which Poggini worked, the various hypotheses art historians have suggested to decipher the message of the impresa are all basically compatible with the medalist's own self-commentary in verse. Nor is this diffraction of proposed explanations simply due to the cultural distance separating modern scholars from their objects of study. In stating the constituent elements of the figuration while remaining silent on their meanings, Poggini's sonnet followed one of the five cardinal rules that Paolo Giovio had established for the invention of an impresa: that it not be "oscura di sorte, c'habbia mistiero [i. e. necessity] della Sibilla per interprete a volerla intendere; né tanto chiara, ch'ogni plebeo l'intenda."[581] In addition to shielding the content of a noble message from the contaminating scrutiny of the masses,[582] maintaining a certain quotient of impenetrable obscurity was functional to the ideal reception envisaged for objects like Poggini's medal. Through its interaction with the image and motto on the reverse of the artwork, the

colle tre Arti sopra, e preso da me per S. E. Ill., la quale dà e porge vigore, forza e nutrimento colle sue sustanze a queste arti, come chiaramente per ognuno s'intende e conosce. Questo è quanto m'occorre dirvi sopra tal cosa, non passando più oltre il mio ingegno e giudicio. E con tal fine a tutti voi altri eccellentissimi ingegni umilmente mi raccomando. Iddio nostro Signore ci presti santa pace e felicità." The letter, whose original appears to have been lost, is undated, but it is undoubtedly from 1563, when twenty-three artists (including Giovann'Angelo Montorsoli, Benvenuto Cellini, and Francesco Salviati) took part in the famous competition for the selection of a new seal for the newly established academic institution: on this, see most recently Luigi Zangheri, Giorgio Vasari e l'Accademia del Disegno, in: Nova and Zangheri 2013 (as in fn. 336), pp. 85–97, pp. 94–97; Alessandro Vezzosi, Il sigillo accademico da Leonardo a Benvenuto Cellini, in: Bert W. Meijer and Luigi Zangheri (eds.), *Accademia delle Arti del Disegno: studi, fonti e interpretazioni di 450 anni di storia*, 2 vols., Florence 2015, 1, pp. 175–183, and Pierguidi 2015 (as in fn. 254).

[579] For the former proposal, see Van Veen 2006 (as in fn. 565), p. 31; for the latter, see Rousseau 2018 (as in fn. 564).

[580] The former hypothesis is formulated ibid., the latter in Jonietz 2017 (as in fn. 344), p. 175. Jonietz makes reference to Bernardo Davanzati's funerary eulogy for Cosimo de' Medici, which compared the ducal campaigns for the reclamation of the territory around Pisa to Apollo's killing of Python (Davanzati, *Scisma d'Inghilterra con altre operette […]*, Padua 1754², p. 147). This interpretation of the myth inspired a number of figurative products in Medici Florence. For instance, Emanuela Ferretti, Cosimo I, la magnificenza dell'acqua e la celebrazione del potere: la nuova capitale dello Stato territoriale fra architettura, città e infrastrutture, in: *Annali di storia di Firenze* 9 (2015), pp. 9–33, p. 22, records how Cosimo's enterprise was celebrated on the occasion of his funeral in the church of San Lorenzo (1574) with a frescoed scene representing Python slain by several arrows.

[581] Quoted from Giovio's *Dialogo dell'imprese militari et amorose*, in Giovio and Domenichi 1556 (as in fn. 564), p. 6.

[582] Luca Contile would insist on this concept, arguing that the arcane forms of the impresa served as "maravigliosi velami della sapientia, usati in confusione dell'ignorantia e della profanità, conciosiaché le vitiose nature sieno d'intendere i concetti divini lecitamente indegne" (Contile, *Ragionamento […] sopra la proprietà delle imprese*, Pavia 1574, c. 30r; on this book, see Caldwell 2004 [as in fn. 576], pp. 98–110).

artist's elusive poem prompted a game of interpretation, encouraging its audience – first and foremost, the lord of Florence – to come up with a variety of hypotheses to decipher the impresa's encomiastic message. This open and plural hermeneutic practice, which most naturally played out in the intellectual world of the courts,[583] is also evident in many passages of the dialogues dedicated in that period to this kind of creation. The learned conversants at the center of these works would typically discuss the imprese of some of the most eminent figures of the time with a profusion of conjectural phrases ("forse," "s'io non m'inganno," etc.), to emphasize the speculative nature of their frequently conflicting theories.[584] In fact, the diffraction of their own interpretative hypotheses reflects the extent to which polysemy was inscribed in such devices from their very invention.

In conclusion, what needs to be underlined is the doubly elitist nature of the rhetoric of imprese. Not only did it exclude the vast lay audience from enjoying these iconotextual nexuses in order to address those who were "dott[i], et scientiat[i]" enough – in the words of Scipione Ammirato – to "penetrar […] ne i lor alti, et profondi concetti," but it required creators to possess a level of *ingegno*, cultural expertise and sophistication that was for the most part considered the prerogative of the finest literati.[585] "Officio d'huomini non solamente dotti, ma capricciosi anchora,"[586] capable of skillfully combining the possible messages that arose from the dynamic interaction between inherently polyvalent images and the words of ancient or modern *auctoritates* that had to partly guide their allegorical interpretation, the invention of imprese in the Cinquecento was often commissioned to the most prominent court poets and writers. It was typically these individuals the prince asked to come up with a visual and verbal message that could communicate the personal qualities or political project

---

[583] See Bolzoni 2004 (as in fn. 576), p. 10, as well as the remarks on the special value that several fifteenth-century and early sixteenth-century sources already ascribed to the plurality of interpretations made possible by the visual and textual enigmas encapsulated in imprese in Pfisterer 2008 (as in fn. 284), pp. 106–129, pp. 112–113. On the courtly destination of the majority of Cinquecento devices, see John Manning, *The Emblem*, London 2004, p. 76.

[584] Such phrasing is particularly recurrent in Domenichi's *Ragionamento*. Compare, for instance, one such passage from his work (Giovio and Domenichi, *Dialogo dell'imprese militari et amorose*, p. 101): "Ar[lenio]: Et quale intentione credete voi che fosse quella di Sua Eccellentia in questa impresa? Lo[dovico]: Io non so, se sarà presuntione a voler mettermi a indovinare, e a penetrare negli altissimi concetti de' principi; pur con questo proposito di non saper nulla di certo vi dico, che a mio giudicio egli ha voluto mostrare."

[585] Scipione Ammirato, *Il Rota overo dell'imprese dialogo* […], Naples 1562, p. 143: "Il volgo dilettisi nella pittura, dalle parole cavi quel senso che può, faccia i sentimenti a suo modo, che noi di ciò non ci curiamo, purché non ci forzi sotto questa legge, che del tutto ci habbiamo a far intender da loro. Che così somiglantemente fanno i poeti, le corteccie de quali come son note et patenti, così la midolla è segreta et occulta. Et bene conviene esser dotto et scientiato colui che penetrar possa i lor alti et profondi concetti". The passage is discussed in Arbizzoni 2002 (as in fn. 576), pp. 52–53. Compare also Bolzoni 2004 (as in fn. 576), p. 7, which stresses that sixteenth-century *imprese* are "in genere inventate da un letterato perché richiedono, oltre che una buona cultura, ingegno, capriccio, fantasia. Si tratta di ricordare i versi dei poeti, di triturarli, di ridurli in frammenti in modo tale che producano accoppiamenti – più o meno giudiziosi – con una immagine."

[586] Quoted from Domenichi's *Ragionamento* in Giovio and Domenichi 1556 (as in fn. 564), p. 131: "Lo[dovico]: Io ò fatto poche imprese a instantia altrui, perché […] questo è uffizio d'huomini non solamente dotti, ma capricciosi anchora."

he wished to highlight, or the success he aimed to emphasize.[587] By inventing imprese for more or less powerful *signori*, men of letters had achieved a hegemonic position in one of the figurative spaces where the issue of *ut pictura poesis* most openly played out at the time: as Paola Barocchi pointed out, those communicative devices were in fact based on a new way of harmonizing the universality and ability to capture a subject's essence that Renaissance artists had often claimed as a prerogative of the visual language with the durability and immateriality that literati recognized as the preserve of poetic words.[588]

Poggini's impresa thus appears to be a telltale of the important new creative fronts that in later sixteenth-century Italy might open to artists who could master the pen. We do not know whether he, too, created his piece in response to a request from the duke or on his own free initiative. His self-commentary in verse on that invention seems however to rule out, or at least deliberately obscure, any participation by a literato in developing the iconography: as a *doctus artifex* with expertise in both medal making and poetry, Poggini presented himself as someone with all the necessary skills for conceiving the kind of savvy rhetorical device that could aptly celebrate the essence of the prince.

---

[587] Compare Arbizzoni 2015 (as in fn. 571), p. 381, highlighting how a prince would typically ask a literato to come up with imprese that would represent him "non nella sua materialità fisica, ma in una sorta di astrazione che vuol palesare la sostanza interiore, pacifica o minacciosa, sempre comunque virtuosa, sulla quale intende fondare la sua legittimazione e proiettare all'esterno una sorta di sintetico programma di governo."

[588] Barocchi 1971–1977 (as in fn. 193), 3, p. 2755.

Appendix

1.
Benvenuto Cellini
… … …
io fo modegli, altrui à l'opre e 'l vanto:
   o mi fusse pur fatto 'l mio dovere!
   Perché diavol m'à ei messo sì da·ccanto?   3
Voi mi terrete fuor d'ogni sapere,
   che come un rinbanbito così canto:
   se tant'io vivo 'l fin potrei vedere.   6

[Cellini 2014 (as fn. 7), fragment 62, p. 188]

2.
Agnolo Bronzino
All'eccellentissimo messer Michelagnolo Buonarroti

O stupor di Natura, Angelo eletto,
   c'havete al virtuoso il Buono arroto,
   né qual più sète, o buono o saggio, è noto,
   sendo in sapere ed in bontà perfetto.   4
Con puro core e con sincero affetto
   fin da' primi anni miei vi feci voto,
   terrestre Dio, di me tutto, e devoto
   vi consacrai la mano e l'intelletto.   8
Apelle e Fidia, il gran Vitruvio, e quanti
   fûr chiari in arte, esser vinti da voi,
   pregio di Febo e di Palla, sapea: 11
ma che fra gli altri in humiltà più santi
   maggior vi prove[1] ancor, vergogna ho poi
   che per più darve, in me più non si crea.   14

Servitore Agnolo Bronzino Pittore
[Florence, Casa Buonarroti, Archivio Buonarroti, ms. XVII, c. 9r;
without subscription also in BNCF, ms. II.IX.10, c. 139v
(hereafter Bronzino, *Canzoniere*)]

3.
Giorgio Vasari

Angel, fra noi più che Michel divino,
    Alle tenebre mie sereno e chiaro
    Lume, solo per cui m'orno e rischiaro
    E di vera virtù scorgo il cammino,   4
Senza te sconosciuto e pellegrino
    Men giva, et or, con te famoso e raro,
    Tanto mi tolgo al volgo empio et avaro,
    Quanto all'alto tuo vol più m'avvicino.   8
Servo e devoto a te, poi ch'a te piacque
    Di rimirar la mia bassa virtute,
    Ho già 'l fato e l'invidia e 'l tempo a scherno: 11
Tu la mia scorta sei, da te mi nacque
    Alto desìo di fam'e di salute,
    E sol per te vivrò chiaro et eterno.   14

[Vasari 2012 (as fn. 7), sonn. 13, p. 53][2]

4.
Id.

Gl'anni che visse quel che fece l'arca,
    Passerai, Bonarroto, in alta via,
    Poggiando a par al gran profeta Elia
    Sovra le nubi in la celeste barca.   4
Ragion non ha più in te la crudel Parca,
    Che la fama mortal e i corpi oblia:
    Resti inmortal fra noi e compagnia
    Farai al divin tuo Dante e Petrarca.   8
Fuggi de i lordi, avari, ingrati preti
    L'orme che 'l tuo disegno alto e divino
    Rompon, l'idee, l'animo e le braccia.   11
Torna e fa' Cosmo e Flora[3] allegri e lieti
    E me, che ho già smarrito il tuo cammino,
    E gl'altri che di te seguon la traccia.   14

[Ibid., sonn. 20, p. 65]

5.
Agnolo Bronzino

Come l'alto Michele Angel, con forte
   mano e felice, asserenando il cielo
   squarciò l'indegno e tenebroso velo
   che men chiara rendea l'empirea corte,   4
tal voi, di nome e d'opre, a noi per sorte
   dato scopriste il ver, cangiaste il pelo,
   e quel confuso, errante, e torto stelo
   che n'avvolgea per vie lunghe e distorte.   8
Oh nobil alma, oh mente alta, ed oh mano
   sovr'ogn'altra felice, a voi si debbe
   quanto han di buono e bel gli studii nostri;   11
chi fia che merti, e che non tenti invano
   lodarvi? E chi tacere anco potrebbe
   di così rari e glorïosi mostri?[4]   14

[Bronzino, Canzoniere, c. 140r]

6.
Benvenuto Cellini

Solo una fronda della tua corona,
   Angel Michel, divin, solo inmortale,
   ricco mi mostra, et d'altro non mi cale,
   ché questa basta in me, sol bella e buona.   4
La gran tua tromba fa che la mia suona
   in bronzi, marmi, e pria Quel che più vale
   (dal qual dipende ogni gran bene et male
   che 'l ciel dispensa), a chi più o men dona: 8
quanto dipinger mai mostrar si puote
   con la tua dotta mano, io gioie et horo
   molti anni spesi, et fra' miglior fé segnio.   11
Non tuo saper né mio: dal ciel dote,
   benignio a noi donate amplio tesoro,
   beato quel che di tal gratie è degnio!   14

[Cellini 2014 (as fn. 7), sonn. 65, p. 196]

7.
Idem
Il Boschereccio loda questi

Virtuosi, gentili spiriti santi,
   che così alto di questo homo degno
   cantate 'l gran sculpir e 'l bel disegno,
qual non fia mai chi d'arrivar si vanti,   4
qual per lodarlo biasmano i pedanti,
   come son questi di Tarsia di legno,
   lodar sta solo a voi quel grande ingegno,
ch'hoggi si ride in ciel de' nostri pianti.   8
Voi sol tenete acceso le virtute
   che quel frà, ser Tarsia, arruota e spegne,
   facendo l'altre lingue sorde e mute;   11
prim'è natura in voi, poi l'arte degne
   vi fa più ch'altre al mondo conosciute,
   portando voi sol di virtù l'insegne.   14

[ibid., sonn. 92, p. 267]

8.
Agnolo Bronzino

Poi che la luce mia da mille chiare
   opre ritrasse l'honorata mano,[5]
   dato allo stile ed ai color sovrano
loco e dimostro quanto arte può fare,   4
in nuova illustre e magna opra, ch'ornare
   dovesse il tempio del gran re toscano,
   la pose, ove cercò sopr'ogn'humano
poter se stessa, e tutti altri avanzare;   8
ma quando, ohimé, non molto lungi al fine
   seguiva intenta il vago, alto lavoro
   d'orror, di meraviglia, e d'arte pieno,   11
soverchii studî a sue voglie divine
   fermarô il corso, e dal terreno coro
   volò al celeste, al vero Lume[6] in seno.   14

[Bronzino, Canzoniere, c. 127r]

9.
Idem

[…]

Piacevi ch'alcun dica che 'l sentiero	145
omai del Buonarroto sia tropp'erto,	
né d'arrivarvi niun faccia pensiero?	
Che questo sia consiglio iniquo è certo,	148
perché l'operar suo ci è guida e insegna	
al vero albergo e ci trae del diserto.	
E questa scusa capricciosa regna	151
tant'oggi, che 'l dipigner si converte	
in frasche e poco si studia e disegna,	
e le semplici turbe poco esperte	154
de' giovani van dietro a questa pesta,	
onde l'arte dal ver cade e diverte.	
E chi ciò dice è cosa manifesta	157
che, come quei che fe' nel cesso il salto,	
cerca trar gl'altri alla medesma festa.	
Pur lo stimo d'ingegno e di cor alto,	160
chi 'n cosa tanto dal dover remota,	
ardisca far al ver sì bravo assalto.	

[excerpt from the *Secondo capitolo delle scuse*: Bronzino 1988 (as fn. 6), pp. 196–197]

10.
Bronzino Pittore

Varchi, ch'a par de' più saggi e migliori	
per la strada d'honor saliste in cima,	
giunto a felice fin, con prosa e rima,	
di mostrar della lingua i frutti e' fiori,	4
già v'inchinava con debiti honori	
l'Adria e 'l Tirreno, e d'eccellenza prima	
vi tenea in pregio; hor sovrumana stima	
spande il bel nome vostro i suoi splendori.	8
Né si poteva, giunta a tanta altezza,	
vostra gloria innalzar senza il mortale	
colpo d'Invidia, al fin di voi pregiona:[7]	11
ben sète hora alto, ove più non si sale	
primo e non pari, onde di voi ragiona	
quanto il sol vede e loda, honora e apprezza.	14

[*De' sonetti di m. Benedetto Varchi colle risposte, e proposte di diversi parte seconda*, Florence 1557, p. 116]

Appendix

11.
Risposta

Bronzino, io cercai sol dietro i migliori
   poter, quando che sia, non dico in cima,
   ma tanto alto salir ch'o 'n prosa o 'n rima
   cogliessi un pur di tanti o frutti o fiori,   4
e più che pago de' secondi honori
   lieto lasciava altrui la gloria prima,
   ma vero amore in voi, non vera stima
   fa parer basse nebbie alti splendori.[8]   8
Né mi debbo io doler, s'a quella altezza
   non si può gir senza il colpo mortale
   di Lei,[9] ch'ogni alma vil sempre ha pregiona: 11
quella è sol vera gloria ove si sale
   per così duri gradi, e chi ragiona
   di te, molto ti loda, e poco apprezza.   14

[ibid.]

12.
M. Francesco Sangallo.

Quei tre spirti del ciel pregiati e chiari,
   che 'l mondo illuminâr con prose e carmi,
   par che preghino ogn'hor che 'n bronzi o 'n marmi
   mostrin ch'a Flora sian graditi e cari,   4
dunque, Varchi gentil, ch'adorni e schiari
   ad Arno l'onde e ch'hai troncato l'armi
   dell'empia Invidia, sì che voce parmi
   sentir: "Pon questi a quei tre primi[10] pari: 8
aiuta quanto puoi sì belle imprese,
   che 'l tuo buon Cosmo, invitto unico duce,
   pe' tuoi preghi a' gran toschi sia cortese."[11]   11
Ei gloria eterna havrà se ciò conduce,
   per te fien sempre tai memorie intese,
   io per quel viverò con maggior luce.   14

[ibid., p. 135]

13.
Risposta

Francesco, se così pregiate e chiari
    fussero al mondo o mie prose o miei carmi
    come i metalli vostri e i vostri marmi
    sono ad ogni gentil graditi e cari,   4
ben porrìa tra gli spirti eletti e rari
    a ricco seggio et honorato alzarmi;
    hor giaccio[12] in terra e mai quindi levarmi
    non spero, non che gir coi primi a pari   8
ma per ciò non fia già che l'alte imprese
    vostre non lodi e non preghi il mio duce
    che voglia ai tre gran toschi esser cortese,   11
il cui valor, che gloria tanta adduce,
    in ogni tempo e per ciascun paese
    via più risplenderà ch'oro non luce.   14

[ibid.]

14.
Al Bronzino dipintore

Nuova casta Ciprigna e nuovo Marte,
    l'alta Isabella e 'l buon Paulogiordano,
    genero e figlia del gran re toscano
    a cui sue grazie il ciel tutte comparte,   4
questa del mondo avventurosa parte,[13]
    a' piè di dolci colli ameno piano,
    rendon sì lieta, o Bronzin mio, che 'nvano
    tento e fatico altrui ritrarla in carte.   8
Voi sol, sol voi, che già gran tempo havete
    la dotta penna al pennel dotto pari,
    farne doppia potete eterna storia: 11
i color vostri, soli omai non rari,
    e i chiari inchiostri mai non vedran Lete,[14]
    ond'a doppio per voi l'Arno si gloria.   14

M. Benedetto Varchi
[Bronzino, *Canzoniere*, c. 185v]

15.
Risposta

Quanto dal vero amor sovente parte
   chi troppo il crede! Hor non son io, sovrano
   d'ogni alto ingegno, da tentare invano,
   quand'io l'ardissi ben, l'una e l'altr'arte?   4
Non è quest'opra da chiamarsi a parte
   molto miglior di me, da voi che 'n mano
   lo scettro havete di Parnaso, e piano
   v'è pur qual servitù da lui mi parte?[15]   8
Di questa al tutto indegno arte vorrete
   chiamarmi all'altra, ond'a mio danno impari
   che sia cercare a' dèi mortal memoria?[16]   11
Beltà divina e vie più che 'l sol chiari
   gesti sol voi ritrar, voi sol potete
   lodar cantando, e pareggiar di gloria.   14

[ibid., c. 186r]

16.
Benedetto Varchi
Al molto reverendo Padre Frate Angelo de' Servi, scultore eccellentissimo

Nunzio e servo di Dio, che queste frali
   cose spregiando e quelle eterne et alme
   curando sole, ognhor co' prieghi l'alme
   e i corpi col martel fate immortali,   4
se ' miei versi o mie prose fusser quali
   le doppie vostre glorïose palme,[17]
   già per cantarle – sì del vero calme –
   havrei spiegate del mio ingegno l'ali.   8
Al pio cor vostro, a vostra dotta mano
   devrà[18] non pur questa presente etate,
   ma quante verran mai di mano in mano: 11
dunque col mio Giorgin del buon toscano
   duce esseguite l'alta mente, e fate
   che 'l tempio surga del gran Pippo Spano.   14

B. V.
[BNCF, Filza Rinuccini 12, c. 373r]

17.
Risposta

Varchi gentil, che le mie poche e frali
   virtù coi vostri versi eterne et alme
   fate, e da freddi corpi e ben nate alme
   lode m'attribuite alte immortali,   4
perché i meriti miei non fûr mai quali
   conviensi a così doppie e chiare palme,
   pregio humil sorte, e sì pocho altro calme
   ch'omai tengo piegati e ' vanni[19] e l'ali,   8
Ben rendo grazie a voi, che cuore e mano
   ponete a darmi in l'una e l'altra etate
   fama e vita maggior di mano in mano,   11
e col buon Giorgio al gran duce toscano
   non resto di lodar, qual voi me fate,
   col tempio i Pippi: un Brunelesco, un Spano.   14

F. G. Angelo Mont'orsoli
[BNCF, Filza Rinuccini 4, c. 458r]

18.
A m. Benedetto Varchi

Chiaro spirto cortese, almo e gentile,
   Varco d'ogni virtute ornato e bello,
   il cui valor non questo monte o quello
   termina[20] o 'l mar degl'Indi o quel di Ide,   4
ma 'l ciel, la terra e le più interne pile[21]
   d'ambiduo gl'hemisperi ara e sacello
   fanno al gran Varchi, e i dèi tutti in drappello
   gli dan di gloria un sempiterno aprile.[22]   8
Le Grazie a pruova ognhor d'eletti fiori
   crescon ghirlande al divin capo vostro,
   tenute pria da pargoletti amori: 11
quai dunque non fien mai lode minori
   de' vostri merti? O qual mai lingua o 'nchiostro
   potran lodarvi? Il ciel convien v'honori.   14

F. Gio. Angelo Mont'orsoli
[ibid., c. 458v]

19.
Risposta

Spirto degno del ciel, c'havendo a vile
   il mondo e quanto 'l volgo avaro e fello
   pregia, sprezzando in sacro e santo hostello[23]
   vi racchiudeste alteramente humile,   4
il puro vostro e sì leggiadro stile,
   che di gloria sen va par al martello,
   può, tanta è grazia e tal virtute in ello,
   chiaro e pregiato huom far d'oscuro e vile.   8
A voi si denno,[24] che dagli alti cori
   tra noi scendeste in questo basso chiostro
   sol per giovar, quei ch'a me date honori,   11
a voi, padre mio buon, che tra ' migliori
   sète per doppia fama a dito mostro
   con doppio grido, d'ogni invidia fuori.   14

[ibid., c. 418r]

20.
Al Bronzino pittore

Bronzin, dove posso io fuggir s'ancora
   in questa sì remota e romita
   profonda valle il Duol[25] sempre m'addita,
   sol perch'io pianga e mi lamenti ogn'hora,   4
lo gran pittor, che dianzi in sì poca hora
   impensata[26] da noi fece partita,
   e me lasciò, perch'io morissi, in vita
   con voi, cui sorte e danno eguale accora?   8
Ohimè, dunque il chiaro vostro e mio
   Puntormo ha spento Morte anzi 'l suo giorno?[27]
   E voi vivete, e 'l Martin vive, ed io?   11
Pur ne consoli, ch'ei non lunge a Dio
   lieto il rimira, e vedrello al gran giorno
   quale il dipinse a noi, tra fero e pio.[28]   14

M. Benedetto Varchi

[Bronzino, *Canzoniere*, c. 118v]

21.
Del Bronzino pittore in risposta

Io sono omai sì di me stesso fuora,
   saggio e buon Varchi, e 'n sì misera vita
   ch'ogni conforto, ogni pietosa aita
   dello[29] sgravarmi il duol, più m'addolora.   4
Lasso, e che più dolor d'uopo mi fora?
   Non basta a far da me l'alma partita
   quel ch'io sento?[30] O si dee, per infinita
   doglia, Morte allungar[31] più d'hora in hora?   8
Anzi pur questo è de' miseri il rio
   sentiero, 'u[32] Morte per più danno e scorno
   fa di sé lungo, ardente e van desìo;   11
ma che rispondo? Anzi perché travìo
   dal pensier giusto e saldo? Ecco ch'io torno
   a trar degl'occhi amaro, eterno rio.   14

[ibid., c. 119r]

22.
Di M. Benedetto Varchi al Bronzino

L'ultimo dì, ch'esser venuto omai
   per me dovea più volte, e da vicino
   o non molto lontan, caro Bronzino,
   tanti ogn'hor provo nuovi affanni e guai,   4
ed io che lieto in fin qui l'aspettai
   certo son hor, non già tristo indovino,
   ch'esser col mio bel Giulio e 'l buon Martino
   desìo più caldo e maggior ho che mai: 8
perché sovente a quell'altezza verde[33]
   mio cor, cui dopo l'Asinaro[34] honora,
   lieto la vista desiosa volve,   11
quivi dich'io, dove tanto si perde
   del volgo, farò io lunga dimora
   quando sarò trite ossa, poca polve.   14

[ibid., c. 133v]

23.
Il Bronzino in risposta

La dura pena, che vince d'assai
   l'human consiglio, il vostro alto e divino[35]
   si sforza traviar dal suo cammino,
   spegnendo in tutto di virtute i rai.   4
Ben vosco hor provo, e sol dianzi provai,
   che voglia il mondo e che possa il destino,
   perso il buon padre e 'l più caro vicino,
   ch'honorai tanto e sì fervente amai.   8
Pur, mal grado di lor, rende e rinverde
   più ch'un non toglie e l'altro discolora
   l'ultimo dì,[36] che dal morir n'assolve: 11
ciò ne conforte, e chi tutto disperde
   non possa il ben,[37] che l'età nostra adora,
   s'unqua di me, di lei, di voi vi dolve.[38]   14

[ibid., c. 134r]

24.
Di M. Benvenuto Cellini scultore

Deh mirabil gran Varchi, e voi, Bronzino,
   troppo gran pianto fate notte e giorno,
   hor del buon Luca, e ier del gran Puntormo;
   e voi, Laura gentile, e 'l mio Crocino: 4
hor non sapete, ch'è fermo il destino
   e l'hora ch'a Dio l'alma ha a far ritorno,
   e lasciar questo rio mortal soggiorno,
   e 'n ciel godersi in Dio santo e divino?   8
Piangalo Cosmo, hor piangalo lui solo,
   c'ha perso un servo tal ch'òmai no 'l possa
   più ritrovar, dall'uno all'altro polo.   11
L'alma in ciel viva, e 'n polve le stanche ossa
   lasciate ha noi,[39] cui io honoro e colo;
   sol piango la mia seco non s'è mossa.   14

[ibid., c. 134v]

25.
Il Bronzino in risposta

Non piange il divin Varchi, alto Cellino,
   od io con seco i duoi ch'or fan sì adorno
   il terzo lume, e ch'hanno il Sarto intorno,
   il Vinci, il Tasso, il Tribolo e 'l Rontino,[40]   4
e tanti altri e sì cari, ch'il confino
   fornito a l'alma patria d'ogn'intorno,
   scorgendo il sommo e vero bene, a scorno
   han questo abisso ad ogni male inchino   8
Di ciò 'l gran Varchi od io non duolsi: il duolo
   nostr'è, che sia da noi tolta e rimossa
   sì nobil coppia, e già levata a volo   11
senza aspettar di noi l'alma riscossa.[41]
   Questo piangeren sempre, insin che solo
   sarà lo spirto ove trovar li possa.   14

[ibid., c. 135r]

26.
Stoldo Lorenzi
Di Stoldo scultore al Bronzino

Tanto m'affligge e mi tormenta il core
   l'interna pena, ohimé, del buon Martino,
   che mi forza, o divin, raro Bronzino,
   prender la penna infra doglia e timore,   4
e con quella sfogar parte il dolore
   che mi conduce a Morte sì vicino,
   che se non fusse o mia sorte o destino
   i' sarei già di questo carcer fore: 8
e forse lui, ch'in ciel si posa lieto,
   vedrei fra le più chiare in grembo a Dio
   alme godere il glorïoso bene;   11
e prego Morte ch'al doglioso mio
   viver dia fine e mi tragga di pene,
   poi che vivendo amari frutti mieto.   14

[ibid., c. 135v]

27.
Il Bronzino in risposta

Che non piangiate in compagnia d'Amore,
    delle Muse e dell'Arte, a cui il divino
    sempre Luca non solo aprìa il cammino,
    ma il seggio era di lor primo e maggiore,   4
Stoldo gentil, già non direi, ch'errore
    troppo il mio fôra, che pianger destino[42]
    finch'al buon padre e al mio maggior vicino
    trarmi harà il pianto il desïato honore.   8
Ben di vostr'arte e verde età discreto
    bramarei in voi quel che far non poss'io,
    ch'omai son tardo a così alta spene,   11
che con opre conformi al voler pio
    cercaste honorar lui qual si conviene,
    che forse il serba a voi divin decreto.   14

[ibid., c. 136r]

28.
Benedetto Varchi
Ad Antonio Crocino

Ben è giusta cagion, non men che forte,
    quella che notte e dì, sera e mattino,
    meco v'affligge ognhor, dolce Crocino,
    né cosa è che v'acqueti o pur conforte: 4
che potea peggio farne empia e rea sorte?
    Che potea nuocer più duro destino,
    poscia che 'l vostro e mio caro Martino
    fera n'ha tolto, invidïosa Morte?   8
Parca crudel, crudel Parca lo stame
    mio, non già il suo già filato era! E pure
    io vivo, lasso, io vivo ed egli è nulla.   11
Troncal, ti prego, omai, troncalo pure,
    che spento lui, ho di morir tal fame
    ch'esser morto vorrei fin dalla culla.   14

[BNCF, Filza Rinuccini 3,[43] c. 266r]

29.
Idem
A M. Bernardo Puccini

Se v'incresce di me, chiaro Puccino,
   come già v'incresceva, e mi portate
   quell'amor dentro che di fuor mostrate,
   ond'io dentro e di fuor v'honoro e 'nchino,   4
con quel che con Atene e con Arpino
   se ne va pari sermon,[44] deh consolate
   mio cor, ch'estrema ogn'hor miseria pate
   per la partita del suo buon Martino!   8
Piange la terra, il sol non par che luca:
   sospirâr[45] d'ognintorno i colli, i fiumi
   ghiacciâr, di smalto si mostraro i prati,   11
l'herbe sfioriro, i fior divenner dumi:[46]
   gridâr l'Osoli[47] e l'Arno: "Oh Luca, oh Luca,
   dove sei gito, e perché n'hai lassati?"   14

[ibid., c. 266r]

30.
Sonetto di m. Bernardo Puccini, in risposta di quello di m. B. V. che incomincia
Se v'incresce di me chiaro Puccino

E' m'incresce di voi, Varchi divino,
   come già m'increscea, e quello Amore
   che di fuor mostro è fisso in mezzo al core:
   voi amo, voi honoro, e a voi m'inchino;   4
non pari ho con Atene o con Arpino
   il mio sermon, ma di poco valore:
   deh potess'ei frenare il gran dolore,
   ch'hor la Morte vi dà del buon Martino!   8
Non più lacrime hormai, non più sospiri,
   ch'ei mortal nacque, onde morir dovea
   e qua lasciare il suo terrestre velo.   11
E ch'altro torgli men Morte potea?
   Non gridi Osoli più, né si martiri
   Arno, che messer Luca è gito al cielo.   14

[ibid., c. 297v]

31.
Idem
A m. Tiberio Calcagni

Quando sovviemmi, e mi sovviene ogn'hora
   caro Tiberio mio, quanto era e quale
   il nostro buon Martin, per minor male
   esser vorrei di questa luce fuora.   4
No 'l suo partir ma 'l mio restar m'accora:
   non di lui già, ma ben di me mi cale,
   e di voi e del danno universale
   ch'ha fatto il mondo, d'ogni ben mondo[48] hora.   8
Oh Carlo mio, oh mio Giovanni,[49] sempre
   piangete pure e sospirate meco,
   ch'io pur sempre con voi piango e sospiro.   11
Almen fuss'io da queste humane tempre[50]
   che son sì dure, oimé, varcato seco!
   Di questo solo e non d'altro m'adiro.   14

[ibid., c. 277v]

32.
Idem
A m. Francesco Moschino

Dopo il mio terno ardor, dopo 'l mio trino
   ghiaccio, dove in un sempre e tremo e sudo,
   altro non haveva io schermo né scudo
   non che più forte che 'l mio buon Martino,   4
ma hor che n'ha[51] di lui, raro Moschino,
   fera Morte spogliato, e destino crudo
   colmo di doglia ognhor, di speme nudo
   piango, e piangendo al valor suo m'affino,   8
che fu sì grande in ogni parte e tanto
   cortese, che di lui chiara memoria
   sarà quaggiù, quant'ei nel regno santo,   11
e se puon nulla i miei versi e 'l mio pianto,
   con lode eterna al mondo e vera gloria
   sarà sempre honorato, e sempre pianto.   14

[ibid., c. 278r]

33.
Idem
A m. Domenico Poggini

Quel ch'a voi si convien, sago[52] Poggino,
   in cui non suol però cadere oblio
   degli amici, non so certo, ma io
dopo 'l quinci sparir del buon Martino   4
   piangere e sospirar mai non rifino,[53]
   e quando penso al danno, non sol mio
   ma d'ogni buon, sì la ragione oblio
che di morir per le mie man destino,   8
   e già sarei di questa carne scemo[54]
   se non fosse che io, come avverrebbe,
perderlo ancor nell'altra vita temo,   11
   e mi consola che 'l mio giorno estremo
   non può stare[55] a venire, e 'n ver sarebbe
pietà sciormi dal fango ov'ardo e tremo.   14

[ibid., c. 278v]

34.
Idem
A m. Bartolomeo Ammannati

In questa mia più d'altra amara sorte,
   null'è che possa e che più debba atarmi[56]
   altro che i vivi bronzi e i vivi marmi
   vostri, che danno vita e tolgon morte,   4
e la pudica vostra alta consorte
   con sue pulite prose e tersi carmi,
   Ammannato gentil, cui[57] veder parmi
   tutto smarrito, ancor che saggio e forte: 8
ma chi tal senno o fortezza hebbe o have,
   moderno o prisco, che bastasse mai
   a schermire o soffrir colpo sì grave?   11
Io, per me, tutto sbigottito e smorto
   divenni, e sono ancor, quando ascoltai:
   "Luca Martin, Luca Martin è morto."   14

[ibid., c. 279r]

35.
Idem
A m. Giorgio Vasari

Ben fu manca cornice[58] e non mancino
   corvo quel che cantò mio fato acerbo,
   poi che Morte spietata ancora acerbo
   per sé volle, e rapinne il buon Martino.   4
Voi, che col sacro vostro e mio Borghino
   l'amaste tanto, il gran dolor ch'io serbo
   dentro il cor sempre, e mai nol disacerbo,
   fate alquanto minor, grande Aretino,   8
che quando scemo fia, quanti mai furo
   passerà di grandezza,[59] e se non pero
   è ch'io bramo il morir, né 'l viver curo.   11
Quel ch'è ver mi par falso e 'l falso vero,
   il sol freddo, il dì notte, il molle duro,
   tal ch'ogni cosa temo e nulla spero.   14

[ibid., c. 281v]

36.
Sonetto di m. Giorgio Vasari in risposta di quello di m. B. V. che incomincia
Ben fu manca cornice, e non mancino

Colpo non tagliò mai dritto o mancino,
   con danno di virtù spietato e acerbo
   in bel spirto ingegnoso d'anni acerbo,
   quanto è quel che diè Morte al mio Martino.   4
Dolente hoggi son io, più 'l mio Borghino
   sospira e freme, e del dolor ch'io serbo
   un sepolcro al cor fo, né 'l disacerbo,
   ch'inmortal non può far spirto aretino.   8
Voi sì, che saper non fia né furo
   ch'aguagli al vostro dir, io so ch'io pero
   perdendo tali, e più di me non curo.   11
Restami il gran Borghin, cui so ch'è vero
   amico, e 'l Varchi, e ciò mi fa men duro,
   e 'l mio duce,[60] nel qual confido e spero.   14

[ibid., c. 293r]

37.
Stoldo Lorenzi
A M. Benedetto Varchi

Varchi divin, che con sì dolci note
   piangete, quasi eterno fonte, ognhora
   il buon Luca Martin, che 'n sì poc'hora
   rendé l'alma a Colui che tutto puote,   4
anco io la notte e 'l dì bagno le gote
   in compagnia di voi, e sì m'accora
   il duol ch'esser vorrei di vita fuora,
   cui già l'ultimo stral sfida e percuote,   8
né so se Morte o destino o Fortuna
   imputar debbo, poi che 'l gran Motore
   tutto dispone e tutto intende e vede.   11
Ben, lasso, so ch'a chi virtù possiede,
   o chi bontate in sé chiude et aduna,
   non potea dare 'l ciel colpo maggiore.   14

Stoldo scultore

[ibid., c. 287v]

38.
Benedetto Varchi
Risposta

Chiunche sia, che dal mortale scuote
   il divin,[61] piacque a lui torne[62] in quell'hora
   il buon Martin, che vive, anzi regna hora
   dove ciò che si vuol tutto si puote,   4
e certo, Stoldo mio, tante e tai dote
   non eran dal dì d'hoggi: il tempo d'hora
   i nomi solo e le ricchezze honora,
   benché di senno e d'ogni virtù vòte.   8
Io, come dite, al sole et alla luna
   per isfogare il duol, che 'n mezzo 'l cuore
   stagna, dove 'l buon Luca estinto siede,   11
come gorgo talor d'alta si vede
   rupe caggiendo far di sé lacuna,
   verso dagl'occhi un rivo a tutte l'hore.   14

[ibid., c. 288r]

39.
Idem
A Messer Baccio Valori

Valor, del gran Cellini l'alta opra visto
   rimasi tutto d'ogni senso privo,
   ch'io non credea ch'un marmo e morto e vivo
   esser potessi, e sì pietoso e tristo.   4
Quanto ha 'l saper colla natura misto
   tanto ivi appare, e men del vero scrivo,
   ch'io tengo certo, e 'l mostrarrò s'io vivo,
   che tal languisse in su la croce Christo.   8
Quanto al gran duce nostro honor s'acquista!
   Quanto s'accresce al nobile Arno gloria
   per così raro arnese,[63] anzi pur solo!   11
La cui sì dolce e mansueta vista
   pregai ch'al sacro signor mio vittoria
   contra l'empio donasse audace stuolo.   14

[BNCF, Filza Rinuccini 5, c. 11r]

40.
Di m. Benvenuto Cellini in risposta di quello di m. B. V. a m. Baccio Valori, che incomincia: Valor, del gran Cellini

Honor d'Italia, che 'spresso hai, non visto,
   il grande Homero e 'l gran Vergilio,[64] e privo
   di speme di seguirti ogn'huom ch'è vivo:
   a chi dài gran tesor, mondo empio e tristo?   4
Se fra tanti tuoi mali un ben sol misto
   si conoscesse in te, certo io che scrivo
   sempre ti lodarei mentre ch'io vivo,
   e pur per te morire elesse Christo.   8
Quei maggior premii che virtù s'acquista
   e che risplendon poi con maggior gloria
   a voi si denno,[65] a voi, buon Varchi, solo.   11
Voi sol mi fate allegro dentro e 'n vista,
   solo da voi mi vien sì gran vittoria,
   che baldanzoso vo tra 'l degno stuolo.   14

[ibid., c. 54r]

41.
Benedetto Varchi
A maestro Pietropaolo Galeotti, orafo[66]

Voi, che solo dei duo primi e maggiori
   celesti messi[67] il sacro nome havete,
   voi, ch'ai piccioli bronzi hoggi rendete,
   col mio caro Poggin, gli antichi honori,   4
se bramate che meco ognhor v'honori
   il mondo tutto e schivar sempre Lete,
   quelle frondi formate, altere e liete,
   che dell'usata via mi trasser fuori,   8
quelle ch'io spero un dì tanto alte e chiare
   veder, ch'al sole e alle superne stelle
   d'altezza andranno e di chiarezza pare: 11
queste, fra tutte l'altre opre più rare
   e di mano e d'ingegno, le più belle
   saran senza alcun dubbio e le più care.   14

[*De Sonetti di M. Benedetto Varchi parte prima*, Florence 1555, p. 252]

42.
Idem
A m. Bartolommeo Ammannati[68]

Poi ch'io non so con mie prose e miei carmi
   (d'amor non già ma sol d'ingegno vizio)
   degnamente honorar Lauro e Fabbrizio,
   par senza pari alcuno o 'n pace o 'n armi,   4
vostro sarebbe, e so che 'l vero parmi,
   nuovo Fidia e Miron, cortese ufizio,
   con quel che gl'altri vince alto artifizio
   scolpirgli in mille bronzi e 'n mille marmi,   8
e della vostra bella, honesta e chiara
   consorte, onde ho nel cor la terza piaga
   e 'l secol nostro ogni virtute impara,   11
con quella dolce sua, che l'alma smaga[69]
   celeste melodia, com'ella rara,
   portargli ovunque il sol girando vaga.   14

[BNCF, Filza Rinuccini 5, c. 48v]

43.
Idem
A m. Alessandro Allori

Eccellente e gentil pittor, ch'havete
   da quella pianta il bel cognome, ch'io
   tant'anni et tanti con doppio disio
   prima, e terza ardo in fiamme altere e liete,   4
s'a me, che v'amo tanto, esser volete
   non dico grato, ma cortese e pio,
   del bello e buon caro Pallante mio
   a formar la sembianza omai movete: 8
a voi gloria, a me gioia, all'Arno honore
   darete tal, ch'ogn'altro è meno assai,
   né spegnerallo il trapassar dell'hore,   11
e se poteste, come il bel di fuore,
   quel di dentro scolpir, pittura mai
   non hebbe il mondo di sì gran valore.   14

[BNCF, Filza Rinuccini 13, c. 456r]

44.
Domenico Poggini
A m. Benedetto Varchi

Varchi, chiaro splendor del secol nostro,
   che quasi sol fra l'altre luci splende,
   perché dal cielo in me virtù non scende
   al mio desire eguale, e al merto vostro,   4
sì ch'io potessi finger quanto ha mostro
   natura in voi nel volto? Ma s'estende
   quest'arte poco in me, che non comprende
   quel ch'è disceso in voi dal santo chiostro.   8
Ma, lasso, alto è il voler, basso il valore,
   perciò, spirto famoso, hoggi fra noi
   mirate il cor, non questo debil dono.   11
Ond'io securo sia, che non v'annoi
   questa rozza opra, ch'io vi sacro e dono,
   col mio divoto insieme e puro core.   14

Domenico Poggini
[BNCF, Filza Rinuccini 4, c. 30r]

45.
Benedetto Varchi
A m. Domenico Poggini risposta

Poggino, il cui desio, le perle e l'ostro
   lasciando a chi l'Egeo turbato fende,
   con metalli e con marmi alzarvi intende
   dove gela Aquilon, dove tepe Ostro,   4
ben s'è nel volto mio per voi dimostro
   che 'l tempo indarno e la fatica spende
   chi d'agguagliarsi a voi stolto contende,
   che vincete il pensier, non pur l'inchiostro,   8
perch'io con lieto e paventoso core
   il vile accetto e prezïoso dono,
   onde fia che né morte ancho m'annoi,   11
e me stesso in eterno hoggi a voi dono,
   ch'havrete vita mai sempre tra noi,
   per doppio honor di gemino valore.   14

Benedetto Varchi
[ibid., c. 30v]

46.
Idem

Dal dì ch'io scorsi in alta, sacra cima
   d'ombroso monte, al bel Parnaso eguale,
   quel sì verde e sì casto almo pedale[70]
   ch'amò tanto il gran tosco, e Febo prima,   4
tutto quel che più d'altro agogna e stima
   il basso e vile stuol posi in non cale,
   e de' suoi rami al ciel fecimi scale,
   dietro quel ben che solo è senza stima,   8
onde quella pietosa e cruda mano,[71]
   che incide tutto e rinovella il mondo,
   stenderà sopra me sua falce invano: 11
e voi, Francesco, al cui chiaro e soprano
   valor Fidia sarebbe hoggi secondo,
   per lui l'oprar di lei farete vano.   14

[BNCF, Filza Rinuccini 3, c. 172r; in Filza Rinuccini 4, c. 62v with the heading *A m. Francesco del Mosca*]

47.
Idem
Al Bronzino Pittore

Voi, che nel fior della sua verde etate
   coll'alto vostro e sì chiaro pennello
   a nome mio, Bronzin, formaste il bello
   di fuor, cui par non fu mortal beltate,   4
se di me punto calvi,[72] o se curate
   di voi, coll'altro stile e non men bello
   formate il buon di dentro, ché con ello
   posta vizio saria mortal bontate:[73]   8
anzi scrivete e dipignete insieme,
   cercondato Avignon da quelle torme
   empie che di Gesù sprezzan le norme,   11
e 'l mio sacro signor che l'urta e preme
   con tal virtù che nel suo sangue immerso
   fugge l'audace e rio popol perverso.   14

[BNCF, Filza Rinuccini 5, c. 19r]

48.
Del Bronzino pittore in risposta di quello di m. B.V. che incomincia: **Voi, che nel**

Tali e tante vid'io grazie adunate
   nel vostro, o nuovo Apollo, angel novello,
   che non che trarne a pieno esempio in quello
   di rimirar perdei le forze usate   4
angel, che di Michel l'armi honorate
   hoggi contra il diabolico e rubello[74]
   stuolo a Gesù si veste, e 'l sacro hostello[75]
   salva della cristiana potestate.   8
Ben troppo ardito, e par ch'ancor ne treme,
   fui (ma chi voi potea negarlo?) a porme
   con l'un stile a ritrar sì rare forme: 11
hor ch'io l'altro ancor muova? E chi non teme,
   se non voi, gir tanto alto? E 'n ira avverso
   il ciel vedersi, e l'Arno in Po converso?   14

[ibid., c. 59v]

49.
Benedetto Varchi

Bronzino, ove sì dolce ombreggia e suona
   quel ch'aguzza al cielo e quasi appunta
   famoso monte, e di sua verde punta
   se stesso intorno intorno alto corona,   4
quivi[76] è 'l Parnaso mio, quivi Elicona,
   quivi di taglio Amor diemmi e di punta,
   per la fronde che mai da me disgiunta
   non fia, e mi farà di sé corona.   8
Hor voi, che nuovo Apelle e nuovo Apollo
   con doppio honore hornate e doppio stile
   hor di rime il bell'Arno, hor di colori,   11
date, prego, con l'uno[77] eterni honori
   all'albor sacro ond'hebbe il sol tal crollo,[78]
   l'altro 'l renda qual è, non pur simile.   14

[Bronzino, *Canzoniere*, c. 116v]

50.
Bronzino
Risposta

L'alma pianta,[79] che Giove quando tuona
   sola prescrive, a tale altezza è giunta
   che la sua verde cima al ciel congiunta
   altrui fama e valor porge e cagiona.   4
Tal di lei penna scrive, e tal ragiona
   lingua, e con tal dolcezza hor canta hor punta,
   ch'ogn'altra a par saria stanca e defunta:
   folle, chi dato il don da lunge sprona.   8
Celeste hor fronda, e già nobil rampollo,[80]
   ricca più ch'altra e più casta e gentile
   hor di buon frutti e già di vaghi fiori,   11
e direi santo allor de' due migliori
   forse 'l premier,[81] ma chi mè[82] scrive, o puollo
   di voi cantar, cui leggo e ascolto humile?   14

[ibid., c. 117r]

51.
Idem
Al medesimo risposta

Ch'io cercarei dove più 'l Nil risuona
   farmi udir lunge in roca voce e munta,[83]
   e dar salute ad alma al cielo assunta,
   e la luce del sol far chiara e buona   4
a lodar lui, che senza arme pregiona,
   con virtù somma a beltà somma aggiunta,
   feo la vostra alma, e pentita e compunta
   se mai lodò cantando altra persona,   8
e che da poi, se bene al cielo alzollo
   e con tal grido, et hebbe ogn'altro a vile
   non però tace o posa i santi ardori.   11
Ahi mondo, hor come a tant'alti rumori
   stai sordo, e a lume tal non drizzi il collo,
   e virtù lasci andar povera e vile?   14

[ibid., c. 117v]

52.
Benedetto Varchi
A messer Benvenuto Cellini

Benvenuto, il tempo è che queste cose
   basse lasciamo a chi dopo noi viene
   e tutta ergiamo al ciel la nostra spene:
   restan le spine sol, còlte le rose.   4
Il ver, che 'n fino a qui colui[84] m'ascose
   che i più dentro sua rete avvolti tiene,
   m'aperse Lui che 'n tanti strazii e pene
   il viver nostro al suo morir prepose.   8
A me, dotto Cellin, prose né carmi
   per far del regno glorïoso acquisto,
   a voi non gioveran bronzi né marmi.   11
Pigliar la croce addosso e seguir Cristo
   bisogna, se vorrete od io salvarmi:
   pigliam dunque la croce, e seguiam Cristo.   14

[*Sonetti spirituali di m. Benedetto Varchi. Con alcune risposte, et proposte di diversi eccellentissimi ingegni*, Florence 1573, p. 45]

53.
Risposta di m. Benvenuto Cellini a 45

Benedetto quel dì che l'alma Varchi,[85]
   lasciando omai la spoglia di lei sazia,
   e reverente a Dio renda ogn'hor grazia
   d'essere scarca di sì grevi incarchi,   4
se ben con doglia par di Lei si scarchi,
   quanto maggior s'a Dio fusse in disgrazia
   sarìa la pena, ch'hor del ben non sazia
   è pur cagion che manco huom si rammarchi.[86]   8
Vostre alte prose, vostre dolci rime,
   che voi fra tutti gl'altri han fatto solo,
   al ciel per dritta via sen vanno prime,   11
e voi ven gite a Dio col maggior volo
   che fesse[87] huom mai e con più ricche stime,
   chiaro dall'uno infino a l'altro polo.   14

[ibid., p. 91]

54.
Benedetto Varchi
A messer Bartolomeo Ammannati

Né l'essere, Ammannato, hor Scopa hor Fidia,
   né co' vostri palazzi al cielo alzarvi
   dagl'inganni di lui[88] potrà guardarvi
   che giorno e notte a l'alme nostre insidia: 4
l'haver voi quasi omai vinto l'invidia
   alle cose di qui forse giovarvi,
   forse bastante fia, non già scamparvi
   dalla sua contra noi sì gran perfidia.   8
Ma la grazia di Lui, che 'n sulla croce
   confitto bevve amaro assenzio e fèle,
   sola ne scampa e salva ogni fedele.   11
Ciò che qui ne diletta, di là nuoce:
   ben è contra sé stesso empio e crudele
   chi sprezza del Signor la santa voce.   14

[ibid., p. 45]

55.
Benedetto Varchi
Al Bronzino pittore

D'ogni cosa rendiam grazie al Signore
   che le ci dà, che così vuole Dio,
   caro e chiaro e cortese Bronzin mio,
   cui hebbi ed haggio ed havrò sempre honore.   4
E se 'l vostro Alessandro al primo fiore[89]
   la bell'opera ha fatto, ove ancor io
   sempre vivrò fuor del comune oblio,
   solo è stata di Dio grazia e favore.   8
Noi siam nulla, Bronzino, e voi che sète
   sì grande Apelle e non minore Apollo
   nulla che vostro sia, nonnulla havete,   11
e che voi, Bronzin mio, come devete,
   ogni ben vostro e suo da Dio tenete,
   il credo certo, anzi per certo sollo.   14

[ibid., p. 46]

56.
Risposta del Bronzino pittore a 46

Ma ben nel farsi ogn'hor vile e minore,
   che nulla senza Lui, l'immenso e pio
   celeste Padre a sé tira il desio
   nostro, ond'esser ne dà caro e maggiore: 4
in Lui sèm, da Lui sèmo, e come fòre
   dell'essere esser puossi? Ahi, folle e rio
   pensier, quando salir per calle invìo[90]
   scendendo pensa e 'n tal s'aggira errore!   8
Quel che credete, anzi del mio sapete
   credere, è certo e vero, e ben dir puollo
   chi meco, ancor che 'n Dio, troppo accrescete: 11
quanto vi deggio, o mia luce? Ch'ardete
   ben hor del trino ardore e me scorgete,
   qual già in Parnaso, al ciel di collo in collo[91]?   14

[ibid., p. 92]

57.
Benedetto Varchi
A messer Giorgio Vasari

Quant'havete maggior l'ingegno e l'arte
   tanto devete più, sublime spirto,
   lodi rendere e grazie a quello Spirto
   Divin che 'n tutte cose ha sì gran parte: 4
Ei sol, non saper vostro vi diparte
   tanto dagl'altri, quanto lauro e mirto
   si pregian più che molle ontano ed irto
   rusco[92] ch'altrui da sé, pungendo, parte.   8
Ben puonno in questa i colori e 'l disegno
   fama darvi tra noi, ma l'altra vita
   per Lui s'acquista, e non per arte o 'ngegno.   11
Fia 'l pennel vostro e la squadra gradita
   col mio chiaro Puccin, ma non è degno
   posporre a breve honor gloria infinita.   14

[ibid., p. 46]

58.
Risposta di m. Giorgio Vasari a 46

Varchi, io cognosco ben l'ingegno e l'arte
   e quel c'haver debb'un gentil spirto
   vien da Colui, che mi diè questo spirto
   troppo da voi amato in ogni parte: 4
sempre ho 'l cor vòlto a Dio, né mai si parte
   vagando per cercare o lauro o mirto
   fra noi, anzi invèr Lui sto intento ed irto[93]
   perché mi dia del ciel sua gloria o parte,   8
e se talhor co' colori o disegno
   il tempo spendo, è[94] ben campar la vita
   a molti ed affinar l'arte e l'ingegno: 11
qui val le seste e la squadra gradita
   a farsi eterno. O qual atto più degno
   ch'ornare il mondo, ed al ciel far salita?   14

[ibid., p. 92]

59.
Risposta del medesimo a 46

Com'a tristo nocchier, governi e sarte
   dall'onde rotte, il mio debole spirto
   sommerso in questo mar d'affanni al spirto
   vostro, saggio huom, si volge, e nuove carte   4
non più dipigne di Giove o di Marte
   ma Gesù, che di palma, oliva, e mirto
   calcò Satan vincendo, e 'ntento ed irto
   salì 'n croce per farci del ciel parte,   8
e chi 'l mondo fallace d'error pregno
   segue, che con inganni ed esche in vita
   perde la luce, e casca al scuro regno;   11
carità benedetta, or che ne 'nvita
   l'ardor vostro a salir, fia mio disegno
   Cristo, che mi darà gloria infinita.   14

[ibid., p. 93]

60.
Benedetto Varchi
A messer Vincenzio Danti

Ben mi credea, dopo mie tali e tante
   colpe, da lungo desto e mortal sonno,
   ringraziar Dio lodando: hor più m'assonno
   che prima e meno ardisco andargli innante   4
perch'è grande il Signore, e sopra quante
   lode mai furo, o sono, od esser puonno;
   formidabile ancor, perch'egli è donno[95]
   di quant'è, quanto fia, quanto fu innante.   8
Voi dunque, Danti, e sì chiaro e sì pio,
   col dolce vostro a me sì caro frate,[96]
   per me lodate e ringraziate Dio.   11
A Lui potenza, a Lui fortezza date:
   qual non è poco, anzi pur nulla fio
   a Chi nacque per noi, visse e morìo?   14

[ibid., p. 47]

61.
Risposta di m. Vincenzio Danti a 47

Beate colpe, che di tali e tante
   lodi e grazie cagion fûr sì che 'l sonno
   (bench'io son quel, ch'ancor vegliando assonno)
   han desto voi, che vegliavate innante,   4
mostrando altera prece, sopra quante
   furon già mai più grate e ch'ognor puonno
   render placato Dio d'ogni ira, e donno
   altrui far sopra a Chi di noi fu limante,   8
col vostro altero stile, hor sacro e pio,
   seguite l'alta impresa, e 'l mio buon frate
   meco di tanto ben ringrazia Dio;   11
ma voi, mentre tal lodi e grazie date,
   prego ch'insieme ogni mio grave fio[97]
   ponghiate avanti a Chi per noi morìo.   14

[ibid., p. 93]

62.
Benedetto Varchi
A messer Domenico Poggini

Nelle cose di qui che tosto han sera,
   anzi son tutte vanitati espresse,
   onde sono in non cal dai saggi messe,
   folle del tutto e cieco è ben chi spera.   4
Non tante arene ha 'l mar, fior primavera,
   e le stelle del ciel son meno spesse
   delle pene di lui, che stolto elesse
   quello onde l'alma insieme e 'l corpo pera,   8
né le vostre o di marmo o di bronzo opre,
   se ben far sanno gl'huomini immortali,
   giovar puonno a schifar[98] gl'eterni mali: 11
la ragion dunque, e non il senso adopre
   in voi, diletto mio Poggin, che fuora
   del cammin dritto non usciste ancora.   14

[ibid., p. 47]

63.
Risposta di m. Domenico Poggini a 47

Ben so che la mondana e folta schiera
   de' suo' dolci pensier fa l'alme oppresse,
   e 'n più modi più reti e lacci tesse
   perché null'alma torni ove prim'era,[99]   4
ma se qui pose la celeste sfera
   l'alma nel corpo, e ch'ei libero stesse
   e tal qual l'opra sua il merto havesse
   (o 'l basso centro o l'alta luce vera),[100]   8
può dunque, e sì conviene, che l'huom s'adopre
   in vari effetti, e chi di virtù l'ali
   spiega, fugge l'oblio qui de' mortali,   11
questi, Varchi, di grazia più 'l ciel cuopre.
   Se dunque il mondo voi cotanto honora,
   quanto fie in ciel più l'alma all'ultim'hora?   14

[ibid., p. 94]

64.
Benedetto Varchi
Al compare Antonio Crocini

Scioglierà 'l cappio omai, non romprà 'l nodo
   che qui mi lega ov'ogni ben si fugge,
   quella[101] ch'ogni mortal biasima e fugge,
   ed io più lieto ogn'hor l'aspetto e lodo,   4
se ben veggo gl'agguati e la voce odo
   di lui, che quasi fero leon rugge
   per divorarmi, e tutto invan si strugge,
   non però temo più suo 'nganno e frodo,   8
ch'io ricorro, Crocin, subito a quella
   croce che mi salvò con tutti loro
   che, battezzati, crederanno in ella.   11
Altro non ho, né voglio haver tesoro
   che lei: ella è sol buona, ella è sol bella;
   habbiansi gli altri perle, argento ed oro.   14

[ibid., p. 48]

65.
Risposta d'Antonio Crocini a 48

Che vale essere di qua con cappio o nodo
   largato o stretto, poi che 'nvan si fugge
   quella che 'l volgo errante biasma e fugge?
   Ma biasmila chi vuol, ch'io pur la lodo: 4
ben tremo tutto quando la voce odo
   dell'avversario universal, che rugge
   qual fier leone e mai sempre si strugge
   per depredarne con suo inganno e frodo.   8
Che farò, Varchi mio? Prenderò quella
   croce c'ha 'n sé virtù tal, che coloro
   sicuri son che sono armati d'ella: 11
dunque di croce, e non d'altro tesoro
   mi pasco, e sento quanto è buona e bella,
   poscia ch'avanza perle, argento, ed oro.   14

[ibid., p. 94]

66.
Tradotto da Cesare da Bagno

Dovea ben porsi di Perseo il segno
   qual del ciel rara gloria fra i celesti,
ma sì sorge alto il ricco e sacro pegno
   a Flora in sen, ch'indi a noi quegli e questi
si mostrin chiari, et ella oh quanto è degno   5
   ch'all'artista Cellin dona e più resti
d'obbligo a Cosmo, che con l'oro il velo
   e 'l maestro con la mano apron del cielo.

Andreae Anguli

Debuerat Persei signum coelestia poni
   inter signa, velut gloria rara poli.
Cernitur erectum tamen id Florentiae, ut inde
   nota homini in terris signa superna forent.
Quantum Cellino artifici debet Florentia, quantum
   praecipue Cosmo debet et illa Duci,
si datur occultas coeli cognoscere formas
   impensis Cosmi dextera, et artificis.

[Florence, Biblioteca Riccardiana, ms. Ricc. 2353, c. 75v]

67.
Del Bronzino pittore

Giovine alter, ch'a Giove in aurea pioggia
   ti veggia nato, alteramente ir puoi
   e più per gl'alti e glorïosi tuoi
   gesti, a cui fama altrui pari non poggia,   4
ma ben pari o maggior fama s'appoggia
   a le tue glorie, hor che rinato a noi
   per così dotta man ti scorgi, e poi
   sovra tal riva e 'n così ricca loggia   8
più che mai vivo. E se tal fosti in terra,
   uopo non t'era d'altrui scudo od ali:
   tal con grazia e beltà valor dimostri.   11
Ma, deh, ricuopri il vago agl'occhi nostri
   volto di lei, che già ne 'mpetra e serra:
   se non, chi fuggirà sì dolci mali?   14

[ibid., c. 156r]

68.
Del medesimo

Ardea Venere bella, e lui che 'n pioggia
   d'oro cangiasti, Amor che tanto puoi,
   chiedeva, ond'egli a' dolci preghi tuoi
   là scese in grembo ove ogni grazia poggia,   4
ma come avvien s'a foco esca s'appoggia
   o qual di neve al sol, quaggiù fra noi
   s'accese e strusse al caldo seno e poi
   seco s'unìo. "Vie più che pietra in loggia   8
starete" disse omai Minerva, "in terra,"
   e fé d'entrambi un sol giovin, ch'a l'ali
   et al tronco gorgon Perseo dimostri,   11
e quinci appar divina agl'occhi nostri
   l'opra ch'il bene e la bellezza serra,
   suprema gloria de' tuoi dolci mali.   14

[ibid., c. 156v]

69.
Di m. Domenico Poggini

Sì come 'l ciel di vaghe stelle adorno,
   delle quai più l'una dell'altra splende,
   con maggior forza sua virtù discende
   a quello amico suo mortale intorno   4
e fa per lui la notte chiara e 'l giorno,
   e coll'immortali alme al ciel l'ascende
   e in sé propria il trasferisce, e rende
   un altro spirto a far poi qui soggiorno   8
così voi qui, Cellin, la propria stella
   che co' bei rai di virtù mostrate
   quanta habbia forza la natura e l'arte,   11
nel grande statuar leggiadra e bella
   opra, che Dio serbò a questa etate
   et a voi serba in ciel la destra parte.   14

[ibid., c. 161v]

70.
Zanobi Lastricati
Al molto magnifico m. Benvenuto Cellini

Quello splendor che 'n voi chiaro riluce,
   e ch'altrui scorge al remirar tant'alto,
   lo scura in guisa di tenebre il manto
   qual chiaro vetro il carro della luce.   4
A questo reverente si conduce
   lo spirto mio da così freddo smalto,
   et a tal col suo lume ogn'hor m'esalto
   che la notte qual giorno a me fa luce: 8
così, la sua merzé, impedite e rotte
   non credo che fien mai molto né poco
   le vie del seguir voi, caro Cellino,   11
se 'l più vien dunque, e 'l mancho in queste grotte
   riman, può minuir del suo ben poco
   se 'l meglio è sempre al suo bel sol vicino.   14

Di Vostra Signoria
Zanobi Lastricati

[Florence, Biblioteca Riccardiana, ms. Ricc. 2728, c. 42r]

71.
Alfonso de' Pazzi

L'Etrusco non ne dice ben né male,
   della nuova bizzarra e gran facciata,
   la qual molto contenta la brigata,
   da quaresima sendo e carnovale.   4
Ivi son le sett'arte liberale,
   e nostra età distinta e consumata,
   i pianeti in cucina il vulgo guata,
   abbasso le virtudi han del triviale.   8
Et Perugia e Fiorenza e tante cose,
   che la mi par del Varchi una letione,
   et simil opre annulla tutte et priva.   11
Un arco trïonfal o prospettiva
   mi sembra ben; ma quella surretione
   discorda fra le cose fabulose.   14
Son la più part'ascose,
   ma tanti brevi che vi son latini
   ne fan capaci insino a' contadini.   17
Et così gli aretini
   pittori e gli accademici hanno cura
   di 'nsegnar le scïenze con le mura.   20
Duolsi l'Architettura,
   che non l'arebbe fat'a pena Cuio,
   per ch'altri vegga rimaner al buio.   23

[text from Celi 2021 (as fn. 448)]

72.
Giorgio Vasari?

Certo, Etrusco, tu sei un huom bestiale,
   per quanto mi dimostra la brigata
   ma più il dir cose contro alla facciata
   che non ne venderebbe lo spetiale.[102]   4
O cervel pazo, o zucca senza sale,
   mente da ogni ben alienata
   et in ogni vituperio transformata,
   peste venuta al mondo per dir male!   8
Taci, alveo pien d'opre vituperose,
   ch'il Varchi è dotto e tu sei un castrone,[103]
   né viver merti, alma d'ogni buon priva.   11

Ché se (poiché la chiami prospettiva)
    farne havessi voluto una a ragione
    te ci havria messo e 'storiate tuo cose,   14
benché son sì famose
    senza più dimostrarle, è noto a tutti
    che le san predicare le donne e ' putti,   17
ch'in te son sì destrutti
    tutti e' buon portamenti e annullati
    quanto il tacere e il sopportar de' frati.   20
Né però son restati
    d'abbracciarti e' contrarii, anzi t'han preso,
    poiché prigione a loro già ti sei reso.   23

A Ampholso de' Pazzi in risposta
[BNCF, ms. Magl. VII.1178, cc. xviiiv–xixr]

73.
Antonfrancesco Grazzini
A m. Benvenuto Cellini quando si scoperse la Cappella de' Montauti nell'Annuntiata. 1564

Hor se ne va, Cellino, la Tarsia,
    la Lasca, la Badia, e l'altra scuola
    tutta smarrita, abbandonata e sola,
    poi che convien ch'il ver[104] di sopra stia   4
ragion coperte di filosofia,
    le quai com'ombra tutte il vero invola:
    restan confuse, e rintuzzate in gola
    dal giuditio del nostro gran Messia,   8
il qual ne' Servi alla nuova Cappella
    alli frati e pittor dimostra quanto
    gran torto fanno alla madre scultura.   11
E se di lor nessun già non favella,
    guardate i visi sbigottiti tanto
    ch'usciti sembran della sepultura: 14
ponetevi ben cura
    che gl'hanno certi ceffi di sentenza
    contro, e bisogn'habbin pacienza,   17
non havendo avertenza
    che del rilievo la pittura è l'ombra
    e la scultura ogni falso disgombra.   20

[BNCF, ms. II.ix.45, c. 125v]

74.
Alessandro Allori?
Al Lasca quando e' disse male della Capella de' Montauti nella Annuntiata. 1564

Vogliomi, Benvenuto, disperare,
   dare alle streghe e far ogni partito
   della mia vita, poi ch'un scimonito
   osa della scultura straparlare.   4
Noi siàn perduti, il mondo ha ' rovinare
   poi che una Lasca, un ranocchio stordito,
   di lische pien, non punto saporito,
   del fango sguizza e vuole indovinare: 8
se pur sapessi almen quest'animale
   se di rilievo o ver dipinto fusse,
   e se i color reggano al martello!   11
Allhor sì, che sciolto il barbazzale
   potrebbe all'ignorantia dar le mosse
   e scinguettar de' subbi e del pennello.   14

[ibid., c. 126r]

75.
Paolo Geri
Dello Scoglio sestina. Pilucca

Per campagne, per boschi, piagge et monti
   cercando vo 'l mio desïato sole,
   chè sol sostegno a questa fragil vita,
   né altro lume ricevon questi occhi,
   né spera altro riposo questo spirto,
   né d'altro sa parlar la stanca lingua.   6
La bocca appena muovo che la lingua
   scioglie parole da muover i monti
   certo a pietà, non ch'un benigno spirto,
   et se talhor fra l'aur veggo 'l sole,
   dico: "Hora remirate, affannati occhi,
   che pena accresce a questa stanca vita."   12
Così meno per lui noiosa vita,
   affaticando questa rozza lingua
   et quinci et quindi rivolgendo gli occhi,
   quanto veder si può in cima de' monti,
   se risprender vedessino e lor sole
   che indarno affaticar fa questo spirto   18

sanza del qual star non può 'l mio spirto,
  né più m'è huopo homai, signor, la vita
  se oscurato se le mostra 'l sole.
  Simil al cigno esser ti convien, lingua,
  che mai non cesserò, di monti in monti,
  andare affaticando te et gli occhi, 24
ma conforto mi prestano ambo gli occhi
  et spene anche ne porgano allo spirto
  che rapparir l'han visto su pe' monti,
  del che molto gioisce lo mio vito,
  sì che l'usato canto prendi, lingua,
  che fuggendo le nube torna il sole. 30
Felici monti, ove apparve 'l mio sole
  che 'l velo mi levò d'ambeduo gli occhi
  et rendette la voce a questa lingua,
  prestando spene di pace al mio spirto
  di condurre a bon fine questa vita
  da' lacci sciolta et da l'errar per monti! 36
Fa', Amor, che i monti più quel chiaro sole
  non celmi, che la vita questo spirto
  conduca a dirvi bel fra gli occhi et la lingua. 39

[BNCF, ms.II.iv.1, c. 43r]

76.
Idem
Sonetto [...] dello Scoglio, un de' fondatori dell'Accademia degl'Humidi fiorentina, dato allo Stradino. Pilucca

Vattene stanco cor, da quel bel sole
  che fu principio a voi d'amaro pianto,
  et tenta di levar lo scuro manto
  che più vuol celi a voi come far suole, 4
et quando se' da lui queste parole
  sciogli, dicendo: "Quel che v'ama tanto
  supplicando mercé vi diede, quanto
  vostra rara beltà promette et vuole." 8
Et quando harà vostre querele intese,
  et tu veggia ver noi pietate spenta
  per haver forse a sdegno l'esser mio 11

non ritornar a me: fermati et tenta,
   quinci et quindi mostrando il mio disio,
   tal che benigno a voi torni et cortese.   14

[ibid., c. 106v]

77.
Idem
Dello Scoglio sonetto. Pilucca

Lieti pastor, che in sulla riva tosca
   del mio bel Arno, che la rena indora,
   felici con gli armenti godete hora
   che più non vi si mostra l'aria fosca,   4
so che non è fra voi chi mi conosca,
   ch'in me l'effigie mia più non dimora,
   ché 'l chiaro sol che mia vita scolora
   l'ha seco e me fuggendo più s'inbosca.   8
Felice laur, che dal mio bel sole
   adornate son tutte le tue fronde,
   tal che l'ha convertite in gemme et oro,   11
le tue vaghe, fiorite et verdi fronde
   desidro sì, ma più d'esse il mio sole,
   che con sua raggi sol mi può far d'oro.   14

[ibid., c. 42v]

78.
Accursio Baldi
Nelle felicissime nozze del Serenissimo Gran Duca di Toscana e della Serenissima Signora Bianca Cappello

Ecco per libertà darne e vittoria
   il cappello e 'l leone, insegne illustri,
   sorgon su l'Arno, et perché mille lustri
   regnin le real palle[105] in pace e 'n gloria;   4
ecco d'Adria la bell'Alba[106] si gloria
   d'altri fior che di rose e di ligustri,
   giunta col sol d'Etruria,[107] onde s'illustri
   per regia prole l'alta lor memoria.   8
Ecco 'l saggio a lei vien padre[108] giocondo
   da le più ricche a le più vaghe sponde
   con chiara scorta, in bel numero eletto;   11

ecco stupisce, ecco gioisce il mondo
   vedendo a gl'alti sposi in dolce affetto
   Flora sacrâr la terra, e Adria l'onde.   14

Accursio Baldi
[BNCF, II.I.397, c. 81r]

79.
Bronzino
Al Duca di Fiorenza e di Siena

Se ben di mille palme,[109] e mille accese
   virtù s'adorna et d'ogni parte splende,
   salito omai dove non pur ascende
   desìr qual vago più d'altere imprese,   4
novellamente il mio signor cortese,
   che sol con seco di valor contende,
   non di tanti honor sazio ad opra intende,
   ch'altri mai non tentò più chiara o intese,   8
onde come Pompei nuovi et Iasoni
   per lui 'l Tirreno,[110] e nuovi Omeri e Plati
   vedrà 'l bel Arno, e girne al cielo il vanto,   11
sì con Apelle i Dedali e i Mironi
   tornare, e i Michelangeli e i Donati:
   oh sovr'ogn'altro eccelso animo e santo!   14

[Bronzino, *Canzoniere*, c. 97v]

80.
Idem

Hor che voi siete, o mio signore, andato
   a riveder la Pietra, che ben oggi
   si può dir Santa al suo signore a lato,   3
vi scorge il mio pensiero hora in sui poggi
   a mirar l'onde salse, hor nelle cave
   dove l'oro e l'argento par ch'alloggi: 6
talora al dolce mormorio soave
   vi contempla d'un rio soave e chiaro,
   atto a scacciare ogn'aspra cura e grave,   9
ond'io che mi sto qua del tempo avaro,
   perch'ei non passi, a mio potere, invano
   e mi sia poi cagion di lungo amaro,   12

cerco così, com'io ne son lontano,
  con queste voci mie, con queste carte
  baciar almen la vostra santa mano, 15
sperando ancor ch'assiso in qualche parte,
  non per ozio fuggir (ch' in cor tant'alto
  la cieca nebbia sua non può haver parte), 18
ma per tornare al glorïoso assalto
  più fresco dei pensier del largo impero,
  ch'arian forza disfare un cuor di smalto, 21
darete, o che m'inganno e troppo spero,
  con l'alme luci e sacre voci ancora
  fors'a queste mie rime il spirto vero: 24
vedrete in queste un servo che v'adora,
  e porge preghi alle beate piante,
  ch'ogni buon segue, e reverisce e honora. 27
Queste non ardiran le tali e tante
  virtù vostre cantar, ch'omai le sanno
  l'austro e l'orse, il ponente e 'l levante, 30
né come dopo grave e lungo affanno
  ch'avea sofferto il bel fiorito nido
  e per altrui ignoranza e per inganno, 33
salito, credo, al ciel de' buoni il grido,
  s'impetrasse lassù ch'a noi scendesse
  Medico al nostro mal sì saggio e fido; 36
né con quanta virtù l'acerbe e spesse
  ferite alla sua Flora medicando,
  più che mai bella e sana la rendesse. 39
Né manco andrò di voi, signor, cantando
  l'honestà, la iustizia, e la pietade,
  ch'eran già tutte, ohimé, del tutto in bando, 42
la continenzia invitta e la bontade,
  l'amor de' buoni e la compassïone
  dei rei, che ignoran le sante pedate,[111] 45
come le sacre leggi e l'opre buone
  tenete salde, e come in vostra corte
  s'osservan pria che per l'altre persone, 48
onde non più il possente, il ricco, o 'l forte
  l'humile opprime, il vile o 'l poverello
  per colpa sol della non pari sorte; 51

né più son tolti a questo cive e a quello
  gli honor debiti a lui, che 'l sangue e 'l senno
  gli diede e chiaro o reverendo fello;   54
né pur mi tacerò, ma non accenno
  l'ardente carità che 'l cor v'incende,
  pur che 'l bisogno altrui vi faccia cenno,   57
ma per dirne o tacer non meno splende
  il sol né più, così di voi, buon duce,
  il valor che per tutto omai risplende: 60
questa v'ha il fianco aperto, e questa sdruce
  qual nuovo Pellican[112] l'acceso core,
  e per esempio in terra vi conduce.   63
O carità celeste, o santo amore,
  pascer non pure il suo ma l'altrui gregge,
  sì come vero universal pastore!   66
A quante pover'alme, ahi dura legge,
  è negato habitar la lor cittade,
  cacciate da colui che sì la regge,   69
ch'hanno trovato e le porte e le strade
  aperte della vostra alma Fiorenza
  per riparar la lor necessitade,   72
e della vostra saggia providenza
  e santa carità godano il frutto,
  e del proprio oro di Vostra Eccellenza.   75
Sarian gli esempii miseri per tutto,
  per l'aspre morti dell'orrenda fame
  da non poter tenerne il viso asciutto: 78
oh quanti ladronecci, oh quante infami
  disonestadi, e quanti inganni e mali
  sarìen seguiti per sì lunghe brame!   81
Quanti esser denno, adunque, i preghi, e quali,
  che salgon dritto alla magion di Dio
  per voi, signor, che fate opere tali?   84
Qual deve il figlio riverente e pio,
  che vede il vecchio suo padre da morte
  per voi scampato, e da tempo sì rio,   87
e quindi volto alla dolce consorte
  da voi la riconosce, e i cari figli,
  tratti di sotto a sì malvagia sorte?   90

E qual priva d'aiuti e di consigli
   la vedovella, a cui la famiglia egra
   lasciò il suo sposo, e fra tanti perigli?   93
Sebbene in veste dolorosa e negra,
   mentre le porge i vostri aiuti santi
   di gran dolcezza piange e si rallegra.   96
E quali i preghi accettabili, e quanti
   dell'innocenti e pure verginelle
   per voi salvate fra perigli tanti?   99
Denn'esser, dico, al gran Re delle stelle
   porti a 'mpetrar per voi vita e contento,
   e mille grazie glorïose e belle.   102
Beati noi, ch'a sì fero spavento
   che c'incontrava minaccioso e crudo,
   faceste il santo e gran provvedimento,   105
e v'opponeste con sì forte scudo,
   faccendo l'opra ch'ognor va crescendo,
   fra 'l popol ch'era d'ogni aiuto ignudo.   108
Ma perché pur mi vo, folle, partendo
   dal cammin primo, e non m'accorgo quanto
   col mio basso lodar forse v'offendo?   111
Ben conosch'io che non può alzarsi tanto
   mio tardo ingegno, e ch'altro stile e rima
   conviensi a nome sì pregiato e santo,   114
ma quand'io porsi a questa penna in prima
   la man, pensai di me, signor, parlarvi
   con humil voci e non tentar la cima,   117
e humilmente così ricordarvi,
   per la vostra bontà cortese e pia,
   quel ch'altra volta m'indusse a pregarvi.   120
Io son, come vedete, della via
   passato il mezzo, e comincia il timore
   a prender forza e speme a fuggir via;   123
il giusto, santo, e lodevole amore
   ch'io hebbi sempre alla mia vaga e bella
   arte mi porge in un gioia e dolore: 126
gioia mi fia potendo seguir quella
   con quelle diligenzie e quelli studi
   che drittamente convengano ad ella,   129

ma come potrò io, s'i colpi crudi
   della miseria (io non dico bisogno)
   mi batteran, d'ogni pietade ignudi? 132
Lasso, che pur a dirlo mi vergogno,
   mi converrà per via volgare e trita
   seguitar quei che fanno opre da sogno, 135
che tanto brama ognuno in questa vita
   salvar la vita, che molti per questo
   ogni strada d'honore hanno smarrita. 138
Aggiugnesi, signor, ch'all'huomo honesto
   troppo accora il dolor, quando la forza
   lo face ai dolci amici esser molesto, 141
e si vede sospinto a poggia ed orza[113]
   e schernito e schivato, ond'ogni saggio
   di non condursi a tal s'ingegna e sforza. 144
Ben lo sa Dio, che nel mio cor non haggio
   una minima stilla d'avarizia,
   né temo che giammai mi faccia oltraggio, 147
ch'io ben conosco che tal vizio vizia
   i buon costumi, le virtudi e l'arti,
   e colma d'ignoranza e di malizia. 150
Ma 'l provveder ch'e' non deggia mancarti
   le cose honeste a mantenerti il grado,
   e gli amici e la vita conservarti, 153
non credo già, che né sovente o rado
   retto giudicio mai danne o riprenda,
   come chi fiume passa e cerca il guado. 156
Ond'io chieggio, signor, tanto ond'io prenda,
   mentre ch'io vivo, al mio viver tal frutto
   che da necessità sol mi difenda, 159
per poter poi di questo resto tutto
   far sacrificio a voi del viver mio,
   fin ch'all'ultimo di sarò condutto. 162
E qualor sia contento il mio desio,
   che fin ad hora esservi esposto credo,
   ogni grave pensier porrò in oblio, 165
e con questo, signor, ch'io pur vi chiedo,
   e con quel che mi date al ricco Creso
   vi do la fede mia che poi non cedo: 168

voi mi vedrete sottentrare al peso
    degli studii dell'arte, e vendicarmi
    di qualche tempo inutilmente speso,   171
intanto a voi verrà voglia di farmi
    far qualch'opra non vile, e non sia manco
    vostra la gloria dell'honesto aitarmi.   174
Voi sapete, signor, ch'io non v'ho stanco
    se non quando il bisogno m'ha constretto,
    e stimolato e l'uno e l'altro fianco: 177
vaglia dunque nel vostro alto conspetto,
    più che l'audacia o prosunzion loquace,
    la reverenzia, la fede e 'l rispetto,   180
e tutto sia però con vostra pace
    detto, perch'io m'accordo finalmente
    a tutto quel ch'a voi diletta e piace.   183
L'alto giudicio e la divina mente
    vostra disponga, e l'humil servo taccia
    alla sua voglia lieto e reverente,   186
e quando al suo signor cortese piaccia
    adempir suo desio, sia ringraziato,
    né men lodato ancor quando li spiaccia.   189
E se questo mio dir forse tediato
    v'havesse, il vostro human quanto gentile
    esser mia indegnitade habbia scusato: 192
questo gli porse ardir, quest'all'humile
    prego l'indusse, e questo in terra chino
    mi fa sperar da voi grazia simile.   195
Qui supplicando all'alto Dio divino
    ch'altezza e stato, e lunga vita e sana
    vi doni, e scampi d'ogni reo destino,   198
insieme con la vostra sopr'humana,
    saggia, honesta, gentil, chiara consorte
    e vostra illustre prole alta e sovrana,   201
resto aspettando un sì, che mi conforte.

Il fine
[ibid., cc. 174r–179v]

81.
Domenico Poggini

Ben fu grande e pregiato il tuo valore,
   o sacro Apollo, contra l'empia fera,
   che gir ne fé tua chiara fronte altera
   tolto ai mortali un sì tremendo orrore,   4
e quel che già ti punse e passò il core
   dorato stral, di che per la riviera
   Dafne seguisti, a te sì dolce e fera,
   al crin ti riportò di Lauro onore   8
Or hai per terza impresa altera e nova
   coronato il celeste Capricorno
   d'oro e di gemme e di virtù fregiato.   11
Maggior è 'l merto tuo, maggior la prova
   rendendo a chi 'l nemica oltraggio e scorno
   per farlo, come in terra, in ciel beato.   14

[*Le imprese illustri con espositioni, et discorsi del S. Ieronimo Ruscelli […]*, Venice 1566, p. 172]

Notes

For the criteria of edition of poems whose transcriptions were based on manuscripts or sixteenth-century editions, see supra, fn. 58.

[1] "You prove to be."
[2] The text follows the earlier, original version of the poem as published in note ibid. A later version, the result of a revision by the bishop of Arezzo Bernardetto Minerbetti, presents a few differences, including an incipit which reads "Angelo, a noi par da Michel divino." As Minerbetti noted in a letter to Vasari, he modified the first line "perché e' mi pareva, che nel primo verso troppo si toccasse la divinità di Michele, per levar occasion di chiacchierar a' frati […], dove Voi dite: Più che Michel divino, scrissi: Par a Michel divino" (quoted ibid.)
[3] Here and elsewhere, the goddess is the personification of Florence.
[4] Here in the sense of "things out of the order of nature," "miracolous things."
[5] I. e., after Pontormo abandoned all other work to dedicate himself to the frescoes of San Lorenzo.
[6] God.
[7] 'Prisoner,' having been vanquished.
[8] I. e., the interlocutor's judgment was clouded by his affection for Varchi.
[9] Envy, here (as in Bronzino's proposta, and in the following poem by Francesco da Sangallo) personified.
[10] Allusion to the three supreme glories of ancient literature, i. e. Homer, Virgil and Cicero.
[11] Here "generous" to the three great men of Tuscan letters.
[12] In the cinquecentina: *ghiaccio*.
[13] "Lucky region" (i. e. Florence).
[14] "Will never be forgotten," the Lethe being the river of post mortem oblivion in classical mythology.
[15] "Which servitude keeps me away from Parnassus and the glory of poetry," with an allusion to the author's chief profession.
[16] "What it means to try to bestow mortal praise on immortal gods."
[17] "Hands."
[18] "Will be indebted".
[19] "Wings," synonym of *ali*.

Appendix

20 "Limits."
21 Here the "stone cippi" that were often placed along roads.
22 "A perennial Spring."
23 Reference is here to the Florentine Servite convent of the Santissima Annunziata, where the friar and sculptor lived.
24 Contracted form for *devono*.
25 Here personified.
26 "Unexpected."
27 Before his time had come.
28 Representing Him unforgiving with the damned and benevolent with the blessed.
29 "Instead of."
30 "Is the pain I feel not enough for me to die?"
31 "Is late."
32 "Where", from the latin *ubi*.
33 The unnamed hill surrounding Florence on which Varchi claimed he wanted to be buried.
34 Mount Senario, close to Florence, which was the naturalistic setting of many of Varchi's compositions.
35 With reference to Varchi's own *consiglio*.
36 The day of death, which rewards those who lived virtuously with the ascent to Heaven.
37 Meaning that death (chi tutto disperde) will not erase the ben made by the deceased.
38 "If you ever cared about me, our age, and yourself."
39 "To us."
40 The Florentine physician Baccio Rontini, who had been Michelangelo's doctor.
41 "Without waiting for our own death."
42 "I plan."
43 This section of the Filza (cc. 263bis–315) preserves the final redaction of the *Sonetti in morte di Luca Martini*: see Brancato 2019 (as in fn. 219), p. 76.
44 A praise of Puccini's rhetorical skills, which Varchi deems equal to the greatest classical examples.
45 I. e. *sospirarono*, contracted form of the simple past (also in the following lines).
46 "Plums."
47 A river in the countryside around Pisa, under the jurisdiction of Martini's activity as *provveditore dei fossi*.
48 "Deprived."
49 Carlo and Giovanni Martini, Luca's brothers.
50 "Condition."
51 I. e. *ci ha*.
52 "Intelligent", "shrewd."
53 "I never stop."
54 "Bereft."
55 "Be late."
56 "Help me."
57 Here used in the function of direct object.
58 "A nefarious jackdow," which was considered a hominous bird.
59 Meaning that even when the author's pain will diminish, it will still be greater than any other pain ever endured by a human being.
60 Duke Cosimo.
61 Here "the soul", as opposed to mortale ("the body".)
62 I. e. *toglierci*.
63 "Object."
64 Allusion to Varchi's lecture at the Accademia Fiorentina *Dei poeti eroici* (1553), which discussed the defining features of the Iliad, the *Odyssey*, and the *Aeneid*.
65 I. e. *debbono*.
66 In the table of contents of the book.
67 Here "apostles," i. e. Peter and Paul.
68 Followed by the number "LXXXVI" on the MS.

69 "Deeply moves."
70 "Trunk," i. e. the laurel, loved by Petrarch and Apollo.
71 Death's hand.
72 "If you care at all about me."
73 Meaning that any mortal goodness would be a vice when joined with Lenzi's inner perfection.
74 "Rebel."
75 I. e. Avignon.
76 On mount Senario.
77 With the stile of poetry, able to eternize its subjects (as opposed to painting's capacity to represent the likeness of its subject).
78 "By which Apollo himself [the god of the Sun] was largely overcome."
79 I. e. the laurel.
80 "Shoot" (with reference to Lenzi's youth).
81 Meaning that Lauro is possibly superior to both Apollo's and Petrarch's laurels.
82 "Better."
83 "Low."
84 Satan.
85 "Blessed is the day of one's death," but with a play on words on the addressee's name.
86 Meaning that the pain that one endures during death is inferior to the suffering of eternal damnation.
87 I. e. *facesse*.
88 Satan.
89 "During his prime youth."
90 "Inaccesible."
91 "From mountain to mountain."
92 "Pliable alder and pricking butcher's broom," to designate worthless plants.
93 "Intent and full of desire."
94 Conjectural emendation to the volume's lesson *e*.
95 "Lord."
96 The friar, astronomer, mathematician and cartographer Egnazio Danti, Vincenzo's brother.
97 "Sin."
98 "Avoid."
99 To the heavens.
100 Ending up among the damned in hell or among the blessed in heaven.
101 Death.
102 A Florentine idiomatic expression that was used to designate bizarre things that were the figment of one's imagination.
103 Literally, a castrated lamb or foal; figuratively, a stupid person.
104 Conjectural emendation to the manuscript's *viver*, which makes the line hypermetrical.
105 The six palle of the Medici coat of arms.
106 Aurora, the pagan god of Dawn, was often compared to Bianca Cappello in Florentine encomiastic verse of the time.
107 The Granduke Francesco.
108 The Venetian Patrician Bartolomeo Cappello, Bianca's father.
109 "Excellences."
110 An allusion to the creation of a maritime fleet that Cosimo had begun to sponsor in 1547, with the intention of controlling the Tyrrhenian sea.
111 "Holy examples."
112 The bird, which was believed to feed its hatchlings with its own blood, was a common symbol of Christ.
113 From every side, with an expression taken from the jargon of navigation.

Bibliography

Primary sources

Aelian. *Historical Miscellany*. Edited and translated by N. G. Wilson. Cambridge, MA: Harvard University Press, 1997.
Agosti, Giovanni, and Dante Isella, eds. *Antiquarie prospetiche romane*. 2nd ed. Milan: Fondazione Pietro Bembo, 2006.
Albèri, Eugenio, ed. *Relazioni degli ambasciatori veneti al Senato, raccolte, annotate ed edite da Eugenio Albèri […]. Serie 2, Volume 2*. Florence: Tipografia all'insegna di Clio, 1841.
Alberti, Leon Battista. *De pictura: redazione volgare*. Edited by Lucia Bertolini. Florence: Polistampa, 2011.
    On Painting and On Sculpture: The Latin Texts of "De pictura" and "De statua." Translated by Cecil Grayson. London: Phaidon, 1972.
Alberti, Leon Battista / Lodovico Domenichi. *La pittura di Leonbattista Alberti tradotta per m. Lodovico Domenichi*. Venice: Appresso Gabriel Giolito de Ferrari, 1547.
Ammirato, Scipione. *Il Rota overo delle imprese dialogo […]*. Naples: Appresso Gio. Maria Scotto, 1562.
Anacreon. *Anacreontis Teji Odae: Ab Henrico Stephano luce et latinitate nunc primum donatae […]*. Paris: Stephanus, 1554.
Anacreontea: Elegy and Iambus, being the remains of all the Greek Elegiac and Iambic Poets […], with the Anacreontea. Edited and translated by J. M. Edmonds. 2 vols. London / New York: Heinemann / G. P. Putnam's Sons, 1931.
Aretino, Pietro. *Lettere sull'arte*. Edited by Ettore Camesasca, Fidenzio Pertile, and Carlo Cordié. 4 vols. Milan: Edizioni del Milione, 1957–1960.
Armenini, Giovanni Battista. *De' veri precetti della pittura*. Edited by Marina Gorreri. Turin: Einaudi, 1988.
Baldini, Baccio. *Orazione fatta nella Accademia fiorentina in lode del serenissimo sig. Cosimo Medici granduca di Toscana gloriosa memoria*. Florence: Nella stamperia di Bartolomeo Sermartelli, 1574.
Baldinucci, Filippo. *Notizie de' professori del disegno da Cimabue in qua […]*. 6 vols. Florence: Per Santi Franchi, 1681–1728.
Bandello, Matteo. *Tutte le opere di Matteo Bandello*. Edited by Francesco Flora. 2 vols. Milan: Mondadori, 1934–1943.
Barocchi, Paola, ed. *Scritti d'arte del Cinquecento*. 3 vols. Milan: Ricciardi, 1971–1977.
    Ed. *Trattati d'arte del Cinquecento, fra Manierismo e Controriforma*. 3 vols. Bari: Laterza, 1960–1962.
Bartoli, Cosimo. *Ragionamenti sopra alcuni luoghi difficili di Dante*. Venice: Appresso Francesco de Franceschi Senese, 1567.
Battiferra, Laura. *Laura Battiferra and Her Literary Circle: An Anthology*. Edited and translated by Victoria Kirkham. Chicago: University of Chicago Press, 2006.
Bembo, Pietro. *Prose e rime*. Edited by Carlo Dionisotti. Turin: UTET, 2013.
Berni, Francesco. *Rime*. Edited by Danilo Romei. Milan: Mursia, 1985.
Berni, Francesco *et alii*. *Secondo libro dell'opere burlesche di Francesco Berni, di Gio. della Casa, del Varchi, del Mauro, di m. Bino, del Molza, del Dolce, e del Firenzuola […]*. Florence: Apresso li Heredi di Bernardo Giunti, 1555.
Billi, Antonio. *Il libro di Antonio Billi*. Edited by Fabio Benedettucci. Anzio (Rome): De Rubeis, 1991.
Borghini, Raffaello. *Il Riposo, in cui della pittura, e della scultura si favella […]*. Florence: Marescotti, 1584.
Borghini, Vincenzio. *Dello scrivere contro ad alcuno, discorso inedito*. Edited by Giuseppe Aiazzi. Florence: Tipografia di Luigi Pezzati, 1841.

Bottari, Giovanni Gaetano, and Stefano Ticozzi, eds. *Raccolta di lettere sulla pittura, scultura ed architettura: scritte da' più celebri personaggi dei secoli XV, XVI e XVII*. Milan: Silvestri, 1822.

Bramante, Donato. *Sonetti e altri scritti*. Edited by Carlo Vecce. Rome: Salerno editrice, 1995.

Bramanti, Vanni ed. *Lettere a Benedetto Varchi, 1530–1563*. Manziana (Rome): Vecchiarelli, 2012.

Britonio, Girolamo. *Gelosia del Sole: edizione critica e commento*. Edited by Mauro Marrocco. Rome: Sapienza Università editrice, 2016.

Bronzino, Agnolo. *I Salterelli dell'Abbrucia sopra i Mattaccini di ser Fedocco*. Edited by Carla Rossi Bellotto. Rome: Salerno editrice, 1998.

Rime in burla. Edited by Franca Petrucci Nardelli. Rome: Istituto della Enciclopedia Italiana, 1988.

Sonetti di Angiolo Allori detto il Bronzino ed altre rime inedite di più insigni poeti. Edited by Domenico Moreni. Florence: Magheri, 1823.

Brunelleschi, Filippo. *Sonetti di Filippo Brunelleschi*. Edited by Domenico De Robertis and Giuliano Tanturli. Florence: L'Accademia della Crusca, 1977.

Caro, Annibale. *Lettere familiari*. Edited by Aulo Greco. 3 vols. Florence: Le Monnier, 1957–1961.

Castiglione, Baldassarre. *Il cortegiano, con una scelta delle opere minori*. Edited by Bruno Maier. Turin: UTET, 1955.

Cellini, Benvenuto. *Due trattati, uno intorno alle otto principali arti dell'oreficeria, l'altro in materia dell'arte della scultura; dove si veggono infiniti segreti nel lavorar le figure di marmo, et nel gettarle di bronzo*. Florence: Per Valente Panizzi et Marco Peri, 1568.

I trattati dell'oreficeria e della scultura novamente messi alle stampe secondo la originale dettatura del codice Marciano. Si aggiungono i discorsi e i ricordi intorno all'arte; le lettere e le suppliche; le poesie. Edited by Carlo Milanesi. Florence: Le Monnier, 1857.

La vita. Edited by Lorenzo Bellotto. Parma: Fondazione Pietro Bembo / Ugo Guanda Editore, 1996.

Opere. Edited by Giuseppe Guido Ferrero. Turin: UTET, 1980.

Rime. Edited by Diletta Gamberini. Florence: SEF, 2014.

Vita di Benvenuto Cellini, orefice e scultore fiorentino. Edited by Francesco Tassi. 3 vols. Florence: Piatti, 1829.

Cennini, Cennino. *Il libro dell'arte*. Edited by Fabio Frezzato. Vicenza: Pozza, 2003.

Cicero, Marcus Tullius. *De officiis*. With an English Translation by Walter Miller. London / Cambridge, MA: William Heinemann LTD / Harvard University Press, 1913.

De oratore. Edited by A. S. Wilkins. Oxford: Oxford University Press, 1902.

Cicero, Marcus Tullius (ps.). *Ad C. Herennium libri IV de ratione dicendi*. With an English Translation by Harry Caplan. London / Cambridge, MA: William Heinemann LTD / Harvard University Press, 1964.

Condivi, Ascanio. *Vita di Michelangelo Buonarroti*. Rome: Antonio Blado stampatore, 1553.

Contile, Luca. *Ragionamento [...] sopra la proprietà delle imprese*. Pavia: Appresso Girolamo Bartoli, 1574.

Dante Alighieri. *La Commedia secondo l'antica vulgata*. Edited by Giorgio Petrocchi. Milan: Mondadori, 1966–1967.

La Comedia. Commentary by Alessandro Vellutello. Venice: Per Francesco Marcolini ad instantia di Alessandro Vellutello, 1544.

Davanzati, Bernardo. *Scisma d'Inghilterra con altre operette del signor Bernardo Davanzati [...]*. 2nd ed. Padua: Presso Giuseppe Comino, 1754.

DellaNeva, JoAnn, ed. *Ciceronian Controversies*. Translated by Brian Duvick. Cambridge, MA: Harvard University Press, 2007.

Dionysius of Halicarnassus. *On Thucydides*. Translated by W. Kendrick Pritchett. Berkeley / Los Angeles / London: University of California Press, 1975.

Doni, Anton Francesco. *Disegno del Doni, partito in più ragionamenti [...]*. Venice: Gabriele Giolito de Ferrarii, 1549.

I marmi. Edited by Carlo Alberto Girotto and Giovanna Rizzarelli. 2 vols. Florence: Olschki, 2017.

Gauricus, Pomponius. *De sculptura*. Edited and translated in Italian by Paolo Cutolo. Naples: Edizione Scientifiche Italiane, 1999.

Gaye, Giovanni, ed. *Carteggio inedito d'artisti dei secoli XIV, XV, XVI*. 3 vols. Florence: Molini, 1839–1840.

Gelli, Giambattista. *Lezioni Petrarchesche di Giovan Battista Gelli [...]*. Edited by Carlo Negroni. Bologna: Gaetano Romagnoli, 1884.

Ghiberti, Lorenzo. *I commentarii: Biblioteca Nazionale Centrale di Firenze, II, I, 333*. Edited by Lorenzo Bartoli. Florence: Giunti, 1998.
Giannotti, Donato. *Dialogi di Donato Giannotti, de' giorni che Dante consumò nel cercare l'Inferno e 'l Purgatorio*. Edited by Deoclecio Redig de Campos. Florence: Sansoni, 1939.
Giovio, Paolo. *Elogia virorum [bellica virt]ute illustrium veris imaginibus [suppo]sita [...]*. Florence: Lorenzo Torrentino, 1551.
   Scritti d'arte: lessico ed ecfrasi. Edited by Sonia Maffei. Pisa: Scuola Normale Superiore, 1999.
Giovio, Paolo, and Lodovico Domenichi. *Dialogo dell'imprese militari et amorose, di monsignor Giovio vescovo di Nocera. Con un Ragionamento di messer Lodovico Domenichi, nel medesimo soggetto*. Venice: Appresso Gabriel Giolito de Ferrari, 1556.
Giraldi, Giovanni Battista. *Gli Ecatommiti ovvero centro novelle*. Florence: Borghi, 1833.
Grazzini, Anton Francesco. *Le cene*. Edited by Riccardo Bruscagli. Rome: Salerno editrice, 1976.
   Le rime burlesche edite e inedite di Antonfrancesco Grazzini detto il Lasca. Edited by Carlo Verzone. Florence: Sansoni, 1882.
   Rime di Antonfrancesco Grazzini detto Il Lasca [...]. Edited by Antonio Maria Biscioni and Francesco Moücke. 2 vols. Florence: Stamperia di F. Moücke, 1741.
Greek Anthology. Translated by W. R. Paton. 5 vols. Cambridge, MA: Harvard University Press, 1916–1918.
Gualterotti, Raffaello. *Feste nelle nozze del Serenissimo Don Francesco Medici Gran Duca di Toscana; et della Serenissima Sua Consorte la Signora Bianca Cappello*. Florence: Giunti, 1579.
   Rime del signor Raffaello Gualterotti. Al serenissimo don Francesco Medici. Florence: Appresso Bartolomeo Sermartelli, 1581.
Hesiod. *Works and Days*. Edited by Martin Litchfield West. Oxford: Oxford University Press, 1978.
Hollanda, Francisco de. *Diálogos em Roma (1538): Conversations on Art with Michelangelo Buonarroti*. Edited by Grazia Dolores Folliero-Metz. Heidelberg: Winter, 1998.
Horace. *Odes and Epodes*. Edited and translated by Niall Rudd. Cambridge, MA / London: Harvard University Press, 2004.
   Satires, Epistles and Ars Poetica. With an English Translation by H. Rusitton Fairclough. London / New York: William Heinemann LTD / G. P. Putnam's Sons, 1926.
Leonardo da Vinci. *Libro di pittura: edizione in facsimile del Codice Urbinate Lat. 1270 nella Biblioteca Apostolica Vaticana*. Edited by Carlo Pedretti. Transcribed by Carlo Vecce. 2 vols. Florence: Giunti, 1995.
Lomazzo, Giovan Paolo. *Idea del tempio della pittura*. In Milano: Per Paolo Gottardo Pontio, 1590.
   Rabisch. Edited by Dante Isella. Turin: Einaudi, 1993.
   Rime ad imitazione de i grotteschi usati da' pittori: con la vita del auttore descritta da lui stesso in rime sciolte. Edited by Alessandra Ruffino. Manziana (Rome): Vecchiarelli, 2006.
   Scritti sulle arti. Edited by Roberto Paolo Ciardi. 2 vols. Florence: Marchi & Bertolli, 1973–1975.
Malvasia, Carlo Cesare. *Felsina pittrice, vite de' pittori bolognesi [...]*. 2 vols. Bologna: Per l'erede di Domenico Barbieri, 1678.
Manetti, Antonio. *Vita di Filippo Brunelleschi*. Milan: Polifilo, 1976.
Martelli, Niccolò. *Il primo libro delle lettere di Nicolo Martelli*. Florence: A instanza dell'auttore, 1546.
Martial. *Epigrams*. Edited by D. R Shackleton Bailey. 3 vols. Cambridge, MA: Harvard University Press, 1993.
Michelangelo Buonarroti. *Il carteggio di Michelangelo*. Edited by Giovanni Poggi, Paola Barocchi, and Renzo Ristori. 5 vols. Florence: Sansoni, 1965–1983.
   Le Rime di Michelangelo Buonarroti, pittore, scultore e architetto. Edited by Cesare Guasti. Florence: Le Monnier, 1863.
   Rime e lettere. Edited by Antonio Corsaro and Giorgio Masi. Milan: Bompiani, 2016.
Pazzi, Alfonso de'. *Nuovi canti carnascialeschi di Firenze: le "canzone" e mascherate di Alfonso de' Pazzi*. Edited by Aldo Castellani. Florence: Olschki, 2006.
Petrarch (Petrarca, Francesco). *Canzoniere*. Edited by Rosanna Bettarini. 2 vols. Turin: Einaudi, 2005.
   Trionfi. Edited by Guido Bezzola. Milan: Biblioteca Universale Rizzoli, 1984.
Piccolomini, Alessandro. *De la institutione di tutta la vita de l'homo nato nobile [...]*. Venice: Apud Hieronymum Scotum, 1542.
Pliny the Elder. *Naturalis Historia (Mineralogia e storia dell'arte: libri 33–37)*. Translated in Italian by Antonio Corso, Rossana Mugellesi, and Giampiero Rosati. Turin: Einaudi, 1988.

Pliny the Younger. *Letters*. Translated by William Melmoth. Revised by W. M. L. Hutchinson. 2 vols. Cambridge, MA: Harvard University Press, 1915.

Plutarch, *Lives*. With an English Translation by Bernadotte Perrin. 10 vols. London / New York: William Heinemann LTD / G. P. Putnam's Sons, 1932.

Moralia, VII: On Love of Wealth. On Compliancy [...]. Translated by Phillip H. De Lacy and Benedict Einarson. Cambridge, MA: Harvard University Press, 1959.

Pontormo, Jacopo da. *Diario, Codice Magliabechiano VIII 1490 della Biblioteca Nazionale Centrale di Firenze. Commentario al facsimile con edizione critica del testo*. Edited by Roberto Fedi. 2 vols. Rome: Salerno editrice, 1996.

Quintilian, Marcus Fabius. *The Institutio Oratoria of Quintilian*. Translated by Harold Edgeworth Butler. 4 vols. Cambridge, MA: Harvard University Press, 1920–1922.

Raffaello da Montelupo. *Vita di Raffaello da Montelupo*. Edited by Riccardo Gatteschi. Florence: Polistampa, 1998.

Ruscelli, Girolamo. *Le imprese illustri con espositioni, et discorsi (etc.)*. Venice: Franciso Rampazetto, 1566.

Sacchetti, Franco. *Il Trecentonovelle*. Edited by Emilio Faccioli. Turin: Einaudi, 1970.

Segni, Bernardo. *Storie fiorentine di messer Bernardo Segni gentiluomo fiorentino, dall'anno 1527 al 1555 [...]*. 3 vols. Milan: Dalla Società tipografica de' classici italiani, 1805.

Varchi, Benedetto. *De sonetti. Colle risposte, e proposte di diversi*. Florence: Lorenzo Torrentino, 1557.

De Sonetti di M. Benedetto Varchi parte prima. Florence: Lorenzo Torrentino, 1555.

Deux leçons sur l'art. Edited and translated in French by Frédérique Dubard de Gaillarbois. Paris: Classiques Garnier, 2020.

Lettere, 1535–1565. Edited by Vanni Bramanti. Rome: Edizioni di storia e letteratura, 2008.

Lezioni sul Dante e prose varie di Benedetto Varchi, la maggior parte inedite [...]. Edited by Giuseppe Aiazzi and Lelio Arbib. 2 vols. Florence: A Spese della Società editrice delle storie del Nardi e del Varchi, 1841.

Lezzioni di m. Benedetto Varchi Accademico Fiorentino, lette da lui publicamente nell'Accademia Fiorentina [...]. Florence: Filippo Giunti, 1590.

L'Hercolano. Edited by Antonio Sorella. Pescara: Libreria dell'Università, 1995.

Liber carminum Benedicti Varchii. Edited by Aulo Greco. Rome: Abete, 1969.

Opere. Edited by Giovanni Battista Busini and Antonio Racheli. 2 vols. Trieste: Sezione letterario-artistica del Lloyd austriaco, 1858–1859.

Orazione funerale di m. Benedetto Varchi: fatta, e recitata da lui pubblicamente nell'essequie di Michelagnolo Buonarroti in Firenze, nella chiesa di San Lorenzo [...]. Florence: Appresso I Giunti, 1564.

Sonetti spirituali di m. Benedetto Varchi. Con alcune risposte, et proposte di diversi eccellentissimi ingegni. Florence: Nella stamperia de' Giunti, 1573.

Varchi, Benedetto, and Vincenzo Borghini. *Pittura e scultura nel Cinquecento*. Edited by Paola Barocchi. Livorno: Sillabe, 1998.

Vasari, Giorgio. *Der literarische Nachlass Giorgio Vasaris*. Edited by Karl Frey and Herman-Walther Frey. 2 vols. Munich: Georg Müller, 1923–1930.

La vita di Michelangelo: nelle redazioni del 1550 e del 1568. Edited by Paola Barocchi. 5 vols. Milan: Ricciardi, 1962.

Le vite de' più eccellenti pittori scultori e architettori: nelle redazioni del 1550 e 1568. Edited by Rosanna Bettarini and Paola Barocchi. 8 vols. Florence: Sansoni, 1967–1997.

Le vite de' più eccellenti pittori scultori e architettori. Edited by Enrico Mattioda *et alii*. Alessandria: Edizioni dell'Orso, 2017–.

Poesie. Edited by Enrico Mattioda. Alessandria: Edizioni dell'Orso, 2012.

Virgil. *Bucolics, Aeneid, and Georgics*. Edited by J. B. Greenough. Boston. Ginn & Co. 1900.

Vitruvius Pollio. *De architectura*. Italian translation and commentary by Antonio Corso and Elisa Romano. 2 vols. Turin: Einaudi, 1997.

Ten Books on Architecture. Translated by Ingrid D. Rowland and Thomas Noble Howe. New ed. Cambridge: Cambridge University Press, 1999.

Secondary literature

Acidini Luchinat, Cristina, and Elena Capretti, eds. *Innocente e calunniato: Federico Zuccari (1539/40–1609) e le vendette d'artista*. Exh. cat. Florence: Giunti, 2009.

Acidini Luchinat, Cristina, and Giacomo Pirazzoli, eds. *Ammannati e Vasari per la città dei Medici*. Exh. cat. Florence: Polistampa, 2011.

Ackerman, James. "Imitation." In *Antiquity and Its Interpreters*, edited by Alina A. Payne, Ann L. Kuttner, and Rebekah Smick, 9–16. Cambridge: Cambridge University Press, 2000.

Adorno, Theodor W. *Notes to Literature, Volume 1*. Edited by Rolf Tiedemann. Translated by Shierry Weber Nicholsen. New York: Columbia University Press, 1991.

Agosti, Barbara. *Giorgio Vasari: luoghi e tempi delle* Vite. Milan: Officina Libraria, 2013.

Agosti, Giovanni. "Scrittori che parlano di artisti, tra Quattro e Cinquecento in Lombardia." In *Quattro pezzi lombardi (per Maria Teresa Binaghi)*, edited by Barbara Agosti, Giovanni Agosti, Carl Brandon Strehlke and Marco Tanzi, 39–93. Brescia: Edizioni L'Obliquo, 1998.

Ahl, Frederick. "The Art of Safe Criticism in Greece and Rome." *The American Journal of Philology* 105 (1984): 174–208.

Albrecht-Bott, Marianne. *Die bildende Kunst in der italienischen Lyrik der Renaissance und des Barock: Studie zur Beschreibung von Portraits und anderen Bildwerken unter besonderer Berücksichtigung von G. B. Marinos Galleria*. Wiesbaden: Steiner, 1976.

Alfie, Fabian. *Dante's Tenzone with Forese Donati: The Reprehension of Vice*. Toronto: University of Toronto Press, 2011.

―――. *Rustico Filippi, 'The Art of Insult.'* Cambridge: Modern Humanities Research Association, 2014.

Alhaique Pettinelli, Rosanna. "Punti di vista sull'arte nei poeti dei *Coryciana*." *Rassegna della letteratura italiana* 90 (1986): 41–54.

Alpers, Svetlana. "'Ekphrasis' and Aesthetic Attitudes in Vasari's *Lives*." *Journal of the Warburg and Courtauld Institutes* 23 (1960): 190–215.

Ames-Lewis, Francis. *The Intellectual Life of the Early Renaissance Artist*. New Haven, CT: Yale University Press, 2000.

Ames-Lewis, Francis, and Paul Joannides, eds. *Reactions to the Master: Michelangelo's Effect on Art and Artists in the Sixteenth Century*. Aldershot: Ashgate, 2003.

Andreoni, Annalisa. *La via della dottrina: le lezioni accademiche di Benedetto Varchi*. Pisa: ETS, 2012.

Angiolini, Franco. "Martini, Luca." In *Dizionario Biografico degli Italiani* 71: 234–238. Rome: Istituto della Enciclopedia Italiana, 2008.

Arbizzoni, Guido. "Giovio, Domenichi e le imprese." *Bollettino storico piacentino* 110 (2015): 9–23.

―――. "Le imprese come ritratto interiore del principe." In *Il principe invisibile: Atti del convegno internazionale di studi (Mantova 27–30 novembre 2013)*, edited by Lucia Bertolini, Arturo Calzona, Glauco Maria Cantarella, and Stefano Caroti, 373–399. Turnhout: Brepols, 2015.

―――. *Un nodo di parole e di cose: storia e fortuna delle imprese*. Rome: Salerno editrice, 2002.

Armour, Peter. "'A ciascun artista l'ultimo suo:' Dante and Michelangelo." *Lectura Dantis* 22/23 (1998): 141–180.

Artico, Tancredi. "Danese Cataneo, 'felicissimo spirito' nelle carte tassiane. *L'Amor di Marfisa* e la *Gerusalemme liberata*." *Italianistica Debreceniensis* 23 (2017): 8–20.

Attwood, Philip. *Italian Medals c. 1530–1600 in British Public Collections*. 2 vols. London: British Museum, 2003.

Auerbach, Erich. *Mimesis: The Representation of Reality in Western Literature*. Translated by Willard R. Trask. Introduction by Edward W. Said. Princeton, NJ: Princeton University Press, 1953.

Avery, Charles. *Studies in Italian Sculpture*. London: Pindar Press, 2001.

Avery, Charles, and Susanna Barbaglia. *L'opera completa del Cellini*. Milan: Rizzoli, 1981.

Baffi, Valentina, and Giacomo Guazzini, eds. *Due pittori tardogotici fiorentini per Pistoia: Mariotto di Nardo e Rossello di Jacopo Franchi*. Pistoia: Gli ori, 2015.

Baffoni, Ingino. *Il conte Giovannadrea Commodi pittore e poeta fiorentino (1560–1638)*. 2nd augmented ed. Gubbio: Tipografia Eugubina, 1955.

Baldassarri, Stefano Ugo. "Alcuni appunti su Giotto e la poesia." *Lettere italiane* 49 (1997): 373–391.

Ballistreri, Gianni. "Bonsi, Lelio." In *Dizionario biografico degli Italiani* 12: 387–388. Rome: Istituto della Enciclopedia Italiana, 1971.

Balsamo, Jean, Franco Tomasi, and Carlo Ossola. *De Dante à Chiabrera: Poètes italiens de la Renaissance dans la bibliothèque de la Fondation Barbier-Mueller*. 2 vols. Geneva: Droz, 2007.

Baracchini, Clara, and Severina Russo. *Arte sacra nella Versilia medicea: il culto e gli arredi*. Florence: SPES, 1995.

Barasch, Moshe. "Character and Physiognomy: Bocchi on Donatello's *St. George*, a Renaissance Text on Expression in Art." *Journal of the History of Ideas* 36 (1975): 413–430.

Bàrberi Squarotti, Giovanni. "Il modello lontano. Arte umana e arte di Dio in alcune immagini del *Paradiso*." In *Pitture di parole: per Barbara Zandrino*, edited by Giovanni Barberi Squarotti and Valter Boggione, 73–91. Avellino: Edizioni Sinestesie, 2012.

Barkan, Leonard. *Michelangelo: A Life on Paper*. Princeton, NJ: Princeton University Press, 2011.

Mute Poetry, Speaking Pictures. Princeton, NJ: Princeton University Press, 2013.

Barletti, Emanuele. "Ipotesi di lavoro su Giovan Battista del Tasso." *Critica d'arte* 6 (1990): 55–61.

Barnes, Bernadine Ann. *Michelangelo and the Viewer in His Time*. London: Reaktion Books, 2017.

Michelangelo's Last Judgment: *The Renaissance Response*. Berkeley: University of California Press, 1998.

Barolsky, Paul. *Giotto's Father and the Family of Vasari's* Lives. University Park, PA: Pennsylvania State University Press, 1992.

Why Mona Lisa Smiles and Other Tales by Vasari. University Park, PA: Pennsylvania State University Press, 2010.

Barriault, Anne B., Andrew Ladis, Norman E. Land, and Jerylden M. Wood, eds. *Reading Vasari*. London: Philip Wilson Publishers, 2005.

Bartoli, Roberta. "Bandinelli contro tutti. L'artista negli occhi dei contemporanei." In *Baccio Bandinelli scultore e maestro (1493–1560)*, edited by Detlef Heikamp and Beatrice Paolozzi Strozzi, 36–59. Exh. cat. Florence: Giunti, 2014.

Bartuschat, Johannes. "Dalla vita del poeta alla vita dell'artista: tendenze del genere biografico nel Quattrocento." *Letteratura & arte* 1 (2003): 49–57.

Bastogi, Nadia. *Andrea Boscoli*. Florence: Edifir, 2008.

Bätschmann, Oskar. "The 'Paragone' of Sculpture and Painting in Florence around 1550." In *Le Vite del Vasari: genesi, topoi, ricezione. Atti del convegno, 13–17 febbraio 2008, Firenze, Kunsthistorisches Institut, Max-Planck-Institut*, edited by Katja Burzer, Charles Davis, Sabine Feser, and Alessandro Nova, 85–96. Venice: Marsilio, 2010.

Battaglia, Salvatore, and Giorgio Bàrberi Squarotti, eds. *Grande Dizionario della Lingua Italiana*. Turin: Unione Tipografico-Editrice Torinese, 1961, 21 vols.

Battisti, Eugenio. *Filippo Brunelleschi: l'opera completa*. Milan: Electa Editrice, 1976.

"La critica a Michelangelo dopo il Vasari." *Rinascimento* 7 (1956): 135–157.

"La critica a Michelangelo prima del Vasari." *Rinascimento* 5 (1954): 117–132.

Michelangelo: fortuna di un mito. Cinquecento anni di critica letteraria e artistica. Edited by Giuseppa Saccaro del Buffa. Florence: Olschki, 2012.

Rinascimento e Barocco. Turin: Einaudi, 1960.

Baumann, Mario. "'Come Now, Best of Painters, Paint My Lover': The Poetics of Ecphrasis in the *Anacreontea*." In *Imitate Anacreon! Mimesis, Poiesis and the Poetic Inspiration in the Carmina Anacreontea*, edited by Manuel Baumbach and Nicola Dummler, 113–130. Berlin / Boston: De Gruyter, 2014.

Bausi, Francesco. "Orcagna o Burchiello? (sul sonetto *Molti poeti han già descritto amore*)." *Interpres* (1993): 275–293.

Baxandall, Michael. *Giotto and the Orators: Humanist Observers of Painting in Italy and the Discovery of Pictorial Composition, 1350–1450*. Oxford: Clarendon Press, 1971.

Words for Pictures: Seven Papers on Renaissance Art and Criticism. New Haven, CT: Yale University Press, 2003.

Bayer, Andrea, ed. *Art and Love in Renaissance Italy*. Exh. cat. New York: Metropolitan Museum of Art, 2008.

Bec, Christian. "Artisti scriventi e artisti scrittori in Italia (secondo Trecento – primo Novecento)." In *Letteratura italiana e arti figurative: Atti del XII Convegno dell'Associazione internazionale per gli studi di lingua e letteratura italiana (Toronto, Hamilton, Montreal, 6–10 maggio 1985)*, edited by Antonio Franceschetti, 3 vols. 1: 81–100. Florence: Olschki, 1988.

Becatti, Giovanni. "Plinio e Vasari." In *Studi di storia dell'arte in onore di Valerio Mariani*, edited by Istituto di storia dell'arte dell'Università di Napoli, 173–182. Naples: Libreria scientifica, 1971.

Beer, Susanna de. *The Poetics of Patronage: Poetry as Self-Advancement in Giannantonio Campano*. Turnhout: Brepols, 2013.

Beltramini, Guido, Howard Burns, and Davide Gasparotto, eds. *Pietro Bembo e le arti*. Venice: Marsilio, 2013.

Beltramini, Guido, Davide Gasparotto, and Adolfo Tura, eds. *Pietro Bembo e l'invenzione del Rinascimento*. Exh. cat. Venice: Marsilio, 2013.

Benassi, Alessandro. "La teoria e la prassi dell'emblema e dell'impresa." In *Letteratura e arti visive nel Rinascimento*, edited by Gianluca Genovese and Andrea Torre, 113–146. Rome: Carocci, 2019.

Benedetti, Stefano. "Poesia funebre nella Roma leonina. Appunti sulle *Lacrimae* per Celso Mellini." In *Il petrarchismo: un modello di poesia per l'Europa*, edited by Loredana Chines, 2 vols., 2: 393–421. Rome: Bulzoni, 2006.

Benini Clementi, Enrica. *Riforma religiosa e poesia popolare a Venezia nel Cinquecento: Alessandro Caravia*. Florence: Olschki, 2000.

Bertelli, Sergio. "Egemonia linguistica come egemonia culturale e politica nella Firenze cosimiana." *Bibliothèque d'Humanisme et Renaissance* 38 (1976): 249–283.

Berti, Ada. *Artisti-poeti italiani dei secoli XV e XVI*. Florence: Seeber, 1907.

Bertolini, Lucia. "Sulla precedenza della edizione volgare del *De pictura* di Leon Battista Alberti." In *Studi per Umberto Carpi: un saluto da allievi e colleghi pisani*, edited by Marco Santagata and Alfredo Stussi, 181–210. Pisa: ETS, 2000.

Bertolini, Lucia, and Francesco Paolo Di Teodoro. "'Al mio gran foco': Raffaello poeta tra passato prossimo, Petrarca e l'antico." In *Raffaello: 1520–1483*, edited by Marzia Faietti and Matteo Lanfranconi, 287–293. Exh. cat. Milan: Skira, 2020.

Beuzelin, Cécile. "Jacopo Pontormo: A Scholarly Craftsman." In *The Artist as Reader: On Education and Non-Education of Early Modern Artists*, edited by Heiko Damm, Michael Thimann, and Claus Zittel, 69–104. Leiden: Brill, 2013.

Białostocki, Jan. "Doctus Artifex and the Library of the Artist in XVIth and XVIIth Century." In *De Arte et Libris: Festschrift Erasmus, 1934–1984*, edited by Abraham Horodisch, 11–22. Amsterdam: Erasmus Antiquariaat en Boekhandel, 1984.

Biffi, Marco, and Raffaella Setti. "Varchi consulente linguistico." In *Benedetto Varchi, 1503–1565: Atti del convegno, Firenze, 16–17 dicembre 2003*, edited by Vanni Bramanti, 25–67. Rome: Edizioni di storia e letteratura, 2007.

Biow, Douglas. *Vasari's Words: The Lives of the Artists as a History of Ideas in the Italian Renaissance*. Cambridge: Cambridge University Press, 2018.

Bizzarini, Marco, and Elisabetta Selmi, eds. *Fortunato Martinengo: un gentiluomo del Rinascimento fra arti, lettere e musica*. Brescia: Morcelliana, 2018.

Blunt, Anthony. *Artistic Theory in Italy, 1450–1600*. Oxford: Clarendon Press, 1956.

Bober, Phyllis Pray. "The *Coryciana* and the Nymph Corycia." *Journal of the Warburg and Courtauld Institutes* 40 (1977): 223–239.

Bolzoni, Lina. "Citazioni letterarie nella Giuntina: per una mappa delle loro funzioni." In *I mondi di Vasari: accademia, lingua, religione, storia, teatro*, edited by Alessandro Nova and Luigi Zangheri, 141–60. Venice: Marsilio, 2013.

Poesia e ritratto nel Rinascimento. Texts edited by Federica Pich. Rome: Laterza, 2008.

Bolzoni, Lina, Barbara Allegranti, Arianna Andrei *et alii*, eds. *Con parola brieve e con figura: libri antichi di imprese e emblemi*. Exh. cat. Lucca: Pacini Fazzi, 2004.

Bolzoni, Marco Simone, Furio Rinaldi, and Patrizia Tosini, eds. *Dopo il 1564: L'eredità di Michelangelo a Roma nel tardo Cinquecento*. Rome: De Luca, 2017.

Bondi, Fabrizio. *Il principe per emblemi: letteratura e immagini del politico tra Cinquecento e Seicento*. Bologna: Il Mulino, 2016.

Bora, Giulio, Manuela Kahn-Rossi, and Francesco Porzio, eds. *Rabisch: Il grottesco nell'arte del Cinquecento*. Exh. cat. Milan: Skira, 1998.

Boström, Antonia. "A New Addition to Zanobi Lastricati. *Fiorenza* or the *Venus Anadyomene*: The Fluidity of Iconography." *The Sculpture Journal* 1 (1997): 1–6.

Bourdieu, Pierre. *Distinction: A Social Critique of the Judgement of Taste*. Translated by Richard Nice. Cambridge, MA: Harvard University Press, 1984.

———. *Outline of a Theory of Practice*. Translated by Richard Nice. Cambridge: Cambridge University Press, 1977.

———. *The Rules of Art*. Translated by Susan Emanuel. Stanford: Stanford University Press, 1996.

Bragantini, Renzo. "Figure e topoi della prestezza." In *Festina lente: il tempo della scrittura nella letteratura del Cinquecento*, edited by Chiara Cassiani and Maria Cristina Figorilli, 15–30. Rome: Edizioni di Storia e Letteratura, 2014.

Bramanti, Vanni. "Corrispondenza e corrispondenti nel secondo libro dei *Sonetti* di Benedetto Varchi." *Italique* 19 (2016): 87–112.

Bramble, J. C. *Persius and the Programmatic Satire: A Study in Form and Imagery*. Cambridge: Cambridge University Press, 1974.

Brancato, Dario. "Ancora sui libri di Benedetto Varchi. Notizie dalle biblioteche inglesi." In *Storia, tradizione e critica dei testi. Per Giuliano Tanturli*, edited by Isabella Becherucci and Concetta Bianca, 2 vols., 1: 47–60. Lecce and Rovato: Pensa Multimedia Editore, 2017.

———. "I componimenti toscani di Benedetto Varchi nelle Filze Rinuccini della Biblioteca Nazionale Centrale di Firenze: genesi, riuso, varietà." *Schriften des Italienzentrums der Freien Universität Berlin* 3 (2019) (*La cultura poetica di Benedetto Varchi*, edited by Bernhard Huß and Selene Maria Vatteroni): 71–89. https://www.geisteswissenschaften.fu-berlin.de/italienzentrum/publikationen/schriften-italienzentrum/Schriften-Band-3/Schriften-des-Italienzentrums-Bd_-3.pdf.

Brock, Maurice. *Bronzino*. Translated by David Poole Radzinowicz and Christine Schultz-Touge. Paris: Flammarion, 2002.

Brucker, Gene A. *Renaissance Florence*. New York: Wiley, 1969.

Brunner, Fernand. "La doctrine de la matière chez Avicébron." *Revue de théologie et de philosophie*, n. s. 6 (1956): 261–279.

Bucchi, Gabriele. "*La Guerra de' topi e de' ranocchi* attribuita ad Andrea del Sarto: un falso di Francesco Redi?" *Filologia italiana* 4 (2007): 1–46.

Butler, Kim E. "La *Cronaca rimata* di Giovanni Santi e Raffaello." In *Raffaello e Urbino: la formazione giovanile e i rapporti con la città natale*, edited by Lorenza Mochi Onori, 38–43. Milan: Electa, 2009.

Calamandrei, Piero. *Scritti e inediti celliniani*. Edited by Carlo Cordié. Florence: La Nuova Italia, 1971.

Caldwell, Dorigen Sophie. *The Sixteenth-Century Italian Impresa in Theory and Practice*. New York: AMS Press, 2004.

Cambon, Glauco. *Michelangelo's Poetry: Fury of Form*. Princeton, NJ: Princeton University Press, 1985.

Cammarella Falsitta, Loretta, and Alessandro Falsitta. *Cellini, Bandinelli, Ammannati: la fontana del Nettuno in Piazza della Signoria a Firenze*. Milan: Skira, 2009.

Campbell, Stephen J. "Bronzino, Aemulatio und die Liebe." In *Aemulatio: Kulturen des Wettstreits in Text und Bild (1450–1620)*, edited by Jan-Dirk Müller, Ulrich Pfisterer, Anna Kathrin Bleuler, and Fabian Jonietz, 193–210. Berlin / Boston: De Gruyter, 2011.

———. "Counter Reformation Polemic and Mannerist Counter-Aesthetics: Bronzino's *Martyrdom of St. Lawrence* in San Lorenzo." *RES: Anthropology and Aesthetics* 46 (2004): 98–119.

———. "Eros in the Flesh: Petrarchan Desire, the Embodied Eros, and Male Beauty in Italian Art, 1500–1540." *The Journal of Medieval and Early Modern Studies* 35 (2005): 629–662.

———. "'Fare Una Cosa Morta Parer Viva': Michelangelo, Rosso, and the (Un)Divinity of Art." *The Art Bulletin* 84 (2002): 596–620.

Campeggiani, Ida. *Le varianti della poesia di Michelangelo: scrivere per via di porre*. Lucca: Pacini Fazzi, 2012.

Campo, Roberto E. "A Poem to a Painter: The *Élégie à Janet* and Ronsard's Dilemma of Ambivalence." *French Forum* 12 (1987): 273–287.

Capecchi, Gabriella, Amelio Fara, and Detlef Heikamp, eds. *Palazzo Pitti: la reggia rivelata*. Exh. cat. Florence: Giunti, 2003.

Capretti, Elena. "Firenze 1575–1579: l'impresa del *Giudizio Universale*, le polemiche, la casa di via del Mandorlo." In *Innocente e calunniato: Federico Zuccari (1539/40–1609) e le vendette d'artista*, edited by Cristina Acidini Luchinat and Elena Capretti, 122–127. Exh. cat. Florence: Giunti, 2009.

Caputo, Vincenzo. *"Dar spirto a' marmi, a i color fiato e vita": Giorgio Vasari scrittore*. Milan: FrancoAngeli, 2015.

Carboni, Fabio. "L'Orcagna e il Frusta." *Cultura neolatina* 69 (2009): 111–165.

Carlson, Raymond. "'Eccellentissimo poeta et amatore divinissimo:' Benedetto Varchi and Michelangelo's Poetry at the Accademia Fiorentina." *Italian Studies* 69 (2014): 169–188.

Carpané, Lorenzo. "Maggi, Girolamo." In *Dizionario biografico degli Italiani* 67: 347–350. Rome: Istituto della Enciclopedia Italiana, 2006.

Carrai, Stefano. "Italian Poetry of the Renaissance: Recent Studies and New Perspectives." *I Tatti Studies in the Italian Renaissance* 17 (2014): 207–215.

L'usignolo di Bembo: un'idea della lirica italiana del Rinascimento. Rome: Carocci, 2006.

Carrara, Eliana. "La nascita dell'Accademia del Disegno di Firenze: il ruolo di Borghini, Torelli e Vasari." In *Les académies dans l'Europe humaniste: Idéaux et pratiques*, edited by Marc Deramaix, Perrine Galand-Hallyn, Ginette Vagenheim, and Jean Vignes, 129–162. Geneva: Droz, 2008.

"Plinio e l'arte degli Antichi e dei Moderni: ricezione e fortuna dei libri XXXIV–XXXVI della *Naturalis historia* nella Firenze del XVI secolo (dall'Anonimo Magliabechiano a Vasari)." *Archives internationales d'histoire des sciences* 61 (2011): 367–381.

"Vasari e Borghini sul ritratto: gli appunti pliniani della *Selva di notizie*; ms. K 783.16 del Kunsthistorisches Institut di Firenze." *Mitteilungen des Kunsthistorischen Institutes in Florenz* 44 (2000, but: 2001): 243–291.

"Vincenzo Borghini, Lelio Torelli e l'Accademia del disegno di Firenze: alcune considerazioni." *Annali di critica d'arte* 2 (2006): 545–568.

Cast, David. *The Calumny of Apelles: A Study in the Humanist Tradition*. New Haven, CT: Yale University Press, 1981.

The Delight of Art: Giorgio Vasari and the Traditions of Humanistic Discourse. University Park, PA: Pennsylvania State University Press, 2009.

Cecchi, Alessandro. "'Famose Frondi de cui santi honori…': un sonetto del Varchi e il ritratto di Lorenzo Lenzi dal Bronzino." *Artista* 2 (1990): 8–19.

"Il Bronzino, Benedetto Varchi e l'Accademia Fiorentina: ritratti di poeti, letterati e personaggi illustri della corte medicea." *Antichità viva* 30 (1991): 17–28.

"Il maggiordomo ducale Pierfrancesco Riccio e gli artisti della corte medicea." *Mitteilungen des Kunsthistorischen Institutes in Florenz* 42 (1998): 115–143.

"Il Tribolo, la corte medicea, i letterati e gli artisti suoi amici." In *Niccolò detto il Tribolo tra arte, architettura e paesaggio*, edited by Elisabetta Pieri and Luigi Zangheri, 29–36. Poggio a Caiano (Prato): Il Commune, 2001.

Celi, Paolo. "'Che non l'arebbe fat'a pena Cuio.' Porte, apparati e facciate fiorentine in tre testi pasquineschi dello Zoppo carrozziere e dell'Etrusco." Forthcoming in: *Mitteilungen des Kunsthistorischen Institutes in Florenz* 63.1 (2021).

"Delle rime del Bronzino pittore Libro primo." PhD diss., Università di Pisa, 2018.

Cerasuolo, Angela. *Literature and Artistic Practice in Sixteenth-Century Italy*. Translated by Helen Glanville. Leiden: Brill, 2017.

Chastel, André. *Arte e umanesimo a Firenze al tempo di Lorenzo il Magnifico: studi sul Rinascimento e sull'umanesimo platonico*. Translated in Italian by Renzo Federici. Turin: Einaudi, 1964.

"L'artista." In *L'uomo del Rinascimento*, edited by Eugenio Garin, 237–270. Rome: Laterza, 1988.

Chiarini, Marco, Alan P. Darr, and Cristina Gianni, eds. *L'ombra del genio: Michelangelo e l'arte a Firenze, 1537-1631*. Milan: Skira, 2002.

Chiodo, Domenico. *Più che le stelle in cielo: poeti nell'Italia del Cinquecento*. Manziana (Rome): Vecchiarelli, 2013.

Chiummo, Carla. "Bronzino e l'Accademia Fiorentina." In *The Italian Academies 1525–1700: Networks of Culture, Innovation and Dissent*, edited by Jane E. Everson, Denis V. Reidy, and Lisa Sampson, 258–76. Abingdon: Routledge, 2016.

"Burlesque Connotations in the Pictorial Language in Bronzino's Poetry." *Renaissance and Reformation/Renaissance et Réforme* 40.1 (2017): 211–237.

"'Sì grande Apelle, e non minore Apollo:' il nonsense del Bronzino manierista." In *"Nominativi fritti e mappamondi." Il nonsense nella letteratura italiana*, edited by Giuseppe Antonelli and Carla Chiummo, 93–124. Rome: Salerno editrice, 2009.

Ciardi, Roberto Paolo, Claudio Casini, and Lucia Tongiorgi Tomasi. *Scultura a Pisa tra Quattro e Seicento*. Florence: Cantini, 1987.

Cicconi, Maurizia. "Lastricati, Zanobi." In *Dizionario biografico degli Italiani* 63: 814–816. Rome: Istituto della Enciclopedia Italiana, 2004.

Ciccuto, Marcello. "Il pregiudizio dell'alterità. Per Benvenuto Cellini biografo 'in figura.'" In *Scritti autobiografici di artisti tra Quattrocento e Cinquecento: seminari di letteratura artistica*, edited by Maria Pia Sacchi and Monica Visioli, 89–99. Pavia: Edizioni Santa Caterina, 2017.

L'immagine del testo: episodi di cultura figurativa nella letteratura italiana. Rome: Bonacci, 1990.

"Un'antica canzone di Giotto e i pittori di Boccaccio. Nascita dell'identità artistica." *Intersezioni* 16 (1996): 403–416.

Clements, Robert J. "Michelangelo on Effort and Rapidity in Art." *Journal of the Warburg and Courtauld Institutes* 17 (1954): 301–310.

Clifton, James. "Vasari on Competition." *The Sixteenth Century Journal* 27 (1996): 23–41.

Cochrane, Eric W. *Florence in the Forgotten Centuries, 1527-1800: A History of Florence and the Florentines in the Age of the Grand Dukes*. Chicago: University of Chicago Press, 1973.

Colasanti, Arduino. "Gli artisti nella poesia del Rinascimento: fonti poetiche per la storia dell'arte italiana." *Repertorium für Kunstwissenschaft* 27 (1904): 193–220.

Cole, Janie. "Cultural Clientelism and Brokerage Networks in Early Modern Florence and Rome: New Correspondence between the Barberini and Michelangelo Buonarroti the Younger." *Renaissance Quarterly* 60 (2007): 729–788.

Cole, Michael W. *Ambitious Form: Giambologna, Ammanati, and Danti in Florence*. Princeton, NJ: Princeton University Press, 2011.

"Cellini's Blood." *The Art Bulletin* 81 (1999): 215–235.

"Grazzini, Allori and Judgment in the Montauti Chapel." *Mitteilungen des Kunsthistorischen Institutes in Florenz* 45 (2001): 302–312.

Cole, Michael W., and Diletta Gamberini. "Vincenzo Danti's Deceits." *Renaissance Quarterly* 69 (2016): 1296–342.

Collareta, Marco. "Benvenuto Cellini ed il destino dell'oreficeria." In *Benvenuto Cellini. Kunst und Kunsttheorie im 16. Jahrhundert*, edited by Alessandro Nova and Anna Schreurs, 161–169. Cologne: Böhlau Verlag, 2003.

"Le arti sorelle: teoria e pratica del 'paragone.'" In *La pittura in Italia. Il Cinquecento*, edited by Giuliano Briganti, 2 vols., 2: 569–580. Milan: Electa, 1988.

"Nouvelles études sur le paragone entre les arts." *Perspective* 1 (2015): 153–160.

"Una restituzione al Tasso legnaiolo." *Paragone* 35 (1984): 81–91.

"Varchi e le arti figurative." In *Benedetto Varchi, 1503–1565: Atti del convegno, Firenze, 16–17 dicembre 2003*, edited by Vanni Bramanti, 173–184. Rome: Edizioni di storia e letteratura, 2007.

"Vincenzo Danti e l'oreficeria." In *I grandi bronzi del Battistero: l'arte di Vincenzo Danti, discepolo di Michelangelo*, edited by Charles Davis and Beatrice Paolozzi Strozzi, 77–85. Exh. cat. Florence: Giunti, 2008.

Conforti, Claudia. "Gli Uffizi e il Corridoio Vasariano nella rifondazione di Firenze ducale." In *Vasari, gli Uffizi e il duca*, edited by Claudia Conforti, Francesca Funis, Francesca De Luca, and Cristina Acidini Luchinat, 61–71. Exh. cat. Florence: Giunti, 2011.

Vasari architetto. Milan: Electa, 1993.

Conforti, Claudia, Francesca Funis, Francesca De Luca, and Cristina Acidini Luchinat, eds. *Vasari, gli Uffizi e il duca*. Exh. cat. Florence: Giunti, 2011.

Conte, Floriana. *Tra Napoli e Milano: viaggi di artisti nell'Italia del Seicento*. 2 vols. Florence: Edifir Edizioni, 2014.

Conte, Gian Biagio. *Genres and Readers: Lucretius, Love Elegy, Pliny's Encyclopedia*. Translated by Glenn W. Most. Baltimore: Johns Hopkins University Press, 1994.
    The Rhetoric of Imitation: Genre and Poetic Memory in Virgil and Other Latin Poets. Translated by Charles Segal. Ithaca, NY, and London: Cornell University Press, 1986.
Contini, Gianfranco. *Varianti e altra linguistica: una raccolta di saggi (1938–1968)*. Turin: Einaudi, 1970.
Corrado, Fabrizio, and Paolo San Martino. *Scherzi d'artista*. Turin: Celid, 2008.
    "Un Buffalmacco del Cinquecento: Paolo Geri detto Pilucca." *Critica d'arte*, 8th ser., 74.51/52 (2012): 113–120.
Corsaro, Antonio. "Dinamiche relazionali nella *Vita* di Benvenuto Cellini." " In *Scritti autobiografici di artisti tra Quattrocento e Cinquecento: seminari di letteratura artistica*, edited by Maria Pia Sacchi and Monica Visioli, 101–19. Pavia: Edizioni Santa Caterina, 2017.
    "Intorno alle rime di Michelangelo Buonarroti: la silloge del 1546." *Giornale storico della letteratura italiana* 185 (2008): 536–560.
Corti, Gino. "Il testamento di Zanobi Lastricati, scultore fiorentino del Cinquecento." *Mitteilungen des Kunsthistorischen Institutes in Florenz* 32 (1988): 580–581.
Costamagna, Philippe. *Pontormo*. Translated in Italian by Alberto Curotto. Milan: Electa, 1994.
Cotensin, Ismène. "De Vasari à Bandello: la nouvelle de Filippo Lippi (I, 58) et la représentation des artistes. Forme celestiali e non asini da vettura." *La Rivista. Études culturelles italiennes Sorbonne Universités* 0 (2013): 39–48. https://etudesitaliennes.hypotheses.org/files/2016/02/Cotensin.pdf.
Cox-Rearick, Janet. *Bronzino's Chapel of Eleonora in the Palazzo Vecchio*. Berkeley: University of California Press, 1993.
    Dynasty and Destiny in Medici Art: Pontormo, Leo X, and the Two Cosimos. Princeton, NJ: Princeton University Press, 1984.
Cremonini, Stefano. "Una topica petrarchesca: i versi in morte di amici, colleghi e mecenati." In *Il petrarchismo: un modello di poesia per l'Europa*, edited by Loredana Chines, 2 vols., 2: 329–347. Rome: Bulzoni, 2006.
Cropper, Elizabeth. "On Beautiful Women: Parmigianino, Petrarchismo, and the Vernacular Style." *The Art Bulletin* 58 (1976): 374–394.
Crum, Roger J. "'Cosmos, the World of Cosimo': The Iconography of the Uffizi Façade." *The Art Bulletin* 71 (1989): 237–253.
Cursietti, Mauro. "Alle radici della poesia burchiellesca: l'Orcagna pittore e lo Za buffone." *La parola del testo* 6 (2002): 109–131.
Curtius, Ernst Robert. *European Literature and the Latin Middle Ages*. Translated by Willard R. Trask. New York: Pantheon Books, 1953.
Dall'Orto, Giovanni. "Socratic Love as a Disguise for Same-Sex Love in the Italian Renaissance." *Journal of Homosexuality* 16 (1989): 33–66.
Dal Poggetto, Paolo. *Le arti nelle Marche al tempo di Sisto V*. Cinisello Balsamo: Silvana, 1992.
Daly, Peter M. *The Emblem in Early Modern Europe: Contributions to the Theory of the Emblem*. Farnham: Ashgate, 2014.
    Literature in the Light of the Emblem: Structural Parallels Between the Emblem and Literature in the Sixteenth and Seventeenth Centuries. 2nd ed. Toronto: University of Toronto Press, 1998.
Damianaki, Chrysa. "Pontormo's Lost Frescoes in San Lorenzo, Florence: A Reappraisal of Their Religious Content." In *Forms of Faith in Sixteenth-Century Italy*, edited by Abigail Brundin and Matthew Treherne, 77–118. Burlington, VT: Ashgate, 2009.
Damm, Heiko, Michael Thimann, and Claus Zittel, eds. *The Artist as Reader: On Education and Non-Education of Early Modern Artists*. Leiden: Brill, 2013.
Danzi, Massimo. *La biblioteca del cardinal Pietro Bembo*. Geneva: Droz, 2005.
Davis, Charles. "Benvenuto Cellini and the Scuola Fiorentina." *North Carolina Museum of Art Bulletin* 13.4 (1976): 1–70.
    "Frescoes by Vasari for Sforza Almeni, 'Coppiere' to Duke Cosimo I." *Mitteilungen des Kunsthistorischen Institutes in Florenz* 24.2 (1980): 127–202.
    "La *Madonna* del Monasterio degl'Angeli: Danti e l'ambiente intorno a Benedetto Varchi, tra la quiete fraterna e la stanza dei *Sonetti spirituali*." In *I grandi bronzi del Battistero: l'arte di Vincenzo Danti,*

discepolo di Michelangelo, edited by Charles Davis and Beatrice Paolozzi Strozzi, 165–203. Exh. cat. Florence: Giunti, 2008.

———. "Michelangelo, Jacone and the Confraternity of the Virgin Annunciate Called 'Dell'Orciuolo.'" *Apollo* 156 (2002): 22–29.

Davis, Charles, and Beatrice Paolozzi Strozzi, eds. *I grandi bronzi del Battistero: l'arte di Vincenzo Danti, discepolo di Michelangelo*. Exh. cat. Florence: Giunti, 2008.

De Girolami Cheney, Liana. *Giorgio Vasari: Artistic and Emblematic Manifestations*. Washington, DC: New Academia Publishing, 2012.

Degl'Innocenti, Luca, Brian Richardson, and Chiara Sbordoni, eds. *Interactions between Orality and Writing in Early Modern Italian Culture*. London / New York: Routledge, 2016.

De Liso, Daniela. *Salvator Rosa tra pennelli e versi*. Florence: Franco Cesati, 2018.

Del Vita, Alessandro. "Giorgio Vasari e Benvenuto Cellini." *Il Vasari*, n. s. 15.4 (1957): 124–134.

De Maio, Romeo. *Michelangelo e la Controriforma*. Rome: Laterza, 1978.

De Marchi, Pietro. "Leonardo da Vinci narratore, o la libertà dell'artista. Su una novella di Matteo Bandello (I, 58)." *Strumenti critici* 114 (2007): 177–191.

Dempsey, Charles. "Some Observations on the Education of Artists in Florence and Bologna during the Later Sixteenth Century." *The Art Bulletin* 62 (1980): 552–569.

Department of Art, Brown University, ed. *Children of Mercury: The Education of Artists in the Sixteenth and Seventeenth Centuries*. Providence, RI: Department of Art, Brown University, 1984.

DePrano, Maria. "'No Painting on Earth Would Be More Beautiful:' An Analysis of Giovanna degli Albizzi's Portrait Inscription." *Renaissance Studies* 22 (2008): 617–641.

De Smet, Ingrid, and Paul White, eds. *Sodalitas litteratorum: Le compagnonnage littéraire néo-latin et français à la Renaissance. Études à la mémoire de Philip Ford = Studies in Memory of Philip Ford*, edited by Ingrid De Smet and Paul White, 11–28. Geneva: Droz, 2019.

Di Benedetto, Arnaldo. "Un'introduzione al petrarchismo cinquecentesco." *Italica* 83 (2006): 170–215.

Di Filippo Bareggi, Claudia. "In nota alla politica culturale di Cosimo I: l'Accademia Fiorentina." *Quaderni storici* 8 (1973): 527–574.

Dionisotti, Carlo. *Geografia e storia della letteratura italiana*. 2nd ed. Turin: Einaudi, 1971.

———. "Leonardo uomo di lettere." *Italia Medioevale e Umanistica* 5 (1962): 183–216.

Donetti, Dario. *Francesco da Sangallo e l'identità dell'architettura toscana*. Milan: Officina Libraria, 2020.

Dressen, Angela. *The Intellectual Education of the Renaissance Artist 1450–1550*. Cambridge: Cambridge University Press, 2021.

Dubard de Gaillarbois, Frédérique. "A proposito del *Capitolo in lode della prigione*, di un bernismo celliniano e di una scrittura materiale." *Studi italiani* 45 (2011): 5–38.

———. "De la 'beffa' comme l'un des beaux-arts ou l'inquiétante esthétique de Lasca." *La Rivista. Études culturelles italiennes Sorbonne Universités* 0 (2013): 109–123. https://etudesitaliennes.hypotheses.org/files/2016/02/Dubard-.pdf.

———. "Le *cagnaccio* et le *botolo*: dialogue d'artistes ou portrait croisé de Cellini et de Vasari." *Chroniques italiennes web* 16 (2009). http://chroniquesitaliennes.univ-paris3.fr/PDF/web16/DUBARDweb16.pdf.

Edelstein, Bruce. *Eleonora di Toledo and the Creation of the Boboli Gardens*. Forthcoming.

———. "Le sculture nel Giardino di Boboli ai tempi di Cosimo I. Una passeggiata con il Principe." In *La prima statua per Boboli. Il Villano restaurato*, edited by Alessandra Griffo, pp. 77–87. Livorno: Sillabe, 2019.

Emiliani, Andrea, and Giorgio Cerboni Baiardi. *Il Bronzino*. Busto Arsizio: Bramante editrice, 1960.

Emison, Patricia A. *Creating the "Divine" Artist: From Dante to Michelangelo*. Leiden: Brill, 2004.

EpistolART. Les correspondances artistiques à la Renaissance. Database: http://web.philo.ulg.ac.be/epistolart_bd/.

Everson, Jane E., Denis V. Reidy, and Lisa Sampson, eds. *The Italian Academies 1525–1700: Networks of Culture, Innovation and Dissent*. London: Routledge, 2016.

Fabretti, Magda, and Anna Guidarelli. "Ricerche sulle iniziative dei Medici nel campo minerario da Cosimo I a Ferdinando I." In *Potere centrale e strutture periferiche nella Toscana del '500*, edited by Giorgio Spini, 139–217. Florence: Olschki, 1980.

Falaschi, Enid T. "Giotto: The Literary Legend." *Italian Studies* 27 (1972): 1–27.

Falciani, Carlo. *Pontormo*. Cinisello Balsamo: Silvana, 2014.
⸻. "Della pittura sacra, ma anche di 'fianchi, stomachi ec.'" In *Bronzino: Pittore e poeta alla corte dei Medici*, edited by Carlo Falciani and Antonio Natali, 277–295. Exh. cat. Florence: Mandragora, 2010.
Falciani, Carlo, and Antonio Natali, eds. *Bronzino: Pittore e poeta alla corte dei Medici*. Exh. cat. Florence: Mandragora, 2010.
Falletti, Franca, and Jonathan K. Nelson. *Filippino Lippi e Pietro Perugino: la* Deposizione *della Santissima Annunziata e il suo restauro*. Livorno: Sillabe, 2004.
Fane-Saunders, Peter. *Pliny the Elder and the Emergence of Renaissance Architecture*. Cambridge: Cambridge University Press, 2016.
Fantuzzi, Guia. "Giovanni da San Giovanni e il cinismo." *Artista* (2003): 130–149.
Fasano Guarini, Elena. "Cosimo I de' Medici, duca di Firenze, granduca di Toscana." In *Dizionario Biografico degli Italiani* 30: 30–48. Rome: Istituto della Enciclopedia Italiana, 1984.
Fedi, Roberto. "La cultura del Pontormo." In *Pontormo e Rosso: atti del convegno di Empoli e Volterra*, edited by Roberto P. Ciardi and Antonio Natali, 26–46. Venice: Marsilio, 1996.
Feinberg, Larry J. *From Studio to Studiolo: Florentine Draftsmanship under the First Medici Grand Dukes*. Seattle: University of Washington Press, 1991.
Fenech Kroke, Antonella. *Giorgio Vasari: la fabrique de l'allégorie. Culture et fonction de la personification au Cinquecento*. Florence: Olschki, 2011.
Feo, Michele Arcangelo. Review of Benedetto Varchi, *Liber carminum Benedicti Varchii*, edited by Aulo Greco, Rome: Edizione Abete, 1969. *Annali della Scuola Normale Superiore di Pisa. Classe di lettere e filosofia* 3 (1973): 1193–1200.
Ferrari, Oreste, and Ferruccio Ulivi. *Salvator Rosa, pittore e poeta nel centenario della morte (1615–1673)*. Rome: Accademia nazionale dei Lincei, 1975.
Ferretti, Emanuela. "Cosimo I, la magnificenza dell'acqua e la celebrazione del potere: la nuova capitale dello stato territoriale fra architettura, città e infrastrutture." *Annali di storia di Firenze* 9 (2015): 9–33.
Ferrone, Silvano. "Dialoghi poetici fra i Tasso e il Varchi." In *Scritti in memoria di Dino Pieraccioni*, edited by Michele Bandini and Federico G. Pericoli, 148–188. Florence: Giuntina, 1993.
⸻. "Indice universale dei carmi latini di Benedetto Varchi." *Medioevo e Rinascimento* 8 (1997): 125–195.
⸻. "Materiali varchiani." *Paragone / Letteratura* 48–50 (2003): 84–113.
Ferroni, Giovanni. "*Carmina conversa*. Appunti su traduzioni e auto-traduzioni liriche di Benedetto Varchi." *L'Ellisse. Studi storici di letteratura italiana* 13.1 (2018): 29–52.
⸻. "'Si ricerca ancora dottrina non picciola.' Varchi, la poesia pastorale e i *Sonetti* del 1555." *Italique* 20 (2017): 211–259.
Ferroni, Giulio, ed. *Poesia italiana del Cinquecento*. New ed. Milan: Lampi di stampa, 1999.
Fidanza, Giovan Battista. *Vincenzo Danti (1530–1576)*. Florence: Olschki, 1996.
Fiore, Francesco Paolo. "Danti, Vincenzo." In *Dizionario Biografico degli Italiani* 32: 667–673. Rome: Istituto della Enciclopedia Italiana, 1986.
Firpo, Massimo. *Gli affreschi di Pontormo a San Lorenzo: eresia, politica e cultura nella Firenze di Cosimo I*. Turin: Einaudi, 1997.
Flemming, Victoria von. "Gezähmte Phantasie. Cellinis Entwürfe für das Akademie-Siegel." In *Benvenuto Cellini. Kunst und Kunsttheorie im 16. Jahrhundert*, edited by Alessandro Nova and Anna Schreurs, 59–98. Cologne: Böhlau Verlag, 2003.
Folliero-Metz, Grazia Dolores. *Le Rime di Michelangelo Buonarroti nel loro contesto*. Heidelberg: Winter, 2004.
Fragnito, Gigliola. "Censura ecclesiastica e pasquinate." In *Ex marmore: Pasquini, pasquinisti, pasquinate nell'Europa moderna. Atti del colloquio internazionale Lecce, Otranto, 17–19 novembre 2005*, edited by Chrysa Damianaki, Paolo Procaccioli, and Angelo Romano, 181–186. Manziana (Rome): Vecchiarelli, 2006.
Franceschini, Chiara. "Giudizi negativi e stime d'artista nel mondo di Vasari e Michelangelo." Forthcoming in: *Mitteilungen des Kunsthistorischen Institutes in Florenz* 63.1 (2021).
Franci, Beatrice. "Le sculture di Simone e Francesco Mosca nel transetto del duomo di Orvieto." In *Le cattedrali, segni delle radici cristiane in Europa*, edited by Laura Andreani and Alessandra Cannistrà, 225–236. Orvieto: Opera del Duomo di Orvieto, 2010.

Frangenberg, Thomas. *Der Betrachter: Studien zur florentinischen Kunstliteratur des 16. Jahrhunderts.* Berlin: Mann, 1990.

———. "The Art of Talking about Sculpture: Vasari, Borghini and Bocchi." *Journal of the Warburg and Courtauld Institutes* 58 (1995): 115–131.

———. "The Notion of Beauty in Francesco Bocchi's *Bellezze Della Città Di Fiorenza*." In *Concepts of Beauty in Renaissance Art*, edited by Francis Ames-Lewis and Mary Rogers, 191–198. Aldershot: Ashgate, 1997.

Franklin, David. *Painting in Renaissance Florence 1500–1550.* New Haven, CT: Yale University Press, 2001.

Freedberg, David. *The Power of Images: Studies in the History and Theory of Response.* Chicago: University of Chicago Press, 1989.

Freedman, Luba. *Titian's Portraits through Aretino's Lens.* University Park, PA: Pennsylvania State University Press, 1995.

Fumagalli, Elena. "On the Medici Payroll: At Court from Cosimo I to Ferdinando II (1540–1670)." In *The Court Artist in Seventeenth-Century Italy*, edited by Elena Fumagalli and Raffaella Morselli, 95–136. Rome: Viella, 2014.

Furlan, Francesco. "*In familiæ patriæque absentia* ossia D'illigittimità e sradicamento." In *Exil und Heimatferne in der Literatur des Humanismus von Petrarca bis zum Anfang des 16. Jahrhunderts: L'esilio e la lontananza dalla patria nella letteratura umanistica dal Petrarca all'inizio del Cinquecento*, edited by Francesco Furlan, Gabriel Siemoneit, and Hartmut Wulfram, 139–159. Tübingen: Narr Francke Attempto Verlag, 2019.

Furlotti, Barbara. *A Renaissance Baron and His Possessions: Paolo Giordano I Orsini, Duke of Bracciano (1541–1585).* Turnhout: Brepols, 2012.

Furno, Albertina. *La vita e le rime di Angiolo Bronzino, studio.* Pistoia: Flori, 1902.

Gallucci, Margaret Ann. *Benvenuto Cellini: Sexuality, Masculinity, and Artistic Identity in Renaissance Italy.* New York: Palgrave Macmillan, 2003.

Gambarota, Paola. *Irresistible Signs: The Genius of Language and Italian National Identity.* Toronto: University of Toronto Press, 2011.

Gamberini, Diletta. "A Bronze Manifesto of Petrarchism: Domenico Poggini's Portrait Medal of Benedetto Varchi." *I Tatti Studies in the Italian Renaissance* 19 (2016): 359–383.

———. "'Antica purezza e dantesca gravità': forme dell'appropriazione della poesia di Michelangelo nella Firenze di Cosimo I." *Italique* 21 (2018): 199–233.

———. "Benedetto Varchi, Giovann'Angelo Montorsoli e il Tempio dei 'Pippi:' un inedito dialogo in versi agli albori dell'Accademia Fiorentina del Disegno." *Mitteilungen des Kunsthistorischen Institutes in Florenz* 57.1 (2015): 139–144.

———. "'Divine' or Not? Poetic Responses to the Art of Michelangelo." In *Tributes to David Freedberg*, edited by Claudia Swan, 431–441. Turnhout: Brepols, 2019.

———. "I colloqui poetici degli artisti con Benedetto Varchi." *La Rivista. Études culturelles italiennes Sorbonne Universités* 5 (2017): 61–69. https://etudesitaliennes.hypotheses.org/files/2017/05/4GamberiniFini-1.pdf.

———. "La 'concucia nana' di Federico Zuccari: critica d'arte in versi all'ombra del *Giudizio Universale* per la cupola di Santa Maria del Fiore." *Mitteilungen des Kunsthistorischen Institutes in Florenz* 59.3 (2017): 362–387.

———. "Nel nome del fratello: Pietro Vasari e la memorializzazione poetica dell'arte nell'Italia di fine Cinquecento." *Italique* 22 (2019): 81–104.

———. "The Artist as a Dantista: Francesco da Sangallo's Dantism in Mid-Cinquecento Florence." *Dante Studies* 135 (2017): 169–191.

Garavelli, Enrico. "Riflessi polemici, difesa del fiorentino e culto di Dante in una lettera inedita di Luca Martini a Vincenzio Borghini." *Neuphilologische Mitteilungen* 108 (2007): 709–727.

Gardner Coates, Victoria C. "'Sculpsit Cellinius Neptunam:' The Biography of the *Neptune* Fountain in Cellini's *Vita*." *Renaissance Studies* 19 (2005): 604–618.

Gareffi, Andrea. "Le *Esequie del divino Michelangelo* o del manierismo consacrato: la misura dell'eternità." *Biblioteca Teatrale* 23/24 (1979): 39–69.

Gasparotto, Davide. "La barba di Pietro Bembo." *Annali della Scuola Normale Superiore di Pisa. Classe di Lettere e Filosofia* 4 (1996): 183–206.

Gaston, Robert W. "Towards a Post-Modernist Bronzino?" In *Agnolo Bronzino: Medici Court Artist in Context*, edited by Andrea M. Gáldy, 107–127. Newcastle upon Tyne: Cambridge Scholars Publishing, 2013.

———. "Vasari and the Rhetoric of Decorum." In *The Ashgate Research Companion to Giorgio Vasari*, edited by David J. Cast, 245–260. Burlington, VT: Ashgate, 2014.

Geremicca, Antonio. *Agnolo Bronzino: 'la dotta penna al pennel dotto pari.'* Rome: UniversItalia, 2013.

———. "'Damone' per 'Crisero' e gli altri: Benedetto Varchi e gli artisti (prima e dopo l'Accademia Fiorentina)." In *Intrecci virtuosi. Letterati artisti e accademie nell'Italia Centrale tra Cinque e Seicento*, edited by Carla Chiummo, Antonio Geremicca, and Patrizia Tosini, 11–26. Rome: De Luca, 2017.

———. "Inedite corrispondenze in versi tra Benedetto Varchi e Agnolo Bronzino." *Italique* 22 (2019): 59–80.

———. "Sulla scia di Agnolo Bronzino, Alessandro Allori sodale di Benedetto Varchi. Un ritratto 'misconosciuto' del letterato e un suo sonetto inedito." *La Rivista. Études culturelles italiennes Sorbonne Université* 6 (2017): 87–113. https://etudesitaliennes.hypotheses.org/files/2017/05/6GeremiccaFiniNouveau.pdf.

Giachino, Luisella. *Al carbon vivo del desio di gloria: retorica e poesia celebrativa nel Cinquecento*. Alessandria: Edizioni dell'Orso, 2008.

Giannotti, Alessandra. *Il teatro di natura – Niccolò Tribolo e le origini di un genere: la scultura di animali nella Firenze del Cinquecento*. Florence: Olschki, 2007.

———. "Pericoli, Niccolò, detto il Tribolo." In *Dizionario Biografico degli Italiani* 82: 379–386. Rome: Istituto della Enciclopedia Italiana, 2015.

Gilson, Simon A. *Reading Dante in Renaissance Italy: Florence, Venice and the 'Divine Poet.'* Cambridge: Cambridge University Press, 2018.

Giontella, Massimo, and Riccardo Fubini. "L'uomo con il compasso e la sfera: note sulla recente edizione delle *Antiquarie prospetiche romane* attribuite a Bramante." *Archivio storico italiano* 164 (2006): 325–334.

Girard, René. *Deceit, Desire, and the Novel: Self and Other Literary Structure*. Translated by Yvone Freccero. Baltimore: Johns Hopkins Press, 1965.

Girardi, Enzo Noè. *Studi su Michelangiolo scrittore*. Florence: Olschki, 1974.

Girotto, Carlo Alberto. "Le accademie di Anton Francesco Doni." In *Intrecci virtuosi: letterati, artisti e accademie tra Cinque e Seicento*, edited by Carla Chiummo, Antonio Geremicca, and Patrizia Tosini, 27–37. Rome: De Luca, 2017.

Giunta, Claudio. *Versi a un destinatario: saggio sulla poesia italiana del Medioevo*. Bologna: Il Mulino, 2002.

Goffen, Rona. *Renaissance Rivals: Michelangelo, Leonardo, Raphael, Titian*. New Haven, CT: Yale University Press, 2002.

Goldhill, Simon. "The Naïve and Knowing Eye: Ecphrasis and the Culture of Viewing in the Hellenistic World." In *Art and Text in Ancient Greek Culture*, edited by Simon Goldhill and Robin Osborne, 197–223. Cambridge: Cambridge University Press, 1994.

Gombrich, Ernst H. "The Leaven of Criticism in Renaissance Art." In *Art, Science, and History in the Renaissance*, edited by Charles S. Singleton, 3–42. Baltimore: Johns Hopkins University Press, 1967.

———. "The Renaissance Concept of Artistic Progress and Its Consequences." In *Actes du XVIIme Congrès International d'histoire de l'art*, 291–307. La Haye: Imprimerie Nationales del Pays-Bas, 1955.

Goodchild, Karen Hope. "Bizarre Painters and Bohemian Poets: Poetic Imitation and Artistic Rivalry in Vasari's Biography of Piero di Cosimo." In *The Ashgate Research Companion to Giorgio Vasari*, edited by David Cast, 129–144. Farnham: Ashgate, 2014.

Gordon, Dillian. "Two Newly Identified Panels from Mariotto Di Nardo's Altarpiece for the Da Filicaia Chapel in S. Maria Degli Angeli, Florence." *The Burlington Magazine* 155.1318 (2013): 25–28.

Gordon, Lewis Hall. "Burchiello Inedito (A Propos of M. Messina: Domenico Di Giovanni Detto Il Burchiello. Sonetti Inediti. Firenze, Olschki, 1952)." *Italica* 33 (1956): 121–139.

Graul, Jana. "'Particolare Vizio de' Professori di Queste Nostre Arti': On the Concept of Envy in Vasari's *Vite*." *I Tatti Studies in the Italian Renaissance* 18 (2015): 113–146.

Greenblatt, Stephen. *Renaissance Self-Fashioning: From More to Shakespeare*. Chicago: University of Chicago Press, 1980.

Greene, Thomas M. *The Light in Troy: Imitation and Discovery in Renaissance Poetry*. New Haven, CT: Yale University Press, 1982.

Gregory, Sharon. "The Unsympathetic Exemplar in Vasari's Life of Pontormo." *Renaissance Studies* 23 (2009): 1–32.
    "Vasari on Imitation." In *The Ashgate Research Companion to Giorgio Vasari*, edited by David J. Cast, 223–243. Farnham: Ashgate, 2014.

Guassardo, Giada. "Una nota sul tema del carcere nella *Vita* e nelle liriche di Benvenuto Cellini." *Rassegna europea di letteratura italiana* 48 (2016): 91–109.

Guidetti, Fabio. "'Quo nemo insolentius.' La 'superbia' di Parrasio e l'autoaffermazione dell'artista nella Grecia classica." *Opera Nomina Historiae* 1 (2009):1–50.

Guthmüller, Bodo, Berndt Hamm, and Andreas Tönnesmann, eds. *Künstler und Literat: Schrift- und Buchkultur in der europäischen Renaissance*. Wiesbaden: Harrassowitz, 2006.

Hajnóczi, Gàbor. "Principî vitruviani nella teoria della pittura di Leon Battista Alberti." In *Leon Battista Alberti: teorico delle arti e gli impegni civili del* De re aedificatoria. *Atti dei convegni internazionali del Comitato Nazionale VI centenario della nascita di Leon Battista Alberti: Mantova, 17–19 ottobre 2002, Mantova, 23–25 ottobre 2003*, edited by Arturo Calzona, 189–202. Florence: Olschki 2007.

Hall, Marcia B. *After Raphael: Painting in Central Italy in the Sixteenth Century*. Cambridge: Cambridge University Press, 1999.
    Renovation and Counter-Reformation: Vasari and Duke Cosimo in S.ta Maria Novella and S.ta Croce, 1565-1577. Oxford: Clarendon Press, 1979.

Hansen, Morten Steen. "Butchering the Bull of St. Luke: Unpublished Writings by and about the Painter-Poet Giovanni Da San Giovanni." *Analecta Romana Instituti Danici* 40/41 (2016): 63–89.
    In Michelangelo's Mirror: Perino Del Vaga, Daniele Da Volterra, Pellegrino Tibaldi. University Park, PA: Pennsylvania State University Press, 2013.
    "'Pro bono malum:' Francesco Furini, Ludovico Ariosto, and the Verso of Painting." *The Art Bulletin* 99.3 (2017): 62–92.

Hardison, O. B. *The Enduring Monument: A Study of the Idea of Praise in Renaissance Literary Theory and Practice*. Chapel Hill: University of North Carolina Press, 1962.

Heffernan, James A. W. *Museum of Words: The Poetics of Ekphrasis from Homer to Ashbery*. Chicago: University of Chicago Press, 1993.

Hegener, Nicole. *Divi Iacobi Eqves: Selbstdarstellung im Werk des Florentiner Bildhauers Baccio Bandinelli*. Munich: Deutscher Kunstverlag, 2008.

Heikamp, Detlef. "Federico scandalista." In *Innocente e calunniato: Federico Zuccari (1539/40–1609) e le vendette d'artista*. Exh. cat. Edited by Cristina Acidini and Elena Capretti, 46–77. Florence: Giunti, 2009.
    "Federico Zuccari e la cupola di Santa Maria del Fiore: la fortuna critica dei suoi affreschi." In *Federico Zuccari: le idee, gli scritti*, edited by Bonita Cleri, 139–157. Milan: Electa, 1997.
    "Luca Martini, i suoi amici artisti e Pierino da Vinci." In *Pierino da Vinci: Atti della giornata di studio, Vinci, Biblioteca leonardiana, 26 maggio 1990*, edited by Marco Cianchi, 67–71. Florence: Becocci, 1995.
    "Poesie in vituperio del Bandinelli." *Paragone / Arte* 15 (1964): 59–68.
    "Rapporti fra accademici ed artisti nella Firenze del '500 da memorie e rime dell'epoca." *Il Vasari* n. s. 1, 15 (1957): 139–163.

Hendler, Sefy. *La guerre des arts: le Paragone peinture-sculpture en Italie XVe–XVIIe siècle*. Rome: L'Erma di Bretschneider, 2013.
    Un mostro grazioso e bello: Bronzino e l'universo burlesco del Nano Morgante. Florence: Maschietto, 2016.

Hermans, Lex. "Going Local: Three Sixteenth-Century Florentine Views on Donatello's *St. George*." In *Transformation of Vernacular Expression in Early Modern Arts*, edited by Joost Keizer and Todd M. Richardson, 99–122. Leiden: Brill, 2012.

Hessler, Christiane J. "'Ne supra crepidam sutor!' [Schuster, bleib bei deinem Leisten!]: Das Diktum des Apelles seit Petrarca bis zum Ende des Quattrocento." *Fifteenth-Century Studies* 33 (2008): 133–150.
    Zum Paragone: Malerei, Skulptur und Dichtung in der Rangstreitkultur des Quattrocento. Berlin / Boston: De Gruyter, 2014.

Hughes, Anthony. "'An Academy for Doing.' I: The Accademia Del Disegno, the Guilds and the Principiate in Sixteenth-Century Florence." *The Oxford Art Journal* 9.1 (1986): 3–10.

Huß, Bernhard. "'Cantai colmo di gioia, e senza inganni.' Benedetto Varchis *Sonetti* (*parte prima*) im Kontext des italienischen Cinquecento-Petrarkismus." *Romanistisches Jahrbuch* 52 (2001): 133–157.

Hutton, James. *The Greek Anthology in Italy to the Year 1800*. Ithaca, NY: Cornell University Press, 1935.
Iacopozzi, Stefania. "Il ciclo scultoreo degli Uffizi: genesi e sviluppo di un progetto non solo celebrativo." In *Gli uomini illustri del loggiato degli Uffizi: storia e restauro*, edited by Magnolia Scudieri, photographs by Aurelio Amendola, 15–33. Florence: Edifir, 2001.
Le statue degli "illustri toscani" nel loggiato degli Uffizi. Florence: Alinea, 2000.
Ijsewijn, Jozef, ed. *Coryciana*. Rome: Herder, 1997.
Iordanou, Ioanna. *Venice's Secret Service: Organizing Intelligence in the Renaissance*. Oxford: Oxford University Press, 2019.
Isella, Dante. *Lombardia stravagante: testi e studi dal Quattrocento al Seicento tra lettere e arti*. Turin: Einaudi, 2005.
Iser, Wolfgang. *The Act of Reading: A Theory of Aesthetic Response*. 7th printing. Baltimore: Johns Hopkins University Press, 1997.
Jakobus, Fredrika H. "Vasari's Peremina: The Paradigmatic Academician." In *Reading Vasari*, edited by Anne B. Barriault, Andrew Ladis, Norman E. Land, and Jeryldene M. Wood, 101–115. London: Wilson, 2005.
Joannides, Paul. *The Drawings of Michelangelo and His Followers in the Ashmolean Museum*. Cambridge: Cambridge University Press, 2007.
Jonietz, Fabian. *Das Buch zum Bild: Die "Stanze nuove" im Palazzo Vecchio, Giorgio Vasaris "Ragionamenti" und die Lesbarkeit der Kunst im Cinquecento*. Berlin: Deutscher Kunstverlag, 2017.
"Poggini, Domenico." In *Dizionario Biografico degli Italiani* 84 (2015). Only available in digital edition: https://www.treccani.it/enciclopedia/domenico-poggini_%28Dizionario-Biografico%29/.
Kettering, Sharon. *Patrons, Brokers, and Clients in Seventeenth-Century France*. Oxford: Oxford University Press, 1986.
Kirn, Paul. "Friedrich der Weise und Jacopo de' Barbari." *Jahrbuch der Preußischen Kunstsammlungen* 46 (1925): 130–134.
Komorowski, Marek. "Donatello's *St. George* in a Sixteenth-Century Commentary by Francesco Bocchi: Some Problems of the Renaissance Theory of Expression in Art." In *Ars auro prior: Studia Ioanni Białostocki sexagenario dicata*, edited by Juliusz A. Chrościcki, 61–66. Warsaw: Państwowe Wydawnictwo Naukowe, 1981.
Koomen, Arjan de. "Aristotle's *Poetics* into Art Criticism: Francesco Bocchi in Praise of Donatello's *Saint George*." In *Officine del nuovo: sodalizi fra letterati, artisti ed editori nella cultura italiana fra Riforma e Controriforma. Atti del simposio internazionale, Utrecht 8–10 novembre 2007*, edited by Harald Hendrix and Paolo Procaccioli, 89–103. Manziana (Rome): Vecchiarelli, 2008.
Koos, Marianne. "'Amore dolce-amaro.' Giorgione und das ideale Knabenbildnis der venezianischen Renaissancemalerei." *Marburger Jahrbuch für Kunstwissenschaft* 33 (2006): 113–174.
"Petrarkistische Theorie oder künstlerische Praxis? Zur Malerei des Giorgionismo im Spiegel des lyrischen Männerporträts." In *Stumme Diskurs der Bilder: Reflexionsformen des Ästhetischen in der Kunst der Frühen Neuzeit*, edited by Valeska Rosen, Klaus Krüger, and Rudolf Preimesberger, 53–84. Berlin: Deutscher Kunstverlag, 2003.
Kreytenberg, Gert. *Orcagna, Andrea di Cione: Ein universeller Künstler der Gotik in Florenz*. Mainz: P. von Zabern, 2000.
Kusch-Arnhold, Britta. *Pierino da Vinci*. Münster: Rhema, 2008.
Lambin, Gérard. *Anacréon: Fragments et imitations*. Rennes: Presses Universitaires de Rennes, 2002.
Lanciarini, Vincenzo. *Dei pittori Taddeo e Federigo Zuccari di S. Angelo in Vado*. Jesi: Spinaci, 1893.
Land, Norman E. "Leonardo Da Vinci in a Tale by Matteo Bandello." *Discoveries* 23 (2006): 9–17.
The Viewer as Poet: The Renaissance Response to Art. University Park, PA: Pennsylvania State University Press, 1994.
Lanza, Antonio. *Polemiche e berte letterarie nella Firenze del primo Rinascimento (1375–1449)*. 2nd ed. Rome: Bulzoni, 1989.
Latini, Francesca. "Edizione e commento di cinque capitoli in burla del Bronzino." 2 vols. PhD diss., Università Europea di Roma, 2015.
Lazzaro, Claudia. "Michelangelo's Medici Chapel and Its Aftermath: Scattered Bodies and Florentine Identities under the Duchy." *California Italian Studies* 6.1 (2016): 1–35.
Lecchini Giovannoni, Simona. *Alessandro Allori*. Turin: Allemandi, 1991.

Lee, Rensselaer W. "'Ut Pictura Poesis': The Humanistic Theory of Painting." *The Art Bulletin* 22.4 (1940): 197–269.

Lejeune, Philippe. *Je est un autre: l'autobiographie de la littérature aux médias*. Paris: Seuil, 1980.

Lingo, Stuart. "Looking Askance: Agnolo Bronzino's *Martyrdom of San Lorenzo* between the Medici, Mercury and Machiavelli." *Rivista di letterature moderne e comparate* 68.3 (2015): 217–242.

Lippincott, Kristen. "'Un gran pelago': The Impresa and the Medal Reverse in Fifteenth-Century Italy." In *Perspectives on the Renaissance Medal*, edited by Steven K. Scher, 75–96. New York: Garland, 2000.

Lohr, Wolf-Dietrich. "*E nuovi Omeri, e Plati*: Painted Characters in Portraits by Andrea del Sarto and Bronzino." In *Poetry on Art: Renaissance to Romanticism*, edited by Thomas Frangenberg, 48–100. Donington: Shaun Tyas, 2003.

Lo Re, Salvatore. "Gli amori omosessuali del Varchi: storia e leggenda." In *Extravagances amoureuses: l'amour au-delà de la norme à la Renaissance. Actes du colloque international du groupe de recherche "Cinquecento plurale," Tours, 18–20 septembre 2008 = Stravaganze amorose: l'amore oltre la norma nel Rinascimento*, edited by Elise Boillet and Chiara Lastraioli, 279–295. Paris: Champion, 2010.

——. *Politica e cultura nella Firenze cosimiana: studi su Benedetto Varchi*. Manziana (Rome): Vecchiarelli, 2008.

——. "Varchi, Doni e l'Accademia Fiorentina." In *Dissonanze concordi: temi, questioni e personaggi intorno ad Anton Francesco Doni*, edited by Giovanna Rizzarelli, 171–197. Bologna: Il Mulino, 2013.

——. "Varchi e Michelangelo." *Annali della Scuola Normale Superiore di Pisa. Classe di Lettere e Filosofia* series 5, 4 (2012): 485–516, 613–614.

Long, Pamela O. "Multi-Tasking 'Pre-Professional' Architect/Engineers and Other Bricolagic Practitioners as Key Figures in the Elision of Boundaries between Practice and Learning in Sixteenth-Century Europe: Some Roman Examples." In *The Structures of Practical Knowledge*, edited by Matteo Valleriani, 223–246. Cham: Springer, 2017.

Longhi, Silvia. *Lusus: il capitolo burlesco nel Cinquecento*. Padua: Antenore, 1983.

Louvel, Liliane. *Poetics of the Iconotext*. Edited by Karen Jacobs. Translated by Laurence Petit. Farnham: Ashgate, 2011.

Love, Harold. *The Culture and Commerce of Texts: Scribal Publication in Seventeenth-Century England*. Amherst: University of Massachusetts Press, 1998.

Lucas Fiorato, Corinne. "Appunti sulle immagini negli scritti di Giraldi Cinthio." *Studi giraldiani. Letteratura e teatro* 5 (2019): 265–294.

——. "Cellini, Vasari et Borghini: un trio problématique." *Chroniques italiennes web* 16 (2009). http://chroniquesitaliennes.univ-paris3.fr/numeros/Web16.html.

Macola, Novella. *Sguardi e scritture: figure con libro nella ritrattistica italiana della prima metà del Cinquecento*. Venice: Istituto Veneto di Scienze, Lettere ed Arti, 2007.

Mangone, Carolina. "Like Father, Like Son: Bernini's Filial Imitation of Michelangelo." *Art History* 37 (2014): 666–687.

Manning, John. *The Emblem*. London: Reaktion Books, 2004.

Marani, Pietro C. *La Vergine delle Rocce della National Gallery di Londra: maestro e bottega di fronte al modello. Quarantaduesima lettura vinciana*. Florence: Giunti, 2003.

Marongiu, Marcella. "'…Perché egli imparassi a disegnare gli fece molte carte stupendissime…' I disegni di Michelangelo per Tommaso de' Cavalieri." *Horti Hesperidum. Studi di storia del collezionismo e della storiografia artistica* 4.1 (2014): 11–55.

Masi, Giorgio. "Le statue parlanti del cavaliere e altri prodigi pasquineschi fiorentini (Bandinelli, Cellini, Michelangelo)." In *Ex marmore: Pasquini, pasquinisti, pasquinate nell'Europa moderna. Atti del colloquio internazionale Lecce, Otranto, 17–19 novembre 2005*, edited by Chrysa Damianaki, Paolo Procaccioli, and Angelo Romano, 221–274. Manziana (Rome): Vecchiarelli, 2006.

——. "Pazzi, Alfonso de', detto l'Etrusco." In *Dizionario biografico degli Italiani* 82: 1–3. Rome: Istituto della Enciclopedia Italiana, 2015.

——. "Politica, arte e religione nella poesia dell'Etrusco (Alfonso de' Pazzi)." In *Autorità, modelli e antimodelli nella cultura artistica e letteraria tra Riforma e Controriforma. Atti del seminario internazionale di studi, Urbino–Sassocorvaro, 9–11 novembre 2006*, edited by Antonio Corsaro, Harald Hendrix, and Paolo Procaccioli, 301–358. Manziana (Rome): Vecchiarelli, 2007.

"Un sonetto inedito sull'Ercole e Caco di Baccio Bandinelli, con ipotesi attributive (e il topos burlesco del dimissionario)." *Italique* 16 (2013): 79–109.

Massinelli, Anna Maria. "Accursio Baldi e la statua di Sisto V a Fermo." In *Le arti nelle Marche al tempo di Sisto V*, edited by Paolo Del Poggetto, 232–235. Cinisello Balsamo: Silvana, 1992.

Mauriello, Adriana. "Artisti e beffe in alcune novelle del '500 (Lasca, Doni, Fortini)." *Letteratura & arte* 3 (2005): 81–91.

Mazzoni, Guido. *Sulla poesia moderna*. Bologna: Il Mulino, 2005.

McCrory, Martha. "Cesare Federighi Da Bagno: Medalist, Gem Engraver and Sculptor in the Workshop of Cellini." In *Coming About… A Festschrift for John Shearman*, edited by Lars R. Jones and Louisa C. Matthew, 227–234. Cambridge, MA: Harvard University Art Museums, 2001.

McHam, Sarah Blake. *Pliny and the Artistic Culture of the Italian Renaissance: The Legacy of the* Natural History. New Haven, CT: Yale University Press, 2013.

McLaughlin, Martin L. *Literary Imitation in the Italian Renaissance: The Theory and Practice of Literary Imitation in Italy from Dante to Bembo*. Oxford: Oxford University Press, 1995.

Menchini, Carmen. "Sguardi incrociati. Rappresentazioni di Firenze e Venezia all'epoca di Anton Francesco Doni." In I marmi *di Anton Francesco Doni: la storia, i generi e le arti*, edited by Giovanna Rizzarelli, 3–26. Florence: Olschki, 2012.

Mendelsohn, Leatrice. *Paragoni: Benedetto Varchi's* Due Lezzioni *and Cinquecento Art Theory*. Ann Arbor, MI: UMI Research Press, 1982.

Merleau-Ponty, Maurice. *Signs*. Translated by Richard C. McCleary. Evanston, IL: Northwestern University Press, 1964.

Middeldorf, Ulrich, and Friedrich Kriegbaum. "Forgotten Sculpture by Domenico Poggini." *The Burlington Magazine for Connoisseurs* 53 (1928): 9–17.

Mitchell, Barbara Irene. "The Patron of Art in Giorgio Vasari's *Lives*." PhD diss., Indiana University, 1975.

Moroncini, Ambra. *Michelangelo's Poetry and Iconography in the Heart of the Reformation*. London: Routledge, 2019.

Mozzati, Tommaso. "'È dunque Artista vocabolo non Latino, ma Toscano': Michelangelo poeta nelle lettere fiorentine da Francesco Berni a Benedetto Varchi." In *Il Cinquecento a Firenze: "Maniera moderna" e Controriforma*, edited by Falciani Carlo and Antonio Natali, 41–51. Exh. cat. Florence: Mandragora, 2017.

Giovanfrancesco Rustici: le Compagnie del Paiuolo e della Cazzuola. Arte, letteratura, festa nell'età della Maniera. Florence: Olschki, 2008.

Mulas, Luisa. "L'Aretino e i Medici." In *Pietro Aretino nel cinquecentenario della nascita: Atti del convegno di Roma-Viterbo-Arezzo (28 settembre–1 ottobre 1992), Toronto (23–24 ottobre 1992), Los Angeles (27–29 ottobre 1992)*, 2 vols., 2: 535–572. Rome: Salerno editrice, 1995.

Müller, Jan-Dirk, Ulrich Pfisterer, Anna Kathrin Bleuler, and Fabian Jonietz, eds. *Aemulatio: Kulturen des Wettstreits in Text und Bild (1450–1620)*. Berlin / Boston: De Gruyter, 2011.

Murphy, Caroline. *Isabella de' Medici: The Glorious Life and Tragic End of a Renaissance Princess*. London: Faber and Faber, 2008.

Murphy, Stephen. *The Gift of Immortality: Myths of Power and Humanist Poetics*. Madison: Fairleigh Dickinson University Press, 1997.

Nagel, Alexander. "Gifts for Michelangelo and Vittoria Colonna." *The Art Bulletin* 79 (1997): 647–668.

Nalezyty, Susan. *Pietro Bembo and the Intellectual Pleasures of a Renaissance Writer and Art Collector*. New Haven, CT: Yale University Press, 2017.

Nava, Marco. "Note in corso d'opera sugli autografi di Alessandro Allori." *Theory and Criticisim of Literature & Arts* 5.1 (2021): 115–128.

Nelson, Jonathan K. "Creative Patronage: Luca Martini and the Renaissance Portrait." *Mitteilungen des Kunsthistorischen Institutes in Florenz* 39 (1995, but 1996): 282–303.

"Luca Martini, *dantista*, and Pierino da Vinci's relief of the Death of Count Ugolino della Gherardesca and His Sons." In *Pierino da Vinci: Atti della giornata di studio, Vinci, Biblioteca leonardiana, 26 maggio 1990*, edited by Marco Cianchi, 39–43. Florence: Becocci, 1995.

"The High Altar-Piece of SS. Annunziata in Florence: History, Form, and Function." *The Burlington Magazine* 139 (1997): 84–94.

Nesi, Alessandro. *Ciano profumiere: un personaggio stravagante della corte di Cosimo de' Medici*. Florence: Maniera, 2015.

———. "Le amichevoli sfide di Pierino da Vinci e Stoldo Lorenzi, per conto di Luca Martini." *Erba d'Arno* 126–127 (2012): 54–71.

———. "Tra classicismo e modernità: un'identificazione e una proposta per gli esordi di Zanobi Lastricati." *Bollettino d'arte* 114 (2000): 79–86.

———. "Zanobi Lastricati tra i cantieri medicei fiorentini e la cattedrale di Pistoia." In *Giorgio Vasari: tra capitale medicea e città del dominio*, edited by Nicoletta Lepri, Simona Esseni, and Maria Camilla Pagnini, 69–78. Florence: Edifir, 2012.

Nesi, Alessandro, Piero Frizzi, and Chiara Piani, eds. *Il Cacciatore di Zanobi Lastricati nel Giardino di Boboli: storia e restauro*. Florence: Associazione Per Boboli, 2013.

Niccoli, Ottavia. "Anticlericalismo italiano e rituali dell'infamia da Alessandro VI a Pio V." *Studi storici* 43 (2002): 921–965.

Nigro, Salvatore Silvano. *L'orologio di Pontormo: invenzione di un pittore manierista*. Milan: Rizzoli, 1998.

Orvieto, Paolo, and Lucia Brestolini. *La poesia comico-realistica: dalle origini al Cinquecento*. Rome: Carocci, 2000.

Osborne, Mary Tom. *Advice-to-a-Painter Poems, 1633–1856: An Annotated Finding List*. Austin: University of Texas, 1949.

Ostrow, Steven F. "The Discourse of Failure in Seventeenth-Century Rome: Prospero Bresciano's *Moses*." *The Art Bulletin* 88.2 (2006): 267–291.

Panofsky, Erwin. *Idea: Contributo alla storia dell'estetica*. Translated by Edmondo Cione. Florence: La Nuova Italia, 1952.

Paolino, Laura. "Il 'geminato ardore' di Benedetto Varchi. Storia e costruzione di un canzoniere 'ellittico.'" *Nuova rivista di letteratura italiana* 7 (2004): 233–314.

Paolozzi Strozzi, Beatrice. "Gli 'Sposi' del Museo di Strasburgo: un'appendice al catalogo del Bronzino." In *Opere e giorni: studi su mille anni di arte europea dedicati a Max Seidel*, edited by Klaus Bergdolt and Giorgio Bonsanti, 505–512. Venice: Marsilio, 2001.

Paris, Jean. *Lisible/visible: Six essais de critique générative*. Paris: Seghers/Laffont, 1978.

Parker, Deborah. "Bronzino and the Diligence of Art." *Artibus et historiae* 25.49 (2004): 161–174.

———. *Bronzino: Renaissance Painter as Poet*. Cambridge: Cambridge University Press, 2000.

———. *Michelangelo and the Art of Letter Writing*. New York: Cambridge University Press, 2010.

———. "The Poetry of Patronage: Bronzino and the Medici." *Renaissance Studies* 17 (2003): 230–245.

———. "Towards a Reading of Bronzino's Burlesque Poetry." *Renaissance Quarterly* 50 (1997): 1011–44.

———. "Vasari's *Ritratto di sei poeti toscani*: A Visible Literary History." *Modern Language Notes* 127.1 (2012): 204–215.

Parma Armani, Elena. *Perin del Vaga: l'anello mancante. Studi sul manierismo*. Genoa: Sagep, 1986.

Parnotte, Alexandre. "Simeoni, Gabriele." In *Dizionario Biografico degli Italiani* 92: 686–689. Rome: Istituto della Enciclopedia Italiana, 2018.

Passignat, Émilie. *Il Cinquecento: le fonti per la storia dell'arte*. Rome: Carocci, 2017.

———. "The Order, the Itinerary, the Beholder. Considerations on Some Aspects of the *Ragionamenti del Sig. Cavalier Giorgio Vasari*." In *Giorgio Vasari and the Birth of the Museum*, edited by Maia Wellington Gahtan, 151–162. Burlington, VT: Ashgate, 2014.

Pasti, Stefania. "La produzione letteraria." In *Bronzino*, edited by Claudio Strinati, 201–237. Rome: Viviani, 2010.

Patetta, Luciano. *Bramante e la sua cerchia: A Milano e in Lombardia 1480–1500*. Milan: Skira, 2001.

———. "La celebrazione degli artisti e degli architetti negli scritti poetici e letterari del Rinascimento." In *Lettere e arti nel Rinascimento. Atti del X convegno internazionale (Chianciano–Pienza, 20–23 luglio 1998)*, edited by Luisa Secchi Tarugi, 603–624. Florence: Franco Cesati, 2000.

Pedrotti, Giorgio. *Alfonso de' Pazzi, accademico e poeta*. Pescia: Tipografia E. Cipriani, 1902.

Pellegrini, Rosa Maria Galleni. "'Ut sculptura poësis:' Danese Cattaneo 'non meno ne lo scrivere che ne lo scolpire eccellente.'" In *Danese Cattaneo da Colonnata, scultore, poeta, architetto: Collezione = Sculptor, Poet, Architect: Collection (Colonnata 1512–Padova 1572)*, edited by Giovanna Baldissin Molli, Rosa

Maria Galleni Pellegrini, Cristina Andrei, and Luisa Passeggia, 2 vols., 1: 320–345. Fosdinovo (Massa Carrara): Associazione culturale PerCorsi d'arte, 2013.

Pellegrino, Francesca. "Elaborazioni di alcuni principali topoi artistici nei *Coryciana*." In *Visuelle Topoi: Erfindung und tradiertes Wissen in den Künsten der italienischen Renaissance*, edited by Ulrich Pfisterer and Max Seidel, 217–262. Munich / Berlin: Deutscher Kunstverlag, 2003.

———. "La poesia sull'arte: il caso di Giovan Battista Marino nella tradizione della poesia sulle arti figurative." PhD diss., Università degli Studi di Salerno, 2003.

Pepe, Mario. "Svolgimenti nella concezione del disegno in Anton Francesco Doni: dalla *Diceria* al Montorsoli del 1546 al trattato del 1549." In *Disegno e disegni: per Luigi Grassi*, edited by Anna Forlani Tempesti and Simonetta Prosperi Valenti Rodinò, 123–132. Rimini: Galleria, 1998.

Perini, Giovanna. "Carmi inediti su Raffaello e sull'arte della prima metà del Cinquecento a Roma e Ferrara e il mondo dei *Coryciana*." *Römisches Jahrbuch der Bibliotheca Hertziana* 32 (1997/98, but 2002): 367–407.

———. "Poems by Bolognese Painters from the Renaissance to the Late Baroque." In *Poetry on Art: Renaissance to Romanticism*, edited by Thomas Frangenberg, 3–28. Donington: Shaun Tyas, 2003.

Pfisterer, Ulrich. *Donatello und die Entdeckung der Stile 1430–1445*. Munich: Hirmer, 2002.

———. *Lysippus und seine Freunde: Liebesgaben und Gedächtnis im Rom der Renaissance, oder, Das erste Jahrhundert der Medaille*. Berlin: Akademie Verlag, 2008.

———. "Phidias und Polyklet von Dante bis Vasari: Zu Nachruhm und künstlerischer Rezeption antiker Bildhauer in der Renaissance." *Marburger Jahrbuch für Kunstwissenschaft* 26 (1999): 61–97.

———. *Raffael. Glaube, Liebe, Ruhm*. Munich: Beck, 2019.

———. "'Soweit die Flügel meines Auges tragen.' Leon Battista Albertis Imprese und Selbstbildnis." *Mitteilungen des Kunsthistorischen Institutes in Florenz* 42 (1998): 205–251.

———. "Subject to Mood Swings: Michelangelo, Titian and Adrian Willaert on Creativity." In *Senses of Sight: Towards a Multisensorial Approach of the Image. Essays in Honor of Victor I. Stoichita*, edited by Henri de Riedmatten, Nicolas Galley, Jean-François Corpataux, and Valentin Nussbaum, 151–66. Rome: L'Erma di Bretschneider, 2015.

Pich, Federica. *I poeti davanti al ritratto: Da Petrarca a Marino*. Lucca: Pacini Fazzi, 2010.

———. "La poesia e il ritratto." In *Letteratura e arti visive nel Rinascimento*, edited by Gianluca Genovese and Andrea Torre, 57–84. Rome: Carocci, 2019.

Pierguidi, Stefano. "Francesco Salviati e il concorso per il sigillo per l'Accademia del Disegno." *Atti e memorie dell'Accademia Toscana di Scienze e Lettere "La Colombaria"* 80 (2015): 191–203.

———. "Il *Disegno* di Doni e la disputa sul 'paragone': alle origini dell'Accademia del Disegno." In *Dissonanze concordi: temi, questioni e personaggi intorno ad Anton Francesco Doni*, edited by Giovanna Rizzarelli, 199–213. Bologna: Il Mulino, 2013.

Piermei, Alessandro Filippo. *Memorabilium sacri ordinis Servorum B. M. V. breviarium: Nunc primum fine appropinquante saeculi septimi a fundatione ejusdem ordinis, editum ac notulis adauctum*. 4 vols. Rome: Castaldi, 1927–1934.

Pietropaoli, Antonio. *Poesie in libertà: Govoni, Palazzeschi, Soffici*. Naples: Guida, 2003.

Pigman, G. W. "Versions of Imitation in the Renaissance." *Renaissance Quarterly* 33.1 (1980): 1–32.

Pilliod, Elizabeth. *Pontormo at San Lorenzo: The Making and Meaning of a Lost Renaissance Masterpiece*. Turnhout: Brepols, 2021.

———. *Pontormo, Bronzino, Allori: A Genealogy of Florentine Art*. New Haven, CT: Yale University Press, 2001.

———. "Representation, Misrepresentation, and Non-Representation: Vasari and His Competitors." In *Vasari's Florence: Artists and Literati at the Medicean Court*, ed. Philip Joshua Jacks, 30-52. Cambridge: Cambridge University Press, 1998.

———. "The Influence of Michelangelo: Pontormo, Bronzino and Allori." In *Reactions to the Master: Michelangelo's Effect on Art and Artists in the Sixteenth Century*, edited by Francis Ames-Lewis and Paul Joannides, 31–52. Aldershot: Ashgate, 2003.

Pinelli, Antonio. "Vivere 'alla filosofica' o vestire di velluto? Storia di Jacone fiorentino e della sua 'masnada' antivasariana." *Ricerche di storia dell'arte* 34 (1988): 5–34.

Pirotti, Umberto. *Benedetto Varchi e la cultura del suo tempo*. Florence: Olschki, 1971.

Pizzorusso, Claudio. *A Boboli e altrove: sculture e scultori florentini del Seicento*. Florence: Olschki, 1989.

———. *Ricerche su Cristofano Allori*. Florence: Olschki, 1982.

Plaisance, Michel. *L'Accademia e il suo principe: cultura e politica a Firenze al tempo di Cosimo I e di Francesco de' Medici*. Manziana (Rome): Vecchiarelli, 2004.

Plazzotta, Carol. "Bronzino's Laura." *The Burlington Magazine* 140 (1998): 251–263.

Plon, Eugène. *Benvenuto Cellini, orfévre, médailleur, sculpteur: recherches sur sa vie, sur son oeuvre et sur les pieces qui lui sont attribuees*. Paris: Plon, 1883.

Poirier, Richard. *The Performing Self: Compositions and Decompositions in the Languages of Contemporary Life*. New York / Oxford: Oxford University Press, 1971.

Pozzi, Giovanni. "Il ritratto della donna nella poesia d'inizio Cinquecento e la pittura di Giorgione." In *Giorgione e l'umanesimo veneziano*, edited by Rodolfo Palluchini, 2 vols., 1: 309–341. Florence: Olschki, 1981.

Pozzi, Mario, and Enrico Mattioda. *Giorgio Vasari storico e critico*. Florence: Olschki, 2006.

Presa, Giovanni, and Alessandra Uboldi. *I rimari italiani*. Milan: Vita e pensiero, 1974.

Previtali, Giovanni. *La fortuna dei primitivi dal Vasari ai neoclassici*. Turin: Einaudi, 1964.

Proctor, Anne E. "Vincenzo Danti at the Medici Court: Constructing Professional Identity in Late Renaissance Florence." PhD diss., University of Texas at Austin, 2013. https://repositories.lib.utexas.edu/bitstream/handle/2152/25889/PROCTOR-DISSERTATION-2013.pdf.

Prodan, Sarah R. *Michelangelo's Christian Mysticism: Spirituality, Poetry, and Art in Sixteenth-Century Italy*. Cambridge: Cambridge University Press, 2014.

Prunai Falciani, Maria. "Manoscritti e libri appartenuti al Varchi nella Biblioteca Riccardiana di Firenze." *Accademie e biblioteche d'Italia* 53 (1985): 14–29.

Quiviger, François. "Benedetto Varchi and the Visual Arts." *Journal of the Warburg and Courtauld Institutes* 50 (1987): 219–224.

——. "Célébrations académiques et débats sur l'art Benvenuto Cellini et l'*Oratione in lode della pittura* di Lionardo Salviati." In *Les académies dans l'Europe humaniste: Idéaux et pratiques*, edited by Marc Deramaix, Perrine Galand-Hallyn, Ginette Vagenheim, and Jean Vignes, 187–96. Geneva: Droz, 2008.

——. "The Presence of Artists in Literary Academies." In *Italian Academies of the Sixteenth Century*, edited by David Chambers and François Quiviger, 105–112. London: Warburg Institute, 1995.

Quondam, Amedeo. *Il naso di Laura: lingua e poesia lirica nella tradizione del Classicismo*. Modena: Panini, 1991.

Rapino, Daniele, ed. *La* Crocifissione *di Giorgio Vasari nella chiesa di Santa Maria del Carmine a Firenze: studi e restauro*. Florence: Polistampa, 2012.

Reilly, Patricia L. "Drawing the Line: Benvenuto Cellini's *On the Principles and Method of Learning the Art of Drawing* and the Question of Amateur Drawing Education." In *Benvenuto Cellini: Sculptor, Goldsmith, Writer*, edited by Margaret A. Gallucci and Paolo L. Rossi, 26–50. Cambridge: Cambridge University Press, 2004.

Residori, Matteo. "Sulla corrispondenza poetica tra Berni e Michelangelo (senza dimenticare Sebastiano del Piombo)." In *Les années trente du XVIᵉ siècle italien*, edited by Daniel Boillet and Michel Plaisance, 207–224. Paris: Centre Interuniversitaire de Recherche sur la Renaissance Italienne, 2007.

Ricci, Antonio. "Lorenzo Torrentino and the Cultural Programme of Cosimo I de' Medici." In *The Cultural Politics of Duke Cosimo I de' Medici*, edited by Konrad Eisenbichler, 103–119. Aldershot: Ashgate, 2001.

Riccò, Laura. "Tipologia novellistica degli artisti vasariani." In *Giorgio Vasari tra decorazione ambientale e storiografia artistica*, edited by Giancarlo Garfagnini, 95–115. Florence: Olschki, 1985.

——. *Vasari scrittore: la prima edizione del libro delle* Vite. Rome: Bulzoni, 1979.

Richardson, Brian. *Manuscript Culture in Renaissance Italy*. Cambridge: Cambridge University Press, 2009.

Richardson, John G. *Handbook of Theory and Research for the Sociology of Education*. Westport, CT: Greenwood Press, 1986.

Richelson, Paul William. *Studies in the Personal Imagery of Cosimo I de' Medici, Duke of Florence*. New York: Garland, 1978.

Rijser, David. *Raphael's Poetics: Art and Poetry in High Renaissance Rome*. Amsterdam: Amsterdam University Press, 2012.

——. "The Sculptor as Philologist: Interaction between Scholarship and the Arts in the Goritz Chapel and the *Coryciana*, Rome 1512–1527." In *Officine del nuovo: sodalizi fra letterati, artisti ed editori nella cultura italiana fra Riforma e Controriforma. Atti del simposio internazionale, Utrecht 8–10 novembre 2007*, edited by Harald Hendrix and Paolo Procaccioli, 257–265. Manziana (Rome): Vecchiarelli, 2008.

Rilli, Jacopo. *Notizie letterarie ed istoriche intorno agli uomini illustri dell'Accademia Fiorentina.* Florence: Matini, 1700.

Rizzarelli, Giovanna. "Disegnare con le parole. La doppia creatività di Benvenuto Cellini." *Italique* 22 (2019): 39–58.

Roeck, Bernd. *Gelehrte Künstler: Maler, Bildhauer und Architekten der Renaissance über Kunst.* Berlin: Wagenbach, 2013.

Rosen, Mark S. "The Cosmos in the Palace: The Palazzo Vecchio Guardaroba and the Culture of Cartography in Early Modern Florence, 1563–1589." PhD. diss., University of California, Berkeley, 2004.

Rosenmeyer, Patricia A. *The Poetics of Imitation: Anacreon and the Anacreontic Tradition.* Cambridge: Cambridge University Press, 1992.

Roskill, Mark W. *Dolce's Aretino and Venetian Art Theory of the Cinquecento.* New York: New York University Press, 2000.

Rossi, Carla. "Nuove indagini attorno ai due maggiori codici latori delle rime burlesche del Bronzino." *Theory and Criticisim of Literature & Arts* 5.1 (2021): 104–114.

Rossi, Massimiliano. "Furini poeta" and "Testi editi e inediti di Francesco Furini." In *Un'altra bellezza: Francesco Furini*, edited by Mina Gregori and Rodolfo Maffeis, 107–119 and 295–306. Exh. cat. Florence: Mandragora, 2007.

"Il tempo ritrovato di Sebastiano Mazzoni." *Paragone* 51 (2001): 64–78.

La poesia scolpita: Danese Cataneo nella Venezia del Cinquecento. Lucca: Pacini Fazzi, 1995.

"Le réseau des arts. Les artistes en tant que poètes face au portrait." In *Florence: Portraits à la cour des Médicis*, edited by Carlo Falciani, 149–155. Exh. cat. Brussels: Fonds Mercator, 2015.

"'… Quella naturalità e fiorentinità (per dir così).' Bronzino: Lingua, carne e pittura." In *Bronzino: Pittore e poeta alla corte dei Medici*, edited by Carlo Falciani and Antonio Natali, 177–193. Exh. cat. Florence: Mandragora, 2010.

Rossi, Sergio. *Dalle botteghe alle accademie: realtà sociale e teorie artistiche a Firenze dal 14° al 16° secolo.* Milan: Feltrinelli, 1980.

Rossi, Vittorio. *Il Quattrocento.* Rev. ed. Milan: Vallardi, 1938.

Rousseau, Claudia. "Astrological Imagery and Rulership Propaganda in the Art of Cosimo I de' Medici." In *Astrology as Art: Representation and Practice*, edited by Nicholas Campion and Jennifer Zahrt, 63–85. Ceredigion: Sophia Centre Press, 2018.

Rubin, Patricia Lee. *Giorgio Vasari: Art and History.* New Haven, CT: Yale University Press, 1995.

Ruffini, Marco. *Art without an Author: Vasari's* Lives *and Michelangelo's Death.* New York: Fordham University Press, 2011.

Sabbatino, Pasquale. "'Imparare sotto la bella maniera di Michelangelo:' L'imitazione nelle opere di Benvenuto Cellini." *Chroniques italiennes web* 16 (2009). http://chroniquesitaliennes.univ-paris3.fr/PDF/web16/Sabbatinoweb16.pdf.

La bellezza di Elena: l'imitazione nella letteratura e nelle arti figurative del Rinascimento. Florence: Olschki, 1997.

Saller, Richard P. *Personal Patronage under the Early Empire.* Cambridge: Cambridge University Press, 1982.

Sapori, Giovanna. "Lo specchio di Perino. La biografia di Perino del Vaga nell'edizione delle *Vite* di Vasari del 1550." In *Giorgio Vasari e il cantiere delle* Vite *del 1550*, edited by Barbara Agosti, Silvia Ginzburg Carignani, and Alessandro Nova, 75–89. Venice: Marsilio, 2013.

Satolli, Alberto. "Una recente scoperta nell'attività orvietana di Francesco Mosca detto il Moschino (e qualche considerazione sui ritratti nel '500)." In *Le cattedrali, segni delle radici cristiane in Europa*, edited by Laura Andreani and Alessandra Cannistrà, 255–274. Orvieto: Opera del Duomo di Orvieto, 2010.

Savarese, Gennaro. *Indagini sulle arti sorelle: studi su letteratura delle immagini e ut pictura poesis negli scrittori italiani.* Edited by Stefano Benedetti and Gian Piero Maragoni. Manziana (Rome): Vecchiarelli, 2006.

Scapecchi, Piero. "Ricerche sulla biblioteca di Varchi con una lista di volumi da lui posseduti." In *Benedetto Varchi, 1503–1565: Atti del convegno, Firenze, 16–17 dicembre 2003*, edited by Vanni Bramanti, 309–318. Rome: Edizioni di storia e letteratura, 2007.

Scardamaglia, Vittorio. "Benedetto Varchi e Michelangelo 'scultore di versi.'" *La Rivista. Études culturelles italiennes Sorbonne Universités* 5 (2017): 113–135. https://etudesitaliennes.hypotheses.org/files/2017/05/7ScardamagliaFiniNouveau.pdf.

Schiavone, Oscar. "Luca Martini as an Art Consultant and Patron of Artists in Pisa (1547–1561)." In *Essere uomini di "lettere": segretari e politica culturale nel Cinquecento*, edited by Antonio Geremicca and Hélène Miesse, 145–153. Florence: Franco Cesati, 2016.

———. "Luca Martini filologo dantesco: collazioni, annotazioni e committenze (1543–1551)." In *La filologia in Italia nel Rinascimento*, edited by Carlo Caruso and Emilio Russo, 117–132. Rome: Edizioni di Storia e Letteratura, 2018.

———. *Michelangelo Buonarroti: forme del sapere tra letteratura e arte nel Rinascimento*. Florence: Polistampa, 2013.

Schiesaro, Jonathan. "*Contra Baccium*. Sonetti, sonettesse ed epigrammi in scherno del Bandinelli." *Theory and Criticisim of Literature & Arts* 5.1 (2021): 50–103.

Schlosser, Julius von. *Die Kunstliteratur, ein Handbuch zur Quellenkunde der neueren Kunstgeschichte*. Vienna: A. Schroll, 1924.

Schmidt, Hans-Werner. "Vasaris Fassadenmalerei am Palazzo Almeni." In *Miscellanea Bibliothecae Hertzianae*, edited by Franz Graf, Wolff Metternich, Leo Bruhns, and Ludwig Schudt, 271–274. Munich: Schroll, 1961.

Schwarz, Michael Viktor, and Pia Theis. *Giottus pictor*. 2 vols. Vienna: Böhlau, 2004.

Settis, Salvatore. "Luci e ombre di Zeusi (Plin. nat. 35,62)." *Materiali e discussioni per l'analisi dei testi classici* 60 (2008): 201–204.

Shearman, John K. G. *Only Connect: Art and the Spectator in the Italian Renaissance*. Princeton, NJ: Princeton University Press, 1992.

Siekiera, Anna. "Benedetto Varchi." In *Autografi dei letterati italiani. Il Cinquecento*, edited by Matteo Motolese, Paolo Procaccioli, and Emilio Russo, 3 vols., 1: 337–357. Rome: Salerno editrice, 2009.

Simon, Anita. "Letteratura e arte figurativa: Franco Sacchetti, un testimone d'eccezione?" *Mélanges de l'école française de Rome* 105 (1993): 443–479.

Simoncini, Stefano. "Lenzi, Lorenzo." In *Dizionario Biografico degli Italiani* 64: 387–392. Rome: Istituto della Enciclopedia Italiana, 2005.

Smick-McIntire, Rebekah J. "Vivid Thinking: Word and Image in Descriptive Techniques of the Renaissance." In *Antiquity and Its Interpreters*, edited by Alina Payne, Ann Kuttner, and Rebekah Smick, 159–73. Cambridge: Cambridge University Press, 2000.

Sohm, Philip L. "Giving Vasari the Giorgio Treatment." *I Tatti Studies in the Italian Renaissance* 18 (2015): 61–111.

Soussloff, Catherine M. *The Absolute Artist: The Historiography of a Concept*. Minneapolis: University of Minnesota Press, 1997.

———. "Imitatio Buonarroti." *The Sixteenth Century Journal* 20 (1989): 581–602.

Spagnolo, Maddalena. "Barn-Owl Painters in St Peter's in the Vatican, 1604: Three Mocking Poems for Roncalli, Vanni and Passignano (and a Note on the Breeches-Maker)." *Journal of the Warburg and Courtauld Institutes* 73 (2010): 257–296.

———. "Effimere saette: Sfide e limiti di una Kunstliteratur satirico-burlesca." Forthcoming in *Mitteilungen des Kunsthistorischen Institutes in Florenz* 63.1 (2021).

———. "Filze di frasche e fogli volanti su Palazzo Bartolini Salimbeni." In *Arte e politica: Studi per Antonio Pinelli*, edited by Novella Barbolani di Montauto, Gerardo de Simone, Tomaso Montanari, Chiara Savettieri, and Maddalena Spagnolo, 49–52. Florence: Mandragora, 2013.

———. "'Pasquino' al bivio: La statua, la piazza e il suo pubblico nel Cinquecento." In *Skulptur und Platz*, edited by Alessandro Nova and Stephanie Hanke, 253–281. Munich: Deutscher Kunstverlag, 2014.

———. *Pasquino in piazza: una statua a Roma tra arte e vituperio*. Rome: Campisano Editore, 2019.

———. "Poesie contro le opere d'arte: arguzia, biasimo e ironia nella critica d'arte del Cinquecento." In *Ex marmore: pasquini, pasquinisti, pasquinate nell'Europa moderna. Atti del colloquio internazionale Lecce, Otranto, 17–19 novembre 2005*, edited by Chrysa Damianaki, Paolo Procaccioli, and Angelo Romano, 321–354. Manziana (Rome): Vecchiarelli, 2006.

———. "Ragionare e cicalare d'arte a Firenze nel Cinquecento: tracce di un dibattito fra artisti e letterati."

In *Officine del nuovo: sodalizi fra letterati, artisti ed editori nella cultura italiana fra Riforma e Controriforma. Atti del simposio internazionale, Utrecht 8–10 novembre 2007*, edited by Harald Hendrix and Paolo Procaccioli, 105–128. Manziana (Rome): Vecchiarelli, 2008.

"Vasari e le 'difficultà dell'arte.'" In *Percorsi vasariani tra le arti e le lettere*, edited by Maddalena Spagnolo and Paolo Torriti, 89–108. Montepulciano: Le Balze, 2004.

Spallanzani, Marco. "The Courtyard of Palazzo Tornabuoni-Ridolfi and Zanobi Lastricati's Bronze *Mercury*." *Journal of the Walters Art Gallery* 37 (1978): 6–21.

Spear, Richard E., and Philip L. Sohm, eds. *Painting for Profit: The Economic Lives of Seventeenth-Century Italian Painters*. New Haven, CT: Yale University Press, 2010.

Spitzer, Leo. "Note on the Poetic and the Empirical 'I' in Medieval Authors." *Traditio* 4 (1946): 414–422.

Squire, Michael. "Making Myron's Cow Moo? Ecphrastic Epigram and the Poetics of Simulation." *The American Journal of Philology* 131 (2010): 589–634.

Sricchia Santoro, Fiorella. *Mu.le.di Pisa e sotto i Medici 1555–1609*. Exh. cat. Rome: De Luca, 1980.

Steinmann, Ernst. *Michelangelo e Luigi del Riccio: con documenti inediti*. Florence: Vallecchi, 1932.

Stimato, Gerarda. *Autoritratti letterari nella Firenze di Cosimo I: Bandinelli, Vasari, Cellini e Pontormo*. Bologna: Bononia University Press, 2008.

Stoichiţă, Victor. "La sigla del Pontormo: il programma iconografico della decorazione del Coro di San Lorenzo." *Storia dell'arte* 38–40 (1980): 241–256.

Strinati, Claudio, ed. *Bronzino*. Rome: Viviani, 2010.

Struhal, Eva. "La semplice imitazione del naturale: Lorenzo Lippi's Poetics of Naturalism in Seventeenth-Century Florence." PhD diss., John Hopkins University, 2007.

"Reading with *acutezza*: Lorenzo Lippi's Literary Culture." In *The Artist as Reader: On Education and Non-Education of Early Modern Artists*, edited by Heiko Damm, Michael Thimann, and Claus Zittel, 105–127. Leiden: Brill, 2013.

Summers, David. *Michelangelo and the Language of Art*. Princeton, NJ: Princeton University Press, 1981.

"The Chronology of Vincenzo Danti's First Works in Florence." *Mitteilungen des Kunsthistorischen Institutes in Florenz* 16.2 (1972): 185–198.

The Judgment of Sense: Renaissance Naturalism and the Rise of Aesthetics. Cambridge: Cambridge University Press, 1987.

Suthor, Nicola. *Bravura: Virtuosität und Mutwilligkeit in der Malerei der Frühen Neuzeit*. Munich: Fink, 2010.

Taddeo, Edoardo. "I grilli poetici di un pittore: le 'Rime' di G. P. Lomazzo." *Il contesto* 3 (1997): 140–181.

Talini, Giulio. *Le guerre di Cosimo I de' Medici, granduca di Toscana*. Florence: Angelo Pontecorboli, 2019.

Tanfani Centofanti, Leopoldo. *Notizie di artisti tratte dai documenti pisani*. Pisa: Spoerri, 1897.

Tanturli, Giuliano. "Formazione d'un codice e d'un canzoniere: *Delle rime del Bronzino pittore libro primo*." *Studi di filologia italiana* 62 (2004): 195–224.

"Il Bronzino poeta e il ritratto di Laura Battiferri." In *La parola e l'immagine: studi in onore di Gianni Venturi*, edited by Marco Ariani, Arnaldo Bruni, Anna Dolfi, and Andrea Gareffi, 2 vols., 1: 319–32. Florence: Olschki, 2011.

"Rapporti del Brunelleschi con gli ambiente letterari fiorentini." In *Filippo Brunelleschi: la sua opera e il suo tempo*, edited by Guglielmo De Angelis d'Ossat, Franco Borsi, Giovanni Spadolini, and Arnaldo Bruschi, 2 vols., 1: 125–144. Florence: Centro Di, 1980.

"Una gestazione e un parto gemellare: la prima e la seconda parte dei *Sonetti* di Benedetto Varchi." *Italique* 7 (2004): 43–87.

Targioni Tozzetti, Giovanni. *Relazioni di alcuni viaggi fatti in diverse parti della Toscana per osservare le produzioni naturali e gli antichi monumenti di essa (etc.)*. Florence: Stamperia imperiale, 1752.

Tazartes, Maurizia. *Bronzino*. Milan: Rizzoli, 2003.

Testaverde, Anna Maria. "L'editoria fiorentina della festa e la memoria storica preventiva." In *La Vérité. Vérité et crédibilité: Construire la vérité dans le système de communication de l'Occident (XIIIe–XVIIe siècle)*, edited by Jean-Philippe Genet, unpaginated. Paris and Rome: Éditions de la Sorbonne, 2015. https://books.openedition.org/psorbonne/6691?lang=de.

Thomas, Ben. "'Artefici' and 'huomini intendenti:' Questions of Artistic Value in Sixteenth-Century Italy". In *Revaluing Renaissance Art*, edited by Gabriele Neher and Rupert Shepherd, 43–56. Aldershot: Ashgate, 2000.

Thompson, Wendy. "Federico Zuccaro's Love Affair with Florence: Two Allegorical Designs." *Metropolitan Museum Journal* 43 (2008): 75–97.

Tinagli, Paola. "The Identity of the Prince: Cosimo de' Medici, Giorgio Vasari and the *Ragionamenti*." In *Fashioning Identities in Renaissance Art*, edited by Mary Rogers, 189–196. Aldershot: Ashgate, 2000.

Toderi, Giuseppe, and Fiorenza Vannel. *Le medaglie italiane del XVI secolo*. 3 vols. Florence: Polistampa, 2000.

Torre, Andrea. *Vedere versi: un manoscritto di emblemi petrarcheschi (Baltimore, Walters Art Museum, ms. W476)*. Naples: La stanza della scrittura, 2012.

Tosi, O. C. "Una lettera inedita del Bronzino." *Arte e storia* 27.1–2 (1907): 8–9.

Tramelli, Barbara. "Artists and Knowledge in Sixteenth Century Milan: The Case of Lomazzo's Accademia de la Val di Blenio." *Fragmenta* 5 (2011): 121–138.

Trento, Dario, ed. *Benvenuto Cellini opere non esposte e documenti notarili*. Florence: Museo nazionale del Bargello, 1984.

——— "Pontormo e la corte di Cosimo I." In *Kunst des Cinquecento in der Toskana*, edited by Monika Cämmerer, 139–145. Munich: Bruckmann, 1992.

Trucchi, Francesco, ed. *Poesie Italiane inedite di dugento autori: dall'origine della lingua infino al secolo decimo-settimo*. 4 vols. Prato: Guasti, 1846–1847.

Tylus, Jane. "Cellini, Michelangelo and the Myth of Inimitability." In *Benvenuto Cellini: Sculptor, Goldsmith, Writer*, edited by Margaret A. Gallucci and Paolo L. Rossi, 7–25. Cambridge: Cambridge University Press, 2004.

Ugolini, Paola. *The Court and Its Critics: Anti-Court Sentiments in Early Modern Italy*. Toronto, Buffalo, and London: University of Toronto Press, 2020.

Utz, Hildegard. "Pierino da Vinci e Stoldo Lorenzi." *Paragone / Arte* 18 (1967): 47–69.

——— "Sculptures by Domenico Poggini." *Metropolitan Museum Journal* 101 (1976): 63–78.

Van Rosen, Valeska. "*Celare artem*. Die Ästhetisierung eines rhetorischen Topos in der Malerei mit sichtbarer Pinselschrift." In *Visuelle Topoi: Erfindung und tradiertes Wissen in den Künsten der italienischen Renaissance*, edited by Ulrich Pfisterer and Max Seidel, 323–350. Berlin / Munich: Deutscher Kunstverlag, 2003.

Vantaggiato, Silvia. "'Non fate enigmi o poesie storpiate:' alcune osservazioni di Antonfrancesco Grazzini sul 'parlar fiorentino.'" *Annali di critica d'arte* n. s. 1 (2017): 123–143.

Van Veen, Hendrik Thijs. *Cosimo I De' Medici and His Self-Representation in Florentine Art and Culture*. Cambridge: Cambridge University Press, 2006.

Vatteroni, Selene Maria. "Dal *Beneficio di Cristo* ai *Sonetti. Parte prima*: tracce di Spiritualismo nel canzoniere di Benedetto Varchi." *Schriften des Italienzentrums der Freien Universität Berlin* 3 (2019): 90–111. https://www.geisteswissenschaften.fu-berlin.de/italienzentrum/publikationen/schriften-italienzentrum/Schriften-Band-3/Schriften-des-Italienzentrums-Bd_-3.pdf.

——— "I testi proemiali nei *Sonetti. Prima parte* di Benedetto Varchi." *La Rivista. Études culturelles italiennes Sorbonne Universités* 5 (2017): 13–22. https://etudesitaliennes.hypotheses.org/files/2017/05/2VatteroniFini-1.pdf.

——— "Le sezioni pastorali e la codifica del 'doppio amore' nel canzoniere di Benedetto Varchi." *Italienisch* 40, no. 79 (2018): 12–26.

Venturi, Lionello. *Storia della critica d'arte*. 2nd ed. Florence: Edizioni U, 1948.

Vezzosi, Alessandro. "Il sigillo accademico da Leonardo a Benvenuto Cellini." In *Accademia delle Arti del Disegno: studi, fonti e interpretazioni di 450 anni di storia*, edited by Bert W. Meijer and Luigi Zangheri, 2 vols., 1:175–183. Florence: Olschki, 2015.

Vignau-Wilberg, Thea. "*Pictor Doctus*: Drawing the Theory of Art around 1600." In *Rudolph II and Prague: The Court and the City*, edited by Eliška Fučíková, 179–188. London: Thames and Hudson, 1997.

Voelker, Franz. "I cinquanta componimenti funebri di Michelangelo per Luigi del Riccio." *Italique* 3 (2000): 23–44.

Wackernagel, Martin. *Der Lebensraum des Künstlers in der florentinischen Renaissance: Aufgaben und Auftraggeber, Wekstatt und Kunstmarkt*. Leipzig: E. A. Seemann, 1938.

Waldman, Louis Alexander, ed. *Baccio Bandinelli and Art at the Medici Court: A Corpus of Early Modern Sources*. Philadelphia: American Philosophical Society, 2004.

"'Miracol' Novo et Raro': Two Unpublished Contemporary Satires on Bandinelli's 'Hercules.'" *Mitteilungen des Kunsthistorischen Institutes in Florenz* 38 (1994): 419–427.

Wallace, William E. *Michelangelo: The Artist, the Man and His Times*. Cambridge: Cambridge University Press, 2010.

Waźbiński, Zygmunt. "Artisti e pubblico nella Firenze del Cinquecento: a proposito del topos 'cane abbaiante.'" *Paragone / Arte* 28 (1977): 3–24.

L'Accademia medicea del disegno a Firenze nel Cinquecento: Idea e istituzione. 2 vols. Florence: Olschki, 1987.

"Lo studio: la scuola fiorentina di Federico Zuccari." *Mitteilungen des Kunsthistorischen Institutes in Florenz* 29.2/3 (1985): 275–346.

Wellen, Sanne. "*La Guerra de' topi e de' ranocchi*, Attributed to Andrea del Sarto: Considerations on the Poem's Authorship, the Compagnia del Paiuolo, and Vasari." *I Tatti Studies in the Italian Renaissance* 12 (2009): 101–132.

"'Ricco di tanto ardire.' A contextual study of Agnolo Bronzino's portrait of Lodovico Capponi." Forthcoming.

Williams, Robert. *Art, Theory, and Culture in Sixteenth-Century Italy: From Techne to Metatechne*. Cambridge: Cambridge University Press, 2010.

Raphael and the Redefinition of Art in Renaissance Italy. Cambridge: Cambridge University Press, 2017.

Wilson, Blake. *Singing to the Lyre in Renaissance Italy: Memory, Performance, and Oral Poetry*. Cambridge: Cambridge University Press, 2019.

Wittkower, Rudolf, and Margot Wittkower. *Born under Saturn: The Character and Conduct of Artists. A Documented History from Antiquity to the French Revolution*. London: Weidenfeld and Nicolson, 1963.

eds. *The Divine Michelangelo: The Florentine Academy's Homage on His Death in 1564*. London: Phaidon Press, 1964.

Woods–Marsden, Joanna. "Introduction: Collective Identity/Individual Identity." In *Fashioning Identities in Renaissance Art*, ed. Mary Rogers, 1–16. Aldershot: Ashgate, 2000.

Zaccarello, Michelangelo. "Ingegno naturale e cultura materiale: i motti degli artisti nelle *Trecento Novelle* di Franco Sacchetti." *Italianistica* 38.2 (2009): 129–140.

Zangheri, Luigi. "Giorgio Vasari e l'Accademia del Disegno." In *I mondi di Vasari: accademia, lingua, religione, storia, teatro*. Edited by Alessandro Nova and Luigi Zangheri, 85–97. Venice: Marsilio, 2013.

Zanrè, Domenico. *Cultural Non-Conformity in Early Modern Florence*. Aldershot and Burlington, VT: Ashgate, 2004.

Plates

Plates

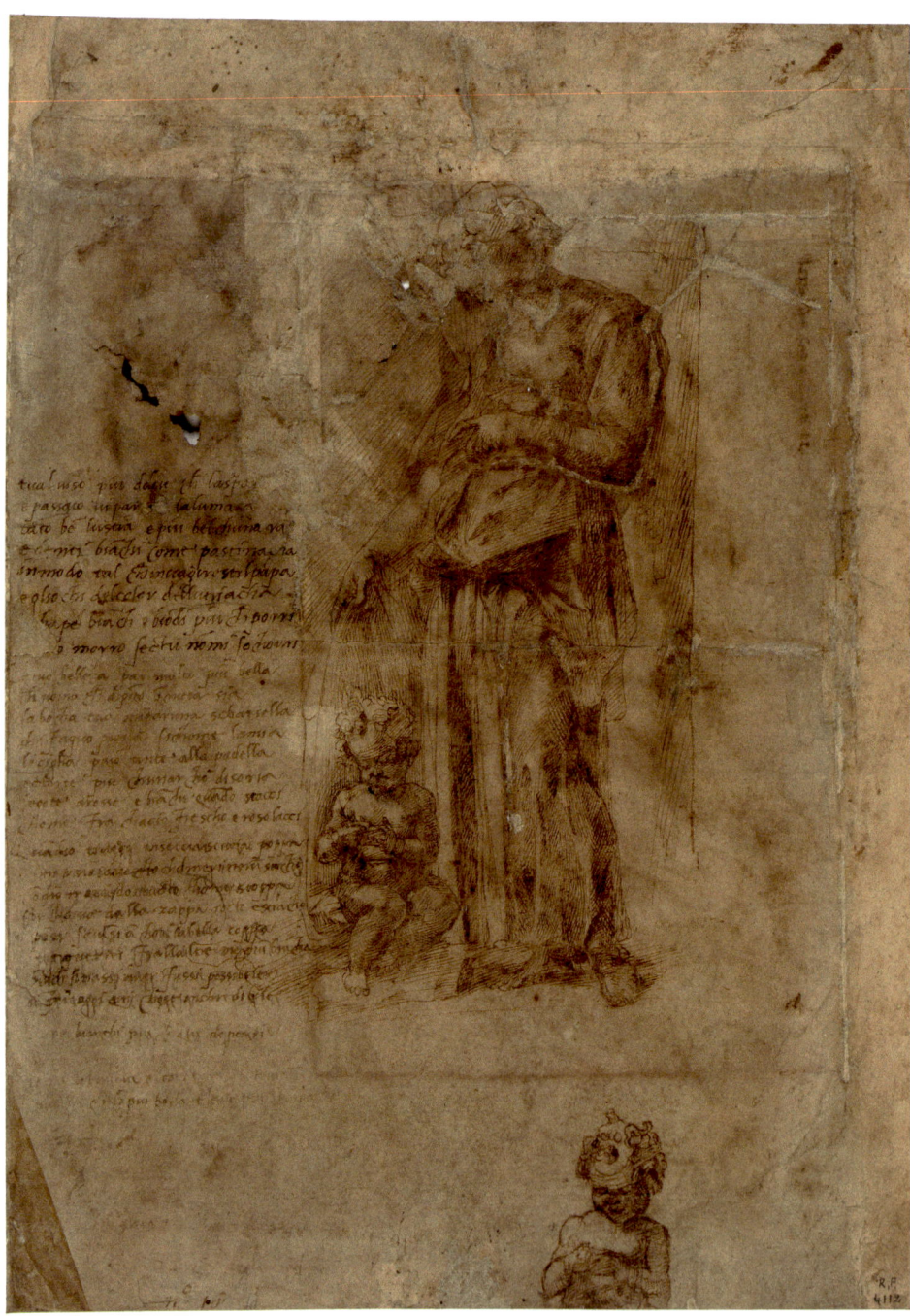

I Michelangelo, paper with drawings and the ottava poem *Tu ha 'l viso più dolce che la sapa*, probably after 1523, Paris, Musée du Louvre, R. F. 4112.

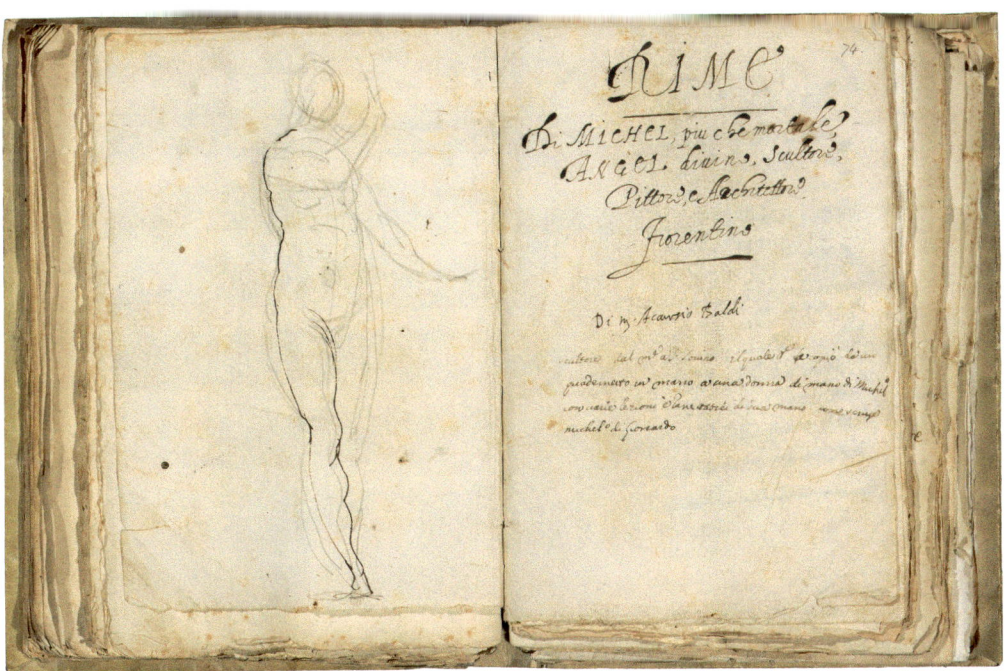

II Accursio Baldi, female figure and title of a manuscript anthology of Michelangelo's poetry, c. 1580–1590, Florence, Archivio di Casa Buonarroti, Biblioteca, ms. XIV.4 ("Codice Baldi"), cc. 73v–74r.

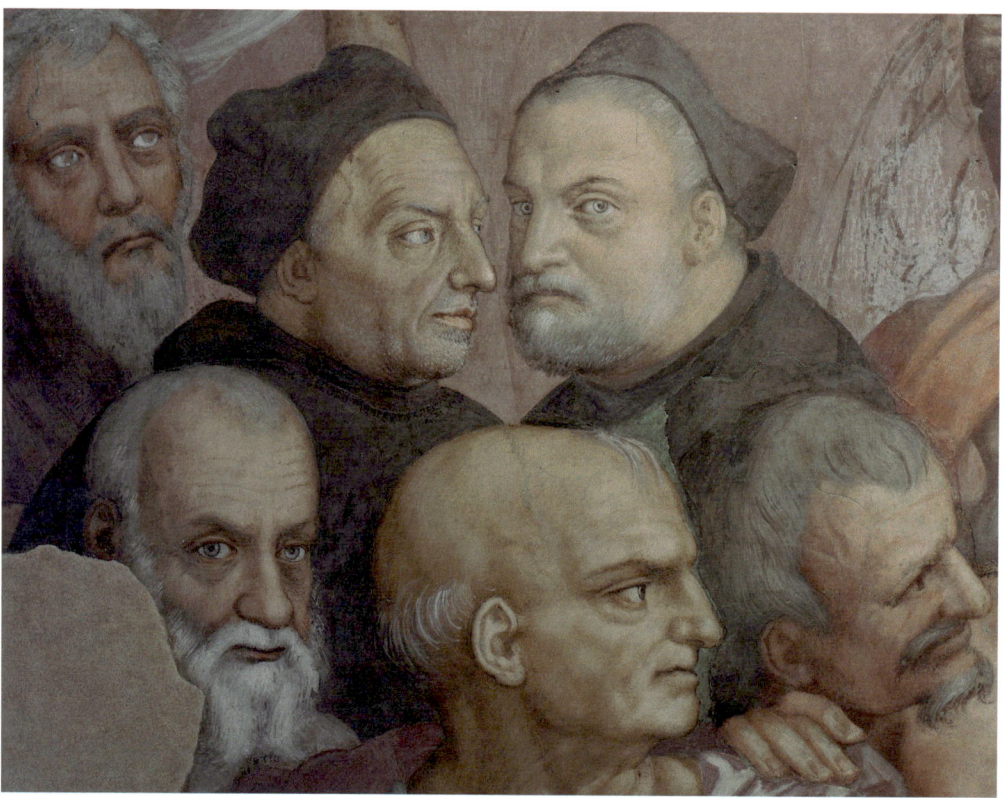

III Alessandro Allori, Christ's Dispute with the Doctors (detail with the portrait of Benedetto Varchi, identified with the bearded man on the far left of the second row of the Doctors), fresco, 1560–1564, Florence, Santissima Annunziata, Montauto Chapel.

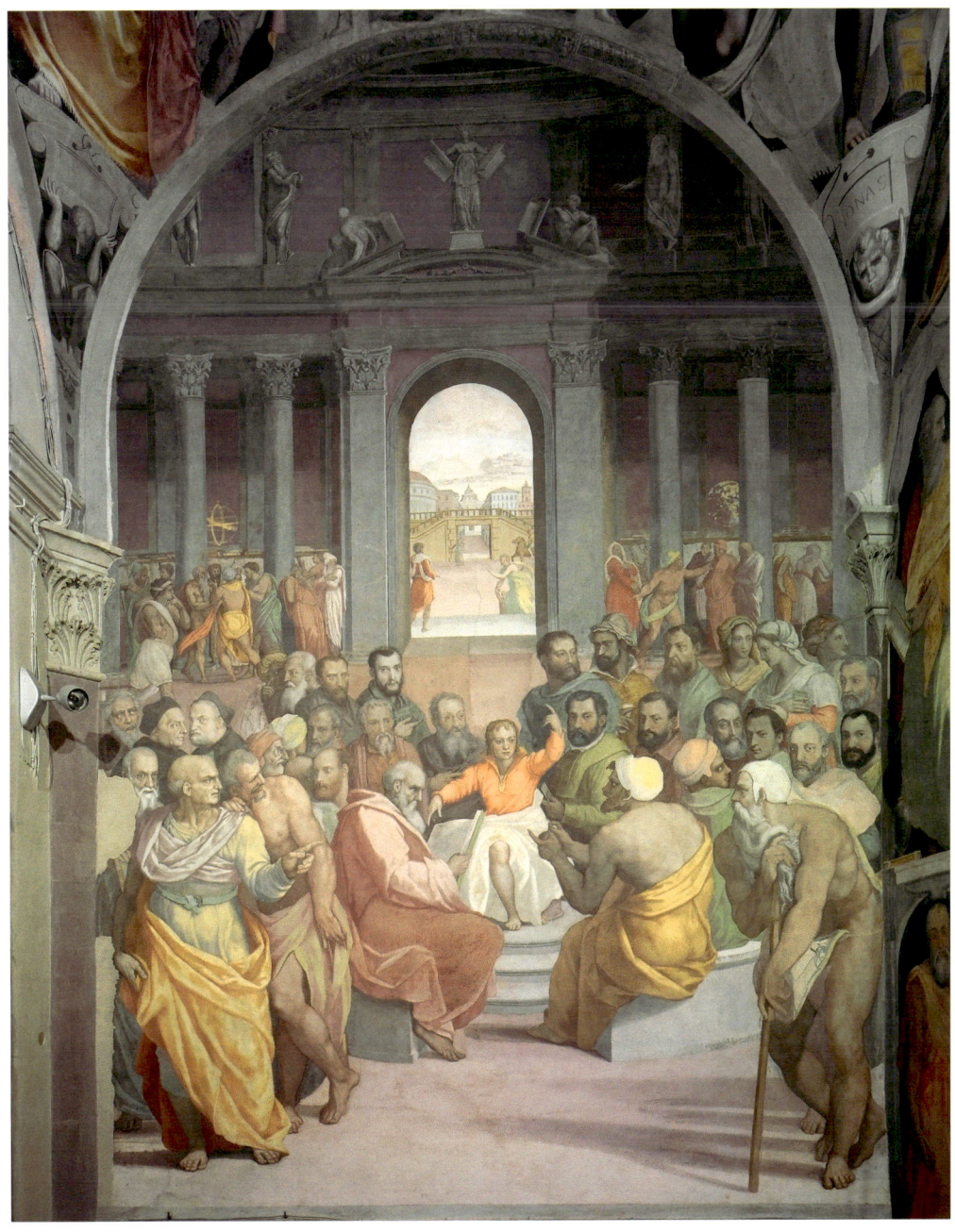

IV Alessandro Allori, Christ's Dispute with the Doctors, fresco, 1560–1564, Florence, Santissima Annunziata, Montauto Chapel.

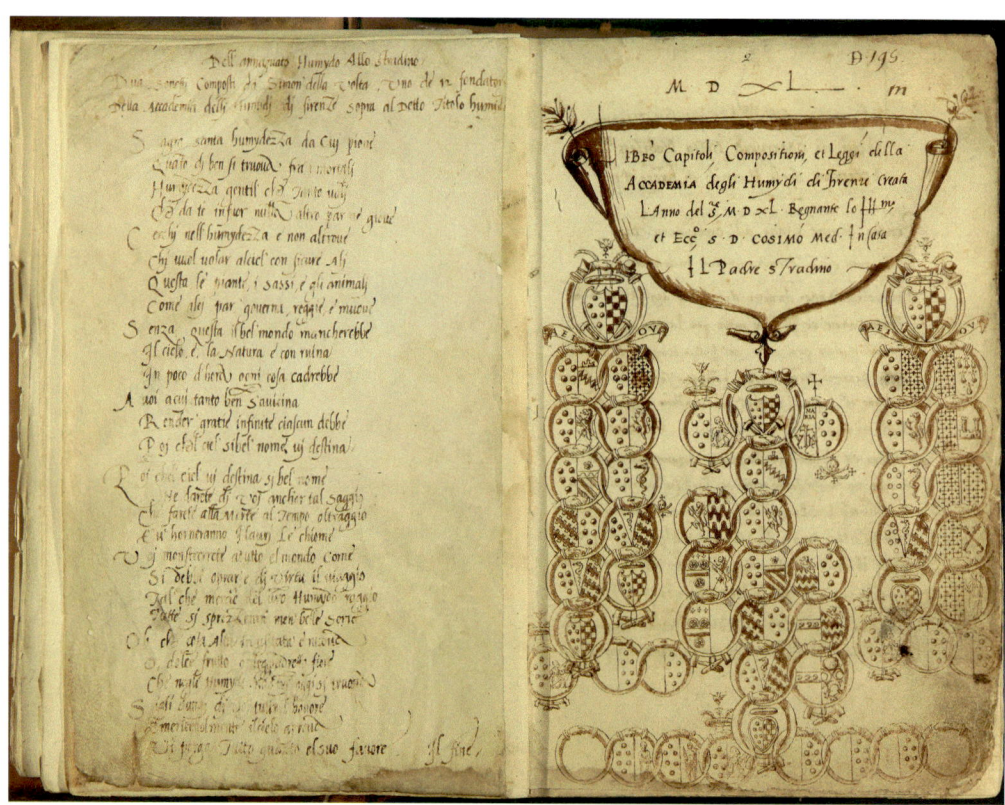

V Paolo Geri (?), Coats of arms, 1540, in Capitoli, Compositioni, et Leggi della Accademia degli Humydi di Firenze, Biblioteca Nazionale Centrale di Firenze, Fondo Nazionale II.iv.1, cc. 1v–2r.

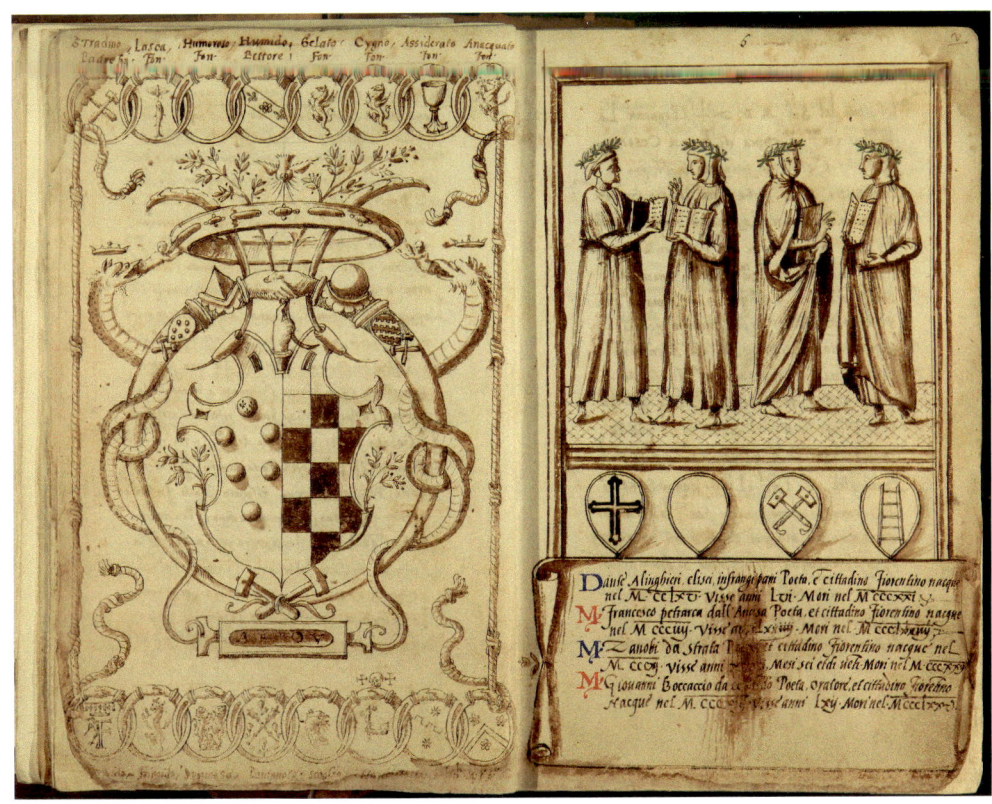

VI Paolo Geri (?), Coats of arms and "Four Crowns" of Tuscan Letters (Dante, Petrarch, Boccaccio, Zanobi da Strada), 1540, in Capitoli, Compositioni, et Leggi della Accademia degli Humydi di Firenze, Biblioteca Nazionale Centrale di Firenze, Fondo Nazionale II.iv.1, cc. 5v–6r.

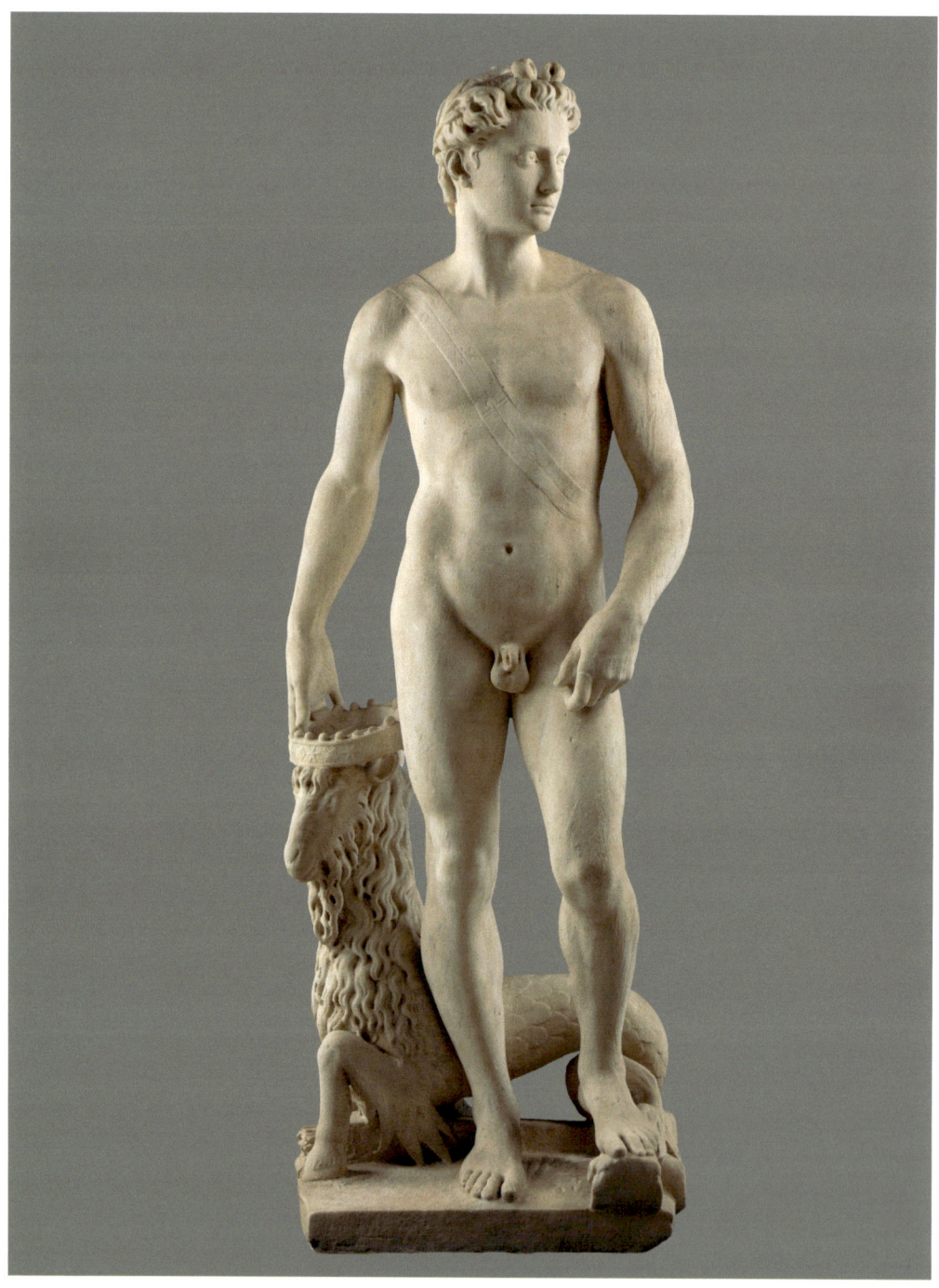

VII Domenico Poggini, Apollo and Capricorn, marble, 1559, Florence, Boboli Gardens, Kaffeehaus.

Credits

Cover ©Fototeca Musei Civici Fiorentini; Fig. 1 La basilica della Santissima Annunziata, dal Duecento al Cinquecento, ed. Carlo Sisi, Florence 2013, p. 206; Fig. 2 Vernon Hyde Minor, Baroque & Rococo Art and Culture, London 1999, p. 159; Fig. 3 Santa Maria Novella. la basilica, il convento, i chiostri monumentali, ed. Umberto Baldini, Florence 1981, p. 245; Fig. 4, 5, 12 , 19, 20 Tables V, VI: Ministero della Cultura; Fig. 6 Pontormo, Bronzino and the Medici. The Transformation of the Renaissance Portrait in Florence, ed. Carl Brandon Strehlke, Philadelphia 2004, frontispiece; Fig. 7 Photo Musées de Strasbourg, A. Plisson; Fig. 8, 9, 15 Wikimedia Commons; Fig. 10 from Francesco Sansovino, L'historia di casa Orsina [...], Venice 1565, c. 90v; Fig. 11 ShAlike, Wikimedia Commons; Fig. 13, 14, 17 Tables III, IV, VII: Kunsthistorisches Institut in Florenz; Fig. 16 The Metropolitan Museum of Art; Fig. 18 Gunther and Christel Thiem, Toskanische Fassaden-Dekoration in Sgraffito und Fresko 14. bis 17. Jahrhundert, Munich 1964, p. 36; Fig. 21 Andrea Alciato, Emblematum Libellus, Venice 1546, c. Aiiiir; Table I: Photo © RMN-Grand Palais (musée du Louvre) / Thierry Le Mage; Table II: Fondazione Casa Buonarroti, Photo Claudio Giusti.

Index of Names

A

Adriani, Giovan Battista   88, 108
Aelian   127, 251
Agostini, Ippolito   48
Alamanni, Luigi   35
Alberti, Leon Battista   17, 37, 40, 41, 122, 123, 124,
    125, 126, 128, 152, 154, 188, 251, 257, 266
Albizzi, Benedetto   88
Alciato, Andrea   196
Aldobrandini, Jacopo   88
Alessandro de' Medici   148
Alessi, Galeazzo   80, 97
Alexander the Great   65
Allori, Alessandro   26, 44, 45, 50, 67, 68, 75, 80,
    90, 94, 95, 97, 99, 106, 114, 115, 116, 118, 120, 160,
    161, 162, 163, 222, 238, 252, 260, 265, 267, 271
Allori, Cristofano   24, 45, 271
Almeni, Sforza   87, 156, 157, 158,
    159, 160, 191, 261, 274
Altoviti, Bindo   195
Ammannati, Bartolomeo   26, 44, 49, 88,
    90, 91, 92, 94, 97, 114, 115, 117, 118, 152,
    153, 154, 217, 221, 227, 255, 258
Ammannati, Giacomo degli   170
Ammannati, Laura Battiferri degli   45
Ammirato, Scipione   199, 251
Anacreon   95, 96, 99, 103
Andrea del Sarto   15, 25, 166, 258, 268, 277
Angeli or Angelio, Piero   88
Angeriano, Girolamo   96
Anguli, Andrea   132, 133, 233
Anonimo Fiorentino   196
Antonio da Pisa, don   88
Antonio di Meglio   21, 22
Apelles   19, 33, 34, 44, 45, 50, 56, 65, 122, 123, 124,
    125, 130, 146, 150, 185, 186, 201, 259, 260, 266
Apollodorus   27, 145
Aquilano, Serafino   19, 105
Aretino, Pietro   20, 21, 37, 42, 43, 64, 65, 77,
    128, 158, 172, 174, 175, 251, 264, 269, 273
Ariosto, Ludovico   24, 47, 122, 177, 266
Aristotle   44, 161
Armenini, Giovan Battista   22, 185, 186, 251

Athenaeus   145
Augustus   193, 197
Avalos, Ferrante d'   178

B

Bacci, Niccolosa   53
Baccio d'Agnolo   145
Baccio del Bianco   24
Baffo, Battista   20
Bagno, Cesare da   80, 131, 132, 133, 233, 269
Baldi, Accursio   47, 48, 176, 240, 241, 269
Baldini, Baccio   88, 111
Baldini, Bernardone   150
Baldinucci, Filippo   25, 183, 251
Bandello, Matteo   189, 251, 261, 262, 267
Bandinelli, Baccio   16, 26, 49, 73, 74, 75,
    121, 127, 136, 137, 141, 142, 144, 146, 147,
    148, 149, 153, 154, 155, 168, 178, 256,
    258, 266, 268, 269, 275, 276, 277
Barbiere, Alessandro del   118
Bardi, Antonio de'   79
Bargagli, Scipione   48
Bartoli, Cosimo   40, 55, 73, 77, 153, 156,
    166, 174, 251, 252, 253, 256
Bartolini, Giovanni   146
Bartolini, Onofrio   154
Bartolomeo da Bagnacavallo   88
Bastiano di Francesco di Jacopo
    Ciano profumiere   72
Battiferri degli Ammannati, Laura   15, 45, 79,
    83, 84, 86, 88, 94, 100, 105, 109, 275
Beccadelli, Ludovico   110
Bellini, Gentile   148
Bellini, Giovanni   122
Belli, Valerio   100, 101
Bembo, Pietro   35, 55, 56, 57, 59, 60, 62,
    65, 66, 67, 71, 73, 92, 96, 100, 101, 113,
    122, 251, 252, 257, 259, 261, 264, 269
Berni, Francesco   33, 34, 39, 42, 44,
    45, 156, 178, 251, 269, 272
Bernini, Gian Lorenzo   52, 268
Bettini, Bartolomeo   62
Betussi, Giuseppe   173

Index of Names

Billi, Antonio 23, 39, 251
Boccaccio, Giovanni 23, 110, 111, 169, 170, 260
Bocchi, Francesco 135, 143, 256, 264, 267
Bonsi, Lelio 88
Bordone, Paris 128
Borghini, Vincenzio 38, 58, 59, 75, 76, 77, 78, 79, 81, 82, 83, 88, 89, 90, 114, 127, 130, 131, 132, 135, 136, 142, 143, 144, 150, 151, 161, 163, 185, 251, 254, 259, 264, 268
Boscoli, Andrea 24, 256
Botti, Matteo 117
Botti, Simone 117
Bracci, Cecchino 100
Bramante, Donato 17, 19, 21, 22, 33, 38, 252, 262, 265, 270
Brambilla, Ambrogio 21
Britonio, Girolamo 170
Bronzino, Agnolo 15, 16, 21, 22, 26, 29, 31, 39, 42, 43, 44, 45, 50, 51, 52, 54, 55, 61, 62, 64, 65, 66, 67, 68, 69, 71, 72, 73, 74, 75, 77, 79, 80, 81, 82, 83, 84, 85, 86, 87, 88, 89, 90, 91, 92, 93, 102, 103, 105, 106, 107, 108, 109, 113, 114, 116, 118, 119, 120, 121, 122, 131, 132, 133, 134, 135, 136, 140, 151, 152, 161, 163, 166, 176, 177, 178, 179, 180, 181, 182, 185, 186, 187, 188, 189, 190, 191, 201, 203, 204, 205, 207, 210, 211, 212, 213, 214, 224, 225, 228, 234, 241, 247, 252, 258, 259, 260, 261, 262, 263, 264, 265, 266, 267, 268, 270, 271, 272, 273, 275, 276, 277
Brunelleschi, Filippo 23, 24, 28, 38, 39, 112, 145, 166, 252, 253, 256, 275
Buffalmacco, Buonamico 39, 168, 169, 188, 189, 261
Buonarroti, Filippo 47
Buonarroti, Michelangelo di Leonardo 47
Buontalenti, Bernardo 46
Burchiello, Domenico di Giovanni called 23, 256, 265
Busini, Giovan Battista 35, 71, 88, 254
Butteri, Giovanni Maria 45, 161

C

Calamis 56
Calcagni, Tiberio 88
Callimachus 186
Camilliani, Santi 55
Campani, Giovanni 88
Campano, Giannantonio 170, 173, 257
Canachus 56
Cappello, Bianca 48, 176, 240, 249, 253
Capponi, Ludovico 106
Capri, Michele 45
Caravia, Alessandro 20
Caro, Annibale 75, 83, 88, 91, 94, 108, 252
Carpaccio, Vittore 148
Casa, Giovanni della 122
Castelvetro, Ludovico 86, 101
Castiglione, Baldassarre 40, 77, 186, 252
Cataneo, Danese 14, 255, 273
Caterina de' Medici 90
Cattani da Diacceto, Francesco 88
Cattani da Montevarchi, Francesco 88
Cavalieri, Tommaso dei 101, 268
Cavalori, Mirabello 69
Cellini, Benvenuto 15, 16, 20, 26, 27, 28, 30, 41, 49, 50, 57, 58, 59, 60, 61, 65, 69, 73, 77, 80, 81, 83, 87, 88, 89, 90, 91, 92, 110, 113, 114, 116, 119, 120, 121, 122, 123, 126, 128, 129, 130, 131, 132, 133, 134, 136, 138, 139, 140, 141, 142, 144, 146, 147, 148, 149, 150, 151, 152, 153, 154, 155, 157, 160, 161, 162, 163, 171, 176, 182, 195, 198, 201, 203, 212, 220, 226, 227, 235, 237, 252, 255, 258, 260, 261, 262, 263, 264, 266, 268, 269, 272, 273, 275, 276
Cennini, Cennino 40, 252
Cesati, Alessandro 80, 262, 270, 274
Charles V 197
Cicero, Marcus Tullius 39, 56, 59, 60, 66, 124, 247, 252
Cini, Giovan Battista 88
Cino da Pistoia 111
Clement VII 178, 182
Clovio, Giulio 80, 127
Colonna, Vittoria 35, 88, 101, 178, 269
Comanini, Gregorio 183
Commodi, Andrea 24, 255
Compagni, Ciano 80
Concini, Giovan Battista 88
Condivi, Ascanio 59, 63, 252
Contile, Luca 198, 252
Coppi, Jacopo 118
Correggio, Niccolò da 96, 105
Cort, Cornelis 156
Cortesi, Paolo 59, 60, 63, 66, 67
Cosimo I de' Medici, duke of Florence 14, 16, 24, 25, 26, 30, 31, 35, 42, 49, 52, 54, 61, 62, 66, 71, 72, 77, 78, 85, 86, 87, 88, 89, 90, 93, 94, 107, 110, 111, 112, 113, 117, 118, 119, 121, 122, 127, 129, 132, 133, 141, 149, 152, 153, 154, 155, 156, 165, 166, 167, 168, 170, 171, 172, 173, 174, 175, 176, 177, 178, 179, 180, 181, 185, 186, 187, 188, 189, 190, 191, 192, 193, 194, 195, 196, 197, 198, 248, 249, 251, 261, 262, 263, 264, 265, 266, 270, 272, 273, 275, 276
Cosini, Silvio 39
Crivelli, Paolo 20
Crocini, Antonio 80, 81, 85, 88, 232, 233
Crocini, Antonio di Romolo 81, 85, 90, 153, 214

D

da Canossa, Ludovico 186
dal Colle, Raffaellino 188
Dante Alighieri 17, 19, 21, 34, 35, 38, 48, 53, 55,
    56, 73, 75, 77, 82, 88, 89, 94, 99, 110, 111, 113,
    137, 138, 140, 150, 170, 173, 196, 251, 252, 253,
    254, 255, 256, 262, 264, 265, 267, 269, 271
Danti, Egnazio 113
Danti, Vincenzo 15, 26, 44, 58, 81, 110,
    113, 115, 116, 138, 152, 153, 193, 230, 231,
    249, 260, 261, 262, 263, 272, 275
da Rovezzano, Benedetto 38
Davanzati, Bernardo 88, 198, 232
de' Barbari, Jacopo 40
dell'Altissimo, Cristofano 181
Della Robbia, Girolamo 174
delle Macchie, Matteo 190
del Piombo, Sebastiano 34, 39, 156, 182, 272
del Riccio, Luigi 34, 47, 100, 275, 276
del Tasso, Giovan Battista di Marco 72,
    80, 85, 87, 89, 90, 256, 260, 263
De Luca, Giovan Battista 150
Desiderio da Settignano 168
de Vigenère, Blaise 186
di Meglio, Antonio 39
Dionysius of Halicarnassus 60, 130, 252
Dolce, Ludovico 64, 65, 128, 129, 186, 193, 273
Dolci, Carlo 183
Domenichi, Ludovico 40, 41, 94, 108, 123, 152,
    188, 192, 194, 197, 198, 199, 251, 253, 255
Domitian 177
Donatello 23, 134, 135, 136, 142, 143,
    145, 152, 256, 266, 267, 271
Donati, Forese 150
Doni, Anton Francesco 26, 30, 127, 128, 129, 165,
    166, 167, 169, 173, 252, 265, 268, 269, 271
Dossi, Dosso 122

E

Eleonora di Toledo, duchess of Florence 51,
    54, 90, 92, 172, 176, 261, 262
Ennius, Quintus 41
Ercolani, Cesare 100
Estienne, Henri 95, 96
Everaerts, Johann Nico 192

F

Fabrini, Giovan Francesco 128
Ferrari, Gaudenzio 21
Ferrini, Tommaso 88
Figino, Ambrogio 183
Filippi, Rustico 150, 255
Fortini, David di Raffaello 85, 269

Francavilla, Pietro 193
Francesco di Sandro 80
Francesco I da Carrara 125
Francesco I de' Medici, grand duke of
    Florence 24, 26, 68, 149, 185
Francesco Ubertini
    Bachiacca 20, 80
Franchini, Gianfrancesco 174
Francia, Francesco 19, 20
Francis I Valois 46
Friedrich the Wise, Elector of Saxony 40
Furini, Francesco 24, 25, 266, 273

G

Gabriele, Trifone 25, 82, 258, 270, 275
Galani, Giuseppe Leggiadro 96
Galeotti, Pietro Paolo 80, 93, 94, 97, 98, 221
Garzia de' Medici 90, 176
Gauricus, Pomponius 40, 196, 252
Gelido, Piero 175
Gelli, Giovan Battista 73, 104, 252
Genga, Bartolomeo 39
Geri, Paolo alias il Pilucca 20, 31, 168, 169,
    170, 171, 172, 173, 174, 175, 176, 238, 261
Gherardi, Cosimo 156, 158
Ghettini, Selvaggio 173
Ghiberti, Lorenzo 40, 132, 253
Ghirlandaio, Benedetto del 71, 95
Ghirlandaio, Domenico 105
Giambologna 44, 47, 260
Giambullari, Pier Francesco 73, 77
Giancarli, Gigio Artemio 20
Giannotti, Donato 34, 47, 71, 168, 172, 253, 265
Gilio, Giovanni Andrea 67
Giordano, Luca 93, 106, 107, 108, 183, 264
Giotto di Bondone 22, 54, 57, 113, 125,
    128, 196, 255, 256, 260, 262
Giovanna d'Austria 185
Giovanni dalle Bande Nere 172
Giovanni da San Giovanni 24, 263
Giovanni de' Medici 90, 146, 176
Giovanni di Francesco
    Piloto 80
Giovio, Paolo 39, 132, 188, 192, 194,
    197, 198, 199, 253, 255
Giraldi Cinzio, Giovan Battista 186
Goethe, Johann Wolfgang 140
Goritz, Johann 133, 148, 272
Gosellini, Giuliano 96
Graziano da Perugia 20
Grazzini, Anton Francesco
    Lasca 79, 88, 94, 149, 156, 157, 160, 161,
    162, 163, 168, 169, 237, 253, 260, 276

Gualterotti, Raffaello   47, 48, 176, 253
Gualtieri, Felice   88
Guidetti, Lorenzo   88

H
Hesiod   150, 181
Hollanda, Francisco de   127, 253
Homer   63, 96, 247, 266
Horace   14, 91, 122, 151, 177, 184, 253
Hurtado de Mendoza, Diego   21

I
ibn Gabirol, Salomon
   Avicebron   140
Isabella de' Medici   93, 106, 107, 269
Isabella d'Este   19

J
Jacone   158
Jerome   125

L
Lancillotti, Francesco   13
Lanfredini, Giovanni   128
Lapini, Pier Francesco   88
Lappoli, Giovanni
   Pollastra   79
Lastricati, Alessandro   139
Lastricati, Zanobi   72, 131, 139, 140, 235, 258, 260, 261, 270, 275
Lenzi, Lorenzo   66, 77, 80, 81, 90, 91, 93, 94, 95, 97, 98, 99, 100, 103, 105, 106, 108, 249, 259, 274
Lenzoni, Carlo   73
Leonardo da Vinci   17, 21, 22, 27, 39, 57, 126, 132, 188, 189, 195, 198, 253, 262, 265, 267, 276
Leoni, Leone   80, 92
Leo X   165, 178, 261
Leo X, pope   146
Lionardo d'Urbano artefice   71
Lippi, Filippino   143
Lippi, Lorenzo   24, 25, 275
Lomazzo, Giovan Paolo   13, 14, 21, 22, 38, 39, 195, 253, 275, 276
Lorenzetti, Ambrogio   168
Lorenzi, Stoldo   86, 87, 88, 89, 213, 219, 270, 276
Lorenzo de' Medici   128
Lotti, Cosimo   24
Lottini, Giovan Francesco   88
Lottini, Giovanni Angelo   24, 25
Luini, Bernardino   21
Lysippus   56, 101, 271

M
Macchietti, Girolamo   68, 118
Maderno, Girolamo   21
madonna Diamante, mother of
   Benedetto Varchi   71
Maecenas, Gaius   177
Maggi, Girolamo   174
Malvasia, Carlo   19, 20, 253
Manetti, Antonio   23, 39, 145, 253
Mantova Benavides, Marco   117
Marignolli, Lorenzo   85
Mariotto di Nardo di Cione   23, 255
Marsili, Sebastiano   48, 176
Marsuppini, Jacopo   61
Martelli, Andrea   133
Martelli, Nicolò   173
Martial, Marcus Valerius   95, 100, 105, 122, 151, 170, 177, 253
Martinengo, Fortunato   165, 257
Martini, Carlo   88
Martini, Giovanni   88
Martini, Luca   71, 72, 75, 81, 82, 85, 86, 87, 88, 89, 90, 169, 248, 255, 264, 266, 269, 270, 274
Martini, Simone   104, 105, 122
Masaccio   144
Mazzoni, Sebastiano   24, 25, 273
Medici, Tommaso de'   181
Mellini, Domenico   88
Metrodorus   37, 41
Michelangelo Buonarroti   14, 17, 21, 26, 28, 29, 33, 34, 35, 36, 37, 38, 39, 41, 42, 43, 44, 45, 46, 47, 48, 49, 50, 51, 52, 53, 54, 55, 56, 57, 58, 59, 60, 61, 62, 63, 64, 65, 66, 67, 68, 69, 71, 72, 75, 76, 77, 78, 80, 82, 86, 100, 101, 105, 106, 110, 115, 121, 127, 130, 135, 136, 137, 138, 141, 142, 144, 153, 154, 156, 158, 160, 161, 163, 166, 186, 188, 189, 248, 252, 253, 254, 255, 256, 257, 258, 259, 260, 261, 262, 263, 264, 265, 266, 267, 268, 269, 270, 271, 272, 273, 274, 275, 276, 277
Michelangelo Buonarroti il Giovane   46, 47
Michieli, Andrea called lo Squarzola   148
Mini, Antonio   46, 88
Mini, Paolo   136
Mochi, Nicolò   17, 136, 258
Molza, Francesco Maria   82
Montauto, Isidoro   114
Montorsoli, Giovann'Angelo   25, 82, 83, 92, 111, 112, 127, 198, 264, 271
Moretto   165
Mosca, Francesco
   Moschino   88, 98, 223, 263, 273
Moschino   88
Myron   94, 122, 140, 275

N

Naldini, Battista   66, 118
Nascimbeni, Baccio   88
Navazzotti, Orazio   96
Nicolini, Domenico   107
Nicomachus of Tebes   186
Nobili, Giulio de'   88

O

Oderisi da Gubbio   113
Ombrone da Fossombrone   148
Oradini, Lucio   88
Orcagna, Andrea di Cione called   17, 23, 24, 38, 39, 256, 259, 261, 267
Orsilago, Achille   88
Orsini, Paolo Giordano   93, 106, 107, 264
Ovid   71, 170, 193

P

Pacuvius   37, 41
Parrhasius   27, 145
Pastorini, Pastorino de'   155
Paulus Silentiarius   105
Pazzi, Alfonso de'   42, 43, 44, 119, 127, 128, 149, 157, 158, 159, 165, 236, 253, 268, 270
Pazzi, Giovanni de'   88
Pazzi, Luigi de'   43
Penni, Giovan Francesco   20
Perin del Vaga   166, 183, 270
Perino del Vaga   143, 183, 273
Perugino, Pietro   142, 143, 144, 263
Petrarch   14, 18, 35, 84, 86, 103, 104, 110, 111, 113, 122, 125, 140, 170, 171, 173, 249, 253
Phidias   94, 98, 99, 271
Philip II of Habsburg   92
Pico, Giovan Francesco   56, 57, 62, 65
Pindar   61
Pino, Paolo   185, 186, 188
Plato   34, 41, 44, 161
Pliny the Elder   27, 37, 38, 41, 102, 122, 123, 125, 126, 136, 145, 146, 147, 185, 253, 254, 261, 263, 269
Pliny the Younger   125, 254
Plutarch   14, 128, 185, 254
Poccetti, Bernardino   107
Poggini, Domenico   15, 31, 39, 45, 80, 81, 88, 94, 97, 98, 101, 115, 116, 119, 131, 136, 137, 138, 139, 140, 161, 192, 193, 194, 195, 196, 197, 198, 200, 222, 223, 231, 232, 235, 247, 264, 267, 269, 276
Poggini, Giovan Paolo   138
Poliziano, Agnolo   59, 66, 67
Polverini, Jacopo   190, 191
Polyclitus   127
Polygnotus of Thasus   56

Pontormo, Jacopo   16, 26, 44, 61, 62, 64, 65, 68, 75, 80, 83, 84, 85, 86, 87, 89, 90, 114, 119, 132, 165, 166, 247, 254, 257, 261, 263, 266, 270, 271, 275, 276
Pontormo, Jacopo da   121
Porcacchi, Tommaso   79
Portigiani, Zanobi di Pagno   139
Priuli, Lorenzo   167
Prospettivo Milanese   13
Protogenes   125, 130, 181, 185, 186
Pseudo-Cicero   108
Puccini, Bernardo   88, 113, 115, 215, 248
Pyrrho   41

Q

Quintilian, Marcus Fabius Quintilianus   67, 124, 125, 129, 177, 254

R

Raffaello da Montelupo
   Sinibaldi, Raffaele   72, 80, 254
Raphael   17, 19, 22, 36, 57, 63, 64, 68, 93, 133, 161, 184, 265, 266, 272, 277
Razzi, Silvano   85, 86, 88, 112
Redi, Francesco   25, 258
Ricasoli, Giovan Battista   80, 88
Ricciarelli, Daniele
   Volterra, Daniele da   52, 59
Ricci, Bartolomeo   61, 272
Ridolfi, Lucantonio   88
Romano, Gian Cristoforo   19, 40, 77, 142, 194, 254, 263, 268, 274
Romano, Giulio   20
Romena, Bernardino   88
Rondinelli, Alessandro di Giovanni   191
Rosa, Salvator   14, 22, 260, 262, 263, 270
Rosi, Zanobi   45
Rossi, Giovan Girolamo   13, 14, 15, 16, 20, 21, 23, 24, 25, 50, 88, 105, 106, 107, 155, 175, 252, 257, 272, 273, 276
Rossi, Vincenzo de'   153, 154
Rosso Fiorentino   51, 75, 166, 258, 263
Rucellai, Palla or Pallante iuniore   94, 97, 99, 100
Rufinus   105
Ruscelli, Girolamo   192, 193, 197, 247, 254
Rustici, Giovan Francesco   25, 183, 193, 269

S

Sacchetti, Franco   169, 188, 189, 254, 274, 277
Salvetti, Cesare   81
Salvetti, Giovan Battista   81
Salviati, Francesco   16, 58, 64, 73, 80, 91, 166, 198, 271, 272

Index of Names

Salviati, Jacopo 91
San Friano, Maso da 161
Sangallo, Francesco Giamberti called da 74, 75, 81, 110, 111, 127, 156, 206, 247, 262, 264
Sansovino, Andrea 48, 133
Santi di Tito 69, 118
Santi, Giovanni 13, 17, 19, 118, 251, 258
Santini, Giovan Battista 88
Santini, Niccolò di Francesco 154
Scala, Lorenzo 47, 72, 75
Scheggia, Raffaello 169
Sclarici del Gambaro, Tommaso 19
Sellori, Cavalier 45, 79
Serbelloni, Fabrizio 90, 91, 94, 97, 103, 108
Sertini, Tommaso 88
Sevaiuolo, Baccio del 173
Severo, Marco Antonio 48
Simeoni, Gabriele 172
Simonides of Ceos 14
Sixtus V 48
Socrates 41
Spano, Pippo
   Scolari, Filippo Buondelmonti degli 112
Spencer, Edmund 102
Spini, Gherardo 79, 90, 109, 130, 262
Stampa, Gaspara 96
Stati, Cristofano 46
Stradano, Giovanni 118
Strozzi, Alessandro 118
Strozzi, Carlo 169
Stufa, Giulio della 133
Stufa, Pandolfo della 154
Stufa, Piero della 79, 88, 99, 100

T

Tacitus 75
Tanini, Girolamo 88
Tarsia, Giovan Maria 45, 160, 161
Tasso, Bernardo 108
Tebaldeo, Antonio 96, 178
Timanthes 56, 65
Tiziano 105, 122
Tornabuoni, Giovanna 105
Tornabuoni, Giovanni 95
Torrentino, Lorenzo 36, 52, 54, 63, 79, 81, 172, 254, 272
Tribolo, Niccolò Pericoli called 71, 72, 77, 80, 85, 86, 90, 133, 161, 166, 168, 169, 172, 259, 265

U

Ubaldini, Agostino 24

V

Valori, Baccio 71, 73, 88, 91, 220
Varchi, Benedetto 15, 30, 34, 35, 36, 37, 38, 39, 42, 44, 45, 46, 48, 50, 51, 59, 71, 72, 73, 74, 75, 76, 77, 78, 79, 80, 81, 82, 83, 84, 85, 86, 87, 88, 89, 90, 91, 92, 93, 94, 95, 96, 97, 98, 99, 100, 101, 102, 103, 104, 105, 106, 107, 108, 109, 110, 111, 112, 113, 114, 115, 116, 117, 121, 127, 130, 132, 136, 137, 138, 157, 158, 161, 166, 167, 192, 193, 205, 207, 208, 209, 210, 211, 214, 218, 219, 221, 222, 223, 225, 226, 227, 228, 229, 230, 231, 232, 247, 248, 252, 254, 255, 257, 258, 259, 260, 261, 263, 264, 265, 268, 269, 270, 271, 272, 273, 274, 275, 276
Vasari, Giorgio 15, 16, 23, 25, 26, 27, 33, 36, 37, 38, 39, 40, 41, 44, 45, 49, 50, 52, 53, 54, 55, 56, 58, 59, 61, 62, 63, 64, 65, 66, 67, 69, 72, 74, 75, 79, 81, 83, 85, 87, 88, 89, 90, 91, 99, 107, 111, 112, 113, 115, 116, 117, 118, 122, 125, 126, 128, 130, 131, 134, 135, 136, 142, 143, 144, 145, 146, 147, 148, 149, 150, 151, 152, 153, 154, 155, 156, 157, 158, 166, 168, 169, 174, 177, 178, 182, 183, 184, 185, 187, 188, 189, 195, 198, 202, 218, 229, 236, 247, 254, 255, 256, 257, 259, 260, 261, 262, 263, 264, 265, 266, 267, 268, 269, 270, 271, 272, 273, 274, 275, 276, 277
Vecchietti, Bernardo 88
Vellutello, Alessandro 137, 252
Vettori, Maddalena 106, 107
Vettori, Piero 114
Vicario di Firenze 88
Vinci, Pierino da 22, 39, 80, 85, 86, 89, 90, 126, 189, 253, 262, 266, 267, 269, 270, 276
Vinta, Emilio 88
Virgil 53, 56, 101, 103, 181, 247, 254, 261
Visconti, Gasparo 33
Vitruvius, Marcus Pollio 40, 122, 195, 196, 254

Z

Zeuxis 27, 130, 145, 146, 185
Zuccari, Federico 149, 155, 156, 255, 259, 264, 266, 267, 277